DREAM

ROUTES OF THE WORLD

Contents

Overview of routes

EUROPE

ASIA

AUSTRALIA

AFRICA

AMERICAS

About this book

There is a Far Eastern proverb that says, "You can't see the plains if you don't climb the mountain." People have been traveling for very different reasons since time immemorial, and their rewarding experience was simply discovering another part of the world. Once it was merchants, soldiers, pilgrims and explorers who endured long distances and hardships; today we often track these legendary routes following in their footsteps just for the sheer pleasure of it.

Traveling along these fifty routes of the world, we are taken to the most fascinating travel destinations on earth – to grand natural landscapes, unique cultural sites, vibrantly pulsating cities and quiet dreamy villages. The routes range from the St James' Way in northern Spain and the Romantic Road in Germany to the Friendship Highway in the Himalayas; from the Garden Route in South Africa and the Pacific Highway in Australia to the Alaska Highway and Route 66 in the United States on down to the Inca Trail in Peru and Bolivia.

The route descriptions:

There is an introduction at the beginning of each chapter providing an overview of the travel route and a short preamble about the country and regions in question as well as its specific natural features and historical and cultural sites. In addition, each chapter includes a map and a number of beautiful color photos pointing out important places and sights.

Extra pages featuring detailed comprehensive information are dedicated to selected cities and metropolises through which the routes pass.

Important travel information specifying the length of each tour, travel time, local traffic regulations, the climate, best season to travel and useful addresses are all listed in the Travel information box.

The touring maps:

The course of each route and the most important places and sights are clearly marked on special tour maps at the end of each chapter in addition to an extra supplement reporting on interesting excursions.

Eye-catching symbols (see list opposite) mark the location and the type of attractions along each route. There are short intros in the margins of each map presenting interesting facts and superb color photos highlight particularly fascinating destinations.

Remarkable landscapes and natural monuments

- Mountain landscape
- Extinct volcano
- Active volcano
- Rock landscape
- Ravine/Canyon
- Cave
- Glacier
- Desert
- River landscape
- Waterfall/rapids
- Lake country
- Geyser
- Oasis
- National Park (fauna)
- National Park (flora)
- National Park (culture)
- National Park (landscape)
- Nature Park
- Cultural landscape
- Coastal landscape
- Island
- Beach
- Coral reef
- Underwater Reserve
- Zoo/safari park
- Fossil site
- Wildlife reserve
- Whale watching
- Protected area for sea-lions/seals
- Protected area for penguins
- Crocodile farm

Remarkable cities and cultural monuments

- Pre- and early history
- The Ancient Orient
- Greek antiquity
- Roman antiquity
- Etruscan culture
- Indian reservation
- Indian Pueblo culture
- Places of Indian cultural interest
- Mayan culture
- Inca culture
- Other ancient American cultures
- Places of Islamic cultural interest
- Places of Buddhist cultural interest
- Places of Hindu cultural interest
- Places of Christian cultural interest
- Places of Jainist cultural interest
- Places of Abor. cultural interest
- Aborigine reservation
- Phoenician culture
- Prehistoric rockscape
- Early african cultures
- Cultural landscape
- Castle/fortress/fort
- Palace
- Technical/industrial monument
- Memorial
- Space telescope
- Historical city scape
- Impressive skyline
- Festivals
- Museum
- Theatre/theater
- World exhibition
- Olympics
- Monument
- Tomb/grave
- Market
- Caravanserai
- Theater of war/battlefield
- Dam
- Remarkable lighthouse
- Remarkable bridge

Sport and leisure destinations

- Race track
- Skiing
- Sailing
- Diving
- Canoeing/rafting
- Mineral/thermal spa
- Beach resort
- Amusement/theme park
- Casino
- Horse racing
- Hill resort
- Deep-sea fishing
- Surfing
- Seaport

Iceland

Fire and ice: archaic landscapes on the world's largest volcanic island

This legendary island in the North Atlantic delivers spectacular natural encounters with primordial force: formidable basalt mountains, vast lava fields, mighty glaciers, meandering glacial streams, thundering waterfalls, and much more. All the more comforting, then, when you encounter villages with a centuries-old cultural tradition on the periphery of seemingly infinite, untouched expanses.

Fishing boats in the port at Ólafsvik on Snæfellsnes peninsula.

Iceland, the largest volcanic island on earth, is just 300 km (186 mi) from Greenland, but nearly 1,000 km (621 mi) from western Scandinavia. The "wayward end of the world" is what the Vikings called these inhospitable shores close to the Arctic Circle when they settled here in the 9th century and set up one of their first free states.

Today, this island measuring 103,000-sq-km (3,976-sq-mi) has 270,000 inhabitants who live primarily off fishing, cattle and horse breeding, sheep farming, aluminum production, and vegetable farming in greenhouses heated by geothermal energy. Iceland offers visitors unique encounters with nature in its original state, where elemental forces still reign free.

The capital of Iceland, Reykjavík, is full of charm and does boast a number of interesting things to see, but the real destinations on the "Island of Fire and Ice" are outside of the city. The other small towns, such as Akureyri and Húsavík in the north or Egilsstadir on the east of the island, are set in very picturesque locations but their buildings are mostly recent or even totally new. Masonry, concrete and corrugated iron have long since replaced the old peat bricks and the traditional

thatched roofs of the scattered individual homesteads. Significant cultural monuments are not to be found anywhere on the island. Iceland's most outstanding attraction is its stunning landscape. Admittedly, it is no image of pastoral tranquility, but rather one of dramatic activity, extreme wilderness and tremendous diversity.

The four essential elements dominate the island with breathtaking intensity. The air is so fresh and clear that when the weather is good – which is fortunately much more often the case than one would expect here – you can see for over 100 km (62 mi).

Water is available in excess and seems to be absolutely everywhere you look, from meandering rivers, powerful waterfalls, cold and warm lakes located atop hot and cold springs, and of course the famous geysers. More than ten percent of the

Massive gurgling mud baths such as this one in Namarskard on Lake Mývatn are typical of Iceland.

On the south coast a 25-m-wide (82-ft) glacial river from the Myrdalsjökull in Skógafoss plunges 62 m (203 ft).

island is covered in glaciers, with one quarter of the total ice surface alone belonging to Europe's largest glacier, Vatnajökull. Indeed, the island owes its name to its numerous ice-covered glaciers.

Given all of that, however, the earth element is still the most spectacular. Vast areas of land are covered with recently cooled lava, transforming Iceland into an open-air geology museum that reveals how our planet looked during the different phases of its early development. As a result, however, the inhabitable areas are limited to a few coastal regions. The rest of the island is shaped by steep cliffs and fjords that extend into the interior, which in turn features expansive plateaus, lava fields, deserts of stone, sand and ash,

table mountains, glaciers, and active and extinct volcanoes.

Today, Surtur, the mythical leader of the fire giants, still leaves fascinating traces of his

Steam rises from the boiling hot fumaroles at Haverarond in Lake Mývatn.

work all around the island. By stoking the fires deep within the earth, he makes the glowing, viscous magma rise from the depths, melt the earth's

crust and erupt in furious explosions. The island itself is actually the tip of a submerged mountain that forms part of the Mid-Atlantic Ridge, where the American and Eurasian tectonic plates drift apart. For visitors, it is a sort of sample gallery of geological shapes, from volcanic craters and cinder fields to tuff cones and countless other whimsical lava formations. Geysers discharge their fountains of scalding water at regular intervals while mud baths bubble away and fumaroles and solfataras smolder. The plentiful thermal springs provide relaxation for Icelanders and their guests all year round and many houses have a bathing pool with volcanically heated water right outside the door.

1

Iceland's ring road: Anyone circling the island of fire and ice on the roughly 1,500-km-long (932-mi), almost completely paved, coastal road (Route 1) will become acquainted with most of the facets of this unique natural paradise, but a number of detours from the ring road into the interior are certainly worthwhile.

1 **Reykjavík** Iceland's capital, which is also the country's cultural, transport, and economic center, is on the northern edge of a peninsula on the southwest coast. Its climate benefits from the mild currents of the Gulf Stream. When it was granted its charter at the end of the 18th century, there were just 200 people settled in the "smoky bay" ("Reykjavík" in Icelandic). Now, including suburbs and outlying towns, the population has grown to around 160,000 – roughly sixty percent of the country's inhabitants.

The city tour begins at the main square, Austurvöllur, which is home to the oldest parliament in the world, a cathedral, and the time-honored Hotel Borg. The city's most prominent feature is the Tjörnin, a small lake in the city center. The new city hall, the National Gallery and some upscale residential villas line its shores. To the south are the National Museum and the

Árni Magnússon Institute, home to the medieval saga manuscripts. The council buildings, originally designed as a prison, and the bronze statue of Ingólfur Arnarson, one of Reykjavík's first settlers, are located closer to the port.

On a hill to the south-east of the town, Hallgríms church watches over the city with the Leif Eríksson monument standing tall before it. Right next door is the Ásgrímur Jónsson Collection, donated to the state by the Icelandic landscape artist who died in 1958. The Natural History Museum, Einar Jónsson's collection of sculptures, as well as the Laugardalslaug swimming pool and the Árbaer Open Air Museum are also worth a visit.

2 **Hraunfossar** Roughly 25 km (15 mi) north of the town of Borganes it is worth taking a detour along the Hálsasveitar-vegur (Route 518) to a great

natural spectacle not far from the Húsafell country estate: the Hraunfossar "lava waterfalls", a multitude of small springs that cascade over a basalt lip into the Hvítá glacial river. Nearby, there is a similar natural attraction called the Barna-foss Waterfall.

3 **Akureyri** With 15,000 inhabitants, this "pearl of the north" is located at the end of the Eyjafjördur and is the country's third largest town. It is also the transport center for the north coast thanks to its ship-yard, airport and port. The local history museum and botanical

Travel Information

Route profile
Length: 1,400 km (870 mi), without detours
Time required: min. 8–10 days
Start and end: Reykjavík
Route: Reykjavík, Akureyri, Mývatnsee, Egilsstadir, Stafafell, NP Skaftafell, Vík, Skogar, Thingvellir

---

Traffic information:
Many gravel roads. Be careful of varying depths when crossing rivers. The following laws are very strictly enforced for drivers: 0.0 mg alcohol limit for drivers; maximum speed limit in towns 50 km/h (30 mph), on gravel roads 80 km/h (50 mph), on tarred roads 90 km/h (60 mph). The majority of the roads in the interior of Iceland are first opened in July.

For more information on road conditions call:
0354/17 77 (8am–4pm)
or go to:
www.vegag.is
If you are driving a diesel vehicle you will be required to pay a weight tax on arrival.
www.icetourist.de

When to go:
Summer is the best time, but don't expect very high temperatures.
Weather in English:
Tel: 0902 / 06 00
www.vedur.is

Other information:
Here are a few sites to help you prepare for your trip:
www.icelandtouristboard.com
www.iceland.org

gardens provide an introduction to the history, flora and fauna of the surrounding region. The Nonnáhús, a monument to local children's book author Jón Sveinsson, alias Nonni, may be interesting for literature fans. The city also serves as a starting point for hiking trips into the fascinating interior, for example to the region around the Hlidarfjall at an elevation of up to 1,200 m (3,937 ft).

4 Goðafoss Some 40 km (25 mi) east of Akureyri, the roaring Skjálfandaðfljót River makes its way from the stony expanse of the Sprengisandur plain down towards the ocean over a 10-m (33-ft) escarpment. Despite the relatively short drop, the width and sheer quantity of water make Goðafoss one of the most impressive and deservedly famous falls in Iceland.

Its name, "Waterfall of the Gods", comes from Thorgeir, the speaker of the Althing. He is said to have thrown the statues of his former house gods into the river here in the year 1000 because the Icelandic parliament decided that Icelanders should convert to Christianity. Norwegian King Olaf exerted pressure on Iceland – he threatened a timber embargo, which would have crippled shipbuilding, an essential industry for the island.

5 Mývatn Located about 30 km (19 mi) east of Goðafoss, Lake Mývatn was formed only about 3,500 to 2,000 years ago by lava discharged during two volcanic eruptions. It measures 37 sq km (14 sq mi) in surface area but is only 4–5 m (13–16 ft) deep and fed by hot springs.

The diversity of plant life here is nearly singular on the planet for such northern latitudes. Mosses, grasses, ferns, herbs and birch trees grow along the shore and on the numerous islands. During the summer months, huge swarms of midge flies form over the warm water. Together with the insect larvae, they provide food for the wealth of fish and waterfowl here, thousands of which nest in the many bays, making the region a veritable paradise for birdwatchers.

The Lake Mývatn area is one of Iceland's most spectacular landscapes. It is also located right in one of the island's most active volcanic zones. Beautiful lava formations are scattered all along the very well-signposted hiking trails. The Dimmuborgir, meaning "Dark Fortresses", consist of bizarrely shaped formations with small caves and arches. The best view over the pseudo-crater in and around Lake Mývatn can be enjoyed from the rim of the Hverfjall crater, a 170-m-high (558-ft) cinder cone.

6 Krafla The area surrounding the 818-m (2,683-ft) volcano just a few miles north-east of Lake Mývatn is one of Iceland's most tectonically unstable zones. Considered extinct at the beginning of the 18th century, the 2,000-year-old Krafla suddenly buried the entire region under a thick layer of lava and ash following a violent eruption. The ultimate result was a dazzling, emerald green tuff cone with a crater lake some 320 m (1,050 ft) in diameter.

In 1975, the volcano came to life again for nearly a decade. Its bubbling, steaming sulfur springs have since remained a very popular attraction and are the most visible indication of ongoing volcanic activity.

7 Húsavík/Tjörnes Instead of following the shortest route along the ring road east of Lake Mývatn, it is worth taking a detour around the Tjörnes Peninsula, which is especially fascinating from a geological point of view. A good 30 km (19 mil) after the turnoff near Reykjahlið you will pass Grenjadarstadur, a peat homestead built in around 1870. It was abandoned in 1949 before being transformed into a folk museum. The little town of Húsavík, which mainly survives off fishing and fish-processing, has managed to make a name

for itself as a tourist destination with a particular focus on whale watching. With commercial whaling a thing of the past in Iceland, local fishermen now take seaworthy holidaymakers out on their cutters for a day's worth of whale watching in the summertime.

8 Jökulsárgljúfur and Dettifoss Compared to the rest of Iceland, the climate around Ásbyrgi, the "Fortress of the Gods", is mild and the contours of the landscape quite gentle. A birch forest covers the valley where, legend has it, Odin's six-legged horse shaped a mighty, semi-circular cliff with its hoof. There are the two roads from here that follow the canyon upstream along the edge of the escarpment towards Dettifoss. The eastern of the two is in better condition, while the western one is bumpier and thus less crowded. Jökulsárgljúfur National Park, founded in 1973, encompasses the canyon-like Jökulsá á Fjöl-

1 The river feeding the Goðafoss begins far to the south.

2 The bizarre Dimmuborgir cliff landscape at Lake Mývatn.

3 Volcanic landscape at Reykjahlið, north-east of Lake Mývatn.

lum valley section between Ásbyrgi and the Dettifoss Waterfall. With a length of 206 km (128 mi), the "glacier river from the mountains", as its name translates, is Iceland's second-longest. It is fed from the northern edge of the Vatnajökull Glacier and intersects the ring road at Grímsstadir. About 20 km (12 mi) upstream is where it plunges into the Dettifoss Waterfall over five formidable rock faces into a deep gorge.

Iceland has a number of magnificent waterfalls, but few will make the same impression as Dettifoss. With a span of about 100 m (328 ft), the gray-brown floodwaters of the Jökulsá á Fjöllum drop 44 m (144 ft) into a canyon between vertical basalt walls. In the summer the flow rate is up to 1,500 cu m/sec (52,972 cu ft/sec). This makes the Dettifoss Waterfall the mightiest in Europe by a long shot. A drive from here to the Herðubreið volcano and the Askja caldera makes for a very worthwhile detour. You'll come to the turnoff about 36 km (22 mi) after Reykjahlið.

9 **Egilstaðir / Fjorde** Eastern Iceland's administrative and commercial center is on the ring road in a mostly agricultural area of the country. It is also a heavily wooded area. A worthwhile destination in these parts is the more than 100-m-high (328-ft) Hengifoss Waterfall on the northern

shore of the long and narrow Lake Lögurinn. The ring road follows the coast once you pass Reydarfjördur and affords spectacular views of the wild ocean.

10 **Stafafell** A historical homestead stands on the edge of the Jökulsá á Lóni Delta about 30 km (19 mi) before Höfn, the only port on the entire south coast. Once a vicarage, it now serves as a youth hostel from which you can set off on hikes into the varied landscapes of the Lonsöraefi wilderness region.

11 **Jökulsárlón** About 70 km (43 mi) beyond Höfn, where the impressive ice tongue of the Breidarmerkurjökull Glacier extends to within a few hundred yards of the sea, the ring road takes you right past the island's glacial lake. Glistening a blue-white hue in the lagoon, giant icebergs from the edge of the glacier evoke an atmosphere akin to Greenland.

12 **Skaftafell National Park** Skaftafell National Park, established in 1967, extends from the area around Vatnajökull, Iceland's largest glacier, to the south as far as the ring road and provides a multitude of scenic attractions. Within the national park, signposted hiking trails take you into dense forests such as the one in Núpstadaskogar, along extensive wetlands and marshes to dilapidated but intact homesteads, and to the Svartifoss Waterfall, which is

surrounded by basalt pillars. Between Fagurhólsmri and Kirkjubaejarklaustur the ring road now traverses the black sand and scree expanse of the Skeiðarársandur. A glacier run here was caused by an eruption of the Lóki volcano below the Vatnajökull Glacier. The melted glacial ice under the Vatnajökull ice cap then surged into the sand in a giant flood wave.

13 **Vík** The big attraction at Iceland's "southern cape" are the bird cliffs at Dyrhólaey, around 20 km (12 mi) away. A number of common North Atlantic seabird species live here at varying levels of the cape. Right at the top are the Atlantic puffins, which hide their tunnels in the grass tufts. On the cliffs beneath them are the kittiwakes and fulmars. You can take a boat tour from the black sand beach. A lighthouse 100 m (328 ft) up on the cliffs is a popular viewing point.

14 **Skógafoss** The catchment area of the Skógar river, which crosses the road south-east of the mighty Mýrdalsjökull is a good stopover for two reasons. The first is the Skógafoss, a waterfall that is 62 m (203 ft) high surrounded by meadows. You can see the falls from above and below, which is what makes it a special place. Secondly, the precisely detailed folk museum in Skógar deserves a visit.

About 7 km (4 mi) beyond Hella it is worth taking a detour

to the Hekla volcano and through the Landmannalaugar thermal region. Back on the ring road, instead of taking the direct route back to Reykjavík, take a detour via Route 30, which passes by the Gullfoss Waterfall and the Strokkur Geyser. Route 35 will then take you directly back to the ring road. Before that, however, you should to take a look at the church in Skálholt, which was a Viking center in the Middle Ages and boasts lovely glass windows. The main road takes you past Lake þingvallavat towards þingvellir, the last stop.

15 **þingvellir** The renowned Thingfeld lies on the northern shore of Lake þingvallavatn. The lava plateau bordering the All Men's Gorge to the west is a very interesting geological area and the historical heart of the country. It was this "Holy Free State" that became the former Icelandic Free State in the year 930 and it was here that the legendary Althing, the oldest democratic parliament in the world, met annually all the way up until 1798. It was also here that the Icelanders declared themselves a republic on June 17, 1944.

1 Glaciers reflected on a lake in the Skaftafell National Park.

2 The water from Svartifoss, "The Black Waterfall", plunges over an impressive basalt cliff into a basin shaped like an amphitheater.

Hraunfossar An underground river appears as if out of nowhere over a 1-km (0.6-mi) stretch on the outskirts of Reykjavík and cascades over a basalt escarpment into the Hvítá, a glacial river. Not far upstream from this "lava rock waterfall" is the equally intriguing Barnafoss ("Child's Waterfall"), the subject of an eerie Icelandic saga.

Goðafoss The Skjálfanda-fljót River, rising from the edge of the Vatnajökull Glacier, forms the "God's Waterfall" east of Akureyri on its way to the ocean. Its breadth and the volumes of water it drops are impressive.

Mývatn This lake was formed just a few thousand years ago when spring water was dammed by lava. It boasts a surface area of 37 sq km (14 sq mi), is very shallow, and has an unusual wealth of flora and fauna.

Herðubreið/Askja The region to the west of the Jökulsá á Fjöllum River is wild and spectacular but can really only be discovered in a four-wheel drive vehicle. The view of the fire mountains is breathtaking.

Reykjavík The sightseeing attractions in Iceland's small capital city are all close together: the National Gallery, the National Museum, the Árni Magnússon Institute (home to a number of historical manuscripts), the world's oldest parliament and a lively port.

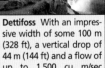

Dettifoss With an impressive width of some 100 m (328 ft), a vertical drop of 44 m (144 ft) and a flow of up to 1,500 cu m/sec (52,972 cu ft/sec), Dettifoss is by far Europe's mightiest waterfall.

Svartifoss Waterfall It may not be the tallest, but its sensational basalt columns make it one of the most unusual waterfalls in Iceland.

The Hekla Volcano Iceland's most famous volcano is 1,491 m (4,892 ft) high and easy to reach. Make a stop at the Leirubakki Information Center where you can learn some fascinating details about the mountain, considered a symbol of evil in the Middle Ages.

Strokkur The Geysir thermal region (after which all such springs are named) is impressive particularly because of the Strokkur Geyser, which shoots its stream of boiling water up to 25 m (82 ft) into the sky every 5 to 10 minutes.

The Skaftafell National Park This national park was founded in 1967, and encompasses parts of the Vatnajökull Glacier. With an area of 1,600 sq km (616 sq mi), it boasts marshes, fens, scree and sand landscapes and birch forests, all against the magnificent backdrop of the Vatnajökull Glacier, which has more ice than all of the alpine glaciers together.

The round Doonagore watchtower on the coast of County Clare.

Ireland

Out and about in the land of the Celts

Ireland is a natural phenomenon in itself. The sandy beaches, striking cliffs, moor landscapes, glistening lakes and green hills are the core of its attractions. But Ireland is much more than a natural history museum. It also possesses a rich folk tradition that is testimony to the island's vibrant spirit.

Ireland is both an island and a divided nation. The Republic of Ireland (Éire) makes up about four-fifths of the island, while the smaller Northern Ireland is still part of the United Kingdom. As different as they might be, both parts of the island have their very own appeal. The spectrum of landscapes is broad and the natural environment is largely pristine. The central lowlands are fringed by modest mountain ranges that rise to peaks of more than 1,000 m (3,281 ft) only in the south-west. Despite their relatively small size, however, many of these mountains rise quite strikingly out of the ocean. The Carrauntoohil (1,038 m/3,406 ft), for example, offers magnificent views of fjord-like bays on the west coast that even appear to change shape in the rapidly shifting light. Lighthouses there defy the relentless pounding of waves on desolate craggy peninsulas. On the flatter coastal sections the sandy beaches provide a contrast to the steep cliffs that surround them. Moorland and countless lakes disappear behind the buttes and green hills of the interior. Indeed, Ireland shows its calmer side on the east coast where the shore is less fragmented, the ocean more tranquil and the surf more placid.

In general, it is not without good reason that Ireland has earned epithets like such as "The Green Island" or the more ostentatious "Emerald Isle". Of course, the island does not possess any precious stone mines, but after one of the frequent rain showers, the green appears to take on a special luminosity in the sunlight.

The moors in the interior of the island are scattered with individual fields and meadows. According to a Gaelic saying, the grass in the Irish meadows

One of the many pubs in the little villages on the Dingle Peninsula.

A sensational view of the Cliffs of Moher, one of Ireland's most impressive scenic attractions.

Cutters waiting to put to sea in the port of Dingle on the peninsula of the same name.

grows so quickly that if you leave a stick lying in the grass you won't be able to find it again the next day. These fertile areas have been targeted by invaders and opportunists since the island's discovery. Word quickly reached mainland Europe of the cows in Ireland having enough food in their pastures the whole year round, making winter storage of fodder unnecessary. To be certain, agriculture remains the backbone of the Irish economy today, with statistics attributing one sheep to each one of the roughly 5.1 million inhabitants. Irish lore and music provide a window into the soul of the Irish people. The Irish harp, for example, is the national instrument, hence its appearance on all Irish Euro coins. It is also a very well-read society, in keeping with a long literary tradition. There are libraries and bookshops on almost every street corner. The renowned Trinity College Library in Dublin comprises some 2.8 million volumes and one of its greatest treasures is the 9th-century Book of Kells, one of the loveliest medieval Irish manuscripts. Ireland's cultural tradition is also characterized by a wealth of myths and sagas in which fairies and hobgoblins often play starring roles. Even today, the Giant's Causeway, a craggy portion of Ireland's north coast, is shrouded in legend. You can hear all about it over a pint of Guinness or an Irish whiskey in one of the cozy pubs.

Part of Ireland's special attraction also lies in its contrasts. While time appears to stand still in the more remote coastal regions, and the howling wind makes you wonder how those rustic, thatched-roof cottages can withstand the harsh elements, things in Dublin and Belfast are entirely different. There, visitors who are interested in getting a taste of the country's urban culture are certainly in for a treat as well.

In the south and west of Ireland, the coast is rocky and rugged and has many secluded bays.

Once around the island: The circular route takes you along wide roads following the coast, from Dublin clockwise around the whole of Ireland, including the counties of Northern Ireland. Fascinating landscapes, lively towns and historical buildings invite visitors to linger a while.

① **Dublin** (see page 17)

② **Powerscourt Estate Gardens** An impressive park with lovely Italian and Japanese gardens, areas of untouched nature and man-made lakes directly on the southern outskirts of Dublin. The ambiance here is further augmented by a castle-like country home, which was fully restored following a fire in 1974. From here, a side trip to the Powerscourt Waterfall is well worth it. The clearly signposted route leads you to Ireland's highest falls, where the Dargle River plunges 130 m (427 ft) over a granite cliff.

③ **Glendalough** About 30 km (19 mi) south of the waterfall, one of Ireland's most wonderfully situated monasteries has stood the test of time amidst the scenic surroundings of the "Valley of the Two Lakes". Known for his reclusive ways, St Kevin founded this isolated monastery in the 6th century. Despite his efforts, other pilgrims followed soon after and the complex grew. The focal

point of the former settlement is now the 33-m-high (108-ft) round tower, which is visible from a distance and was both a lookout post and a place of refuge. Most tourists limit their visit to the ruins on the lower lake, but those on the upper lake are no less interesting yet more peaceful to explore. From Glendalough there is a road leading west toward the heart of the Wicklow Mountains, which peak at 924 m (3,032 ft). There are scenic hiking trails leading to the mountain lakes of Lough Dan and Lough Bray. From the mountains you return to the coastal road, then continue southward to Enniscorthy, 50 km (31 mi) away.

④ **Jerpoint Abbey** At Enniscorthy, which features a towering fortress close to the island's southern tip, it is worth leaving the coastal road to take a side road westward into the interior. The Cistercian Jerpoint Abbey (12th century) on the shores of Little Arrigle is one of Ireland's best-preserved monastery ruins. The route then continues to the

north-west to what is perhaps the loveliest town of Ireland's interior, Kilkenny.

⑤ **Kilkenny** The 17,000 residents of Kilkenny enjoy life in a medieval jewel of a town with narrow alleyways, half-timbered stone houses and myriad historical buildings. The town's main landmark is the tower of St Mary's Cathedral (19th century),

which stands 65 m (213 ft) tall. Kilkenny Castle, a fortress built by the Normans, towers high above the River Nore and is one of the most famous in Ireland. The ostentatious Long Gallery has antique furniture and portraits of former lords of the

1 The gentle, rolling landscape reflected in the port at Ballycrovane in County Cork.

Travel Information

Route profile
Length: approx.
1,200 km (746 mi)
Time required: 2–3 weeks
Route (main locations):
Dublin, Kilkenny, Cashel, Cork, Killarney, Ring of Kerry, Limerick, Cliffs of Moher, Galway, Clifden, Westport, Ballina, Sligo, Donegal, Londonderry, Giant's Causeway, Belfast, Dublin

Traffic information:
The Irish drive on the left. Four-wheel-drive vehicles are required only in very remote areas.

Weather:
In keeping with the motto "The only guarantee with Irish weather is that it's constantly changing", you are

advised to take both warm and rain-proof clothing. The mild-Atlantic climate keeps winter temperatures from sinking below 5°C (40°F), while July and August have an average temperature of 16°C (60°F).

Accommodation:
There are myriad options for bed and breakfast establishments in Ireland. They are a popular form of accommodation and can be found just about everywhere, even in the most remote corners.

Information
Here are a few sites to help you prepare for your trip:
www.discoverireland.com
www.travelireland.org
www.travelinireland.com

Dublin

The capital of the Republic of Ireland is over 1,000 years old and has always been worth a visit, albeit more for its celebratory flair than for its artistic treasures.

The Vikings, who were the first to settle in what is now Dublin, called their settlement Dyfflin, which basically meant "black puddle". Sound like a bad omen? Well, it must be said that Dublin's long history has indeed been largely determined by outside influences, particularly those of the neighboring English, whose first "colony" was, you guessed it, Ireland. Dublin was selected as the repre-

sentative center of the Anglo-Irish administration, and yet, despite hundreds of years of rule, the city never fully gave in to British hegemony. Gaelic traditions of music, poetry, storytelling and debate have been ardently upheld in Ireland. It is no surprise, then, that the battle for Irish independence began in Dublin in 1916 with the Easter Uprising. And although today's vibrant, trendy Dublin is no longer Irish enough for some, it is still a very interesting city. The center of the metropolis on the Liffey boasts wide shopping streets. A ride on a double-decker bus is a good laugh – although best not in the rush hour. Among the other must-see attractions are: the Gothic Christ Church Cathedral; the Gothic St Patrick's Cathedral; the historical

Temple Bar nightlife area; Trinity College and lively university district; the National Gallery with a collection of Irish paintings; the National Museum of Irish cultural history; and the National Botanic Gardens with its 19th-century greenhouses.

Top: The library at Trinity College, Ireland's oldest university, founded in 1592.

Below: The O'Connell Bridge over the River Liffey in Dublin.

manor. Even the buildings in Kilkenny's main streets are not short on grandeur, and some of the pubs with their stained-glass windows seem to be in competition with the churches for attention. From Kilkenny the route continues westward to Cashel.

6 Cashel The Irish are well aware of the cultural importance of this town of just 2,500 residents. The theater and music events at the Brú Ború Heritage Center are renowned throughout the country. Most visitors to Ireland, however, are drawn to the Rock of Cashel, an imposing limestone cliff with the ruins of a fortress towering over the broad Tipperary plains. Starting in the 5th century, the fortress was the seat of the kings of Munster whose dominions extended for centuries over large areas of southern Ireland. At the end of the 11th century, the complex passed into the hands of the Catholic Church. It was later plundered by English troops under Oliver Cromwell in 1647 before being abandoned some 100 years later. In addition to the cathedral, its mighty walls also house the Cormac's Chapel, a true masterpiece of romanesque architecture, and the 28-m (92-ft) round tower. Another of Cashel's attractions is the Folk Village, an open-air museum that documents the region's history. From Cashel the route continues south-west toward Cork, which is about 60 km (37 mi) away.

7 Cork The Republic's second-largest city after Dublin has about 125,000 people and is noticeably more "continental" than the capital. It also boasts a range of architectural treasures dating from the 18th and 19th centuries. The old town is situated on an island between two channels of the River Lee. The narrow alleyways, quaint canals and bridges lined with townhouses are reminiscent of Dutch towns.
Cork's landmark is St Ann's Shandon, a church built in 1722. The weather vane in the shape of a salmon on the top of the tower is visible from afar and is a good orientation point. A climb up to the top of the tower is rewarded with great panoramic views.
From Cork it is worth taking a detour to the town of Midleton, just 20 km (12 mi) to the east, or to Ballycrovane in the direction of Killarney.

8 Jameson Heritage Center Midleton is known primarily as the site of the island's largest whiskey distillery. A number of famous whiskey brands, such as Jameson, Tullamore Dew and Hewitts, are distilled here. On the guided tour you'll learn a bit about the history and techniques of whiskey production.

9 Blarney Castle A second detour takes you along the bypass road north of Cork to Blarney Castle (15th century). Visitors from all over the world flock to the ruins of this castle

10 km (6 mi) north-west of Cork to not just see the legendary Blarney stone but also give it a kiss. According to the legend, anyone kissing the stone will be endowed with eloquence and the power of persuasion, the word "blarney" being a synonym for flattery.
With its many handicraft and souvenir shops, the village of Blarney is particularly tourist-oriented. The route back to the main road heading west, the N 22, follows some sections of the Lee River.

10 Killarney This town is a popular starting point for one wishing to explore south-west Ireland. You won't be able to overlook the many horse-drawn coaches plying the roads and inviting visitors to take a tour of the town. Killarney's sightseeing attractions include the National Museum of Irish Transport, with a collection of vintage cars, as well as a life-like model railway.
Most guests don't linger long in the town, though, for nearby awaits the spectacular landscape of Killarney National Park, which covers an area of about 100 sq km (39 sq mi) and features three scenic lakes: Upper Lake, Muckross Lake and Lough Leane, the largest of the three. The many small islands appear like dabs of green paint in the blue water, while the densely wooded hills rise gently from the shores. At a few locations, however, the mountains rise abruptly enough from the

lake's edge to create sizable falls. One of these is the Torc Waterfall, which drops 18 m (59 ft) into Muckross Lake, marking the end of the Owen-garriff River. A number of monasteries and fortress ruins dot the surrounding lake landscape as well, including Muckross Abbey (ca. 1448) and Ross Castle (ca. 1420).
Up until the mid-17th century, some of these buildings formed the last of the Irish bastions in their fight against the English under Oliver Cromwell.
From the lake district, a number of roads lead to the Macgillcuddy's Reeks, a mountain chain that includes the Carrauntoohil, a 1,041-m (3,416-ft) peak.

11 Ring of Kerry In addition to the scenery of the Iveragh Peninsula, there are a number of picturesque locations in County Kerry that are worth a stopover. In Sneem, near the south coast, for example, the colorful houses of this picturesque town make a charming impression.
Only a few miles farther to the west is a 3-km-long (2-mi) road leading from the main road up to Staigue Stone Fort, a Celtic fortification dating from the 3rd/4th centuries.
Caherdaniel beach, 3 km (2 mi) long, has a Mediterranean atmosphere, with scenic sand dunes and boats for hire. The Derrynane House, a feudal country home in the Derrynane National Historic Park, commemorates Daniel O'Connell,

an Irish national hero, for his efforts in liberating Catholics from oppressive British laws. After the road takes a turn to the north, a famous postcard scene awaits you behind the Coomakista Pass: a lonely row of houses on a cliff in Waterville that defies the strong winds blowing up from the ocean. From the main road, head westward to the fishing village of Portmagee where boats take you to the monastery island of Skellig Michael. The village is linked by a bridge to Valentia Island off the coast to the north. Accordion music emanating from the pubs is typical of the island's main town, Knight's Town.

Back on Iveragh you soon come to the main town on the peninsula, Cahersiveen, which has retained much of its charm despite the heavy tourism in the area. The village of Glenbeigh boasts the 5-km-long (3-mi) Rossbehy Beach, which seems to be neverending and proudly flies the sea-blue environmental flag indicating especially clean water. The Kerry Bog Museum nearby has an interesting exhibition on the history of the now defunct peat cultivation trade. The town of Killorglin to the north-east nicely rounds off your visit to the Ring of Kerry with a choice of more than twenty pubs.

🄬 **Dingle Peninsula** A drive around the 48-km-long (30-mi) Dingle Peninsula is equally stunning as the Ring of Kerry, and

you'll need to plan at least half a day for it. The alternating craggy cliffs and sandy bays are what make this coastal landscape particularly appealing. Coming from the south, you leave the main road at Castlemaine heading west. The sandy Inch Spit is a perfect beach for a swim. The main road continues past several old fortresses and monasteries. The tiny Gallarus Oratory stone church, with an unusual shape reminiscent of a capsized boat, is one of the best-preserved early churches in Ireland. The Blasket Islands, just off the coast, can be visited by ferry from Dingle Marina.

🄭 **Tralee** The main attractions in Tralee are the Kerry County Museum and the Blennerville Windmill, situated just outside of town and the largest still functioning windmill in Ireland. From Tralee the route heads north to Tarbet, where the road then follows the course of the Shannon River. On the way to Limerick it is worth making a stop in Glin and the Georgian Glin Castle, built in 1780.

🄮 **Limerick** Several bridges span the mighty Shannon River at Limerick. Although the town does not appear particularly inviting at first glance, it does have a number of sights worth seeing. The oldest structure in Limerick, which was founded by the Vikings in the 9th century, is the proud St Mary's Cathedral, built on a hill in 1172. No less imposing, King John's Castle,

from 1200, boasts five round towers and impressive ramparts. The Hunt Museum has antique relics from all over Ireland.

🄯 **Bunratty Castle und Folk Park** North-west of Limerick, Bunratty Castle is yet another must for any Ireland visitor's itinerary. The most famous lords of this manor, from the 15th century, were the O'Briens. The castle's rooms are magnificently appointed with antique furniture and tapestries, creating a very special atmosphere. Medieval-style banquets still take place here in the evenings. From the stout battlements to the dark dungeons, the castle complex provides a graphic portrayal of aristocratic life in Ireland. An entire medieval Irish farming village has also been reconstructed in front of the castle in the Folk Park.

Continuing north for a mile or so you will come to the 12th-century Augustine Clare Abbey shortly before reaching the town of Ennis. Ennis Abbey (13th/14th centuries) was once one of Ireland's largest and it features some high-quality medieval styling.

The small town is characterized by winding alleys and a lively music scene. Indeed, folk music seems to be everywhere here. From Ennis, the road continues south-west through the interior before reaching Kilrush, one of Ireland's largest yachting ports, just before the Shannon widens and flows into the ocean. From here you continue along the

west coast to one of the region's main attractions.

🄰 **Cliffs of Moher** The Cliffs of Moher are an absolutely breathtaking feat of nature. These vertical cliffs can be more than 200 m (656 ft) high and stretch over a length of 8 km (5 mi). The spectacular backdrop is accompanied by the cackle of countless sea birds. Visitors can venture up to the edge of the cliffs along the paths but the lack of protective barriers means that caution needs to be exercised.

🄱 **The Burren** In Lisdoonvarna the R 476 heads south-east toward Leamaneagh Castle (17th century).

You will pass through a unique landscape on the way north known as the Burren, whose name is derived from the Irish word for "great rock" (boire-ann). In the 17th century, this limestone plateau, with its many rifts and cleavages, was somewhat grimly described by

1 County Kerry in the south-west of Ireland is a paradise for botanists and ornithologists.

2 The Cliffs of Moher are among the many popular attractions in the west of Ireland. They extend over 8 km (5 mi) between Hags Head in the south and Aillensharragh in the north.

3 The town of Limerick is divided into three parts by the Shannon and Abbey Rivers.

one English military commander as follows: "No water for drowning, no trees for hanging, no soil for burying". Stone circles and other traces of settlement in this desolate region remain an enigma today.

The excavation of human remains, however, has proven that the Poulnabrone dolmen, a collection of large monoliths, served as a burial ground in around 2500 to 2000 BC. The Burren is also known for its caves. One of them, the Aillwee Cave, can be visited and is set back somewhat from the road. Bring a jacket as the temperature in the caves is only 10 °C (50 °F) all year round.

18 Galway With a population of about 66,000, Galway is the largest town in western Ireland. It is also a university town and is characterized not only by its cozy alleyways and stone buildings with wooden façades, but also for its pub and music scene. For car drivers the center of the town at Corrib is a nightmare, but for pedestrians it is a paradise. In fine weather, street cafés get busy and musicians and artists display their skills. The renovated suburbs along the river attest to a high standard of living, a result of the high-tech boom of recent years. The town's best-known buildings include the St Nicholas Church, built by the Normans in 1320, and the 1965 St Nicholas Cathedral, on the north bank of the river. From Galway, a good road heads east to Clonmacnoise Monastery, 65 km (40 mi) away.

19 Aran Islands The ferries to the craggy Aran Islands depart from Galway. The archipelago's main island, Inishmore, is a mountain bikers' paradise, but tours of the island are also offered via minibus or horse-drawn carriage. Recommended stops are the steep cliffs as well

as the monastery and fortress ruins like Dun Aengus. The *Men of Aran*, a silent film from the 1930s, portrays the fishermen doing what would appear even then to have been a tedious job.

20 Kylemore Abbey The landscape west of Galway is defined by coastline, mountains and stark moorlands, all protected in part by the Connemara National Park. The route from Galway towards the west and north-west closely follows the coast and features many bays as well as Clifden Castle. Kylemore Abbey is an enchanting 19th-century Benedictine abbey, idyllically situated on Kylemore Lough. Part of the present-day national park land actually used to belong to the abbey. En route to the north it is also worth taking a detour at Bangor to Blacksod Point.

21 Donegal Castle A mighty 15th-century fortress dominates the small town of Donegal. After several renovations, it now looks more like a castle, and the banqueting hall alone is worth the entrance fee. Preserved in the style of the Jacobean era, it boasts a fireplace dating from this time. You leave the coast road at Donegal and head across the northern tip of Ireland toward Londonderry.

22 Londonderry You reach the walled town of Londonderry shortly after crossing the border into Northern Ireland. The city is known as Londonderry to Protestants here, while

Catholics and residents of the Republic refer to it as Derry, a name derived from the Irish "Daire", meaning "oak grove". Houses in pastel hues mark the cityscape. The walls of Derry, up to 9 m (30 ft) wide in places, are some of the most intact town fortifications in all of Europe. The Tower Museum details the town's history and the Bloody Sunday Center tells of the Northern Ireland conflict.

23 Giant's Causeway The innumerable basalt stones of the Giant's Causeway are the undisputed highlight of the very scenic Antrim north coast. They are also shrouded in legend. One story tells of a giant who built a causeway so that his mistress, who lived on the Scottish island of Staffa, would be able to reach Ireland without getting her feet wet. No one knows the exact number of the many mostly hexagonal basalt columns, but some measure up to 25 m (82 ft) in height.

The route then continues along the north-east coast of the North Channel, past Dunluce Castle, heading to Belfast and then leaving Northern Ireland again south of Newry.

24 Belfast The Northern Irish capital has been the subject of

largely negative headlines in recent decades but they are quickly forgotten when you arrive in Belfast. The city is situated at the mouth of the Lagan River in a bay known as Belfast Lough. Belfast is the political, economic and cultural center of Northern Ireland. The lively seaport, with a population of 300,000, has everything that makes a vibrant town into a city – a wealth of shopping opportunities, myriad restaurants for all budgets, theaters and cinemas, and some architectural highlights.

25 Bend of the Boyne Before reaching Dublin, it is worth stopping in the Boyne Valley near Slane. The valley features neothlithic passage graves. The grave built near Newrange in 3200 BC remained untouched until 1960. It has a 19-m-long (62-ft) passage leading to the 6-m-high (20-ft) burial chamber with three side chambers.

1 Giant's Causeway: Some 35,000 hexagonal basalt columns rise out of this coastal formation to heights of up to 25 m (82 ft).

2 A prehistoric stone circle at Blacksod Point on the southern tip of the Mullet Peninsula.

Blacksod Point The Mullet Peninsula is connected to the north-west Irish mainland by a narrow, sparsely inhabited spit of land. On the west, it is a wide rocky plateau with pebble beaches. A granite lighthouse stands at the southernmost tip of the island.

Giant's Causeway The roughly 35,000 step-like basalt columns, most of which have a hexagonal shape and rise to heights of up to 25 m (82 ft), are the natural scenic highlight of Northern Ireland. Their origins are shrouded in legend but they are in fact a completely natural form of cooled, slow-flowing lava.

Dunluce Castle The well-preserved 13th-century castle ruins are located on a high cliff on the north coast of Antrim, only about 10 km (6 mi) west of the Giant's Causeway. As defiant as the former headquarters of the lofty MacDonnels and Lords of Antrim may appear today, the castle was in fact powerless in the face of the harsh coastal winds.

Connemara The area in the north-west of County Galway is a barren landscape of stone walls and moors where traditional rural culture has been well preserved. Its white beaches provide a stark contrast, and the Victorian resort town of Clifden is an ideal base from which to explore the area.

Bend of the Boyne Due to its ring-like fortifications, passage graves and cairns, this river valley in the Midlands near Dublin is considered to be the cradle of Irish civilization.

Belfast The numerous Victorian buildings here make the Northern Irish capital and the port at the mouth of the Lagan River well worth a visit. The Grand Opera House is a main attraction.

Clonmacnoise This especially attractive monastery on the Shannon was founded in the mid-6th century. It has been in ruins since its destruction by English soldiers in 1552.

Dublin Christ Church and St Patrick's cathedrals, as well as Dublin Castle, Trinity College, the National Gallery and the National Museum are all worth a visit in the Irish capital.

Cliffs of Moher The sandstone and shale cliffs, some of which are up to 200 m (656 ft) high, extend over 8 km (5 mi) from Hags Head to Ailllensharagh.

Rock of Cashel, County Tipperary On the lower reaches of the Shannon, this county is rich in farmland. St Patrick is alleged to have picked three-leaf clover on the Rock of Cashel.

Skellig Michael The monastery shelters on the island of Great Skellig are examples of Irish architecture. The 700 steps give an indication of how tough monastic life must have been.

County Kerry This southern Irish county is known for its prehistoric and early Christian sites as well as the panoramic Ring of Kerry. The decrees from Dublin were also willingly ignored here such that the county is also known as "The Kingdom".

County Cork The hinterland of this popular southern Irish resort region is full of lakes and hills. Cork's rocky coastline is very fragmented and richly endowed with islands, peninsulas, bays and idyllic seaports. The city of Cork – the second-largest in Ireland – is situated on an island in the River Lee. It is a typically Irish city with numerous steps, bright cottages, attractive pubs and even a vineyard!

The summit of Buchaille Etive Mor is a challenge for mountain climbers.

Scotland

Clansmen, whisky and the solitude of the Highlands

Whether you're a romantic, a lover of the outdoors or a culture connoisseur, Scotland's raw beauty rarely fails to move the souls of people who make the journey there. Those who choose to experience the rugged, often solitary landscape of the Highlands and the rich history and tradition of this country will be rewarded with unforgettable memories.

Jagged escarpments covered in a lush carpet of green grass, deep lakes in misty moorlands, and torrential rivers tumbling down craggy valleys often um up our image of the Highlands and Scotland in general. But there is more to Scotland than the Highlands in the north, notably the interesting groups of islands to the west and a couple of lovely cities.

'Clansmen' in Scottish with bag-pipes and in national costume.

Glasgow and the capital, Edinburgh, offer modern city living, with cultural events, attractive shopping possibilities and internationally renowned festivals, while idyllic sandy beaches await discovery, for example on the Western Isles. On the mainland, Scotland's first national parks were recently opened around the Cairngorm Mountains and Loch Lomond.

Poets such as Sir Walter Scott and the 'national poet of Scotland', Robert Burns, have written of this country's unique beauty. The modern revival of Gaelic music and language has long since spread beyond Scotland's borders, and customs like caber tossing and wearing kilts may seem peculiar to outsiders, but to the Scots they are part of their identity. If you take one

insider tip, make it this one: Scottish cooking. Once you have tried Angus steak, grouse or Highland lamb, you will no longer limit your praise of the country to single malt whisky. Having said that, there are about 110 whisky distilleries in Scotland, mainly spread around the Highlands and on the Western Isles. These world-famous single malt elixirs age for up to thirty years in old whisky and sherry barrels.

Scotland's territory covers a total area of 78,000 sq km (30,014 sq mi), roughly the top third of the island of Great Britain. Most of its many islands are part of either the Hebrides (Inner and Outer), the Orkneys or the Shetlands. During the last ice age, glaciers formed deep valleys throughout the

Eilean Donan Castle lies on Loch Duich in Glen Shiel and is linked to the mainland by a small dam and a bridge. The castle was rebuilt last century from its former ruins.

Kilchurn Castle on the northern edge of Loch Awe dates from the 15th century.

region. When they melted, they left behind lochs (lakes) and firths (fjords) along the country's 3,700 km (2,300 mi) of coastline.

Among the characteristics of the Highlands, the most sparsely populated area of Scotland, are steep rock faces, heath-covered moors, deep lochs and rushing mountain streams. The Great Glen valley divides the Highlands into two parts. To the south of the Highlands are the Lowlands, a fertile and densely populated area containing both Glasgow and Edinburgh. The Southern Uplands make up the border with England.

Despite what one might think, Scotland's oceanic climate rarely produces extreme weather conditions – but the weather really can change from sun to rain in a hurry. Wide areas of Scotland are renowned for their characteristic flora (heather, pine trees, ferns) and a wide variety of wildlife.

The Scots are the descendants of a mix of different peoples including the Picts, the Scots, who gave their name to the country, as well as the Scandinavians and the Anglo-Saxons. It was in the 9th century, under Kenneth MacAlpine, that Alba was founded, the first Celtic Scottish kingdom. From then on Scotland's history was beset with struggles for independence and resistance against the ever-mightier forces of England. In 1707, the 'Acts of Union' created the Kingdom of Great Britain and with that came the end of Scotland's independence. Things unfortunately went from bad to worse after that. The characteristic solitude of the Scottish landscape was a direct result of the Highland Clearances, a move by the Scottish clan chiefs and aristocratic land owners in the 18th century to run small Highland and island farmers off their plots in order to make room for more lucrative sheep breeding. As a result, many people emigrated.

After 300 years, Scotland now has its own parliament again, in Edinburgh, and some 5.1 million people. Although the official language is English, many Scots in the Highlands and on the Hebrides speak Scottish Gaelic, a Celtic language.

Tobemory with its colourful houses lies on the northern end of the Isle of Mull.

A journey through Scotland: venerable buildings, mysterious stone circles and the occasional whisky distillery line your route, which begins in Edinburgh, takes you through the Highlands and ends in Glasgow. Detours to the Hebrides are highly recommended and can be easily organized from the various port towns.

1 Edinburgh (see page 25). Your route begins in the cultural metropolis of Edinburgh, travelling initially north-westward towards Stirling.

2 Stirling The charming city of Stirling, roughly 58 km (36 miles) west of Edinburgh, is built on the banks of the Forth at the point where it first becomes part of the tidal firth (fjord). It is often called the 'Gateway to the Highlands' and is dominated by a large castle. The oldest part of Stirling Castle dates back to the 14th century. The Church of the Holy Rood (cross), which was built in the 13th century, is historically significant in that it is one of the very few churches from the Middle Ages to have survived the Reformation in Scotland.

3 Fife Peninsula The Fife Peninsula juts out between the Firth of Forth and the Firth of Tay. In the 4th century the region here made up one of the seven Scottish kingdoms.
The northern coast of the Firth of Forth leads to Culross, a

small town that blossomed as a trading center in the 16th century. Wealthy trade houses nd historic buildings have remained intact and make for an enchanting atmosphere here.
About 11 km (7 mi) to the east of Culross you'll come to Dunfermline, once a longstanding residence or 'burgh' of the Scottish kings. The ruins of the old castle, abbey and monastery can still be seen atop a hill to the south-west of the town. A little further east, between the coastal towns of Elie and Crail and behind the Chapel Ness headland, is a series of picturesque fishing villages, castle ruins and old churches.

4 St Andrews Continuing on around the north-east side of the peninsula you will come to the proverbial golfing mecca of the world, St Andrews, about 10 km (6 miles) north of Crail. This, the first ever golf club, was founded here in 1754, and it is still possible to play on the famous Old Course. The 16th-century ruins of the Blackfriars Chapel, at one time Scotland's

1 View from the Nelson Monument of the Old Town and castle in Edinburgh.

2 Glamis Castle was the childhood home of the late Queen Mother.

Travel Information

Route profile
Length: approx. 1,200 km (745 miles), excluding detours
Time required: 2–3 weeks
Start: Edinburgh
End: Glasgow
Route (main locations): Edinburgh, Stirling, Dundee, Dunottar Castle, Ballater, Inverness, John o'Groats, Durness, Fort William, Inveraray, Glasgow

Traffic information:
Drive on the left in Scotland. Ferries connect the mainland with the various islands:
www.northlink-ferries.co.uk
www.scottish-islands.com

Weather:
The weather in Scotland is generally 'unsettled':

summers are relatively cool, winters on the coast are mild, but in the Highlands bitterly cold, and it can rain at any given moment.

When to go:
Between April and October is the best time. You can check weather forecasts at:
www.onlineweather.com

Accommodation:
An interesting option is a private bed & breakfast:
www.bedandbreakfast scotland.co.uk
www.aboutscotland.com

Information:
wikitravel.org/en/ Scotland
www.visitscotland.com
www.scotland.org.uk

Edinburgh

Both the Old Town and New Town of Scotland's capital have been listed as UNESCO World Heritage Sites, and both are a fascinating display of architectural unity and its exceptional cultural activity. Summer is especially lively during the renowned Edinburgh Festival weeks. The city has been the cultural center of the north since the 18th and 19th centuries, with famous authors such as Robert Burns and Sir Walter Scott making it their home.

The oldest core of the city, inhabited since the Bronze Age, is Castle Rock, a volcanic outcrop upon which King Edwin built the first castle in the 7th century – hence the name Edinburgh. The castle is still the city's eye-catcher but other higher buildings from the 17th century rise up around it like battlements.

The attractions most worthy of a visit in the Old Town include Edinburgh Castle, a large edifice with buildings from numerous eras, of which St Margaret's Chapel (11th century) is the oldest; the Scottish royal insignia in the castle's Crown Room; the Palace of Holyroodhouse, the Queen's official residence in Scotland; and the Royal Mile between her residence and the castle with its many side streets, pubs and eateries.

The New Town, built at the end of the 18th century, is home to the National Gallery of Scotland with one of Europe's most important collections of paintings, the Museum of Antiques for early and art history, and the Scottish National Gallery of Modern Art (20th-century art), all of which are worth a visit.

Edinburgh Castle has served as a fort, a royal residence and a prison in the course of centuries. It dominates the skyline of the city of Edinburgh from its position atop the volcanic Castle Rock.

The Whisky Trail

The famous 110-km-long (68-mile) Speyside Malt Whisky Trail, which sets off from Tomintoul, is a well-signposted route leading visitors past seven whisky distilleries. Among them are some very well-known names such as Glenlivet, Glenfiddich and Glenfarclas.

largest church, are also worth a visit if golf isn't your cup of tea. There is a fabulous view of the grounds from the top of St Rule's Tower.

The route now follows the coast through Dundee to Montrose, about 12 km (8 miles) north of Arbroath. A worthy detour here takes you to Blair Castle, roughly 65 km (40 miles) inland from Arbroath.

5 Montrose This port town and 'burgh' is built like a defensive wall on the peninsula of a natural bay. The House of Dun Mansion, built in 1730, stands on the bank of the Montrose Basin. The coastline north and south of Montrose impresses with long sandy beaches and steep cliffs.

6 Dunnottar Castle Following the A92 to the north you'll reach one of Scotland's most fascinating ruins just a few kilometers before Stonehaven – Dunnottar Castle. Built on a rock more than 50 m (60 yds) out to sea, the fortress is connected to the mainland only by a narrow spit of land.

In the 17th century, the Scottish imperial insignia were stored here. Nowadays, only the ruins of the turret, a barrack and the chapel remain of the once formidable construction.

7 Aberdeen This town is the capital of Europe's oil industry and one of the largest European ports. Despite its industrial leanings, however, there are a number of historic highlights to visit, including Kings College, the Maritime Museum, St Andrew's Cathedral and St Machar's Cathedral.

From Aberdeen the route leads inland to Ballater. Here a detour to Balmoral Castle, about 50 km (31 miles) away, is recommended. The mountain road (A939) then goes from Ballater through Colnabaichin to Tomintoul, the starting point of the whisky trail, before heading to Dufftown and Keith.

You then go west through the Spey Valley to Aviemore where the A9 takes you to Inverness.

8 Inverness This modern-day industrial center at the northern tip of Loch Ness is the ideal starting point for trips to the home of 'Nessie', Urquhart Castle and into the wild and romantic Highland landscape. Due to its exposed location, Inverness was often involved in military disputes, to the extent that few of its old buildings remain standing today. Most of the present structures were erected in the 19th century.

9 East Coast of the Northwest Highlands From Inverness the A9 (and the A99) snake northward along the striking east coast. Various sites like

3

Dunrobin Castle, Helmsdale Castle or the mysterious Bronze-Age rock lines near Greg Cairns are worth short visits on your way. One option is to take a long walk from the former fishing village of Wick out to the picturesque cliffs of Noss Head. Near-by are the ruins of Sinclair and Girnigoe Castles.

⑩ John o'Groats The village of John o'Groats is about 17 km (11 miles) north of Wick on the north-eastern tip of Caithness. Just before you get there, Warth Hill will offer an excep-

tional view of the area. Ferries travel between John o'Groats, the Orkneys and the coastal seal colonies.

⑪ North Coast The A836 then takes you from John o'Groats along the north coast towards Bettyhill past deserted beaches that are often only accessible by short footpaths. Dunnet Head is the most northern point of the Scottish mainland. The popular holiday resort of Thurso, which is also the ferry port for travel to the Orkney Islands, was the scene

of a memorable battle between the Scots and the Vikings in 1040. To the west of the village of Bettyhill in the county of Sutherland, the A836 leads over the impressive Kyle of Tongue Fjord and on to Durness. Shortly before Durness you'll find the Cave of Smoo, which was used as shelter first by the Picts, then the Vikings, and later still by Scottish smugglers.

Organized trips to Cape Wrath, the rocky outcrop on the north-westernmost point of Scotland, with a lighthouse and a café, are offered from Durness.

⑫ North-west Coast up to Ullapool The wild north-west portion of Sutherland is not your typical holiday destination. Its steep mountains and fjords, deep blue lakes and glistening waterfalls are too secluded for the average traveller. The impassable valleys and deserted coastlines have thus become a paradise for hikers, hunters and fishermen. Naturalists can observe seabirds, dolphins and seals and sometimes even whales from these remote environs. Innumerable small alcoves are perfect for a relaxing break. A narrow road, the A838, then leads from Durness towards the south-west. Just before Scourie you can take the A894, which branches off towards Handa Island, a seabird sanctuary with imposing cliffs where puffins and guillemots nest.

From Kylesku, which is further south, you can take boat trips to seal colonies and to Great Britain's highest waterfall along Loch Glencoul (200 m/ 656 ft). If you want to follow the tiny roads along the coast, turn off after Kylesku on to the B869. Otherwise follow the wider roads, A837 and A835, south to Ullapool. This beautiful stretch passes Loch Assynt and the ruins of Ardvreck Castle.

If you are interested, you can take the ferries that travel from Ullapool on Loch Broom to Lewis in the Outer Hebrides,

1 The once strategic position of Dunnottar Castle is unmistakable: built on a solid rock promontory, a deep ravine separates the castle from the mainland.

2 View from the port over Aberdeen.

3 Mighty waves from the Atlantic crash against the cliffs of Cape Wrath on the north coast of Scotland. The lighthouse was built in the year 1828.

1

The Outer Hebrides

The Atlantic islands to the west of Scotland are made up of the southern Inner Hebrides, near the Scottish mainland, and the Outer Hebrides (Western Isles) farther out toward the north-west. The main islands of the Outer Hebrides are, from north to south, the double islands of Lewis and Harris, North Uist and South Uist, joined by a dam, and Barra. You can reach the Western Isles by ferry from Ullapool or from Skye, the largest of the Inner Hebrides islands, which also include Rum, Coll, Tiree, Mull, Jura and Islay.

The Hebrides have a long and varied past. In 563 the Irish minister Columban the Elder (who later became St Columba) established a Celtic monastery on the small island of Iona and began the process of Christianizing Scotland. In the 8th century the islands were invaded by the Norwegian Vikings, who kept their rule over much of the region for many hundreds of years. It was only in 1266, after the signing of the Treaty of Perth, that the Scots regained the upper hand and the islands were henceforth run by the clans MacDougall and MacDonald. Their rulers were thereafter called 'Lord of the Isles'.

Today's visitors are met by a world in which life is still greatly influenced by natural forces and the isolation of the Atlantic. History and time have left some clear traces in the partly undulating moor and heath landscape. In geological terms the islands consist of the oldest rocks in the entire British

Isles. Stone-Age graves, Celtic Christian ruins, Viking settlements and Scottish forts can all be found around the various Hebrides islands.

In addition to the historical attractions, the stunning natural environment includes lakes and valleys, pristine white sand beaches, and rich animal and plant life that all help to attract a good number of adventurous tourists each year.

The Isle of Lewis and Harris

The two halves of the island of Lewis and Harris are connected by an isthmus and are not just the largest of the Western Isles, but the largest island around Great Britain after Ireland. Lewis and Harris have very different landscapes: Lewis is littered with rocky hill ranges, fjords and bays, while Harris is covered with moors and heath. The A859 leads from the main town of Stornoway to south Harris, which is noteworthy for its fabulous sandy beaches. Don't miss the mysterious stone circles of Callanish on Lewis, which, like Stonehenge, were built thousands of years ago, presumably for cult rituals.

North Uist und South Uist

North and South Uist, and the island of Benbecula between them, are covered with countless lakes. Deep ocean bays line the east coast to such an extent that it resembles a series of islands that have grown together.

The Stone-Age burial chambers on North Uist and the low, reed-covered crofters' houses, some of which have

2

3

survived hundreds of years of wind and weather, are worth visiting.

The A865 leads all the way around North Uist and down to the southern tip of South Uist, conveniently passing the prettiest areas of the island on the way. The east coast of South Uist has two 600-m (2,000-ft) peaks – Beinn Mhór and Hecla.

Barra

Ferries from Ludag on South Uist to the small island of Barra, the most southerly island of the Outer Hebrides, only take about 40 minutes. Barra's small neighbouring islands include Berneray with it tall lighthouse.

The island, named after St Finbarr, is regarded as one of the prettiest islands of the Outer Hebrides due to the thousands of colourful flowers that grow there. Kisimuil Castle, the old residence of the MacNeils, dominates the port of the main town,

Castlebay. The ring road, the A888, goes as far as Cille Barra in the north, with ruins of a monastery built in the 12th century. A 12th-century chapel has been restored and houses some sacred objects. On the hill is a cemetery.

1 Isle of Lewis: the monumental 'Standing Stones of Callanish' form a 13 m by 11 m (40 ft by 35 ft) circle and were erected around 1800 BC.

2 The Taransay Sound separates the island of Taransay from the south-west coast of Harris. This island of beautiful beaches and dunes is uninhabited.

3 Lovers of treeless, wild landscapes will be contented on the Isle of Lewis in the north of the Outer Hebrides.

If you are short on time, travel directly from Eilean Donan Castle eastward on the A87 and then turn south onto the A82 at Invergarry to reach Fort William.

⑮ **Ben Nevis** The highest mountain on the British Isles, at 1,344 m (4,409 ft), rises magnificently from the Grampian Mountains above Fort William. While the north-western face of the mountain is relatively easy to hike, the 460-m-high (1,509-ft) north-eastern rock face is reserved for experienced climbers. Before travelling on to Glencoe, take the A828 15 km (9 miles) to Castle Stalker near Portnacroish.

⑯ **Loch Rannoch** Fort William is the starting point for a small detour by train into the otherwise intractable Rannoch Moor. Rannoch Station, a tiny house in the wide landscape of the moor, is one of the most isolated stations in Great Britain. Small ponds and trout-rich streams cross the boulder-scattered moor and marshland. To the east of the moor lies the impressively calm Loch Rannoch.

⑰ **Glencoe** The Glencoe Valley begins roughly 16 km (10 miles) to the south of Fort William and is one of Scotland's must-see destinations. After the Jacobite Risings of the 17th century, the English tried to take control over Scotland by exploiting clan rivalries and dis-

putes. So it was that in 1692, soldiers led by the Clan Campbell of Glencoe and loyal to the new king, William of Orange, massacred the opposing Clan MacDonald almost in its entirety. Women and children were apparently left to perish in the elements. An impressive monument marks this gruesome event.

Following the A82 you will soon cross the A85 at Tyndrum. If you are planning a trip to the Isle of Mull, follow the A85 west to Oban, a port on the Firth of Lorne. Ferries sail from here to Mull and the other islands of the Inner Hebrides.

⑱ **Kilchurn Castle** If you turn east from the A82 onto the A85, you will reach the northern tip of Loch Awe where you will find the ruins of the 15th-century Kilchurn Castle. The ruins were hit by lightning in the 18th century and completely abandoned. One of the turrets still lies upside down in the courtyard. Restored steamboats navigate Loch Awe, the longest freshwater loch in Scotland.

1 Eilean Donan Castle, a Jacobite stronghold, was destroyed in 1719 by the English.

2 View from Loch Eil to the east with Ben Nevis.

3 Mountain stream in the snow-covered Highlands near Glencoe.

and the steamers that travel to the nearby Summer Isles.

After Ullapool, stay on the A835 until shortly after Corrieshalloch Gorge (61 m/200 ft), a spectacular ravine with waterfall and a fine example of a box canyon, where you will turn onto the A832.

⑬ **Inverewe Gardens** After Little Loch Broom and Gruinard Bay you come to Loch Ewe and the Inverewe Gardens. These gardens were planted in 1862 and exhibit a wonderful collection of rhododendron and hibiscus bushes. Next you will come to Kinlochewe, in the Torridon Mountains, where the road to Shieldaig on the coast follows the Liathach Ridge out to a seabird sanctuary. Thrill seekers can then follow the tiny coastal road south from Shieldaig.

⑭ **Eilean Donan Castle** A bit further along the A87 is Eilean Donan Castle, a picturesque natural stone castle rising up from St Donan Island in Loch Duich. This edifice, which was badly damaged by the Jacobite Wars, was only rebuilt at the start of the 19th century.

Around 5 km (3 miles) from the castle, the A890 feeds into the A87, which leads to Kyle of Lochalsh. A toll bridge from there takes you over to the Isle of Skye. From Ardvasar in the south-west of Skye there is a ferry back to Mallaig on the mainland. Take the 'Road to the Isles' (A830) 40 km (25 miles) to the east to reach Fort William.

19 Inveraray The town of Inveraray, 15 km (9 miles) south of Loch Awe, was constructed alongside Loch Fyne according to plans drawn up in the 18th century by the Duke of Argyll. He had his castle built in artistically arranged gardens. A prison museum in the old Inveraray Jail is also worth a visit. You can appear in court there, and even be locked up.

20 Loch Lomond The A83 leads further east to the holiday resort of Loch Lomond, Scotland's largest loch in surface area. The area is well loved by hikers, water-sports enthusiasts and families looking to take a steamboat trip to the islands.

In 2002, Loch Lomond and the Trossachs National Park was opened to the east of the lake. It is the fourth largest in Britain.

21 Glasgow For culture fans this city is one of Europe's hot destinations. Renowned museums and galleries as well as countless cultural programs vie for your attention. The million-strong city on the Clyde River is also an important industrial center. To get an overview of Glasgow's various highlights and attractions, take a double-decker bus tour. Only a few of the buildings in Scotland's largest city date back to before the 18th century. Among them are the Gothic St Mungo's Cathedral and the classical Pollok House. The Hunterian Museum (with works by the Scottish artists Charles Rennie Mackintosh, for example), the Burrell Collection (art and craft-work from all periods) and the Gallery of Modern Art with permanent and temporary exhibitions are all well worth a visit. A little way out of town is the New Lanark textile mill from the 18th century, which was recently listed as a UNESCO World Heritage Site – one of four in Scotland. This interesting museum town provides insight into factory life at the start of the 19th century.

1 Kilchurn Castle in the shadow of the 1,125-m-high (3,691-ft) Ben Cruachan.

2 The inaccessible Rannoch Moor is Britain's largest uninterrupted moor. The landscape is made up of wild streams, crippled trees and thousands of boulders carried here by a glacier.

3 View over the industrial city and port of Glasgow.

The Isle of Skye The largest of the Inner Hebrides islands is a craggy refuge for all kinds of animals: otters, sheep, cattle and seals all find their home here.

The Hebrides Islands Most of the islands off the west coast of Scotland in the Atlantic are raw, isolated and covered with ancient flora and fauna. Because of the great distances between them, the Outer Hebrides are vastly different from the Inner Hebrides in this respect. The Hebrides are also the home to most of Scotland's native Gaelic-speaking population.

The Orkney Islands Only eighteen of the seventy islands off Scotland's north-eastern coast are actually inhabited, despite the fact that the Gulf Stream blesses them with an exceptionally mild climate, which helps farming, fishing and tourism. The island of Mainland is interesting due to its many prehistoric finds, including the Stone-Age grave Maes Howe.

Eilean Donan Castle This formidable castle sits on the island of St Donan in Loch Duich. It was destroyed in 1719 and reopened in 1932.

Dunrobin Castle The earls and dukes of Sutherland were among the most powerful landowners in Europe when they built 'Scotland's Neuschwanstein' in the middle of the 19th century. Many of the 150 rooms can be visited.

Dufftown This town, referred to historically as early as AD 566, is home to several well-known whisky makers including the Glenfiddich Distillery.

Stalker Castle This 15th-century castle stands alone on a small island in Loch Laich. Due to its situation, it was well-protected from attacks.

Dunottar Castle This castle from the 14th century was home of the Scottish insignia in the 17th century. Although thought of as impenetrable due to its prime location, today it lies in ruins.

Glencoe An important event in Scottish history took place here in the Glencoe Valley: in 1692 faithfuls to the new king, William of Orange, massacred the Clan MacDonald. The North Lorn Folk Museum provides more information.

Rannoch The large (130 sq km/50 sq mi) and nearly impassable Rannoch Moor is home to Rannoch Station, one of Britain's most isolated train stations. East of the moors is the tranquil Loch Rannoch.

Edinburgh Scotland's capital captivates visitors with its architectural consistency and cultural diversity. Edinburgh Castle (11th century), the royal residence of Holyrood Palace and the lanes around the Royal Mile are but three of the highlights of this incredible city.

St Andrews This town in the region of Fife is the home of golf, and it was here that the first golf club was founded in 1754. Its course is still playable. The view here is from St Rule's Tower in the church ruins of Blackfriars Chapel, once Scotland's largest religious building. St Andrews on the North Sea is also home to Scotland's oldest university, founded in 1410.

The most famous prehistoric structure in Europe – Stonehenge, erected around 3000 BC.

England

Magical locations in southern Britain

Ancient trading routes crisscross the south of England, and monumental stone circles bear witness to prehistoric settlements in the region. The Celts, the Romans, the Anglo-Saxons and the Normans came after the original inhabitants of the island and eventually transformed the magnificent natural environment here into a diverse cultural macrocosm with monuments, cathedrals, quaint fishing villages, parks and country houses.

Generally, the 'South of England' refers to the region along the south coast, extending northwards to Bristol in the west and London in the east. For some, however, the south only includes the coastal counties south of London – East and West Sussex, Hampshire and Dorset. Others think of just the south-east including London,

Bodiam Castle near Hastings.

while others of the south-west with Cornwall and Devon.

In some references, the south even reaches up to the middle of England. Some areas, like Greater London (with around eight million inhabitants) are densely populated, whereas others like Dartmoor in Devon appear at first glance to be deserted. In the end, the South of England is unspecific, but Britons look at it as an area 'steeped in history' and known for its contrasts: picturesque cliffs and small sailing villages, busy seaside resorts and modern port towns, green pastures and barren moorland.

Indeed, the bustling metropolis of London dominates the south-east, while the more relaxed south-west has a real holiday feel to it. The area has

always attracted writers and artists: Shakespeare, Jane Austen, Turner and Constable all lived here, or at least gave the south a recognizable face in their various works. Numerous nature reserves and magical, manicured gardens invite you to take peaceful walks.

Geologically speaking, the British Isles 'separated' from the continent roughly 700,000 years ago. At the time, there had been a land bridge connecting what is now England to the mainland, with a river running through (now the English Channel). The water trapped in the ice at the end of the ice age about 10,000 years ago was then released, causing sea levels to rise and gradually wash away the land bridge. The characteristic white lime-

The natural arch of Durdle Door on the Jurassic Coast of Dorset is the result of erosion by the pounding sea.

The western façade of Wells Cathedral is decorated with countless sculptures from the medieval period.

stone cliffs that we now see in places along the south coast like Dover and Eastbourne are the result of this 'river' flooding through the weakest point in the now divided land masses. The West Country consists mostly of granite, whereas the limestone is typical of the south-east. At the narrowest point in the channel, the Dover Strait, the distance between the United Kingdom and the European continent is only around 32 km (20 miles).

Demographically, countless generations have created a rich landscape in Britain. Due to the geographical proximity to the continent, the south has always been the arrival point for immigrants, invaders and traders. In about 3500 BC, farmers and livestock breeders migrated to the island. The fortuitously warm Gulf Stream provided them and their modern-day descendants with a relatively mild climate and even some subtropical vegetation. Natural resources like tin and copper also attracted invaders to the south over the centuries.

England has not been successfully subdued by an enemy power since 1066, when the Normans under William the Conqueror emerged victorious at the Battle of Hastings. The vulnerability of the south coast is revealed by countless castles and fortresses, and also by installations from World War II. The varied history of settlements also features in the endless stories and myths that originate here. King Arthur and his Knights of the Round Table are among the prominent characters in these tales.

Castles, cathedrals and grand old universities testify to the historical importance of the south while small fishing villages on the coast have developed into significant port towns and naval bases that enabled the British Empire's rise to maritime dominance. In return there arrived from faraway places exotic goods and even peoples, changing yet again the cultural fabric of the traditional island inhabitants.

'High society' discovered the south coast in the 19th century, and from then on vacationed in fashionable resort towns like Brighton and Eastbourne. Today the coastal economy relies primarily on the service industries and on tourism.

Tower Bridge is a masterpiece of Victorian engineering completed in 1894.

This dream route through the South of England begins in London and heads down to the coast, which it then follows west until bending northwards at Land's End back towards Oxford and eventually back to the capital, London. Along the way you will experience everything from fashionable seaside resorts and Roman ruins to awe-inspiring cathedrals, desolate moors and craggy cliffs.

1 London (see pp. 36–37 for a detailed description of the sights and sounds that await you in England's capital).

2 Hastings Around 40 km (25 miles) south of London (A21) lies possibly one of the most important battlefields in the long, distinguished and bloody history of the British Isles: Hastings, scene of the legendary battle in 1066 between Duke William of Normandy and the Saxon army under King Harold of England. The outcome of the Battle of Hastings was the coronation of the victorious Duke of Normandy as the third king of England in Westminster. The first building he commissioned was the Battle Abbey on the site of the historic struggle. Nearby Bodiam Castle is also worthy of a visit. Purportedly intended as a fortress to protect against French attacks during the Hundred Years War, it has come to light that it was actually all show, a purpose it fits well: the castle is guarded by eight mighty towers and is

artistically placed in the middle of a spring-fed moat.

3 Eastbourne and the Seven Sisters The traditional seaside resort of Eastbourne, 17 km (11 miles) west of Hastings, is noteworthy for its wonderful sandy beaches and Victorian architecture. Just beyond Eastbourne is the fascinating Seven Sisters Country Park, named after seven bright limestone cliffs on the coast. A short walk leads to the South Downs Way, which meanders along the shore and over the remarkable limestone landscape.

From Beachy Head, the highest limestone cliff in Britain at 163 m (535 ft), you get a breathtaking view over the English Channel and the 100-year-old lighthouse out in the sea. The postcard panorama of the Seven Sisters, however, is only visible from the next cliff along, South Hill.

4 Portsmouth and the Isle of Wight The narrow coastal

Travel Information

Route profile
Length: approx. 1,200 km (746 miles), excluding detours
Time required: 2–3 weeks
Start and end: London
Route (main locations): London, Hastings, Brighton, Portsmouth, Salisbury, Weymouth, Exeter, Torquay, St Austell, Land's End, Barnstaple, Bridgwater, Bath, Stratford-upon-Avon, Oxford, Windsor, London

Traffic information:
Drive on the left in Great Britain. The green insurance card is necessary.
Info: *www.theaa.com*

When to go:
Thanks to the Gulf Stream, the weather in southern

Britain is better than reputed with warm summers and mild winters. Recommended travel season: April to October. Further information available at:
www.onlineweather.com

Accommodation:
As well as hotels and guesthouses, bed-and-breakfast accommodation (B&B) is in private houses recommended. Useful information:
www.bedandbreakfast nationwide.com
www.accommodation britain.co.uk

Information:
British Tourist Office
www.visitbritain.com
London sights and travel
www. visitlondon.com

road now travels past the elegant seaside resort of Brighton toward Portsmouth, an old port and trading port that is home to the Royal Navy. Some of the attractions here include Lord Nelson's flagship from the Battle of Trafalgar (the most significant naval victory of the Napoleonic Wars), the Sea Life Center and the house where Charles Dickens was born.

Ferries sail from Portsmouth to the Isle of Wight, the smallest county in England at 381 sq km (146 sq mi), once inhabited by the Romans. The island benefits from a varied landscape thanks to the warm Gulf Stream, which gives it a mild climate and allows colourful subtropical plants to blossom here between palm trees.

Off the west coast are three limestone formations – The Needles. At the base of the last rock outcrop, a lighthouse defies the constant pounding of the waves.

Back on the mainland, we continue inland to Winchester, which was the capital of Eng-land until 1066, and then on to the town of Salisbury. About 16 km (10 miles) to the north of the town lies Stonehenge.

5 **Stonehenge** It should come as no surprise that the most famous prehistoric site on the British Isles has been listed as a UNESCO World Heritage Site. Stonehenge is believed to have been erected in four stages between 3100 BC and 1500 BC by successors of the Bell-Beaker culture. The incredible 'engineering' and building capacity of these Stone-Age peoples inspires awe to this day: they transported eighty-two gigantic building blocks from the Welsh mountains, nearly 160 km (100 miles) away, presumably using rivers and rollers of some sort, all the way to Stonehenge. Later, at the start of the Bronze Age, these blue stones were replaced by even larger sandstone blocks measuring 7 m (23 ft) high.

Indeed, the site was modified a number of times. Today two concentric stone circles make up the middle section. The outer circle, with a total diameter of about 30 m (98 ft), is made up of seventeen trilithons and two vertical monoliths with a horizontal stone.

The inner circle is made up exclusively of monoliths. It is a point of debate as to whether the site was used as a place of worship, an observatory or for monitoring the sun's behaviour. On the day of the summer solstice, the sun rises exactly over the Heel Stone, following the axis of the entrance, and throws its light through a stone window. Stonehenge has been a magical place for thousands of years. Celtic druids also used the site for their rites.

6 **Shaftesbury** About 20 km (12.5 miles) to the west of Salisbury, one of Britain's rare medieval hill towns continues to enchant visitors. Time seems to have stood still in Shaftesbury: ancient town walls and Gold Hill are reminiscent of a long forgotten time. The steep, cobbled lanes are lined with small, sometimes thatched houses and were at one time part of the pilgrimage route to the grave of Edward the Martyr, whose bones are now kept in Westminster Abbey in London. In the Middle Ages there was a prosperous Benedictine monastary here, but it was disbanded in 1539 and for the most part demolished.

The oft-photographed Gold Hill is classified today as Britain's prettiest street. From the top of the hill you get a view over green, undulating pastureland that is interrupted only by lush, dark-green hedges.

The A350 then leads south, back to the coast, past Blandford and on to the coastal town of Swanage on the lovely Purbeck Peninsula.

1 The white lighthouse of Godrevy, which sits atop an isolated rock, is not far from Gwithian in Cornwall. The lighthouse inspired Virginia Woolf's famous novel *To the Lighthouse*.

2 One of England's most recognizable medieval streets: Gold Hill in Shaftesbury.

3 The limestone cliffs of the Seven Sisters between Seaford and Eastbourne are visible from far away.

4 The Needles and lighthouse west of the Isle of Wight.

5 The yacht port of Torquay on the 'English Riviera' in Devon.

London

England's capital, London, is the seat of the British government and an international financial center of massive proportions, but above all it is a cosmopolitan city in the truest sense of the word. For a few centuries, London was the heart of the British Empire, and this is still very much perceptible in its dynamic atmosphere. Due to numerous restrictions for cars in the city center, use of the excellent public transport network or a tour on a red sightseeing double-decker bus is recommended.

The western part of central London is typified by diversity – the administrative center of Whitehall in the historic district of Westminster; posh residential and business districts like Knightsbridge and Belgravia; busy squares like Piccadilly Circus and Trafalgar Square; and the fabulous parks like St James's and the Kensington Gardens. Starting with the district of Westminster, here is a handful of things to see, the first two being UNESCO World Heritage Sites: Westminster Abbey, the mighty Gothic church where English kings are crowned and buried (not to be confused with nearby Westminster Cathedral, a Catholic church from the 19th century), and the neo-Gothic Houses of Parliaclock tower housing Big Ben (1858). Westminster Bridge spans the Thames. After that we have Buckingham Palace (early 18th century), the city residence of the Queen, Green Park and St James's Park, and the Tate Gallery with a first-class collection of British and foreign art from 1500.

In Whitehall you'll find 10 Downing Street, residence of the Prime Minister; the Palladian-style Banqueting House, opposite Horse Guards Parade for the Changing of the Guard; Trafalgar Square with the Nelson's Column; the National Gallery with works from the 16th to 20th centuries, the National Portrait Gallery; Hyde Park, a public park from the 17th century with Speaker's Corner;

Top: Buckingham Palace – London residence of the Queen.
Bottom: Bustling Trafalgar Square with Nelson's Column.

ment on the Thames. Then we have the only remaining part of the original medieval building, Westminster Hall, and standing next to that the Madame Tussaud's Wax Museum. In Knightsbridge are the Victoria and Albert Museum, the largest arts and crafts museum in the world; the Natural History Museum, with a famous dinosaur section; the Science and Technology Museum; the legendary Harrods department store; and the younger and less staid Harvey Nichols department store.

London's districts

In the City district of London you should take time to visit St Paul's Cathedral (1674–1710), a Renaissance masterpiece designed by Christopher Wren, with the Whispering Gallery, a walkway that goes all the way around its dome. North of here are the futuristic Barbican towers and the internationally important London Stock Exchange from 1773.

In the West End you'll find countless theaters, cinemas, pubs and restaurants around Piccadilly Circus. Covent Garden, once a market, is now a pedestrian zone with the Royal Opera House. The British Museum, with a number of world-famous collections, is also in the West End.

Interesting places in Southwark, on the south side of the Thames, include the cathedral, the oldest Gothic church in London. It has a memorial for Shakespeare, whose Globe Theater was rebuilt nearby. The Tate Modern is a striking modern art museum in a disused power station. The Docklands and Canary Wharf feature modern architecture – Canada Tower and Canary Wharf Tower, respectively. The latter is the tallest building in the UK at 244 m (800 ft). Greenwich boasts the Royal Maritime Museum, the historic Cutty Sark clipper, and the observatory, which crosses the prime meridian.

Top: Walls from the 13th century protect the Tower of London.
Bottom: Houses of Parliament with Big Ben.

7 Corfe Castle and Swanage On your way to Swanage it is worth stopping at Corfe Castle, a wild and romantic set of ruins out on a high promontory. In 1646 the fort fell through a betrayal on the part of Oliver Cromwell's soldiers and was almost totally destroyed.

Swanage is a charming seaside town at the end of the narrow Purbeck Peninsula. The Old Harry Rocks, named after the devil, are just a walk away from here. Like the Needles on the Isle of Wight, the chalk stacks rocks in this formation were formed by the emergence of the Alps over thirty million years ago.

8 The Jurassic Coast The coast between Swanage and Weymouth is not called the Jurassic Coast for nothing. The cliff formations here date from the Jurassic period and because of their location are only partially accessible by car. In 2001 this stretch of coastline was classified a Natural World Heritage Site by UNESCO – the first site to be listed as such in the UK – because it records 185 million years of the earth's history, a geological walk through time.

The beaches and the cliffs here bear witness to periods within the Mesozoic Era, effectively the geological 'Middle Ages'. Ever since the spectacular find of an Ichthyosaurus, an enormous fish dinosaur, in the 19th century, this area has also become world-famous among hobby fossil hunters.

Yet the region is also perfect for walks with breathtaking views. Shortly before the town of Weymouth is the enchanting Lulworth Cove, a natural port with steep cliffs and golden sands. A footpath then leads you along the cliff edge to the impressive Durdle Door, a natural bridge that extends out into the ocean. St Oswald's Bay, with its shingle beach, can also be reached from here by a steep and precarious path.

Between Weymouth and Exeter there are many small coastal villages that invite you for a break. In the dreamy village of Abbotsbury, the Swannery swan colony is home to about 1,000 swans, a sight to behold. Chesil Bank is a gravel bank that is over 80,000 years old and stretches more than 29 km (18 miles). It resembles a pebble dune. Beyond the dune is a bird sanctuary in the brackish water of the lagoon.

9 Torquay Torquay is around 40 km (25 miles) south of Exeter on what is commonly known as the English Riviera. This 30-km-long (19-mile) stretch of coast has been so named because of its numerous idyllic bays, palm-fringed beaches, mild climate and its urbane atmosphere. Three towns – Torquay, Paignton and Brixham – have become known as Torbay, though they have kept their own individual styles. Elegant hotels, Victorian villas and countless bars and restaurants around the port give the area a holiday feel.

After the impressive mountain road through Dartmoor National Park (with grades of up to twenty-five per cent), the A390 leads from Liskeard back down toward the coast and St Austell.

10 St Austell and the Eden Project Since the discovery of kaolin in the 18th century, the economic welfare of the town has been closely linked to the mining of this important base product used in the manufacture of porcelain. The story of china clay or 'white gold' is retold in St Austell's museum. The Eden Project was laid out on 14 ha (35 acres) on a disused kaolin quarry near Bodelva. In two gigantic greenhouses, gar-

deners have reproduced two climatic zones – tropical rainforest and Mediterranean. The greenhouses are densely populated with plants from these respective regions in order to allow a natural ecosystem to develop. In another area, a cool zone was set up, in which indigenous plants from Britain and exotic plants from temperate Cornwall flourish. The larger of the greenhouses, the Humid Tropics Biome, is the largest greenhouse in the world, covering an area of 1,559 ha (4 acres) at a height of 55 m (180 ft).

11 Mevagissey Every bit as fascinating as the Eden Project are the Lost Gardens of Heligan north of Mevagissey – strange, prehistoric fallen tree trunks lie amid a subtropical landscape with giant bamboo, ancient tree ferns and mysterious ponds. The gardens were initially planted in the 18th and 19th centuries, but then fell into a long dormant phase.

In 1990, the developer Tim Smit cut through the 5-m-thick (16-ft) thorn bushes and discovered a site that had been forgotten for nearly a hundred years. After a painstaking reconstruction of the original gardens, the microenvironment was saved.

The 32-ha (80-acre) site includes a ravine, an enchanting Italian garden, a grotto and ancient rhododendron bushes. Lost Valley, a jungle environment with a view over Mevagissey, and a Victorian productive garden are among the other highlights of the gardens.

12 Penzance The largest town in Cornwall lies 50 km (31 miles) to the west of here. A drive over the Penwith Peninsula to Land's End is definitely recommended. Due to its temperate climate, this striking region is also called the 'Cornish Riviera'. Penzance was an important tin trading point for the Roman Empire and medieval Europe. The center of town, between Chapel Street and Market Jew Street, is the oldest part of Penzance, where the long since vanished times of the seafarers can still be felt. The Barbican, which is an old storage house, and the Egyptian House (1830) are both worth visiting.

Opposite the town stands the old castle of St Michael's Mount on top of a granite island in the bay of the same name. This former Benedictine monastery came into the Crown's possession in 1535 and was then converted into a fortress. Historians

3

date the founding of the monastery back to the 8th century. At that time Celtic monks had built a monastery on Mont St-Michel in Normandy, which bears a remarkable, but not coincidental, resemblance to its Cornish counterpart. At low tide you can cross the bay on foot. At high tide there is a boat service. If you climb to the top of the 70-m-high (230-ft) outcrop, you'll get a fabulous view over Penwith Peninsula. From Penzance, there is a 35-km (22-mile) road that leads round the peninsula to Land's End and then on to St Ives.

13 Land's End The westernmost point of England is covered with an open moor and heath, and is absolutely riddled with archaeological treasures. Headstones from the ice age and Bronze Age, Celtic crosses and entire villages that date back to times before the birth of Christ all bear witness to thousands of years of settlement in the area. The continual breaking of the waves from the Atlantic over the mighty rocks led the Romans to christen the place Belerion – Home of the Storms.

14 Scilly Isles About 40 km (25 miles) off the coast to the south-west lie the 140 Scilly Isles, which are reachable by ferry from Penzance. The 2,000 inhabitants, who live mostly from tourism and the export of flowers, are spread over only seven inhabited islands. With their rough granite rocks, white sandy beaches and turquoise bays, the Scilly Isles are best discovered on foot or by bicycle. A collection of the exotic palms and plants that traditionally flourish in this mild climate can be seen in the Abbey Garden at Tresco. Back on the mainland, the often steep coastal road then follows the Atlantic coast around to St Ives. Ornithologists come here to find rare visitors like egrets or New World warblers and vireos that have come over from America accidentally on the omnipresent Westerlies. Some of the best observation points are the lighthouses.

15 St Ives Grey granite houses populate this former fishing village, which also happens to have one of Cornwall's most beautiful beaches. Numerous artists and sculptors have been coming here since the last century, fascinated by the light and landscape. The Tate Gallery has even opened a 'branch' high above Porthmoor Beach where works by artists from St Ives are on display including paintings by Patrick Heron and Ben Nicholson, who lived here with his artist wife Barbara Hepworth. The village of Gwithian and its sandy beach just up the road are also worth a stop.

The tiny fishing village of Port Isaac is near by, just off the A30. It has been spared a lot of the mass tourism that has become rampant in these parts, which makes it a refreshing alternative. The extremely steep streets probably put off a lot of visitors, so the best bet is to park the car above the village, and walk to Kellan Head on the coast.

16 Tintagel The legendary ruins on Tintagel Head are said to be the birthplace of King Arthur. Beyond the village of Tintagel a path leads over the cliffs to a green outcrop on the Atlantic that is crowned with crumbling ruin walls and can be reached via the steep staircase. As digs have proven, a Celtic monastery from the 5th century once stood here with a library, chapel, guest house, refectory and even a bath house.

The castle, however, whose ruins are also still visible, only dates back to the 13th century, a fact that would cast a doubt over the speculation of it being the birthplace of the legendary king of England.

And yet he who stands in the fog on the cliffs looking down at waves crashing by the dark entrance to Merlin's Cave can easily feel himself transported back to the times of King Arthur. The Norman church graveyard has a number of half-buried tombstones telling tales of dead seamen and grieving widows.

The A39 leads further north from Tintagel along the coast, passing between Blackmoor Gate and Dunster across Exmoor National Park. In order to fully appreciate the coast and the moorland here, you should walk a section of the Somerset and Devon Coastal Path, from Bossington for example.

17 Glastonbury and Wells At Bridgwater, the coastal road A39 finally turns inland and leads to Glastonbury, a mythical place that attracts countless esoteric types. There are many reasons for the concentration of mystical and supernatural activity here: the remains of King Arthur are thought to be buried under the ruins of Glastonbury Abbey, and Glastonbury is often thought to be the legendary Avalon – a paradise to which Arthur was carried after his death. Each year, the largest open-air music and performing arts festival in the world also takes place here.

Historical facts date the foundation of the first monastery back to the 7th century while the construction of England's largest abbey came around the year 1000 and the dissolution of the monastery in 1539.

The small city of Wells, on the other hand, is known for its glorious cathedral, the first Gothic building in all of England. The main section was completed in 1240, but the western tower and chapel came much later. The western façade was at one time covered with 400 figures, testimony to the skill of the medieval masons here – one picture book carved into the stone relates biblical and world history. Adjacent to

1 Street in the picturesque town of St Ives.

2 A great boulder near Lower Slaughter in the Cotswolds.

3 The cove of Port Issac on the west coast of Cornwall.

the cathedral is the Bishop's Palace, which is still used by the Bishop of Bath and Wells.

Bath, your next stop, is the cultural center of the county of Somerset and is located around 30 km (19 miles) north of Wells on the A367.

18 Bath The Romans knew this hot-springs town as Aquae Sulis. They built magnificent swimming pools, Turkish baths and saunas, and turned the town into a meeting place for the Roman elite. Oddly, the unique baths were only rediscovered in the 18th century.

Bath's rebirth as a health resort began in earnest in the 19th century when the city's grandiose Georgian architecture, concerts and balls enticed London's upper class to enjoy the recuperative benefits of its historic facilities. Visitors could also admire the dignified limestone buildings such as those

on Queen Square, Royal Crescent and Pulteney Bridge. Today, you can taste the healing waters and take in the atmosphere in the Pump Room. A short detour of about 12 km (7.5 miles) via Chippenham leads you to the archaeological site at Avebury in Wiltshire. Avebury is home to the remains of England's largest and most impressive stone circle, made up of over 100 stones erected around 3,500 years ago. Nearby, the 40-m-high (130-ft) Silbury Hill looks like a pyramid, but it was not used as a burial site.

19 The Cotswolds The A429 takes you through the deep, wooded valleys and gentle hills of the Cotswolds, an area that has been populated since prehistoric times. After the Roman occupation, the Cotswolds once again bloomed through the Middle Ages thanks to the local wool production. The region

then sank into a long period of dormancy before finally being reawakened by tourism.

The typical Cotswolds architectural style and fairy-tale charm can be best seen in places such as Bouton-on-the-Water where golden stone buildings stand side-by-side with little bridges crossing streams in quaint and vivid meadows.

The beautiful town of Stow-on-the-Wold with its stone market hall sits atop a hill and was once a thriving sheep market. On the other side of the hill are the tiny villages of Upper Slaughter and Lower Slaughter, whose

miniature appearance have made them into much-loved postcard images.

20 Stratford-upon-Avon The birthplace of the famous playwright, William Shakespeare (1564–1616), is the northernmost point of your route. In 1594, the 'Bardof Avon' left for London, where he was able to establish his legendary reputation as actor and writer in one of the leading theater companies of the time. In 1610 he returned to his home town of Stratford, where he also died. Despite thousands of tourists

Wells This town was originally founded by the Romans. Its cathedral was begun in AD 700, and the Bishop's Palace is over 800 years old.

Bath 2,000 years ago the Romans established a bath complex that was later rediscovered in 1870. In the 18th century, Bath became a fashionable health resort.

Stonehenge This world-famous prehistoric site was erected between 3100 and 1500 BC by a late Stone-Age people and given some detailed inscriptions in the Bronze Age. Some of the artistically sculpted stones originate from mountains in 'nearby' Wales.

Blenheim Palace This controversial baroque palace completed in 1722 was a gift from Queen Anne to the Duke of Marlborough for winning the Battle of Blenheim (1704). .

Scilly Isles Fabulous bays and an exceptionally mild climate make the Scilly Isles a popular holiday destination. Only seven of the 140 islands are inhabited.

The Cotswolds Typical of this wooded, hilly area are the constructions of Cotswold stone used in bridges, cottages, churches, country houses and walls.

St Ives Two museums in St Ives show works by a group of landscape-inspired artists who 'discovered' the fishing village at the end of the 1920s.

Land's End The stunning scenery from here, the westernmost point of England, has made it into a popular destination for visitors and artists alike.

St Michael`s Mount Its resemblance to Mont St-Michel in Normandy was the inspiration for this isle's name.

East Devon Coast The lovely coastline of Devon is seemingly endless, quite diverse and littered with holiday resorts.

Shaftesbury Ruins of a cloister and Gold Hill, the most picturesque street in England, make this a charming town.

walking in the footsteps of the poet every year, Stratford has been able to retain some of its Shakespearian atmosphere.

Visitors can tour the house where the playwright was born, learn about his life and work in the Shakespeare Center, or watch the renowned Royal Shakespeare Company perform one of his plays in the Swan Theater. A boat trip on the Avon rounds off the visit.

The A44 toward Oxford passes the impressive Blenheim Palace at Moreton-in-Marsh.

21 Blenheim Palace This impressive palace near Oxford was finished in 1722 and is Britain's largest private home. It was originally a gift from Queen Anne to John Churchill, the 1st Duke of Marlborough, after his defeat of Ludwig XIV in Blenheim, Bavaria (actually Blindheim near Höchstädt on the Danube). Blenheim Palace

is recommended for a relaxing afternoon walk followed by tea. Many garden-lovers come here to visit the palace park, created by landscape gardener Lancelot 'Capability' Brown in typical English style.

22 Oxford The many spires of Oxford, especially Tom Tower of Christ Church and Magdalen Tower, are visible from the approach road. Oxford is known throughout the world as England's most prestigious university town. Its cathedral and the Picture Gallery, containing masterpieces from the Renaissance and baroque era, are worth a visit. Don't miss the Radcliffe Camera (which houses the Radcliffe Science Library), Sheldonian Theater and the Bodleian Library with its five million books.

The college tour is a classic, and leads around the buildings of Merton College, Corpus Christi

and New College, among others. Take a relaxing walk through the University of Oxford Botanic Gardens as well, which has old glasshouses and a walled garden to breathe fresh air and get prepared for the last stop before London.

23 Windsor and Ascot Windsor Castle is located in the Thames Valley west of London, and has been the primary residence of the English royal family since the Middle Ages. The fort, built in the 12th and 13th centuries, has been frequently remodelled over the years.

Many sections of Windsor Castle, one of the largest inhabited castles in the world, are open to the public. A trip to St George's Chapel and the Albert Memorial Chapel to view the burial sites of the monarchs is highly recommended. The Round Tower offers a wonderful view of the castle and the Windsor Great

Park. Opposite Windsor Castle stands Eton College, founded in 1440–41. This very exclusive private school favours a traditional English education with an emphasis on both, the Classics and sport.

Windsor and Ascot, the famous racetrack, are separated only by a few kilometers. The Hippodrome, built in 1711 by Queen Anne, is one of the most famous tracks in the world. From 1825 until 1945, the four-day Royal Meeting race was the only event that was staged there. Today twenty-five races take place each year.

The final stop on this tour is London, with its numerous historical monuments, its world-renowned museums and its famous churches.

1 Winston Churchill was born in 1874 in Blenheim Palace (UNESCO World Heritage Site), a baroque masterpiece.

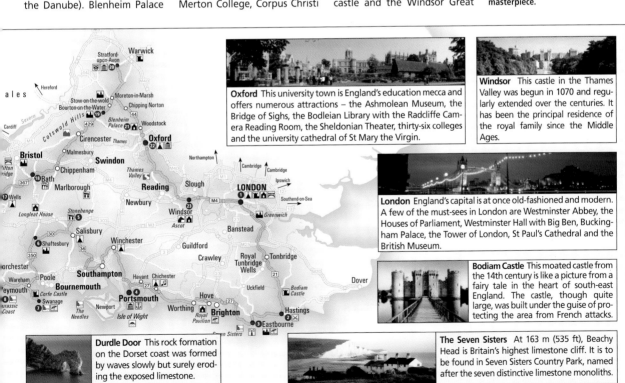

Oxford This university town is England's education mecca and offers numerous attractions – the Ashmolean Museum, the Bridge of Sighs, the Bodleian Library with the Radcliffe Camera Reading Room, the Sheldonian Theater, thirty-six colleges and the university cathedral of St Mary the Virgin.

Windsor This castle in the Thames Valley was begun in 1070 and regularly extended over the centuries. It has been the principal residence of the royal family since the Middle Ages.

London England's capital is at once old-fashioned and modern. A few of the must-sees in London are Westminster Abbey, the Houses of Parliament, Westminster Hall with Big Ben, Buckingham Palace, the Tower of London, St Paul's Cathedral and the British Museum.

Bodiam Castle This moated castle from the 14th century is like a picture from a fairy tale in the heart of south-east England. The castle, though quite large, was built under the guise of protecting the area from French attacks.

Durdle Door This rock formation on the Dorset coast was formed by waves slowly but surely eroding the exposed limestone.

The Seven Sisters At 163 m (535 ft), Beachy Head is Britain's highest limestone cliff. It is to be found in Seven Sisters Country Park, named after the seven distinctive limestone monoliths.

Historic warehouses in Bergen, member of the Hanseatic League.

Norway

Over fjord and fell:
the spectacular natural world of northern Europe

Norway shares its borders with Russia, Finland and Sweden and is enveloped by the Norwegian Sea, the North Sea and the Skagerrak. It is a natural realm of truly unmatched beauty – alternately wild and delicate. One tip – make sure you allow plenty of time for the enormous distances.

As you might expect from industrious Scandinavians, the Norwegian mainland has an astonishingly well-maintained road infrastructure. In places where the rugged terrain would have you think the onward journey has come to an end, there appears a ferry, a tunnel or a bridge. Even the smallest hamlets and remote coastal villages are generally easy to reach. And yet progress in this expansive land inevitably takes much longer than you've planned, mainly due to the unusual physical geography and strict speed limits. But, on the other hand, you won't have to worry much about traffic jams and red lights.

The *Hurtigruten* is Norway's legendary passenger ship, which has been plying the 2,500 nautical miles between Bergen in the south and Kirkenes on the Russian border in the very north for well over a hundred years. It was originally used to transport post and supplies. Nowadays the permanent route, known as 'Imperial Road No. 1', has become famous as one of 'the world's most beautiful sea voyages'.

From a geographical point of view, Norway is unlike any other European country. No other country in Europe is longer (1,752 km/1,089 miles), almost none is as narrow, and despite its odd shape it is (without its polar provinces) three times the size of England.

Almost half of Norway is over 500 m (1,640 ft) above sea level. Its mountains are not particularly high – the highest does not even measure 2,500 m (8,200 ft) – yet nearly a quarter of the country is covered by alpine or high-alpine landscape, glaciers or treeless plateaus at

Mountain landscape in Kjerringøy in the north.

View from the mountain of Aksala over Ålesund past the town center to the port.

Autumn tundra in the Finnmark Province of Norway's far northern expanse.

over 1,000 m (3,280 ft) altitude. The generally barren, high-level plateaus – known as fjells, or fells – are an upland tundra, covered in snow for a large part of the year, and consist mainly of moors, lakes and rivers.

Above the Arctic Circle and in the highland areas of the interior there is often no sign of human life at all. With the exception of Oslo, Bergen, Trondheim and Stavanger there is no town with more than 100,000 inhabitants in this relatively large country. Four out of five people live on the coast or the banks of a fjord. Norway's very craggy coastline, including the fjords and bays, is over 28,000 km (17,398 miles) long – more than half the circumference of the earth.

The country is very sparsely populated and, thanks to the Gulf Stream, free of ice all year. Were it not for these warm ocean currents, the Norwegian mainland would be covered with a crust of ice, as is the case in large areas of the Norwegian polar provinces. On the other hand, the Gulf Stream is also to blame for the high level of summer rainfall, which is common. The fjords – the most famous of which are Geirangerfjord, Hardangerfjord and Sognefjord – are the Number One tourist attraction in Norway. Former valleys and canyons of various sizes and shapes, they were carved out by massive glaciers and ultimately flooded by rising sea levels following the last ice age. The short summer in Norway are quite mild. North of the Arctic Circle – in the 'Land of the Midnight Sun' – summer days actually don't end and the special atmosphere during this time of year often inspires wild parties. The opposite is the case during the cold period, which is snowy and dark in the very north – no sun for two months straight. Norway is not in the EU and still uses the Norwegian Krone as its currency. After hundreds of years of occupation and invasion by the Danes, the Swedes and the Germans, they feel they have earned this 'exclusivity'. But things are going swimmingly here – fishing and tourism, as well as plentiful oil and natural gas reserves in the North Sea, have made the beautiful 'Land of Utgard' quite prosperous.

Fishing boats in the port of Hamnøy on the Lofoten island of Moskenesøya.

North Cape Route: On the 4,000-km (2,484-mile) trip to the North Cape you get to experience just about everything Norway's fascinating natural landscape has to offer: glaciers, waterfalls, steep mountains, high plateaus, rugged coastline and endless fjords. The cultural highlights include old port and mining towns, stone carvings and charming old churches.

1 **Oslo** At the end of the fjord of the same name, stretching nearly 100 km (60 miles) inland and surrounded by wooded hills, is Norway's capital Oslo, a city dating back to the 11th century. Oslo was called Kristiania until 1925 and had varying political and industrial significance. Although the capital is home to a mere half-million inhabitants, it is one of Europe's largest cities in surface area. It is the largest port in Norway and the country's trading and industrial center.

Worth seeing in the center of the town: the new town hall (1931–1950), the city's trademark with a lavish interior and Europe's highest clock tower; Akershus Fort (from 1300), one of the country's most important medieval buildings; Nasjonalgalleriet, the largest collection of paintings and sculptures in Norway; the royal castle (changing of the guard at 1:30 pm).

Highlights outside the city center include Holmenkollen, a wintersport resort with skiing museum; Munch-Museet; Vigelandpark (Frognerpark) with 200 bronze and stone works by Gustav Vigeland; the Bygdöy peninsular museum with the Vikingskipshuset (three ships from the 9th century); Kon-Tiki Museet with the Thor Heyerdahl Raft (Kon-Tiki, RA I, RA II); Fram-Museet. From Oslo follow the coast to Kongsberg.

2 **Kongsberg** The Mining Museum here casts you back to the times of silver mining, which ceased in 1957 after more than 330 years. In the Saggrenda pit you can see what is probably the world's first ever elevator – it consists of ladders that go up and down.

3 **Heddal and Eidsborg** Norway's first stave church (1147) is in Telemark and has an outer

Travel Information

Route profile
Length: approx. 4,000 km (2,484 miles), excluding detours
Time required: at least 4 weeks, ideally 6–8 weeks.
Start: Oslo
End: The North Cape
Route (main locations): Oslo, Kongsberg, Bergen, Jotunheimen, Trondheim, Fauske, Narvik, Tromsø, Alta, North Cape

Traffic information:
This route requires some driving skill and good planning as the ferries are often fully booked. Drive on the right in Norway. Customs laws are strictly enforced. Headlights are obligatory even during the day. Bridges, tunnels and mountain pass roads mostly charge tolls. Mountain roads are often only opened in June/July.

When to go:
The best time to go is from June to August. Even in these months, snowfall is common in the north and on the plateaus.

Accommodation:
Mountain inns, known as fjellstue or fjellstove, and chalets make for attractive choices.

General information:
www.visitnorway.com
www.norway.org
www.norway.com
Customs:
www.toll.no

rare wildlife. From Skarsmo our route leads north on Road 13. Alongside the road are the wild frothing waters of the Låtefossen. It is definitely worth a short detour (50 km/31 miles) from Kinsarvik, along the Eidfjord to Fossli, to the edge of the Vidda where the Vøringfossen Falls drop 170 m (557 ft) into the depths of Måbø Canyon.

From Kinsarvik, ferries cross the Utne to Kvanndal on the Hardangerfjord. The 'King of the Fjords' reaches far inland at a length of 179 km (111 miles) and a depth of 830 m (2,723 ft). The route then leads over the plateau of Kvamskogen on to the town of Bergen.

⑤ Bergen The most famous street in this Hanseatic League town is Bryggen, a UNESCO World Heritage Site with picturesque warehouses right on the waterfront. The fishing port, the cathedral, the 12th-century church and the Gamle Bergen open-air museum are also worth visiting.

⑥ Viksøyri The E16 passes many lakes on the way to Voss, home of the oldest wooden house in Norway – 'Finneloftet' from the 13th century. Further along the route you should take a detour to Viksøyri (with a charming stave church) where you can see the Sognefjord about 40 km (25 miles) away. It

gallery that was used to protect people from the weather and to store weapons. Road 45 (direction Dalen) splits off towards the Eidsborg stave church at Ofte. The walls of the church are covered with shingles, which is unusual. About 4 km (2.4 miles) beyond Rødal, Road 13 turns off towards Stavanger. The E134 also passes through Hardangervidda further on.

④ Hardangervidda Europe's largest plateau is a fascinating area for hiking and is home to

1 Oslo town hall.

2 UNESCO World Heritage Site: the picturesque wooden houses of Bryggen in Bergen, once a member of the Hanseatic League.

3 The Vøringfossen falls cascade from the Hardanger Plateau into the deep and narrow Måbø Canyon.

4 The 800-year-old stave church of Borgund near Borlaug, deep in the Lærdal Valley.

is Norway's greatest fjord – 180 km (112 miles) long, in some places only 5 km (3 miles) wide, and up to 1,200 m (3,937 ft) deep.

❼ Stalheimskleiva and Nærøyfjord About 13 km (8 miles) past Oppheim, a road leads to the Hotel Stalheim, which has wonderful views. Norway's steepest road leads round thirteen hairpin bends down to the Nærøyfjord. It is the narrowest one in the country with walls up to 1,200 m (3,937 ft) high. Two impressive waterfalls are also on the route – the Stalheimfoss (126 m/413 ft) and the Sivlefoss (240 m/787 ft). The road goes from Gudvangen to

Kaupanger and on to Songdal. The fjord route leads past Nærøyfjord, Aurlandsfjord and Sognefjord, among the most beautiful in Norway.

❽ Borgund The best-preserved stave church in the country can be viewed by taking a short diversion inland after driving through the 20-km (13-mile) Lærdals Tunnel on the E16. The church was erected around 1150 and is known for its ornate carvings. The pagoda-shaped bell tower is next to the church.

❾ Jotunheimen and Sognefjell road Norway's highest and most spectacular mountain

pass runs from Sogndal to Lom. It climbs a steep, winding trail into the Jotunheimen Mountains where over two hundred peaks of at least 2,000 m (6,561 ft) form a bizarre ring. The two highest among them are Galdahøppigen at 2,469 m (8,100 ft) and Glittertind at 2,452 m (8,045 ft). The Sognefjell is a plateau dotted with lakes of all sizes. To the west of the road is Europe's largest mainland glacier, the Jostedalsbree, which is about 100 km (62 miles) long.

❿ Urnes A small single-lane road now leads from Skjolden on the east bank of the Lustrafjord to the town of Urnes and

Trollstigen

Surrounded by waterfalls, deep valleys and mountains as high as 1,760 m (6,316 ft), Norway's most photographed mountain pass, the Trollstigen, snakes its way from Langdal to Åndalsnes at elevations of up to 850 m (2,789 ft). Eleven hairpin bends with a gradient of ten per cent take some skill to master. The road was built in 1936 and winds along almost vertical rock faces. As a result, it is unfortunately closed to camper vans.

an 11th-century stave church, the oldest of twenty-nine listed stave churches and a UNESCO World Heritage Site. The robust design of the exterior is fascinating and inside are lovely carvings of fable characters.

⓫ Geirangerfjord The route continues through some pretty landscape on its way to the

Geirangerfjord, a 15-km (9-mile) arm of the Sunnylvsfjord. Its walls are up to 800 m (2,625 ft) high and many waterfalls feed into the fjord. The panorama from the Dalsnibba viewpoint before Geiranger is fabulous. The winding road 'Ornevein' (Eagle Route) leads up into the mountains offering frequent spectacular views over the fjord.

1 The Jostedalsbreen National Park, the 'Land of the Giants', in southern Norway protects the largest land glacier in Europe, which has four glacial tongues.

2 Picturesque fishing boats reflected in the Lusterfjord, a northern arm of the Sognefjord.

3 South of Oppdal lies the Dovrefjell National Park with Snøhetta (snow cap) in the background (2,286 m/7,500 ft), Norway's highest mountain just outside Jotunheimen.

4 Typical mountainous and fjord landscape in Nordland, the Norwegian province that straddles the Arctic Circle.

After crossing the Nordalsfjord you get your first chance to turn off towards Ålesund Island (80 km/50 miles).

The main route then continues through the Gudbrands Gorge to the Trollstigen mountain road and on to Åndalsnes. Here you have a second possibility to head towards Ålesund about 120 km (74 miles) down the E136. The E136 continues east in Romsdalen to Dombås, and from here through the hilly or mountainous countryside to the Dovrefjell.

⑫ **Dovrefjell** Norway's tallest mountain, Snøhetta, at 2,286 m (7,500 ft) dominates the plateau

and you can get a great view from the road's highest point (1,026 m/3,366 ft). The national park is classified as the only remaining intact high-altitude ecosystem in Europe.

The road passes through Drivdalen to Oppdal with its modest open-air museum. On the way to Trondheim (E06) you will be presented with a diversion to the old mining town of Røros (120 km/74.5 miles), which boasts a massive stone cathedral and some charming historic buildings.

⑬ **Trondheim** Trondheim was Norway's capital for quite some time. To this day, royal corona-

tions still take place in the mighty Nidaros Cathedral, built in 1070 over the grave of Olav the Holy. The western façade of the cathedral has some particularly interesting sculptures. The Tyholt Television Tower, Fort Kristiansen and the cathedral tower all offer wonderful views over the rooftops of Trondheim. The scenic E16 then leads from Trondheim to Grong, following the banks of numerous fjords along the way. In Grong, Road 760 links up with the R17, the Kystriksveien. The E06 goes north towards Fauske, rolling through the charming Namdalen with the Namsen River, an excellent salmon river.

⑭ **Kystriksveien** The 560-km (348-mile) Kystriksveien is in effect the mainland counterpart to the legendary Hurtigruten coastal journey – one of Europe's dream routes. Many ferries ply the fjords and lakes in this region and the landscape is varied. But the coastal road requires a lot of time and money, and waiting times are to be expected for the various ferries. The crossing fees can indeed add up to a considerable sum. A few kilometers beyond Sonja there is a small road to Mo i Rana which has a World War II cemetery. There you can get back on the E06 to the Saltfjellet-Svartisen National Park.

The section of the coastal road north of the turnoff to Mo i Rana is called Helgeland-Salten, the 'Green Road'. A natural tidal spectacle can be seen near Løding – every six hours the water trapped behind the 'Eye of the Needle' forces its way through the strait.

From Løding it is a 43-km (27-mile) drive back to the E06 at Fauske. An interesting alternative is the road through the Saltfjellet-Svartisen National Park, one of the largest in the country. Norway's second largest glacier is high in the Arctic Circle here. The tremendous glacier is hard to reach, however – gravel tracks turn off at Skonseng towards Svartisdalhytta.

Inside the Arctic Circle and above the tree line, only moss and shrubs grow here. The road to Rognan on Saltdalsfjord leads through the high valley of Saltfjells, and then follows the eastern bank to Fauske. The E06 then goes north to Ulsvåg, where you can turn off to Skutvik, the most important Lofoten port.

15 Narvik Swedish iron ore from Kiruna is shipped around the world from the permanent-ly ice-free port of Ofotenfjord. The warehouses and transport systems are best viewed from the panorama point up on Fagernessfjell (656 m/2,151 ft). Ferries also travel to the Lofoten archipelago from Narvik. The E08 turns to Tromsø at the small village of Nordkjosbotn.

16 Tromsø Northern Norway's largest town ironically benefits from a mild climate. The Polarmuseet has interesting exhibits covering various international polar expeditions. The Tromsøbrua connects the island town to the mainland. Next to it is the town's icon – the pointed Arctic Cathedral (1965). The town also boasts the largest number of old wooden houses in Norway. Back on the E06 you drive through some spectacular fjords.

17 Alta This town on the fjord of the same name is a center of Sami culture. The stone carvings of Hjemmeluft, which date back between 2,000 and 6,000 years, are definitely worth a visit. They depict animals, hunting and everyday scenes and are listed as a World Heritage Site. The Alta

Canyon is also a must-see, with impressive depths of up to 500 m (1,634 ft) and a length of 15 km (9 miles).

The route then traverses the tundra landscape of Finnmarksvidda to the port town of Hammerfest. After that, the E06 crosses a plateau before the E69 turns off at Olderford towards the North Cape.

18 North Cape The road now heads past Porsangerfjord to the ferry port of Kåfjord, where ferries travel to Honningsvag on the North Cape island of Magerøya. There is a tunnel to the island. Across the harsh landscape we reach the North Cape, a major tourist attraction and the end of our trip.

1 The Lyngenfjord is over 10 km (6 miles) wide and one of the prettiest in northern Norway. From Skibotn there is a fine view of the west side of the fjord, with the glaciated peak of Jeggevarre beyond the Pollfjell.

2 The midnight sun shines on the North Cape from May 14 to July 30, yet the Cape is often immersed in thick fog, rain or snow. A huge globe sculpture marks Europe's northernmost point.

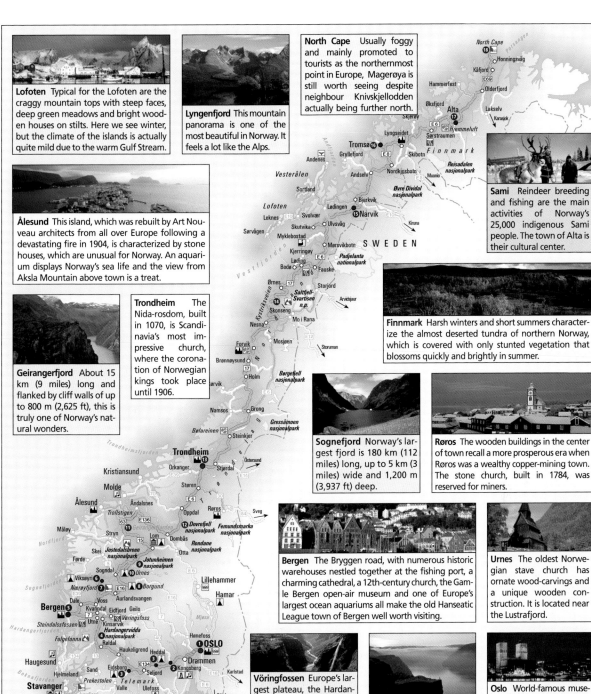

Lofoten Typical for the Lofoten are the craggy mountain tops with steep faces, deep green meadows and bright wooden houses on stilts. Here we see winter, but the climate of the islands is actually quite mild due to the warm Gulf Stream.

Lyngenfjord This mountain panorama is one of the most beautiful in Norway. It feels a lot like the Alps.

North Cape Usually foggy and mainly promoted to tourists as the northernmost point in Europe, Magerøya is still worth seeing despite neighbour Knivskjellodden actually being further north.

Ålesund This island, which was rebuilt by Art Nouveau architects from all over Europe following a devastating fire in 1904, is characterized by stone houses, which are unusual for Norway. An aquarium displays Norway's sea life and the view from Aksla Mountain above town is a treat.

Sami Reindeer breeding and fishing are the main activities of Norway's 25,000 indigenous Sami people. The town of Alta is their cultural center.

Trondheim The Nida-rosdom, built in 1070, is Scandinavia's most impressive church, where the coronation of Norwegian kings took place until 1906.

Geirangerfjord About 15 km (9 miles) long and flanked by cliff walls of up to 800 m (2,625 ft), this is truly one of Norway's natural wonders.

Finnmark Harsh winters and short summers characterize the almost deserted tundra of northern Norway, which is covered with only stunted vegetation that blossoms quickly and brightly in summer.

Sognefjord Norway's largest fjord is 180 km (112 miles) long, up to 5 km (3 miles) wide and 1,200 m (3,937 ft) deep.

Røros The wooden buildings in the center of town recall a more prosperous era when Røros was a wealthy copper-mining town. The stone church, built in 1784, was reserved for miners.

Bergen The Bryggen road, with numerous historic warehouses nestled together at the fishing port, a charming cathedral, a 12th-century church, the Gamle Bergen open-air museum and one of Europe's largest ocean aquariums all make the old Hanseatic League town of Bergen well worth visiting.

Urnes The oldest Norwegian stave church has ornate wood-carvings and a unique wooden construction. It is located near the Lustrafjord.

Vöringfossen Europe's largest plateau, the Hardangervidda, is the starting point for the 170-m-high (557-ft) Vöringfossen, a spectacular waterfall that plummets into the Måbø Canyon.

Prekestolen This 600-m-high (1,969-ft) promontory, 'Preacher's Pulpit', is one of the must-see attractions in southern Norway.

Oslo World-famous museums, plenty of greenery and water make this sprawling metropolis a fascinating experience. The new town hall on the port is the icon of the Norwegian capital.

Many Swedes have second homes on Runn near Falun.

Denmark and Sweden

Where the North Sea meets the Baltic: a journey around the Kattegat

Ever since the bold Öresund Bridge connected Denmark with Sweden, it has been much easier to explore the two "united kingdoms". Indeed, there are many similarities between these Scandanavian countries, but there also many differences to discover. Denmark, the smaller of the two, is known for its seaside holidays, while its larger neighbor features vast tracts of untouched nature.

The most bizarre but perhaps fitting travel recommendation for Denmark came from the royal mouth of its popular and friendly Queen Margrethe II: "There is no other country in the world that is as much like Denmark as Denmark itself." But what is Denmark? Initially it was an island kingdom comprising the divided Jutland Peninsula, the larger islands of

Fünen, Seeland, Falster, Møn, Lolland and Bornholm, and about four hundred smaller islands, of which not even one hundred are inhabited.
Denmark is also a small country that you can cover easily in one day, if you so desire. It is also particularly well suited to those who love the sea. Where else can you choose from 7,400 km (4,598 mi) of largely unspoiled

View of the Blå Jungfrun National Park west of Öland.

and easily accessible coastlines, from the shimmering blue Kattegat strait and the mild Baltic Sea to the rigged Skagerrak and the tidal North Sea? Denmark's interior, characterized by lakes, forests, moors and fields is actually quite hilly. The towns and small villages, with their whitewashed and often slightly dilapidated half-timbered houses, are what the Danes refer to as "hyggelig", meaning cozy. Denmark's cultural assets range from Bronze Age and Viking era archaeological monuments to magnificent manor houses, castles, groundbreaking modern architecture and world-famous museums and art collections.
Beyond the Kattegat strait, the Baltic Sea and the Strait of Öresund, the Kingdom of Sweden –

the skerry coast, as here at Lake

The changing of the guard ceremony in front of Amalienborg Palace in the Danish capital, Copenhagen.

Stockholm: Riddarholmskyrkan on Riddarholmen. The Swedish church is the final resting place of many Swedish monarchs.

ten times larger than Denmark – offers a breathtaking diversity of landscapes and tranquil expanses. But it also attracts tourists accordingly. The south of the country, where little Nils Holgersson's wonderful journeys to the Sápmi region (Lapland) began, will likely remind travelers a bit of Denmark's meadow and field landscape. North of Gothenburg (Göteborg), however, the scenery becomes typically Swedish and is more reminiscent of the film adaptations of books by Astrid Lindgren, a Swedish author best known for creating *Pippi Longstocking*. Swedish houses painted "ox blood red" stand in the middle of lush green meadows surrounded by miles of birch and conifer woodlands. Vänern and Vättern, Sweden's

two largest lakes, almost feel like massive inland seas and are also found in this region.

North of Stockholm, nature takes on an increasingly primal feel. Population decreases, the rivers run more wildly and the forests become denser. The northernmost third of the country, Sweden's Sápmi region, is shaped by almost melancholy beauty and pure tranquility. Only the reindeer herds of the Saami people are able to find enough food in the bleak realm of the midnight sun.

Visitors here should do as the outdoor enthusiastic Swedes do and stay a few summer days in a remote *stuga* as part of their adventures in the countryside. They may even encounter one of the 500,000 Swedish moose along the way. There is

no need to fear the moose, but you should always be on the lookout for trolls lurking in the forests – Sweden is a land of legends, myths and fairy tales. This popular cultural strain is also expressed in the numerous festivals and customs here that are unknown in other parts of Europe. Perhaps the nicest of

these is the "magic" of midsummer night's festival held all over the country in June. Along with Christmas, this longest day (and shortest night) is the favourite holiday in Sweden. People meet up for an evening meal of herring, they drink aquavit (a clear schnapps) or "öl" (Swedish for beer) and enjoy traditional dance and the conviviality.

Egeskov Castle is one of the most beautiful Renaissance water castles in the south of Denmark.

1 The Kalmar Union, which united the kingdoms of Sweden, Denmark and Norway, was signed at Kalmar Castle in 1397.

2 The cathedral in Lund, Sweden, was begun in 1103. with the help of stonemasons from the Rhineland.

3 The baroque Kalmar Cathedral in south-east Sweden was built between 1660 and 1703.

This tour of southern Scandinavia first heads along the southern Swedish Baltic Sea coast to Stockholm, then passes by numerous lakes and through seemingly endless forests to Göteborg. In Denmark, a fairy-tale journey leads through Jutland, Fyn and Seeland with picturesque ports and trading towns before reaching Copenhagen.

1 **Copenhagen** (see page 53) You can get to Malmö from Copenhagen by ferry or via the Öresund Bridge.

2 **Malmö** Canals run through the picturesque Old Town here, which can be discovered either on foot or by boat. The Stortorget is lined with wonderful buildings. The route then continues to Lund, a picturesque university town where the cathedral is the oldest Romanesque church in Sweden.

3 **Ystad** Many imposing half-timbered buildings make Ystad one of the most beautiful cities in Scania. The herring catch brought wealth to the monastery and fishing town back in the Hanseatic era.

After Ystad, it is worth making a detour at Tomelilla to Sweden's only castle complex still to be preserved in its original condition from 1499. Christinehof's ramparts and yard-thick walls meant it had been previously impregnable. Regular ferries depart Ystad to the Danish island of Bornholm.

4 **Karlskrona** Many building complexes in this city were designed for military purposes in the late 17th century and are

Travel Information

Route profile
Length: approx. 2,500 km (1,550 mi) without detours
Time required: 4 weeks
Start and end: Copenhagen
Route (main locations): Copenhagen, Malmö, Karlskrona, Stockholm, Falun, Göteborg, Århus, Odense, Copenhagen

Traffic information:
The Green Insurance Card is recommended. "Shark teeth" on the road replace "Yield" signs in Denmark. The Öresund and Storebælt bridges have tolls of up to 50 euros each way for passenger cars. Watch out for deer crossings in Sweden. They are quite common. Low-beam headlights are automatic in both Sweden and Denmark.

When to go:
May to October (Denmark), June to September (Sweden).

Accommodation:
All price categories are available and in demand Scandinavia, particularly holiday homes.
Typically Danish: "Kros" – royally licenced regional guesthouses/hotels (www.dansk-kroferie.dk).

Information:
Denmark:
www.dt.dk
www.visitdenmark.com
Sweden:
Sveriges Rese- och Turistråd, Box 3030, Kungsgatan 36, S-103 61 Stockholm, www.visit-sweden.com and www.sweden.se

Copenhagen

History and tradition greet travelers at every turn here, in the Danish capital and royal residence on the Strait of Öresund. The atmosphere is relaxed and open-minded, and most tourist attractions can be reached on foot.

The city on the Strait of Öresund has been the capital of Denmark since 1443. It experienced its first heyday in the late Middle Ages as a trading port, and a second boom in the 16th and 17th centuries, particularly under King Christian IV, who greatly expanded and developed the city.

Sights of note here include: the Tivoli Gardens amusement park; the promenade at Nyhavn Canal, lined with old wooden sailing ships and cafés; canal and harbor tours; excursions to the Little Mermaid (Lille Havfrue) on

Left: The Little Mermaid.
Top: Nyhavn, today the oldest port in the city, built from 1671 to 1673.
Bottom: The Tivoli amusement park.

the Langelinie pier; Amalienborg Palace, the royal residence; the Zoological Gardens; Slotsholm island and Christiansborg Castle; works by Danish sculptors at the Thorvaldsen-museum; the antique collection of the Ny Carlsberg Glytotek; Rådhus Pladsen with the town hall; the Carlsberg brewery; and the historical and ethnographic collections of the Nationalmuseet.

listed as UNESCO World Heritage Sites. The Karlskrona's Stortorget is among the largest squares in northern Europe; the admiralty church, built in 1685, and the Trinity church from 1714 are also worth visiting.

⑤ Kalmar The Kalmar Union of 1397 united the kingdoms of Denmark, Norway and Sweden. The castle and cathedral of this city on the Kalmarsund is worth seeing, as are the baroque and Renaissance harbor and the buildings in the Old Town. A 6-km (4-mi) bridge spans the sound from Kalmar to the island of Öland.
Your route then follows the coastal road E22 toward Norrköping. Along the way there are several ferry connections to Gotland from Oskarshamn and Västervik. If you have time, be sure to make a detour to the Swedish skerry coast at Västervik, Valdemarsvik/Fyrudden or St Anna south of Norrköping. At Norrköping, the road continues north past the Hjälmaren to the intersection with the E20, where you follow the E20 to Gripsholm, 20 km (12 mi) beyond Strängnäs.

⑥ Gripsholm Castle The German writer and satirist Kurt Tucholsky created a literary monument out of this castle at Lake Mälaren. He is buried at the nearby village of Mariefred. From Gripsholm Castle, the road follows the south-east bank of Lake Mälaren to the Swedish capital, Stockholm.

⑦ Stockholm (see page 55)

⑧ Uppsala This city is famous for having the oldest university in northern Sweden, founded in 1477, and Scandinavia's largest cathedral, the Domkyrka, which houses the remains of national heroes, kings Erik and Gustav Wasa. The 16th-century

castle and the Carolina Redviva, the largest library in Sweden, are other worthwhile sights in this city on the Frysån River.
To the north is Gamla Uppsala with royal burial mounds and an 11th-century church. It was the country's political center until the 13th century.
From Uppsala, your route leads north to the harbor town of Gävle, marking the start of Highway 80, which you will take west to Falun.

⑨ Falun The Vikings allegedly mined copper in Falun, but the town's heyday as a center for copper processing ended in disaster: The mine collapse here in 1687 created Stora Stöten, said to be the largest hole in the world at 65 m (213 ft) deep, 370 m (1,214 ft) long and 220 m (722 ft) wide. The town's historic copper mine is a UNESCO World Heritage Site.
On Highway 70, you now head north-west to Lake Siljan, which you will almost completely circumnavigate on your trip.

⑩ Siljansee Dalarna province is densely forested and known for the carved wooden Dalarna horses. When travelling around the lake, it is worth stopping in Mora on the northern shore. The town marks the end of the Wasa Track (86 km/53 mi). The "Zorngaarden", a museum by artist Anders Zorn, and the "Zorns Gammelgaarden"open-air museum are worth a visit. From Leksand at the southern end of the lake, you initially follow Highway 70 to Borlänge, where you change to Highway 60 towards Örebro.

⑪ Örebro In addition to the beautiful sculptures and monuments in this old city in central Sweden, it is also worth paying a visit to the 800-year-old castle on an island in the river, the 13th-century St Nicholas church

as well as to the more modern Svampen water tower.
From Örebro, the route now follows the E4 to Vättern via the town of Askersund.

⑫ Vättern Vättern is Sweden's second-largest lake. Plan a stop at the Göta Canal in Motala, which connects Vättern and Vänern, and in the garden city of Vadstena with its interesting minster and castle. At the southern end of the lake is Jönköping. From there the route heads directly west to the port city of Göteborg.

⑬ Göteborg Sweden's second-largest city has a charming Old Town lined with canals. Highly recommended are a stroll down Kungsportsavenyn boulevard, a visit to Lieseberg amusement park and the futuristic new

opera, and a boat ride through the ports, canals and islets.
From Gothenburg, it is not far to Bohuslän, with prehistoric rock carvings at Tanum. Ferries depart Göteborg for Frederikshavn on the Danish Jutland peninsula via the Kattegat. Travel time is around three hours.

1 View of Gripsholm Castle from the beach in Mariefred in Södermanland province. The castle has housed the National Portrait Collection since 1822.

2 Drottningholm Castle (1699) on the island of Lovø in Lake Mälar was modelled on Versailles and has been the residence of the royal family since 1981.

3 A village near Göteborg on the western Swedish coast in Västergötland.

Stockholm

This metropolis, home to 1.6 million people, is spread out over fourteen islands at the southern end of Lake Mälar, on the skerry-rich Baltic Sea coast between fresh- and saltwater zones. Founded in 1252 and capital since 1634, Stockholm has developed into a vibrant, cosmopolitan city. Magnificent buildings, parks, rivers and bridges make it unique among its peers.

Worth seeing in the Swedish capital are: the Royal City Castle (Kungliga Slottet), one of the largest residences in the world with around six hundred rooms; Storkyrkan, Stockholm's oldest church, with a Gothic interior; Tyska Kyrkan, church of the German community with an impressive altar; Riddarholmkyrkan, royal burial site since the Thirty Years War; the baroque Reich Chamber of Corporations Riddarhuset; the picturesque port district

Top: Stockholm in winter.
Left: 17th-century row houses.

between Österlanggatan and Skeppsbron; Stadshus (1911– 1923), an icon of the city with a stunning views; Konserthuset, venue of the annual Nobel Prize ceremony. Worthwhile museums include: the Nationalmuseet and Moderna Museet (modern art); Skansen, the world's first open-air museum; Vasamuseet with the Vasa, Gustav II Adolf's flagship of sunk at its launch in 1628. Also worth seeing are the decorated subway stations ("the longest gallery in the world"); the grand Strandvägen boulevard; the skerry garden and the residence of the royal family, Drottningholm Castle, with fully functional rococo theater.

⑭ Frederikshavn The largest city in northern Jutland, Frederikshavn is famous for the Krudt-tårnet, a 17th-century powder tower with a weapons collection spanning three centuries. Before your journey continues south, it is worth making a small detour to the northern tip of the peninsula in Skagen.

⑮ Skagen About 150 years ago, a number of artists settled here on the northernmost tip of Jutland, formed an artists' colony and began creating what would become icons of Danish painting. Their collective works can be seen in the Skagen Museum and in the Michael and Anna Ancher House. Don't miss the Tilsand-ede Church, which was ultimately abandoned in 1795 due to the incessant sand that blew onshore here.

⑯ Sæby The half-timbered fishing houses, cutter port and minster with 15th-century frescos, this spa town is a quaint little bit of paradise. The Saeby-gaard Manor (the oldest part of which dates back to 1576) is also worth seeing. The nearby Voergaard Renaissance castle houses a world-class art and porcelain collection.

⑰ Aalborg The Limfjord and Aalborg are best viewed from the 105-m (345-ft) Aalborgtårnet tower. The Budolfi Cathedral is dedicated to the patron saint of sailors. Jens Bang's Stenhus, the home of a rich merchant built in 1624, and the North Jutland Museum of Modern and Contemporary Art should also not be missed.

⑱ Viborg The cathedral in Denmark's oldest city had to be completely rebuilt in the 19th century. Its ceiling frescos and the medieval quarter are worth seeing, as are the limestone

mines, which were shut down in the 1950s after nearly one thousand years of mining. They are in front of the city gates.

⑲ Århus Denmark's second-largest city was built on a former Viking settlement. The St Clement's church, begun in 1200, is Denmark's largest cathedral. The Den Gamle By is the first open-air museum for non-royal Danish culture. The architect, Arne Jacobsen, co-designed the Raadhuset, completed in 1942. A 2,000-year-old preserved body found in the marshland is the main attraction of the Moesgård Museum.

⑳ Vejle This "mountain town" has a spectacular location on the fjord of the same name. St Nicolai Church is the oldest building in the town and is home to a 2,500-year-old preserved body found in the marshland and the walled-in skulls of 23 robbers. The graphic art in the museum and the city's landmark, a windmill, are worth seeing. Northwest of Vejle is the UNESCO World Heritage Site of Jelling, with impressive burial mounds and two royal rune stones from the 10th century, which are considered to be "Denmark's baptismal certificates".
The Jutland mainland is connected to Fyn island with a railway road bridge and a highway bridge (Storebæltsbro). The island's capital is the next stop.

㉑ Odense Hans Christian Andersen made this island capital world famous. His childhood home and museum are open to visit, while the Carl Nielsen Museum, the Old Town and the Gothic St Knuds Church are other attractions.
From Odense, Highway 9 leads to the next stop, Egeskov.

㉒ Egeskov This 16th-century castle is one of the best-known moated castles in Europe. It has a cemetery and drawbridge, a park with baroque landscaping and a vintage car museum.
From the south of the island it's on to Nyborg on the east coast, where the 18-km (11-mi) Store-bæltbro bridge spans the Great Belt between Fyn and Sjælland.

㉓ Trælleborg Not far from Slagelse is the Viking fort of Trælleborg, built according to strict geometric theory and dedicated to King Harald Bluetooth (10th century).

㉔ Roskilde This city's cathedral is a UNESCO World Her-

itage Site and the burial site of thirty-eight Danish regents. The five preserved Viking ships displayed in the modern Vikingeskibs Museet were discovered in the adjacent Roskilde fjord, and are worth seeing.
Finally, you pass Frederiksborg castle en route to Helsingör at the northern end of Sjælland.

㉕ Helsingør The main attraction of this city located on the Strait of Öresund is Kronborg castle. Another 50 km (31 mi) or so along the coast and you arrive back in Copenhagen, the end of your journey.

1 The Renaissance Kronborg castle near Helsingør on the strait between Denmark and Sweden.

2 A walk through the open-air museum Den Gamle By in Århus shows you the Denmark of old.

3 Roskilde was the summer residence of the Danish kings from the 11th to the 15th centuries.

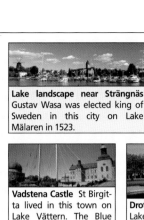

Lake landscape near Strängnäs Gustav Wasa was elected king of Sweden in this city on Lake Mälaren in 1523.

Skerry coast off Stockholm The rock islands that stretch along a 150-km (93-mi) belt are a popular weekend refuge for city dwellers.

Stockholm Magnificent buildings, parks, waterways and bridges make Sweden's capital unique. It stretches over fourteen islands between the Baltic Sea and Lake Mälaren.

Vadstena Castle St Birgitta lived in this town on Lake Vättern. The Blue Church is worth seeing.

Drottningholm Castle This castle on an island in Lake Mälaren is the primary residence of the royal family and has a functional rococo theater.

Uppsala This is the oldest university town in the north (from 1477) and is home to Scandinavia's oldest church.

Bohuslän This region stretches north of Göteborg up to the Norwegian border and features a long coastline with numerous bays.

Gripsholm One of the most popular tourist attractions outside Stockholm is the castle on Lake Mälaren.

Århus Denmark's second-largest city is home to the country's largest place of worship, the St Clemes Kirke. The Den Gamle By open-air museum is the second-largest of its kind in Europe.

Öland This is the second-largest island in Sweden and is connected to the mainland by a bridge.

Gotland Sweden's largest island can be reached by ferry and is popular for its comparatively mild climate. The bizarre rock formations off the coast are a big draw for visitors.

Map labels:

Särna, Mora, Orsa, Malung, Santa world, Leksand, Rättvik, Siljan, Falun, Sundsvall, Gävle, Borlänge, Ludvika, Furnebofjärdens nationalpark, Tierp, Engelsberg, Kopparberg, Nora, Västerås, Uppsala, Norrtälje, Skokloster, Enköping, Karlstad, Birka, Drottningholm, STOCKHOLM, Garphyttans nationalpark, Örebro, Eskilstuna, Gripsholm, Skogskyrkogården, Katrineholm, Askersund, Nyköping, Nynäshamn, Vadstena, Motala, Göta kanal, Norrköping, St.Anna, Linköping, Valdemarsvik, Oslo (N), Svinesund, Bjørnsholm, Bohuslän, Tanumshede, Karlstad, Nordens Ark, Trollhättan, Gränna, Gamleby, Norra Kvills nationalpark, Västervik, Visby, Raukar, Lärbro, Gotland, Stenungsund, Orust, Tjörn, Kungälv, Göteborg, Jönköping, Astrid Lindgren Värld, Oskarshamn, Ljugarn, Hirtshals, Skagen, Borås, Kungsbacka, Store mosse nat.park, Byxelkrok, Burgsvik, Raukar, Fårup Sommerland, Frederikshavn, Småland, Blå Jungfrun nationalpark, Lindholm Høje, Sæby, Läsø, Varberg, Mönsterås, Borgholm, Öland, Aalborg, Np.Rebild Bakker, Nybro, Hobro, Anholt, Kattegat, Kalmar, Viborg, Randers, Färjestaden, Södra Ölands odlingslandskap, Silkeborg, Århus, Kullaberg, Karlshamn, Jämjö, Ottenby, Jutland, Helsingør, Helsingborg, Kristianstad, Stumholmen, Karlskrona, Jelling, Nordby, Frederiksborg, Legoland, Horsens, Samsø, COPENHAGEN, Lund, Stenshuvuds nationalpark, Vejle, Fredericia, Roskilde, Bornholm, Esbjerg, Odense, Trælleborg, Øresundsbro, Malmö, Simrishamn, Kolding, Ringsted, Trelleborg, Ystad, Ales stenar, Hammershus, Ribe, Egeskov, Storebæltsbro, Herlufsholm, Svaneke, Rømø, Svendborg, Valdemars Slot, Rønne, Husum (D), Hamburg (D), Radby Gedser, SWEDEN, DENMARK

Egeskov Castle This moated castle is surrounded by thick oak forests, from which its name is derived. The castle's park and vintage car museum are also worth a visit.

Copenhagen Denmark's capital is busy yet cozy. Its highlights include the Lille Havfrue (Little Mermaid) and the Tivoli Gardens. Pictured here is the Amalienborg Palace.

Landscape near Ystad Fishing (especially for herring) brought wealth to the region around Ystad, which was traditionally focused on agriculture.

Bornholm The "Pearl of the Baltic" is actually quite far from Denmark. It is home to almost all types of Scandinavian scenery as well as many tourist attractions.

Kalmar Castle The union of Denmark, Sweden and Norway, decreed in the Kalmar Union, took place in Kalmar's magnificent castle in 1397. The cathedral is also worth seeing.

Route 7
Finland and Russia

St Petersburg: Smolni Cathedral and

From the empire of the Czars to the land of a thousand lakes

Finland is a quiet country with countless lakes and seemingly endless forests. It is ideal for visitors looking for a bit of peace and seclusion. From Finland's capital, Helsinki, you can also make a detour to St Petersburg, Russia, just a few hours away.

The iconic animal of the Arctic far north, the moose, is very common in Finland. In fact, the very shape of the country is similar to the head of a female elk, and a look at any map of Finland will make it obvious why the "Elk Head" is considered the "Land of a Thousand Lakes": the complex maze of roughly 50,000 to 60,000 bodies of inland water dominates the entire southern half of the country. Approximately 12 percent of "Suomi", the Finnish name for Finland, is covered by freshwater, and about 70 percent by forest. The ever-changing landscape of beautiful waterways, lakes and vast forests make Finland a dream destination for anyone seeking a quiet, relaxing holiday. Having said that, however, the Finnish Baltic Sea coast along the Gulf of Bothnia and the Gulf of Finland is also a very impressive landscape, with offshore skerry (rock) islands, innumerable bays and sandy beaches, picturesque

A 19th-century icon of Konevitsa in Kuopio.

villages perfect for bathing and fishing, and a verdant green hinterland. In addition to that

are the slightly more melancholy fjell and tundra regions north of the Arctic Circle.

Finland offers ideal conditions for winter sports between the months of November and May, but the icy-cold temperatures and the somewhat bleak darkness of the long polar nights may deter. They are also the reason why the Finns are often considered a rather serious and quiet folk. In reality, however, they are a fun-loving and relaxed people who place great value on family and, as soon as summer starts, spend much of their free time outside picking berries, gathering mushrooms, fishing, swimming, boating or just lounging around. They also use the time to "tank up" on

Resurrection Monastery.

St Petersburg: the magnificent baroque building of the Nicholas Naval Cathedral on the Griboyedov canal.

The 150-year-old cathedral behind the statue of Czar Alexader II at Senate Square in Helsinki. An imposing staircase leads to the cathedral, whose interior includes a statue of Agricola, Finland's reformer.

light and warmth for the long winters, forgetting time and space and simply enjoying the relief from the dark time of year. For 1.5 million enthusiasts of music, film, literature, jazz, choir, theater and dance from all over the world, the summer festivals in Finland are the highlight of the year. No other country boasts as many festivals per capita.

Nearly all who visit Finland come for its natural scenic beauty, and less so for its cities. But that is not to say they are without their own charms. And this does not just apply to the neoclassical capital, Helsinki, or Turku, the former capital on the Gulf of Bothnia. Finland's coast is home to plenty of picturesque fishing and resort towns where, not surprisingly, Swe-

dish culture and language are also widespread. Meanwhile, there is a distinct Russian feel in Karelia, Finland's "Wild East". The Sami settlements beyond the Arctic Circle, like the one on Lake Inari, are also fascinating. Even Finland's unique language does not represent a hindrance as far as pronunciation is concerned. Finnish is the one of the few languages in the world to have largely solved the exasperating problem of one sound, one letter. This means you can read "suomalainen" and say it correctly without any overly complex pronunciation rules. Most Finns understand a bit of English and German as well, and only one little Finnish term is actually truly essential: "sauna". Only those who have had the pleasure to partake in this

2,000-year-old Finnish body wellness ritual have experienced the "true" Finland.

From Helsinki, or one of the coastal towns on the Gulf of Finland, it is also worth taking a trip to the Russian cities of St Petersburg and Novgorod to the south, especially during the "White Nights". Both are Han-

seatic cities with unique architectural and cultural treasures. The historic center of St Petersburg, with its beautiful churches, magnificent palaces, museums, canals and bridges, is listed as a UNESCO World Heritage Site, as are the churches of Novgorod with their steep roofs and carvings.

Most of Finland's lakes are concentrated in the south of the country and are connected by rivers and canals.

The Finlandia Route:
the wonders of Finland,
St Petersburg and the
North Cape on one, albeit
long journey. Follow our
route through the diversity
of southern Finland
(Route I) and Lake Saimaa
before connecting with
Route II, which takes you
through Karelia's wild
forests toward the
northern tip of Europe.

Route I – Southern Finland
1 **Helsinki** (see page 61)
Your journey through southern
Finland begins in the capital.

2 **St Petersburg** For more
details, look in the Travel Information box and on page 63.

3 **Raasepori** The "City of
Oaks" is known for the national park just off the coast that
features picturesque skerry, or
rock, islands. Wooden houses
from the 17th and 18th century
can be found in the historic
center of Raasepori, while Alvar
Aalto's bank building showcases modern architecture.
Raasepori Castle, located outside of town, is a curious place:
At the time of its construction in
the 14th century, it could only
be reached by boat; now it is
located in the country's interior.

4 **Hangö/Hanko** The Hangö
headland sits at the western
foothills of the Salpausselkä
mountains and is mostly covered in dense pine forest. Finland's southernmost mainland
point is a sailing, swimming,
fishing and walking paradise
for Finns looking to take it easy
amidst the skerry gardens or on
the many long sandy beaches.
The Art Nouveau villas in the
park were built at the turn of
the 20th century.

Back in Ekenäs, Road 184 leads
to Salo on the Lappdalsfjärden.
From there it heads back to the
unique skerry coast.

5 **Turku/Åbo** The skerry garden off the coast of Turku has
over 20,000 islands of varying
sizes and is one of the Finland's
most popular attractions. Only
a few buildings in the former
capital survived what proved to
be Scandinavia's largest fire in
1827: Turunlinna Castle, a solid
stone building (built in the late
13th century), and Turku's brick
cathedral, the country's national
shrine consecrated in 1290.

6 **Naantali** This town has
managed to preserve its late
18th- and early 19th-century
architectural charm, the main
attraction being the Old Town,
the Minster, and the Kultarnata
Castle, which is the summer residence of Finland's president.
Anyone wishing to experience
the skerry garden up close can

1 The Uspensky Cathedral towers
over the harbor in Helsinki.

2 The skerry gardens off the
Finnish coast near Tammisaari.

Travel Information

Route profile
Length:
Route I: 1,350 km (839 mi),
Route II (from Juva):
1,400 km (870 mi)
Time required: at least two
weeks; do not underestimate
the return journey!
Start and end: Helsinki

Traffic information:
The green insurance card is
recommended. Video devices
must be declared. Vehicle na-
tionality labels are required
and low-beam lights during
the day are compulsory.
Watch out for deer crossings.

When to go:
Route I: June–September
Route II: July–end of August

Accommodation:
Holiday homes, or "mökkis",
with sauna facilities are
popular all over Finland.

Information:
Here are some websites to
help you prepare for your
trip:
www.visitfinland.com
www.alltravelfinland.com

**St Petersburg and
Nizhny Novgorod:**
The best way to arrive in
St Petersurg is to take a
ferry from Helsinki or other
Finnish port towns, or take
a bus from Lappeenranta.
There are also good bus or
rail connections to Russia
from other towns in Finland.

Helsinki

Roughly 500,000 people live in Helsinki, Finland's compact capital, founded in 1550 by Swedish King Gustav Vasa. Following devastating fires, Czar Alexander II ordered Helsinki to be rebuilt in the neoclassical style. Twenty of the buildings erected then still stand today. Combined with Art Nouveau and other contemporary edifices, the metropolis on the Gulf of Finland offers a unique and enjoyable panorama.

Amond the attractions in Helsinki, Engel's Senate Square is considered one of the most beautiful plazas in the world. It includes the cathedral, the government palace, the main university campus and the university library. At its center is the statue of Czar Alexander II. The market square and historic market halls at the southern harbor has ferry piers for ships to Suomenlinna, an old Swedish island fort and UNESCO World Heritage Site, and to the skerry islands. The Katajanokka Peninsula has the best panoramic view of the capital. The beautiful Orthodox Uspenski Cathedral (1868) has a lavish interior. Luotsikatu, one of the most magnificent streets in Helsinki has numerous Art Nouveau buildings. The Esplanade, Helsinki's pedestrian zone, is home to Stockmann department store, the largest in Scandinavia.

Museums include the Ateneum (Finnish), the Kiasma (modern) and the Sinebrychoff (foreign). Take a look at the central station with a 48-m-high (158-ft) clock tower, the Suomalainen brothers' rock church (1969), Alvar Aalto's Finlandia Hall (1970), where the last stage of the CSCE act was signed in 1975. The tower at the Olympic stadium provides a fantastic view over Helsinki.

View of the cathedral from the harbor.

follow a small access road to Pulkkalla. The N8 now leads to Rauma at the Gulf of Bothnia.

7 Rauma Finland's third-oldest city is an important center for top bobbin lace making. The historic Old Town, which has been completely unaffected by any fires over the last 320 years, has been declared a World Heritage Site: 600 wooden buildings form the largest inner city complex of this kind in all of Scandinavia. From Pori take the N8 to the N2, which leads to Forssa, and from there head on to Hämeenlinna.

8 Hämeenlinna The birth house of composer Jean Sibelius (1865–1957), the Häme brick castle from the 13th century, and Aulanko Park are all among the attractions here.

9 Lahti This famous winter sports town is situated on an impressive moraine tuffet with two lakes. It impresses visitors with its six ski jumps and a small ski museum. The Church of the Cross (built in 1978, designed by Alvar Aalto) and the Sibelius Hall are considered architectural gems. Lahti is also the gateway to Finland's lake region, while the Salpausselkä mountains and Vesijärvi and Päijänne lakes offer many leisure options.
The landscape along the N5 to Mikkeli affords visitors everything they would expect of the "Land of a Thousand Lakes".

10 Mikkeli This city is situated in a rolling hills landscape and was built on orders from Czar Nicholas I in 1838. It had already become an important center in eastern Finland in the Middle Ages. A small stone chapel from 1320 in the market square dates back to this time as well. The largest wooden vicarage in Finland – Kenkävero – is in the town center. Roughly 700 lakes

and ponds surround the city, and marshlands stretch off toward the north. Dark-green forests, shimmering lakes, a few villages and some summer homes are scattered along the way to Savonlinna and Kerimäki. Those wanting to travel up to the North Cape must initially stay on the N5 and not turn off toward Savonlinna.

11 Kerimäki The world's largest wooden church is located in the small town of Kerimäki, north of Savonlinna. Its benefactor – an emigrant who found wealth in the United States – provided the building plans in feet, but the Finnish architect built it in metres, hence its unintended dimensions (27 m /89 ft) high with a capacity of 5,000). The tiny village only has about 6,000 people!

12 Retretti and Punkaharju Beyond Savonlinna, it is worth making a stop at the Retretti art center – which is partly above ground and partly in caves – and at the mile-long moraine hill Punkaharju, which stretches between Lakes Pihlajavesi and Puruvesi. The rest of the journey on the N6 from Sääkjsalmi runs between the lake district and the Russian border.

13 Imatra on Lake Saimaa Imatra, a lively garden city on the Russian border, is located in the main basin of Lake Saimaa, the largest in Finland. The "Lake of a Thousand Islands" is known for its population of ringed seals living in freshwater. In Imatra, it is worth visiting the community center, designed by Alvar Aalto, in the Vuoksennista district, as wel as the Vuoksa waterfalls, mostly "subdued" for a power plant.

14 Lappeenranta This old garrison city is located on the

Saimaa canal, which runs for 50-km (31-mi) from the lake district past the Russian border to the Gulf of Finland. All kinds of cruises are available on Lake Saimaa and they depart from Finland's largest inland port. Most of the city's attractions are located outside the old fortress section of Lappeenranta, whose ramparts have been partially reconstructed.
The Orthodox church is the oldest in the country (1785) and is worth a visit. Near Luumäki, Route 25 takes you to Hamina on the Gulf of Finland.

15 Hamina/Vehkalahti The Swedish ramparts here, dating from the early 18th century, are well worth seeing. They were designed to replace the Vyborg Castle that fell to the Russians, but they were again seized by the Russians before their completion. Hamina's charming octagonal market square, in the

center of which is the town hall from 1789, is an urban gem. The fortress is also worth seeing.

16 Kotka The main attractions in Finland's largest export harbor are the Orthodox St Nicholas' Church (1795), a simple edifice with an ornately decorated wall, and the grand buildings from the 19th century (trade union house, town hall, savings bank). The coastal road to Porvoo affords breathtaking views of the deep fjords and the skerry coastline.

17 Porvoo/Borgå This town has two old quarters: the Old

1 The historic center of Rauma, declared a UNESCO World Heritage Site in 1991.

2 An attractive rapeseed field on the way through the southern Finnish countryside.

Detour

St Petersburg

Czar Peter the Great planned his city down to the finest detail. Founded in 1703, St Petersburg was meant to be the Russian "window to the West" and it was here on the banks of the Neva that his vision of progress was realized. The entire city was to be built of stone, an innovation in itself, and since then, it has developed into one of Russia's most important cultural, political and economic centers. Since its founding, the city's name has changed three times: Petrograd, Leningrad and back to St Petersburg. It is well worth paying a visit during the "White Nights" in June when it is still light at midnight.

The square with the mighty Alexander Column (1832) in front of the Winter Palace is a sight along with the magnificently decorated Czars' residence. The Hermitage Museum in the Winter Palace is worth a visit including the adjoining buildings. It has a renowned art collection.

Around the palace square you'll find Alexander Park with the architecturally unique Admiralty (UNESCO World Heritage Site), whose golden spire is one of the city's landmarks; Senate Square with the Peter the Great monument; St Isaac's Cathedral (19th C.), the largest and most lavishly decorated church in Russia with a golden cupola; Yussupov Palace on the banks

of the Moika; St Nicholas' Naval Cathedrawith its shiny gold domes (18th C.); and the Mariinsky Theater, the world-famous opera and ballet playhouse. The historic city center (UNESCO World Heritage Site) includes the Peter and Paul Fortress (18th century) with Peter's Gate; the burial site of the czars in the Peter and Paul Cathedral; the crownwork with artillery museum; the Central Naval Museum in the former stock exchange; the art chamber and Peter the Great's collection of rarities and the Lomonossov

Museum; the 18th-century science academy; the complex of the twelve councils (1721), today a university; and the baroque Menshikov Palace. Around the majestic Nevsky Prospekt stand: Kasaner Cathedral; Resurrection Church (1907); Stroganov Palace (1754); Arts Square with the Michaelmas Palace and the Russian Museum; the Ethnography Museum; Anitshkov Palace; Anitshkov Bridge; and the baroque Belosselsky-Belosersky Palace. Also worth seeing are: the Summer Garden, the city's oldest park with the

Summer Palace from 1710, and the Marble Palace; Alexander Nevsky Monastery with its neoclassical Trinity Cathedral; Tilchvin and Lazarus cemetery and the Smolni Resurrection Monastery with the baroque Resurrection Cathedral; Pushkin Theater and Pushkin Museum, Dostoyevsky Museum; Sheremetev Palace with the Anna Achmatova Museum.

Don't miss the UNESCO World Heritage Site of Novogorod while you are here. The "New City" is some 200 km (124 mi) south-west on Lake Ilmen, on the main road to Moscow. Despite its name, Novgorod is one of Russia's oldest cities, founded in the 9th century. The walled Kremlin of the former city state, which existed from the 12th to the 17th centuries and is protected by nine towers, is imposing. Novgorod's churches, built between the 12th and 14th centuries in a great variety of styles, are also famous. At the time, almost every street and guild had its own ornate church.

1 The Winter Palace: a masterpiece of Russian baroque.

2 St Isaac's Cathedral is the largest and most magnificent church in St Petersburg.

3 The Grand Palace, summer residence of the czars, is in Pushkin (Tsarskoe Selo) near St Petersburg and was built in 1724, for Catherine the Great, wife of Peter III.

Town plastered in header brick with a Gothic brick cathedral, and a "younger" Old Town with neoclassical stone buildings. The red warehouse sheds on the shores of the Porvoonjoki are from the 18th and 19th centuries and worth seeing. The best view of Finland's second-oldest city is from the old bridge. Helsinki, the final stop on the Route I section, is further 51 km (32 mi) from here.

Route II Juva – North Cape

18 Kuopio The city's Orthodox Church Museum shows you how deeply Russian Orthodox beliefs are rooted in the Karelian community. It has one of the most famous collections of its kind in Western Europe.

Not far from the museum, a trailhead leads you up to the Puijo at 232 m (761 ft), where you can enjoy a spectacular view of the university town and the lakes and forests of the Karelian countryside from the 75-m-high (246-ft-) tower.

19 Kajaani This industrial city on the Oulujärvi is particularly worth seeing for its Kajaaninlinna Castle (17th to 20th centuries) and the minuscule town hall. It is also worth taking a detour to see the frescoes in the wooden church (1725) in nearby Paltaniemi.

The road then continues around the Oulujärvi. A vast marshland known as the Käinuunselkä begins on the north side of the road and stretches well into Finland's northern reaches. In the Rokua district, dunes soar 80 m (262 ft) above the plains of northern Finland.

20 Oulu Like so many other Finnish cities, Oulu's medieval townscape was also destroyed by a devastating fire. The main attractions in Northern Europe's second-most important export harbor on the Gulf of Bothnia

are the city's cathedral and the museums, including the fascinating Tietomaa science center. Off the coast of Oulu is the holiday island of Hailuoto, with quaint fishing villages, reed-roof houses, windmills, sandy beaches and an impressively large bird population. In peak summer in the Oulu region, the sun rises at three o'clock in the morning and does not set until after one o'clock at night. As a result, there is plenty of time to observe, for example, the Lapland titmouse or the Arctic diver with its rather eerie call.

21 Kemi Lapland's seaport at the mouth of the Kemijoki is an important lumber trading hub with tourist attractions such as the Sampo ice-breaker and the Isohaara power plant.

22 Rovaniemi The administrative center of Lapland is located just south of the Arctic Circle. After the city was razed to the ground in 1944, Alvar Aalto was given the job of designing its reconstruction. He had the main roads laid out in the shape of reindeer antlers, and also created the "Lappia House". The 320-m (.2-mi) Jätkänkynttilä Bridge is the landmark of this university town. The 172-m (564-ft) glassed-in Arcticum with the Arctic Center and the Lapland Provincial Museum are worth seeing.

23 Sodankylä This village is famous for the oldest wooden church in Lapland (1689) and also has the unfortunate reputation of being the coldest place in Finland. In mid-June, the "Midnight Sun Film Festival" is held here during the long midsummer nights.

24 Vuotso und Tankavaara You can learn a bit about the handicrafts and reindeer breeding of the Sami people in

the Sami settlement of Vuotso. The Gold Prospector Museum in Tankavaara recalls the local gold rush of the 1940s.

In the nearby Urho-Kekkonen National Park, you can go on some wonderful hikes. It is Finland's second-largest nature reserve. Beware of bears and wolves here.

25 Inari It is predominantly the Sami who choose to live through more than 200 days a year with temperatures below zero. The open-air Sami Museum provides information on their ancient culture. A nice hiking trail leads to the Pielpajärvi Wilderness Church (1760). The Inari region is dominated by Lake Inari, which is 80 km (50 mi) long and 40 km (25 mi) wide. The "Holy Lake of the Sami" is Finland's third-largest lake and is only free of ice for three months a year.

26 Karigasniemi After another 100 km (62 mi) through the stark wilderness, you reach the

Norwegian border at the village of Karigasniemi. The Ailigas rises to 620 m (2,034 ft) in the north-east, and not far off is the start of the Kevo Nature Reserve with Finland's mightiest spring, Sulaoja.

27 North Cape The North Cape is another 261 km (162 mi) away across the stark landscape and the dark-grey cliff soaring 307 m (1,007 ft) out of the Arctic Sea is often shrouded in fog. The northernmost point of the European mainland is actually Cape Knivskjellodden.

From the North Cape, it is now another 2,600 km (1,616 mi) by car along the E4 through Sweden along the Gulf of Bothnia to the German cities of Hamburg or Berlin (see Route 5).

1 Shore landscape at Lake Inari, Finland's third-largest lake with over 3,000 islands.

2 The densest brown bear population in Finland lives in the east and south-east.

North Cape This severe rock plateau, soaring 307 m (1,007 ft) out of the Arctic Sea, is the final stop on our tour. The objective is simply to be there, because the landscape itself is not necessarily a highlight. The same applies to the nearby Cape Knivskjellodden, actually the northernmost point of the European mainland.

Lapland The southern part of Lapland is covered in dense forest. A tundra landscape stretches through the north, however, while the north-west is mountainous with peaks of up to 1,324 m (4,344 ft).

The Sami Half of the approximately 17,000 Sami, predominantly found in the Finnish part of Sápmi, speak their own Finno-Ugric language. Only very few still lead a nomadic life, and technology has long been a feature of their community's survival.

Lake Inari The "Holy Lake of the Sami" is Finland's third-largest lake. It is only free of ice for a very short time and for 200 days of the year, temperatures dip below 0°C (32°F).

Kuopio The Orthodox Church Museum is the most famous of its kind in north-eastern Europe.

Finnish lake district This landscape is typical of Finland and consists of a tangle of lakes, bays and islands all connected to each other. Lakes cover around one-tenth of the country's area.

Savonlinna Finland's most beautiful and best-preserved medieval castle complex, Olavinlinna, is reached by pontoon bridge. It dates back to the year 1475.

Rauma Finland's third-oldest city is known for its bobbin trade. Rauma's city center, with its wooden buildings, has fortunately been protected from fires for over 300 years.

Helsinki An architectural highlight of the vast, green capital on the Gulf of Finland is the neoclassical Senate Square with the cathedral pictured here. Helsinki's museums, the underground rock church, Alvar Aalto's Finlandia Hall and the offshore skerry island belt are also worth seeing.

Turku (Åbo) Only very few buildings, including Turunlinna Castle, from the end of the 13th century, and the brick cathedral (consecrated in 1290), survived the major blaze of 1827. The skerry garden is just off the coast.

Peterhof Czar Peter I's oldest and most beautiful summer residence is near St Petersburg, on the southern banks of the Gulf of Finland. The castle is surrounded by a large park.

Finnish skerry coasts The region between Turku, Helsinki and the Åland islands, is particularly rich in skerry formations. Thousands of the islands create a unique habitat for birds and seals.

St Petersburg This 300-year-old city was planned down to the finest detail. Be sure to see the Peter and Paul Fortress, the Hermitage Museum and St Isaac's Cathedral.

Russia

Moscow and the Golden Ring

The Golden Ring is a must-see for enthusiasts of Russian art and architecture. The name itself actually refers to a ring of charming old towns north of Moscow – gems of Old Russia. They are localities that could easily be the setting for Russian novels, and the historic monasteries and churches are indeed testimony to a bygone era.

The old trading city of Nizhny Novgorod and its port on the ice-covered Volga River.

The New Virgin Convent in Moscow

The term Golden Ring, which was first coined in Russia at the start of the 1970s, refers to a series of Old Russian towns north of Moscow, the main ones being Vladimir, Suzdal, Yaroslavl, Rostov Velikiy, Sergiev Posad, Pereslavl-Zalessky and Kostroma. Moscow itself is also included. These Old Russian centers originally evolved from former fortresses built during Medieval times as protection against the Mongo-lians. Their mighty kremlins – defensive complexes – monasteries and churches were endowed with magnificent mosaics, icons and valuable treasures and represented a stark contrast to the misery of everyday life in these rural towns. While "Golden" refers to the striking, gilded domes of the medieval churches, the word "Ring" denotes the close cultural and historical links between individual towns.

Today they still stand as testimony to the "Old Russia" that existed until the October Revolution and which was a deeply religious nation. The towns of the Golden Ring are spread out across the broad, undulating plains which, shaped by the forces of multiple ice ages, extend to the south-east from the Gulf of Finland. The predominantly continental climate is characterized by warm summers and cold winters. Average temperatures in January are -11 °C (14 °F), while July reaches an average of about 19 °C (65 °F). Annual rainfall measures roughly 530 mm (209 in). The landscape along the upper reaches of the Volga and its tributaries, the Oka and Kama, is dominated by sizable rivers and lakes.

What most people would consider Russian history begins in the 10th century on the banks of the Dnepr, in Kiev, home to the Slavic tribes who traded with the passing Varangians

Moscow: the Kremlin with the Great Kremlin Palace, the Cathedral of the Dormition and "Ivan the Great" bell tower.

Red Square is Moscow's largest and most famous square. St Basil's Cathedral at the southern end draws everybody's attention.

from the north. It was only in the mid-11th century that the Russian heartland shifted towards the north-east, to the Golden Ring. The relatively mild climate, navigable rivers and existing trade routes that traversed the region led settlers to establish a series of towns during this period (9th-11th centuries). The population quickly rose to between 10,000 and 20,000.

With the collapse of the first Russian Empire, Vladimir became the successor to Kiev in the mid-12th century. During the same period, many residents of Kiev left the city for the Golden Ring region. The towns there became the capitals of powerful principalities. Rostov, Suzdal and Vladimir, for example, had already become

trading centres as well as hubs of secular and religious power even before the founding and rise of mighty Moscow. At that time, Moscow was part of the principality of Vladimir-Suzdal. In the 13th century, the Mongolians subordinated the Russian Empire and forced substantial tributes from its inhabitants. Moscow, at that time of minimal significance, eventually spearheaded the battle against the "Golden Horde", leaving the other principalities of the Ring to sink into obscurity after the end of the 14th century. Although chased out of the European zone, the Mongolians continued to leave their mark on Russia's Asian territories until the late 15th century. An important and ally of the Russian state at this time was

the Orthodox Church, whose churches, monasteries and monasticism created a unified front. A trip around the Ring usually begins in Moscow, then continues through the large

towns described on the following pages. However, there are also other interesting towns to be found such as Pushkino, Bratovscina, Rachmanowa, Muranovo or Abramtsevo.

Rostov Velikiy: A mighty wall encloses the kremlin and its picturesque churches which are elaborately painted and decorated.

Moscow and the Golden Ring: This poignant journey through the history of Old Russia begins in Moscow, continues via Rostov northwards as far as Kostroma, and then brings you back to Moscow via Ivanovo. During the trip you will be constantly confronted with the feeling that time has indeed stood still.

①　Moscow (see pages 70–71) Your route begins in Moscow before heading north towards Sergiev Posad, known as Zagorsk between 1931 and 1991.

②　Sergiev Posad The Monastery of the Holy Trinity and St Sergius (1340) is without doubt one of Russia's most important religious sites and serves as a pilgrimage destination for Orthodox Christians. It is encircled by a 1,600-m-long (1750 yard) wall that was breached once, albeit ultimately in vain, by Polish troops for sixteen months from 1608–1610.

Sergiev Posad was a national sanctuary even during the Czarist era and enjoyed unfettered support from the ruling class, who had their own residence in the complex, the Chertogi Palace (17th century). Large enough to accommodate a royal entourage of several hundred during official visits, the state converted the monastery into a museum in 1920 and it became a UNESCO World Heritage Site in 1993.

The Monastery of the Holy Trinity and St Sergius contains wonderful examples of paintings from Old Russia. The iconostase in the cathedral, for example, is decorated with works done by famous icon master Andrei Rublov and his assistants. The Holy Trinity was finished by the master himself.

The complex also displays outstanding examples of Russian architecture from the 14th to the 18th centuries. These defensive monasteries originally had several functions, as hospital wards, poorhouses, orphanages and schools. For a long time they were in fact the only institutions of their kind in all of Russia. The hospital building dates from the early 17th century, as do the adjoining churches St Zosima and St Sabbatius.

③　Pereslavl-Zalessky This Old Russian trading town is actually one of the oldest towns in the country and has a wealth of lovely churches and wooden houses. Located on the shores of Lake Pleshcheyevo, the town was founded in the 10th/11th centuries, and its ramparts also date from this time.

The outer walls of the white cathedral on the Red Square, behind the walls of the town's kremlin, are beautifullly decorated with semicircular ornaments called "zakomaras",

Travel Information

Route profile
Route length: 760 km (472 mi)
Time required: 8–10 days
Start and end: Moscow
Route (main locations):
Moscow, Sergiev Posad, Pereslavl-Zalessky, Rostov Veliky, Yaroslavl, Kostroma, Suzdal, Vladimir, Moscow

Special note:
There is a range of operators offering organized tours along the Golden Ring route. If you prefer to travel according to your own schedule, however, you have the option of hiring a car with a driver from Moscow.

Traffic information:
Entering Russia by car is possible, in theory, but it can be very complicated and time-consuming.
Entry visas require a passport, application and passport photograph.

Visiting the monasteries:
There are strict rules of conduct that apply in the various monasteries. Women need to wear a headscarf and a skirt; shorts and bare shoulders are taboo.
A film and photography permit is also required.

Further information:
Here are some websites to help you plan your trip:
www.thewaytorussia.net
www.russia-travel.com
www.geographia.com/russia
www.visitrussia.com
www.moscowcity.com

important stylistic features typical in Old Russian architecture. A few of the older remaining kremlin buildings include: the Church of the Metropolitan Peter from 1585; the 17th-century Annunciation Church with its spacious nave; the Goritsky Monastery dating from the first half of the 14th century; and the Danilov Monastery, located in the lower-lying south-western part of the town, which is from the 16th century.

🟠 **Pereslavsky National Park** This national park protects Lake Pleshcheyevo, the surrounding forest areas and wetlands, and the churches and cathedrals of Pereslavl-Zalessky. The lake is a breeding ground for 180 indigenous and thirty migratory bird species, and is home to brown bears as well. There is also a museum detailing the history of the Russian fleet and it was here that Czar Peter the Great built the first small battleships for mock warfare. It is the birthplace of the Russian navy.

🟠 **Rostov Velikiy** This city affords a panorama of stunning beauty, with its cathedral of seven silver roofs, a kremlin and the towers of the Monastery of Our Savior and St Jacob rising up beyond picturesque Lake Nero.

The name Rostov Velikiy has special historical significance here: In Czarist Russia, only Novgorod and Rostov were entitled to use the adjunct "Velikiy", meaning great. The town, founded in 862, had already developed into a flourishing trading center by the Middle Ages.

The large kremlin in Rostov Velikiy is protected by a wall over 1 km (0.6 mi) long with eleven towers. Silver and gold domes crown the palace here. When Prince Andrei Bogolyubsky conquered the town in the 12th century, it became the largest and most beautiful town in his principality. He had the Cathedral of the Dormition built in 1162. Only fragments of the 12th-century frescoes survived. The five domes of the Church of the Assumption rise opposite the cathedral. The lovely Church of St John (17th century) on the banks of the Ishna River is worth a visit as it is one of the very few surviving wooden churches in the region.

🟠 **Yaroslavl** Prince Yaroslav founded this fortified town at the confluence of the Kotorosl and the Volga rivers in the year 1010, and many of the original historical buildings have been preserved despite the ravages of war. The town enjoyed its golden age in the 17th century and the buildings from this era are among the loveliest in Russia. The Monastery of Our Savior (12th century) houses the Cathedral of the Resurrection of Christ (16th century). Approaching the town from the south you will get a lovely view, with the glittering gold-decorated domes of the cathedral and its masterful frescoes which, together with the Church of the Epiphany (17th century), is the most important building. The town's most magnificent church bears the name of the Prophet Elijah (17th century) and is on the central town square, from which the roads radiate out in a star shape. The church is also decorated with frescoes. The famous Tolchkovo Church with its many domes and towers stands on the other side of the Volga.

1 Moscow's St Basil's Cathedral comprises eight small chapels, each with a tower, grouped around the central church tower.

2 The Monastery of the Holy Trinity and St Sergius in Sergiev Posad is considered a unique gem among Russian monasteries.

3 One of the loveliest monasteries in Pereslavl Zalessky is the Gorizky Monastery founded in 1328.

4 Rostov is one of the smallest towns along the Golden Ring.

Moscow

Russia's capital lies on the Moskva River, which is a tributary of the mighty Volga. Mention was first made of Moscow in 1147, and it became the residence of the Grand Prince in 1325. In 1713, under Czar Peter the Great, Moscow lost its capital city status to the newly founded St Petersburg. In 1918, it was the Bolsheviks who once again made Moscow the political center of Russia's massive realm.

Moscow has been plundered repeatedly during its history, and has suffered a number of major fires. At the beginning of the 20th century, Moscow had 450 churches and twenty-five monasteries as well as 800 charitable institutions. Even after the decline of the Soviet Union, this city of 10 million still boasts impressive cultural statistics.

mausoleum with the mummified body of Soviet leader, Vladimir Ilyich Lenin (1870–1924), as well as the tombs of numerous other political figures and artists, the former artisan district of Kitaigorod and the GUM department store which which is now a shopping mall. Attractions also worth visiting around Red Square

Top: One of seven gingerbread style high-rises. Left: Moscow by night.

With sixty theaters, seventy-five museums, over 100 colleges and 2,300 listed buildings, it deserves its place as one of the world's top-ranking cities.
The sights near Red Square include the enchanting St Basil's Cathedral (begun in 1555 under Ivan the Terrible in memory of the conquest of Kasan, consecrated in 1557, and completed in 1679), the Kremlin (citadel, former coronation venue, seat of power, and a former prison) with twenty towers, the Great Stone Bridge, the Kremlin cathedrals (including the Uspenski Cathedral), the Alexander Garden, the remains of the Manege (former indoor riding arena that almost completely burned down in 2004) and the History Museum, the Kremlin Wall, the

are Yelisseyev deli, the Duma, and the world-famous Bolshoi Theater.
Interesting sights near Arbatskaja Vorota Square include the seat of the Russian government (the "White House"), the Church of Christ the Savior (rebuilt 1994–1997), and the "Stalin high-rise buildings".
Other sights worth visiting include: the palatial Moscow subway stations (begun in the 1930s), the Tretyakov Gallery (Russian and Soviet art), the museums and the former artists' district of Arbat, the Pushkin Museum of Fine Arts (also includes Western European art, the Priamos Treasure), the New Virgin Monastery including the "Celebrity Cemetery", the Lomo-oldest in Russia), Gorky Park's sculpture garden and Kolomenskoye Church of the Ascension.

7 Kostroma Kostroma marks the northernmost point of the Golden Ring and is a classic textbook town. Its current form took shape after a devastating fire in 1773. A number of significant monasteries, such as the Ipatiev Monastery, and the Resurrection Church, are among the few surviving relics of the era before the fire. A collection of wooden buildings which are typical of the region are on display in the Museum of Wooden Architecture, including a windmill, a farmhouse and some churches. The museum is in the Monastery of St Hypathius, which is dominated by the stunning golden towers of Holy Trinity Cathedral.

8 Suzdal This unique museum town with over 100 historical buildings is the best-preserved Old Russian town. The monastery town became the religious center of medieval Russia after the fall of Kiev. In the 11th century, the small town was the seat of the most powerful principality in Russia but the invading Mongolian army destroyed it in 1238. Suzdal, a UNESCO World Heritage Site since 1992, is on the Kamenka River. If you take an early summer morning walk among the whitewashed buildings of this monastery landscape, you will gain insight into the very soul of Russia.

The kremlin, the marketplace, the open-air museum, the traditional wooden houses and the monasteries stand out among the many attractions here. Some of the 18th- and 19th-century structures are decorated with woodcarvings.

The 600-year-old Spaso-Yevfimiev Monastery in the east of town is the largest in Suzdal and is enclosed by a solid stone wall and crowned with twenty towers. Many of Suzdal's churches traditionally stand in

pairs next to one another: the summer church windows were larger while those of the winter church were smaller. Parts of the winter church were even heated. Some of the churches have since lost their counterparts, such as the elegant Our Lady of Smolensk Church.

9 Vladimir This town on the Klyazma River was founded in 1108, by Vladimir Monomakh, the Grand Prince of Kiev and named after himself. The ancient earthen walls and the grand Golden Gate form part of the 12th-century fortifications that still remain today. The town boasts awe-inspiring churches whose magnificence and wealth of treasures easily compete with the glorious sights of Kiev.

Prince Andrei Bogolyubsky built the town's landmark, the Assumption Cathedral, in 1160, with three domes. A two-floor gallery, crowned with four sparkling golden domes, was

erected around the main building. The St Demetrius Cathedral is also well worth a visit. Both cathedrals and the Church of the Intercession have been declared World Heritage Sites. One of the oldest Russian churches, the white Church of the Intercession of the Virgin on the Nerl (1165), is located east of Vladimir. From Vladimir

it is worth taking the detour to Nizhny Novgorod, which is 250 km (155 miles) east.

1 One of several wooden churches in the open-air Museum of Wooden Architecture in Suzdal.

2 The Resurrection Church in Kostroma, the most northerly town on the Golden Ring.

Rostov This once important medieval trading center with a cathedral and the Monastery of Our Savior and St Jacob stands on the shores of Lake Nero. The imposing kremlin in this town founded in 862, is surrounded by a wall with eleven towers.

Yaroslavl The Monastery of Our Savior (12th century) with its Cathedral of the Resurrection of Christ is among the impressive preserved historical sites here.

The Volga Europe's longest river rises in the wooded plateaus northwest of Moscow and flows into the Caspian Sea 3,530 km (2,194 mi) away.

Kostroma This well-planned town was built after a fire in 1773. The Ipatiev Monastery as well as the Resurrection Church existed prior to the fire and are among the town's attractions.

The Goritsky Monastery The Goritsky and Danilov monasteries, dating from the 14th century and the 16th century, respectively, are among the main attractions in the southwestern district of Pereslavl-Zalesskyof, one of the towns along the Golden Ring.

The Pereslavsky National Park This national park is home to hundreds of bird species and even brown bears. It protects forests, wetlands, and the cathedrals and churches of Pereslavl-Zalessky and Lake Pleshcheyevo.

Ivanovo The town of Ivanovo, first mentioned in 1561, lies almost 300 km (186 mi) north-east of Moscow. It later became a textile center and is a cultural focal point today with an art museum. In the 1920s it was also known as the "Red Manchester".

Nizhny Novgorod This old trading center on the Volga is surrounded by swampy forests and vast agricultural lands. Its kremlin is located in the upper town.

Pereslavl'-Zalessky Founded in the 10th/11th centuries on Lake Pleshcheyevo, this town boasts a wealth of churches and wooden buildings. The White Cathedral (1152) is among the gems.

Sergiev Posad The Monastery of the Holy Trinity and St Sergius (1340) in this popular pilgrimage destination is one of the most important religious sites in Russia. The walled sanctuary also houses exquisite paintings.

Vladimir Easter Procession with Russian Orthodox dignitaries. The Assumption Cathedral, built after 1160, is the town's main landmark.

Suzdal Over 100 historical buildings, including numerous monasteries, adorn the best-preserved Old Russian town and former religious center of Old Russia.

The Moscow Kremlin The most important buildings in the former residence of the Czars and patriarchs include the Great Kremlin Palace, the Armory Chamber, the Patriarch's Palace, the Terem Palace, the Faceted Chamber, the Senate, the Arsenal, the Annunciation, the Assumption and the Savior's Cathedrals as well as Ivan Veliky's bell tower.

Moscow There are 2,300 listed buildings in Russia's capital. Attractions include: Red Square, St Basil's Cathedral, the Kremlin, the Lenin Mausoleum, the GUM department store, the Bolshoi Theater, the Tretyakov Gallery, and the Pushkin Museum.

Kolomenskoye This 16th-century town, situated high above the Moskva River south-east of Moscow, used to be the Czars' summer residence. The cathedral's tent-like roof is a special attraction.

Map labels: Vologda, Rybinsk, Kostroma, Yur'yevets, Yaroslavl, Zerkov Bogojavleniya, Privolzhsk, Kineshma, Furmanov, Puchezh, Borisoglebskiy monastyr, Ivanovo, Rodniki, Zavolzhe, Gorodec, Nizhniy Novgorod, Rostov, Petrovskoe, Tejkovo, Shuja, Kaljazin, Gorizkiy monastyr, A113, Kovrov, Vjazniki, Dzerzhinsk, Kazan', Pereslavsky N.P., Suzdal, Zerkov Borisa i Gleba, Pavlovo, Pavlovskoe, Dubna, Dvoriki, Pereslavl-Zalessky, Kolchugino, Vladimir, Murom, Saint Petersburg, Sergiyev Posad, Lakinsk, Klin, Pokrov, Sobinka, Petushki, Losiny ostrov N.P., Mytishchi, Orekhovo-Zuyevo, Velikie Luki, Élektrostal', Moscow, Balashiha, Odincovo, Kolomenskye, Domodedovo, Rjazan', Smolensk, Podol'sk, Novomoskovsk, Orel

Germany, Poland, Baltic States

In the footsteps of the Hanseatic League

The Hanseatic route along the Baltic Sea from northern Germany through Poland and into the Baltic States is unique for its tranquility, impressive scenery and dreamy qualities. Time seems to stand still n this part of the world, creating a magic that is singular to the coast and the villages and cities that line it.

During the last ice age, the Baltic Sea and the Baltic states were buried under a thick sheet of ice. After it melted away, the land, now free from the pressure of the ice, slowly began to rise. The Baltic land ridge – a hilly moraine landscape filled with lakes on the southern coast of the Baltic Sea – is a glacial rockfill region from this last ice age, and the Baltic Sea of course has added its own features to the coastal outline. It created impressive spits, the

Courland Spit being one of the most prominent and beautiful, and carved out lagoons with tranquil inland bodies of water like the Szczecin or Vistula lakes. The famous white chalk cliff coasts owe their current appearance to the surging, post-ice age Baltic Sea.

The Baltic Sea is often known by its Latin name of Mare Balticum. "Balticum" is derived from "baltas", meaning "white" in Lithuanian and Latvian. Indeed, the beaches, dunes and craggy

Picturesque Old Town alleyways in Estonia's capital, Tallinn.

coastal cliffs practically sparkle in brilliant white. The national parks of the Vorpommersche Boddenlandschaft, Jasmund, Slowinsky and Courland Spit protect some of the most beautiful stretches of the Baltic coast. Because the coastlines in Poland and the Baltic states are only sparsely populated, there is still enough room in the forests and marshlands for animals that have long been extinct in other parts of Europe: elks, bears, lynxes and wolves still have a natural habitat here. Storks nest in the many church towers, while cranes brood in the marshlands.

Your journey passes through six of the countries lining the Baltic Sea. In addition to Germany and Poland, these include Lithuania, Latvia, Estonia and Russia – or more specifically,

The towers of the Holsten Gate in Lübeck, built in the mid-15th century, were modelled on Flemish bridge gates.

The Dornbusch lighthouse is located at the northern tip of the sprawling Baltic Sea island of Hiddensee. It is much sandier than Rügen in the east and has no steep banks.

Kaliningrad, a Russian exclave actually separated from Russia proper. The histories of these countries are closely intertwined with the Teutonic Order, and many of the castles and cities in the region were also members of the Hanseatic League. Since the collapse of the Soviet Union, the Baltic States have regained independence and are once again asserting their own cultural traditions.

A journey along the Baltic Sea coast is therefore in some ways a journey through time: back to before World War II – a period that is still tangible in the countryside – and the time of the Hanseatic League.

The League was an association of merchants established in the 12th century as a Germans response to the increasing risk of Baltic Sea trade. It quickly developed into a mighty urban and trading league that eventually ruled northern Europe economically for over 300 years. Many cities received their town charters in the 13th century, and the revolutionary Lübeck Law was adopted by over 100 Hanseatic cities. The Hanseatic League owes much of its success to its organization and vast capital, but also to the design of efficient ships such as the cog. This had a wide hull, was initially oarless and intended as a sailing ship, and had high superstructural parts that allowed it to transport loads over 550 tons. Confident merchants and municipal rulers built magnificent churches, mansions and town halls in the brick Gothic style now typical of the Baltic Sea region, and their robust Hanseatic ships used the church towers as orientation points along the coast. Many churches in the Hanseatic cities are dedicated to St Nicholas, the patron saint of sailors and fishermen; other are dedicated to the pilgrims' patron saint, St James the Elder.

The decline of the Hanseatic League began in the 15th century as decreasing numbers of Germans chose to migrate east, and the Hanseatic League finally lost its supremacy to the ever-more powerful kingdom of Poland and Lithuania.

Sunrise over Gdańsk: St Mary's Church, one of the largest Brick Gothic buildings in Europe. Inside the church is room for 25,000 people.

The Hanseatic route: Passing through the lowlands of northern Germany, along the Bay of Mecklenburg and the Baltic Sea coasts of Poland, Lithuania, Latvia and Estonia, your path mirrors the trading routes of the Hanseatic League, where ports and merchant cities characterized by traditional brick architecture line the road like pearls on a necklace.

1 Bremen (see page 78)
The journey begins in the Free Hanseatic City of Bremen which, with Bremerhaven 50 km (31 mi) north, forms the smallest of the federal German states. On the way to Stade, the B74 leads past Teufelsmoor, north-west of Bremen.

2 Stade This small town on the lower Elbe was an important trading port more than 1,000 years ago, but the Vikings destroyed the castle in 994. Stade became a member of the Hanseatic League in the mid-13th century, but nearby Hamburg soon started to challenge its dominance.
On the way to Hamburg, the road passes through the Altes Land (Old Country). In Germany's largest fruit production region, it is worth seeing the traditional farming villages, particularly in spring when the trees are in

bloom. It was not until the 12th and 13th centuries that an elaborate drainage system allowed the once marshy lower Elbe area to be cultivated.

3 Hamburg (see page 79)
Those not wishing to drive into Hamburg's city center should bypass it and take the A1 to the port city of Lübeck.

4 Lübeck This merchant settlement founded in the 12th century was given the status of Free Imperial City by Emperor Friedrich II in 1226. The city became the voice of "foreign affairs" for the German Hanseatic League when it was founded, and the first General Hanseatic Day was held in Lübeck in 1356. At the end of the 13th century, Lübeck was the most densely populated city in Germany after Cologne and, with 25,000 inhabitants by

Travel Information

Route profile
Route length: approx. 1,700 km (1,056 mi)
Time required: 3–4 weeks
Route (main locations):
Bremen, Hamburg, Rostock, Rügen, Sczeczin, Gdańsk, Olsztyn, Kaliningrad, Klaipèda, Riga, Tallinn

Traffic in formation:
Check the validity of the vehicle's liability insurance before driving into any of these countries!

Visa Russia: You need your visa, international driver's licence, vehicle registration,

and an international green insurance card.
Visa EU countries: All you need for the EU are a valid passport or ID card.

Information:
Here are some websites to help you plan your trip.
Poland:
www.polen.travel/en
Russia:
www.waytorussia.net
Estonia:
www.visitestonia.com
Latvia:
www.latviatourism.lv
Lithuania:
www.tourism.lt

3

4

5

back to Dutch influences. The Gothic St Mary's Church, with its slender tower, was modeled on the church of the same name in Lübeck.

A 30-km (19-mi) detour takes you south to Schwerin, capital of Mecklenburg-Vorpommern.

6 Schwerin Slavic tribes built a castle in this, the "City of Seven Lakes" on the shores of Lake Schwerin in the 11th century. As a royal residence town of the Mecklenburg dukes, the castle, situated beautifully on an island, and large parts of the Old Town were given their present look back in the 15th century by the royal architect, Georg Demmler. He used Chambord Castle in the Loire Valley in France as a model and created one of the most famous works of historicism. The cathedral, which dates back to the 13th–15th centuries, is a masterpiece of German brick Gothic.

From Schwerin, a road leads back to Wismar through Cambs, and then the B105 follows the old trading route between Lübeck and Gdańsk. On the way to Rostock you can make detours to the Cistercian monasteries of Sonnenkampf (13th century) and Bad Doberan (14th century).

1 View of the St Pauli piers on the dry docks in the internationally sigificant Port of Hamburg.

2 The town hall and St Peter's Cathedral standing on Bremen's market square.

3 Merchant houses and sailing ships at Holsten Harbour in Lübeck.

4 A baroque garden surrounds Schwerin Castle on an island in Lake Schwerin.

5 The "Wasserkunst" fountain house on Wismar's market square.

1500, it was also one of the largest cities in Europe.

Some of Lübeck's most important attractions are held in the medieval Old Town, which was extensively rebuilt after the destruction of World War II and which is completely surrounded by moats and the Trave River. The entire Lübeck Old Town was declared a UNESCO World Heritage Site as a main location for German Gothic brick buildings. A series of churches have been preserved or renovated including the cathedral, begun in 1173 and completed in the 13th century, St Mary's parish church, built by the people of Lübeck, St Catherine's Basilica and the brick Gothic churches of Saints Jakobi and Petri. The city's main landmark, however, is the 15th-century Holstentor gate, part of the once-mighty fortifications. The Gothic town hall is evidence of the city's wealth and the confidence of its sponsors. A highlight of a stroll through the Old Town are the medieval burgher town houses, the most attractive of which are located on Mengstraße (also home to the Buddenbrookhaus, a literary museum dediacted to the Mann family), Königstraße, the Große Petersgrube and on Holsten Harbour. Your journey continues east from Lübeck through the Klützer Winkel to Wismar on the Bay of Wismar.

5 Wismar The picturesque old port in this merchant settlement and Hanseatic town is just a fishing port these days. As an international port, Wismar was of national significance for Baltic Sea trading for over 750 years, and the walled city has largely been able to preserve its beautiful medieval look. Wismar has numerous gabled houses dating from the Renaissance and baroque periods (16th to 18th centuries) and a Gothic town house from 1380. The oldest burgher house in the city, the "Old Swede", is located on the market square where you will also find the fountain house, known as the "Wasserkunst" (1602), built in Dutch Renaissance style. The fountain provided the city with water until the end of the 19th century. The royal court from 1555 was modelled on Italian styles and the sculptures can be traced

The Free Hanseatic City of Bremen

The mighty fishing and merchant city on the Weser River was founded in the early Middle Ages, and a bishop's see and cathedral have stood on the fortified dune hill since 787.

Bremen's economic significance was based on its location on the Weser and proximity to the sea just 60 km (37 miles) away. The city had a port and a ford, and was also an important diocesan town. Foreign trade financed the town hall, some religious buildings and a city wall (1129). Bremen joined the Hanseatic League in 1358 and became a Free City in the 17th century. The plagues haunted Bremen several times. In the 15th century, the city flourished, but large parts of the old town were destroyed in World War II.

Sights include: the market square with the famous Roland Column (1404); Schüttung, the merchants' guild house (16th century); the renaissance town hall (15th century); the Gothic Church of Our Lady (13th century); the hall church of St Martin on the Weser; St Peter's Cathedral and museum; the Schnoorviertel, a fishermen's quarter; and the wall complex with a moat. Museums: Overseas Museum with folklore collection; the Kunsthalle with its graphic design collection; the Roseliushaus museum and the Paula Becker Modersohn House; and the Universum Science Center Bremen.

Beautiful view over patrician houses and Bremen's Roland Column, an emblem of city liberties since the Holy Roman Empire.

The Free Hanseatic City of Hamburg

Thanks to its location on the Elbe River and its closeness to the North Sea, Hamburg became an important trade center in the 12th century. The most important German port, it is now a vibrant, cosmopolitan metropolis.

Hamburg was an early member of the Hanseatic League and in the 14th century became the most important link between North and Baltic Seas. The old and new town were united in 1216. Hamburg was ravaged by fires in 1276 and in 1842, and much of the city was destroyed in World War II.

Attractions here include: St Michael's Church with Michel, symbol of the city; St James (14th century); St Catherine (14th/15th century); St Peter (14th century); St Nicholas; the homes of the Shopkeepers' Guild (17th century); the stock exchange (19th century); the old town with town hall (19th century) and town houses (17th/18th century); Inner Alster Lake and Jungfernstieg promenade; the warehouse district of the Old Free Harbour; St Nicholas Fleet (17th/18th century); St Paul's pier (1907–1909); the Kontorhaus district with the Chile House (UNESCO); the Ethnology Museum, the Hamburg Art Gallery, the Planten un Blomen Park; and the zoo.

St Nicholas Church and the town hall from the Lombard Bridge on Hamburg's broadway Jungfernstieg promenade at Inner Alster.

7 Rostock This city was established by German merchants and craftsmen at the end of the 12th century, and experienced its heyday as member of the Hanseatic League in the 14th and 15th centuries. The University of Rostock (est. 1419) is one of the oldest in the Baltic Sea region. Today, the metropolis on the Lower Warnow River mostly survives off its lively port. The Thirty Years War left Rostock in ruins, as did heavy bombing during World War II. Most of its late-Gothic, baroque and classicist homes were destroyed, but many have been carefully restored or rebuilt. The late-Gothic town hall, which actually comprises three buildings, is unique; the city's two parish churches are dedicated to St Nicholas and St Peter. St Mary's Church, with its famous astronomical clock, towers over the north-west corner of the market square.

From Rostock there are numerous possible detours to Warnemünde on the coast or to the beautiful Mecklenburg lake district farther inland.

The Rostock Heath (Rostocker Heide), east of the city, is a pristine moor and woodland. The western part was felled to build "cog" ships during the time of the Hanseatic League, while the eastern section was kept as a ducal hunting reserve.

Nature lovers should visit the fishing town of Wustrow on Fischland, the narrow spit that leads over to the Darss Peninsula in the Vorpommersche Boddenlandschaft National Park.

A lovely road between Bodstedter Bodden and Barther Bodden goes to Barth via Zingst and back to the B105 at Löbnitz.

8 Stralsund This city's former significance as Hanseatic League member is still reflected in the buildings today. It has a network of medieval streets, pri-

marily with brick Gothic architecture, and many of the burgher houses originate from the 15th–19th centuries. This "Venice of the North" is located on the Strelasund, a strait between the mainland and Rügen. In the center of the city, which is a UNESCO World Heritage Site, the town hall towers over the Old Market, while just next door stands a late-Gothic alcove. Not far away you'll find

Rügen Dam

The Rügen Dam was opened in 1937, and connects Rügen with the mainland via the island of Dänholm. The "Ziegelgraben" bascule bridge, between Strelasund and Dänholm, still renders Rügen an island for a few hours each day – but also causes traffic jams. From Dänholm, a 500-m-long (0.3-mi) bridge connects the island with Rügen.

the St Nicholas patrician church, considered one of the most beautiful on the Baltic. The late-Gothic St Mary's Church was built from 1384; the St James' Church was completed in the first half of the 14th century.

9 Rügen Germany's largest island owes much of its popularity to Caspar David Friedrich, whose painting of the Stubbenkammer chalk cliffs on the Jasmund Peninsula is a classic of German Romanticism. The old beech trees on Jasmund, in the Stubnitz forest, and the vast fields of colorful spring flowers in the island's south-west make it a stunning area for hiking. Botanists are fascinated by the rare flora, while the pagan antiquities and burial mounds catch the attention of ancient history enthusiasts.

A trip to Cape Arkona on the Wittow promontory, a chalk cliff with lighthouses and a Slavic fort, 46 m (151 ft) in height, is a must-see. From there, go across the 8-km (5-mi) Schaabe Spit to the Jasmund promontory. The Stubbenkammer, with its 117-m (384-ft) peak, the Königsstuhl, and the surrounding beech forests are protected within the Jasmund Nature Reserve.

From Sassnitz, a road leads along the densely forested Schmale Heide (Narrow Heath) between the Small Jasmunder Bodden and Prorer Wiek out to the Baltic Sea spa town of Binz, with its romantic seaside resort architecture dating back to the 19th century. In 1994, a 370-m

and East Pomerania), Szczecin is today a modern metropolis with an active port that owes its importance to its shipyard and the heavy industries based here. The historic buildings in the badly destroyed Old Town have been partially restored. St James' Cathedral was built in the 14th/15th centuries and the beautiful Gothic St John's Church dates from the 13th century. The late-Gothic Old Town Hall dates from the 14th century and the castle of the dukes of Pomerania is from the 16th/17th centuries. The Piastentor and Hafentor gates are reminders of the mighty belt of fortifications that once protected the city from attack.

From Szczecin, the E28 heads toward Gdańsk. About 20 km (13 mi) into the journey, it is worth making a detour north to the island of Wolin and the Cammin lagoon.

⑬ Polish Baltic Sea coast from Karlino to Gdańsk The route continues now through vast plains where golden cornfields alternate with dense forests and flowering meadows. Those looking to return to the sea, which is lined with deserted sandy beaches, should head to Kołobrzeg or turn off towards Lazy near Koszalin. Lazy is situated between Jamno and Bukow, two lakes that are protected from the Baltic Sea by a spit of land that is often

(0.2-mi) bridge was built, and this area also marks the start of some very nice daytrips to the chalk cliffs along the coast. From Binz, the route heads through Bergen, Rügen's "capital", and the fertile Mutland meadows back toward Strelasund, and from there it continues on to Greifswald.

⑩ Greifswald This city on the Ryck was built on its salt trade and obtained its town charter in 1250. Salt was an important trading commodity for centuries as it was needed to preserve fish and other foodstuffs in the Middle Ages. The St Mary's Church, a hall church from the first half of the 14th century, towers over the Greifswald Old Town. The brick Gothic cathedral of St Nicholas is one of the most beautiful in the entire state of Mecklenburg-

Vorpommern, and many late-Gothic homes still attest to the former wealth of the patrician families who once lived here. The town's most famous icon is the 30-m-long (33-yds) wooden bascule bridge in Wieck. The 12th-century Eldena monastery ruins are depicted in a number of Caspar David Friedrich's paintings; they became a symbol of Romanticism. The complex has housed parts of the university since 1535.

⑪ Usedom An attractive detour takes you through the royal Pomeranian residence town of Wolgast to Usedom, which is connected to the mainland by two bridges. The island is separated from the mainland by the Peene River and from the Polish island of Wolin by the Swina River. The eastern corner, which has the mouths

of the river, is part of Poland. The famous Wilhelminian seaside resort towns of Zinnowitz, Bansin, Heringsdorf and Ahlbeck are interspersed with stunning, extensive, sandy beaches along a 40-km (25-mi) stretch of Baltic Sea coast. Both Heringsdorf and Ahlbeck are home to impressively long wharfs typical of 19th-century resort towns: they are 508-m (0.3-mi) and 280-m (0.2-mi) long, respectively.

From Ahlbeck, the route returns to the mainland at the Hanseatic city of Anklam, past the Ueckermünder Heath to Pasewalk and from there over the border to Sczezcin, Poland.

⑫ Szczecin The Hanseatic City of Szczecin is located on the western banks of the Oder, not far from where it flows into the lagoon. The former capital of Vor and Hinterpommern (West

1 The 280-m (0.2-mi) sea bridge from Ahlbeck (1998) on Usedom.

2 The St Mary's Church towers over Rostock's old town was also used by sailors as a landmark.

3 The famous chalk cliffs in Jasmund National Park on the island of Rügen.

4 The Stralsund marina, with St Mary's Church in the background.

just 200 m wide (219 yds). The area is an important habitat for many breeding birds.

Darłowo has the most beautiful medieval Old Town in the region. Its main attraction is the castle of the Pomeranian dukes, while the port village of Ustka offers long beaches and a relaxing atmosphere.

A day trip into the Slowinski National Park near Leba is a must here. The "Polish Sahara" has shifting sand dunes of up to 40-m (131-ft) high that move some 10 m (11 yds) or so southeast every year.

14 Gdańsk Gdańsk (formerly Danzig) has a history that dates back 1,000 years. In the 12th and 13th centuries, the city had close trading relations with Flanders, Russia and Byzantium. It became a Hanseatic League member in 1361, and as host to the Teutonic Order it gained valuable access to the throne of Poland in 1466. By 1945, some 95 percent of the city had been completely destroyed by the war, but it has now been carefully rebuilt into a modern European metropolis.

The most important tourist attractions in Gdańsk are found in the center, the "Rechtstadt" neighborhood. St Mary's Church is the largest medieval brick work of its kind in Europe and the pride of the city. Its most notable feature is the 82-m-high (269-ft) bell tower. The long lane and the adjacent streets form the historic focal point of Gdańsk, where influential patricians erected magnificent manor houses such as the 17th-century Hans von Eden House in the heart of the Rechtstadt.

The most impressive examples of northern European late-Gothic architecture include the 15th-century Artushof, the Rechtstadt Town Hall, the Golden House and the Torture Chamber. The Crane Gate, which

was once a medieval gate to the city, was rebuilt into a port crane. Still in the Old Town, but north of the Rechtstadt area, it is worth visiting a number of the quaint churches, the old town hall, the big and little mills as well as the old castle. A detour to the northern edge of Gdańsk brings you to the lovely Cathedral of Oliva, with its baroque interior, and to Sopot, once the most glamorous seaside resort and health spa on the Baltic Sea coast.

South of Gdańsk is the Gdańsk River Isle, the northernmost part of the Vistula Delta. This landscape, which is partly submerged in the sea, was for the most part dried out in the 15th century and then reclaimed in the 17th century. Crossing the river island heading south-east you will soon arrive in Malbork.

15 Malbork St Mary's Castle, destroyed in World War II and rebuilt starting in 1961, is on the right bank of the Nogat, which flows north-east at this

point. The mighty castle complex comprises two units separated by a trench and protected by a common moat. Malbork's old German name – Marienburg – refers to its Christian founders: In the second half of the 13th century, the grand master of the Teutonic Order moved his seat of government here from Venice. South-west of the castle is the late-13th-century city of Malbork, whose center is dominated by the impressive town hall. St John's Church, the only preserved medieval building, is to the north from there.

Heading north-east from Malbork you arrive in yet another Hanseatic city.

16 Elbląg When the Teutonic Order began its fight against the "heathen" Prussians, it established a Hanseatic city here in 1237 to assist their cause. Until 1370, this was of greater importance in the area than even Gdańsk. When the medieval Old Town became too small, a new town was designed. It received

its Lübeck rights in 1347. The Elbląg River connects the city to the Gdańsk bay and therefore to the Baltic Sea, and wheat and wood exports originally made the city rich. Some of the many burgher town houeses from the 16th and 17th centuries have been restored and attest to the former wealth of Elbląg, which was a Free Imperial City starting in the early 16th century. In January 1945, shortly before the end of World War II, the city

dates back to the 14th century. The Polish-Russian (Kaliningrad) border is just a few miles further north-east.

You'll cross a few borders before arriving in Lithuania since the Russian exclave, Kaliningrad, lies between the new EU states.

18 Kaliningrad Kaliningrad was the last major city founded by the Teutonic Order, in 1255. Having already been a refuge for Slavic Prussians, with whom the crusading German Catholics had long been in conflict, the newly designed city comprised three central components: the Old Town between the castle and the Pregel River; Löbenicht in the east; and the Kneipphof (1327) on Pregel Island in the south. The city became a member of the Hanseatic League in 1340. Kaliningrad is the former capital of East Prussia and the home of Imannuel Kant who taught at the university from 1755 to 1796. Today, the Kaliningrad Cathedral glistens in its new splendor after being renovated in the 1990s – mostly with German money. Other worthwhile sights include the old German city manor houses on Thälmann and Kutusow streets, while parts of the warehouse district have also remained intact. The New University, constructed from 1844 to 1862, has been rebuilt as well.

The coast near Kaliningrad is known for its amber deposits – it is thought to have about 90 percent of the world's amber. If

was heavily bombed. Attractions include the Market Gate, the Gothic Dominican church, the St Nicholas Church with its 96-m (315-ft) tower, and the Ordensburg ruins.

From Elbląg a detour south on the E77 leads to the important medieval city of Olsztyn.

17 Vistula Lagoon Route 503 heads north-eastward along the Vistula Lagoon to the town of Frombork. The road, which closely skirts the lagoon,

is surprisingly diverse, with sudden climbs to the highlands near Suchacz followed by stretches of forest before the road falls dramatically back down to the lagoon. Further along you'll see the impressive green of the Vistula Spit. This headland stretches north-east, parallel to the coast, and is home to villages whose former names included Vogelsang and Schottland (German for birdsong and Scotland). The town of Tolkmicko, back on the 503

to the west, is at the northern end of Butter Mountain, the highest peak in the Elbląg Highlands: 197 m (646 ft). It has a pretty beach with fine, white-grey sand and a cute little marina with sailboats.

The onward journey takes you down some splendid avenues; gnarled old trees line the road and provide shade from the glaring sunlight. Some of the lanes have such dense treetops that the road underneath even stays dry in light rain.

The town of Frombork is culturally the most interesting city in the Ermland region because of the historic hilltop cathedral complex. The museum, as well as the cathedral itself, is dedicated to the works of Copernicus, who studied astronomy here. The water tower affords great views over the lagoon and port. The route continues along the lagoon to the Hanseatic city of Braniewo, the former residence of a prince-bishop. St Catherine's Church, which was only rebuilt a few years ago,

1 The Crane Gate on the Mottlau in Gdańsk was both a city gate and a port crane.

2 The Renaissance castle of the dukes of Pomerania in Stettin.

3 The famous astronomer, Copernicus, is buried in the Gothic brick cathedral of Frombork.

you are luck, you may even be able to find a piece of this beautiful stone for yourself!

⑲ Courland Spit National Park "The Courland Spit is a narrow strip of land between Memel and Königsberg (now Klaipèda and Kaliningrad), between the Courland Lagoon and the Baltic Sea. The lagoon contains fresh water, which is unaffected by the small connection to the Baltic Sea near Memel, and is home to freshwater fish." These were the words of the author Thomas Mann, who owned a house in this area in the 1930s that is now open to the public, to describe the unique natural paradise here that has been declared a UNESCO World Natural Heritage Site.

The Courland Spit National Park protects the forests rustling in the sea breeze, the dreamy towns with their traditional wooden houses, and the pristine dune and beach landscape along the Baltic Sea and the lagoon. The southernmost town in the Lithuanian part of the Courland Spit is Nida. The dune landscape, with dunes up to 60 m (197 ft) high, is also jokingly known to locals as the "Lithuanian Sahara".

⑳ Klaipèda A series of seaside resorts make this coast the most attractive holiday spot in Lithuania. The Baltic town of Klaipèda, located at the mouth of the lagoon and which seemed to still be in slumber until just a few decades ago, is today one of the country's important industrial centers. Its history also began with the Teutonic Order, and Klaipèda adopted the Lübeck city charter in 1254.

Just a few miles further north is the popular spa resort of Palanga, with its fine white-sand beaches, dunes and vast

pine forests. With a bit of luck, you can experience some spectacular sunsets here after visiting the botanical garden and the fascinating amber museum. From Klaipèda, the A1 takes you through Kaunas to Vilnius, the capital of Lithuania, 300 km (186.5 mi) away. If you would rather head to Riga in Latvia instead, take the A12 east for about 100 km (62 mi).

㉑ Riga The Latvian capital on the mouth of the Daugava joined the Hanseatic League in 1282, and is today one of the most beautiful cities in the Baltic region.

The Old Town of Riga itself was declared a UNESCO World Heritage Site. Within its walls are buildings dating back to numerous eras in European architecture including medieval patrician homes, twenty-four warehouses in the Old Town, and some Art Nouveau houses, which in some cases line entire residential streets.

Apart from the former palace of Czar Peter the Great, it is also worth visiting St John's Church (14th century), which is on the ruins of a diocesan town and was burned to the ground in 1234. The castle of the Teutonic Order, built in 1330, features the Sweden Gate and is home to many museums. The Saints Peter and Paul Cathedral was

built in the late 18th century. German merchants began unifying here in what was called the Great Guild back in the mid-14th century and even constructed their own Great Guild building. The locals were excluded here as well as in the Small Guild, where German craftsmen held secret meetings in the Small Guild House. The Schwarzhäupterhaus, or House of the Black Heads, built by merchants from Riga in 1341, is one of the

most beautiful buildings in the city. It was rebuilt in the 1990s after heavy war-time damage. The red brick construction has several storage levels.

Riga's icon is the 137-m (450-ft) wooden tower of St Peter's. The Latvian parliament building is a replica of the Palazzo Strozzi in Florence. The Arsenal, Riga's old customs house (1828–32), is now a museum and gallery worth seeing. For those interested in architecture and rural

Gothic church spires soaring toward the heavens like giant needles, all make Tallinn a fantastic architectural destination. The towers of the city wall and the baroque domes on the patrician houses are also interesting relics of a world gone by. Many of the narrow lanes are paved with cobblestones.

The Gothic Old Town has been deignated a UNESCO World Heritage Site – it features the oldest town hall in northern Europe (14th/15th centuries). There is also the Town Hall Pharmacy, the Great Guild Hall and the House of the Brotherhood of Black Heads. The nearly intact city walls boast twenty-six towers. Cathedral mountain, which dramatically falls away toward the sea, is the site of the cathedral and Toompea Castle. The view over the rooftops to the historic Old Town is magnificent. The 13th-century Cathedral of the Virgin Mary is one of the oldest churches in Estonia, while the baroque Kadriorg Palace, with its beautiful park, was designed by Nicolo Michetti for Czar Peter the Great in 1718. The Dominican monastery was built in 1246, and is the oldest existing monastery in Estonia.

1 The Courland Spit is 98 km (61 mi) long and in parts only 400 m (0.25 mi) wide. It lies between the Baltic Sea and the Courland Lagoon.

2 Looking out over the distinctive skyline of Riga's Old Town.

3 Riga: The tower of the 13th-century St Peter's Church.

4 With its imposing city walls and watchtowers, Tallinn had one of the best northern European defense complexes of the 16th century.

5 The cathedral – the main church of Kaliningrad – was completely destroyed in 1944, and was not rebuilt until the 1990s.

lifestyles of the 16th to 19th centuries, be sure to visit the 100-ha (247-acre) open-air museum near Rīga.

West of Rīga is the spa resort of Jūrmala, on a headland in the Gulf of Rīga. Fine sandy beaches stretch over 30 km (19 mi) and a handy railway connects the capital with the town. From Riga, it is worth making a small detour to Sigulda, located in the idyllic Gauja National Park about 50 km (31 mi) to the north-east. Aside from sandstone cliffs, forests and lakes, the main attractions in the park include a toboggan run, Turaida Castle, and many caves and wells that can be discovered along the hiking routes.

From Rīga , the E67 leads north along the Gulf of Rīga to the Estonian capital, Tallinn. You'll cross the border at Ainazi.

22 **Pärnu** The Estonian west coast is similarly appealing, with picturesque forests, shimmering water, simple thatched houses, stout castles and old ruins. About 180 km (112 mi) north of Rīga is Pärnu, located on the river of the same name. This quaint old city, which dates back to the 13th century, is an important Estonian port city but is also famous as a health resort thanks to the healing mud found in the area. Homes from the 16th and 17th centuries, as well as the Orthodox St Catherine's Church and the baroque St Elizabeth Church, are also worth seeing.

The last stop on your journey along the Baltic Sea coast is the Hanseatic city of Tallinn.

23 **Tallinn** In the 13th century, the knights of the Teutonic Order advanced as far as the northern reaches of the Baltic territories, right up to the entrance of the Gulf of Finland. Tallinn itself was first documented in 1154. Its Hanseatic League membership, which began in 1284, indeed inspired the city's rapid economic rise, but the collapse of the Order in the 16th and 17th centuries also marked the start of a decline for Tallinn. After 1945, the capital became Estonia's most important industrial city. The many churches on cathedral mountain and in the lower part of town, as well as the

Kaunas and Vilnius

Kaunas was the capital of Lithuania between the world wars. The old city center and the castle are located on a peninsula at the confluence of the Nemunas and Neris Rivers. The Hanseatic League had a branch office here from 1441 until 1532, before the fire of 1537 destroyed large parts of the Old Town. From Kaunas it is roughly 100 km (62 mi) to Vilnius, the current capital on the Vilnia river. That city's landmarks are the many watchtowers scattered through the picturesque Old Town. The "Rome of the Baltic", as this picture-book town used to be called, still contains remnants of its former masters, the Jesuits, champions of the Counter-Reformation in the kingdom of Poland and Lithuania. Vilnius was first documented in 1323, and even then it was already a prosperous trading and merchant settlement. Vilnius surprises most visitors with its superb baroque churches and buildings. The narrow, picturesque cobblestone lanes snake through the Old Town, at the center of which is the university, a Renaissance building with a number of courtyards influenced by Italian styles. Vilnius Cathedral was rebuilt several times before being given its current classicist makeover in the 18th century. The city's main road is the Gediminas Prospekt, a beautiful avenue lined with lime trees. Extensive baroque and classicist palaces attest to the wealth that once flowed through the city.

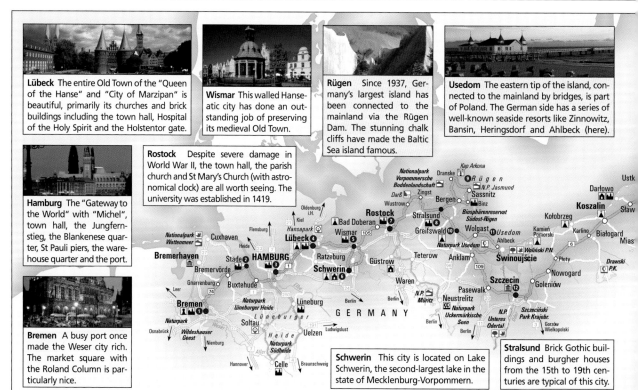

Lübeck The entire Old Town of the "Queen of the Hanse" and "City of Marzipan" is beautiful, primarily its churches and brick buildings including the town hall, Hospital of the Holy Spirit and the Holstentor gate.

Wismar This walled Hanseatic city has done an outstanding job of preserving its medieval Old Town.

Rügen Since 1937, Germany's largest island has been connected to the mainland via the Rügen Dam. The stunning chalk cliffs have made the Baltic Sea island famous.

Usedom The eastern tip of the island, connected to the mainland by bridges, is part of Poland. The German side has a series of well-known seaside resorts like Zinnowitz, Bansin, Heringsdorf and Ahlbeck (here).

Hamburg The "Gateway to the World" with "Michel", town hall, the Jungfernstieg, the Blankenese quarter, St Pauli piers, the warehouse quarter and the port.

Rostock Despite severe damage in World War II, the town hall, the parish church and St Mary's Church (with astronomical clock) are all worth seeing. The university was established in 1419.

Bremen A busy port once made the Weser city rich. The market square with the Roland Column is particularly nice.

Schwerin This city is located on Lake Schwerin, the second-largest lake in the state of Mecklenburg-Vorpommern.

Stralsund Brick Gothic buildings and burgher houses from the 15th to 19th centuries are typical of this city.

1 The neoclassical cathedral of Vilnius, built in the 18th/19th centuries, has a remarkable, free-standing tower.

2 A romantic location: The picturesque town of Trakai with its impressive medieval fortress set on the lakeshore.

Tallinn Estonia's capital is home to a Gothic Old Town and the oldest town hall in northern Europe (1400s). Its landmark is the cathedral mountain, which drops off steeply into the sea.

Sigulda The main attractions of this small town in a densely forested area are Turaida Castle and the nearby "Folk Song Hill" with sculptures depicting traditional Latvian songs.

Rīga The Latvian capital displays some important European architectural styles, from medieval to Art Nouveau, and is one of the most beautiful cities on the Baltic Sea.

Courland Lagoon This nature paradise is home to dunes, forests, fairy-tale towns and a choice of Baltic Sea or freshwater beaches. Famous artists and literary figures (Corinth, Schmidt-Rottluff, Pechstein, Thomas Mann) spent many a holiday here.

Gdańsk Gdańsk was completely destroyed in 1945, but extensive reconstruction work has ensured that the Crane Gate (above) as well as 650 other buildings again shine in their "former glory".

Vilnius Lithuania's capital is peppered with baroque buildings and is located near the border with Belarus. Here: the neoclassical cathedral and its bell tower.

Kaliningrad This city, founded by the Teutonic Order in 1255, was a member of the Hanseatic League from 1340. The cathedral has been restored after being severely damaged in World War II. The former capital of East Prussia and home of Immanuel Kant, a professor here from 1755 to 1796, is rather unsightly, but is located near the Samland coast, which is worth visiting.

Masuria Tiny alleyways and cobblestones, village ponds and migrating storks' nests. A visit to this region is a journey back in time. Dense forests, gentle hills and the beautiful Masuria lake district, home to more than 3,000 lakes, characterize this subtle moraine landscape in north-eastern Poland.

Malbork The Marienburg castle, which was rebuilt after World War II, was the residence of the grand master of the Teutonic Order in the 13th century. The town of Malbork is located near the castle.

Frombork This 14th-century cathedral, located on an impressive embankment, is a model of northern German brick architecture.

The vineyard town of Löf. The tall hills of the Upper Mosel Valley taper off converges with the Rhine at Koblenz.

Germany

Wine, culture and the rolling hills of the Rhine, Mosel and Neckar

The Rhine, the "most German of all rivers" and without doubt one of the most beautiful rivers in Europe, is the subject of countless songs. The Mosel, which flows into the Rhine at Koblenz, is smaller but no less alluring. The Neckar, which joins the Rhine from the east at Mannheim, is a worthy rival on all counts. All three rivers boast enchanting valleys bound by lovely hills dotted with castles, vineyards and quaint villages.

The Rhine, known as Rhenus by the Celts and the Romans, is 1,320 km (820 mi) long, making it one of the longest rivers in Europe, and also one of the most important waterways on the continent.

The Rhine originates in the canton of Graubünden (Grisons), Switzerland, flows into and out of Lake Constance, nips over

Ladenburg on the Neckar.

the Rhine Falls at Schaffhausen, then continues on toward Basel as the Upper Rhine. It then turns northward across the Upper Rhine Plain where it enters its most familiar "German" manifestation. The Neckar joins the Rhine at Mannheim where the latter becomes the Middle Rhine, which cuts spectacularly through the low mountains of central western Germany, accompanied on the left bank by the "peaks" of the Hunsrück and on the right by the Taunus foothills. The Mosel flows into what is now the Lower Rhine at Koblenz and enters the Lower Rhine Basin near Bonn. After passing through the cities of Cologne, Düsseldorf and Duisburg, it leaves Germany just

beyond Kleve and flows into the North Sea in the Netherlands a few river miles later.

In 2002, the Middle Rhine from Bingen to Koblenz was made a UNESCO World Heritage Site, in recognition not only of its natural beauty but also the cultural, historical and, not least, economic significance of this part of the river. The Rhine valley here is inextricably linked with the "Rhine Gold" of Wagner fame and the Nibelung epic. On both sides of the meandering river are steep hillsides with exquisite vineyards and defiant medieval castles.

It seems every castle and every rock formation on the Rhine is linked with a myth or a legend, whether it is of the beautiful

a bit just before the Mosel river

View over the Rhine of the much fêted Loreley rock, which rises 132 m (433 ft) above the river in a bend.

One of Germany's most famous picture-postcard views: the famous university town of Heidelberg on the Neckar.

Loreley, who is said to have lured many a boatsman to his untimely death with her songs, or of the two estranged brothers in the Burg Katz (Cat) and Burg Maus (Mouse) castles.

Perhaps all of these myths and legends were merely inspired by centuries of enjoying the delectable Rhine wine, whose vineyards are as much a part of the culture as the numerous castles that line the river's banks. Whatever the case, the wine is most certainly influential in creating the conviviality of the people in the region, which reaches its climax during Carnival, especially in Cologne. A more recent festivity on the Rhine is the spectacle "Rhine in flames": five times a year, fireworks soar high over the river between Rüdesheim and Bonn.

Wine also plays an important role on the longest and largest of the Rhine's tributaries, the Mosel. Known for its romantic meandering course, the Mosel originates in the southern Vosges Mountains in France and after 545 km (339 mi) flows into the Rhine at Koblenz. With the exception of Trier, which lies on a comparatively broad section of the Mosel, no other large cities have developed on its banks because the river's valley is so narrow. This makes the surrounding countryside, especially between Bernkastel-Kues and Cochem, particularly charming with vineyards, wine-growing towns and medieval castles. The Mosel Valley is a unique cultural landscape with thousands of years of history started by Celtic and Roman settlers.

Farther upstream from where the Mosel joins it, the "Father Rhine" has already collected one of his sons: the Neckar, yet another of the German "wine rivers". The Necker originates at an altitude of 706 m (2,316 ft) in the Schwenninger Moos and flows into the Rhine 367 km (228 mi) later at Mannheim. Along its course, it twists and turns through steep valleys like the one at Rottweil, or meanders through broad meadows like the ones where Stuttgart and Heilbronn are now located. Below Neckarelz, the river cuts through the red sandstone formations of the Odenwald, and beyond the romantic town of Heidelberg it passes through the Upper Rhine Plain.

The Reichsburg above Cochem on the Mosel is one of Germany's most attractive and best-known castles.

Your route along Germany's enchanting rivers begins in Trier and follows the course of the Mosel down to its confluence with the Rhine at Koblenz. It then heads back up through the Middle Rhine Valley past countless castles and vineyards to Mannheim. From there you will travel parallel to the Neckar River to Tübingen.

1 Trier Framed by the forested hills of the Hunsrück and Eifel, Trier sits in one of the few broad valleys along the Mosel. It is a city of superlatives: Northeast of the Roman Porta Nigra is the church of St Paulin (18th century), designed by Balthasar Neumann and the region's most significant baroque structure. The Cathedral of St Peter was begun in the 4th century, making it the oldest cathedral in Germany. The Liebfrauenkirche next door (13th C.) is one of the oldest Gothic churches in the country. And the Hauptmarkt with its Marian cross and the St Peter's Fountain counts as one of Germany's most attractive fairy-tale squares.

From Trier to Koblenz you skirt both sides of the Mosel River among the enchanting hillside vineyard towns.

2 Bernkastel-Kues The half-timbered houses and the Marktplatz here are dominated by the ruins of Landshut Castle, with vineyards climbing up to its stone walls. A bridge connects Bernkastel with Kues, the birthplace of philosopher Nikolaus von Kues (1401–1464).

3 Traben-Trarbach This charming vineyard town straddling the Mosel is distinguished by attractive half-timbered houses

and patrician villas. Fans of Art Nouveau architecture will find some unique specimens here, including the Brückentor, the Huesgen Villa, the small Sonora Villa and the Hotel Bellevue, all reminders of a golden age in the wine trade at the turn of the 20th century.

Towering above the small town is Grevenburg Castle. On Mont Royal, enclosed by a wide loop in the river, are the ruins of a fortress planned by Vauban.

4 Zell This vineyard town on the right bank of the Mosel boasts remnants of very old town walls, the church of St Peter and a former electors' palace. On the road to Bremm you can take a scenic detour to Arras Castle (9th C.) near Alf.

Travel Information

Route profile
Length: approx. 550 km (342 mi)
Time required: 6–7 days
Start: Trier
End: Tübingen
Route (main locations):
Trier, Koblenz, Bingen, Mainz, Frankfurt, Darmstadt, Mannheim, Heidelberg, Heilbronn, Stuttgart, Tübingen, Lake Constance

Traffic information:
Roads in Germany are well maintained and signposted. There are no toll roads. After passing on the autobahn, return to the slow lane.

When to go:
The best time to visit Germany is from April/May to September/October. And don't forget a rain jacket!

Information:
Here are just a few of the many websites for Germany.
Mosel region:
www.mosellandtouristik.de
Rhine region:
www.e-heidelberg.com
Heidelberg region:
www.wikitravel.org/en/Heidelberg
Lake Constance area:
www.bodensee-tourismus.com

Stolzenfels Castle (13th C.), Lahneck Castle and Marksburg Castle. The latter is the only hilltop castle on the Rhine that was never destroyed. In Boppard itself, the remains of the medieval town walls, relics from the Roman Castellum Bodobriga and the church of St Severus (12th/13th C.) are all worth a visit.

⑨ St Goar and St Goarshausen These two vineyard towns are dominated by Rheinfels Castle, once the mightiest fortress on the Rhine. St Goar is on the left bank while St Goarshausen is on the right, and they are linked by ferry. From the latter you can see the ruins of Burg Katz and Burg Maus castles, built by two estranged brothers in the 14th century.

⑩ Loreley Just a few bends downstream, this famous rock rises 133 m (436 ft) above the Rhine, just 133 m (145 yds) wide at this point. It was an historically dangerous strait for boats. Poet Heinrich Heine wrote a romantic song about the rock.

⑤ Mosel Loop at Bremm One of the most famous of the Mosel's many hairpin turns is the one around the wine village of Bremm, whose vineyards on the Bremmer Calmont are among the steepest Riesling vineyards in Europe. The village itself is lovely, with picturesque narrow alleyways and the usual half-timbered houses. Heading downstream, take a trip to legendary Burg Eltz castle.

⑥ Cochem This town is one of the most attractive in the Mosel Valley. It is dominated by the Reichsburg, built in 1070, then destroyed in 1688 and built once again in the 19th century in neo-Gothic style. The Marktplatz is surrounded by lovely old row houses and the town

hall from 1739. Before the vineyard town of Kobern-Gondorf you will see the ruins of Ehrenburg castle near Löf-Hatzenport and in Alken the twin towers of Thuant Castle rise above the Mosel.

From Kobern, it is worth taking the time to visit Maria Laach, culturally perhaps the most important sight in the southern Eifel mountains.

⑦ Koblenz This town on a spit of land at the confluence of the Mosel and the Rhine was of great strategic importance even in Roman times, and in the 11th century it became the residence of the archbishops and electors of Trier. The location is known as the Deutsches Eck (German Corner). At the tip, the stately

equestrian statue of Emperor Wilhelm II guards the rivers.

Aside from the St Castor Basilica, sights worth seeing in Koblenz include the medieval Alte Burg castle, the Münzplatz, the birthplace of Prince Metternich, the Liebfrauenkirche (12th–15th C.) and the church of St Florin (12th–14th C.) as well as the vast Electors' Castle (16th C.) down by the Rhine. On the east bank of the Rhine you'll find Ehrenbreitstein Fortress, one of the largest fortified complexes in all of Europe.

From Koblenz, follow the B9 up the left bank to Bingen.

⑧ Boppard This idyllic town is tucked into a sweeping curve on the left bank of the Rhine. On the way there, you pass

⑪ Kaub A ferry takes you over to this romantic village encircled by a splendid medieval wall. It is one of the most

1 View from Calmont of the wide arch in the Mosel near Bremm.

2 The main square in Trier with Gangolf, the market cross and the Steipe, which also functioned as the town hall until the 18th century.

3 Bernkastel-Kues, a medieval vineyard town and health resort on the Middle Mosel.

4 View across the Mosel towards Cochem and the Reichsburg castle.

5 Burg Landshut, nestled among the vineyards above Bernkastel-Kues, has been a ruin since 1692.

important wine-growing areas on the Rhine. Towering over Kaub is the Gutenfels Castle (13th C.), and on a small rock island in the middle of the river stands the former Pfalzgrafenstein toll tower, known in brief as the Pfalz bei Kaub.

⑫ **Bacharach** This idyllic vineyard town is located on the west bank of the Rhine surrounded by a wall with several towers. It is dominated by Stahleck Castle, which is now a youth hostel. Down by the river near the town stands Sooneck Castle. Heading now towards Bingen you will pass the castles of Reichenstein, one of the oldest, and Rheinstein, both on the west bank.

⑬ **Bingen** The icon of this town at the confluence of the Nahe and Rhine rivers is Klopp Castle, the foundations of which date back to Roman times. At the Binger Loch, the Rhine makes a dramatic entrance into the Rhenish Slate Mountains. On the left bank stands majestic Ehrenfels Castle (13th C.). In the middle of the river is the Binger Mäuseturm (Mouse Tower), a watch and toll tower, along with Ehrenfels Castle. Car ferries cross the Rhine to Rüdesheim here.

⑭ **Rüdesheim** This vineyard town is mainly famous for the Drosselgasse, a street lined with countless wine bars and tourist traps, but old patrician estates like the Brömserhof and the ruins of the Boosenburg, Vorderburg and Brömserburg (10th C.) castles are impressive as well. The latter is home to the Rheingau Wine Museum.
Above town is the Niederwald Memorial, a statue of Germania erected in 1883 to celebrate the founding of the German empire in 1871.

⑮ **Eltville** The journey continues past a number of castles to Eltville, in a similarly picturesque location among vineyards and mountains. The ruins of a castle from the 14th century overlook the Old Town, which has some lovely old manor houses and the church of Saints Peter and Paul (14th C.). Take a short detour to the former Cistercian monastery of Eberbach with Romanesque and early Gothic buildings. Wine has been made here for 850 years.

⑯ **Mainz** This town dates back to Moguntiacum, a Roman fort built in 38 BC, and is one of Germany's oldest

cities. St Boniface made Mainz an archbishopric in 742, and the university was founded in 1476. In the 15th century, one of the modern world's most important technological innovations was made here when Johann Gutenberg invented moveable metal type printing. Of the 200 bibles he ultimately printed, 48 copies are still around. One of these "Gutenberg Bibles" is held at the Gutenberg Museum on the north-eastern side of the Domplatz, along with a reconstruction of his workshop.
The reddish Mainz Cathedral of Saints Martin and Stephen dominates the city center with its six towers. It is a masterpiece of Romanesque architecture. The market fountain on the north side of the Domplatz is one of the most attractive

Renaissance fountains in Germany. The former Electoral Palace down on the Rhine now houses the Roman-Germanic Central Museum.
South-east of the university are the Römersteine, remains of an aqueduct built in the 1st century. Fans of Marc Chagall enjoy the Gothic church of St Stephen, which has nine glass windows painted by the artist between 1978 and 1985, and depicting scenes from the Bible.

⑰ **Wiesbaden** The capital of the state of Hesse is located at the foot of the wooded Taunus Mountains. Thanks to its twenty thermal hot springs, Wiesbaden has been a popular spa resort since the Romans built a fort here in the year 6 AD. The main thoroughfare in town is the

charm. This is especially evident in the historic Old Town around the Römerberg. On the other side of the Main River are half a dozen museums of international renown as well as the Sachsenhausen nightlife district. Sights in the Old Town include: the Römerberg with the Römer Old Town hall (with corbie gables from the 15th–18th centuries); the imperial hall, once a venue for coronation banquets; the Ostzeile, opposite the town hall, with six half-timbered patrician houses; the old St Nicholas Church (consecrated in 1290); the Domplatz and the Kaiserdom cathedral from the 13th–15th centuries, a coronation church from 1562; Paulsplatz and the neoclassical church of St Paul (1796–1833), where the Goethe Prize and the Peace Prize of the German Book Trade are awarded by the City of Frankfurt; the baroque Hauptwache (1729/30); Goethe's birthplace and the Goethe Museum; the neoclassical Börse (stock exchange, 1879); the Eschenheimer Tower (with remains of the old town walls); and the late-neoclassical Old Opera House from 1880.

Important museums in Frankfurt include: Kunsthalle Schirn (German painting from the

stately Wilhelmstrasse, at the northern end of which extends the spa district with the imposing neoclassical Kurhaus (1907) and the Kurhauskolonnade, the longest colonnade in Europe. Diagonally opposite the Kurhaus is the impressive Hessian State Library. West of the spa district you come to the Kochbrunnen, a fountain combining fifteen of a total of twenty hot springs, as well as the Kaiser Friedrich Baths, which are beautifully decorated in Art Nouveau style.

In the center of the city stands the Stadtschloss (municipal palace), completed in 1841, and the seat of the Hessian Landtag (regional government) since 1946. Opposite that is the impressive old town hall from 1610, and the square is domi-nated by the red neo-Gothic Marktkirche church from 1862.

⑱ Frankfurt am Main "Mainhattan" or "Bankfurt" are nicknames often used to refer to Germany's metropolis on the Main. It is not entirely without reason, for the city's numerous skyscrapers do indeed resemble its North American counterpart. Frankfurt is not just Germany's financial center, but second only to London in European finance. The 258-m-tall (846-ft) Commerzbank skyscraper is Europe's tallest office building, and Frankfurt's airport is one of the largest and busiests hubs on the continent. The city is also a major international trade fair and publishing center. As the birthplace of the German writer Johann Wolf-gang von Goethe, it is also not unjustifiably the host of the world's largest book fair.

Indeed, Frankfurt has played an important role throughout the country's history. Its Kaiserpfalz (imperial palace) was first mentioned in 794. In 876, it became the capital of the Ostrogoth empire. From 1356 to 1802, German kings and emperors were chosen and crowned here. In 1848/49, the German National Assembly met at St Paul's Church to defend the merits of democracy before the German court.

As "Mainhattan", Frankfurt has often had a dubious reputation – but unjustly so. Despite large-scale destruction during World War II, and booming construction since, the city has managed to preserve much of its Hessian

1 The picturesque "Pfalz" near Kaub stands on an island in the Rhine. It once served as a toll station. High above towers Gutenfels Castle.

2 Famous poets like Heinrich Heine, Victor Hugo and Clemens Brentano extolled the charms of the vineyard town Bacharach am Rhein.

3 Romantic Rheinstein Castle, built as a toll stronghold, stands at the beginning of the Middle Rhine Valley near Bingen, opposite the popular red wine vineyard town of Assmannshausen.

Renaissance on); Museum for Modern Art; the Jewish Museum housed in the former Rothschild mansion; Nature Museum Senckenberg; the German Architecture Museum; and the Städelsches Art Institut with paintings from the 14th century to the present.

⑲ Darmstadt This former Hesse imperial residence town is distinguished by remnants of life at the royal court. In the city center stands the ducal palace, which was built over the course of more than six centuries. The last extensions were added in the 18th century.

Up on the Mathildenhöhe, evidence of the regional rulers' passion for hunting is on show at the Kranichstein Hunting Lodge. The market square and the old town hall from 1598 testify to the fact that bourgeois life has always played an influential role here. A weekly market takes place on the square around the 18th-century fountain. If you want to go for a stroll, head to the Herrngarten, formerly a park for the regional counts that was transformed into an English-style landscape garden in the 18th century and finally opened to the public in the 19th century. From Darmstadt, the detour to Lorsch is a must. The Königshalle, or royal hall, is a real jewel of Carolingian architecture and one of the oldest completely preserved medieval structures in the country. A slightly longer detour takes you to the former imperial city of Worms, one of the oldest cities in Germany.

⑳ Heidelberg This idyllically situated university town on the Neckar is considered one of the birthplaces of German Romanticism. Towering over the Old Town are the famous castle ruins. The expansive grounds, which are laid out in terraces,

were remodeled and extended several times between the 13th and the 16th centuries. To the modern eye it is a fascinating jumble of castle and chateau, with Gothic as well as Renaissance elements, the latter of which are of particular interest, especially the Ottheinrichsbau from 1566 and the Friedrichsbau from 1607. Superb views of the Old Town below unfold as you make your way around.

At the heart of the Old Town, directly on the market square with its historic fountain, is

the late-Gothic Heiliggeistkirche (Church of the Holy Spirit), which houses the tombs of the regional electors.

The Old Bridge, with its lovingly preserved medieval bridge gate, is another of the city's most recognizable landmarks. Once you get to the other side, it's just a short stroll to the Philosophers' Walk on the slopes of the Heiligenberg, where once the city's philosophers and the university's professors used to walk and talk. It is worth the climb – from here you get the most attrac-

tive views of the Old Town, the Neckar and the castle.

We also recommend another detour while in Heidelberg: the former imperial city of Speyer. After returning, continue along the B37 through the Neckar Valley. From Neckargemünd, the road runs through the narrow valley via Hirschhorn up to Bad Wimpfen past picturesque villages and stout castles.

㉑ Bad Wimpfen This town is divided into Wimpfen im Tal (lower) and Wimpfen am Berg

Versailles" is one of the largest baroque chateaus in Germany, further enhanced by the magnificent gardens, for which Ludwigsburg is famous. During the annual Blossoming Baroque festival, thousands of visitors flock to the 30 ha (74 acres) of beautifully landscaped gardens, which also have an attraction for kids – the fairytale garden. Everyone from Hansel and Gretel to the witch, Sleeping Beauty, Snow White and the Frog Prince reside in this charming little park.

There are a number of other castles in Ludwigsburg as well. Not far from the imperial palace, in the middle of a vast nature and wildlife park, is Favorite, a baroque hunting lodge and maison de plaisance. It was constructed on the orders of Duke Eberhard Ludwig between 1713 and 1723. The Monrepos Palace on the lake was completed in 1768, a rococo building that features an attractive Empire interior and is often used as a venue for concerts, such as the Ludwigsburg Castle Festival.

From Ludwigsburg, a detour to the north-west to the Maulbronn monastery is worthwhile. This Cistercian abbey is

(upper). In the former, enclosed by ramparts, sights include the early-Romanesque Ritterstiftskirche (13th C.) and the adjacent monastery.

The main landmark of Wimpfen am Berg are the Staufen towers of the Kaiserpfalz (imperial palace). Half-timbered houses such as the Bügeleisenhaus, a former bourgeois hospital, the Krone Inn, the Riesenhaus (the manor house of the lords of Ehrenberg), all combine to create an enchanted medieval atmosphere in the upper town.

Also worth a visit are the sumptuously decorated municipal church and the Parish Church of the Holy Cross. The best views of the old town and the Neckar are from the western donjon of the former imperial palace.

㉒ Heilbronn This town is best known as the center of one of Germany's largest wine-growing regions. The Renaissance-style town hall on the market square has an astronomical clock from the 16th century. Construction of the nearby St Kilian's Church

began back in 1278. South-west of the market square you'll find the Deutschhof, the former headquarters of the knights of the Teutonic Order.

㉓ Ludwigsburg This city's founder, Duke Eberhard Ludwig, felt most cities lacked creativity. This inspired him in 1704, to fashion one according to his own personal designs.

Ludwigsburg's most lavish building is the Residenzschloss (palace), still the focal point of the city today. The "Swabian

1 "Mainhattan": the impressive skyline of Frankfurt am Main.

2 The royal hall of Lorsch Monastery, a "jewel of the Carolingian Renaissance".

3 Hirschhorn, the "Pearl of the Neckar Valley", is located just east of Heidelberg.

4 The Kaiserpfalz palace in Bad Wimpfen was built by the Staufer dynasty in the 12th century.

5 Ludwigsburg Palace is one of the largest baroque palaces in Germany and Europe

the most completely preserved medieval monastic complex north of the Alps and has been a declared a UNESCO World Heritage Site. The triple-naved basilica was consecrated in 1178, while the chapter house dates from the 14th century.

㉔ Stuttgart The capital of Baden-Württemberg is charmingly nestled into a valley that opens out towards the Neckar. The historic city center and the rows of houses seem to climb up the often steep slopes.

Originally built around a 13th-century moated castle on the Neckar, Stuttgart quickly developed into a very important trading city. The magnificent Königstraße runs from the impressive, 58-m-high (190-ft) tower of the Stuttgart central station to the grand Schlossplatz. In the middle of the square are the Jubilee Column (1842) and some modern sculptures by Alexander Calder and Alfred Hrdlicka.

The square is dominated by the Neues Schloss (new castle, 1807), which has three separate wings, expansive gardens and the neoclassical Königsbau (1860) opposite, the home of the Stuttgart Stock Exchange. The Altes Schloss (old castle) was completed in the Renaissance style in 1578. Today, it houses the highly reputed Württembergisches Landesmuseum (state museum).

Also on Schillerplatz, one of Stuttgart's most attractive squares, is the Gothic collegiate church with two towers (12th–15th centuries), the old chancellery, completed in 1544, and the "Fruchtkasten" (fruit box), an old grain silo from the 16th century.

Other interesting sights include the Akademiegarten next to the new castle, the Staatstheater (state theater) and the Staatsgalerie (state gallery).

Roughly 10 km (6 mi) southwest of the city center stands Solitude, an extravagant rococo palace built on a hill in 1767, for Duke Karl Eugen.

North of the city center, not far from the Killesberg with its 217-m-high (712-ft) television tower, you'll find the Weissenhof artists' colony, designed by renowned architects including Le Corbusier, Mies van der Rohe, Walter Gropius and Hans Scharoun. In the present district of Bad Cannstadt stands the Wilhelma, one of the most attractive and diverse botanical and zoological gardens in Germany.

㉕ Tübingen A university town since 1477, the "Athens on the Neckar" is still defined by the overwhelming student culture and the accompanying vibrant bar scene. Tübingen's picturesque and meticulously maintained Old Town, which climbs up in terraces from the banks of the Neckar, has a number of half-timbered houses surrounding a charming market square. From the 16th-century Schloss Hohentübingen, which you can reach via the delightfully scenic Burgsteige lane, you get mag-

nificent views of the Old Town and the Hölderlin Tower on the opposite side of the river. The famous poet lived there from 1807 until 1843. Other sights nearby worth visiting include the Alte Aula and the Burse (1478–1482), Tübingen's oldest university buildings, as well as the Evangelisches Stift (1536). From Alte Burse you will also be able to see the Collegiate Church, built around 1470, the old auditorium and the town hall, dating back to the 15th century. Tübingen has always had a hint of Venice about it, especially when the "Stocherer" (pokers) punt on the Neckar

with their longboats, often making the boat trip into an evening's entertainment.

From Tübingen, a detour to Lake Constance brings you back to the Rhine, which flows into the lake west of Bregenz in Austria, and leaves it again near Stein, where it is referred to as the Upper Rhine.

1 View across the Neckar to Tübingen and its Stiftskirche with the remarkable spire.

2 Villa Solitude in Stuttgart was built between 1763 and 1767 on the orders of Duke Carl Eugen.

Mosel Loop at Bremm The slopes on the loop are the steepest Riesling vineyards in Europe. Bremm delights visitors with its alleyways and half-timbered houses.

Cochem To see the main feature of this town on the Lower Mosel you have to look up: Reichsburg Castle was built in 1070 and renovated in the 19th century.

Eltz Castle This picturesque fortified castle with fairy-tale towers and decorative balconies was built back in 1160.

The Rhine near Kaub This small romantic town on the right bank of the Rhine is surrounded by a medieval town wall and is one of the most important wine-growing villages on the Middle Rhine. Kaub is dominated by Gutenfels Castle from the 13th century. On an island in the river is the former Pfalzgrafenstein toll tower from 1326.

Trier Germany's oldest city boasts buildings dating from Roman times to the present. The market square is a charming centerpiece.

Mainz This bishops' town was founded by the Romans and is one of Germany's oldest cities. Sights include the Gutenberg Museum, the cathedral and the half-timbered houses in the Old Town.

Bacharach Situated on the left bank of the Rhine, this little half-timbered wine village is enclosed by turreted town walls from the 16th century and dominated by Stahleck Castle.

Bingen Among the sights here at the confluence of the Nahe and the Rhine are Klopp Castle and the Mouse Tower.

Frankfurt Europe's tallest office building distinguishs the skyline of "Mainhattan". The airport is one of the largest on the continent too. Goethe's birthplace is also importance for its international trade fairs and many banks. In addition, it boasts a very attractive Old Town.

Heidelberg This venerable university town is the epitome of German romanticism. The castle ruins (13th–16th centuries) rising high above the beautiful Old Town and the Old Bridge (1786–1788) are the most recognizable icons of Heidelberg. The best views are from the Philosophenweg.

Tübingen This old university town (since 1477) boasts a picturesque and almost entirely preserved Old Town.

Speyer Located on the high banks of the Rhine, Speyer Cathedral was begun in the year 1025. It is Germany's largest Romanesque building. This is a view of the crypt, built in 1041.

Ludwigsburg This county seat is known for its ducal palace, the largest baroque palace complex in Germany, also known as the "Swabian Versailles".

Stuttgart Baden-Württemberg's capital city is situated at the bottom of the Neckar River valley. The elegant Königstraße leads up to Schlossplatz and the New Palace. Also worth seeing are the Königsbau and the Old Palace.

Lake Constance With an area of 538 sq km (207 sq mi), Constance is the second-largest lake in the Alps. Romantic villages, orchards and vineyards thrive on its shores. The mild climate even supports subtropical plant life on Mainau.

Germany

A fairy-tale journey – the Romantic Road

From the vineyards of Mainfranken through the charming Tauber Valley, to the geologically unique meteor-crater landscape of Ries and along the Danube, into the foothills of the Alps and the limestone mountains of Bavaria, the Romantic Road leads past myriad cultural sites from different centuries while giving you a glimpse of Germany's diverse natural landscape.

For the millions of visitors who travel the Romantic Road each year, it is a route that makes the cliché of charming and sociable Germany a reality. The stress of modern living seems to have had no effect in towns like Rothenburg ob der Tauber, Dinkelsbühl or Nördlingen, where the Middle Ages are still very much a part of the atmos-

Four city gates and fourteen towers surround the medieval fortress town of Dinkelsbühl.

phere. Yet they are dynamic towns that have understood the value of preserving the relics of their great past and carefully rebuilding those that were destroyed in World War II. Plenty of culture awaits the traveller along this route. Alongside the well-known highlights there are numerous architectural gems that are also

King Ludwig II by Ferdinand von Piloty. (1845-1886)

worth viewing if time permits. Some examples of these are Weikersheim Castle, the small church in Detwang with its Riemenschneider altar, Schillingsfürst Castle, the old town and castle at Oettingen, Harburg high above the Wörnitz

Valley, the convent in Mönchsdeggingen, the churches in Steingaden and Ilgen, the little church of St Koloman near Füssen and other treasures along the way that have – perhaps luckily – not yet been discovered by the tourist hordes. And yet the natural highlights should not be forgotten either as you cruise the Romantic Road to places like Würzburg, Rothenburg, Dinkelsbühl, Nördlingen, Donauwörth, Augsburg, Landsberg, the Wieskirche or Füssen, whose unique beauty is underscored by their rustic settings in romantic valleys, enchanting forests or impressive mountains.

Two of the most visited buildings on the route have been classified as UNESCO World Heritage Sites: the Würzburger

Donauwörth with its Gothic parish church and 15th-century Tanzhaus. The once 'free city' has an incredible medieval old town.

The St Koloman Pilgrimage Church stands in a field against the backdrop of the Schwangauer Mountains.

Residenz and the Wieskirche, important baroque and rococo works. A trip to Munich, the charming and cosmopolitan capital of Bavaria, or to the Werdenfels region with its famous sights such as Oberammergau, Linderhof Castle, Ettal Monastery and the twin villages of Garmisch-Partenkirchen enhances this aspect of your German experience.

For those who have the time, a visit to one of the numerous festivals that take place along the Romantic Road is highly recommended. Some are based around regional history like the Meistertrunk in Rothenburg ob der Tauber, a re-enactment of a drinking contest from the 17th century, or the Kinderzeche in Dinkelsbühl, a children's festival originating in the 17th-cen-

tury Thirty Years War. Classical music lovers should try to obtain tickets for the Mozart Festival in Würzburg, the Jeunesses Musicales concerts in Weikersheim, the Mozart Summer in Augsburg or the Richard Strauss Days in Garmisch. The Cloister Theater performances in Feuchtwangen are staged before a magnificent backdrop. In addition to all this, there are festivals where anybody can participate, like the Free Town Festival in Rothenburg ob der Tauber or the Peace Festival in Augsburg. All these events take place in summer. Then of course there is the world-famous Oktoberfest in Munich, unmatched on the entire planet in its degree of debauchery and its sheer size. In winter the Christmas markets set up stalls

that invite you to stroll, shop and drink a mulled wine with gingerbread cookies and other delicacies. To sum it up, the Romantic Road has myriad attractions throughout the entire year, and takes you through

the prettiest regions of Bavaria and Baden-Württemburg. Like no other road in Germany, it connects regional history with broad cultural landscapes, and brings the country's rich past fabulously to life.

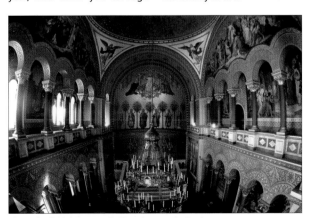

The majestic throne room in Neuschwanstein Castle.

The Romantic Road – The fascinating route between Würzburg and Füssen is lined with picturesque towns, forts, castles and priceless works of art. The road starts in the Main River Valley on its way through the charming Tauber Valley into the Wörnitz Valley and then crosses the Danube to follow the Lech towards the impressive Alps.

① **Würzburg** The Romantic Road begins with a sensation: the majestic Würzburger Residenz (1720), a baroque masterpiece. Despite the devastating bombings of 16 March 1945, which left even the most optimistic people with little to be optimistic about, this city on the Main offers many sights: the late-Gothic chapel of Mary and the rococo Haus zum Falken blend nicely on the market square.

The cathedral, which was consecrated in 1188, has unfortunately lost some of its character due to war damage. Near the baroque Neumünster lies the tranquil Lusamgärtlein, where the minstrel Walther von der Vogelweide lies buried. And all of this is dominated by the mighty fortress (13–18th cen-

turies) on the Marienberg with its Main-Franconia Museum containing many works by Tilman Riemenschneider.

② **Tauberbischofsheim** This town in the Tauber Valley is famous for its history in the sport of fencing. It is distinguished by the Kurmainzisch Castle, whose storm tower is a masterpiece from the turn of the 16th century. The Riemenschneider School altar in St Martin's Parish Church is also worth seeing.

③ **Bad Mergentheim** The Old Town in this health resort is

dominated by the Castle of the German Knights (16th century). Don't miss the baroque castle church designed by B. Neumann and François Cuvilliés. A small detour to see 'The Madonna' by Matthias Grünewald in Stuppach Parish Church is worth it.

④ **Weikersheim** Continuing through the Tauber Valley, Weikersheim invites you to visit its Renaissance castle and baroque gardens, which are among Germany's prettiest. The small former royal capital is surrounded by numerous vineyards.

Travel Information

Route profile
Length: approx. 350 km (217 miles), excluding detours
Time required: 7–10 days
Start: Würzburg
End: Füssen
Route (main locations): Würzburg, Tauberbischofsheim, Bad Mergentheim, Rothenburg ob der Tauber, Dinkelsbühl, Nördlingen, Donauwörth, Augsburg, Landsberg, Schongau, Füssen

Traffic information: Drive on the right in Germany. There is a 420-km (261-mile) cycle path that runs parallel to the Romantic Road. More information about this route can be found on the

Internet at:
www.bayerninfo.de.

Information:
There is a lot of information available on the Romantic Road but no definitive site for the entire route. The following sites might help you get an idea of how to organize your trip.

General:
www.romantischestrasse.de
en.wikipedia.org/wiki/Romantic_Road

Town sites:
www.rothenburg.de
www.dinkelsbuehl.de
www2.augsburg.de
www.fuessen.de

⑨ **Nördlingen** Ideally you would approach fabulous Nördlingen from above in order to fully appreciate the nearly perfectly circular city center. Its original town walls have been masterfully preserved and its five town gates are still in use today.

St Georg is one of the largest late-Gothic German hall churches, its icon being 'Daniel', the 90-m (295-ft) bell tower. On a clear day from the tower you can make out the rim of the Ries crater, especially towards the south-west, the south and the east.

⑩ **Donauwörth** This 'free town' developed from a fishing village on the Wörnitz island of 'Ried' at the confluence of the Wörnitz and the Danube. Most of its attractions are located along the main road, the Reichsstrasse: the Fuggerhaus from 1536, the late-Gothic Maria Himmelfahrt Parish Church, the Tanzhaus from around 1400, the town hall and the baroque Deutsch-ordenshaus. The baroque church of the old Benedictine monastery Heiligkreuz is also worth visiting.

⑪ **Augsburg** 'Augusta Vin-delicorum' was the original name given to Augsburg by its Roman founders. By the 16th century the 'free town' was one of the most important cultural and financial metropolises

⑤ **Creglingen** The Tauber Valley houses many of the works of the wood sculptor Tilman Riemenschneider. The altar in the Creglingen Herrgottskirche is among the most beautiful. The Old Town here is a lovely mix of half-timbered houses and medieval fortresses.

⑥ **Rothenburg ob der Tauber** This small town is synonymous around the world with German medieval Roman-ticism. A walk along the well-preserved town walls offers an overview of the place and great views across the Tauber Valley. The market square is dominated by the town hall, which has Gothic and Renaissance wings. You can also view more works of Tilman Riemenschneider here. In fact, the triple-nave St Jakob Basilika houses his Holy Blood Altar. Further along the route heading south you'll cross the Frankenhöhe, the European watershed between the Rhine and Danube.

⑦ **Feuchtwangen** This one-time collegiate church, part Romantic, part Gothic, is worth a visit any time of the year. The marketplace has an attractive mix of bourgeois town houses.

⑧ **Dinkelsbühl** The main attraction of this town in the idyllic Wörnitz Valley is the perfect medieval town center with its town walls. Other highlights include the Deutsches Haus, a fabulous half-timbered house, and the St Georg Parish Church (second half of the 15th century). The town is more than 1,000-years-old.

1 View of the Würzburger Residenz from Residenzplatz with the Franconia Fountain (1894).

2 The town hall in Augsburg with its remarkably symmetrical facade and 78-m (256-ft) Perlach Tower.

3 View from 'Daniel' over the Nördlingen market square.

101

1

north of the Alps. The town hall was built between 1615 and 1620 and was designed by Elias Holl, as was the Zeughaus of 1607. Stained-glass windows depicting the five prophets in St Maria Cathedral are among the oldest in the world. The streets are lined with many patrician houses like the Schaezler and Gignoux palaces. A few towers and gates (such as the Red Gate) are left over from the old town defenses.

From Augsburg it is a quick half-hour drive to Munich (see p. 104). From there you can take the Lindau motorway straight to Landsberg.

12 Klosterlechfeld This monastery was built on the site of an historic battlefield from the year 955. Elias Holl was the architect of this pilgrimage church, which was erected in 1603. It was based on the Pantheon in Rome.

13 Landsberg am Lech The first wall surrounding the Old Town between the Lech River

and the Lech bluff was built in the 13th century. It included the Schmalzturm at the top end of the triangular main plaza, which is dominated by the town hall. The stucco facade of the town hall was designed by Dominikus Zimmermann in 1719.

The Bayer Gate, built in 1425, is part of the third wall and is one of the most beautiful of its kind in southern Germany. The four churches in Landsberg am Lech are especially noteworthy: the Gothic, late-baroque Maria Himmelfahrt; the Johanniskirche by Dominikus Zimmermann; the Ursuline Convent Church by J.B. Gunetzrhainer (begun in 1740) and the Heiligkreuz Monastery church. Portions of the 15th-century Landsberg town wall are also quite well-preserved.

14 Altenstadt St Michael's is one of Upper Bavaria's most significant Romantic churches. It was built in the early part of the 13th century and is surrounded by a mighty protective

2

wall. It houses frescoes from the 14th and 15th centuries as well as the 'Grosser Gott von Altenstadt', a Romanesque crucifix from around 1200. Because of its enormous size, it is one of the most important works of art of its type, radiating an expressive calm in the church.

15 Schongau The drive to Schongau follows the Lech River through Claudia Augusta. The Gothic Ballenhaus of 1515 bears witness to its previous importance as a trading town. The town walls with their bat-

tlements are still conserved in part, as are five towers and the Frauen Gate to the west (14th century). The Maria Himmelfahrt Parish Church, which was remodelled by Dominikus Zimmermann in 1748, has frescoes by Matthäus Günter and is well worth a visit.

If time permits, you can continue from here into the Werdenfels area to enjoy some wonderful mountain scenery.

16 Rottenbuch The old Augustine canonical church in Rottenbuch was remodelled between 1737 and 1742 and

3

17 Wieskirche One of this route's best highlights is the Wieskirche, built by Dominikus Zimmermann in 1745. Against the backdrop of the Trauchberge Mountains, the ceiling frescoes and a large part of the stucco here were done by Johann Baptist Zimmermann. The white and gold interior appears light and cheerful, as if music had been turned to stone. The Wieskirche near Steingaden is visited by hundreds of thousands of tourists every year. It is considered to be a complete work of art.

18 Hohenschwangau and Neuschwanstein These two royal castles are picturesquely set in a striking mountain scene. Crown Prince Maximilian gave Castle Hohenschwangau (12th century) a neo-Gothic facelift in 1833 – Ludwig II, the man behind nearby Castle Neuschwanstein, had spent part of his youth here in Hohenschwangau. Neuschwanstein is the idealized image of a medieval castle with towers,

battlements, royal gardens and majestic rooms.

19 Füssen The Romantic Road comes to an end in this small town on the Lech River. Don't miss the St Mang Monastery or the baroque St Magnus Parish Church. The medieval edifice here was also given a generous baroque remodel. The trompe l'oeil on the facade of the Hohen Schloss castle courtyard is particularly noteworthy. The facade of the Heilig-Geist-Spital Church (1748–1749) is sumptuously painted. To finish off the trip, how about a wild nature experience: take a gander at the nearby Lechfall.

1 Neuschwanstein Castle with the Allgäuer Alps as a backdrop.

2 The pilgrimage church of the Gegeißelter Heiland auf der Wies lies in the Pfaffenwinkel and is a UNESCO World Heritage Site.

3 The two-tiered choir in the Wieskirche with the painting of Christ in the center.

now shines with baroque cheerfulness. Stucco artist Joseph Schmuzer and painter Matthäus Günter were responsible for the wonderful interior. In this area it isn't hard to stumble over one charming baroque

church after another. Add the natural environment of the area and you've got a delightfully attractive combination for walks such as the one leading through the Ammerschlucht to Wieskirche.

Munich

Munich exudes the magic of an old city that still manages to remain youthful, multicultural and very much itself.

Munich was originally founded by Guelph Heinrich the Lion, but the royal Wittelsbacher family controlled the city until 1918 and played a much greater role in its history. They are to be thanked for most of the city's monuments and works of art and the prettiest stretches of road. Ludwig I was particularly energetic, claiming that he wanted to build 'Athens on the Isar'. The Old Town lies between the Isartor, Sendlinger Tor, Karlstor and the Feldherrnhalle. Schwabing, the university and museum district, gives Munich its reputation for being a fun-loving and cultured city of the arts.

The Munich of artists

Important paintings and sculptures are on display in the large and impressive Munich museums: the Alte and Neue Pinakothek, Pinakothek der Moderne and Haus der Kunst. The Lenbachhaus and the Villa Stuck show how successful artists lived in Munich at the end of the 19th century. The Lenbachhaus was designed by the architect Gabriel von Seidl in 1887 for the painter Franz von Lenbach and is today home to the municipal gallery which contains

major works by the Blaue Reiter group. The Villa Stuck was designed by the aristocratic painter Franz von Stuck in 1897–98 and hosts a variety of exhibits. A wander into the heart of Schwabing is also part of any trip on the trail of artists – at the beginning of the 20th century, 'bohemian Munich' used to gather near Nikolaiplatz. Schwabing has been able to preserve some of its old flair.

Green Munich

For those who have had enough of the city it is also easy to find a bit of nature in this wonderful city. The first and foremost of the green oases is of course the Englischer Garten. At 4 sq km (1.5 sq mi) it is the world's largest city park – even larger than Central Park in New York. Beyond the vast lawns and brooks that flow through this wonderful park there are a few architectural highlights as well: the Chinese Tower, the Monopteros and the Japanese teahouse. The best way to explore the Englischer Garten – and Munich in general – is by bike. Take a break along the way at one of the beer gardens or stroll along the river banks. The Isar River runs straight through Munich and on a summer day can be a nice way to cool down. To get there just walk to

the Deutsches Museum. In the center of town, just a few steps from Karlsplatz (also known as Stachus), is the old botanical gardens park. Take a tram to Nymphenburger Park, another oasis of relaxation where you'll a baroque castle and royal gardens.

Munich theater town

For theater lovers, Munich offers interesting shows and fantastic theater architecture. The majestic Cuvilliés Theater next to the National Theater is part of the former royal Residenz. François Cuvilliés designed the fabulously ornate rococo structure. A second building that attracts also architecture enthusiasts is the Kammerspiele in the Maximilianstrasse. Richard Riemerschmid and Max Littmann allowed their art-nouveau fantasies free rein here. Another building with a bit of history

is the Prinzregenten Theater, which was badly damaged during World War II and not reopened until the renovation was completed in 1996. It was built in 1901 to celebrate the works of Richard Wagner.

1 Munich by night: View over the Frauenkirche with its imposing spires and the neo-Gothic town hall tower. To the far right is the Olympia Tower.

2 The Cuvilliés Theater is the city's oldest surviving opera house. Only the interior remains of the original building.

Bad Mergentheim The Old Town here is dominated by the Castle of the German Knights (16th century). Its church was designed by B. Neumann and F. Cuvilliés.

Weikersheim This precious royal town in the Tauber River Valley has a Renaissance castle and a baroque garden, one of Germany's prettiest.

Würzburg Despite the bombings of 1945, this wine city on the Main offers a number of attractions. The most important of these are St Kilian Cathedral (opened in 1188), the old Main bridge and Fort Marienberg (13th–18th centuries).

Würzburger Residenz The majestic construction, started in 1720, was supposed to replace Fort Marienburg. Its scale is amazing, both inside and out.

Feuchtwangen This former 'free town' with rows of pretty houses has a collegiate church that is part Romantic and part Gothic. There is also a handful of museum collections worth seeing.

Rothenburg Once a Franconian 'free town', Rothenburg has hardly changed since the Thirty Years War. The town offers spectacular views over the Tauber River Valley.

Dinkelsbühl More than 1,000 years of history bless this town in the Wörnitz Valley, perhaps the best example of medieval architecture. Surrounded by formidable walls, its main attractions are the Deutsches Haus and St Georg Cathedral.

Nördlingen St Georg is one of Germany's largest late-Gothic hall churches. From the bell tower 'Daniel' you can get a good view of this almost perfectly circular town.

Augsburg The Renaissance town hall and Perlach Tower are highlights in this 2,000-year-old city.

Wieskirche This pilgrimage church is considered in its entirety to be one of the major works of Bavarian rococo art.

Nymphenburg This baroque castle in Munich is a majestic site indeed. The expansive grounds make for a lovely walk or picnic. The state porcelain factory is next door.

Linderhof Castle The only one of Ludwig II's three castles to be finished during his lifetime is surrounded by a park with unusual buildings, some of which are derived from Wagner's operatic fantasy world.

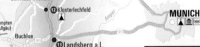

Füssen/Neuschwanstein The old city between the Ammergau and Allgäu Alps awaits you with two royal castles: Hohenschwangau (12th century, transformed to neo-Gothic in 1837) and the world-famous fairy-tale castle of Disney fame, Neuschwanstein (1869–86).

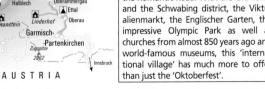

München A detour into the Bavarian capital should be part of any trip along the Romantic Road. With the Old Town and the Schwabing district, the Viktualienmarkt, the Englischer Garten, the impressive Olympic Park as well as churches from almost 850 years ago and world-famous museums, this 'international village' has much more to offer than just the 'Oktoberfest'.

Route 1 2

In the heart of Europe

Schönbrunn Palace in Vienna – a
with extensive gardens.

The Route of the Emperors: Berlin – Prague – Vienna – Budapest

On this journey along the ancient European transport and trade arteries of the Elbe, Vltava and Danube rivers, Europe presents itself in all its historical and cultural diversity. On the various riverbanks, cities like Dresden, Prague, Vienna and Budapest show off their abundant monuments of art, and everywhere along the route are palaces, castles and urban gems surrounded by unique natural scenery.

No emperor could ever have imagined that at the beginning of the 21st century you would be able to travel all the way from the Spree River (Berlin) to the Danube without any complicated border checks, particularly after the centuries of mini-states in the region and the tragic rift of the 20th century.

What happened to the days when autocratic despots jealously erected border checkpoints and threw up 'iron curtains' to protect their territories? When the Viennese knew nothing of Budweis or Bratislava, and to the people of West Berlin, Dresden might as well have been further away

than the Dominican Republic? Gone inddeed are those days. These days, the road is free to explore what is so close and yet still quite unfamiliar, and there really is a lot to discover.

The landmark of Vienna: St Stephen's Cathedral.

Berlin, Germany's old and new capital, is its very own unique tourist cosmos. It would take weeks to see even a fraction of its museum treasures, its continuously changing skyline with so much contemporary architecture, an art and restaurant scene that is just as dynamic as that of any other cosmopolitan city, and its large green parks. On this route, however, Berlin is but the starting point of a fascinating journey across Europe. In Brandenburg and Saxony, both core regions of German intellectual history, one highlight seems to follow the next. Potsdam, the royal residence of the Prussian kings, provides a magnificent overture to the

Hradčany Castle above the Charles Bridge, Prague's most famous bridge, on the Vltava River.

former Habsburg summer palace

Charlottenburg Palace in Berlin, the summer residence of Sophie Charlotte, wife of Frederick I.

Lutheran town of Wittenberg, to Weimar, the focal point of German classicism, and to the porcelain metropolis of Meissen, your next stops.

Dresden is simply irresistible as a tourist destination. The capital of Saxony, which rose like the proverbial phoenix from the ashes (and from the floodwaters in 2002), enchants with its baroque and rococo buildings and its art galleries. Music lovers flock to highlights like the Semper Opera, the Staatskapelle orchestra and the famous Kreuzchor choir.

Attempting to describe in words the exquisite beauty of Prague is often an exercise in futility. The views across the Vltava River towards Hradčany Castle are some of the most unforgettable city sights any-where on earth. And just like one of Mozart's melodies, the magic hovering above the picturesque alleyways in the Small Quarter and around the Old Town Square will leave no soul untouched.

From the splendidly restored spa towns of Karlovy Vary and Mariánské Láznû, to Litoměřice, Hrad Karlštejn, České Budějovice and Český Krumlov – the number of five-star attractions in Bohemia is just incredible.

There are just as many amazing sights on the journey through Upper and Lower Austria – Freistadt, Linz, Enns, Grein and Krems, not to mention the Melk and Klosterneuburg monasteries. Away from urban attractions, nature will also spoil you along the route – the heathlands of lower Fläming and Lower Lausitz, the sandstone mountains on the River Elbe, the Vltava Valley, the Bohemian Forest, the Mühl Quarter, Wachau and the Viennese Forest. On top of that, you can always sample the tasty delicacies that the local cuisine has to offer. An almost exotic piece of scenery awaits you at the Hortobágy National Park, a real piece of the idyllic Hungarian Puszta at the end of the tour.

East of Budapest's Matthias Church is the Halászbástya, the Fisherman's Bastion in neo-Gothic and neo-Romanesque style on the Buda bank.

1

From the Spree in Berlin to the Danube in Budapest – a journey through the European heartland of old empires is now possible without border checks, through five countries from the German capital to the Hungarian capital. It will give you a comprehensive overview of its cultural depth and scenic beauty.

1 Berlin (see pp. 110–111).

2 Potsdam Our first stop outside the city limits of Berlin is Potsdam, the state capital of Brandenburg. It is famous mainly for the beautiful baroque and neoclassical buildings and its magnificent parks dating from the era of the Prussian kings.

The best-known attraction of this town, which is 1,000 years old and has been partially declared a UNESCO World Heritage Site, is Frederick III's pompously decorated summer palace. Its park covers 300 ha (740 acres) and was designed by Lenné. It is an architectural gem in itself, full of statues and monuments such as the neighbouring park of Charlottenhof.

In Potsdam's Old Town, the Old Market with the St Nicholas Church and the former town hall, the Marstall stables, the Dutch Quarter and the old Russian colony of Alexandrowka are all worth a visit. Another must-see is the New Garden with its Marble Palace and Cecilienhof Castle. From Potsdam, drive to the old town of Beelitz, and from there east to the B101 south towards Luckenwalde.

3 Luckenwalde At first glance, this medieval market town may seem dull and industrial, but its interesting historical center has been well preserved. Its landmark is the steeple of St Johannskirche with its Gothic frescoes and important altar statues. A former hat factory, built at the beginning of the 1920s by Erich Mendelsohn, is also remarkable.

4 Jüterbog This town, located 15 km (9 miles) further south at the edge of the lower Fläming heathlands, still has most of its original fortifications, including three beautiful gates. Sites here include the Liebfrauenkirche, the Nikolaikirche and the town hall, but the main attraction is really 5 km (3 miles) to the north: the ruins of the Cistercian mona-

Travel Information

Route profile
Length: approx. 1,100 km (700 miles), excluding detours
Time required: at least 2 weeks
Start: Berlin, Germany
End: Budapest, Hungary
Route (main locations): Berlin, Potsdam, Dresden, Prague, České Budějovice, Linz, Krems, Vienna, Bratislava, Komárno (Komárom), Budapest

---

Traffic information:
Drive on the right in all the countries on this trip. Speed limits are signposted. If not, 50 km/h (35 mph) in built-up areas, 90–100 km/h (55–60 mph) outside of towns. Autobahns in Germany have no speed limit

unless otherwise indicated. In the other countries, 130 km/h (80 mph) is usually the limit. Roads are typically good in all five countries.

When to go:
Central Europe is typically quite warm in summer, cold in winter, and inconsistent in spring and autumn. Always have a rain jacket, regardless of season.

General travel information:
Here are some sites that may help get you started with planning:
wikitravel.org/en/Berlin
www.saxonytourism.com
www.czech.cz
www.aboutaustria.org
www.oberoesterreich.at
www.hungary.com

Today the town is more famous for its 'white gold' than for its 1,000 years of history. Home of Europe's first hard porcelain, Meissen has produced this valuable product since Augustus the Strong founded the factory in 1710. It continues to be exported all over the world.

Past Radebeul, the route along the B26 takes us to Dresden, the Saxon state capital 25 km (16 miles) away.

6 Dresden This former elector's residence, which has also been praised as the 'Florence of Germany' or the 'Baroque Pearl', is doubtless one of Europe's major cultural centers. In 1485 it became the seat of the Albertinian government, and during the 17th and 18th centuries, Augustus the Strong and his successors turned it into one of the most magnificent baroque residence cities in all of Germany.

The devastating bomb raids in February 1945 were unfortunately fatal for the city, destroying the Old Town almost beyond recognition. However, many of the famous buildings have either already been restored or are still works in progress, chief among them being the Zwinger, housing the 'Old Masters' art gallery; the Semper Opera; the castle; the Frauenkirche; the Japanese Palace; the Albertinum, housing the 'New Masters' art gallery; the Green Vault; and the Brühl Terraces high above the riverbank. You should definitely visit the important attractions in the surrounding area, above all Pillnitz Castle, Moritzburg Castle and the so-called Elbe Castles.

If you are not intending to do the detour to Weimar and Wartburg Castle, you now follow the B172 upriver from Dresden. You'll pass Pirna, with its picturesque center and the interesting Großsedlitz baro-

que gardens, and enter the spectacular Elbe Sandstone Mountains.

7 Elbe Sandstone Mountains In order to get the best possible views of these bizarre sandstone rock formations, you would really have to do a boat trip on the meandering river. Barring that, you can get some magnificent views from the road. Most of the area is now included in the 'Saxon Switzerland' National Park, with its monumental plateaus. Königstein Castle and the bastion in the spa town of Rathen are quite popular. Bad Schandau is the starting point for hiking and climbing tours to the Schrammsteine rocks and through Kirnitz Valley up to the Lichtenhain waterfalls.

8 Děčín The rocky sandstone scenery continues in all its grandeur here on the Czech side of the border. From the town of Hřensko, for example, there is a beautiful 4-km (2.5-mile) walk to the spectacular Pravčická Gate stone formation. An ideal starting point for trips into the park area is Děčín, where the famous 'Shepherd's Wall' towers 150 m (492 ft) over the river.

On the way to the Ústí nad Labem region you'll find another magnificent rock formation, crowned by the ruins of Strekov

1 Dresden owes its nickname, the 'Florence of Germany', to its baroque cityscape, which includes the Semper Opera and the Frauenkirche Church.

2 View of Sanssouci Palace, Friedrich II's summer residence, considered a rival to Versailles.

3 Moritzburg Castle was used by the Elector Friedrich August II of Saxony as a hunting lodge.

stery of Zinna, with important Gothic wall paintings.

Driving along the edge of the Lower Lausitz heathlands for about 100 km (62 miles) on the B101, you will pass Elsterwerda and Großenhain before you reach the Elbe River and the porcelain center of Meissen.

5 Meissen In the 12th century, this 'Cradle of Saxony', where the German emperors

founded the first settlement on Slavic soil, was a royal residence of the House of Wettin. Until the devastations of World War II it was able to preserve its medieval imprint, with the Gothic cathedral and Albrecht Castle representing both religious and worldly power. These are still visible from the historic Old Town with its market square and half-timbered buildings.

Berlin

Things have been changing incredibly rapidly in Berlin since the Berlin Wall came down in 1989. Now it seems the whole world knows that the lively German capital on the rivers Spree and Havel is a cosmopolitan city on a par with the likes of New York, Tokyo and London.

Berlin, whose history began in the 13th century, is not one of Germany's older cities. It was Prussia's rise to a great European power in the 18th century that made the capital significant. Berlin then became larger and more beautiful, finally being named the capital of the German Empire in 1871.

Under the National Socialists, terror and annihilation spread from the capital, but in 1945 it was reduced to rubble. After being divided in 1961, it went on to inspire the reunification of East and West Germany in 1989 with the opening of the Berlin Wall. Since then it has changed dramatically. Today, Berlin is still not one entity but rather a grouping of districts. In a way, however, this is a blessing – for it is the city's variety and its contrasts that define this metropolis.

In the Charlottenburg district visit: Kurfürstendamm, the city's principal shopping boulevard, the ruins of the Emperor William Memorial Church and the Zoological Gardens.

Outside the city center visit the Charlottenburg Castle and Park, the 'German Versailles', palace of the Prussian kings (built 1695–1746); the Egyptian Museum with Nefertiti; and the Museum Berggruen with great modern art.

In the Tiergarten district check out Berlin's largest city park with Bellevue Castle and Park, the residence of the German president; the Cultural Forum with the Philharmonic, the Museum of Musical Instruments, the Arts and Crafts Museum, a gallery with European paintings to the 19th century, the New National Gallery with 20th century art, the memorial

Brandenburg Gate, built in the late 18th century, is considered the most important landmark of Berlin and of the German Reunification.

to the German Resistance in the former Wehrmacht headquarters; the Road of 17 June with Victory Column (67 m/220 ft) between Brandenburg Gate and Ernst-Reuter-Square.

West of city center go to Grunewald, Berlin's forest, the Wannsee, and the Dahlem Museum with an outstanding collection of ethnological exhibits. In Kreuzberg see the ruins of Anhalt Station, the Martin Gropius Building, the Jewish Museum by star architect Daniel Liebeskind, the German Technology Museum, and Victoria Park with Kreuzberg Memorial.

Berlin 'Mitte' (center): the Brandenburg Gate (1791); 'Unter den Linden' historic boulevard with a memorial of Frederick the Great; the New Guard by Schinkel; St Hedwig's Cathedral from the 18th century; the neoclassical public opera house, the baroque Zeughaus with the German Historical Museum; the Crown Prince's Palace (18th century); Humboldt University; the Gendarmes Market; the French and German Cathedral (18th century); the Schinkel Theater (1821); the Reichstag (Parliament) with glass dome by Sir Norman Foster; Potsdam Square's modern architecture, Museum Island with Pergamon Museum, the Old Museum (antiquities), the New Museum, the Old National Gallery, the Bode Museum and Lustgarten. Beyond that is the Berlin Cathedral (late 19th century), 'Alex' TV tower (365 m/1,198 ft), old Checkpoint Charlie with the Berlin Wall museum; St Mary's Church (13th century); historic Nikolai Quarter; Märkisches Museum of the city.

In the Scheunenviertel go to the Hamburger Bahnhof Gallery (modern art), the New Synagogue with its center on the history of Berlin's Jewish community, and the Hackesche Höfe from 1906, once the largest working and living compound in Europe.

castle. From here you can take a detour heading west on the N13 via Most and Chomutov to the renowned spa towns of Karlovy Vary and Mariánské Lázně.

⑨ Litoměřice At the confluence of the Eger and the Elbe (Labe), where the Bohemian hills flatten out towards the plains, is the ancient town of Litomůfiice surrounded by vineyards and orchards. Its Old Town is among the most beautiful in Bohemia. At its center is the market square, which is around 2 ha (5 acres) in size. Don't miss the 'Kelchhaus', the town hall and St Stephen's Cathedral on Cathedral Hill.

About 4 km (2.5 miles) to the south, Terezín invokes memories of darker times. In World War II, the German occupation was not good to this town, which was originally built by Emperor Joseph II (1741–90) as a fortification against Prussia. There was a large concentration camp here.

⑩ Mělník High above the junction of the Vltava and Elbe Rivers is the much-visited town of Mělník, with its market square surrounded by beautiful stately houses. The town's most eye-catching sight, however, is its castle, a cherished possession of the local nobility for more than 1,100 years. The terrace of the castle restaurant has some fantastic views over the idyllic river valley.

From Mělník it is ca. 40 km (25 miles) to Prague, the fairy-tale city on the Vltava River, and only 30 km (18 miles) to what is considered Bohemia's most famous castle.

⑪ Prague For detailed information see p. 113.

⑫ Karlštejn After 16 km (10 miles) on the R4, you head westbound at Dobřichovice for around 40 km (25 miles) until you get to this monumental castle perched majestically on a limestone rock 72 m (236 ft) above the Berounka Valley. It

was built in the mid 14th century by Emperor Charles IV as his royal residence and a depository for the treasures. Its highlight in terms of art history is the Chapel of the Cross in the Great Tower with its gold-plated arches.

Back on the R4, you go to Příbram, which is located 50 km (31 miles) south-west of Prague, just off the main road.

⑬ Příbram This industrial and mining town, where silver has been mined since the 14th century and uranium since 1945,

would not be worth mentioning if it were not for one of the Czech Republic's most visited pilgrimage destinations at its south-eastern edge – the Church of Our Lady of Svatá Hora with its baroque additions.

1 View over Prague's Charles Bridge with the Old Town bridge tower and the church of St Franciscus in the background.

2 Hrad Karlštejn was used as a summer residence by Charles IV.

Prague

For centuries, the 'Golden City' has been an important intellectual and cultural center, characterized by unique and beautiful architecture throughout the entire city.

Although Prague escaped destruction in World War II, time has still taken its toll on the city's buildings over the centuries. Thanks to an expertly managed restoration, however, Prague can once again show off the magnificence of more than 1,000 years of history.

The Czech people can be proud of their capital, which is the former residence of Bohemian kings and Habsburg Emperors. Hradčany Castle, where they used to reside, provides you with the best views of this masterpiece of historical urban architecture – the entire city is designated a UNESCO World Heritage Site.

In the Old Town go see the Altstädter Ring with rows of historic houses; the baroque Týn Church and Jan Hus Memorial; the art-nouveau Representation House; St Wenceslas Square with buildings from the 19th and 20th centuries; the Gothic town hall with its astronomical clock; and the late-Gothic gunpowder tower.

In the Castle Quarter on the Hradčany visit the castle (royal residence since the 10th century); the Golden Alleyway; the King's Palace with Renaissance Hall; the St Veit's Cathedral, with relics from St Wenceslas, the national saint; St George's Basilica (12th century).

In the Josefov district see the Old Jewish cemetery, the Old New Synagogue, and the Pinkas Synagogue. In the Lesser Quarter visit the Charles Bridge (14th century); St Nicholas Church, Prague's most important baroque church and the Waldstein Palace of the commander Wallenstein.

Gothic town hall with astronomical clock and the Church of Our Lady before Týn with the oldest pipe organ in Prague.

South-east of Příbram, not far from the B4, are two imposing castles on the bank of the Vltava River, which actually forms a reservoir more than 100 km (62 miles) long in this area. One of them is Zvíkov Castle, built in the 13th century on a towering rock outcrop; this former royal residence is worth a visit for its Chapel of St Wenceslas and the late-Gothic frescoes in its Great Hall. Orlík Castle, owned by the Schwarzenberg family for more than 700 years and reconstructed in neo-Gothic style in the 19th century, captivates with its richly decorated interior.

⑭ Písek On your way south on Road 20 you'll cross the Otava River after 50 km (31 miles). The well-manicured center of this little town used to be an important stopping point on the so-called Golden Path, the trade route between Prague and Passau. Deer Bridge recalls the town's importance as an ancient traffic hub. The bridge, which was built in the second half of the 13th century, is Bohemia's oldest stone bridge.

⑮ České Budějovice Another 50 km (31 miles) on, you come to České Budějovice, which is world-famous for its breweries. Since Ottokar II founded the town in 1265, its center has been the market square. The most dramatic sight on this huge square, which covers an area of 133 by 133 m (145 by 145 yds) and is surrounded by arcades on all sides, is the Samson Fountain.
From the viewing platform of the steeple (72 m/236 ft), you can easily spot the other sights of the town – the baroque cathedral of St Nicholas, the town hall, the Dominican Monastery and the Church of Our Lady, as well as the Salt House. Around 10 km (6 miles) to the

north, the battlements of Hluboká Castle appear on the horizon. Considered 'Bohemia's Neuschwanstein', this lavishly furnished castle was also owned by the Schwarzenberg family until 1939.

⑯ Český Krumlov Upriver from České Budějovice, it is another fifteen minutes by car along the Vltava River to the famous town of Český Krumlov. UNESCO certainly had its reasons for declaring this gem of more than 700 years as a World Heritage Site.
Its location on both sides of a narrow hook in the river is incredibly scenic, and the labyrinthine alleyways of the Old Town and the Latrán with its shingled roofs are almost unsurpassably quaint. Highlights of every city tour are the Gothic St Vitus Church and the Schiele Center. The painter Egon Schiele worked and lived

in Český Krumlov in 1911. The defining attraction of the town, however, is its castle. It is Bohemia's second-largest, and is surpassed only by the Hradčany in Prague. It was originally owned by the Rosenberg family for 300 years, then by Emperor Rudolph II before landing in the hands of the counts of Schwarzenberg in the early 18th century. A guided tour of the castle shows you the

living quarters, gallery, chapel, the Masque Hall with frescoes and a fine rococo open-air theater. It has been a designated UNESCO World Heritage Site since 1992.

⑰ Freistadt Right across the border in Austria you'll come to the next delightful example of medieval town planning. The center of the northern Mühl District, developed under

and technology available, now defines Linz's cultural identity. The Lentos Museum of Modern Art, the Ars Electronica Festival and the Design Center all pay their tribute to modern times. Every year, the bigwigs of computer art turn up for the Ars Electronica Festival, and a multimedia wave of sound and light descends on the city.

Beyond all this modernism is also the neatly restored historic center around the town square, which includes the Renaissance Landhaus (house of the provincial government), the castle, the Church of St Martin, the parish church and the old and new cathedrals, as well as a number of interesting galleries and museums. An integral part of any sightseeing trip should also be a boat ride on the Danube with the Linz City Express, or a journey up the Pöstlingberg mountain on the ancient mountain railway.

the Babenberg Dynasty, quickly became the most important trading post between Bohemia and the Danube. To this day it has kept its 14th-century fortifications. Take a stroll through the narrow alleyways between the Linz Gate and the Bohemia Gate, past the town's handsome mansions and the huge town square to the church. Make sure not to miss the Mühl District House in the castle, which has a superb collection of reverse glass painting.

Your next stop is Linz, the capital of Upper Austria, and from there our route follows the northern banks of the Danube (B3) towards Vienna.

⑱ Linz In the last couple of decades, Linz, which had long endured a bad reputation as an unattractive industrial town, has radically polished up its image. Contemporary art, using the most modern media

⑲ Enns This attractive town near the Danube dates back to a Roman fort called Lauriacum and is one of the most ancient towns in Austria. Its landmark is the city's free-standing tower, which measures 60 m (197 ft). Antiquity is brought to life in the Museum Lauriacum, which is located on the town square. On the left bank of the Danube, some miles north of Enns, lies the market town of Mauthausen.

A monument in the local granite quarries commemorates the fact that the Germans ran a

1 View of Český Krumlov castle and the Old Town.

2 Samson Fountain on the square in České Budějovice, also known as Budweis of Budweiser fame.

3 The old cathedral on Linz's central square.

concentration camp here, where around 100,000 people lost their lives.

Around 30 km (18 miles) downriver, at the start of the 'Strudengau', a stretch of river that is feared for its strong currents and dangerous sandbanks, is the little town of Grein. It originally became wealthy because local mariners would guide voyagers through the dangerous waters. It also has a very delightful rococo theater. Close by, the castle ruins of Klam are also worth seeing.

20 Ybbs This traditional market and toll location marks the beginning of the next section of the valley, the so-called 'Nibelungengau'. North of the power station (1958), the historic castle of Persenbeug keeps vigil over the valley. The castle remains the property of the Habsburg family and can only be viewed from outside. A little further east, there are two reasons for a short excursion up to Maria Taferl, a Lower Austrian market town with no more than a thousand inhabitants. In addition to the baroque pilgrimage church, whose exuberant hues and shapes are truly beguiling, it is mainly the view from the terrace that is so captivating – the entire Nibelungengau of Burgundian legend sprawled out at your feet. In good weather, you can even see large parts of the Eastern Alps.

21 Melk A real baroque icon salutes us from a rock outcrop 60 m (197 ft) above the south bank across the river, around 10 km (6 miles) east of the pilgrimage church. It's the Benedictine abbey of Melk with a church, two steeples and a facade of more than 360 m (393 yds) – undoubtedly one of the most magnificent of its kind in the world. This religious for-

tification, which was built in the early 18th century, impressively symbolizes the euphoria among the clerics and the nobility after their dual triumph – over the Reformation and over the Turks. There is exuberant splendour everywhere in the edifice: in the Emperor's Wing with the Emperor's Gallery, which is nearly 200 m (219 yds) long; in the marble hall with its frescoes by Paul Troger; in the vast library with approximately 100,000 volumes; and also in the church, with ceiling frescoes by Johann Michael Rottmayr.

Back on the northern riverbank, the B3 takes us past the Jauerling Nature Park via Aggsbach, Spitz, Weißenkirchen and Dürnstein to the spectacular transverse valley of the Wachau River. Many of these places have an interesting history, like the Aggstein Castle on a rock outcrop high above the Danube. It is said that a series of unscrupulous men abused the castle's position on the river to rob passing Danube boats and charge exorbitant tolls. The

ruin of Dürnstein tells the tale of the capture of Richard the Lionheart and Blondel, the singer, who recognized him.

22 Wachau The transverse valley of the Danube, between Melk and Mautern and Emmersdorf and Krems, is the very image of a central European cultural landscape. No surprise, then, that it has been listed as a UNESCO World Heritage Site. Blessed with a sunny

climate and surrounded by picturesque, painstakingly terraced vineyards, it is just as famous for its good wines and fruit, especially its apricots, as for its history and stone memorials.

In addition to the historic treasures of Krems, Stein, the old Kuenringer town of Dürnstein and the monasteries at Göttweig and Melk, the many small towns with their Gothic churches, covered arcades on

Danube, it takes just under thirty minutes to get to Tulln.

㉔ Tulln This town on the Danube, which started out as a Roman fort called Comagenis, has an impressive architectural ensemble of parish churches and a former charnel house. A visit to the mighty salt tower with its Roman core is also worth doing, and can easily be combined with a stroll along the riverside promenade. A museum with around ninety original paintings commemorates Egon Schiele, the town's beloved son and groundbreaking expressionist.

㉕ Klosterneuburg This small town right outside Vienna on the southern bank of the Danube is world-famous thanks to its Augustinian monastery. The monumental building was built in the early 12th century by the Babenberg Duke Leopold III and soon after donated to the order. For centuries, it was the scientific center of the country. The dazzling emperor's rooms, the emperor's staircase and the marble hall are the

1 The Melk Abbey, founded c. 1000 AD, received its distinguished baroque makeover between 1702–39.

2 The icon of Wachau – the baroque monastery at Dürnstein contains a Renaissance castle, a former Augustinian monastery and a former Clarissan nunnery, all forming a unique ensemble on the bank of the Danube.

3 High above the Danube, not far from Aggsbach, is the Schönbühel Castle dating from the 12th century.

4 Impressions of Wachau – Weißenkirchen, the local wine-growing center, with its mighty Gothic parish church.

the vineyards and medieval castles are among the highlights of a drive through this region 'wrapped in the silver band of the Danube'.

Must-sees along the northern river bank are Spitz with the Museum of Navigation, St Michael with its bizarrely decorated parish church in Aggsbach Markt, traditional little wine-growing towns of Weißenkirchen, Joching and Wösendorf, and last but not least,

Dürnstein with its monastery and legendary castle.

㉓ Krems This town is located on the exact spot where the Danube trade route meets one of the main routes between the Alpine foothills and the Bohemian Forest, and where traders and mariners as far back as the early Middle Ages came to exchange their goods. This mercantile center at the eastern entrance to the Wachau is

not only one of the oldest, but also one of the most beautiful towns in the whole area. As a way into its restored alleyways, take the Steiner Tor ('Stone Gate'). From here, there is a circular walk across Corn Market to the Dominican Church, which houses the wine museum, and on to Gozzoburg on the High Market. From the gunpowder tower you have a beautiful view onto the more modern districts, the port and the Danube over to Göttweig Monastery. On the way back you go along the road, past such architectural gems as the Bürgerspitalkirche, Gögl House and the town hall.

At the western end of Krems is the town of Stein. Must-sees here are the Minorite and St Nicholas Churches and a number of magnificent buildings as well as a former monastery which now houses the 'House of Lower Austrian Wines'.

Driving along the Wagram, a steep slope where lovely vineyards drop colourfully and abruptly down towards the

117

primary attractions. Don't miss the enamel Verdun Altar by Nicholas of Verdun in Leopold's Chapel. The monastery also houses the largest religious library in the country, a museum and a treasury.

㉖ Vienna (see p. 119). After ample time in Vienna, the capital of Austria, you can take an interesting excursion to Lake Neusiedl. Your best option is the A4 to Neusiedl on the lake's northern shore. Alternatively, carry on along the Danube.

㉗ Carnuntum Around 35 km (22 miles) east of Vienna, where the 'Amber Road' (between the Baltic Sea and the Mediterranean) and the East-West Route along the Danube meet, are the Roman remains of Carnuntum, south of the river. Nowhere else in Austria have archaeologists found such rich ancient heritage.

The excavation site, officially made into an 'archaeological park' in 1996, comprises the whole of the civilian town with its network of ancient walls and streets, a reconstructed Diana Temple and a long piece of the original Roman Limes Road (Border Road). A little further away are the ruins of a palace, baths, an amphitheater and the Heathen's Gate. Many of the rich findings are on display in the Museum Carnuntinum in Bad Deutsch-Altenburg.

㉘ Bratislava When the Turks conquered Budapest in the middle of the 16th century and kept it for nearly 150 years, Bratislava, now the capital of Slovakia, was called Pozsony and was the capital of free Hungary until 1848.

In modern times it was behind the Iron Curtain until 1989. Since then, it has not only forged closer ties to the Western world, but also undergone

a radical beautification and rejuvenation.

The sins of socialist town planning cannot be undone, and the prefabricated tower blocks in Petržalka on the southern bank of the Danube, for example, will continue to be an eyesore for quite some time. Staré Mesto, by contrast, the largely car-free Old Town, has done itself up rather nicely. Its most important sights are St Martin's Cathedral, the archbishop's palace, the Slovak National Gallery, the National Theater and Museum and the castle residing above the river.

East of Bratislava, Road 63 (E575) takes you down into the Danube Plains (Podunajsko), which are completely flat and extremely fertile. During the summer months fresh fruit and vegetable stands are everywhere.

During World War II, this region was particularly hard hit. Reconstruction led to local towns looking very much alike. This route, however, now takes us away from the Danube to the south – back through Austria to Fertöd in Hungary.

㉙ Fertöd/Esterházy Palace Around 5 km (3 miles) east of Fertö-tó (the Hungarian name

of Lake Neusiedl), we come to Fertöd and Esterházy Palace. The Esterházys are an old Hungarian dynasty from which many politicians and military men have come.

㉚ Győr This large city has an important port on the Danube and is worth seeing for its 12th-century cathedral which was given a baroque makeover in the 17th century.

1 The classical Austrian Parliament Building in Vienna (1874–84) with the Pallas-Athene Fountain.

2 The ceremonial hall, the main hall of Vienna's National Library, was begun by Johann Bernhard Fischer von Erlach in 1719; his son finished it.

3 Esterházy Castle in Fertöd was the royal residence of the Esterházy princes and the workplace of the composer Joseph Haydn.

Vienna

Located on the 'beautiful blue Danube', the Austrian capital has a uniquely charming atmosphere and seems still to radiate the Old World feel of the Dual Monarchy.

Vienna, the old royal city and former center of the 'multicultural' Habsburg Empire, has architecture and art treasures from all eras of its long history. As a result, you will need some time to explore this city, especially if you want to catch a bit of its famous atmosphere, which is largely communicated through the pleasures of food and drink. Your best bet is in the 'Heurigen' wine taverns, in the coffee houses or on the traditional 'Naschmarkt' (literally 'Nibbles Market').

Definitely visit the Stephansdom with Romanesque, Gothic and late-Gothic sections, a richly ornate facade and precious interior; the Hofburg, until 1918 the imperial residence with treasure chamber, emperor's rooms and palace chapel; the Art History Museum with its collection of European paintings; and the baroque Josefsplatz with National Library; the Gothic Augustinerkirche with its baroque Capuchin crypt of the Habsburg emperors; the Spanish Riding School; the Karlskirche, the most beautiful baroque building in Vienna; the Museum of Applied Art; Belvedere Castle with Lower Belvedere (baroque museum) and Upper Belvedere (19th- and 20th-century paintings); Schönbrunn, a baroque Versailles imitation with park, Gloriette classical arcades with a beautiful view of the castle and town. The historic center and Schönbrunn Palace are UNESCO World Heritage Sites.

Top: Karlskirche by Fischer von Erlach.

31 Komárno/Komárom Located where the River Váh meets the Danube, the town has always been of the utmost strategic importance. The Romans even had a fort here called Brigetio. In the course of the 19th century, the Habsburg Dynasty turned the town into a 'city of fortifications' like no other in the monarchy. After Ferenc I, King of Hungary, had found shelter from Napoleon's army in Komárno in 1809, it was made the central defense post of the Habsburg Empire. Ever since the Treaty of Trianon (1920) marking the Danube as the border of the realm, the city has been divided into two parts. The former Old Town on the northern shore is now part of the Slovakian town of Komárno. On the Hungarian side, three fortifications are an interesting attraction for military history enthusiasts.

Monostor, the largest of the forts with 640 rooms and 4 km (2.5 miles) of underground shelters, is sometimes nicknamed 'Gibraltar of the Danube' and there are guided tours around it. The Igmánd fort, which is significantly smaller, houses a Roman museum.

32 Tata This spa town at the bottom of Gerecse Hill gives off an atmosphere of cosiness and charm with its lakes and complex labyrinth of rivers and canals. But its location and its history have not been kind to the 'City of Water' – for 150 years it was situated on the border between the territories of the Habsburgs and the Ottoman Empire, which resulted in consistent large-scale devastation of its buildings

In around 1730, the Esterházy princes, then rulers of the town, initiated the reconstruction of the Tata, whose myriad baroque architectural ensembles shape the town to this day.

Be sure to visit the ruins of the castle, built in the 14th century and later expanded into a magnificent Renaissance Palace by Matthias Corvinus. Don't miss Esterházy Castle and the former synagogue, which houses about 100 plaster-of-Paris copies of famous antique sculptures.

Halfway between Tata and Budapest – you can see it from the M1 motorway – is an apogee of Hungary's Romance architecture reaching high up into the sky. The Zsámbék Church itself actually collapsed in the middle of the 18th century, along with the adjacent Premonstratensian priory, a truly spectacular sight.

33 Budapest The Magyar metropolis has around two million inhabitants on a location where the Romans had already founded a town called Aquincum. Like many others, the two medieval communities of Ofen and Pest were devastated by the Mongols in 1241.

After the reconstruction, Ofen became Hungary's most important city, but was overtaken in the early 19th century by its sister town of Pest. The two cities were finally united in 1872. In the early 20th century, Budapest was considered the 'Paris of the East', a reputation it is still hoping to regain despite

the devastation of World War II and more than four decades of Soviet rule. The first thing on a long list of things to do just has to be the castle mountain. It is here on this limestone rock, nearly 1.5 km (0.9 miles) long, above the right bank of the Danube that the country's historical heart has been beating ever since the first king's castle was constructed upon it by Béla IV. Combining the Matthias Church, the Fisherman's Bastion and the castle, which houses several first-rate museums, this quarter has some of the most important sights in the city. And there are also some unforgettable panoramic views down to the city and to the river. The view from the neighbouring Gellért Mountain is just as scenic. The majority of the city's sights are located on the left bank of the Danube, in the Pest district. Once you leave behind the narrow Old Town center,

the cityscape is typified by extensive Wilhelminian ring and radial roads.

You can visit St Stephen's Basilica, the National Opera, the National Museum, the Grand Synagogue and, directly by the river, the large market hall and the even larger houses of parliament. Out in the city forest are Vajdahunyad Castle, the Széchenyi Baths and the Museum of Fine Arts. A must-see is, of course, the baroque palace in Gödöllő 30 km (18 miles) north-east of the city center, where Emperor Franz Joseph I and his wife Elizabeth ('Sisi') lived.

1 Budapest – the Houses of Parliament on the banks of the mighty Danube. In the foreground is the city's suspension bridge.

2 Hungarian grey cattle in Hortobágy National Park.

Sanssouci The rococo ensemble, whose name means 'Carefree', is the most visited attraction in Potsdam, capital of Brandenburg, where you can take a carefree stroll through the summer residence of Friedrich II.

Berlin The old and new German capital has become even more attractive since the Berlin Wall came down. Located on the Spree and Havel rivers, it has a lot of greenery, vibrant nightlife and myriad cultural highlights. Pictured is the Charlottenburg Palace.

Meißen The center of this porcelain town and 'Cradle of Saxony' has a medieval atmosphere. Above it is the towering cathedral and the Albrecht Castle.

Wartburg Legend has it that the castle was founded in 1067. Located at the edge of the Thuringian Forest it was probably the site of the German minstrels' contest. Luther translated the bible into German here.

Dresden Buildings like the Zwinger and the Semper Opera House, as well as precious collections like the Old Masters Gallery, have made Dresden a leading European cultural metropolis.

Saxon Switzerland Whether you prefer hiking or a boat trip on the Elbe River, the bizarre plateaus, rock outcrops and gorges of the Elbe Sandstone Mountains near Dresden are fascinating. Most of the area has been made into a national park.

Prague The Czech capital is located on the Vltava River and has an unusual skyline. Hradčany Castle, Charles Bridge and the art-nouveau buildings of this 'Golden City' are unique. This photograph is of Týn Church.

České Budějovice The center of this world-famous city of breweries and beer is the market square with Samson Fountain.

Karlovy Vary This spa town on the Eger River has some healing springs as well as historical and modern spa facilities.

Český Krumlov Its location on a curve in the Vltava River, its dreamy Old Town, and the huge castle on the hill make the Bohemian town of Krumlov a real gem.

Wachau The forest and wine-growing area of Wachau extends from Melk to Krems – a transverse valley of the Danube that is 30 km (18 miles) long.

Melk The Benedictine abbey high above the Danube is baroque architecture in all its perfection.

Budapest One of the landmarks of the Hungarian capital is the mighty suspension bridge (1839–1849). The list of further sights in the metropolis on the Danube is a long one – from Fisherman's Bastion and the crown of St Stephen in the National Museum to the neo-Gothic Houses of Parliament and the terrific art-nouveau bath houses.

Vienna The Austrian capital is always worth a visit. The number and quality of the sights in this metropolis on the Danube is simply overwhelming. Pictured here is the Austrian Parliament Building.

Fertőd, Esterházy Palace The 'Hungarian Versailles' in Fertőd used to belong to a family of princes. There is even an opera house and a puppet theater inside.

The Alps

Switzerland's most photographed icon: the Matterhorn, at 4,478 m (14,692 ft).

Spectacular mountain scenery between Lake Geneva and the Salzburg region

Looking at any map, it is immediately clear that the Alps form a sort of backbone for the European landmass. This route will take you on a journey of exploration through every facet of this complex terrain, from the shores of Lake Geneva to a world of rock and ice around Zermatt and Grindelwald, from glamorous winter resorts to the fairy-tale scenery of the Dolomites, and from the Grossglockner High Alpine Road to the Salzburg region and the birthplace of Mozart.

For many, the Alps are the "most beautiful mountains in the world". All told, this high Central European range covers an area of 200,000 sq km (77,200 sq mi). The western section alone is home to about fifty peaks rising over 4,000 m (13,124 ft). There are many more in the 3,000 and 2,000 m (9,843 and 6,562 ft) range – nearly 2,000 in Austria alone. The range features the jagged limestone spikes of the Dolomites, bulky gneiss and granite massif, and lower layers made of sandstone, slate and flysch. It stretches from mighty Mont Blanc, at 4,810-m (15,782-ft) the tallest peak in the Alps, to the gentle knolls of the Wienerwald (Vienna Woods).

Salzburg: Residenzplatz with a majestic fountain.

Famous rivers such as the Rhine and the Rhône, the Po and the Save, the Drava and the Inn originate in the Alps, and vast lakes such as Lake Constance, Lake Geneva and Lake Lucerne are all nestled in their valleys. Immense waterfalls like the ones in Krimml, Lauterbrunnen, Gastein or on the Tosa thunder down granite faces, while glistening glaciers continue to hold their own in the highest and more remote areas – though the effects of climate change can be seen.

The main charm of the area lies in the juxtaposition of contrasts; the Côte d'Azur is just a stone's throw from the foothills of the Maritime Alps, and the glaciers of the Bernese Oberland are not far from the Wallis (Valais) wine region. An hour's

The distinctive hallmark of South Tyrol: the Three Peaks, in the Sexten Dolomites. The highest peak rises to 2,999 m (9,840 ft).

Evening ambience in Salzburg: Looking out over the Salzach to the Old Town with Hohensalzburg Fortress.

drive will take you from the rocky peaks of the Dolomites to the cypress-lined lanes of Lago di Garda, and it wouldn't take much longer to get from the icy cold cirque lakes of the Hohe Tauern to the warm swimming lakes of Carinthia.

The mightiest mountain ranges in the world, such as the Himalayas or the Andes, might have more exalted reputations and are more sparsely populated, but what sets the Alps apart is indeed their human dimension. Extreme mountaineers do not need permits, visas or porters to indulge in their passion. When it comes to infrastructure, accommodation and dining, people seeking a more comfortable experience will be delighted by the ease of travel and the plethora of options. Even the

desire for a more urban environment can be satisfied in cities such as Grenoble, Bolzano and Innsbruck. And yet those seeking temporary refuge from civilization will also find more than enough solitude on hikes, climbs or just relaxing in a meadow all day long – all without bumping into another single person. However, what makes the journey along the backbone of Europe so fascinating is not just the spectacular scenery, but rather the distinctive and diverse cultural traditions that seem to change as often as the landscape, and the undeniable natural charm of the Alps. Rural architecture, customs and handicrafts form an "alpine heritage" that is once again being enthusiastically promoted in many places – without necessar-

ily being motivated by tourism. Aside from the dominant peaks like the Matterhorn, the Jungfrau, the Eiger, the Mönch, Bernina, Marmolada, the Tre Cime di Lavaredo and the Grossglockner, mention should certainly be made of the fruit and wine growers along the Rhône or

Adige, the anonymous architects of the Engadine or East Tyrolean manors, the thousands and thousands of alpine dairy farmers and dairymaids, and the creators of all the frescos, sgraffiti, shingle roofs, and carved altars in the village churches, castles and manors.

Rustic farmhouses are still common in the high valleys of Switzerland.

Those exploring the Alps will quickly discover the charms of this historically significant and culturally diverse region: from elegant resort towns to quaint hamlets, and from the Mediterranean-like shores of Lake Geneva to remote mountain stations among the high glaciers and peaks.

① Geneva Your journey begins at the south-western-most point of Switzerland at the end of Lake Geneva, known by French-speaking locals as Lac Léman. Geneva is nestled among the Jura and Savoy Alps and sits on one of the lake's many bays. The city's most famous landmark is the Fontaine du Jet d'Eau, which shoots its water up to 145 m (476 ft) into the air.

The "Protestant Rome", where Jean Calvin preached his rigorous reform ideas some 450 years ago, and Henri Dunant founded the Red Cross in 1864, is today a truly international city. One-third of its residents are foreigners, and 200 international organizations, including the United Nations (UN) and the World Health Organization (WHO), are based here.

But apart from the diplomats, the expensive clocks and fancy cigars, there are also a number of other attractions: St Peter's Cathedral with its archaeological burial site, the adjacent Place du Bourg-de-Four, the ornate Museum of Art and History, the Palais des Nations – today UN headquarters – and the monument to native son, Jean-Jacques Rousseau, one of the most influential thinkers during the Enlightenment.

Follow the A1 along the northern shores of Lake Geneva toward the next Swiss city on the lake, Lausanne.

② Lausanne The metropolis of Vaud is a reputable university and trade fair city as well as the home of the International Olympic Committee. Tucked in among exclusive residential neighborhoods and spanning several hills, the Cité, or Old Town, is best accessed by the funicular railway from the port district of Ouchy. The main attraction there is the early-Gothic cathedral with its rose window, while the most interesting of the many museums are the Art Brut Collection and the Pipe Museum.

③ Vevey and Montreux These two resort towns form the center of the wine-indulged "Vaud Riviera" and have enjoyed international prominence since the early 19th century.

Travel Information

Route profile
Length: approx. 1,150 km (715 mi), without detours
Time required: at least 12–14 days
Start: Geneva
Finish: Salzburg
Route (main locations):
Geneva, Lausanne, Zermatt, Interlaken, Andermatt, Chur, St Moritz, Merano, Bolzano, Cortina d'Ampezzo, Lienz, Heiligenblut, Werfen, Salzburg

Traffic information:
Motorways in both Switzerland and Austria require vignettes that you can buy at most petrol stations. French motorways require tolls.

Roads in all countries are well maintained. Check weather conditions for higher passes.

Travel weather:
www.alpineroads.com
www.weatheronline.co.uk

Information:
Here are some websites to help you plan your trip.
Switzerland:
www.myswitzerland.com/en
www.graubuenden.ch/en
www.nationalpark.ch
South Tyrol:
www.suedtirol.info (top EN)
Austria:
www.austria-tourism.info
www.hohetauern.at/english
www.nationalpark.at

and the 150-year-old Hotel Monte Rosa.

A ride on the Gornergrat Railway, the highest cog railway on the continent, is unforgettable. In forty minutes, it climbs up to 3,089 m (10,135 ft) over a stretch of 10 km (6 mi) before you continue another 400 m (1,312 ft) by cable car. The mountain station provides a 360-degree panoramic view of twenty-nine peaks in the 4,000 m (13,124 ft) range.

⑤ Brig Back in the Rhône Valley, follow the river upstream to the capital of the Oberwallis region. Once an important trading hub for goods being transported over the Simplon, Furka and Grimsel passes, Brig experienced its heyday in the 17th and 18th centuries.

The main attraction in Brig is Stockalper Castle, an extensive late-Renaissance complex whose imposing towers and golden onion domes can be seen from afar. In the suburb of Glis, it is worth paying a visit to the lavish St Mary's pilgrimage church. From here, head west again along the Rhône as far as Höge Steg, then take the car on the train through the 14.6-km-long (9-mi) Lötschberg tunnel. From Kandersteg you will go through Thun, along the northern shore of Lake Thun, past

Vevey, where the first Swiss chocolate was made at the start of the 19th century, is also the home of Nestlé, the largest foodstuffs corporation in the world. Montreux is known primarily for the annual TV awards show, the "Golden Rose", its world-famous jazz festival and the Château de Chillon, located on the shores of the lake just 3 km (2 mi) to the south-east of town. Heading away from the lake, your route follows the Rhône Valley through Martigny and Sion to Visp, where the road turns right into the Matter Valley. Park the car in Täsch about 30 km (19 mi) further on, as the most famous Swiss mountain town can only be reached by railway, bus or taxi.

④ Zermatt and Matterhorn The most renowned village in the Wallis region owes its fame to the 4,478-m-high (14,692-ft) Matterhorn, the primary icon of the Swiss Alps. The region's popularity was developed predominantly by daring mountaineers from the British Isles in the mid-19th century who became the first to conquer the imposing four-sided pyramid in 1865, led by locals. Today, 3,000 people flood the "summit of all European summits" every summer. In the town itself, a number of old houses attest to the pioneer days. Particularly worth seeing are the Alpine Museum,

1 Swiss mountain paradise: the Matterhorn at 4,478 m (14,692 ft) with its pyramid-shaped peak.

2 View of Geneva's boardwalk from Lake Geneva.

3 The "Top of Europe" funicular station on the Jungfraujoch at 3,445 m (11,303 ft) provides a spectacular view over the Aletsch Glacier.

4 Oberhofen Castle (12th century) was built right on Lake Thun.

1

Oberhofen Castle and into the town of Interlaken.

It is especially worthwhile making a detour beforehand to the Swiss capital of Bern, roughly 25 km (16 mi) from Thun. You can easily explore the perfectly preserved Old Town on foot.

6 Interlaken Situated between Lake Thun and Lake Brienz on the "Bödeli", the Aar River floodplain, Interlaken was named after the inter lacus monastery, founded in the 12th century. It has long been one of the cornerstones of Swiss alpine tourism as the starting point for excursions into the Jungfrau region. The Höhenweg, lined with hotel mansions from the turn of the 20th century, affords breathtaking panoramic views of the snow-capped peaks to the south.

7 Grindelwald A 20-km (12 mi) detour will take you to

2

Grindelwald, even closer to the Jungfrau region, the first alpine landscape to become a UNESCO World Natural Heritage Site, in 2001, as home to forty-seven peaks over 4,000 m (13,124 ft) and the Great Aletsch Glacier. The Grindelwald climatic spa resort is encircled by the three mighty peaks of the Eiger at 3,970 m (13,026 ft), the Wetterhorn at 3,701 m (12,143 ft) and the Schreckhorn at 4,078 m (13,380 ft). It has been the greatest tourist draw in the Bernese Oberland for over 150 years. Don't miss a ride on the

Jungfrau railway from the Kleine Scheidegg pass through Eigerwand and Mönch to Europe's highest train station – the Jungfraujoch at 3,454 m (11,333 ft).

From Grindelwald, it's back to Interlaken and then south along Lake Brienz over the Grimsel Pass (2,165 m/7,103 ft) and the Furka Pass (2,431 m/7976 ft) to Andermatt.

8 Andermatt The highland resort town of Andermatt is at the junction of the north-south route between Lake Lucerne

3

and St Gotthard, where Wallis (Valais) turns into the Upper Rhine Valley region. It has a lovely rococo church and a carefully designed valley museum, and is an ideal starting point for hikes and mountain tours. For travelers, however, it is primarily a traffic hub.

Continuing east, you have to cross the Oberalp Pass (2,044 m/6,706 ft), before skirting the Upper Rhine tributary to Flims. The Furka-Oberalp railway, a nice alternative to the passes connecting the valleys Rhine and Rhone, is the heart of the

4

experienced from the old road built in the early 19th century (a branch off the A13 about 1 km/0.6 mi beyond Rongellen). At the south end, in Zillis, pay a visit to St Martin's Church for its painted wooden ceiling.

Back in Thusis, the route now heads to Tiefencastel, in the Albula Valley, and then through parts of the very steep Albula Pass (2,321 m/7,615 ft) into the Upper Engadine region.

12 St Moritz This glamorous resort town in the heart of the Upper Engadine is considered the cradle of winter tourism and, along with Davos, the most upscale address in Graubünden. It hit the world stage as the two-time host of the Winter Olympics (1928 and 1948). Located at the gateway to unique lake scenery (Lake St Moritz, Lake Silvaplana, and Lake Sils), it offers a wide range of outdoor sporting options in both winter and summer. The Cresta Run, or "skeleton sled run", and the bob run to Celerina are legendary.

A varied programme of nightly entertainment meets the needs of the guests, who are as famous as they are wealthy.

From St Moritz, the B27 takes you down the Inn River

1 Even beginners can enjoy some impressive hikes from Grindelwald below the north face of the Eiger.

2 Schreckhorn and Finsteraarhorn, both over 4,000 m (13,000 ft), reflected in the Bachsee above Grindelwald.

3 The Kleine Scheidegg at the foot of the Jungfrau Massif is a popular ski area in winter.

4 Lake Silvaplana, at a height of approximately 1,800 m (5,906 ft), is the largest of the three Upper Engadine lakes and is a popular windsurfing spot in summer.

large alpine narrow gauge network between Engadine and Matterhorn.

9 Flims This spa resort, where Rhaeto-Romanic dialects are still spoken, is situated on a ledge in a sunny high valley that owes its existence to a massive landslide during prehistoric times. It comprises the old Flims-Dorf center and the new Flims-Waldhaus hotel complex. The town and its romantic surroundings offer a variety of sporting activities in summer, and in winter it joins Laax and

Falera to form a vast ski area known as the "White Arena". Before heading to the mountains of Graubünden (Grisons) take the 10-km (6-mi) detour at Reichenau to Chur.

10 Chur This cantonal capital, which obtained its Roman town charter in the 3rd century and was the first diocesan town north of the Alps in the 4th century, puts off many newcomers with its unsightly strip of highrise buildings. But a charming Old Town with a number of historic treasures lies hidden

behind this unfortunate blemish. The most important of these are the St Mary's Cathedral and museum, the Winegrowing and Rhaetian museums, the Bündner Art Museum with works by Chur painter, Angelika Kauffmann.

11 Via Mala Back in Reichenau, you route initially heads upstream along the Lower Rhine. Over the millennia, this tributary cut a 6-km-long (4 mile) and up to 600-m-deep (1,969 ft) gorge into the rock. The romantic Via Mala is best

1

through Samedan and Zuoz to the Lower Engadine region – a worthwhile detour for those who appreciate the old-world charm of Graubünden villages. The main route now heads from St Moritz over the Pontresina and Bernina Pass at 2,323 m (7,622 ft), past the dream-like panorama of the glaciated Bernina Group, into the valley of the upper Adda, the Veltlin, and into Italy. From here, the spectacular Stilfser Joch pass rises to 2,578 m (8,458 ft) at the foot of the Ortler (Ortles) peak and heads to Bormio before taking you through the Trafoi Valley down to the Etsch (Adige), where it is worth making a detour through Schludern (Sluderno) to St John's Monastery in the Val Müstair. Continue east to Merano in the Vintschgau Valley.

⑬ Merano This city on the Passer River blossomed under the rule of the counts of Tyrol until the mid-14th century. After the Habsburgs took over

co-rule in South Tyrol and moved the residence to Innsbruck, Merano's significance waned. It did not return to the spotlight until the 19th century, when word spread about the healing effect of the local springs and mild climate. Reputable figures began coming in droves from all over Europe to seek rest and recuperation.
The main sites in the Old Town, with its narrow lanes, quaint arcades and old burgher houses, include the Gothic St Nicholas Church (with the St Barbara Chapel), the Hospital Church and the sovereigns' castle with 15th-century frescos in the chapel. It is also worth taking a walk through the elegant residential area of Obermais.

⑭ Bolzano The capital of South Tyrol is located at the confluence of the Isarco and the Adige rivers and is not only the economic center of the region, but also a hub of alpine art and culture. A stroll through the narrow lanes between

2

Lauben, the Kornplatz and the Obstmarkt reveals a charming Old Town that dates back to the Middle Ages. Highlights include the Dominican and Franciscan monasteries, Maretsch Castle, Runkelstein Fort, the City Museum, and the old parish church in the Gries district, with part of an altar by Michael Pacher. South-east of Bolzano, the SS241 takes you into the dreamy landscape of the Dolomites, littered with breathtaking limestone towers and peaks. The Karer Pass (with a view of the Rose Garden), the Fassa Valley and Passo Sella are

the next stops, and the jagged rock formations here never fail to impress.

The road heads along the twisting SS242 with a view of Sassolungo toward the Val Gardena through Ortisei until you reach the vast Val d'Isarco. Continuing north, you will arrive in

Klausen. From there you can take a short detour to get a stunning view of the Funes Valley. On the way back through the Isarco and Gardena valleys, turn off on SS243 after the town of Plan and head towards the Passo Gardena. A breathtaking backdrop of giant rock walls unfolds as you pass the Sella Group via Colfosco and Corvara. As you cross the Passo di Campolongo you will be further delighted by the geological wonders here before

reaching the "Great Dolomite Road" which leads to Cortina d'Ampezzo.

🟤 **Cortina d'Ampezzo** This famous spa and winter sports resort is surrounded by some of the most beautiful 3,000-m-high (9,843 ft) peaks in the region. Indeed, they contain the very epitome of Dolomite magnificence, the Tre Cime de Lavaredo, which come into view as you make your way toward Misurina.

The next stops are Schluderbach and Toblach. You are in the Drava Valley here, but will soon cross into Austria and arrive in Lienz just under 40 km (25 mi) away.

🟤 **Lienz** The capital of East Tyrol is surrounded by splendid mountains and is home to a number of charming buildings including St Andreas Parish Church, with the tomb of the last count of Görz, and the baroque St Michael's subsidiary church. Bruck Castle has Tyrol's

1 Evening ambience at the Langkofel Massif (3,181 m/10,437 ft), west of the Sella Group.

2 After the Tre Cime de Lavaredo, the Vajolet Towers are the most beautiful in the Dolomites and are part of the Rose Garden at the Karer Pass.

3 The Grossglockner High Alpine Road affords spectacular views of the Alp summits.

largest homeland museum, and the city's Roman roots are evidenced by the graveyards of its predecessor, Aguntum.

17 Heiligenblut Over the Iselsberg at 1,204 m (3,950 ft) and through the Upper Möll Valley (B107), you arrive in the ever popular pilgrimage and mountaineering town of Heiligenblut. The church here, with its pointed tower standing against the stunning backdrop of the Grossglockner, Austria's highest peak at 3,798 m (12,461 ft), is a long-time favorite among photographers.

From here, you follow one of the most impressive mountain roads in the world, the Grossglockner High Alpine Road, which has run from Carinthia through the main alpine ridge to the Fusch Valley near Salzburg since 1935. It is also in the Hohe Tauern National Park which is the biggest of Austria.

18 Werfen From the end of the valley at Bruck-Fusch (Lake Zeller is just a few miles away), follow the Salzach upstream through Lend and the Pongau to Bischofshofen and Werfen. The picturesque Hohenwerfen Fort is perched above the quaint 12th-century market place here. The fort was erected by Archbishop Gebhard around 1077, to ensure control over the Lueg Pass. Those who climb the steep path from the parking lot into the inner ward will get a good feeling for how daunting this fortress must have once been for would-be attackers.

Another must-see here is the Eisriesenwelt or "World of the Ice Giants", the largest ice caves in the world.

19 Hallein The "small Hall", about 25 km (16 mi) down the Salzach, was a center for salt production from the 13th cen-

Chillon This castle, located near Montreux on an island in Lake Geneva, has twenty-five interconnected buildings.

Bern The impressive "Zytgloggeturm" clock tower (15th century) is the icon of the Swiss capital.

Lake Thun Mediterranean-like vegetation characterizes the Lake Thun area, at an altitude of roughly 560 m (1,837 ft). Oberhofen Castle on the north shore is worth a visit.

Bernese Alps Eiger, Mönch and Jungfrau are the best-known mountains in the western Alps. Many peaks of the "Bernese Alps" reach heights of over 4,000 m (13,124 ft) and have impressive glaciers.

Geneva Numerous international companies and organizations are based here. The city's attractions include St Peter's Cathedral, the Museum of Art and History, the Palais des Nations and the 145-m-high (476-ft) Fontaine du Jet d'Eau.

Matterhorn The 4,478-m (14,692-ft) mountain is an icon of Swiss alpinism and has few rivals when it comes to perfect proportions. It was first climbed in 1865, but its northern face was not conquered in winter until 1962.

Lake Geneva Sixty percent of Lake Geneva is in Switzerland and the rest is in France. It is some 72 km (45 mi) long and lies at an altitude of 370 m (1,214 ft) above sea level.

Aletsch Glacier The largest glacier in mainland Europe: 170 sq km (66 sq mi) and 25 km (16 mi) long.

20 Salzburg Finale furioso on the Salzach: You actually get the impression that the Creator and his earthly helpers wanted to demonstrate clearly to the people here that it is possible to create a beautiful harmony between the European spiritand a benevolent natural environment. The cathedral, residence, collegiate church, St Peter's Abbey, Nonnberg Monastery, the Getreidegasse and, above all, mighty Hohensalzburg Fortress certainly speak for it.

Salzburg, on the left bank of the Salzach, with its large squares and narrow lanes, myriad fountains and statues, and the vivid marble and stucco work, all form a unique combination of urban design that continues to inspire artists and admirers from all over the world. Long in the shadow of the prince-bishop center on the left bank, however, is the district located on the east bank, with Mirabell Park and Castle, Mozart's home, the Marionette Theater, the St Sebastian Cemetery and the tiny alleyways at the foot of the Kapuzinerberg mountain. It offers a multitude of first-class tourist attractions, and you should not miss a visit to Hellbrunn Castle and Anif Water Castle. Those wanting to experience another alpine gem should head along the B305 from Salzburg to Berchtesgaden and the national park of the same name, located just 20 km (12 mi) away.

tury to 1989. The precious substance has been mined from the Dürrnberg for 4,500 years now. The Celts were specialists at this, and their culture is today documented at an open-air museum, the Celts Museum, down in the valley on the edge of this lively city with its charming Old Town. The mine has been converted into an ornate display that is open year-round.

1 Salzburg at sunrise with a view of the bridges and towers of the Old Town and the Hohensalzburg Fortress in the background.

2 The Anif Water Castle near Salzburg dates back to the 17th century. It can only be viewed from the outside.

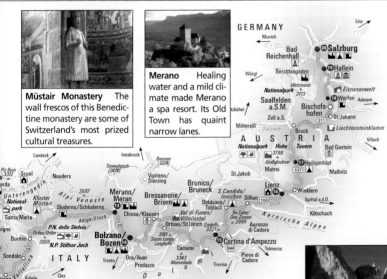

Müstair Monastery The wall frescos of this Benedictine monastery are some of Switzerland's most prized cultural treasures.

Merano Healing water and a mild climate made Merano a spa resort. Its Old Town has quaint narrow lanes.

Stilfser Joch This alpine pass at 2,757 m (9,046 ft) runs along the border of Lombardy, Trentino and South Tyrol and affords fantastic views.

Grossglockner High Alpine Road This 48-km-long (30 mile) road, which has been constantly upgraded since 1930, is one of the most impressive high mountain roads in Europe. It follows a Roman alpine pass.

Salzburg The City of Mozart on the Salzach is a very popular destination, and for good reason. The cathedral, residence, collegiate church, St Peter's Abbey, Nonnberg Monastery, Mirabell Park and Castle and Hohensalzburg Fortress are impressive.

Tre Cime di Lavaredo These natural obelisks in the Sexten Alps are up to 2,999 m (9,840 ft) high and have been a challenge for mountaineers ever since the first ascent in 1933.

Dolomites The rocky peaks in the Italian limestone Alps were created by erosion from the elements.

Funes Valley The "Val di Funes" is primarily an agricultural region that is only sparsely populated due to its isolation by the Geisler Peaks. Tiny hamlets form the valley's tight community.

The Keizersgracht canal in Amsterdam

Netherlands, Belgium

Medieval guilds and burgher cities from Amsterdam and Bruges

Flatlands, canals, dykes, windmills, clogs, and medieval houses reflected in the canals and waterways – these are all the things we associate with the Netherlands and Belgium, along with charming landscapes covered in vibrant fields of tulips, famous sea ports and bustling cities with old markets, squares and town halls.

When we think of the Netherlands, there are certain pictures that come to everyone's mind: world-famous Dutch cheeses; the stately old windmills that were once used to drain the countryside and now dot the landscape like beautiful gems; or the countless dykes that have become an essential element in protecting the country against ocean tides.

For centuries, the Dutch have been trying to conquer new land from the North Sea: they build levies and embankments, pump it dry, and then settle and farm it. In fact, two-thirds of all Dutch people today live in the "lower" lands, which are up to 7 m (23 ft) below sea level. This is made possible by canals and drainage ditches that are often located higher than the

roads, fields or villages. In contrast to "life on the seafloor", the sprawling metropolitan areas are home to six million people – 40 percent of the total

Rembrandt, self-portrait from 1669.

population. However, the cities at the edge of the "Randstad" chain, which includes Amsterdam, Leiden, Haarlem, The Hague and Rotterdam, only make up a mere tenth of the country's area and are surrounded by a wonderfully green landscape of croplands, marshes and moors.

In many cities, it is still easy to get a sense of how successful the Netherlands was over the centuries as a world trading power whose colonies brought great wealth to the country. That wealth is reflected in the ornate buildings of the Old Towns, which line the quaint canals. Today, more than 55,000 houses in the Netherlands are listed buildings.

The wealth of earlier times has also naturally also benefited

is spanned by fourteen bridges.

Ghent, with its medieval townscape of proud patrician houses on the Graslei mirrored in the water.

The network of windmills in Kinderdijk is a listed UNESCO World Heritage Site. The successful technical innovation was developed in the 18th century.

the arts. Painters like Rembrandt, Franz Hals, Jan Vermeer and Piet Mondrian are synonymous with the Netherlands. Ultimately, this historically seafaring nation's experiences with distant lands and foreign cultures has created an atmosphere of open-mindedness that has been preserved until the present day.

There is also an extra special ambience in the land of the Flemings and Walloons, who united to form the kingdom of Belgium some 160 years ago. Although Belgium has some first-class references in men like George Simenon and Jacques Brel, and is loved for its Brussels lace, Ardennes ham and a highway that is lit up at night, it is not a classic holiday destination – but that is short-sighted.

The coastal resorts along the North Sea, the wide sandy beaches and the spectacular dune landscapes alone are worth making the trip. And it's not just romantics who go into rapture over the ornate façades and wonderful buildings that reflect off the canals and waterways, or the church spires that soar high above the historic Old Towns of Bruges and Ghent.

Brussels, which proudly calls itself the Heart of Europe, is home to one of the most beautiful market squares in the world – the Grand' Place – and the stunning Museum of Fine Art displays works by masters from Rubens to Magritte.

On an unusual note: no other country has a higher population of comics illustrators per square

mile – which means that comic strips, along with Brussels lace, Antwerp diamonds and Belgian pralines, are among the most commonly exported Belgian products. At every turn, it is apparent that Belgians know how to live. Surprising as it may seem, no other country in Euro-

pe has as many award-winning restaurants. The most popular drink in Belgium is beer, and there are almost five hundred types produced in over hundred breweries. And as far as snacks go, well, pommes frites (french fries or chips) are said to have been invented here.

Every two years in August, a spellbinding carpet of flowers covers the Grand' Place in Brussels.

Along the Dutch and Belgian coast: In Holland, the route heads through the "nether lands", with their seemingly endless fields of flowers, and then to the bustling metropolises. In Belgium you visit cities with charming, medieval Old Towns and priceless works of art.

① **Amsterdam** (see page 136) Your journey begins in Amsterdam. From there, you can initially take a day trip to Zaandam just 15 km (9 mi) north to the Zaanse Schans open-air museum and the cheese town of Alkmaar a bit further north.

② **Haarlem** This city is about 20 km (12 mi) west of Amsterdam and was officially mentioned in the 10th century. It has a picturesque Old Town quarter whose Grote Markt was once a sports arena. The beautifully decorated 17th-century gabled houses are evidence of the wealth the city once achieved as the stronghold of the drapery and fabric bleaching guild.

At the south end of the square is the Grote or St Bavokerk, a late-Gothic cruciform basilica.

The nursing home where painter Frans Hals spent his final years was converted into a museum in 1912, with important works by the great artist.

③ **Keukenhof** The Bollenstreek between Haarlem and Leiden takes you through a sea of flowers. It is home to the fields of around 8,000 nurseries that specialize in wholesale flowers. The Tulip Route leads to the most important of these nurseries; the mecca among them for all flower lovers is the world-famous Keukenhof.

The information center was jointly founded by a community of flower growers in 1949.

④ **Noordwijk aan Zee** In the height of summer, this seaside resort after the turnoff at Sassenheim attracts tens of thousands of beachgoers with 13 km (8 mi) of strand and vast sandy

Travel Information

Route profile
Length: approx. 400 km (249 mi)
Time required: at least 8–10 days
Start: Amsterdam
Finish: Bruges
Route (main locations):
Amsterdam, Leiden, The Hague, Rotterdam, Breda, Antwerp, Mechelen, Brussels, Ghent, Bruges

Traffic information:
Speed limit in the city is 50 km/h (30 mph); on rural roads it's 80 km/h (50 mph) (in Belgium it is 90 km/h (56 mph)); and on highways 120 km/h (75 mph). The legal alcohol limit for drivers is 0.05, and it is strictly enforced. Remember to

bring a warning triangle in case of emergencies.

When to go:
Generally from May to October. Holland is typically at its most beautiful in late spring when everything is in bloom.
From June to late August, southerly winds bring sunny and mostly dry days. At that time, the average maximum temperature is around 20°C (68°F). Only in high summer is swimming really an option.

Information:
Holland:
www.holland.com
www.traveltoholland.org
www.visitbelgium.com

3

4

5

well as the headquarters of the International Court of Justice with the UN War Crimes Tribunal. The city's history goes back roughly 750 years and began with a few houses built around the hunting grounds of the Count of Holland. One of these houses, the Binnenhof or "Inner Court", was built in the 13th century and is still home to the nation's politics – it is the seat of government and the Parliament. The city's most important tourist attraction is the Mauritshuis, a neoclassical building with an art gallery featuring priceless works by famous Dutch painters from the "Golden Age" as well as Flemish Mas-

1 Around 1,300 bridges span Amsterdam's countless canals.

2 The Gravenstenenbrug bridge in Haarlem spans the Spaarne River.

3 Night view of the port city of Rotterdam.

4 The Binnenhof or "inner court" (13th century) in The Hague is seat of Parliament and other governmental institutions.

5 Beach boardwalk in Scheveningen, a seaside resort in front of the gates of The Hague.

dunes. Just like Katwijk ann Zee a few miles further south, Noordwijk has a style that is reminiscent of English seaside resorts. From here it's another 20 km (12 mi) to Leiden.

5 **Leiden** The oldest university town in the Netherlands was already home to 11,000 students back in the mid-17th century. The most beautiful view over the town and its canals can be seen from the Burcht or fort, a mound fortified with brick

curtain walls over 1,000 years ago that was built to protect against Holland's most persistent enemy: flooding. The Pieterskerk, a Gothic cruciform basilica with five naves, is worth seeing and, of course, the city's most famous native son is Rembrandt Harmensz van Rijn, born here in 1606. A few of his works are on display in the Stedelijk Museum de Lakenhal.

6 **Scheveningen** The center of this North Sea coastal resort

is the magnificent old Art Nouveau health spa establishment that is today a luxury hotel. The 3-km-long (2-mi) beach boardwalk and the Scheveningen Pier, which extends 400 m (437 yds) out into the North Sea, are also well-known features of the town. The International Sand Sculptures Festival is held here every year in May.

7 **The Hague** The third-largest city in the Netherlands is the seat of government as

Amsterdam

The capital of the Netherlands is one of the smallest and most manageable metropolises in Europe. It is tolerant and cosmopolitan, but also characterized by a rich history, so it is no coincidence that Amsterdam, the headstrong city at the mouth of the Amstel, is a popular tourist destination.

Amsterdam is the world's largest pile-dwelling settlement. The foundations for the buildings in the entire Old Town district are formed by countless logs beaten up to 30 m (98 ft) into the ground, creating some seventy man-made islands.

Amsterdam's Golden Century (17th century marked the beginning of construction on the crescent-shaped Three Canals Belt. In the historic center alone, four hundred bridges span the canals. Water levels are maintained at a constant height by locks and pumps. Hundreds of houseboats are moored at the docks of the 160 canals in the Canal Belt and are just as much part of the townscape as the numerous cyclists, flower stands with the "tulips from Amsterdam". Amsterdam's cityscape resembles a bustling open-air museum, and its open-mindedness, cultural diversity, international cuisine, and the count-

less options for all types of accommodation suit every budget and every standard.

The tourist attractions in the Old Town include: the oldest church, the Oude Kerk (14th century, rebuilt in the 16th); the late-Gothic Nieuwe Kerk where Queen Beatrix was crowned; Dam, once a market place with a Nationaal Monument; the 17th-century town hall, Koninklijk Paleis, whose façade frieze is dedicated to sea trade; Museum Amstelkring, an original canal house; Beurs van Berlage, the 19th-century merchants' stock exchange; Montelbaanstoren, the former city tower (1512); the seven-towered Waag; and the Rembrandt House. In the former Jewish quarter: the Portuguese synagogue (1675) and Joods Historisch Museum;

the neo-Gothic Central Station (19th century); Amsterdam's historic museum; and the Begijnhof, a former Beguine convent. In the Canal Belt: Westerkerk (17th century); the Anne Frank House; and the historic working quarter of Jordaan with the beautifully renovated Hofjes, historic residential complexes.

In the museum quarter: The Rijks-museum, the world's most famous collection of Dutch Masters; the Van Gogh Museum; Stedelijk Museum for Modern Art; and the Vondelpark landscaped gardens.

Top: Patrician houses along a romantically lit canal.
Bottom: The Magere Brug is the most famous of Amsterdam's bridges.

ters. The Mesdag Panorama, a cylindrical painting created by Hendrik Willem Mesdag in 1881, is 120 m (131 yds) long and 14 m (46 ft) high and hangs in a building at Zeestraat 65. It gives visitors the impression of standing in the middle of the Scheveningen dune landscape. The nearby Mesdag Museum has additional paintings from the Hague School of the late 19th century. Another building that constantly makes headlines is the Vredespalais in the Carnegieplein. This half neo-Gothic, half neoclassical Peace Palace is the venue for the controversial meetings of the International Court of Justice.

8 Delft Halfway between The Hague and Rotterdam is Delft, with its historic Old Town and charming canals. It is particularly famous for its pottery.

9 Rotterdam Container terminals, trans-shipment centers, warehouses and silos all line up beside one another over 20 km (12 mi) along the Nieuwe Waterweg at the world's largest port. All kinds of goods are moved through this port at the mouth of the Maas and Rhine rivers.

It is not difficult to see that emphasis is placed on modern high-rise architecture in "Maashattan". One of the most amazing sights is the Erasmusbrug, a suspension bridge over the Nieuwe Maas constructed by Ben van Berkel in 1996. The city museum, which has an interest-ing display of the history of Rotterdam, is in the Het Schielandshuis, a former administrative building that managed the 17th-century dyke systems. The Boijmans van Beuningen Museum at the Museumspark is home to a sizeable collection of Old and New Masters. A variety of artwork is also exhibited at the Rotterdamer Kunsthal.

From Rotterdam it's roughly 20 km (12 mi) north-east to the country's most famous "cheese town", Gouda. Just a few miles south of Rotterdam, the route leads to one of the country's iconic landmarks – the windmills of Kinderdijk.

10 Kinderdijk It really is an impressive sight: nineteen old polder mills lined up in a tidy row along the town's drainage canals. The ingenious constructions at the confluence of the Noord and Lek rivers once drove pumping stations that regulated water levels. These days, the blades, which are covered in canvas and have a span of up to 28 m (92 ft), only rotate on Saturday afternoons. The mills were declared a UNESCO World Heritage Site in 1997, and are particularly impressive in the second week of September when they are illuminated at night by floodlights.

11 Breda With its numerous barracks and military facilities, this garrison city at the confluence of the Mark and Aa rivers has a lot to offer visitors. Beautiful burgher houses on the Old Town market square, for example, date back to the 18th and 19th centuries and include the Stadhuis. And, as is often the case, the Old Town is surrounded by charming canals. The Kasteel van Breda is encircled by moats and features four corner towers. It is considered the ancestral castle of the House of Orange, the Dutch royal family. Breda is also home to another moated castle, Kasteel Bouvigne, and the city's most important building is the Gothic Onze Lieve Vrouwe Kerk (Church of

1 The current design of the Ooidonk water castle south-west of Ghent dates back to 1595.

2 Kasteel Bouvigne water castle near Breda in North Brabant was used as a hunting lodge in the 17th century.

Our Lady) with a spire 97 m (318 ft) tall. Those looking to head back to the North Sea before continuing on to Belgium are advised to visit the islands of Walcheren and Beveland. They are connected to the mainland by a series of dams and bridges.

From Breda, the N263 takes you through green, flat and sparsely settled landscapes towards Antwerp, the first real metropolis on this journey.

⑫ Antwerp The port here in Belgium's second-largest metropolitan area is the lifeblood of the city and home to a number of automotive and chemical industry companies. The port is the second-largest in Europe after Rotterdam, a fact that has created an open-minded attitude and contributed greatly to Antwerp's rise as the center of the diamond trade. The 1993 European Capital of Culture is home to historic monuments and a vibrant cultural scene. Most of its tourist attractions are in the inner city, which forms a semicircle on the right bank of the Schelde. The most striking part of Antwerp is the Steen, the former fort complex whose oldest section dates back to the 9th century. It now houses the National Shipping Museum, with a 15th-century Flemish warship as its centerpiece. The fort's lookout platform provides an amazing view over the Schelde – which is 500 m (547 yds) wide at this point – the bridges, the old wharf, and the sea of countless cargo derricks along the horizon at the modern port.

The Museum of Municipal History is housed in the late-Gothic meat market, while the Diamond Museum on Lange Herentalsestraat in the Jewish Quarter lets you watch diamond polishers at work.

The Rubens House, a symbolic city palace reminiscent of an Italian palazzo, was home to Peter Paul Rubens from 1610 to 1640. The master's lavish quarters, studio and art cabinet as well as some works by the painter and his students are on display.

⑬ Mechelen This city south of Antwerp has a rich history. It experienced its heyday when Margarethe of Austria ruled the country from here and her statue at the Grote Markt, which marks the city center, commemorates this time. The square is encircled by the town hall, a Gothic palace and the former cloth hall from the 14th century.

Mechelen aimed high throughout its history, in fact. In the second century, the 97-m-tall (318-ft) spire of the Romboutskathedraal was designed as the highest symbol of Christianity, and its carillon of forty-nine bells still charms listeners today. From Mechelen, it's just a half-hour drive to the Belgian capital. Those wanting to head towards the North Sea after that will initially pass through Aalst, the "Gateway to Flanders", on the way to Bruges.

⑭ Brussels (see page 140)

⑮ Aalst This city is heavily influenced by industry and, well, flowers. Every morning there is a flower market at the Grote Markt, and beautiful Gothic row houses line the square.

⑯ Ghent A center of the textile industry since the Middle Ages, Ghent has continued to remain true to this tradition even today. Fruits, vegetables and even flowers play only a supporting role. The most important attractions are found in the well-preserved historic city center between the Count's Castle and the St Bavo Cathedral (14th century). The cathedral is on a rise and is visible from afar. Its most valuable treasure is the *Ghent Altarpiece*, also known as the *Adora-*

tion of the Mystic Lamb, completed by the van Eyck brothers, Hubert and Jan, in the 15th century. The cathedral tower once housed thirty-nine bells, but only seven remain now. The others were sold or destroyed.

The Belfort bell tower, opposite the cathedral, is 91 m (312 ft) high and was considered the symbol of the aspiring middle classes in the 14th century. The Belfort is 88 m high (289 ft) and has forty-seven bells. It has also served as a municipal treasure chamber and a watchtower.

The cloth hall, the Great Meat Market, the Count's Castle, and the town hall are also worth visiting while downtown.

About 15 km (9 mi) from Ghent, between Deinze and Ghent, is the 17th-century Ooidonk

castle complex. The moated castle's name means "high location in a swampland", which can be traced back to an older Low Franconian word "hodonk". Both Flemish and Dutch are creations of a linguistic root dating back to the Franconian empire.

On the way to Bruges, you will pass through Eeklo, where jenever (gin) is made in the historic van Hoorebeke distillery. The jenever is spicier than its English counterpart and the oude genever, or old-style jenever, is yellower in hue.

⑰ Bruges With its semicircular Old Town full of canals, the capital of Western Flanders is a perfect example of medieval city architecture and, in those days, was considered the richest

and most magnificent city in the known world after Venice. All major trading houses were based in Bruges, the dukes of Burgundy held court here, and art was of the utmost importance. Artists such as Jan van Eyck and Hans Memling were dedicated city painters.

The best way to discover Bruges is on a circle tour. The Grote Markt, which was the scene of lively jousting competitions in the Middle Ages, continues to form the city center, which is also home to the 83-m-high (272-ft) Belfort tower.

From the Grote Markt, Vlamingstraat heads to the "Hanseatic Bruges" with its beautiful patrician homes and trading houses from the 14th and 15th century; the Old Customs House; and then the Burgplein before continuing on to the Groeninge Museum with Belgian contemporaries; and finally the 15th-century Gruuthuse-palais, a lavish palace that was home to rich patricians who earned their money by taxing the brewery for their ingredients, the "Gruute".

The Gothic Onze Lieve Vrouwe-kerk, or Church of Our Lady, has a spire 122 m high (400 ft) that is in an atypical position on the left side of the church. It is home to the city's greatest artis-

tic gem: the Bruges Madonna from 1503, the first of Michaelangelo's works to make it across the Alps during his lifetime. The old sluice-house at the southern end of Wijngaardplaats is also interesting. It is used to regulate the water levels of the city's canals. The Minnewater, behind the house in a park, was the city's main dock in the Middle Ages.

After all of this journeying back in time to the Middle Ages, the charming coastal resorts on the North Sea may be calling: Knokke, Zeebruges, Blankenberge and Ostend are all just a few miles away from Bruges.

1 The northern end of the Grand' Place in Brussels shows the Hotel de Ville (1401–1459) on the left.

2 The 88-m-high (289-ft) Belfort (city tower) in Ghent was the city's commercial center in the Middle Ages. It has forty-seven bells.

3 The southern end of the Grand' Place in Brussels is characterized by the neoclassical Maison des Ducs de Brabant in the middle.

4 The historic town of Bruges takes you on a journey through time to the Middle Ages. Here: the Belfort tower reflected in the waters of the Dijver.

Brussels

Belgium's confident metropolis awaits visitors with grandiose cultural monuments and special culinary treats. It calls itself the Capital of Europe, which is true at least as far as the institutions of the European Union.

Brussels has been a wealthy city for centuries. Between the Middle Ages and the baroque period, it was primarily the middle classes who adorned their city with majestic row houses. The 19th century saw some wonderful additions to the unique townscape. The EU's ambitious buildings claimed many architectural victims e. g. the Quartier Léopold. Luckily, numerous Art Nouveau works remained intact. At the turn of the 20th century, Brussels was one of the focal points of this architectural style, and artists such as Victor Horta, Henry van de Velde and Philippe Wolfers enriched the city with a series of unique edifices.

Brussels is Belgium's most important cultural city and scientific center, with a university, the polytechnic, the Royal Academy and numerous technical colleges and art schools. The city is at the crossroads of major transport routes. Furthermore, Brussels is the second largest industrial city in the country after Antwerp. "Fine goods" such as the famous Brussels lace, cotton and silk goods, carpets and even porcelain are all produced here. World-famous culinary products such as exquisite chocolates, pralines, and even beer – virtually a given in the hometown of fabled King Gambrinus – keep visitors coming back for more. Although Brussels has a number of tourist attractions and gets a lot of attention as the "Capital of Europe" and the headquarters of NATO, the Belgian capital is overshadowed by metropolises like Paris, London and Amsterdam. However, it's an insider's tip: slightly chaotic, not always pleasant, easy to access and never overrun. Particularly worth seeing are: the Manneken Pis, the famous peeing boy statue and icon of the city from 1619; Grand' Place, one of the most beautiful squares in Europe and a World Heritage Site with the Hôtel de Ville and the Gothic town hall; the Cathédrale St Michel; the Center Belge de la Bande dessinée, a comics museum in an Art Nouveau building; the "Old England" Grand Magasin; Musées Royaux des Beaux Arts with an outstanding collection of old and new masters from Brueghel to Magritte; Hôtel van Eetvelde, a magnificent building from the late 19th century; Hôtel Hannon, Maison Cauchie and Maison St Cyr, three examples of Brussels Art Nouveau residential architecture; Musée Charlier, 20th-century art; Place du Grand Sablon with galleries and antique stores, and an antiques market on weekends; and Place du Jeu de Balle in the multicultural Marolles (Dutch: Marollen) district.

Top: The Grand' Place with the Maison du Roi, home to the municipal museum. Bottom: The Atomium was built for the 1958 World Exhibition.

Haarlem The Old Town quarter of this bulb-growing city features gabled houses and the mighty Grote Kerk church.

Alkmaar The traditional "cheese market" includes weighing and tasting down at the quaint market square. It is held every Friday in summer.

Amsterdam Despite its historic appearance, the capital of the Netherlands is a youthful city built on several islands and criss-crossed by crescent-shaped canals. It has myriad attractions including world-class museums and fantastic art collections.

Hoorn Cape Horn owes its name to a sailor from Hoorn, but this cute town on Lake IJssel is significantly less rugged than the South American headland.

The Hague The Dutch government, the International Court of Justice and the UN War Crimes Tribunal hold meetings in famous historic buildings while the museums exhibit some fine art.

Keukenhof A community of florists display their plants over an area of 28 ha (69 acres).

Edam The cheese trade has been booming in Edam since the 17th century, and a lovely cheese market is held every Wednesday from July to August. This small town on Lake IJssel was made famous by its cheese balls encased in red or yellow packaging.

Rotterdam This city in the estuary region of the Maas and Rhine rivers is characterized by modern architecture, such as the Erasmus Bridge, and the world's largest port where the facilities along the Nieuwe Waterweg stretch over 20 km (12 mi).

Gouda This city is not just worth visiting for the cheese of the same name. It is also has a picturesque Old Town with a Gothic town hall.

Map labels:
Afsluitdijk, Leeuwarden, Westfriesland, IJsselmeer, Alkmaar, Enkhuizen, Heerenveen, Droogmakerij de Beemster, Hoorn, Markermeer, IJmuiden, Zaandam, Edam, Lelystad, Haarlem, Zandvoort, AMSTERDAM, Almere, Noordwijk aan Zee, De Keukenhof, Katwijk aan Zee, Loosdrechtse Plassen, Scheveningen, Leiden, Utrecht, Apeldoorn, The Hague, Delft, Hoek van Holland, Gouda, Arnhem, Rotterdam, Ridderkerk, Nijmegen, Hellevoetsluis, Kinderdijk, Spijkenisse, Dordrecht, Oosterscheldedam, Zierikzee, NETHERLANDS, Domburg, Walcheren, 's-Hertogenbosch, Middelburg, Goes, Bergen op Zoom, Roosendaal, Breda, Efteling, N.P.Loonse en Drunense Duinen, Eindhoven, Beveland, Tilburg, Eindhoven, Zeebrugge, Knokke-Heist, Terneuzen, Blankenberge, Oostende, Brugge, Dunkerque, Aalter, Eeklo, Zelzate, Turnhout, Eindhoven, Calais, Lokeren, Antwerp, Lier, Liège, Kortrijk, Gent, BELGIUM, Mechelen, Maastricht, Kortrijk, Aalst, Oudenaarde, Leuven, Ninove, BRUSSELS, Liège, Waterloo, Six Flags, Tournai, Ste-Gertrude, Namur, Charleroi

Delft The Grote Markt, the Nieuwe Kerk, and the Stadhuis make the city of blue-and-white porcelain tiles one of the prettiest in the Netherlands.

Kinderdijk A picture-perfect panorama unfolds at the confluence of the Lek and Noord rivers: a row of nineteen polder mills that once drove a pumping station to drain the fields for agriculture.

Bruges The Old Town in Bruges has numerous canals, grand squares and patrician houses from the 14th and 15th centuries, as well as churches and museums that cannot be matched anywhere in Europe.

Ghent Most of Ghent's medieval attractions are found between the Count's Castle and the St Bavo Cathedral and include the Belfort tower, the cloth hall, meat market, St Nicholas Church and more.

Brussels The Belgian capital (and Capital of Europe) is known around the world for its excellent cuisine. World-famous symbols of Brussels also include the vast Grand' Place and the Atomium, the 60-cm-tall (2-ft) Manneken Pis (peeing boy), the city's Art Nouveau buildings, museums, palaces and, of course, fine Brussels lace.

Mechelen The treasures of the Rombout-skathedraal include a van Dyck painting and the glockenspiel. The spire is 97 m high (318 ft) and was originally supposed to reach a height of 167 m (548 ft).

The fishing ports of Saint-Guénolé on

France

Limestone and granite: natural and cultural landscapes of the French Atlantic coast

The territory extending out into the Atlantic and the English Channel in north-western France is not exactly hospitable in terms of weather, but the romantic windswept coast and the luscious green interior radiate a sense of magic that captivates even the most unsentimental visitors. Indeed, across the entire region between Le Havre and Nantes, every stone seems to have a story to tell.

Powerful Atlantic surf, jagged windy bluffs, and shimmering white limestone cliffs scattered with the long, deserted sandy beaches. These are the elements that define the coastlines of Normandy and Brittany, where dynamic forces of nature are unfettered and the aesthetic is that of an ancient world. Augmenting the scene are sleepy fishing villages and busy port cities, elegant seaside resorts and cozy holiday towns. Thousands of years of human history here have left so much behind that the entire region could be considered an open-air museum. Castles and manors, abbeys and cathedrals, meticulously preserved Old Town centers, half-timbered row houses and stone buildings all attest to eras of power and wealth.

Stout fortifications and sentry towers are reminiscent of darker times. Normandy was ruled by the Celts, Romans and Germanic tribes until the 5th century, before the Vikings and Normans claimed the area as theirs. The war between England and France lasted for centuries before the Huguenots devastated the land. But all of this was nothing compared to the German occupation in 1940. Within four years, all of Normandy had become a battlefield until allied troops landed on Calvados and Cotentin beaches on June 6, 1944, "D-Day". The territory was eventually liberated in September of 1944, but many of the cities lay under soot and ash.

Today, Normandy is experiencing what is arguably the most peaceful era in its long history. The roughly 30,000-sq-km (11,580-sq-mi) region is primarily involved in agriculture, and is characterized by grasslands with stone walls, fields of grain and apple plantations.

Fort La Latte on the Brittany Côte d'Armor west of St Malo

142

The impressive limestone cliffs (falaises) of the Normandy coast near Étretat, north of Le Havre. It is definitely worth seeing the Falaises d'Amont and the Falaises d'Aval not far from the city.

the Bigouden Peninsula form the south-western tip of Brittany.

The coast, which is about 600 km long (373 mi), transforms Normandy a popular holiday destination in July and August, whith ovely resorts and stunning beaches. From here, it is possible to make interesting detours to places such as the famous rock island monastery of Mont Saint-Michel.

Before the Common Era, Brittany was home to a culture that continues to mystify the scientific world: Who were the people of the megalith culture? Were the menhirs, the stone monuments from between 5000 and 2000 BC, used as solar or lunar calendars? Were they fertility symbols or cult sites? There are still no explanations for any of these exciting questions. After 500 BC, the history becomes clearer. Around this time, the Celts came and settled in the area, which they called "Armor" or "Land by the Sea". Although they were evangelized around AD 500, they preserved many of their "pagan" customs and legends, as well as their Breton language. Certain Celtic elements still thrive here: fantasy and defiance are particularly defined, fuelled on by a healthy dose of pride. Brittany, which covers an area of roughly 27,200 sq km (10,499 sq mi), is one of France's most important agricultural regions. It is a fishing center and almost every sea bass (loup de mer) or monkfish you eat in Europe comes from its waters. It also specializes in early vegetable exports as well as meat and dairy processing. With its 1,200-km (746 mi) coastline, it is second only to the Côte d'Azur among tourism regions in Europe.

The wind and the stones, the green the meadows and the wild Atlantic ocean spray – Brittany is defined by all of this. That said, it did not achieve true international fame until the emergence of the comic book, *Asterix and Obelix*. Indeed, they are the best-known Bretons after King Arthur and have delighted readers around the world since the first strip by René Goscinny and Albert Uderzo appeared in 1959, but their village does not exist anywhere Brittany.

Saint-Malo on the northern coast of Brittany is situated on an island of granite, not far away from Mont Saint-Michel.

A tour of the Norman-Breton coast takes you first from the urban jungle of Paris to the wildly romantic limestone cliffs of Normandy and the beaches where Allied forces landed in 1944. Brittany then offers a unique natural and scenic experience and confronts visitors with the mysteries of prehistoric cultures and myths.

1 Paris (see Tour No. 16) Highway N 15 is a good way to get to Normandy from Paris, and leads you along the impressive Seine River valley.

2 Rouen This Norman city is home to one of France's largest sea ports, despite its inland location. However, what really fascinates visitors is the historic Old Town, with its quaint alleyways snaking between crooked half-timbered houses, churches with extravagant ornamentation, the magnificent Notre-Dame Cathedral and the rest of the massive fortifications.

3 Fécamp This is where the road meets the Côte d'Albâtre, the Alabaster Coast, where the bizarre limestone cliffs drop more than 110 m (361 ft) down to the sea. Fécamp was once famous for two things: its booming fishing port and its tasty Bénédictine cordial. The Sainte-Trinité Church of the Benedictine abbey has been lovingly preserved.

4 Étretat This village was one of the fishing villages that was particularly popular among artists in the 19th century. It is situated in a bay enclosed on both sides by romantic cliffs. The Notre-Dame Church from the 13th century is astonishingly large

for such a small town, and is well worth visiting.

5 Le Havre This city at the mouth of the Seine was occupied by the Germans in World War II and bombed by the Allies for an entire week in an attempt to win it back. The important port and center were rebuilt, but it is more modern and functional than it is picturesque. The most impressive site is Europe's longest suspension bridge, inaugurated in 1988. The art museum houses a collection of impressionist and cubist works.

6 Honfleur This port city is steeped in tradition and considered the most beautiful city on the Côte Fleurie, the Floral Coast. The architectural gems of the old port, the wharfs lined with narrow row houses, and the steep, hilly Ste Catherine quarter exude fishing village romanticism and an artistic flair. The Musée de la Marine is housed in the oldest church of St Étienne, dating back to the 14th century.

7 Deauville This town is the epitome of sophisticated seaside resorts. In the mid-19th century, the rich and famous

Travel Information

Route profile
Length: approx. 1,400 km (870 mi)
Duration: 10–14 days
Start: Paris
Finish: Nantes
Route course: Paris, Rouen, Le Havre, Honfleur, Caen, Brest, Quimper, Lorient, Nantes

Traffic information:
The blood-alcohol limit for drivers is 0.05 and it is strictly enforced.
The speed limit in cities is 50 km/h (30 mph), on rural roads 90 km/h (55 mph), on expressways 110 km/h (70 mph) and 130 km/h (80 mph) on the motorways. Motorways require tolls.

When to go:
Spring and autumn are ideal, because it the peak season at most resorts is in high summer. Extreme heat is not an issue in this region. Temperatures average around 15°C (59°F) in May and October, while June to September you can expect about 18-20°C (64-68°F). Regardless of the season, the weather here is very active and it can rain at any time.

Information:
Here are some websites to help you plan your trip.
www.franceguide.com
www.brittanytourism.com
www.discoverfrance.com

was rebuilt to its original condition after 1945. The Ville Close, the Old Town with its granite houses from the 17th and 18th centuries, as well as the promenade along the ramparts are but a few of the highlights.

The road to Dinard heads over the 750-m-long (0.5 mile) dam cum bridge of the tidal power station over the Rance. Its lock is 65 m (213 ft) long.

⑫ Dinard The second-largest seaside resort in Brittany is a garden city nestled neatly into a hilly landscape. A walk along the Promenade du Clair de Lune is a must. Dinard was and still is a favorite meeting place for the international jet set.

A great detour from here takes you 22 km (14 mi) south towards Dinan, a picturesque little town perched high above the Rance River. Anyone wishing to skip this side trip can head along the scenic coastal road past Cap Fréhel to the capital of the Côte d'Armor, St-Brieuc, some 3 km (2 miles) inland.

⑬ St.-Brieuc This city has a nicely preserved Old Town with gorgeous half-timbered houses, including the Hôtel des Ducs de Bretagne. The twin-spired cathedral from the 13th century, which was modified over the 18th and 19th centuries, looks almost like a fort.

1 Six-storey row houses from the 17th century line the beautiful port of Honfleur.

2 Mont Saint-Michel, an icon of Normandy and a famous abbey, is an unrivaled synthesis of monastery and fortress architecture.

3 Looking out over the city wall of St Malo, which encloses the restored Old Town quarter.

came in droves to the expensive luxury hotel, part of which still exists today. Deauville's town center comprises the casino, which served as inspiration for Ian Fleming's *Casino Royal*, and the stylish squares include the Promenade de Planches, which is constructed of wooden planks.

⑧ Caen Nearly completely destroyed in World War II, Caen is now a modern city. Its historic features are the two abbeys of Abbaye-des-Dames and Abbaye-aux-Hommes.

It is worth making a detour out to the Cotentin Peninsula, which includes Cherbourg and other villages such as Barfleur. From Coutances at the southwestern end of the peninsula, continue south on the D971.

⑨ Granville The "Monaco of the North" is today a mix of

medieval city and fishing village. The impressive Old Town is perched high above the center on a cliff. As in Deauville, one of the most famous buildings is the casino, opened in 1910. Couturier, Christian Dior, spent his childhood in the pinkish house with exotic garden. Today, it is the Dior Museum. Heading towards Avranches on the D911 you will get magnificent views of the Bay of Mont Saint-Michel, which runs right along the coast.

⑩ Mont Saint-Michel France's most frequently visited attraction is not necessarily a place of peace and quiet, but you can still feel the magic of this town. Its location on a conical mountain in the middle of a tidal bay renders the monadnock either isolated as an island in the ocean or as a rock island

surrounded by sand. It is simply sensational.

Hermits lived in the first houses of worship in the area until, according to lore, Saint Aubert was charged in the 8th century by Archangel Michael to build a sanctuary on the mountain. Further development on the structure began in the 13th century. The church of Notre-Dame-sous-Terre, the new abbey church, the three-levelled monastery complex, the cloister and the Salle de Chevaliers are the most interesting areas.

The D155 heads out of the Bay of Mont St-Michel towards the Côte d'Emeraude, the Emerald Coast, which is home to probably the most beautiful town of the Breton north coast.

⑪ Saint-Malo This medieval city of the corsairs was badly destroyed in World War II but

145

Côte de Granit Rose Off the coast from the fishing port of Paimpol is the Ile-de-Bréhat, a birdlife reserve with red granite rock formations like the rest of the neighboring eighty-six islands. It is of course this stone that gave the entire coast the name Côte de Granit Rose. Also worth seeing is the fishing town of Ploumanach just a few miles further north, as well as Plougrescant at the mouth of the Jaudy River north of Tréguier. The windswept chapel in the small seaside resort of Perros-Guirec is also made of red granite.

From Lannion, the road continues along the coast to Finistère, the "end of the earth", and it is here that Brittany showcases its most attractive side: the Atlantic crashing along the wild, craggy cliffs, and lighthouses balancing precariously on promontories and islands surrounded by the ocean. The picturesque fishing villages feature houses of solid stone and walled church courtyards.

Morlaix This port city is home to an Old Town that is well worth seeing for its carefully preserved medieval houses, but the townscape is actually dominated by a massive railway viaduct. Those interested in the vicarages and calvaires should turn off here onto the N 12 into the Elorn Valley and head towards St.-Thégonnec (see left margin).

Roscoff There is a regular ferry connection to England and Ireland from this heavily frequented spa resort. The town has a number of beautiful old fishermen's houses, and the laboratory for oceanographic and marine biology research here is world renowned.

Brest This city was transformed into France's largest naval port by Cardinal Richelieu in the mid-17th century, and it remained so until being reduced to rubble during World War II. Since its reconstruction, it has become one of the most modern cities in the country and is once again an important naval base. The Pont de Recouvrance, with pylons 64 m (210 ft) high and a total length of 87 m (285 ft), is the longest drawbridge in Europe. Brest's research center and Océanopolis maritime museum are located at the Moulin Blanc yacht harbor. A short detour west takes you to the Pointe de St-Mathieu, famous for the lighthouse located within the ruins of an old

monastery. From Brest, take the N165 along the Bay of Brest to Le Faou, a town with interesting medieval houses made of granite. The D791 will take you to the Crozon Peninsula with its stunning coastal cliffs.

18 Crozon The main town on the peninsula of the same name is a popular holiday destination. Gorgeous beaches are tucked between breathtaking cliffs, and you can take boats to explore the picturesque coastal grottos. Four headlands extend out into the sea here. Perched atop one of them is Camaret-sur-Mer, at one point the most important lobster and crayfish port in France. It is worth going to see the Château Vauban, a fort built according to designs by Louis XIV's master military engineer, the Marquis de Vauban.

West of Camaret-sur-Mer are the Alignements des Lagatjar, quartzite menhirs arranged in a U-shape in three rows. You can get a spectacular view of this prehistoric wonder from the peninsula's most beautiful cape, Pointe de Penhir.

19 Douarnenez This city has an interesting Old Town and is one of the most important fishing ports in Brittany. The maritime museum displays a collection of boats and all sorts of information on shipbuilding. Popular spa resorts in the area invite you to spend a day on the beach.

1 View from the cliffs of the Pointe du Raz in Finistère over the stormswept lighthouses.

2 Ile-de-Bréhat on the Côte de Granit Rose, the Pink Granite Coast, far away from the crowds.

3 A Breton stone house at the northern tip of Brittany near Plougrescant, not far from Tréguier.

4 Château de Brest from the 12th–17th centuries and the city's natural habour.

20 **Pointe du Raz** This cliff drops 70 m (230 ft) to the sea and is the westernmost point of France. It is also one of the most visited places in Brittany. Countless holidaymakers do the half-hour climb over the rocky ridge every day. And for good reason: the view of this rugged landscape amidst the surging waves of the Atlantic is spectacular. Offshore is the small tiny Ile de Sein. It is flat and has hardly any vegetation, but the charming white houses shimmer invitingly. Far out at sea, the mighty lighthouse of Phare d'Ar-Men, built on a ledge in 1881, helps ships navigate the dangerous waters from up to 50 km (31 mi) away.

21 **Quimper** The capital of Finistère is a pretty old town with pedestrian zones, quaint medieval row houses and towering church spires. It is definitely worth seeing St-Correntin Cathedral with its magnificent 15th-century Gothic windows

and twin 76-m-high (249 ft) spires. Local history and culture is exhibited at the well frequented Musée Départemental Breton. Point-l'Abbé, south of Quimper, is a small town whose ornate lacework and embroidery made it famous well beyond Brittany. On the way to Quimperlé you will pass Pont Aven, where Paul Gauguin painted and developed his unique expressionist style with

Emile Bernard between 1886 and 1889. The Musée de Pont-Aven provides an insight into this time. A well signposted footpath heads from the banks of the Aven River to the painters' favorite spots.

22 **Quimperlé** This small town has a lower section as well as an upper section picturesquely situated on a headland between the Isole and Ellé rivers. It

has some charming old houses and the circular Ste-Croix Church is also worth seeing. Your route now heads into the southern part of Brittany. The port city of Lorient has no less than five ports, including one of the most important fishing ports in France. In Auray,

St. Thégonnec The pulpit and calvaire of the village church here are masterpieces of 17th-century Breton art.

Brest France's largest naval port was almost completely destroyed in World War II. Today, Brest is one of the country's most modern cities.

Pointe du Raz This dramatic lighthouse is on a 70-m-high rock formation in the Atlantic.

Côte de Granit Rose Picturesque pink and reddish rocks characterize the northernmost tip of Brittany. They have been beautifully shaped by the wind and waves.

Pointe de Saint Mathieu Looks can be deceiving: the lighthouse 20 km (12 miles) west of Brest is not on top of the old monastery walls (12th–16th centuries), but behind them.

Quiberon This peninsula is popular among watersport enthusiasts, while families prefer the more sheltered east coast.

Cap Frehel On a clear day you can see as far as Saint Malo and the Channel Islands from the reddish cliffs of the cape. You can get a panorama view of the 70-m-high (230-ft) cliffs while on a boat tour.

Carnac Now a spa resort, this location was even popular in prehistoric times: 3,000 menhirs (from 4000–2000 BC) and other stone monuments attest to human settlements.

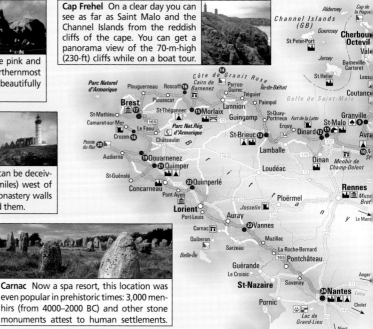

roughly 18 km (11 mi) before Vannes, you should not miss the detour to the approximately 3,000 menhirs of Carnac. From there continue along the peninsula to Quiberon.

㉓ Vannes The capital of Morbihan is a worthwhile destina-

tion for anyone with a romantic streak. The medieval alleyways, the partially preserved Old City wall with its quaint towers, and the charming half-timbered houses attract thousands of visitors every year.

Archaeological relics from the region are displayed in the Musée d'Árchéologie du Morbikau, in the 15th-century Château Gaillard. Anyone who does not want to go directly to

Nantes from Vannes on the highway should take the 30-km (19 mi) detour to the French coast, for example to Le Croisic, at La Roche-Bernard.

㉔ Nantes The journey ends in Nantes, which vied for centuries with Rennes to be the capital of Brittany, It eventually lost in the late 19th century.

This city at the mouth of the Loire River was once the most

important port city on the Loire, and magnificent buildings in the Old Town attest to this. The Château des Ducs de Bretagne is an impressive fort surrounded by a moat.

In addition to the impressive cathedral, the Old Town's Art Nouveau plazas and elegant 18th-century arcades enchant visitors to Nantes.

1 The coastal landscape on the Quiberon Peninsula is breathtaking: the shimmering cliffs, electric blue-white skies and the crashing waves are conducive for a stroll.

2 Half-timbered row houses in front of St Corentin Cathedral in Quimper. This capital of the Département Finistère is also a episcopal see.

3 Hundreds of yachts bob up and down in the marina of Le Croisic on the headland west of St Nazaire. The popular holiday resort offers a wide range of watersports in summer for adventure tourists.

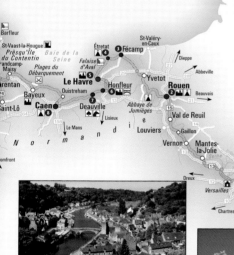

Honfleur The city on the Côte Fleurie, the Floral Coast, emanates port romanticism. The Musée de la Marine is inside Honfleur's oldest church, while the Musée Satie remembers the city's great composer.

Limestone coast near Étretat This village lined with glorious cliffs ("falaises") was a favorite among artists like Monet and Courbet in the 19th century.

Deauville This elegant seaside resort was already popular in the mid-19th century. Luxury hotels, casinos and the Promenade des Planches still prosper here.

Paris The capital of France is also the country's cultural center. If you want to explore the city's numerous museums and enjoy its special flair, make sure you allow plenty of time.

Dinan A mighty castle towers over Dinan, considered one of the most idyllic towns in Brittany. Miles of walls with sixteen gates surround the Old Town quarter on the left bank of the Rance River.

St. Malo The granite houses in the Old Town quarter and the boardwalk on the ramparts are impressive here. The city has been restored to its original state.

Mont St Michel This cone-shaped monadnock with its magical location in a tidal bay, is one of the country's most popular attractions. Additions were made in the 8th century, and again from the 13th century onwards. Three million visitors come to the small monastery island every year.

The old port of La Rochelle and the watchtowers of St-Nicolas and Tour de la Chaîne. Arcaded streets are hiding behind the Porte de la Grosse Horloge.

France

Via Turonensis – on the old pilgrimage route from Paris to Biarritz

The Via Turonensis was mainly travelled by pilgrims from the Netherlands and northern France on their way to Santiago de Compostela in Galicia, the far north-west corner of Spain. They mostly went on foot to their imminent salvation. Today, there are still pilgrims who follow the Camino de Santiago (St James' Way) and its various 'side streets' for religious purposes, but most people these days are simply interested in seeing the wonderful sights along the way.

Four different trails originally led pilgrims through France to the tomb of St James in Santiago de Compostela – the Via Tolosana from Arles through Montpellier and Toulouse to Spain; the Via Podensis from Le Puy through Conques, Cahors and Moissac to the border; the Via Lemovicensis from Vézelay through Avallon, Nevers and Limoges; and finally, the fourth route, the Via Turonensis, known as the 'magnum iter Sancti Jacobi' (the Great Route of St James).

The route's name comes from the city of Tours, through which it passed. The pilgrims started at the tomb of St Dionysius in St-Denis before heading through Paris, down the Rue St-Jacques to the church of the same name, where only the tower still stands on the right bank of the Seine. The tomb of St Evurtius was the destination in Orléans, while the tomb of St

Jeanne d'Arc Arriving at Orléans, a painting by Jean Jacques Scherrer.

Martin, who was often compared to St James, awaited pilgrims in Tours. In Poitiers, there were three churches on the intinerary: St-Hilaire, Notre Dame la Grande and Ste-Radegonde. The head of John the Baptist was the object of worship in St-Jean-d'Angély, and pilgrims would pray at the tomb of St Eutropius in Saintes. Bordeaux was also the custodian of important relics like the bones of St Severin and the Horn of Roland.

The pilgrims of the Middle Ages would most certainly have been amazed and would have shaken their heads at the buildings that the modern pilgrims along the Via Turonensis today find so fascinating. While

Château de Chambord, in the middle of a large forest, is a structure of fairy-tale proportions.

The modern glass pyramid by I.M. Pei in front of the magnificent Louvre building has been the museum's main entrance since 1989. It has become a landmark of the city of Paris.

the largest and most beautiful buildings in the Middle Ages were erected to honour and praise God, modern man seems obsessed with himself and his comforts. 'Pilgrims' nowadays are most interested in visiting the castles along the Via Turonensis, drawn to the extravagance as if by magic.

Perfect examples of this absolutism are just outside Paris in the Île-de-France – the enormous palace complex of Versailles and the castle of Rambouillet which, as the summer residence of French presidents, continues to be a center of power. Many other magnificent buildings are scattered along the Loire River and its tributaries, the Indre, Cher and Vienne, including the colossal Château de Cham-

bord, a dream realized by King Francis I, the Château de Chenonceaux, and others like Beauregard, Chaumont, Valençay, Loches, Le Lude and Langeais.

The area around Bordeaux is home to a completely different kind of château. Médoc, Bordeaux and Entre-Deux-Mers are names that make the wine-lover's heart skip a beat. This region is the home of myriad great wines, in particular red wine. The wineries around Bordeaux, most of which look like real castles in the middle of vast vineyards, are referred to as châteaus and include internationally renowned names such as Mouton-Rothschild, Lafitte-Rothschild and Latour.

Last but not least, today's 'car pilgrims' are attracted to desti-

nations that are far off the beaten track and would have seemed rather absurd as a detour to the pilgrims of the Middle Ages – namely, those on the Atlantic coast. The sandy beaches and coves of the Arcachon Basin and the sections of coast further south on the Bay of Biscay provide wind and

waves for passionate wind-surfers and surfers. The elegant life of the 19th century is celebrated in the charming seaside resort of Biarritz and, from here, it's not much further to the Aragonian section of the Camino de Santiago, which stretches along the northern coast of Spain.

The Médoc on the left bank of the Gironde, close to Bordeaux, is one of the best red wine regions in the world, including grands crus classes guide.

The Via Turonensis follows one of the four major French routes of the St James' pilgrimage trail. Starting in the Île-de-France, you'll head to Orléans on the Loire, continue downstream past some of the most beautiful and famous Loire châteaus and then, from Saumur onwards, make your way south into the Gironde to Bordeaux. Prior to arriving in Biarritz, you stop in St-Jean-Pied-de-Port, the former last stop for pilgrims before crossing the Pyrenees.

1 St-Denis The actual pilgrim route begins in St-Denis, north of Paris. During the heyday of the Camino de Santiago (St James' Way) pilgrimages, this town was located north of the former city border and was the meeting place for the pilgrims coming from Paris. The French national saint, Dionysius, is buried in the city's cathedral. The basilica, where almost all of France's kings are entombed, is considered the first masterpiece of Gothic architecture.

2 Paris (see pp. 154-155). South-west of Paris is Versailles. The name of the palace is intrinsically tied to the Sun King, Louis XIV, and is a symbol of his display of absolutist power.

3 The Palace of Versailles Louis XIII first had a small hunting lodge built on the site where this magnificent building now stands. Under Louis XIV, the lodge was gradually expanded to the immense dimensions we know today, followed by some 'insignificant' extensions like the opera, built under Louis XV.

During the reign of the Sun King, Versailles was the place where anyone who wanted to have any sort of influence in the State had to stay. Apart from the large, opulent reception rooms such as the Hall of Mirrors, the Venus Room, the Hercules Room or the Abundance Salon, there were also the king and queen's lavishly furnished private chambers. The opera is a real gem, completed in 1770.

Beyond the water features of the Bassin d'Apollon is the vast park complex, which is home to the Grand Trianon, Petit Trianon and Le Hameau. The Grand Trianon was built under the orders of Louis XIV – one wing for him and the other for his beloved, Madame de Maintenon. The Petit Trianon was built for Louis XV's mistresses. Le Hameau is almost an absurdity – a small village with a homestead, dairy farm, mill and pigeon loft, where Marie

Travel Information

Route profile
Length: approx. 1,100 km (684 miles), excluding detours
Time required: 10–14 days
Start: Paris
End: Bayonne
Route (main locations):
Paris, Versailles, Orléans, Blois, Tours, Saumur, Poitiers, Saintes, Cognac, St-Émilion, Bordeaux, St-Jean-Pied-de-Port, Bayonne

Traffic information:
Drive on the right in France. The speed limit in built-up areas is 50 km/h (31 mph), 90 km/h (56 mph) on rural roads, 110 km/h (68 mph) on expressways and 130 km/h (81 mph) on highways. Headlights are required when driving in foggy, rainy or snowy conditions.

Weather:
The best seasons to visit the Île-de-France and the Loire Valley are spring and autumn, when the Loire Valley shows off its most beautiful side and is ablaze with all shades of yellow and red. For more information go to:
www.meteofrance.com

Information:
General
www.francetourism.com
www.franceguide.com
www.theviaturonensis.com
Paris
en.parisinfo.com
Loire Valley
www.westernfrancetourist board.com
Bordeaux
www.bordeaux-tourisme. com

Antoinette played 'peasant', a game that did not win her any fans among supporters of the revolution – she wound up under the guillotine on the Place de la Concorde.

④ Rambouillet Although the palace is the summer residence of the French president, it can be visited most of the time. The building consists of wings designed in different architectural styles including Gothic, Renaissance and baroque.

This castle only became royal property in 1783, when Louis XVI acquired it as a hunting lodge. The park and the adjacent Rambouillet forest are ideal places to take a relaxing stroll. On the way to Orléans to the south of Paris, it's worth making a detour to Chartres, whose name is automatically associated with its Gothic cathedral, the largest in Europe.

⑤ Orléans This city's cathedral, Ste-Croix, is built in Gothic style, though only very small parts of it date back to the Gothic period. The original building, destroyed during the French Wars of Religion, was rebuilt under Henry VI, and the architects of the 18th and 19th centuries continued to use the Gothic style.

The city's liberator lived in a house named after her – the Maison de Jeanne d'Arc. The half-timbered house, which was destroyed in World War II, was reconstructed identically to the original. Only very few of the beautiful old houses and noble palaces were spared

from the severe attacks of the war, but the Hôtel Toutin, with its gorgeous Renaissance interior courtyard, is one that was. Of course, Orléans wouldn't be complete without the statue of Jeanne d'Arc, erected on the Place du Martroi in 1855.

Before heading on to Blois, it's well worth making a detour to the beautiful moated castle of Sully-sur-Loire, some 40 km (25 miles) south-east of Orléans.

From Orléans, you have two options for reaching Chambord, which is somewhat outside of the Loire Valley – either along the right bank of the Loire to Merand and across a bridge, or along the left bank of the Loire on small rural roads.

⑥ Chambord King Francis I had this château built on the site of an older hunting lodge. Lost among the vast forests, the result was a vast dream castle with an incredible 440 rooms, seventy staircases, corner towers, a parapet and a moat. Leonardo da Vinci was apparently involved in its construction as well, designing the

elaborate double-helix staircase whose two spirals are so intertwined that the people going up cannot see the people going down, and vice versa.

One of the château's real charms is its unique roof silhouette with its numerous turrets and chimneys. Francis I did not live to see the completion of his château, and work was not continued on it until the reign of Louis XIV. Louis XV gave it as a gift to the Elector of Saxony, who had it gloriously renovated. The château fell into temporary neglect after his death.

1 View of the Eiffel Tower lit up at night from one of the many bridges along the Seine.

2 The Palace of Versailles – the Cour de Marbre courtyard is paved with marble slabs.

3 The oldest bridge in Paris, the Pont Neuf, spans the Seine on the north and south sides of the Île de la Cité. Despite its name 'New Bridge', the Pont Neuf was opened in 1607 and connected the city to the island in the river, its medieval center.

153

Paris

The French capital is a city of thrilling contrasts – rich in tradition and at the same time avant-garde, enormous in size and yet captivatingly charming. Paris is also a university city and the place of government, a global center for fashion and art, in-credibly multicultural and yet still very much the epitome of all things French.

Throughout its long history, Paris has continually been in a state of expansion. Today, greater Paris covers an area of about 105 sq km (40 sq miles) and is home to some twelve million people – more than twenty percent of the entire population of France. This city's non-stop growth is not least due to the fact that Paris does not accept any rivals. The capital has always been unchallenged in its political, econom-ic and cultural significance.

On the south side of the Seine you won't be able to miss the Eiffel Tower, the symbol of Paris built in 1889 for the World Fair. The iron con-struction, rising up to 300 m (984 ft), took engineer Gustav Eiffel just six-teen months to be completed. The viewing platform, accessed by elevator, is one of the city's major attractions. The Hôtel des Invalides, a complex crowned by the Dôme des Invalides, was built by Louis XIV for the victims of his numerous wars.

North of the Seine is probably the most magnificent boulevard in the world, the Champs-Elysées, with the Arc de Triomphe providing a great view of the streets emanating from its center. Be sure to see the Place de la Concorde, an excellent example of wide boulevards and geometric plazas that gave the French capital its 'big city' look during its renovation in the 19th century. Also visit the park complex Jardin des Tuileries, which leads up to the Louvre; the Place Vendôme with its upmarket shop-ping; the Palais Garnier, an opulent 19th-century opera house; and the 17th-century Palais Royal.

Montmartre, on the north side of town, is great for exploring both day and night. Things to see include the historic Moulin de la Galette with its outdoor garden restaurant; the Sacre Coeur basilica up on the hill, with fan-tastic views of the city; the Père Lachaise Cemetery (east, outside city center), one of three large cemeteries built around 1800 with the graves of numerous celebrities (Oscar Wilde, Jim Morrison, Edith Piaf, Eugène Delacroix and Frédéric Chopin, for example). All the cemeteries have detailed maps available at the main entrance.

In the northern suburb of St-Denis you will find the early-Gothic church of St-Denis, the burial place of the French kings, and the Stade de France. The historic center of the 'City of Light' is relatively easy to navigate, and many sights can be reached on

foot. You could spend days just wan-dering around the Louvre. During the Middle Ages, when Paris was arguably the most important city in Europe, three factors determined the city's development and status – the church, its royalty and the university, all of which have left their mark on the historic city center. Out on the Île de la Cité – the city's oldest core settle-ment where the Romans, Merovin-gians and Carolingians based their dominions – stands one of France's most splendid cathedrals: Notre Dame.

As of 1400, medieval royalty focused their power on the northern banks of the Seine at the Louvre, which was begun in 1200 as part of a first ring of fortifications and developed into a magnificent residence over the cen-turies. On the other side of the river, in the Latin Quarter, professors and stu-dents united to establish the Sor-bonne at the end of the 12th century. The riverbank, with its grand build-ings, is a UNESCO World Heritage Site. On the Île de la Cité, don't miss the early-Gothic Cathédrale Notre Dame (12th/13th centuries), where you can climb both 68-m-high (223-ft) towers; the former palace chapel of Ste-Chapelle, a high-Gothic masterpiece; the Conciergerie, part of the medieval royal palace; Pont Neuf, one of the most beautiful bridges on the Seine; and the idyllic Île St-Louis, south-east of the Île de la Cité, with its Renais-sance buildings. North of the Seine visit the Louvre, first a medieval castle, then the royal residence until the 17th century, then rebuilt and made into one of the largest art museums in the world; the Centre Pompidou, a cultur-al center with exemplary modern architecture; the Hôtel de Ville, the 19th-century town hall at the Place de Grève; the Marais quarter with the romantic Place des Vosges, the avant-garde Opéra National de Paris, the Gothic church of St-Gervais-et-St-Pro-tais, the Picasso museum, and the Hôtel Carnavalet's museum on the city's history.

South of the Seine go to the famous Latin Quarter; the St-Germain-des-Prés and Montparnasse Quarters and the Jardin du Luxembourg park.

Left: The illuminated Louvre pyra-mid was built at the end of the 20th century as part of the costly modernization of the largest art museum in the world.
Top: The striking Arc de Triomphe on the Champs-Elysées by night.

7 **Blois** In the first half of the 17th century, Blois was the center of France's political world. The town revolves around its castle, where the individual building phases are very easily recognized. The oldest section is Louis XII's wing, constructed in red brick with white limestone decorations. The Francis I wing is far more lavish, built in Renaissance style with traces of French Gothic in parts. The king would often have his heraldic animal, the salamander, displayed in certain areas. What really catches your eye is the Renaissance-style staircase tower in the interior courtyard, where the royal family could attend events.

Noble palaces such as the Hôtel Sardini, the Hôtel d'Alluye and the Hôtel de Guise are proof that, apart from royalty, numerous other aristocrats also had their residences along the Loire. The St-Louis Cathedral is not Gothic and only dates back to the 17th century, the previous building having been extensively destroyed by a hurricane. An especially lovely half-timbered house, the Maison des Acrobates, is located on the cathedral square. If you are interested in Gothic churches, pay a visit to the 12th-century St-Nicolas.

8 **Cheverny** This castle, built between 1620 and 1634, is still owned by the family of the builder, Henri Hurault. It is also probably thanks to this fact that the castle still contains a large part of the original, opulent interior decor. The ceiling frescoes in the dining hall and bedroom are particularly worth inspecting.

9 **Chenonceaux** Powerful women played a large role in the history of this romantic pleasure palace. For example, Cathérine Briçonnet supervised

its construction in the early 16th century while her husband was in Italy. After Thomas Bohier's death, the building fell into the hands of the king and Henry II gave it as a gift to his beloved, Diane de Poitiers, who extended it to include a bridge over the Cher. Following Henry's death, his wife, Catherine de Medici, kept the castle for herself, and it is thanks to her idea that the Florentine-style bridge was built, including its own gallery.

After Catherine de Medici, the widow of the assasinated Henry III, Louise de Lorraine, proceeded to live a life of mourning in what was actually a very bright and cheerful-look-

ing castle. This spirit returned in the 18th century with the arrival of middle-class Louise Dupin, who saved the castle from the destruction of the revolution. Only very little remains of the original decor, but Renaissance furnishings have been used to give an impression of what the interior may have been like.

Located on the bridge pier is the gorgeous kitchen, where copper pots and pans still hang in an orderly fashion.

10 **Amboise** Perched on a hill sloping steeply into the Loire is France's first major Renaissance château. Although only parts of the construction have been

preserved, they are still very impressive in their size and grandeur.

Following an expedition to Italy in 1496, Charles VIII brought back with him Italian artists, craftsmen and works of art to decorate the palace. The interiors of the mighty towers were constructed in such a way that a rider on a horse could reach up into the storey above. The Chapelle-St-Hubert is a good example of Gothic architecture. Not far from the château is the Le Clos-Lucé mansion, where Leonardo da Vinci spent the final years of his life. Francis I had originally arranged for the Italian universal genius to come to France, and a small museum

it be beds of flowers or vegetables, everything is laid out artistically and trees and hedges are perfectly trimmed into geometric shapes.

⑬ Azay-le-Rideau This castle on the Indre, built between 1519 and 1524, captivates visitors with the harmony of its proportions and its romantic location on an island in the river. However, it did not bring its builder, the mayor of Tours, Gilles Berthelot, much luck. Like other French kings, Francis I could not tolerate his subjects openly displaying their wealth. Without further ado, he accused the mayor of infidelity and embezzlement, and seized the castle.

⑭ Ussé The Château d'Ussé was built on the walls of a fortified castle in the second half of the 15th century. With its turrets and merlons, as well as its location at the edge of the forest, it's easy to see how it was the inspiration for authors of fairy tales. The Gothic chapel houses an important work of art from the Italian Renaissance, a terracotta Madonna by the Florentine sculptor Luca della Robbia.

1 After Versailles, the fantastic 16th-century water palace in Chenonceaux is the most visited château in France.

2 A stone bridge crosses the Loire in Amboise, home to the grand château of the same name.

3 Located on the left bank of the Indre, the 15th-century Château d'Ussé is like a fairy-tale castle made into reality.

4 Saumur – a view over the Loire to the Château de Saumur and the church tower of St-Pierre.

ent styles. The St-Gatien Cathedral is the city's most important historic church. The two-storey cloister provides a great view of the towers' tracery and the finely carved flying buttresses. In some parts of the Old Town, like the Place Plumereau, you could be forgiven for thinking you were back in the Middle Ages. Charming half-timbered houses with pointed gables and often ornately carved balconies are proof of the wealth of the traders at the time. A waxworks cabinet is located in the historic rooms of the Château Royal (13th century).

⑫ Villandry The last of the great castles to be built in the Loire during the Renaissance (1536) fell into ruin in the 19th century and its Renaissance gardens were then made into an English-style park. The Spanish Carvallo family eventually bought it in 1906 and it is thanks to them that the castle has been renovated. More importantly, the gardens were remodelled in the original Renaissance style. This explains why a lot of the people who visit the castle today are lovers of historic landscaping. Whether

displaying models of Leonardo's inventions pays homage to this influential man.

The small town located below the château, a row of houses, and the clock tower all date back to the time of this region's heyday. From Amboise, a small road leads through the middle of the Loire Valley to Tours.

⑪ Tours This is the town that gave the Via Turonensis its name, and the tomb of St Martin here was an extremely important stop for St James pilgrims. Revolutionaries demolished the old St-Martin Basilica at the end of the 18th century. The new St-Martin Basilica, in neo-Byzantine style, contains the tomb of the saint, consecrated in 1890. It is an example of the monumental church architecture of the time, one that made use of many differ-

15 Saumur Horse lovers around the world should be very familiar with the name Saumur. The cavalry school, founded in 1763, is still France's national riding school. The castle was built in the second half of the 14th century and is located on a hillside above the city. Today, it houses two museums, an art museum and the Musée du Cheval. In the Old Town, half-timbered houses like the town hall on the Place St-Pierre, which was created in 1508 as a patrician palace, and the numerous 17th-century villas are all worth a look. In the Gothic church of Notre Dame de Nantilly, the side aisle, which Louis XI had built in a flamboyant style, is home to a prayer chapel that an inscription identifies as being the royal oratorio. On rainy days there are two interesting museums worth visiting: a mask museum (Saumur produces a large quantity of carnival masks) and a mushroom museum. These precious fungi are grown in the surrounding area in numerous limestone caves.

From Saumur, the westernmost point of the journey through the Loire, the road heads 11 km (7 miles) back towards Fontevraud-l'Abbey.

16 Fontevraud-l'Abbaye This abbey was founded in 1101 and existed as such until the 19th century. In the tall, bright church (consecrated in 1119) is the tomb of Eleonore of Aquitania. South-west France 'wedded' England when she married Henry Plantagenet, later Henry II of England. Eleonore's husband and their son, Richard the Lionheart, are also buried in Fontevraud.

The 16th-century cloister is the largest in all of France. However, the abbey's most original building is the monastery kitchen, which almost looks like a chapel with six arches.

17 Chinon This castle-like château high above the banks of the Vienne played an important role in French history. This is where Jeanne d'Arc first met Charles VII and recognized him despite his costume, his courtiers, who were hiding him, and the fact that she had never seen him before. It is for this reason that the large tower, the Tour de l'Horloge, houses a small museum dedicated to her. Other parts of the castle, originating from the 10th to 15th centuries, are only ruins now. A highlight of any visit to the castle is the view over the Vienne valley.

18 Châtellerault This town, no longer of much significance, was once an important stop for pilgrims on the Camino de Santiago. Pilgrims would enter the town, as did Jeanne d'Arc, through Porte Ste-Cathérine. The church of St-Jacques, the destination of all pilgrims on the Camino de Santiago, was furnished with an ornate set of chimes. Some of the houses, such as the Logis Cognet, enable you to imagine what life was like in the 15th century.

19 Poitiers This old city, which was an important stop for pilgrims on the Camino de Santiago, found an important patron in Duke Jean de Berry. In the second half of the 16th century, it became a center of spiritualism and science and its churches still show evidence of this today.

20 Marais Poitevin The marshland located west of Poitiers and stretching all the way to the coast seems to have remained stuck in time. The most important and often the only means of transport in the 'Venise Verte' (Green Venice) is one of the flat-bottomed boats. The Romanesque churches of Parthenay-le-Vieux, some 50 km (31 miles) west of Poitiers, are well worth a visit. You have to return to Poitiers before continuing on to St-Jean-d'Angély.

21 St-Jean-d'Angély Although it has now paled into insig-

nificance, this town was once an important destination for St James pilgrims as it was here that they had the opportunity to pay their respects to John the Baptist. Only ruins remain of the Gothic church, but a row of beautiful half-timbered houses, the Tour de la Grosse Horloge (clock tower) dating from 1406, an artistic fountain (1546), and the 17th-century

brandy, which takes between five and forty years to mature. Some of the distilleries offer interesting tours of their facilities.

You head south-west from here to Pons before continuing on to Libourne.

24 Libourne This small town is a typical bastide, a fortified town, built at the time when South-West France was an apple of discord between England and France (1150–1450). Every bastide is surrounded by a wall and has a grid-like layout and a large market square. Libourne was founded in 1270 and was for a long time a very important port for shipping wine out of the region. Today, it's worth taking a stroll around the Place Abel Surchamp.

25 St-Émilion Soaring out of the sea of vineyards that belong to the St-Émilion appellation, which produce very high-quality wines, is the small town whose beginnings trace back to a monastery. The sizeable rock-hewn church here (9th–12th centuries), whose understated facade faces towards the pretty market place, is a special attraction. The collegiate church was built in the 12th century and its main aisle is Romanesque. By no means should you miss having a look at the very well-preserved cloister.

The donjon, a relic from the royal fort, towers high above St-Émilion where the 'Jurade'

The Abbaye aux Dames, for example, was founded in 1047, and the Romanesque church was built in the 11th and 12th centuries. The Gothic St-Pierre Cathedral was constructed in the 13th and 14th centuries and the tower was added in the 17th century. The church of St-Eutrope, dating from the late 11th century, was one of the destinations of the St James pilgrims. They prayed here in the spacious crypt at the tomb of the city's saint, Eutropius.
From Saintes you head southeast towards Cognac.

23 Cognac This town, on the banks of the Charente, today very much revolves around the drink of the same name, which expert noses will be able to catch whiffs of as they stroll through the town. The Valois Castle, from the 15th and 16th centuries, has a cognac distillery.
An exhibition at the town hall allows you to get a better understanding of the history and production of the precious

abbey enable modern visitors to take a trip back in time.
From here, it's worth making a detour to the port town of La Rochelle on the Atlantic, where you can make an excursion out to the Île de Ré.

22 Saintes The capital of the Saintonge looks back on a long history, traces of which can still be seen today. The Arc de Ger-

manicus, which was originally the gateway to a bridge, dates back to Roman times. When the bridge eroded, it was saved and rebuilt on the right bank. The ruins of the amphitheater, dating back to the 1st century and today overgrown with grass, once seated 20,000 people. There are also some impressive remains from the Middle Ages.

1 Storm clouds over the port of La Rochelle with its 15th-century Tour de la Lanterne.

2 With its medieval houses, squares and streets, St-Émilion is a charming little town in the middle of the lovely wine region of the same name.

wine confrèrie meets to test the new wines. Every year, from the tower platform, the members ceremoniously declare the grape harvest open.

㉖ Bordeaux This old city on the Garonne has long been dominated by trade – predominantly the wine trade. An historic event had a profound effect on the city – in 1154, Bordeaux fell under English rule and, thanks to their huge interest in the region's wines, trade boomed. Even when Bordeaux was again part of France, it still maintained a close relationship with the British Isles.

The Place de la Comédie, with the classical columned facade of the Grand Théâtre, is an ideal place to start a stroll through the city. The Esplanade des Quinconces here is considered the largest square in Europe. You shouldn't miss seeing the city's churches. The St-André Cathedral was built between the 13th and 15th centuries and fascinates visitors with its Porte Royale, a magnificent door lavishly decorated with sculptures. Apart from the church, there is the Tour Pey-Berland, a free-standing tower. St-Michel was constructed somewhat later, in the 14th/16th centuries, and is furnished in 17th-century baroque style.

Those following in the footsteps of Camino de Santiago pilgrims should pay a visit to St-Seurin. Worshipping St-Severin (St-Seurin) was an important part of the route. The early-Romanesque crypt dates back to this time.

Bordeaux has a lot more to offer than just St James relics – the city gates of Porte de Cailhau, Porte d'Aquitaine, Porte de la Monnaie and Porte Dijeaux, for example. The Pont de Pierre (a stone bridge) and the tall, modern bridge, Pont d'Aquitaine, dating from 1967,

are also worth a look. Those interested in seeing the region's world-famous vineyards should make the 50-km (31-mile) journey along the Gironde to the Château Mouton-Rothschild in Pauillac.

㉗ Les Landes This is the name given to the landscape typical of the area south of Bordeaux – flat, sandy earth with sparse pine forests. The forests are planted by hand and are still used for their lumber by-products, predominantly for the extraction of resin.

The region's capital is Mont-de-Marsan, located somewhat off the beaten track in the southeast and home to some interesting Romanesque houses, the 15th-century Lacataye donjon and some very pretty parks.

㉘ Dax This small town on the Adour is one of France's most frequently visited thermal baths. Water at a temperature of 64°C (147°F) bubbles out of the Fontaine de la Néhé.

The 17th-century cathedral here is also worth seeing. The apostle gate from the earlier Gothic building is significant in an art-history context. A visit to the Musée Borda in a beautiful city palace and a stroll along the banks of the Adour round

off the visit. If you want to go to the seaside, you can can drive 40 km (25 miles) from Dax to the southern end of the Côte d'Argent and then further on to the Côte des Basques around Biarritz.

On the other hand, those wanting to get a whiff of the mountain air in the Pyrenees should continue south-east along the spectacular route to Orthez.

㉙ St-Jean-Pied-de-Port In the Middle Ages, this mountain town was already an important stop for pilgrims – and the last before the strenuous crossing of the Pyrenees over the Roncesvalles Pass and across the Spanish border. 'Saint John at the Foot of the Pass' manages to preserve its medieval character even today. The banks of the Nive River are lined with houses

from the 16th and 17th centuries and the Gothic church of Notre Dame du Bout du Pont.

㉚ Bayonne The capital of the Pays Basque is a densely settled area but it has managed to retain much of its charm in its center with bridges on two rivers, large squares and rows of houses packed closely together around the Gothic cathedral of Ste Marie. Its city festival is famous, held every year on the second weekend in August.

1 The Bay of Biarritz with its tiny port and the main beach.

2 The Pont du Pierre crosses the Garonne in Bordeaux, with the striking tower of the Cathédrale St-André in the background.

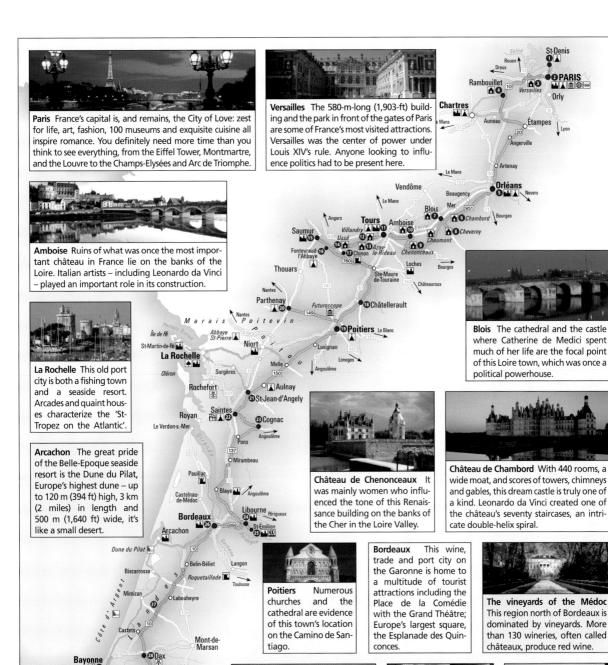

Paris France's capital is, and remains, the City of Love: zest for life, art, fashion, 100 museums and exquisite cuisine all inspire romance. You definitely need more time than you think to see everything, from the Eiffel Tower, Montmartre, and the Louvre to the Champs-Elysées and Arc de Triomphe.

Versailles The 580-m-long (1,903-ft) building and the park in front of the gates of Paris are some of France's most visited attractions. Versailles was the center of power under Louis XIV's rule. Anyone looking to influence politics had to be present here.

Amboise Ruins of what was once the most important château in France lie on the banks of the Loire. Italian artists – including Leonardo da Vinci – played an important role in its construction.

La Rochelle This old port city is both a fishing town and a seaside resort. Arcades and quaint houses characterize the 'St-Tropez on the Atlantic'.

Arcachon The great pride of the Belle-Epoque seaside resort is the Dune du Pilat, Europe's highest dune – up to 120 m (394 ft) high, 3 km (2 miles) in length and 500 m (1,640 ft) wide, it's like a small desert.

Blois The cathedral and the castle where Catherine de Medici spent much of her life are the focal point of this Loire town, which was once a political powerhouse.

Château de Chenonceaux It was mainly women who influenced the tone of this Renaissance building on the banks of the Cher in the Loire Valley.

Château de Chambord With 440 rooms, a wide moat, and scores of towers, chimneys and gables, this dream castle is truly one of a kind. Leonardo da Vinci created one of the château's seventy staircases, an intricate double-helix spiral.

Poitiers Numerous churches and the cathedral are evidence of this town's location on the Camino de Santiago.

Bordeaux This wine, trade and port city on the Garonne is home to a multitude of tourist attractions including the Place de la Comédie with the Grand Théâtre; Europe's largest square, the Esplanade des Quinconces.

The vineyards of the Médoc This region north of Bordeaux is dominated by vineyards. More than 130 wineries, often called châteaux, produce red wine.

Biarritz Winter guests made this former whaling town on the Basque coast popular in the 19th century. Its beaches and promenades still enjoy huge popularity.

Bayonne This town is the heart and soul of the French Basque region. Its Gothic cathedral, famous for its folk festival in August, is definitely worth a visit.

St-Émilion Amid the vineyards are the fortress complexes of St-Émilion, with its famous cathedral and rock-hewn church.

France and Spain

Lavender fields – a symbol of Provence. scented oil purifying the air.

The 'Land of Light' – from Côte d'Azur to Costa Brava

The coastline along the Côte d'Azur, the Golfe du Lion and the Costa Brava could hardly be more diverse or enticing. At the southern edge of the Alps, the Côte d'Azur showcases a landscape of breathtakingly unique beauty. Provence is a paradise for nature lovers and culture enthusiasts, while the Camargue is a near pristine delta landscape. The Costa Brava gets its name from the mountains which drop away steeply into the sea.

An incredibly varied stretch of coast between Menton on the Côte d'Azur and Barcelona on the Costa Brava greets visitors with all the beauty the French Midi and the north-eastern Spanish coast have to offer.
Directly behind Monte Carlo's sea of houses and apartments are the captivating mountains of the Alpes-Maritimes, which only begin to flatten out near

Nice, allowing trendier cities like Cannes and Antibes to sprawl a bit. The foothills of the Massif des Maures once again straddle the coast beyond St-Tropez where there is really only enough room for small, picturesque villages – your search for sandy beaches will be in vain. But not to worry, you'll find them again around Hyères and the off-

The Calanques cliffs near Cassis.

shore islands in the area. Wine-lovers will get their money's worth between Toulon and Cassis – the wines grown between Bandol and Le Castellet are some of the best in the Midi. Marseille then presents

itself as the port city with two faces. Founded by the Greeks, and later a stronghold of the Romans, its cultural history dates back 2,500 years. At the same time, it was long the gateway to the cultures on other Mediterranean shores – Europe, North Africa and the Near East are all well represented in Marseille's multicultural population.
West of Marseille, in the delta between the two mouths of the Rhône, sprawls a breathtakingly beautiful wetland of ponds, marshes, meadows and plains abundant with springs, grass, and salt fields – the Camargue. North of here is where you'll discover the heart of Provence. Cities such as Arles, Avignon

The plants are cultivated for their

Isolated bays along the rocky coast of the Costa Brava near Cadaqués.

St-Tropez: The international jet set discovered this idyllic fishing town in the 1950s and since then there have been more yachts than fishing boats anchored in the port.

and Nîmes are strongholds of European cultural history with their unique examples of Roman architecture.

The Languedoc-Roussillon region begins west of the Rhône delta and stretches to the Spanish border with a mix of long beaches and mountainous hinterland. The Languedoc is home to the troubadours, and the Roussillon was part of Spain until the 1659 Treaty of the Pyrenees. The Catalán legacy in this region can still be seen at every turn. Even traditional bullfights are still held here. The Languedoc was also home to the Cathars, who broke away from the Catholic Church in the 13th century.

Between Narbonne and Carcassone in the hills of Corbières, where an invitation to taste wine should never be refused, are numerous ruins of the proud castles that once stood here. With its fortress complexes, Carcassonne takes you back in time to the Middle Ages. South of Narbonne, near Leucate, marks the start of long, brilliantly white sandy beaches stretching to the Franco-Spanish border and the eastern foothills of the Pyrenees.

The last of the French villages before reaching Spain are self-assured fishing villages virtually embedded into the mountains. The Costa Brava, as this coastline is called, owes its name to the steep seaside cliffs at the eastern end of the Pyrenees. Bravo also means 'brave' or 'outstanding' in Spanish, so travellers should expect much more than just a wild coast. The

further south you go, the bigger the beaches become and the more towns and villages appear. The Catalán capital, Barcelona, is Spain's second-largest city. Carthaginians, Romans, Visigoths and Moors have all left their legacy here,

making the city into a European metropolis with a special Catalán charm. The numerous art-nouveau buildings by Gaudí and Domènech i Montaner are quite spectacular. Life pulses day and night on the Ramblas, Barcelona's pedestrian zone.

The Old Town of Carcassonne enclosed by a double wall.

1

Along the north-western Mediterranean coast – our dream route from Menton to Barcelona takes you on forays into the hinterland of Provence, leads you along impressive rocky coasts, white beaches, the Rhône delta and the foothills of the Pyrenees, and passes through famous seaside resorts on a journey that includes 2,000-year-old towns in a region with unmatched cultural history.

① Menton Rich Englishmen discovered the pleasant climate of the Côte d'Azur quite late – around 1870. But they didn't waste any time. Villas and magnificent hotels from this Belle Époque recall the glory days of their 'winter residences' between the Alps and the sea.

The most beautiful view over Menton and the bay here can be seen from the cemetery above the city. Its attractions include the baroque Church of St-Michel, the Register Office in the town hall with frescoes by Jean Cocteau, and the Musée Cocteau in a 17th-century fort. Just a few kilometers beyond Menton is the Principality of Monaco, where a steep street heads into the mountainous interior towards Èze.

② Èze This tiny village sits on the top of a 427-m-high (1,401-ft) rock formation overlooking the Mediterranean Sea as if from a throne. It is one of Provence's most beautiful medieval fortified villages, the

so-called 'villages perchés'. A thick stone wall surrounds the houses, which are clustered around a castle donjon high in the mountains. An exotic garden was created around the former fort, and the view from here reaches as far as Corsica on a clear day. Following the N7 towards Nice, the route heads back along the sea to Villefranche-sur-Mer.

③ Cap Ferrat In the shadows of mighty pines and hidden behind high walls, the magnificent villas of millionaires cling to the coastline of Cap Ferrat, which drops steeply into the sea. The Fondation Ephrussi de Rothschild, probably the most beautiful villa on the Cap Ferrat peninsula, is even open to the public. The stately building, in gorgeous gardens, displays the furnishings bequeathed by Baroness Rothschild.

④ Nice The 'unofficial' capital of the Côte d'Azur is a city of contrasts – the grand boule-

2

Travel Information

Route profile
Length: approx. 1,300 km (808 miles), excluding detours
Time required: 2–3 weeks
Start: Menton, France
End: Barcelona, Spain
Route (main locations): Menton, Monaco, Nice, Toulon, Marseille, Aix-en-Provence, Arles, Avignon, Orange, Nîmes, Camargue, Narbonne, Carcassonne, Perpignan, Barcelona

---

Traffic information:
Drive on the right in both countries. The speed limit for urban areas is 60 km/h (37 mph), 90 km/h (56 mph) on rural roads, and 130 km/h (80 mph) on highways (120 km/h/75 mph in Spain). In rainy conditions, the speed

limit for rural roads is 80 km/h (50 mph) and 100 km/h (62 mph) for highways. The 'right before left' rule almost always applies in built-up areas in both France and Spain!

When to go:
Spring and autumn are the best seasons for the Mediterranean coast. Summer is often very hot, while winter can be quite cold, rainy and even snowy, particularly higher up.

Information:
France
General: *www.france.com*
Provence: *www.beyond.fr*
Spain
General: *www.spain.info*
Costa Brava:
www.costabrava.org

3

4

gorges, wild rivers and secluded bays.

7 Fréjus The Roman legacy of this settlement, founded by Julius Caesar in 46 BC, is still clearly visible in the cityscape. Parts of the Roman city wall, the aqueduct and, most importantly, the amphitheater have all been very well-preserved. The area around the Cathédrale St-Léone is also worth seeing.

The fortified church and the monastery were founded in the 12th century, and the older baptistry dates back as far as the 5th century.

8 St-Tropez Between Fréjus and Hyères, thick pine, oak and chestnut forests line the coast, and the hills drop away steeply into the sea, leaving no room for townships of any size on the Corniche des Maures. The coastal road is nothing less than spectacular here, and although it winds partly into the hills it continually provides stunning views of the sea. Small villages that were once dedicated to fishing are nestled tidily into the small bays, many of them retaining most of their original charm.

St-Tropez is no exception. In this town – which first became famous after the film *And God Created Woman* (1956) with

vards try to rekindle the memories of the Belle Époque while parts of the Old Town are still like an Italian village. The Greeks founded Nikaia here, the 'Victorious City', in the 5th century BC, but the Romans preferred the hills further up for their township of Cemenelum, today Cimiez.

The most powerful icon of Nice is the Promenade des Anglais, which is directly on the sea. Wealthy British made Nice their retirement home in the mid 19th century and the most impressive mansions from that era are the famous Hotel Négresco and the Palais Masséna.

The main square in the Old Town, with its maze of small alleyways and Italian-style hou-

ses, is the Cour Saleya, with a remarkable flower and vegetable market. The castle hill provides a great view over the Old Town and the sea.

The city's most interesting museums are the Musée d'Art Contemporain, the Musée Chagall and the Musée Matisse in Cimiez, which displays works by the artist, who moved to Nice in 1916. Some of the most impressive Roman ruins in Nice make up the 67-m-long (220-ft), 56-m-wide (184-ft) arena, which used to hold some 5,000 Romans. The city's most exotic landmark is the Cathédrale Orthodoxe Russe St-Nicolas (1912).

After passing the airport, the route now leaves the coastal road for a trip into Provence's

hilly interior. For art lovers, it is worth taking the 10-km (6-mi) detour into St-Paul-de-Vence, a medieval town where the Fondation Maeght displays modern artwork. From the coast, the D2085 heads to Grasse, a perfume manufacturing center.

5 Grasse Perfume brought this town its early prosperity, traces of which can still be seen in the medieval alleys and streets of the Old Town. The International Perfume Museum will tell you everything you wanted to know about the manufacture of these valuable essences, and the large factories hold daily tours.

From Grasse, the N85 heads back to the sea towards Cannes, one of the swankier places on the already swanky Côte d'Azur.

6 Cannes This city is of course known for its annual film festival, where the world's rich and famous gather on the Boulevarde la Croisette. Cap d'Antibes, with the holiday resorts of Juan-les-Pins and Antibes, is just 11 km (7 miles) from here. The N98 heads from Cannes to Fréjus along the Corniche d'Esterel, which is undoubtedly one of the highlights of the journey with its marvellous red rocks, rugged cliffs, many

1 The marina in Menton on the eastern Côte d'Azur.

2 The famous Promenade des Anglais is 8 km (5 miles) long and separates the beach from the Old Town of Nice.

3 The château in Mandelieu-la-Napoule, a spa resort west of Cannes, dates back to the 14th century.

4 The view of the Old Town in Cannes on the slope of Mont Chevalier.

Brigitte Bardot – it's all about seeing and being seen. The image of the extravagant life in the film captivated the youth of the world and ultimately drew mass tourism to the sleepy coastal town.

9 **Hyères** This small town east of Toulon is the oldest seaside resort on the coast. The medieval Vieille Ville, with its Place Massillon, is delightful. The old castle ruins provide an amazing panoramic view of the coast. Offshore from Hyères are the Iles d'Hyères, a group of islands that President Pompidou ordered the French state to make into a nature preserve in 1971. A visit to Porquerolles allows you to imagine how the entire Côte d'Azur must have looked before tourism began.

10 **Toulon** The capital of the Département Var owes its importance to the large natural port here, which continues to be an important marine base. Architect Vauban built Toulon into a war port in the 17th century under King Louis XIV.

11 **Route de Crêtes** La Ciotat is the starting point for a trip over the Route des Crêtes to Cassis. The 'Mountain Ridge Road' leads over the steep slopes of the Montagne de la Canaille and provides magnificent views of both the sea and the country.
The small port town of Cassis has been able to retain much of its early charm, particularly in the old alleys directly behind the port. The shops and businesses give an insight into the original Midi way of life. West of Cassis, white limestone walls rise straight out of the crystal blue waters. You can take an adventurous boat ride to the cliffs from Cassis. If you take the rural road N 559 direct towards Marseille and turn left, you'll

see narrow access roads leading to three bays that are worth seeing – Port Miou, Port Pin and En-Vau.
To drive into the heart of Provence, take the highway or the N559 to Aubagne and then the N96 to Aix-en-Provence.

12 **Marseille** The second-largest city in France and the country's most important port town boasts a long history of 2,500 years. Its significance as an important gateway to North Africa is reflected in its multi-cultural population.
Marseille was originally founded as Massalia by Greeks from Asia Minor who built the city on the hill where Notre Dame de la Garde now stands. It then came under the yoke of the Romans, with Caesar eventually

conquering the Greek republic in 49 BC. The port city experienced its first big boom in the 12th century when legions of crusaders embarked from here on their journeys to Jerusalem and the Holy Land. For the next few centuries, Marseille was the most important port in the entire Mediterranean.
The heart of Marseille continues to beat in the old port quarter. It marks the beginning of the city's main road, the Canebière, which connects the port with the rest of the city and was once the icon of a lively town. The entrance to the old port is flanked on the north side by the Fort St-Jean and on the south side by the Fort St-Nicolas. Other attractions include the Basilique St-Victor, a 5th-century church with early-

Christian sarcophagi and sculptural fragments in its crypt; Basilique de Notre Dame de la Garde (19th century), a neo-Byzantine church with a gold-plated figure of Mary on the bell tower and mosaics inside and the Chateau d'If (1516–28) on the rock in front of the port, accessed from the Quai des Belges. The citadel was the state jail from 1580. Museums include Vieille Charité, Musée des Docks Romains, Musée du Vieux Marseille, and Musée Grobet-Labadié with relics of the 19th century.

13 **Aix-en-Provence** The Romans originally founded the colony of Aquae Sextiae Saluvorium on the former Celtic-Ligurian township of Entremont in 122 BC – what is now

Aix-en-Provence. This spa and university town eventually became the capital of Provence at the end of the 12th century and remained so for hundreds of years. It also developed into a city of artists and academics.

The Old Town is tucked between the Cours Mirabeau, an avenue of sycamores with a gorgeous 18th-century city palace, and the Cathedral of St-Sauveur with a baptistry from the Merovingian era.

Other attractions include the town hall (17th-century), the Musée des Tapisseries and the Atelier de Paul Cézanne. A popular source of inspiration of the city's most famous son was the Mont St-Victoire in the eastern section of the town, which is also worth a detour to see for yourself.

The shortest connection to Arles heads along the A8 and A7 to Salon-de-Provence and from there crosses the eastern part of the Rhône delta.

⑭ Arles The gateway to the Camargue was an area settled by the Celts, the Greeks and the Romans. Emperor Constantine had a splendid residence here, where he once summoned a council in AD 314.

Today, Arles is still home to impressive and important buildings from Roman times – the amphitheater, a grandiose oval structure about 137 m (446 ft) by 107 m (351 ft) wide with a capacity of 20,000; and the theater, which could fit an impressive 12,000 people into its semicircle. The tidy Romanesque Church of St-Trophime is a masterpiece of Provencal stonemasonry, with a portal that dates back to 1190. The Romanesque-Gothic cloister adjacent to the church is considered the most beautiful in all of Provence.

From Arles, a rural road heads north-east to one of Provence's best-known villages, Les Baux.

⑮ Les Baux-de-Provence This stone village is perched on a 900-m-long (2,953-ft) by 200-m-wide (656-ft) rocky ridge that rises dramatically out of the modest Alpilles range. In the Middle Ages, troubadours performed their courtly love songs in the once proud fort of Les Baux. The fort's unique location on a rock combined with the gorgeous view over the expanses of the Camargue and the Rhône delta draw countless visitors to this car-free town every year.

From Les Baux, the road crosses the Alpilles to St-Rémy, a 24-km-long (15-mile) mountain range between Rhône and Durance.

⑯ St-Rémy-de-Provence Nostradamus was born in this quintessential Provencal town in 1503, and van Gogh painted his picture of the cornfield and cypresses here in 1889. St-Rémy's predecessor was the old city of Glanum, about 1 km (0.6 miles) south of the present-day center. An 18-m-high (59-ft) mausoleum dates back to this time and the Arc Municipal traces back to the time of Emperor Augustus.

⑰ Avignon This former papal city dominates the left bank of the Rhône and is still surrounded by a 4.5-km-long (3-mile) city wall. The Rocher des Doms and the enormous Palais des Papes (Papal Palace) are an impressive sight even from a distance.

Seven French popes resided here between 1309 and 1377, the time of the Papal Schism. The last 'antipope' did not flee his palace until 1403. The

1 Les Arènes, a former Roman amphitheater in Arles.

2 The view of St-Tropez from the walls of the citadel.

3 The centerpiece of Marseille is the Vieux Port (old port), which is protected by two mighty forts.

4 View from the far side of the Rhône across to Avignon, capital of the Département of Vaucluse.

mighty fort-like Palais des Papes was built during this century-long schism, but next to nothing remains of the once ostentatious interior decor. The famous bridge, Pont St-Bénézet (also known as Pont d'Avignon), was built in 1177, and four of its original twenty-two arches still stand today. From Aix, the journey heads north to two more of Europe's most beautiful Roman constructions.

Near Sorgues, the D17 turns off towards Châteauneuf-du-Pape. The popes of Avignon built yet another castle here in the 14th century. Today, the wine from this region is one of the best in the Côtes du Rhône region. If you have enough time, you should make a detour into the Luberon or Villeneuve-les-Avignon on the way to Orange.

18 Orange Emperor Augustus founded this location as Arausio in 35 BC. The theater was built soon after, and today it is one of the most beautiful Roman works in Provence. The large stage wall is 103 m (338 ft) wide and 38 m (125 ft) high.

On the north side of the city is the third-largest triumphal arch of its kind, with a height of 22 m (72 ft), a width of 21 m (69 ft) and a thickness of 8 m (26 ft). Driving south-west along the A9 you reach the Pont du Gard, a famous Roman aqueduct.

19 Nîmes This city of temples, public baths and theaters was founded in AD 16, also by Emperor Augustus. The Romans' most impressive building is the amphitheater, with an oval arena and tiered stone benches that seated 25,000 guests. The Maison Carrée, from the second and third centuries AD, is one of Europe's best-preserved Roman temples, with columns and decorative friezes. Many public baths, temples and a theater (today a

1

2

park) are concentrated around the Jardin de la Fontaine. About 20 km (12 miles) northeast of Nîmes is the Pont du Gard. From Nîmes, the route heads along the north-western edge of the Camargue to Aigues-Mortes.

20 Aigues-Mortes This town impresses visitors with the mighty walls of its fort, which are still completely intact. Aigues-Mortes, or 'Place of Dead Water', was constructed by Louis XI in the 13th century to consolidate his power on the Mediterranean coast. One part of the city wall can still be accessed. The Tour de Constance provides the best view over the city and the Camargue.

21 Saintes-Maries-de-la-Mer A 30-km-long (19-mile) road heads through the Camargue to the département capital, Les

Saintes-Maries-de-la-Mer, well-known for the gypsy pilgrimage held every year in May. The Roman church here looks like a medieval castle with its battlements and crenellated platform.

22 Montpellier The capital of the Département Hérault is home to France's oldest Botanic Garden, among other things. The focal point of the city is the Place de la Comédie, with a 19th-century opera house. Its most important attractions include the 17th-century patrician houses.

23 Béziers The route now heads through Montepellier to this lovely city on the Canal du Midi. The town's most recognizable landmark is the massive Cathédrale St-Nazaire (14th century), which is perched like a mighty fort on a mountain above the city.

24 Narbonne This town was once the most significant Roman port in the area. The Horreum, an underground granary built in the first century BC, is visible evidence of this time.

The Cathédrale St-Just, with its beautiful sculptures and vivid stained-glass windows, dates back to the 13th century. The Palais des Archevêques is a fort-like complex with massive towers (14th century). Some 60 km (37 miles) west of Narbonne is Carcassonne, a prime example of medieval fortress architecture.

1 Along with the Cathédrale St-Nazaire, the historic fort town of Carcassonne has been listed as a UNESCO World Heritage Site.

2 Some of France's best wines are grown in the mountainous hinterland of the Languedoc.

Barcelona

The capital of Catalonia, with its striking monuments, exciting nightlife and beautiful walks along the port and the sea, combines cosmopolitan flair with independent local tradition. Of course, it is also the city where Antoní Gaudí erected his largest and most compelling architectural feats.

Madrid's eternal competitor has a history that spans more than 2,000 years. Founded by the Romans, it was later conquered in 236 BC by the Carthaginian Hamilka Barcas, who named it Barcino. Control over this Mediterranean city changed hands between the Visigoths in 415, the Arabs in 713 and the Franks in 803.

When the kingdoms of Catalonia and Aragon were united (1137), it rose to become an important Spanish port and trading city. It unsuccessfully tried to become independent from Spain in the 17th century, and during the Spanish Civil War in the 20th century, Barcelona sided with the Republicans – against the eventual victor, Franco. Towards the end of the 19th century, a completely new style of art and architecture developed in Barcelona, especially in the Eixample quarter – The Catalán version of art nouveau, which has shaped the city's contemporary image was largely influenced by Antoní Gaudí.

Particularly worth seeing are the Barri Gòtic, the oldest, elevated part of the city; the medieval square; fabulous places and palaces; Las Ramblas, Catalonia's most famous pedestrian and shopping strip; the nostalgic market hall of La Boqueria (the 'gorge'); Museu Nacional d'Art de Catalunya, whose collection of Romanesque frescoes is internationally reputed; Museu Picasso and the Museu Maritim, a maritime museum in old shipbuilding halls as well as Antoní Gaudí's Palau Güell and Casa Milà; both are UNESCO world Heritage Sites.

La Sagrada Familia by Gaudí.

169

25 Carcassonne This city on the steep bank of the Aude is visible from quite a distance. Its double walls with distinctive merlons and towers date back to King Louis IX, who began construction in the 13th century. Porte Narbonnaise takes you to the Old Town, where the most important buildings are the Château Comtal and the Basilique St-Nazaire, home to France's most beautiful stained-glass windows. The castle, a mighty fort inside a fort, was constructed in the 12th century and has five defense towers.

The next part of the journey heads towards Perpignan along the D118 as far as Quillan, and it's worth making a detour on the D117 to the Château de Peyrepertuse, probably the most impressive Cathar castle ruins in the Corbières hills.

26 Perpignan The capital of Roussillon had its heyday under the kings of Mallorca in the 13th and 14th centuries. The fortified Palais des Rois de Majorque, picturesquely built around an arcaded courtyard, is evidence of this time. The two-storey chapel, a Gothic masterpiece with Moorish elements, is also a real dazzler. The Cathédrale de St-Jean was begun in 1324 and completed in 1509 and the houses on the palm-lined River Têt promenade are painted in vivid hues. Catalán influence is particularly noticeable in summer in Perpignan.

The Place de la Loge becomes a stage for Sardana, a Catalán dance in which both young and old participate. You'll also find the most beautiful building in the city here, the Loge de Mer, built in 1397.

At the point where the Pyrenees meet the Mediterranean, the coastal road snakes along the red (vermillion) rocks of the Côte Vermeille, where ancient fishing villages are tucked into picturesque bays. The most significant of these old towns are Argelès-Plages, Cerbère and Banyuls on the French side and Portbou on the Spanish side.

27 Cadaqués One of the most beautiful fishing villages on the Costa Brava, which stretches

1

from Empordà to Blanes, is hidden behind the Coll de Perafita and can only be reached on a

Béziers This city, dominated by the Cathédrale St-Nazaire (14th century), has an interesting regional museum.

Pont du Gard The 49-m-high (161-ft) bridge was built by the Romans over 2,000 years ago and also served as a water channel. It supplied the citizens of Nîmes with cool mountain water.

Arles This city, located at the gateway to the Camargue, was Vincent van Gogh's temporary place of residence and has many Roman buildings. The amphitheater has a capacity for 20,000 people.

Carcassonne This city is encircled by two protective walls dating back to the 13th century. It is also home to the 12th-century Château Comtal Castle.

Nîmes The most impressive buildings in this city, which was founded in the 16th century, are the amphitheater with a former seating capacity of 25,000, and the Maison Carrée, one of Europe's best-preserved Roman temples. Other sites include the Romanesque Cathédrale Notre Dame et St-Castor and the 18th-century Jardin de la Fontaine.

Tossa de Mar This former Roman city is located in one of the most beautiful areas on the Costa Brava. Below the town is a lovely bay and beach.

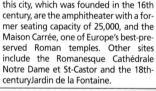

Cadaqués This fishing village on the Costa Brava captivates visitors with its white houses and a mighty baroque church.

Barcelona Catalonia's proud capital has a Gothic old town as well as numerous quarters in the characteristic Modernism style – art nouveau. Here we see the Museu Nacional d'Art de Catalunya (1929).

Avignon A mile-long wall encircles this city on the Rhône River – the city of the Papal Schism (13th–14th centuries). Behind it tower the Rocher des Doms and the enormous Palais des Papes.

Camargue Black bulls, semi-wild white horses, huge mountains of salt and flocks of flamingos and other unique birds are typical of the vast Rhône delta.

Map labels:
FRANCE
Castres, Toulouse, Carcassonne 25, Limoux, Quillan, Couiza, Château de Peyrepertuse, St-Paul-de-Fenouillet, Bourg-Madame, Pic du Canigou 2784, Port-Vendres, Lézignan-Corbières, Coursan, Narbonne 24, Leucate-Plage, Salses-le-Château, Perpignan 26, Pézenas, Béziers 23, Agde, Cap d'Agde, Sète, Frontignan, Montpellier 22, La Grande-Motte, Aigues-Mortes, Saintes-M-de-la-M, Nîmes 19, Clermont-Ferrand, Alès, Abbaye de Fontfroide

SPAIN
Ripoll, Figueres, Sant Pere de Rodes, Cap de Creus, Cadaqués 27, l'Escala, Vic, Girona, Pals, Palafrugell, Palamós, Sant Feliu de Guíxols, Tossa de Mar, Lloret de Mar, Blanes, Malgrat de Mar, Mataró, BARCELONA, València, Lleida, Berga, Parc Natural de Montseny, Circuit de Catalunya, Monestir de Sant Cugat, Llagostera, Pyrénées

pean art from the 15th to 20th centuries.

North of Cadaqués, the cape of Creus is the last of the Pyrenees foothills and also the easternmost point of the Iberian Peninsula. The Parc Natural del Cap de Creus combines nature and sea and is a vast uninhabited region. The Greeks were some of the first to recognize the beauty of the Badia de Roses with its long beaches. From here it's worth making a detour to the Dalí museum in Figueres. Continuing south, you cross a plain where there is an amazing view of the eastern Pyrenees rising high.

28 Costa Brava Pals, the most beautiful village on the entire Costa Brava, is located just north and inland of Palafrugell. It enchants visitors with its quaint back alleys. Back on the coast is one holiday resort after another. Around Palamós are some isolated bays and beaches, but Platja d'Aro is lined with high-rise hotels. The medieval old town of Tossa de Mar is a great place for a stroll while the famous Botanical Gardens of Mar i Murtra rise high above the town of Blanes.

29 Barcelona (see p. 169). Our journey ends here, in Spain's second-largest city.

Barcelona (see p. 169).

1 Cadaqués on the Costa Brava. Dalí spent many years of his life in the Port Llegat area.

narrow side road by car. Cadaqués is home to tidy white houses and a stunning 16th-century baroque church. The Museu Perrot Moore has an astonishing collection of Euro-

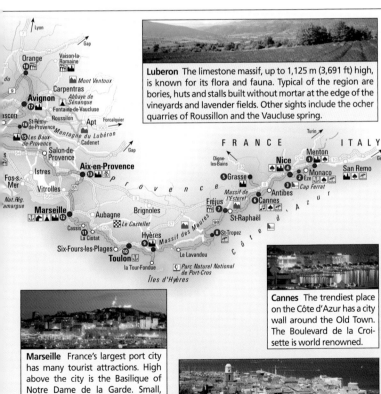

Marseille France's largest port city has many tourist attractions. High above the city is the Basilique of Notre Dame de la Garde. Small, stepped streets, idyllic squares and the lively port and fish market lend the city its charm. The Château d'If is located on an island offshore from the city and offers great views.

Luberon The limestone massif, up to 1,125 m (3,691 ft) high, is known for its flora and fauna. Typical of the region are bories, huts and stalls built without mortar at the edge of the vineyards and lavender fields. Other sights include the ocher quarries of Roussillon and the Vaucluse spring.

Cannes The trendiest place on the Côte d'Azur has a city wall around the Old Town. The Boulevard de la Croisette is world renowned.

St-Tropez This fishing village, located on a little peninsula, has been a popular Côte d'Azur seaside resort since the 1950s. The former citadel dates back to the 16th/17th centuries.

Menton Grand villas and hotels in Belle Époque style define the 'winter residence' once so prized by the English. Its attractions are the baroque Church of St-Michel, the Register Office in the town hall with frescoes by Jean Cocteau, and the Musée Cocteau in a 17th-century fort.

Monaco The principality is a mix of high-rise and grand buildings including the famous casino, the cathedral and the Grimaldi palace. 'Monte Carlo' is actually a rock formation that juts out into the Mediterranean on a headland below a rock.

Antibes Pablo Picasso used the 12th-century Château Grimaldi as his studio in 1946. Many of his works can be seen here.

Nice The Promenade des Anglais, the Hotel Négresco and the Palais Masséna are symbols of the 'unofficial' capital of the Côte d'Azur. Also worth seeing are the maze-like old town, the flower and vegetable market, the Musée d'Art Contemporain and the Musée Chagall.

Esterel Red rock, steep cliffs and gorges, and very remote bays distinguish this coastal area between Cannes and St-Raphaël: a secluded location on the southern French coast.

Spain

A picturesque village crowned with a pilgrimage church along the Camino de Santiago in Galicia.

Camino de Santiago and Costa Verde – a journey through verdant Spain

Since the Middle Ages, pilgrims from all over the world have been drawn to the shrine of the apostle St James in Santiago de Compostela. Picturesque villages and towns, monasteries and castles, and the mighty cathedrals of Burgos and León line the 'Camino', which stretches from the Pyrenees on the border with France to Galicia in the north-western corner of Spain. The return journey skirts the rugged northern Spanish coast.

Legend has it that the apostle St James was beheaded in Palestine in the year AD 44 and his remains were sent by boat to the extreme north-west of Spain, where he had previously taught the gospel. It was not until much later, after the apostle's grave was discovered in the early 9th century, that the first St James' Basilica was built. Subsequently, in 950, Gotescal-

co, the Bishop of Le Puy, became one of the first to make the pilgrimage to Compostela with a large entourage. Cesareo, the Abbot of Montserrat, followed suit in 959. The stream of pilgrims grew so much that in 1072 Alfonso VI suspended the toll for the Galician Trail. Just one century later, Aymeric Picaud, a priest from Poitou, wrote the first guidebook for

the pilgrimage to Compostela, which was published throughout all Europe's monasteries as *Codex Calixtinus*.
Paris, Vezelay, Le Puy and Arles became the main meeting

Running with the bulls in the arena of Pamplona, Navarre.

points from which the groups of pious travellers would continue on their way. Before starting their journey, the pilgrims and their equipment – a hat and coat to protect against the weather, a gourd for water and a staff for defence – were ceremoniously blessed. The seashells that the first pilgrims brought back from Galicia quickly became the symbol for future pilgrims. Those who arrived in Santiago and could prove the pilgrimage by showing their pilgrim book to the cathedral's secretary received the 'compostela', an official pilgrim certificate. To this day, every pilgrim who travels along the Camino de Santiago for at least 100 km (62 miles) either

The Cuevas del Marbei Llanes beach lies on the Costa Verde at the foot of the Sierra de Cuera. To the north of Spain , between Cantabria and Galicia , lies this beautiful coast, also known as the Asturias coastline.

Every pilgrim's goal – the Cathedral of Santiago de Compostela. According to legend, the remains of the apostle St James were brought to Galicia from Jerusalem and were later found in the city on this site.

by walking or riding a bicycle or a horse also receives such a certificate.

Picaud described the meeting points in France: the two trails over the Pyrenees and the main trail from the Puente la Reina. Pilgrims coming from Paris, Vezelay and Le Puy would go over the Puerto de Ibaneta (1,057 m/3,468 ft), and those coming from Arles would go over the Puerto de Somport (1,650 m/5,414 ft). In his trail guide, Picaud even describes the townships, hospitals and accommodation options along the way in great detail – the classic pilgrim trail still follows these today.

Nowadays, the thousand-year-old trail is signposted with blue signs depicting hikers or yellow St James shells. You can also experience the beauty along the way as an 'independent pilgrim', perhaps learning even more about the country, the people, the art and the culture of this stunning area. The rugged mountains stretch from the western Pyrenees to the Cantabrian Mountains, over the plateaus of the northern Meseta, mostly moorland, to the semi-desert area of the Navarran Bardenas Reales. While the pilgrims' destination is Santiago, you have the option of heading back along the northern Spanish coast, which partly corresponds to the Aragonian pilgrim route, and experiencing the charming interplay of mountains and sea on the rugged, craggy Atlantic coast between Galicia and the Basque country (País Vasco).

On the way to the Basque country, the tour passes through the historic province of Asturias, with its mountain pastures, and Cantabria, with its impressive Atlantic coniferous forests. The mountains then go east into the Pyrenees. Both routes also offer a multitude of art and culture, with historical relics dating back 1,500 years. From the treasures hidden in the tiniest of village churches to the lavishly filled chambers of major cathedrals, St James' Way will not disappoint.

Chaparral scenery along the Camino de Santiago, from the Pyrenees to Galicia.

The Camino de Santiago and the northern Spanish coast are home to several pilgrim trails that lead from the Pyrenees to the shrine of St James in Galicia. This particular route starts in Roncesvalles and heads through Burgos and León to Santiago de Compostela. The return trip along the Atlantic coast unleashes the beauty of the Galician, Asturian, Cantabrian and Basque coastline.

1 Roncesvalles In the year AD 778, this small village below the Ibañeta Pass decided the fate of one Marquis Roland, who in the wake of Charles the Great had tried to expel the Moors from Zaragoza. When the armies retreated, Roland led the rearguard but got caught in an ambush and was killed. The heroic sagas surrounding his death became the 'Song of Roland' in 1080.

The historic Augustine Hostel in Roncesvalles is one of the oldest along the pilgrimage route and the collegiate church dates back to 1127. The Gothic Church of Santa Maria was built in the 13th century and is home to the Madonna of Roncevalles, a silver-plated statue with a core of cedar wood.

2 Pamplona The city of the San Fermines, with the famous 'Running of the Bulls', was founded by the Roman General Pompeius in 75 BC. The Moors ruled here in the 8th century, but starting in 905 it became the capital of the Kingdom of Navarra, which transformed into the Castillian Empire in 1512. Today, the Plaza del Castillo, with its rows of houses from the 18th and 19th centuries, is the lively center of the city. The facade of the town hall at the Plaza Consistorial is really quite impressive with its interesting Doric, Ionic and Corinthian features. Opposite the plaza is the Church of San Saturnino, once a military church, and next door is the hostel for pilgrims travelling the Camino de Santiago.

The symbol of Pamplona is, however, the Santa Maria Cathedral, with its 50-m-high (164-ft) towers. Behind its classical facade is a French-style Gothic interior. The dominating feature of the cathedral is the Virgen del Sagrario, who looks over the main altar. In the Middle Ages, the kings of Navarra were crowned here under the Romanesque statue of Mary. Make sure not to miss the Gothic cloister, built in 1472, with its numerous tomb slabs.

3 Puente la Reina This town's name traces its origins to the Puente Regina, the five-arched pedestrian bridge built in the 11th century that was a donation from Doña Mayor, the wife of the Navarran King Sancho el Mayor. The Romanesque pilgrim bridge over the Río Arga is the most beautiful on the entire pilgrimage route.

Right at the entrance to the town, next to the old pilgrim hospital, is the Iglesia del Crucifijo, built in the 12th century by the Knights Templar and housing a crucifix from the 14th century. This parish church has a Romanesque facade with a baroque interior and contains the interesting little carving Santiago Beltza, the 'Black James'.

4 Estella In its heyday, this old royal residence included no less than twenty churches, monasteries and chapels, the most beautiful of which is San Pedro de la Rúa (12th century). Its three Gothic naves each have Roman-esque arches, and

Travel Information

Route profile
Length: approx. 1,800 km (1,119 miles), excluding detours
Time required: at least 2 weeks
Start: Roncesvalles
End: San Sebastián
Route (main locations):
The main Camino de Santiago including Roncesvalles, Pamplona, Logroño, Burgos, León, Astorga, Ponferrada, Santiago de Compostela, then back through La Coruña, Gijón, Santander, Bilbao, San Sebastián.

Traffic information: Drive on the right in Spain. The speed limit in urban areas is 50 km/h (31 mph), 90 km/h (56 miles) on rural roads, 100–120 km/h (62–75 mph) on expressways and 120 km/h (75 mph) on freeways. Important: you must carry two warning triangles and a set of spare bulbs for the vehicle lights in the car at all times.

Accommodation:
The pilgrim hostels along the Camino de Santiago are reserved for hiking pilgrims with an official pilgrim book. Pilgrims are only accepted on bicycles if they have vacancies. Drivers are not normally accepted. You may only stay once in each hostel, except in Santiago itself, where three nights are allowed.

Information
www.aragonguide.com
www.euskadi.net (Basque)
www.galiciaguide.com
www.turismodecantabria.com
www.visitasturias.co.uk
St James' Way:
www.caminodesantiago.me.uk

baroque altar is a wonderful image of Mary. However, the most beautiful feature is the magnificently decorated late 15th-century choir stalls.

⑦ Santo Domingo de la Calzada The main attraction of the local cathedral is an ornate chicken coop where a white hen and a white rooster have been kept for centuries. According to legend, the two birds are said to have saved the life of an innocent boy who was condemned to the gallows.

The church itself was founded by St Domingo, who rendered outstanding services to the pilgrims along the Camino de Compostela in the 11th century. An impressively high altar dating back to 1540 fills the Romanesque choir of the church.

⑧ Burgos Over the centuries, this city was one of the most important stops on the Camino de Santiago. At the end of the 15th century it had no less than thirty-two hostels for those making their way to or from Galicia. Its importance was also due to the cathedral, the construction of which began in 1221 under the auspices of Bishop Mauricio. Work continued on this, the third-largest cathedral in Spain, for more than three centuries – 108 m (354 ft) long and 61 m (200 ft) wide with a central arch measuring 20 m (66 ft) in height. Its Gothic towers, completed in the 15th century, soar to 80 m (262 ft) while its main, lavishly decorated facade displays eight statues of kings. All four entrances are sculptural masterpieces and the interior is similarly awe-inspiring.

Art lovers will be blown away by the nineteen chapels, thirty-eight altars and numerous sculptures, reliefs and paintings. The chapels, in particular, house many centuries' worth of individual works of art. In the center of the opulent high altar stands the silver statue of Santa Maria la Mayor, patron saint of Burgos. A visit to the 13th-century cloister and the adjacent chapels is also not to be missed. The city's most famous son, El Cid (1043–99), who retook Valencia from the Moors in 1094 and was immortalized through the poem *El Cantar del mio Cid,* is buried in the cathedral.

Those who are short of time to see all the many interesting churches the city has to offer should at least visit the old Carthusian monastery of Cartuja de Santa María de Miraflores in the east of the city.

The Gothic minster, which was completed in 1499, contains a masterful Renaissance choir stall, a high altar decorated in gold, and the alabaster tomb of Juan II and Isabel of Portugal.

⑨ Frómista This tiny town is home to what is probably the most beautiful, stylistically sound Romanesque church on the entire Camino de Santiago. Begun in 1066, both the eight-cornered intersecting tower and the two round towers in the west look almost like defence fortifications. The eaves extending out over the walls were decorated with more than three hundred mythical creatures, animals, plants and designs.

1 The Puente la Reina over the Río Agra was built as a pedestrian bridge in the 11th century.

2 The Gothic cathedral of Burgos was inaugurated in 1221.

3 San Pedro de la Rua in Estella, an important stop on the Camino de Santiago.

4 The cloister in the Gothic cathedral of Pamplona.

the main arch was completed in the 17th century. The most precious pieces are the figure of Mary dating from the 12th century and one of Christ from the 14th century. The finely crafted column capitals in the ruins of the cloister are also interesting.

⑤ Logroño The most beautiful part of La Rioja's capital is its old city center around the Plaza del Mercado, where you will find the Cathedral of Santa Maria la Redonda. Its baroque towers are visible from quite a distance. The building dates back to the 15th century, and its most precious piece is an image of the crucifixion by Michelangelo.

⑥ Nájera This small town, which was the capital of La Rioja and Navarra until 1076, experienced its heyday under King Sancho el Mayor until 1035. The monastery of Santa María la Real also dates back to this time. The Knights Cloister in the monastery was built in the 16th century and the church of Santa Maria in the 15th century. At the center of the golden

Inside the sacred building is a 14th-century portrait of St Martin, and another of St James from the 16th century. The column capitals are also unique, ornately decorated with animal motifs and biblical scenes.

⑩ **León** The old royal city of León on the Río Bernesga was founded in the 1st century. It quickly became an important stop along the Camino de Santiago, and its grand churches were built accordingly. The best of these is the Gothic Cathedral of Santa María de la Regla, begun in the 13th century, with its two 65- and 68-m-high (213- and 223-ft) towers.

The lavishly decorated western facade is impressive with its rose window and three entrances adorned with exquisite relief work. The southern facade also has a large rose window and the ruins of Roman baths under glass casing.

The cathedral's main treasure, however, is its more than a hundred stained-glass windows covering an area of about 1,800 sq m (19,368 sq ft). The oldest of these dates back to the 13th century, with the most recent dating back to the 20th century, and all of them cover a variety of themes from mythical creatures to plant motifs.

Similarly significant is the royal collegiate church of San Isidoro, tracing back to the 11th century. It is an example of Spanish Romanesque architecture and has housed the relics of St Isidor of Seville since 1063.

Next to the church is the Panteón Real (Royal Pantheon), which can be visited as a museum and is the final resting place of no fewer than twenty-three kings and queens. The ceiling was painted with unique Romanesque frescoes as early as 1160, which gave the Pantheon its nickname, the 'Sistine Chapel of Spain's Romanesque Art.'

Go through the cloister to get to the actual museum with its countless artistic treasures. Catholic kings were responsible for the Monastery of San Marcos, which was founded at the start of the 16th century. Behind the monastery's ornate facade – considered one of the most impressive examples of the Spanish Renaissance style – is a hotel. If you are are interested in seeing the beautiful cloister of the old monastery you can go into the hotel hall and take the second door on the right.

⑪ **Astorga** This city's finest treasures can all be seen from the Avenida de las Murallas – the impressive city wall dating back to Roman times, the Episcopal Palace built by Antoni Gaudí, and the Santa María Cathedral.

Gaudí's palace, completed in 1913, was never actually used by the bishops and today serves as an interesting Camino de Santiago museum (Museo de los Caminos).

Construction on the late-Gothic Santa María Cathedral began in

1471 but wasn't completed until the 18th century. Its main altar dates back to the mid 16th century, as does the richly decorated choir stall.

⑫ **Ponferrada** The Knights Templar built this enormous castle with a surface area of 160 m by 90 m (525 ft by 295 ft) on the 'Pons Ferrata', an 11th-century iron bridge, to protect pilgrims travelling on the Camino de Santiago. The attractions of the old town include the Mozarabic Iglesia de Santo Tomás de las Ollas, with its horseshoe arches. It's worth taking a trip out of Ponferrada to the

ancient gold-mine of Las Médulas (see sidebar left).

⑬ **Cebreiro** This tiny village is home to the oldest little church on the Camino de Santiago. It was built in the 9th century and its well-fortified walls house a painting of the Madonna from the 12th century.

⑭ **Santiago de Compostela** In the Middle Ages, the tomb of St James was the most important Christian pilgrimage site outside of Rome and Jerusalem. In 1075, after the Moors were expelled, Bishop Diego Pelaez began building a cathe-

dral to reflect the importance of this pilgrimage destination, although it was not completed until the mid 18th century. In fact, the two solid exterior towers were only finished in 1750. The long construction time meant that simple Romanesque styles and opulent baroque touches existed side by side. This fusion also dominates the facade. The Pórtico de la Gloria, with its ornate sculpture work, is now within a late-baroque building placed in front of it, and the mix of styles continues inside as well. The impressive Romanesque design of the building is partially covered in the most lavish of baroque decor, and the entire structure is crowned with a golden high altar with a 13th-century silver-plated figure of St James in the center. Under the high altar is the mausoleum of the saint, whose remains rest in a silver shrine.

The cathedral museum includes the treasure chamber, the chapter house and the cloister from the 16th century. The city itself practically grew around the cathedral and is today similar to an historic open-air museum. Countless churches, particularly ones built in baroque style, await the eyes of connoisseurs, while picturesque old town alleys offer recreation of all kinds to both tourists and religious pilgrims.

In addition to the journey along the historic Camino de Santiago, it is worth heading further out to the Galician coast. The road then heads back along the shores of northern Spain to the Basque town of San Sebastián back near the French border.

⑮ Carnota The 7-km-long (4-mile) sandy beach on Spain's north-west coast is a surfer's paradise. The small village itself is home to the longest (over

1 The Cathedral at León illuminated at night.

2 A typical mountain landscape north of León.

3 The core of the Cathedral Santiago de Compostela is unchanged since the 11th century.

4 The Palace of Astorga was designed by Antoni Gaudí.

5 The Knights Templar built the Castle of Ponferrada between the 12th and 14th centuries to ensure the safety of pilgrims on the 'Camino'.

30 m/98 ft) and probably also the most beautiful granary in Galicia, built out of granite at the end of the 18th century. To protect the grain from mice, the granary stands on two rows of pillars, secured with a corbel.

16 Cabo Finisterre The *finis terrae*, the end of the world, is a peninsula that towers above the Costa da Morte. Even today, the Atlantic tides and the dangerous cliffs mean numerous ships are wrecked on this 'Coast of Death'. The westernmost point of continental Europe is further north at Cape Touriñana. Both places are hauntingly beautiful and were important cult sites for the Celts.

17 La Coruña The Romans built this, the second-largest city in Galicia, into an important port city. The Torre de Hércules on the western side of the peninsula dates back to those Roman times. Begun in AD 100, it is said to be the oldest lighthouse in the world. Today, the tower is 60 m (197 ft) tall and can be climbed in summer.
The Old Town of La Coruña grew out of the former pescaderia, the fishmongers' quarter. Apart from Romanesque and baroque churches, two museums are of particular interest – the Museum of Archaeological History in the San Antón Castle displays findings from Celtic and Roman times as well as

medieval sculptures; and the Fine Arts Museum at the Plaza de Zalaeta exhibits world-famous works from Rubens to Picasso.

18 Rías Altas Those following the coastal road between La Coruña and Ribadeo will see picturesque estuaries, small holiday and fishing towns, ancient farmhouses and even older granaries. Flat coastal plains are interspersed with steep coastal mountains and striking promontories and headlands. The interior is dominated by pine and eucalypt forests and the weather is dictated by the windy and wet Atlantic.

19 Ribadeo This is the easternmost town in Galicia. It is situated on the Ría, the Atlantic mouth of the Río Eo, which cuts deep into the interior like a Scandinavian fjord. Old manors surround the Plaza de España, and the Convento de Santa Clara dates back to the 14th century.

20 Luarca This port town on the Costa Verde is undoubtedly one of the most beautiful parts of the Asturias region. The fishing port is so tightly jammed in between the rock faces and the rows of houses that there is only a tiny bit of room for the fishing boats to come in and out. The fish mar-

Picos de Europa. The Desfiladero de la Hermida Gorge starts after Panes, with some nearly vertical rock faces that reach 600 m (1,969 ft) in height. Potes is the main town in the eastern Picos de Europa.

㉕ Santillana del Mar This small town, located slightly away from the sea, owes its existence to the remains of St Juliana. Monks built a monastery around her remains and its Romanesque collegiate church is the area's most important building even today. The town's main points of interest are, however, its picturesque alleys, the variety of lovingly tended flowerpots, and the old walls, romantically overgrown with ivy. Hidden about 2 km (1 mile) up from the village is the world-famous Altamira Cave.

㉖ Santander Cantabria's capital, jutting out on a long peninsula, is a port city, seaside resort and secret 'Capital of Promenades'. The city grew from a small fishing port into a relatively large trading port. In 1941, however, many of its buildings went up in flames. That's why walkers are again in demand in Santander, and their main destination should be the La Magdalena Peninsula. King Alfonso XIII chose the Palacio de la Magdalena, built in English style at the start of the 20th

ket quarter is especially picturesque, and you'll get the best view from the city hill of Atalaya.

㉑ Costa Verde The coast between Ribadeo and Santander showcases a series of spectacular, as well as very isolated, sandy bays and impressive cliffs that are only interrupted once by the long Rías. The town of Cudillero has a gorgeous fishing port, cosy pubs and, more importantly, a number of isolated and often empty beaches. Turning off from the coastal highway, there are plenty of peaceful spots for everyone to take break. It's worth taking a detour inland at Avilés to visit

Oviedo, the beautiful capital of Asturias.

㉒ Luanco North-west of the industrial city of Gijón, this beach town has its own oceanography museum. A vast beach sprawls from Banugues to the windy and exposed Cabo de Peñas. Swimming can be dangerous along some sections of this coast.

㉓ Ribadesella The Old Town at the mouth of the Río Sella and the long promenade around the fine sandy beach are what make this town so attractive. It also has a point of interest worth seeing – the cave of Tito Bustillo, which was

discovered in 1968. This dripstone cave contains Stone Age rock paintings that are around twenty thousand years old depicting red and black deer and horses. For preservation purposes, the number of visitors allowed in per day has had to be limited, similar to the caves in Altamira.

㉔ Cueva del Pindal Beneath the small farming village of Pimiango, the Pindal cave also contains prehistoric rock paintings. It is best to come in the early morning, as only 200 people are admitted each day.

In Unquera it's worth taking a detour away from the coastal road to head south into the

1 The view of the port of Castro Urdiales between Santander and Bilbao.

2 Cabo Finisterre above the vast Atlantic.

3 Closely-packed fishing boats at the port of La Coruña.

4 A view of the port in Ribadesella on the Costa Verde.

century, to be his summer residence.

Sprawling north-west of the peninsula are the beautiful beaches of Primera Playa and Segunda Playa. Following the coastal road further east you will eventually come to Castro Urdiales, an attractive port town dominated by a Knights Templar castle.

27 Bilbao Now an industrial town, Bilbao originally grew out of a fishing village started back in the 11th century. Steelworks were eventually established here in the second half of the 19th century, which brought considerable wealth to the city. Only the Old Town is really worth seeing, in particular its Siete Calles, the 'Seven Streets', between the cathedral and the river. The 14th-century cathedral was completely burnt down in 1571 so its current

form and its cloister date back to the 16th century. A more elegant life is reflected in the 19th-century neoclassical Plaza Nueva. North of the square you should visit the 15th-century church of San Nicolas. It has a gorgeous Gothic carved altar, as well as some interesting sculptures.

Always worth a visit is the Museum of Fine Arts with important works by El Greco, Goya and Gaugin. The gigantic Guggenheim Museum, designed by Frank O. Gehry, is an absolute must. It alone attracts over one million people a year to the city. Besides, the futuristic airport by Santiago Calatrava and the metro stations by Norman Foster are some of the most important additions.

28 Costa Vasca The 176-km-long (109-mile) Basque coast is defined by bays and estuaries

lined by numerous cliffs. The landscape of the hinterland is one of wooded hills. Travellers stumble across heavenly beaches near Algorta on the eastern coast of the Ría of Bilbao.

Far more interesting, however, is the chapel of San Juan de Gaztelugatxe, west of Cape Machichaco, perched on a protruding rock in the middle of wildly romantic, windswept cliffs. It is only accessible on foot up a uniquely beautiful set of steps formed out of the rock. The 11th-century sailors' chapel on the rock is also of interest. Whalers set off from Bermeo towards Iceland and Labrador. The Museo del Pescador in the 16th-century Ercilla military tower has all the answers on the topic of fish.

29 Guernica This city is evidence of one of the darkest chapters in Spanish-German

1

history. During the Spanish Civil War, an air raid by the German Condor Legion on 26 April 1937 destroyed virtually the entire city. Some two thousand people died in the inferno, but the world did not see it as a precursor to the disaster that was World War II. Only Pablo Picas-

---

Cabo Finisterre This cape is feared by sailors because of its cliffs, but it is a popular viewpoint for the mighty Atlantic.

La Coruña This Galician port city is home to the only Roman lighthouse left in the world. It also has astonishing rows of houses enclosed in glass to withstand the harsh elements.

Picos de Europa Homecoming sailors gave this massif its name, which appears to soar out of the sea. Part of the mountains form Europe's largest national park. The highest peak is the Torre Cerredo (2,648 m/8,688 ft).

Santiago de Compostela The capital of Galicia is one of the world's most important Christian pilgrim destinations. The entire old town and the cathedral are works of art built of stone.

Las Médulas The Romans made their slaves dig for gold here, creating a bizarre landscape left over from excavations.

Ponferrada The 11th-century Templar castle was built to protect the pilgrims. Worth seeing are the baroque town hall and the Iglesia de Santo Tomás de las Ollas.

Astorga This city's main attraction is the Episcopal Palace and the Santa María Cathedral built by Antoni Gaudí.

León Churches like the Santa María de la Regla show León's importance along St James' Way.

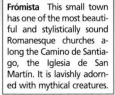

Frómista This small town has one of the most beautiful and stylistically sound Romanesque churches along the Camino de Santiago, the Iglesia de San Martín. It is lavishly adorned with mythical creatures.

Aristocracy from all over Europe would stay in the mansions from this era that still dominate the cityscape. The Monte Urgull and the Cas-tillo de la Mota tower above the Old Town, at the center of which is the Plaza de la Constitución. Bullfights used to be held in this square – the large number of balconies is evidence of this. The other attractions of the Basque city include the aquarium, the Museo de San Telmo in a 16th-century monastery, and the Palacio del Mar – and of course the best tapas in Spain. On the west side is an enormous bay with two popular beaches.

so captured the horror in his world-famous *Guernica* painting which had been commissioned by the Spanish Government for the World Fair of Paris in 1937. It now hangs in Madrid's Museo Nacional Centro de Arte Reina Sofía. Guernica is considered the 'holy city of the Basques' because the Basques held their regional meetings here in the Middle Ages. When the Basque region became part of Castile, the Spanish kings had to swear that they would forever respect the rights of the Basques. Everything worth knowing about the Basques can be found in the Museo Euskal Herria.

30 San Sebastián The journey across northern Spain ends in this beautiful seaside town from the Belle Époque, which was for a long time the summer resort of the Spanish kings.

1 The glittering façade of Gehry's Museo Guggenheim in Bilbao was covered in 60 tonnes (66 tons) of titanium. Its exterior shell is just 3 mm (0.1 in) thick.

Altamira When the cave was discovered, the images of hunting and animals on the walls were first thought to be fakes. A replica of the cave now means that everyone can experience artwork from the Old Stone Age.

Castro Urdiales This lively fishing town is a good starting point for visiting Cantabria's beaches and historical sites. It is home to a natural port with elegant riverside walks while above it all are the Gothic Iglesia de Santa Maria and a castle built by the Knights Templar.

Bilbao The old town of this industrial Basque city has mostly understated buildings. But the Museum of Fine Arts with major works by El Greco, Goya and Gaugin, as well as the glinting silver Guggenheim Museum (1997) by Frank O. Gehry, are definitely worth a look.

Burgos Construction started on Spain's third-largest cathedral in 1221 and took three centuries to complete. The Carthusian monastery is another attraction here.

Estella Many of its attractions lie on the other side of the Ega Bridge. The most beautiful church in Estella is the lavishly decorated San Pedro de la Rúa (12th century).

Puente la Reina This stone bridge was built in the 11th century as a donation from the wife of the king of Navarra.

Pamplona This city was made famous by Hemingway's novel *Fiesta*, in which he called this the 'Running of the Bulls'.

Palacio Real de Aranjuez, the king's summer residence south of Madrid.

Spain

Castile: On the road in Don Quixote country

Castile is not only the geographical center of Spain, but also its historical heartland and the birthplace of Castilian Spanish. Vast, ochre-colored plains, magnificent cities and monumental castles distinguish the region surrounding Madrid.

In modern-day Spain, the Castilian highlands contain two of the country's autonomous regions: Castilla y León in the northwest and Castilla-La Mancha in the south-east. This political division largely reflects the natural geography, with the Cordillera Central, or the Castilian Dividing Range, running straight through the two regions and separating them from each other.

On either side of the mountain range extends the Meseta Central, an expansive, slightly arid plateau where vegetation is sparse and only solitary pine and eucalyptus trees dot the landscape. Despite the relative aridity, however, the ground is fertile and supports the cultivation of grains, sunflowers, chickpeas (garbanzo beans) and wine grapes. In winter, the predominantly treeless landscape is more or less fully exposed to the strong winds and cooler temperatures, while in the summer the sun beats

Easter processions ("Semana Santa") in Zamora.

down mercilessly on the hot plains.

The large La Mancha plateau to the south-east of the meseta owes its name to the Moors, people of Arab and Berber (North African) descent who conquered much of Iberia for several hundred years. They named it *manxa*, meaning "parched land", but in present-day Spanish *mancha* simply means "spot".

In the Middle Ages, Castile was actually still densely forested, but the former world power needed every available tree to build its extensive fleet of ships. In the bare countryside that resulted, grassland fortunately took hold in some areas and is able to sustain a modest living for goat and sheep farmers. The animals supply milk for the region's bestselling export product – savory and rich Manchego cheese. Some parts of the countryside here seem

Iconic windmills and a castillo near Consuegra overlooking over the plains of La Mancha.

Built onto a rock, the Alcázar defiantly stands guard over the Old Town of Segovia.

almost uninhabited. While the landscape is often monotonous at first glance, however, this is what makes it so fascinating. The sunsets are unique, the sky dowsed in a range of reddish hues.

The most important chapters of Spanish history were written in the heart of this region. In the 11th century, for example, it was here that the Reconquista gained momentum and Christian forces massed in order to reclaim the southern half of Iberia from the Moors. It is as such the birthplace of the Spanish nation, a fact that is reflected in the seemingly non-stop historical sites. Generals and kings erected great fortified castles that became monuments to their victories in the Christian reclamation of the area.

On a journey through Castile, it is these old cities that receive the lion's share of your attention. Some Old Towns, such as those in Ávila, Salamanca, Segovia, Cuenca and Toledo have been declared UNESCO World Heritage Sites due to their historical importance. The city of Salamanca is home to the oldest university in Spain; the charming Plaza Mayor in Valladolid became the model for similar squares in other cities. Few other cities possess such perfectly preserved medieval town walls as Ávila; and stunning Toledo awaits visitors with countless architectural treasures from the Convivencia (coexistence), a period when Jews, Christians and Muslims lived peacefully together and the city experi-

enced a period of unrivalled prosperity. Not only the larger cities, but in particular the smallest villages proudly celebrate their cultural treasures and landmarks, be they architectural, in the form of majestic castles, old churches or "simply" windmills, or cultural in the

form of festivals. One literary figure of the region gained world-wide fame through his struggle with the windmills – Don Quixote de la Mancha. He mistook the windmills for giants, wildly flailing about, and he rode to attack them with his lance drawn.

The library of the Monasterio San Lorenzo de El Escorial, north of Madrid.

The 1,200-km (746-mi) journey through the high plains of Castile begins in Madrid before taking you first north-west across the Castilian Dividing Range into the Castile and León region. You return to Madrid after crossing the Sierra de Guadarrama and visiting the cultural and scenic highlights of the Castile-La Mancha Region.

1 Madrid (see pages 186-187)

2 El Escorial From Madrid your journey heads out towards the 500-km-long (311-mile) Castilian Dividing Range (Cordillera Central), which forms a natural border between Old and New Castile. The scenic C505 begins at Las Rozas. The water in the reservoirs along the road is used to irrigate the olive groves.

El Escorial, King Felipe II's impressive palace, lies in the Sierra de Guadarrama, which is part of the Cordillera Central. Beyond the northern foothills of the mountains you come to Ávila at an elevation of 1,130 m (3,708 ft).

3 Ávila This tranquil town provides insight into life in Castile in the Middle Ages. With 50,000 inhabitants, Ávila rises abruptly from the plains, its stunning walls visible from afar. They are considered the most magnificent medieval fortifications in Europe and their dimensions are difficult to fathom: 2,500 m (2,734 yds) long, an average of 12 m (39 ft) high and 3 m (3 yds) thick. Some of the eighty-eight towers are open to the public and can be climbed.

Inside, the city has managed to preserve its medieval appearance. In the heart of the Old

Town is the Plaza Mayor where once the bullfights took place. East of the square is the cathedral, which has been integrated into the town walls (11th–14th centuries). Other evidence of the town's heyday in the 16th century are the many aristocratic palaces and bourgeois mansions.

4 Peñaranda de Bracamonte North-west of Ávila, halfway to Salamanca, is the small town of Peñaranda de Bracamonte. On the plaza it is worth checking out the pharmacy, which has antique interior fittings.

The church of San Miguel features a unique high altar.

5 Salamanca Continuing over the virtually treeless plains you arrive in Salamanca, one of Castile's main cultural centers and the European Capital of Culture in 2002.

The main sights of the city – the Plaza Mayor, two cathedrals and the university – are all in the Old Town. The trapeze-shaped Plaza Mayor was created in the middle of the 18th century.

Travel Information

Route profile
Length : approx. 1,200 km (745 mi)
Time required: 8–10 days
Start and finish: Madrid
Route (main locations):
Madrid, Ávila, Salamanca, Zamora, Valladolid, Cuéllar, Segovia, Guadalajara, Cuenca, Alcázar de San Juan, Toledo, Aranjuez, Madrid

Traffic information:
There is an extensive network of maintained roads throughout Spain. The motorways require tolls but are therefore also well maintained. The best seasons to visit the hot

central region of Spain are spring and autumn, when temperatures are not as extreme.

Where to stay:
A Spanish specialty is the Paradores, upscale hotels in beautiful historic buildings such as castles, monasteries or palaces.
www.parador.es

Further information:
Here are a few websites to help you plan your trip.
www.spain.info
www.whatmadrid.com
www.justspain.org

in the Middle Ages thanks to its trade in wool and features a handful of historic buildings. The most important sacral building is Santa María de Mediavilla (16th century), which boasts a beautiful star-vaulted ceiling.

8 Valladolid The capital of the Castilla y León region is spread across fertile plains on the banks of the Río Pisuerga, which flows into the Río Duero to the south-west of the town. Valladolid has 320,000 inhabitants, making it one of the largest cities in Central Spain, but only a few historic buildings have been preserved in the Old Town.

Some 500 m (547 yds) east of the Plaza Mayor, which instantly became a model for similar plazas in Madrid and other cities, is the city's cathedral. Construction began in the year 1580, but the church remains unfinished. The cathedral combines a relatively plain architectural style with sheer size: the interior is 122 m (133 yds) long and 62 m (68 yds) wide. The oldest place of worship in Valladolid is the Church of Santa María la Antigua (13th/14th centuries).

Behind the cathedral is the university, which was founded in 1346, and features an attractive baroque façade. One of the gems in the city's sea of houses is the Casa de Cervantes. Another treasure is the small Casa

Significant buildings in the university district include the Palacio Anaya, a Renaissance palace, and the famous Casa de las Conchas of 1514, the most prestigious example of theQueen Isabella Renaissance style.

The university was founded in 1218 by King Alfonso IX, and the ornately adorned façade of the Patio de las Escuelas is a classic example of the famous picaresque style.

Salamanca boasts not just one but two cathedrals. The Romanesque Catedral Vieja (old cathedral), which dates from the 12th century, has some priceless frescoes. If you go out the Patio

Chico you can go straight over to the Catedral Nueva (new cathedral), a mostly Gothic structure from the 16th–18th centuries that also features other architectural styles.

6 Zamora About 65 km (40 mi) north of Salamanca is Zamora, a medieval town with about 160,000 inhabitants that is considered an open-air museum of Romanesque architecture. Its heritage of buildings from this style period is unrivalled in Spain. Two very old and stylistically important bridges here span the Río Duero. One, the Puente Viejo, was built in the 14th century on

Roman foundations, has sixteen pointed arches, and is the more prominent. However, the undisputed architectural highlight here is the cathedral, built in just twenty-three years in the 12th century and standing on a rise in the Old Town. The cathedral museum exhibits a collection of very precious tapestries and superb goldsmiths' works. Following the valley of the Rio Valderaduey for a bit, the journey now leads to Medina de Ríoseco, the northernmost point of the trip through the highlands.

7 Medina de Ríoseco This charming little town flourished

1 The Plaza de Cibeles with its enormous fountain, Fuente de Cibeles, is one of the Madrid's most attractive squares.

2 The Old Cathedral of Salamanca, built in the 12th century.

3 The Old Town of Ávila and the churches outside the town walls have all been declared UNESCO World Heritage Sites.

Madrid

The capital of Spain is not only the geographical center of the Iberian Peninsula, but was once the center of an empire upon which the "sun never set". Dynasties like the Habsburgs and the Bourbons have all had an influence on the city, and its urban landscape is accordingly very heterogeneous, even within the city center. Since the end of the Franco dictatorship in 1975, Madrid has undergone a rapid transformation and developed from a sleepy administrative center into a vibrant and pulsating metropolis.

As the capital of Spain, Madrid began attracting both artists and merchants back in the 16th century. Velazquez and Goya, for example, were called to the Spanish Court as royal painters. An extensive collection of their works as well as those of other artists can today be admired in the Museo del Prado. It is one of the most famous collections of classic works of art with more than 9,000 paintings, 5,000 etchings and 700 sculptures. Aside from the Prado, Madrid is home to other museums of world renown: the Museo Thyssen Bornemisza provides an overview of more than 700 years of European art history, with an important collection of modern classics; the Museo Nacional Centro de Arte Reina Sofia mainly has Spanish modern art with works by Dalí, Miró, Tàpies and Picasso, including *Guernica*.

Madrid also offers a wide variety of architecture styles, from Renaissance and "Madrid de los Austrias" (the Monasterio de las Calzas Reales) to baroque, neoclassicism, Art Deco and Postmodernism (Urbanización AZCA).

With the so-called "Movida", the avant-garde art and fashion scene of the 1980s, a rich cultural scene developed after the stagnation of the Franco era, with plenty of activity in all areas of art, music, film,

theater and fashion. One expression of this phenomenon is an extremely lively nightlife scene with a vibrant bar and restaurant culture.

Especially worth seeing: Museo del Prado; Museo Nacional Centro de Arte Reina Sofía; Monasterio de las Descalzas Reales, a Renaissance monastery with a rich collection of art treasures (16th century) that was reserved for women from the upper aristocracy; the Museo Arqueológico Nacional, with outstanding collections from early Iberian history; Museo Thyssen Bornemisza; Parque del Retiro, a green oasis in the middle of the capital fashioned in neoclassical style; Palacio Real, the royal palace built in late-baroque and neoclassical styles; Plaza Mayor (17th century), the imposing main square in the capital and the model for similar squares around Spain; Rastro, the flea market that takes place every Sunday in the Old Town district of Lavapiés, the Madrid of the "little people", where 19th-century tenement blocks known as corralas have picturesque inner courtyards and wooden balconies; Real Academia de Bellas Artes de San Fernando, with works by Spanish masters (16th–19th centuries) in a baroque city palace.

No capital without a boulevard: the Gran Via was begun in 1910, north of the center. Its splendid bourgeois villas exude a certain charm.

A bit farther away, the original Madrid can be seen in the Malasaña and Chueca barrios, former artisan districts and now the lively gathering point of a more youthful scene in the evenings.

Top: The Plaza Mayor in Madrid, dating back to the 17th century

Bottom: The Prado displays one of the most important collections Old Masters.

1

de Colón, the house where Christopher Columbus died.

A visit to the Museo Nacional de Escultura north of the city center is a must. This sculpture museum, housed in the Colegio de San Gregorio (15th century), has the most important collection of religious woodcarvings in Spain.

⑨ Medina del Campo This small town to the south-west of Valladolid on the Río Zapardiel was the royal residence of the Spanish kings in the 15th and 16th centuries. Catholic Queen Isabella I died here in 1504.

A reminder of this period is the Castillo de la Mota, originally a Moorish fortress that towers over Medina del Campo. Built in 1440, it is among the most beautiful in all of Spain.

From Medina, the C112 continues east to Cuéllar, where you can see more fascinating castle fortifications.

⑩ Cuéllar The castillo de Cuéllar (15th century) is situated on a barren hill and dominates its surroundings. The

castle, which is fearsome to look at from the outside, also served as a residence for the Castilian kings. Its walls contain a magnificent palace, a Gothic chapel and a lovely Renaissance courtyard. If you have the time before continuing on to Segovia, make a detour to the fascinating castles in the villages north-east of Segovia. To get there, leave the N601 at Navalmanzano and continue northeast. The first stop is Turégano, home to the partial ruins of a once imposing castillo.

About 14 km (9 mi) north-east, in Cantalejo, turn onto a minor road that takes you to Sepúlveda about 20 km (13 mi) away. The village, located high above a curve in the Río Duratón, has preserved the remains of Roman town walls. From there, the route heads south to the Moorish castles of Castillo Morisco and Castillo de Castilnovo. The last stop before returning to the N601 is Pedraza de la Sierra, with a monumental castle atop a prominent rock. From Pedraza, Segovia is another 25 km (16 mi) on the N110.

⑪ Segovia Situated on a rocky promontory that is about 100 m (328 ft) wide is the provincial capital of Segovia. The heart of its Old Town is the Plaza Mayor where Segovia presents itself from its most vibrant side. The center of the square even has a music pavilion where, in the evening street entertainers of all kinds jibe for the attention of passersby.

The Roman aqueduct, which still carried the city's water supply as late as the 19th century, counts as one of the most magnificent Roman structures in all of Spain. The cathedral, which dominates the city center with its 100-m-high (328-ft) steeple, stands on the highest point of the Old Town and is protected by a wall with eighty-six towers. Its cloisters are adorned with 17th-century Brussels tapestries and paintings by old masters.

Among the other churches in Segovia, the church of San Martín from the 12th century stands out. Its Romanesque columned hall is decorated with flower patterns and Bibli-

2

cal scenes. San Miguel achieved historical significance as the coronation church of Isabella II as Queen of Castile and León. "Old Segovia" is bordered in the north by the Alcázar. The fortress, which has been altered several times, is adapted to the shape of the rock on which it stands. Dating back to the 11th century, it is an outstanding example of Old Castilian castle architecture.

⑫ Guadalajara The special jewel of Guadalajara on the Río

Henares is the Palacio del Duque del Infantado. The influential Mendoza Family had this palace built between the 14th and 17th centuries, the façade of which is from the 15th century and is richly adorned with exceptionally beautiful diamond-shaped blocks and filigreed columns. It is one of the most flawless examples of the Mudéjar Gothic style. The palacio houses the Museo de Bellas Artes, which holds a collection of valuable paintings from the 15th–17th centuries.

Aside from several churches, including the church of Santa María de la Fuente, which was erected on the remains of a Moorish mosque, the 16th-century Convent of La Piedad is one of the most famous sights in Guadalajara. It is framed in by double arcades.

⓭ **Cuenca** The Old Town here was built on a steep rock that drops away suddenly on both sides to the gorges of the Río Júcar and the Río Huécar. Famous for its *casas colgadas*

("hanging houses"), Cuenca originally achieved prosperity with the wool and fabric trade and is one of the most picturesque in the country.

In one of the *casas colgadas* is the Museo de Arte Abstracto Español. With more than seven hundred paintings, it is one of the largest collections of Spanish modern abstract art. Not far away is the Museo Arqueológico, which has valuable finds from the region.

The Old Town has largely managed to preserve its medieval character. The Gothic cathedral, built in the 12th–13th centuries on the site of a former mosque, has Norman influences and was rebuilt after collapsing in the early 20th century; the interior had been largely undamaged. The Plaza Mayor is also lined with noteworthy old mansions that feature wooden balconies and wrought-iron balustrades. On the highest point of the rocky plateau is the Torre de Mangana, the former fortress watchtower that affords panoramic views over the roofs of Cuenca and its surroundings.

⓮ **Carrascosa del Campo** West of Cuenca, the N400 leads to the 1,166-m-high (36,636-ft) high Puerto de Cabrejas via tight hairpin turns before continuing through several smaller towns and past the ruins of several castles to Carrascosa del Campo. This village features a Gothic church with a beautiful baroque portal as well as the remains of an old fortress.

Some steep inclines and bends have to be navigated during the onward journey to Tarancón. From Tarancón, a detour to Uclés is worthwhile for one of the most beautiful monasteries in the province of Castile-La Mancha. The Monasterio de Uclés dates back to the 16th–18th centuries, and is often jokingly called "El Escorial de la Mancha". It is known for its valuable wood carvings and the crypt contains the tomb of writer Jorge Manrique. The remarkable patio is richly adorned with a sea of plants. If you do not wish to return to Tarancón, you can continue via Saelices (which contains the remains of a Roman aqueduct) directly to Quintanar de la Orden, some 50 km (31 mi) to the south-east.

This region, which is dominated by vineyards and fields of grain, was immortalized by Miguel de Cervantes as the backdrop for the adventures of his knighterrant Don Quixote.

From Mota del Cuervo, it is worth taking the 35-km (2-mi) detour to Belmonte.

1 Two structures tower over the Old Town of Segovia: the Gothic cathedral in the town center and the Alcázar on the westernmost edge of the city.

2 These "hanging houses" are the most recognizable icon of the picturesque Old Town of Cuenca.

⑮ Mota del Cuervo and Belmonte An entire hillside here is covered with the windmills that are typical for La Mancha. On a hill above Belmonte, which was the birthplace of the poet Fray Luis de León, stands the Castillo Villena, built in the 15th century. One of its three gates is decorated with a scallop shell and a crucifix, symbols of the St James' pilgrims on their way to Santiago de Compostella. A double ring of walls encircles the star-shaped late-Gothic complex with six round towers. The three sections of the castle are grouped around a triangular inner courtyard.

From here, we return on the same route to Mota del Cuervo and then continue towards Alcázar de San Juan.

⑯ La Mancha (south-east of Toledo) To the south-west of Mota del Cuervo, a number of castle ruins can be seen on both sides of the road and in the hills of the Sierra de Molinos near Campo de Criptana, a number of windmills have small museums with local exhibits.

The Alcázar de San Juan houses a real treasure and the Museo Arqueológico has a beautiful display of Roman mosaics. The charming church of Santa María dates back to the 13th century.

⑰ Consuegra From here, the journey continues to follow the road to Toledo until you reach Consuegra, about 40 km (24 mi)

away. The town is also dominated by castle ruins, which afford lovely views of the southern Mancha. Staying on the same road and passing the Montes des Consuegra and the Embalse de Finisterre, you eventually arrive in Mora, about 30 km (19 mi) away. It has the remains of some interesting Roman structures.

⑱ Toledo The Middle Ages still seem omnipresent in this city on the Tajo. Its location alone is absolutely superb: the Old Town is spread out over a rock promontory that is surrounded on three sides by the Río Tajo in a deep gorge. The first panoramic view from the opposite bank of the river allows visitor to admire the splendor of the cityscape. The cathedral, the Alcázar and countless medieval buildings combine to form a magnificent urban architectural ensemble while narrow alleyways with nooks and crannies characterize the Old Town, all surrounded by a medieval wall with numerous towers.

Toledo is a veritable treasure trove of Spanish and Moorish architecture. The city's most recognizable icon is the cathedral, which dates from the 13th–15th centuries and was erected on the site of a former late-Gothic church and an even older Moorish mosque. While the exterior is pure early French Gothic, the interior is a perfect example of late Spanish Gothic.

The three portals on the main façade are richly adorned with reliefs and sculptures. The interior measures a stately 110 m (120 yds) and features the Capilla Mayor, a depiction of a number of Biblical scenes using life-sized figures carved from wood that are either painted or gilded.

The Alcázar stands on the highest point of town. The façade of the virtually square building is predominantly from the 16th century. The way up to the fortress begins at the Plaza de Zocodover. This triangular plaza is the actual center of town.

Other attractions include the Franciscan Monastery San Juan de los Reyes (15th–17th centuries) and the Casa El Greco. The famous painter lived in Toledo for almost forty years and created many works here. The journey then takes you along the Río Tajo to the west, past extensive fields that are irrigated with water from the river. As a last stopping point before you return to Madrid, be sure to visit Aranjuez.

⑲ Aranjuez This town, which has been well-known at least since Rodrigo's Concierto de Aranjuez, is laid out on a geometric grid and is most famous for its lovely gardens.

The largest area of the park is the Jardín del Príncipe in the north-east. Inside the park, which was created by French landscape gardeners in 1763, you will find the Casa del Labrador, a small palace that is worth a look. In another building, the Casa de Marinos, you will find six royal barges on display. The Palacio Real (the royal palace) south of the gardens was rebuilt in the 17th century after two fires. Its main façade combines elements of Renaissance and baroque styles.

1 Most of the windmills in the La Mancha region south-east of Madrid (here near Consuegra) are no longer in operation.

2 The preciously appointed interior of the summer residence in Aranjuez can be admired on a guided tour.

Salamanca This town's university was founded back in 1254. Buildings in yellow stone characterize the Old Town, which can boast not just one but two beautiful medieval cathedrals.

Valladolid The most significant sight in this town is the cathedral, begun in 1580, but still an unfinished project today. Equally impressive is the baroque façade of the university.

Medina del Campo This town was the residence of the Spanish kings in the 15th and 16th centuries. The Castillo de la Mota was once a Moorish fortress.

Semana Santa Easter week here begins with a procession on Palm Sunday for which palm fronds, woven sculptures and oversized representations of the Passion of Christ are carried around town.

Segovia This provincial capital is a mixture of Moorish and secular medieval buildings, towers, squares, churches, a cathedral, impressive town walls and a famous Roman aqueduct with more than one hundred stone arches. In the north of the Old Town stands a perfect example of an Old Castilian castle, the Alcázar.

Madrid The highest capital in Europe is a city of extreme weather and mixed architectural styles. Churches, monasteries, palaces and breathtaking modern buildings convey a fantastic impression of old and new. The art museums of Madrid also enjoy worldwide reputations, especially the Museo del Prado and the Museo Thyssen-Bornemisza.

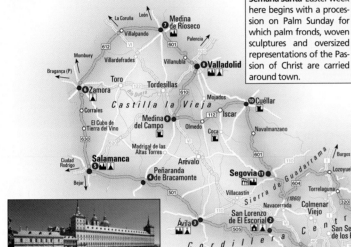

Cuenca The Old Town here is situated atop a rocky cliff that is surrounded by two rivers. The "hanging houses" cling for survival on the cliff's edge.

El Escorial Spain's most visited sight is only about 50 km (31 mi) from Madrid. The residence, including a royal palace, basilica, monastery and a library was built during the reign of King Felipe II.

Ávila This medieval town boasts one of the mightiest fortifications in Europe. The heavily castellated complex, up to 12 m (39 ft) high and 3 m (3 yds) thick, was built in the 11th century and served as a bulwark against Moorish conquest.

Belmonte The late-Gothic Castillo Villena from the 15th century dominates Belmonte. The heavily fortified complex is surrounded by a double ring of walls.

Aranjuez Laid out on a strictly geometrical grid, this town is famous for its gardens and the splendidly appointed palace with its cabinets and galleries.

Toledo This former residence of the Castilian kings was also the religious center of the country and for a long time the home of painter El Greco. Toledo is perched a mighty promontory surrounded by the Río Tajo. The Gothic cathedral and the Alcázar look over the Old Town and its alleyways.

La Mancha Castle ruins and windmills are typical of the expansive landscape south-east of Toledo. Also worth visiting are the museums of Alcázar de San Juan and the castle of Consuegra. The views across the distant southern La Mancha are wonderful.

Puerto Banus near Marbella, one of the best-known yacht ports on the Costa del Sol.

Spain

Andalusia – a Moorish legacy in southern Europe

Andalusia is a region filled with passion and culture. The fertile agricultural land here is blessed with plentiful sun where olives trees grow against a backdrop of snow-covered mountains and the tidy whitewashed houses recall Moorish architectural styles. This natural setting coupled with the local aromas of leather and sherry and the rhythms of the castanets and flamenco all combine to create a truly unforgettable experience.

'Al Andaluz' – the 'Land of Light' – is what the Arabs called this sunny southern part of Spain. Interestingly, it was not meant as a metaphor. This region, where two continents and two seas meet, actually possesses a unique light that seems not to exist anywhere else in the world, and whose clarity never ceases to amaze its inspired visitors. Andalusia covers an area of more than 87,000 sq km (33,582 sq mi). Its landscape is defined by the Sierra Morena Mountains and the Betic Cordillera Range, whose 3,481-m-high (11,421-ft) Sierra Nevada Mountains are covered in snow almost all year long.

The area is home to ancient settlements that pre-date the Romans, including Cadiz, which was first settled by the Phoenicians in around 1100 BC. Since then, Greeks, Romans, Vandals and Visigoths have taken turns settling and farming the sun-

Flamenco "art" – a dance and a way of life, since the 19th-century.

drenched land in the south of Iberia. It wasn't until the 8th century that the Arabs ended the reign of the Visigoths and took control of the area.

It turns out to have been an easy campaign for the Arabs to gain their foothold in Andalusia. When they secretly crossed the Strait of Gibraltar under Tariq ibn Ziyad, and later Musa ibn Nusair in 711, they only needed gradually to seize the already deteriorating kingdom of Roderic, the Visigoth ruler. After that, virtually no one else stood in their way and their expansion reached as far as Galicia and the Pyrenees. They were only halted by Charles Martell in 732 at the Battle of Tours in France.

The Puente Nuevo across the rock gorge in Ronda, which is more than 100 m (328 ft) deep, is a technical masterpiece dating from the 18th century.

The 'White Village' ('Pueblo Blanco') of Zaharade la Sierra is a national monument.

In Spain, however, the Arabs reigned supreme for over half a century. Abd ar-Rahman I made Córdoba the capital of his Caliphate and adorned the city with an exquisite mosque. In Granada, Islamic culture developed with consummate splendour. Over the centuries, the Moors erected some truly magnificent buildings all throughout this region, in architectural styles that remain the defining element of Andalusia even to this day.

In the 13th century, the Christian 'Reconquista' of the Iberian Peninsula began in earnest and a huge victory was won for the Catholic monarchs Ferdinand and Isabella when Seville fell in 1248. When Granada was taken as well in 1492, the last Muslim minorities were expelled, mark-ing the start of a new Andalusia that would not just ride the tide of good fortune that came with the discovery and conquest of the 'New World', but even dictate its development. Following the conquests of Mexico and Peru, the city of Seville became the most important trading center in all of Spain.

Today, the autonomous region of Andalusia, which enjoys 3,000 hours of sun a year and where oranges, olives, wine and almonds all flourish, is home to some seven million people and has around 760 towns and communities. Traditional festivals and religious life are of extreme importance to Andalusians, and these are celebrated with full fervour and devotion especially during the Semana Santa, or Holy Week, when numerous pil-grimages and processions take place.

Community culture is reflected in the local festival weeks, the ferias, as well as in the bullfights and diverse flamenco styles. These events show the true Andalusia, the land of bold caballeros, beautiful señoritas, formidable black bulls – the land that gets your blood pumping like no other place. And the natural landscape is breathtaking and diverse, from the glorious beaches of the Costa del Sol to the magnificent snow-covered peaks of the Sierra Nevada.

The famous stone pillars in the lion courtyard of the Alhambra in Granada.

Your Andalusian excursion takes you 1,600 km (994 miles) through the mountains of the Sierra Nevada Range, across the fertile plains of the Guadalquivir River and on down towards the Costa del Sol and the Costa del Luz. You'll visit the charming 'white villages' and the magnificent cities that are home to Moorish architectural masterpieces.

① Seville For detailed information see p. 195.

② Vega del Guadalquivir After leaving Seville on the C431 towards Córdoba you will emerge onto the flat, green and fertile plains known as the Vega del Guadalquivir. It is one of Andalusia's primary agricultural regions, with orange plantations, cornfields and sunflower fields sprawling across a wide valley formed by the river that made Seville a world power in the days of the explorers. Small villages pop up along the route, with tidy white houses perched on top of lush hills. Most of the people in the area live off the rich agricultural bounty.

③ Palma del Río Its prime location at the confluence of the Guadalquivir and Genil is romantic enough. Add to that the verdant green surroundings and you've got two good reasons why this area is called 'Andalusia's Garden'.

The impressive 12th-century city walls have been well preserved in parts and recall the town's rich history, which goes back to the Romans who founded it. Palma del Río then played a special role in Spain's history from the 16th to 18th centuries when the Convento de San Francisco regularly sent missionaries to the New World. One of them was Brother Junípero Serra, who was

1 The mighty Moorish bell tower of La Giralda overlooks the Gothic cathedral and the Archivo General de Indias in Seville.

Travel Information

Route profile
Length: approx. 1,600 km (994 miles), excluding detours
Time required: at least 8–10 days
Start and end: Seville
Route (main locations): Seville, Córdoba, Granada, Almería, Málaga, Ronda, Olvera, Arcos de la Frontera, Cádiz, Sanlúcar, Jerez, Seville

Traffic information:
Drive on the right in Spain. The speed limit in built-up areas is 50 km/h (31 mph), 90 or 100 km/h (56 or 62 mph) outside built-up areas, and 120 km/h (75 mph) on highways (generally tolls are required).

When to go:
The recommended times to travel are spring (around 26°C/79°F) and autumn (up to 32°C/90°C in September). Summer can be brutally hot.

Accommodation:
Paradores are state-run hotels in historic buildings. Bookings and reservations are made through Ibero Hotel (*www.iberotours.de*).

Information:
www.tourspain.es
Info on Andalusia:
www.andalusien-web.com

Seville

To experience Spain you simply have to visit Seville, the capital of Andalusia.

Seville is one of the country's most charming cities, rivalling with Granada, Andalusia's second Moorish treasure. After America was discovered, Seville had its heyday as a river port on the Guadalquivir and as a commercial hub where goods from Spanish colonies overseas were unloaded and transported to the interior. This brought extreme wealth and a breath of fresh air from the New World to this old city!

Particularly worth seeing here are the 15th-century Santa María Cathedral, a complex with lavishly designed porticos, the Patio de los Naranjos, the former mosque courtyard with early medieval marble bowls, and the Giralda bell tower, built as a minaret in the 12th century; the Reales Alcázares, built in the 12th century by the Almohadas, and used as a Christian royal palace. Highlights of any visit also include the exquisitely decorated interior courtyards, as well as the gardens (the cathedral and the Alcázares are UNESCO World Heritage Sites); the

Left: Ceramic works on the Plaza de España.
Top: The Santa Maria Cathredal

Barrio de Santa Cruz, the Jewish quarter; the Casa de Pilatos, a private palace; the Hospital de la Caridad, a gem of baroque architecture; the Museo de Bellas Artes with Spanish baroque art; the Plaza de España, a dazzling structure with ceramic paintings in the city park, and Parque de María Luisa. Outside the city are the ruins of the Roman Itálica.

1

2

responsible in large for the fabulous mission churches that can still be seen in California. But those times have long passed and the monastery has been given a new purpose now – beautifully renovated, today it is used as a hotel.

④ Medina Azahara Just before reaching Córdoba, a road turns off towards the ruins of Medina Azahara, the old palace city built on three terraces where the caliphs lived together with their royal suite between the mid 10th and early 11th centuries. Parts of the complex have been renovated and give you a pretty good idea of the former beauty of the 'Flower City', a masterpiece of Islamic architecture.

⑤ Córdoba This city was an important political and cultural center as early as Roman times – one of its most famous sons is the philosopher, Seneca, from the 3rd century BC. By AD 929, Córdoba had risen to become one of the Caliphate's most resplendent metropolises on

Spanish soil, competing even with the likes of the former cosmopolitan city of Baghdad. Jews, Arabs and Christians lived in harmony with each other. Science and philosophy flourished like never before.

In the old city center, traces remain of this heyday when the mighty Caliphate city had over a million inhabitants. It has now become a provincial capital with a population of just 300,000, but Córdoba remains a gem indeed: the Old City's narrow little alleyways, white-washed houses and inner courtyards decorated with flowers all create an idyllic scene.

At the center of it all is the Mezquita – previously a mosque and now a cathedral – standing strong like an old fortification.

The enormous building, with the magnificent prayer hall supported by 856 ornate columns, was declared a UNESCO 'Legacy of Mankind'. Nineteen naves and thirty-eight transepts, exquisite Oriental decorations and light casting mysterious shadows on the pillars make the Mezquita a truly unforgettable sight.

Just next to the Mezquita is the Judería, the former Jewish quarter with narrow streets

adorned with flowers. One of the most beautiful of these is the aptly named Calleja de las Flores. The former synagogue and the bullfighting museum, which incidentally is one of the most interesting in all of Spain, are also worth a visit.

The Alcázar de los Reyes Cristianos, a royal residence built as a fort in the 14th century, has really lovely gardens. The Museo Arqueológico Provincial, located in a Renaissance palace, has a number of Roman, Visigoth and Arabic exhibits. In the quarter around the Christian churches, Córdoba has another tourist attrac-

Nasrids for 250 years, and it was during this time that its most magnificent edifice was built – the Alhambra.

A total of twenty-three sultans from the Nasrid Dynasty contributed to this tour de force of Spanish-Arabic constructions. Now the castle, at once fortress-like and elegant, is the pearl of the city of Granada.

The Alhambra, whose name 'The Red One' derives from the reddish ochre of its walls, is an enormous complex of fortifications, towers, royal residential palaces, mosques and gardens. It comprises four main sections – the defences, or Alcazaba, on the western tip of the hill; the Palacio Árabe (Alhambra Palace); the Palacio de Carlos V, a Renaissance palace with the Museum of Fine Arts in the center of the hill; and the gardens of the Generalife in the east. Apart from the gardens, which were part of a summer residence, all other buildings are surrounded by fortified walls with towers.

The Palacio de los Leones, with its arcade passage adorned with filigree work, and the lion fountain are two of the most impressive parts of the Alhambra, along with the water features in the gardens, which have a real oasis feel. But the Alhambra is not all that this splendid city has to offer.

1 To get the most beautiful view of the Alhambra in Granada and the Sierra Nevada Mountains, go to the Mirador de San Nicolás in Albaicín.

2 The prayer room of the former Umayyad Mosque in Córdoba has 856 columns.

3 The churches of Iglesia de la Villa (16th century) and Iglesia de la Encarnación (18th century) tower over Montefrio.

tion in store – the Palacio de Viana, a mansion with twelve inner courtyards and spectacular gardens.

The two most important centers during Spain's Moorish period, Córdoba and Granada, are connected by the Caliphate Route. Today it is known as the N432, a slightly less romantic name, but it still passes through a hilly region with relatively little settlement, some small homesteads and a handful of well-fortified castles and towers.

At the town of Alcalá la Real, nestled in the shadow of the Moorish Castillo de la Mota,

you leave the N432 for a leisurely drive through the villages of the fertile highlands of the Vega.

6 Montefrio This town lies in a unique mountain landscape and is known for its castle, Castillo de la Villa, which was built around 1500 on the walls of an old Moorish fort.

After some 20 km (12 miles) you come to the A9 heading towards Granada.

7 Granada The geographic location of this city is fascinating in itself – bordered in the west by a high plateau, in the

south by the northern bank of the river Genil, and with the snowcapped peaks of the Sierra Nevada as a background setting. However, what really gives Granada its 'One-Thousand-and-One-Nights' feel is the extensive Moorish legacy that has defined this city for more than seven hundred years now.

Granada experienced its heyday between the 13th and 15th centuries, before the Moors were pushed south by the gathering armies of the Christian 'Reconquista'. At that point the city had been the capital of the independent Kingdom of the

The Albaicin is also something to behold – the whitewashed Moorish quarter is an architectural gem in its own right, with tiny alleyways and the mirador, the San Nicolás lookout. In addition, there is the area around the 16th/17th-century cathedral, the Capilla Real, the late-Gothic royal chapel and the Carthusian monastery, founded in the early 16th century – each and every one of them worth a visit.

A must for poetry-lovers after all this is the small detour from Granada to Fuente Vaqueros, the birthplace of García Lorca, 17 km (11 miles) away on the plains. From there it is up into the mountains for a detour into the Sierra Nevada over Europe's highest pass.

As you leave Granada heading east on a small road parallel to the A92, the landscape becomes sparser and wilder. This effect is enhanced when you see the first cave dwellings dug into the rocky hillsides.

8 Guadix This truly ancient city with grand Moorish ruins and a history that dates back to Roman times also has a section with cave dwellings – some five thousand gitanos (gypsies) live here underground in the Barrio de Santiago. Their homes, painstakingly carved into the steep loess slopes and actually comprising multiple rooms, are even connected to the city water supply and electricity network.

The landscape remains sparse for a while now. After Guadix, the castle of La Calahorra is worth a detour. The Gulf of Almería soon comes into view.

9 Almería This fine city has always benefited from its spe-

cial geographic location. Protected from the mainland by mountain ranges, the vast Gulf of Almería fulfills all the right conditions for a nice port and a good center for trade. The Phoenicians even recognized this and built a port that became the foundation for the Roman Portus Magnus. Pirates later found it to be an ideal hideout, too.

During the time of the caliphs, Almería experienced yet another rise as an important trading center, becoming the capital of a kingdom to which the likes of Córdoba, Murcia, Jaén and even parts of Granada temporarily paid allegiance. In 1489, the city was reconquered by the Christians and from then on only played a secondary role.

Today, Almería is very much an agricultural town. The sur-

rounding area is home to rows of enormous greenhouses where fruit and vegetables are grown for export. The nearby Andarax Valley is home to the region's orchards and vineyards.

Almería is a predominantly modern town with wide, palm-lined streets dominated by the massive alcazaba (fort), which sits on top of a hill as if on its own throne. Construction began on the alcazaba in the 10th century and it is one of the most powerful and best-preserved fort complexes in all of Andalusia.

The Old Town, with its picturesque fishing and gitano quarter on the castle hill, La Chanca, still has an undeniable Moorish feel to it. The colourful cubic houses and the cave dwellings look like relics from distant times.

the other by steep terrain; sprawled at its feet is the San Francisco Quarter, with a street network lined with farms; and on the other side of the 'Tajo' gorge is the modern area El Mercadillo, where most of Ronda's 35,000 inhabitants live.

One of the most important attractions here is the Casa del Rey Moro in the La Ciudad. Inside the rock, a staircase with 365 steps leads down from this Moorish palace into the gorge. The cathedral, the Palacio de Mondragón and the Casa del Gigante with their Arabic ornamentation and decorative elements are worth seeing.

Then there is the bullfighting arena. Built in 1785, it is one of the oldest in Spain. Ronda was also the place where bullfights were given a sort of 'constitution' in the 18th century.

It is absolutely essential to do day trips around Ronda where the 'white villages' are charmingly tucked into the rugged mountains and valleys – Prado del Rey, with its neatly planned streets; Ubrique, capital of the Sierra de Cádiz, known for its leather products; Zahara or Setenil, which look like large eyries with their houses clinging to the rock; and of course Olvera, a town whose architecture is still entirely Moorish and whose walled upper city is dominated by a 12th-century castle.

For the next part of the journey there is an alternative route to the highway – the very picturesque 332/348, which take you inland through the mountains of the Sierra Nevada and then back down the coast.

Passing through Motril, the road continues towards the Costa del Sol through the fertile plains where tropical fruits are a speciality. Along the way, a good place to stop is Nerja, about 50 km (31 miles) before reaching Málaga. Perched on a ridge, this town is home to the amazing Cueva de Nerja dripstone cave.

⑩ **Málaga** Málaga is a very important economic center, Andalusia's second-largest city with over half a million inhabitants, and the second-largest Spanish port on the Mediterranean after that of Barcelona.

It is the main trading center for the agricultural products from the nearby plains, in particular wine and raisins.

In terms of tourist attractions, Málaga does not have a lot to offer. However, it is well worth climbing up to the Gibralfaro, the Moorish citadel and lighthouse that gives you a beautiful view of the semicircular expanse of land.

Today, next to nothing remains of the splendour of the alcazaba – often compared to the Alhambra in Granada – and the cathedral, whose construction started in the 16th century but was not completed: the middle section of the tower, 'La Manquita', (the missing one) is still open for all to see.

From Málaga, the Costa del Sol continues along coastal road 340 with its large holiday resorts. After Marbella, the

main road turns off into San Pedro de Alcántara. For those who want to enjoy some beautiful scenery, however, drive another 30 km (19 miles) west and take the route at Manilva that heads up into the Serranía de Ronda. If you wish to to visit Gibraltar you can do so by continuing another 40 km (25 miles) from Manilva along the coastal road.

⑪ **Ronda** If for nothing else, this town is worth seeing for its adventuresome location. It lies at the edge of a high plateau divided by the Río Guadalevín, which flows by in a gorge that is up to 200 m (656 ft) deep. Its houses and numerous mansions are built right up to the edge of the cliff.

The 98-m-high (322-ft) Puente Nuovo, built in the 18th century, spans the gorge. Ernest Hemingway was as fascinated with the city, the deep gorge, the houses and the cliffs as was the poet Rainer Maria Rilke, who once wrote: 'I have searched everywhere for my dream city and I have found it in Ronda.'

Ronda is divided into three sections. The oldest, La Ciudad, lies in the middle of the limestone plateau and is bordered on one side by a Moorish wall and on

1 The view over the port city of Málaga on the Costa del Sol.

2 White houses in Ronda look out over the abyss on the high plateau.

3 Setenil, one of the 'white villages' around Ronda.

4 Casares, west of Marbella, was founded by Julius Caesar.

5 The mountain town of Arcos de la Frontera captivates visitors with its Moorish quarter.

12 Arcos de la Frontera The route now continues towards the Atlantic coast, passing by Embalse de Zahara. This town has a population of 30,000 and sits on a rocky ridge basically in the middle of the Guadelete River. Its whitewashed houses still create a Moorish atmosphere, while the church of San Pedro is most definitely worth a look, perched directly on a cliff with an impressive view of the gorge and the plains with their seemingly endless olive groves.

The route now follows Highway 328 towards the Atlantic coast, although it is worth making a detour to Cádiz beforehand.

13 Cádiz This city is considered the oldest in Spain; the Phoenicians were already making good use of its narrow, 10-km-long (6-mile) peninsula as a storage yard. Much later, after America was discovered, the city became extremely wealthy. Cádiz is still the second most important shipyard in Spain after El Ferrol. Fish is also an important source of revenue, as is salt, which is obtained from enormous salt refineries in the south-east of the city.

The best way to discover Cádiz is to take a taxi ride around the Old Town, which is especially picturesque with the golden cupola of the Catedral Nueva towering over the tiny square houses. The treasures of its church include the largest and most precious processional monstrance in the world. The Church of San Felipe Neri downtown is also worth a visit as the location where the Cádiz Cortes government in exile declared Spain's liberal Constitution in 1812. The Museo de Bellas Artes has some beautiful works by Spanish masters such as Francisco de Zurbarán and Murillo.

North of Cádiz on the Atlantic coast is a series of lovely resort towns – Puerto Real, Puerto de Santa Maria, Rota and Chipiona all have long, wide, fine sandy beaches.

14 Sanlúcar de Barrameda This dignified city, located at the mouth of the Guadalquivir, is the export hub for the famous Manzanilla sherry. The Fino variety is only produced here in Sanlúcar.

The city is divided into two sections, the upper and lower city. Be sure to pay a visit to the palace of the once influential dukes of Medina-Sidonia and the superb Mudejar portico of the Church of Santa Maria. Another attraction is the royal equestrian school, the Real Escuela Andaluza de Arte Ecuestre, where you can witness Spanish dressage riding styles.

This famous port saw Columbus begin his third voyage to America, and Magellan also set off from here on the trip on which his ship became the first to circumnavigate the globe.

Long before that, the Holy Virgin is said to have appeared

here, hence the name Coto de Doñana (Coast of the Mistress). Today, you can take a boat to the Parque Nacional de Coto de Doñana from the quay.

From Sanlúcar the C440 'Ruta del Vino', or Wine Road, leads into the home of jerez (sherry).

15 Jerez de la Frontera A visit to one of the most wonderful bodegas – wine cellars – is a must in this charming city so rich in tradition. Many of these bodegas also have something special to offer apart from sherry. The Bodega Domecq in Calle Ildefonso, for example, enchants visitors with its Moorish interior, while the ironwork in the Bodega González Byass was done by none other than Gustave Eiffel. Those still keen on

seeing more sights after the enticing bodegas should head to the Old Town and have a look at the 17th/18th-century Church of San Salvador, the 11th-century Alcázar and the 'Cartuja', somewhat outside the city, whose Gothic church is particularly ornate.

From Jerez, highway E05 then heads back to your starting point, Seville.

1 Jerez de la Frontera: in the vaults of the Bodega Pedro Domecq, sherry matures painstakingly in hundreds of barrels until it can be bottled and drunk.

2 The Catedral Nueva offers a magnificent view of the Cádiz headlands.

Seville The capital of Andalusia and host of the 1992 EXPO lies on the banks of the Guadalquivir. It was an important trading center after the discovery of the Americas. The 15th-century cathedral, with Moorish elements from the 12th century, the former royal palaces, the museums and the Plaza de España all make this city an absolute must.

Córdoba The hometown of the philosopher, Seneca, was already of importance during Roman times and in 929 became the center point of the Spanish Caliphate. There are still traces of this around the great Mezquita – once a mosque, now a cathedral.

Granada Surrounded by the Sierra Nevada and the Río Genil, Granada's greatest treasure is the Alhambra, a sultan's residence with fortress walls, towers, residential palaces, mosques and gardens, inhabited by twenty-three Nasrid rulers over the centuries.

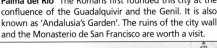

Palma del Río The Romans first founded this city at the confluence of the Guadalquivir and the Genil. It is also known as 'Andalusia's Garden'. The ruins of the city wall and the Monasterio de San Francisco are worth a visit.

Montefrío A lovely view of Montefrio from the south with its white houses, quaint churches and Moorish ruins all clinging to the jagged slopes.

The Sierra Nevada National Park The country's highest mountain range is home to excellent ski slopes and is often covered in snow until well into summer.

Guadix Some 1,300 of this village's dwellings are caves, the first of which were created in pre-Roman times. Today they are equipped with modern comforts.

Jerez de la Frontera Upon arriving in the 'Sherry City', the first things to see are the Church of San Salvador (17th/18th century) and the 11th-century Alcázar – before you pay an inevitable visit to the bodega.

Casares A 13th-century Moorish fort towers over this village, originally founded by Julius Caesar in the Sierra Bermeja.

Ronda Hemingway was one of many famous artists and writers to have spent long periods of time in this fascinating town.

La Calahorra The protective walls and towers of the Renaissance castle south of Guadix surround a two-storey interior courtyard made of the finest marble.

Arcos de la Frontera Whitewashed houses give the town a slightly Arabic feel. The views from the village over the area and the gorge are fantastic.

Zahara 'White villages' like Zahara are scattered throughout the area between Ronda and Arcos de la Frontera.

Gibraltar A trip up the 425-m-high (1,394-ft) rock inhabited by the famous Barbary apes is worth it: the view of the British outpost and North Africa is spectacular.

Costa del Sol The 150-km-long (93-mile) 'Sunshine Coast' is a charming part of Andalusia with loads of long sandy beaches.

Almería This coastal city has a picturesque Old Town and a mighty cathedral, towered over by the Alcazaba (10th century), the largest Moorish fort in Spain.

Portugal

The Santa Maria da Vitória monastery in Batalha was built partly in the Manueline style.

The land of fado and peaceful matadors: a journey to the "edge of the world"

When it was still a province of the Roman empire, what is now Portugal was once called Lusitania. In the sixth century it was part of the Visigothic empire. In the 8th century the Moors took over, but as a result of the "Reconquista" to take back Iberia, it became a kingdom separate from Galicia and León. Portugal finally gained independence in around 1267, and takes its name from the port city of Porto (Latin: porto cale).

Portugal was known in Antiquity and in the Middle Ages as the "edge of the world" and, even in the 20th century, its location on the edge of the continent had both advantages and disadvantages. It is a relatively narrow country, roughly 150 km (93 mi) wide and 550 km (342 mi) in length, but it has 832 km (517 mi) of coastline characterized by steep coastal cliffs and miles of glorious beaches. The mighty Tagus River (Tejo) divides the mountainous north, the Montanhas, from the rolling south known as Planícies, or plains. In the north you journey through what is still largely an untouched forest and mountain landscape with abundant water resources, the Costa Verde with its pine groves, the fertile Minho region with the vineyards of the Douro Valley, and the remote "land behind the mountains", Trás-os-Montes.

Central Portugal has a very different character, with the Serra da Estrela range rising to an altitude of almost 2,000 m (6,562 ft), with vineyards dotting the river valleys and the flood plains of the Tagus. Southern Portugal is dominated by Alentejo, Portugal's "breadbasket", with its vast landed estates that were dissolved after the "Carnation Revolution" of 1974. It is a flat, open region extending as far as the Serra de Monchique. Portugal's best-known region, of course, is Algarve, with its rocky cliffs and sandy beaches.

The population distribution is uneven throughout the country. While the sparse mountain regions are largely empty, there are almost three million people in Lisbon and almost one million in the greater Porto region. Cork is one of Portugal's best-known agricultural products: the country has more than eighty-six million cork oaks and they have to be twenty years old before the bark can be peeled for the first time. Today one in three of the world's wine corks still comes from Portugal. As with most European countries, Portugal, too, has a diverse historical and cultural heritage to look back

Bragança Citadel enjoys a strategic location on top of a knoll and once served as a place of refuge.

The dream destination for many holidaymakers is situated in the south of Portugal: the Algarve, with its magnificent beaches and deep blue ocean.

on. Unique throughout all of Europe, however, is the Manueline architectural style, which enjoyed its heyday during the reign of King Manuel I (1495–1521), arguably Portugal's "golden age". The Manueline is a mixture of Gothic and Renaissance elements, supplemented with frenzied decoration inspired by exploration. The cultural influence of the Portuguese voyages of discovery saw the development of exotic, maritime ornaments that were utilized in abundance everywhere. The azulejos, the usually blue and white tiles that can be found almost everywhere in Portugal, are a Moorish legacy and, in addition to their aesthetic function, they protect against heat, provide sound insulation, reflect light and liven up surfaces.

Those hoping to immerse themselves in the world of the Portuguese will not be able to avoid *saudade*, a word that somehow defies translation because it denotes a sentiment that seems to exist only in Portugal and that is also intricately linked to the language's long development. The word derives from the Latin "solus", meaning loneliness, and therefore also expresses feelings such as solitude, yearning, melancholy, mourning, pain, and a restrained joy of life. *Saudade* is best expressed in *fado*, the traditional Portuguese folk song alleged to originate from Lisbon's Alfama district and from Coimbra. They are tristful songs mostly concerned with unfulfilled longing, lost love or despair. In Lisbon, *fado* is primarily performed by female

singers accompanied by two guitarists, while in Coimbra it is typically young men who convey this sense of "fatum" (fate) deriving from social and political circumstances, like Jose Afonso with his fado number "Grandola", which accompanied the 1974 Carnation Revolution leading to the overthrow of the Salazar dictatorship.

The Portuguese style bullfighting, called "tourada", is also quite peaceful but less practised here. The bulls don' t die in the arena.

On the outskirts of Lisbon, in Benfica: the Palacio Fronteira boasts magnificent gardens with a big variety of sun tolerant mediterranean plants.

This circuit of Portugal begins in Lisbon and takes you west from the capital as far as Cabo da Roca before heading north to the culturally exciting cities of Porto and Braga. After a detour to the ancient town of Bragança, it then turns to the south passing through the Ribatejo and Alentejo regions on the way to Faro in the Algarve before returning to Lisbon along the coast.

①　Lisbon　(see page 205)

②　Cascais　The long beaches here have transformed this fishing village into a popular destination with plenty of cafés and boutiques. The daily fish auction provides something of a contrast to the main sightseeing attractions, which include the Parque da Gandarinha as well as the ornate azulejos in the old town hall and in the Nossa Senhora de Nazaré chapel.
A scenic coastal road takes you to Europe's western-most point north of Cascais. Cabo da Roca rises up 160 m (525 ft) out of the pounding Atlantic.

③　Sintra　This former Moorish town and later summer residence of the Portuguese kings and aristocracy lies at the base of a rocky outcrop with dense vegetation. It is characterized by winding alleyways, picturesque street corners and charming quintas. In the town center is the Paço Real, the Manueline city palace (15th/

16th century) that offers a mixture of diverse architectural styles. Its oversized chimneys are the landmark of the town. The Palácio is visible from a distance and dominates the town of Sintra from atop the highest of its rocky promontories.

④　Mafra　North of Sintra is Mafra, home to a colossal palace completed in 1750, with which King João V once aimed to overshadow the Spanish El Escorial. Behind the 220-m-long (241-yd) façade are 880 rooms, a chapel the size of a cathedral and a sizable basilica.

⑤　Óbidos　From Mafra, you continue north along the coast as far as Peniche, one of Portugal's largest fishing ports. Situated on a prominent headland

1　The view over the old part of Lisbon from Largo das Portas do Sol.

2　The picturesque village of Azenhas do Mar is north of Praia das Maçàs near the Cabo da Roca.

Travel Information

Route profile
Length: approx. 1,250 km (775 mi)
Time required: 14–16 days
Start: Lisbon
End: Setúbal/Lisbon
Route (main locations):
Lisbon, Cascais, Sintra, Peniche, Óbidos, Leiria, Coimbra, Porto, Braga, Guimães, Vila Real, Guarda, Marvão, Estremoz, Évora, Moura, Mértola, Faro, Portimão, Lagos, Sagres, Setúbal, Lisbon

Traffic information:
The speed limit on the motorways is 120 km/h (75 mph), on national roads 90 km/h (55 mph), in towns 60 km/h (35 mph). The legal blood alcohol limit is .05 and it is strictly enforced. Seatbelts are compulsory.

The motorways are also subject to tolls.

When to go:
The best times to visit Portugal are spring and autumn. Summer can be gruellingly hot.

Accommodation:
State-run hotels, or *pousadas*, in historic buildings and/or scenic locations, are a popular form of accommodation in Portugal. Check this site for more information: *www.pousadas.pt*

Further information:
Here are some websites to help you plan your trip.
www.justportugal.org
www.travel-in-portugal.com
www.portugal.com

Lisbon

The sea of buildings in the "white city" extends from the wide mouth of the Tagus River up the steep hills of the Barrio Alto. Lisbon's wonderful location attracts visitors from all over the world who, like the locals, navigate the hilly city in eléctricos, creeky old trams.

Sights particularly worth seeing in Lisbon include: Alfama, the oldest and most picturesque district with labyrinthine streets on a fortified hill, dominated by the ruins of the Castelo de São Jorge; the two (of many) lovely miradouros, or viewing terraces, that make Lisbon so enjoyable, are tucked between the ruined fortress and the medieval Sé Cathedral; the Avenida da Liberdade, a 90-m-wide (98-yd) boulevard from the 19th century; the Barrio Alto (upper town), an entertainment district with countless bars, restaurants and fado taverns; Baixa, the lower town rebuilt in a regimented fashion following the devastating earthquake of 1755, today a banking and shopping district; Chiado, the former intellectuals' district in Belle Époque style; the Elevador de Santa Justa (1901) between the upper and lower town; the Museu do Azulejo in the Madre de Deus monastery; the Museu Calouste Gulbenkian, an oil magnate's foundation with top-ranking European art; the Museu de Arte Antiga, the largest museum of Portuguese art; the Oceanário, a magnificent aquarium; and the Palácio dos Marqueses da Fronteira, a castle complex with a magnificent baroque garden.

Top: Rossio, the center of the Baixa. The area was primarily constructed after the 1755 Lisbon earthquake. Bottom: The Torre de Belém, built in the 16th century as a monument to Portugal's Age of Discovery.

jutting out into the sea, Peniche has an 18th-century maritime fort that is worth visiting before heading inland toward Óbidos. Óbidos, also known as the Queen's Village, is a must-see in Portugal. The fortified hilltop village boasts charming alleys with tidy white houses decorated with flowers, all contained within a picturesque medieval town wall that is up to 15 m (49 ft) high in places.

6 Alcobaça It is hard to believe that one of Christianity's largest sacral buildings – the former Cistercian Mosteiro de Santa Maria de Alcobaça – was built in this town of just under 6,000 inhabitants north of Caldas da Reinha. Founded in the late 12th century and completed in about 1250, it was the first Gothic edifice in Portugal.

The three-storey baroque façade (18th century) is 220 m (241 yds) wide and 42 m (138 ft) high. The three naves of the Gothic interior are also impressive due to their unusual dimensions: 106 m (16 yds) long, 20 m (66 ft) high, but just 17 m (19 yds) wide.

Many of the visitors here are pilgrims visiting the tombs of King Pedro I and his murdered mistress Ines de Castro, who is buried directly opposite him so that, "at the resurrection, each of them should see the other first of all". The complex is a UNESCO World Heritage Site.

7 Batalha This simple country town is on the way to Leiria and is also a UNESCO World Heritage Site for the world-famous Santa Maria da Vitoria monastery. Construction began in 1388, following João I's historical victory at Aljabarrota (1385), but it was not completed until 1533. The complex has become a kind of national shrine for the Portuguese as a symbol of the coun-

try's independence from Spain. A 15-m-high (49-ft), elaborately decorated Manueline portal invites you to enter the cathedral, which is nearly as long as a football field and 32 m (105 ft) high. It is adjoined by the "royal" cloister and contains the tomb of King João I.

8 Leiria Portugal's coat of arms contains the images of seven castles. One of these is in Leiria and it is one of Portugal's most beautiful. The history of its construction begins with the Romans, is influenced by the Moors, and continues through to the crusaders. The complex is

now a mix of Gothic and Renaissance styles and affords a magnificent view of Portugal's largest pine forest.

From Leiria it is worth taking a detour to the south-east, first to Fátima, a pilgrimage site about 30 km (19 mi) away, and then to the Templar castle in Tomar.

9 Coimbra This town on the steep banks of the Rio Mondego is one of Europe's oldest university towns (12th century) and in fact was the only one in Portugal until 1910. The center boasts a fortress-like cathedral (Sé Velha, the largest Roman-

esque church in Portugal), also dating from the 12th century. Behind the cathedral you then continue up to the old university, which is the former royal palace. The highlight here is the library (1716–1728), Portugal's loveliest baroque construction featuring gilded wood and fresco ceilings by Portuguese artists. Not far from the library, in the former bishop's palace, is the Museu Machado de Castro, with the Sé Nova (new cathedral), a former Jesuit church (1600) high on the slope above it.

A short walk takes you through a maze of alleys to the Mosteiro

collide – the stock exchange is juxtaposed with narrow, dingy alleyways.

11 Braga This old episcopal city is inland and to the north-east of Porto and is home to twenty churches closely packed together. The originally Romanesque cathedral was frequently remodeled over the centuries and has two massive towers. Other sites include the 18th-century Palácio dos Biscainhos, surrounded by a magnificent garden; the Oratorio São Frutuoso (7th century) is located 4 km (2.5 mi) outside town; the baroque pilgrimage church of Bom Jesus do Monte, 7 km (4 mi) away, is also famous for its elaborate staircase designed to match the Stations of the Cross (18th century). It is Portugal's second-most important pilgrimage destination after Fátima.

12 Guimarães This town 22 km (14 mi) south-west of Braga proudly claims to be the "Cradle of Portugal". It was here that the founder of the Kingdom of Portugal, Afonso Henriques, was born in 1111. His Romanesque castle with its mighty 27-m (89-ft) tower stands high on the "holy hill"

1 The "royal cloister" in the Santa Maria da Vitória Monastery, Batalha.

2 The Ponte de Dom Luís I in Porto was designed in Gustave Eiffel's office. To the left of the picture is the former bishop's palace; behind it to the right is the Torre dos Clérigos and the cathedral.

3 The University of Coimbra is located on the Alcácova and is the oldest in Portugal.

4 The monumental baroque stairway up the Bom Jesus do Monte pilgrimage church in Braga.

de Santa Cruz, a former Augustinian monastery. Take a break in the Parque de Santa Cruz, part of the monastery grounds. The Quinta das Lágrimas estate was the setting for the love story between Spanish Crown Prince Pedro and his mistress Ines that ended in such tragedy. The Fonte las Lágrimas (Fountain of Tears) supposedly originated with Ines' tears after her death.

Life in Coimbra is heavily influenced by the 20,000 students who still wear the traditional *capa* gown, and not just for special occasions like the Queima das Fitas festival.

10 Porto It was no coincidence that Portugal's second-largest town on the Costa Verde was the European Capital of Culture in 2001. The port at the mouth of the Rio Douro has a great deal to offer visitors. Five bridges now link Porto with Vila Nova de Gaia, where a majority of the port wineries are based.

The streets and rows of houses in Porto's Old Town seem to cling precariously to the steep granite cliffs. At the lower end of the Avenida dos Aliados is the Praça Liberdade with the Torre dos Clerigos, the highest church tower in Portugal at

75 m (246 ft). At the other end is the town hall with its 70-m-high (230-ft) bell tower. The huge azulejo scenes on the wall of the São Bento railway station are especially worth seeing as well.

En route to the Ponte de Dom Luis I you come to the cathedral with its sacrament altar made from 800 kg (1,764 lbs) of silver. From here you can go down into the Bairro da Sé district, the oldest part of Porto, or to the Largo do Colegio. The Praça da Ribeiro and the Praça Infante Dom Henriques make up the heart of the Ribeira district, where wealth and poverty

above town, and the palace of the dukes of Bragança (15th century) is in the charming Old Town. Nossa Senhora da Oliveira Church is also worth seeing. From Guimarães, the scenic N206 heads to Bragança in the north-east of Portugal. It is a worthy detour despite the distance (230 km/143 mi).

If you are wanting to head south, the road branches off to the south at Vila Pouca de Aguiar and brings you to Vila Real and the Palácio de Mateus.

⑬ Vila Real This "royal town" on the Rio Corgo has a number of palaces and is famous for its black pottery. The baroque wine estate belonging to the Mateus family is located 4 km (2.5 mi) to the east. Not far from Vila Real is also the magnificent Solar de Mateus country estate.

⑭ Viseu This town's history goes back to the Romans and the Visigoths, whose last king, Roderich, was defeated here by the Moors. A stroll through the picturesque Old Town will bring you to the cubic proportions of the cathedral with its two-storey 13th-century cloister. The Manueline vaults are remarkable. The Museu Grão Vasco documents the history of

the famous "Viseu" school of painting.

The scenic N10 now brings you to Guarda 100 km (60 mi) away.

⑮ Guarda Portugal's highest town is situated on a cliff 1,056 m (3,465 ft) up in the Serra de Estrela range and was one of Portugal's most important border fortresses for a long time. The older forts and the cathedral in particular are testimony to this history. It is well worth taking a stroll through the picturesque Old Town.

⑯ Castelo Branco The next stop is the capital of the Beira Baixa, a town which was a political bone of contention for centuries due to its proximity to Spain. Only the ruins of the 13th-century fortress remain. The somewhat bizarre Jardim Episcopal, which belongs to the

bishop's palace, is considered to be one of the loveliest baroque gardens in Portugal.

Taking the N18 now to the south, you then turn off at Alpalhão and head for the mountains in the east.

⑰ Marvão This mountain village dating back to the Moors perches like an eagle's nest on the 870-m-high (2,854-ft) cliff. Its mighty fortress once played an important role in the border wars with Spain. You get a magnificent view of the small town ringed by the old town walls, the Serra de São Mamede, the Serra de Estrela and you can even see Spain. With its palaces, townhouses, monasteries, castle, cathedral and medieval town walls, the small town 16 km (10 mi) to the south, Estremoz, is like a open-air museum.

⑱ Estremoz In the Middle Ages this town was home to one of the most important fortresses in Alentejo, of which only the massive keep (13th century) survives today. It is known for its pottery, which is sold on the large marble-paved marketplace on Saturdays and Sundays.

From Estremoz, we highly recommend an excursion to Elvas, situated around 30 km (19 mi) east of Estremoz close to the Spanish border.

⑲ Évora The largest and most scenic town in Alentejo has been declared a UNESCO World Heritage Site because of its historical Old Town, its plazas, 16th- and 17th-century townhouses, palaces, churches and its medieval town wall. From the Praça do Giraldo, with its lovely Renaissance fountains and San-

to Antão Church (1557), you will come to the cathedral, a Gothic church building completed in the 14th century. This fortress-like edifice combines both Romanesque and Gothic elements along with having a Renaissance portal and a baroque altar. Today it adjoins the Museu de Arte Sacra and the Museu Regional. North of the cathedral is the Templo Romano (2nd century) with fourteen Corinthian pillars. Their reliefs

are in surprisingly good condition despite centuries of misappropriation.

The Casa dos Ossos in São Francisco Church is a somewhat macabre attraction: the walls are "adorned" with five thousand skulls.

20 Monsaraz and Mourão
The medieval village of Monsaraz about 50 km (31 mi) east of Evora features an intact town wall, a Castelo (14th cen-

tury), a Gothic parish church and a *pelourinho*, or pillory, from the 17th century. On the opposite side of the Rio Guardiana, the road takes you to Mourão, situated on Europe's largest reservoir lakes, the Barragem do Alqueva. It serves as a catchment for the Rio Guadiana. Small country roads lead to the next stop, Moura.

21 Moura The name of this thermal hot springs resort alone (with its well-maintained spa gardens and music pavilion) is indicative of its Moorish origins. A castle (13th century) is also testimony to that fact. The old Moorish district with its simple white houses and curious chimneys is worth a stroll.

22 Beja Passing through Vidigueira you then reach Beja, the second-largest town in Alente-

jo and one of the hottest towns in Portugal. Originally a Roman settlement, it was then declared a diocesan town under the Visigoths before being ruled by the Moors for 400 years.

It is worth visiting the Old Town for its maze of alleyways, the Convento Nossa Senhora da Conçeição with a cloister decorated with lovely old azulejos, and Santo Amaro Church, which dates back to the Visigoth era. The Castelo (1300) is dominated by the highest keep in Portugal.

23 Mértola The terraces of this scenic little town on the right bank of the Rio Guadiana nestle up against the slope beneath the Castelo dos Mouros.

1 A wonderful view from the Castello de Vide in Marvão.

2 The World Heritage Site of Evora: the Roman Diana Temple.

3 Monsaraz is a commanding mountainous location near Spain, dominated by 13th-century castle.

4 Olive trees and fields of sunflowers near Moura.

5 Mértola's attractions include the castle ruins and a Moorish church.

209

The snow-white Igreja Matriz was a mosque up until 1238.

㉔ Faro Today the "Gateway to the Algarve" is a rather unappealing fishing and industrial town situated on a large lagoon, but it has an attractive Old Town around the cathedral at Largo da Sé and is enclosed by a medieval town wall.
The Carmo Church (18th century) with the Capela dos Ossos (skulls) is also worth seeing. You have the option of taking an excursion from Faro to the fishing port of Olhão with its market halls. The Ria Formosa nature reserve extends between Olhão and Faro, with the Cabo de Santa Maria, the southernmost point in Portugal, at its southern tip.

㉕ Albufeira This former fishing village west of Faro does not have many sightseeing attractions to offer but its favorable Algarve location makes it a tourist stronghold nonetheless. To some extent it is the Saint-Tropez of the Algarve, boasting countless beaches and bizarre cliffs combined with bars and nightlife to suit all tastes.
The buildings in the attractive Old Town sprawl up the steep, scenic coastal slopes.

㉖ Portimão The second-largest tourist stronghold on the Algarve is primarily known for its 1.5-km-long (1-mi) Praia da Rocha beach, which features beautiful and bizarre cliffs. If you have time, it is possible to take an excursion from here to Silves, a town in the interior that has a striking castle complex and a lovely Gothic cathedral (13th century).
In addition to a cork museum, it also boasts the only museum dedicated to Portugal's Moorish era. At that time Xelb, the present-day Silves, served as the capital city.

㉗ Lagos This was the port from which the droves of Portuguese seafarers used to put to set sail in their caravels. In fact, Lagos has been a shipbuilding center since the time of Henry the Navigator (1394–1460). The slave trade forms part of the darker side of the town's history: Lagos was a market and trans-shipment center for the trade in African slaves, the first of whom were auctioned on the Praça da Republica in 1443. The town is dominated by the Ponta da Bandeira fortress, which dates back to the 17th century. The sandy and rocky beaches around Lagos are a very popular destination for water sports enthusiasts.
The fortified walls and the baroque Santo Antonio Church (17th century) are worth seeing, as are the magnificent cliffs on the Ponta Piedade around 2 km (1.2 mi) to the south.

㉘ Sagres This port played a significant role in the 15th and 16th centuries as it is alleged to have been the location of Henry the Navigator's legendary navigation school, a fact that is documented by the giant stone compass on the rocky ledge of the Ponta de Sagres, close to the Fortaleza de Sagres. The rose-shaped compass has a diameter of 43 m (47 yds).
The Cabo de São Vicente is close by and has 24-m-high (79-ft) lighthouse that protrudes out of the sea, marking the south-westernmost point in Europe. The 60-m-high (197-ft)

cliffs were once considered to be "World's End".

㉙ The west coast of the Algarve From Sagres, the road back to Lisbon largely follows the Atlantic coast. The first stop is the village of Vila do Bispo, where the Ermida de Nossa Senhora de Guadelupe chapel is worth a visit.
From there, the journey continues to Aljezur where the ruins of the Castelo afford a magnificent view. Nearby Carrapateira is to be recommended for anyone wanting to make a short detour to the beach. From Aljezur, the road leads to Odemira, a small country town on the Rio Mira, which is controlled by the 44-km (27-mi) lake above the Barragem de Santa Clara dam 30 km (19 mi) to the south-east.
The next stop is Vila Nova de Milfontes, with sandy beaches and water sport options. The road initially heads inland after Sines, before turning back toward the coast after the fortress-liked town of Alcácer do Sol with its Moorish castle, towards Setúbal.

㉚ Setúbal Portugal's third-largest port was already an important fishing port during Roman times and the bay formed by the mouth of the Rio Sãdo is dominated by the port facilities, sardine factories and dockyards. The lively fishing port is an attractive setting as is the Old Town with its winding alleys. Setúbal is also called the "Manueline jewel", and the Igreja de Jesús (1491) with its elaborate columns and magnificent 18th-century azulejosis is a real gem.
You can get a wonderful view over the town from the Castelo São Filipe to the west. For the beach you can take the ferry over to the Tróia Peninsula. Otherwise, the journey now takes you directly back to the capital of Lisbon.

1 Albufeira, with its charming whitewashed buildings, is one of the most popular tourist resorts on the Algarve, retaining its old fishing village flair.

2 The 60-m-high (197-ft) Cabo de Sao Vicente is the weather-beaten south-western tip of Europe.

Porto With a hillside location at the mouth of the Douro and some striking bridges, the European Capital of Culture 2001 is without comparison. Most of the port wineries are in Vila Nova de Gaia on the opposite side.

Guimarães This town is known as the "Cradle of Portugal" because Afonso Henriques, the kingdom's founder, was born here in 1111.

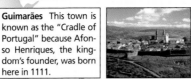

Bragança The approach to this ancestral seat of the ruling dynasty of the same name is absolutely stunning, and the castle and the Torre de Menagem are equally lovely. The cathedral has an unusual brickwork cloister.

Braga This town is famous for the Bom Jesus do Monte church with its elaborate stairway (18th century).

Coimbra Fado bars, the largest Romanesque church in Portugal and a former royal palace are what make this old university town special.

Vila Real This town is rich in palaces and famous for its pottery. The nearby Mateus family manor and wine estate are good for excursions.

Batalha The Santa Maria da Vitoria monastery was built between the 14th and 16th centuries. It is a symbol of independence from Spain.

Castello de Vide Even the Romans valued this mountain village's mineral springs, but the health resort near Marvão close to the Spanish border is also worth visiting for its magnificent view.

Évora Impressive squares, palaces and churches are what make this the loveliest town in Alentejo, Portugal's largest province.

Óbidos This town boasts picturesque alleys, white buildings, a medieval town wall and a large castle. The Romans and the Moors had settlements here.

Monsaraz This medieval town has an intact town wall, the Castelo (14th century), a parish church and the Pelourinho (17th century). It is on the Rio Guardiana near Barragem do Alqueva, a dam reservoir.

Sintra The Palácio Nacional da Pena (1840) and the Paço Real (15th/16th centuries) here used to be summer residences for the aristocracy.

Mértola This scenic small town is on the right bank of the Rio Guardiana, with its terraces nestling up against the slopes beneath the Castelo dos Mouros. The Igreja Matriz was a mosque until 1238.

Lisbon Portugal's capital enjoys a unique location on top of several hills around the mouth of the Tagus and is easily explored by means of the trams (*eléctricos*).

Algarve The best known and most frequently visited region of the country is famous for its bizarre coastal cliffs, magnificent sandy bays and pleasant climate all year round. The water quality is also excellent.

Italy

The area north of Siena is the traditional wine growing region for Chianti Classico, a well defined zone between Florence and Siena.

From Riviera di Levante fishing villages to famous Renaissance cities

From golden rolling hills, aromatic pine forests and stylish cypress boulevards to extraordinary art treasures and mouth-watering cuisine – Tuscany is a perfect holiday destination for nature lovers, art connoisseurs and gourmets. With rustic villages, a rich history and unique landscapes, this attractive region presents itself as one of Europe's 'complete artworks'.

Travelling in Tuscany is simply an intoxicating experience for the senses. Your eyes feast on the magnificently cultivated landscape, the delicate hints of rosemary and lavender please the nose, and your palate is spoilt for choice with world-famous Chianti wines and a cuisine that, with great help from the Medici family, had already begun conquering the world during the Renaissance.

If that were not enough, nearly all Tuscany's charming ancient towns offer abundant art treasures as well.

Historically, central Italy is a region that has been inhabited for thousands of years, and proof of that fact is not hard to find. The ubiquitous remains of Etruscan necropolises, ruins from Roman settlements or the medieval town of San Gimignano make the point clear enough. Tuscany reached its zenith primarily during the medieval and Renaissance periods, and rightly regards itself as the 'Cradle of European culture'. Modern art, including

Michelangelo's *David* in Florence.

painting, sculpture and architecture, can be traced back to this region.

The most important role in the region's rise to glory was played by the Medici, a Florentine family of vast wealth and influence that decisively dictated politics and the arts in that city for almost three hundred years, between 1434 and 1743. The pronounced cultural interest of the Medici drew the renowned artists of the time into their fold and, as patron of the arts, the family commissioned some of the most important works of the Renaissance period.

The cultural bounty of Tuscany attracts a great number of

Cypresses, wine, an isolated farmhouse in the rolling hills – Tuscany presents a unique cultural landscape.

View from Pienza across the Tuscan plain with the cathedral tower in the background.

tourists every year. But a visit to Tuscany should include not only the well-known towns but also the countryside, as Tuscany is as famous for its ancient rural aesthetic as it is for its urban culture. This extraordinary countryside was planned in incredible detail and cultivated for centuries, with the landed gentry as well as the farmers playing a part in the development. The farms, with a geometrical layout unchanged over the years, were placed on hilltops and all boasted a cypress-lined drive to their entrances. These splendid, centuries-old cypress lanes indicate their penchant for precise planning here.

Geographically, Tuscany stretches from the Apennine Mountains in the north to the Monte Amiata in the south, offering a varied landscape with rugged mountains, gentle rolling hills, the fertile coastal area of the Maremma and the green valleys of the Arno river. Southern Tuscany differs considerably from other Tuscan regions, being much hotter and having a less lush vegetation, dominated by maquis – dense, evergreen shrubs.

Industry and tourism are the economic backbones of Tuscany. Agriculture's main product is olive oil, but agriculture nowadays only supports a small part of the population. As a holiday destination, Tuscany is almost perfect all year round – between May and June an abundance of plants blossom in an extraordinary range of colours, while summer is dominated by the radiant red of the poppies and the glowing yellow of sunflower fields. Autumn is the time of the grape harvest, when the chestnut trees and the beeches change colour in late October and transform the landscape into a sea of mellow golden and red.

Your tour also enters the Emilia, a region between the river Po and the Apennine Mountains where Bologna is the city of note. On the west coast you reach Liguria with the Riviera di Levante and the tourist mecca, La Spezia. And from the hills of eastern Tuscany you finally reach Umbria.

Built on cliffs, the coastal village of Rio Maggiore in Cinque Terre.

Tuscany – your tour through this magnificent region is also a journey through the Middle Ages and the Renaissance, starting in the lovely city of Florence. A highly recommended day trip leads to three towns on to the Ligurian coast, and the romantic country roads offer you a unique chance to get to know the varied Tuscan landscape in all its glory.

① Florence (see p. 215). Your circular tour through Tuscany begins in beautiful Florence. Only 8 km (5 miles) north of there is the village of Fiésole.

② Fiésole Founded in the 6th century BC by the Etruscans, this hilltop village is a far cry from the hustle and bustle of the big city and offers a fantastic panoramic view of Florence. In centuries past it was an ideal summer retreat for Florence's aristocracy, who were looking for respite from the city's heat and dust. The wide Piazza Mino da Fiesole with the San Romolo Cathedral (begun in 1028) is the center of the village. North-east of the cathedral, remains of some partially well-preserved Roman settlements were discovered, including the ruins of a theater that seated up to three thousand people. Continuing via Florence you come to lively Prato, Tuscany's third-largest town.

③ Prato With its daring mixture of medieval buildings and modern architecture, Prato is a city of stark contrasts. As it was the metropolis of textile manufacture, wool-weavers began settling here in the Middle Ages. Medieval ramparts enclose the historic town center, which has a cathedral modelled on the cathedrals of Pisa and Lucca. The imposing Castello dell' Imperatore, built by Emperor Frederick II between 1237 and 1248, is a remarkable sight.

④ Pistóia Following the SS64, an often very winding road that negotiates considerable differences in altitude, you reach Pistóia, a lively town

1 The Ponte Vecchio was built in 1345 and is the oldest bridge in Florence. Since 1593, goldsmiths and jewellers have been working in the bridge's workshops.

2 The Romanesque church of San Sepolcro houses the tomb of Saint Petronius and is one of Bologna's many artistically and historically significant ecclesiastical buildings.

Travel Information

Route profile
Length: approx. 1,200 km (745 miles), excluding detours
Time required: at least 2 weeks
Start and end: Florence
Route (main locations): Florence, Bologna, Parma, La Spézia, Livorno, Piombino, Siena, Arezzo, Florence

Traffic information:
Drive on the right in Italy. There is a toll-charge for Italian motorways, but these are rarely used on this trip. Tuscany's roads are well-planned and free of charge.

Accommodation:
Tuscan farmhouses and wine estates (generally known as agriturismo) offer modest to luxury accommodation and are a great alternative to hotels. Try: *www.agrotourismo.net*

Weather:
Italy is dry and hot in the summer, mild in the winter. The rain falls in the autumn, October and November mainly, and July and August can be oppressively hot. The recommended travel season for Tuscany is therefore spring (20–22°C/68–72°F).

Information:
There is an abundance of information on travelling in Italy. Here are a couple of helpful resources:
www.enit.it
www.toskana.net
www.anitalyattraction.com

Florence

Florence's influence on the history of Western civilization is unequalled – it is considered the birthplace of the Renaissance. The city boasts a long list of famous sights, and attracts a phenomenal number of tourists each year. If you want to see the city from above, go to the Piazzale Michelangelo, situated 104 m (341 ft) above the historic town center – the view of Florence stretching picturesquely over both sides of the Arno river is breathtaking.

Almost all the sights in the old part of town are within walking distance of one another. Florence's architectural jewel, the 'Duomo' (Santa Maria del Fiore, built 1296–1436), dominates the Old Town with its magnificent octagonal dome by Brunelleschi. Opposite that is the Baptistry of San Giovanni (11th–13th centuries) with its three sets of bronze doors by Pisano and Ghiberti, and the famous 'Gates of Paradise' doors.

The Uffizi Gallery houses one of the oldest and most important art collections in the world, including masterpieces by Giotto and Botticelli. Nearby, the Ponte Vecchio, Florence's oldest bridge, is famous for the goldsmiths' and jewellers' shops built on it in the 16th century. Back on the Piazza del Duomo, be sure to take a stroll along the Via Calzaiuoli to the Piazza della Signoria, Florence's most beautiful square and home to the 14th-century Palazzo Vecchio, the city's massive town hall with a slim, crenellated tower.

A visit to the Giardino di Boboli is then a lovely finish to your leisurely stroll through town.

Duomo Santa Maria del Fiore.

steeped in tradition that is surrounded by nurseries and colourful flora. The picturesque markets and the beautiful 9th-century church of Sant'Andrea is worth a visit with its legendary pulpit by Pisano (1298).

⑤ Bologna Tuscany is not alone in the area as a custodian of Italy's art treasures. The SS64 leads you to the neighbouring province of Emilia-Romagna and three cities that are as richly steeped in history as any Tuscan locations.

Like so many of the cities in this area, Bologna, the capital of Emilia-Romagna, was founded by the Etruscans. It lies in a fertile plain in the foothills of the Apennines and is home to one of Europe's oldest universities, dating back to 1119.

Important churches, arcaded lanes, towers and palaces bear witness to Bologna's period of prominence back in the Middle Ages. Among other sights, the Church of San Petronio is worth visiting. Its interior ranks up there with the most exemplary of Gothic architectural works. The two 'leaning towers', built in brick for defense purposes, are the hallmark of the city.

The SS9 now leads you on to the town of Módena, about 40 km (25 miles) to the north-west.

⑥ Módena Located in the Po river valley, Módena is worth a visit for its magnificent cathedral and celebrated art treasures. The center of town boasts extensive squares and leafy arcades. The Cathedral San Geminiano (1184), with its impressive 88-m (288-ft) bell tower, and the Piazza Grande have been given joint status as a UNESCO World Heritage Site.

⑦ Réggio nell'Emília Like Módena, Reggio nell'Emília was founded by the Romans and mainly belonged to the

House of Este. The town is situated on the edge of Italy's northern plain, a fertile area with great agricultural yields. The cathedral, whose construction began in the 9th century, the 16th-century San Próspero Church and the Church of the Madonna della Ghiaira, a baroque edifice featuring stucco and frescoes (1597–1619), are all well worth visiting.

⑧ Parma The city of Parma, near the Apennine Mountains, was founded by the Etruscans, but now has a modern layout due to reconstruction after devastating bombings in World War II. The Piazza Garibaldi, with the Palazzo del Governatore, marks the center of town. On the Piazza del Duomo stands the 12th-century Romanesque cathedral with its famous frescoes, while further west you'll find the Palazzo della Pilotta. Inside this unfinished brick edifice is a beautiful inner courtyard and some museums,

such as the Galeria Nazionale. The journey continues now across the 1,055-m (3,460-ft) Cento Croci Pass (SS62 and SS523), a very curvy road with breathtaking scenery that runs from Varese Ligure via Rapallo along the Riviera di Levante.

⑨ Cinque Terre These five legendary coastal villages built on the cliffs of the Riviera di Levante have become one of the most popular tourist areas in all of Italy. Ever since the

4

11 Carrara Here in the north-west of Tuscany, Carrara marks the beginning of the Versilia Coast, a beautiful stretch scattered with white sandy beaches and the Apuan Alps providing the film-set backdrop.

The road takes you through a unique marble region where exhausted marble quarries have left rather bizarre formations that now seem to dominate the landscape. Even in Roman times, Carrara was famous for its fine-grained white and grey marble. Today, Carrara is home to an academy for sculptors, where artists have the luxury of learning to work with the rock directly at its source.

In the workshops of the Old Town of Pietrasanta, you can see stonemasons at work, happy to let tourists watch while they create. It is also well worth taking a stroll through the historic town center to admire the 13th-century Cathedral San Martino with its charming brick campanile.

12 Viaréggio Even in the coastal resort town of Viaréggio, people's livelihood depends to an extent on the marble industry. Other options, however, include shipbuilding and, of course, tourism. Europe's high society discovered this picturesque fishing village in the 19th century, as the art

steeply terraced landscape in the area was made accessible to automobiles, the villages – Monterosso, Vernazza, Corniglia, Manarola and Riomaggiore – are practically household names. However, visitors are strongly recommended to leave their cars in Levanto and take the train instead. The roads leading to the villages are very steep and winding – and often full of traffic.

To be able to enjoy the natural beauty of this place to the full, you need to take the five-hour walk on the footpath that links the five villages. Italy's most beautiful walking trail offers absolutely awe-inspiring views of the Mediterranean and the magnificent cliffs.

After a short excursion to Portofino, another elegant former fishing village, the journey continues south to La Spézia.

10 La Spézia One of Italy's most beautiful bays is located at the southernmost point on the Gulf of Genoa, with the spectacular Apennine Mountains as a backdrop. La Spézia, Liguria's second-largest town, is one of Italy's most important military and commercial ports, a fact that has rendered the town less attractive over the years. However, its charming shopping streets date back to the 19th century and the museum of archaeology and the shipping museum make a visit worthwhile. A short trip south leads to Lerici.

1 Baptistry on the Piazza del Duomo in Parma.

2 Módena's Romanesque cathedral also has a leaning tower – the Torre Ghirlandina.

3 A medieval castle rises above Lerici's marina.

4 Vernazza on the Italian Riviera, one of the five villages of beautiful Cinque Terre.

217

deco villas and audacious rococo-style cafés will illustrate.

From Viaréggio it is only 25 km (15 miles) to Lucca, which is not to be missed on your trip. The road now leaves the coast and runs parallel to the regional nature reserve, Parco Naturale Migliarino-Massaciúccoli, which stretches all the way down to Livorno.

⑬ Pisa About 21 km (13 miles) south of Viaréggio is Pisa, well-known for its unique buildings around the Campo dei Miracoli, the 'Field of Miracles'. Among the masterpieces here are the Duomo (the cathedral) and the Baptistry – and most important of all, the Leaning Tower of Pisa, which began leaning to the south-east almost immediately after construction began in 1775. Although these structures were built at different times, they were all erected with white Carrara marble and

therefore have the effect of being one harmonious entity. Pisa's role as an important commercial and naval port earned the city the epithet of 'Queen of the Sea', and its influence was considerable. Its decline

came when Pisa was defeated by powerful rivals from Genoa and Venice, and the port silted up. The only leading institution remaining in Pisa is its university, proof of a deep-rooted educational tradition. If you wish

to relax, visit the romantic botanic gardens, established in 1543.

⑭ Livorno One can hardly believe that Livorno is part of Tuscany, its ambience is so dif-

town. Only fifteen are standing now, but these perfectly preserved 14th-century towers, the iconic skyline of San Gimignano, make you feel as if transported back to the Middle Ages.

Returning along the same route, you reach the coast again about 72 km (45 miles) further along. Follow the old Via Aurelia south to San Vincenzo, and continue on a small coastal road until you get to a series of beaches that look inviting for a dip.

⑰ Piombino The ferries for Elba leave from Piombino, a port town with an interesting port promenade and charming views of the old anchorage and the island of Elba. Populonia, an ancient Etruscan port town with the impressive necropolis of San Cerbone, is nearby and worth a visit.

Getting back on the S1 at San Vincenzo, continue to Follónica, where the SS439 turns inland.

⑱ Massa Marittima Roughly 26 km (16 miles) from the sea, the small town of Massa Marittima lies on the edge of the Maremma, a former marshland that was drained in the 19th century. From the upper part of town – in particular the Torre del Candeliere – you can get a magnificent view of the Old Town's red roofs and the surrounding Tuscan countryside. A diocesan town in the 12th and 13th centuries, Massa Marittima boasts magnificent medie-

1 View across the plains of the Maremma, from Massa Marittima on the hills of the Colline Metallifere. The Romanesque-Gothic cathedral is the town's icon.

2 Pisa's famous symbols – the Baptistry, Duomo and 'Leaning Tower' in the Field of Miracles.

ferent. But this is probably due to the late construction of the town. It was not until 1571 that this small fishing village was expanded into a port by Cosimo I (see the Medici sidebar p. 268) because Pisa's port was in

danger of silting up. The dyke protecting the port here was built between 1607 and 1621. Today, Livorno is Tuscany's most important port. At the seaside visitors can admire the 'Old Fortress' (1521–23) and the 'New Fortress' (1590) and enjoy a visit to the aquarium.

South of Livorno the route continues along the cliffs to San Pietro in Palazzi, past some sandy bays. From here you take the exit onto the SS68 heading east and continue for another 33 km (20 miles) inland until you get to Volterra, high above the road on a hillside.

⑮ Volterra Medieval ramparts surround Volterra's historic town center with its narrow and dark little alleyways and tall rows of houses. The town's livelihood comes mainly from the alabaster industry. The Etruscan Museum, containing thousands of funer-

ary urns and sarcophagi, is a must for anyone interested in this ancient culture.

The view from the top of the city hall's tower is breathtaking – on clear days you can even see the sea. The old town has been left intact for a rather dramatic reason – Volterra is in danger of subsiding because the steep hill it is built on frequently suffers landslides, making the town unattractive to developers.

A turn-off from the SS68 leads onto a small road of outstanding natural beauty – this is the heart of Tuscany, with its typical landscape of vineyards and olive groves.

⑯ San Gimignano For a time, the merchant families of San Gimignano built tall towers to display their wealth – the taller the tower, the richer the family. Seventy-two of them guarded the dreamy Piazza della Cisterna in the historic center of

val buildings such as the Duomo San Cerbone (1228–1304). Stay on the SS441 and SS73 for 75 km (46 miles) to Siena.

19 Siena Siena's red-brick palaces and extraordinary flair often give this town a more authentic ambience than its great rival Florence. The 'Gothic City' stretches over three hillsides in the heart of the rolling Tuscan countryside. Its historic center has long been designated a UNESCO World Heritage Site. Siena is also home to what is arguably Italy's most beautiful square, the shell-shaped Piazza del Campo, surrounded by Gothic palaces. Twice a year it hosts the legendary Palio horse race, which attracts up to fifty thousand spectators and causes total chaos throughout the city.

The Duomo (12th century) is Siena's cathedral and one of the jewels of the Gothic period. It should not be missed. Other architectural treasures include the Palazzo Pubblico (1288–1309) and the slim 102-m (334-ft) Torre del Mangia, one of the most daring medieval towers. The center of the Chianti area is north of Siena. From here, small roads lead to the domain of Chianti Classico, carrying the emblem 'Gallo Nero' (black cockerel) as proof of its outstanding quality. The vineyards advertise 'Vendita diretta' for

wine tasting and direct sales. Follow the S222, S249 and S408 in a clockwise direction to visit a number of quaint villages – Castellina in Chianti, Radda in Chianti, Badia a Coltibuono, Moleto and Brolio with its castle Castello di Brolio.

20 Montepulciano About 70 km (43 miles) south-east of Siena is Montepulciano, a Renaissance town of outstanding beauty on top of a limestone hill. The small town, with its lovely brick buildings, is a Mecca for wine and art connoisseurs.

Just outside Montepulciano you'll find San Biagio, an architectural treasure dating back to the 16th century. The pilgrimage church is laid out in the form of a Greek cross and is surrounded by cypresses – in perfect harmony with the landscape.

From Montepulciano the S146 leads to Chiusi and south-east to the junction of the S71,

which runs along the west side of the Lago Trasimeno before bringing you to Cortona 40 km (25 miles) away. From the lake we recommend a detour of about 75 km (46 miles) to visit Assisi on the S75 – birthplace of the legendary St Francis of Assisi.

21 Cortona Cortona, one of the oldest Etruscan settlements, is another Tuscan hill town situated above the plains of Chiana. We recommend a stroll through the maze of the Old Town, full of alleyways and steps. The Piazza Garibaldi offers a spectacular view of the Lago Trasimeno.

22 Arezzo Arezzo, 80 km (50 miles) south-east of Florence, is the last port of call on your journey. The palaces of rich merchants and influential families dominate the scene, along with the ubiquitous religious buildings. The town is wealthy, partly due to its world-

wide gold jewellery export industry.

The Gothic Basilica of San Francesco has become a Mecca for art lovers. The main attraction is the *History of the True Cross*, a series of frescoes by Piero della Francesca. *La Leggenda della Vera Croce* (The Legend of the True Cross) is also one of Italy's most beautiful frescoes. Its theme is the wood from the tree of knowledge in the Garden of Eden that became the cross on which Christ was crucified. The colour and the perspective are extraordinary.

1 The pilgrimage church of Tempio di San Biagio (1518–34) is a masterpiece by architect Antonio da Sangallo just outside Montepulciano.

2 The Duomo and the 102-m (334-ft) bell tower of the Palazzo Pubblico dominate the modest skyline of Siena.

Parma This town is famous for its food – the delicious prosciutto di Parma and of course Parmesan cheese. After being destroyed during World War II, the Old Town was not restored. The Lombardian-Romanesque Duomo (12th century) and the Palazzo della Pilotta are the only remains.

Módena A Duomo (1184) with an 88-m-high (29-ft) bell tower and leafy arcades are the prominent features of this town.

Bologna This university town in the province of Emilia-Romagna is steeped in history and well worth a visit. The Church of San Petronio, with its two famous leaning towers, and the interesting alleys and palaces keep you wandering.

Prato The historic part of this textile industry hub is surrounded by medieval fortifications. Prato is home to its own Duomo and the Castello dell'Imperatore, built by Emperor Frederick II from 1237 to 1248. The rest of the Old Town is an interesting mix of ancient and modern buildings.

Portofino This seaside town in the Gulf of Rapallo is surrounded by olive and cypress groves. The quaint fishing village has long attracted the rich and famous, who have built luxury villas here.

Florence A trip to Florence should start at the Piazzale Michelangelo, to get a perfect view of the 'Birthplace of the Renaissance', before visiting the other main attractions – the Duomo Santa Maria del Fiore, the Uffizi, the Ponte Vecchio and the Palazzo Vecchio.

Cinque Terre The villages of Monterosso, Vernazza, Corniglia, Manarola and Riomaggiore on the Riviera di Levante are among Italy's most photographed.

Assisi This town on the western flank of Monte Subasio is the birthplace of the famous St Francis (1182–1226).

Lucca Seven arches open onto the historic center of this walled town, to the Duomo San Martino (11th century) and to many merchants' houses, towers and villas.

Volterra This ancient city is famous for its alabaster products, and its History and Etruscan Museum ranks among Italy's best.

Elba Italy's third-largest island offers an amazingly varied landscape with mountains, lowland plains, olive groves, pine forests and bays for swimming. In the northern part of the island is Napoleon's summer residence, the Villa Napoleonica – a must-see.

Massa Marittima The upper part of town offers a breathtaking view over the historic center's red roofs, with the Duomo San Cerbone (1228–1304), and the surrounding Tuscan countryside.

San Gimignano Many of the medieval buildings here have been expertly preserved, among them fifteen of the original seventy-two medieval towers, which offered shelter against enemy attack.

Pisa Not only the Leaning Tower, but all the buildings on the Campo dei Miracoli (the Field of Miracles), including the Duomo and Baptistry, are worth visiting. Although these edifices in elegant Carrara marble were constructed at different times, they convey perfect architectural harmony.

Siena Florence's eternal rival is defined by the Gothic period. The Piazza del Campo, one of Italy's most beautiful squares, is a perfect example. Also visit the Duomo and the bold Torre del Mangia.

Italy

The Temple of Hera, also known as the 'Basilica', was built around 530 BC, and is the oldest surviving temple in Paestum.

On the Via Appia from Rome to Brindisi

In the time of the Imperium Romanum, the motto of the day was 'All roads lead to Rome', when Romans saw their capital as the cradle of not only their own empire but of the civilized world. Large parts of Europe and the entire Mediterranean were ruled from here, and military roads ensured the necessary logistical infrastructure. Probably the best known of these ancient roads is the Via Appia Antica, the basis for your journey.

Relatively little remains of the brilliant splendour of ancient Rome, but what is left is indeed impressive enough – the Colosseum, the Baths of Caracalla, the Pantheon, Domus Aurea, the Arch of Titus, Forum Romanum, the emperors' forums and the Capitol. Contemporary Rome, on the other hand, is defined more dramatically by the unremitting desire of the popes to build magnificent churches, palaces, squares and fountains using the best architects of their times. The popes were particularly active during the Renaissance and baroque periods. To this day, St Peter's Square and St Peter's Cathedral remain the heart of the city and of the Catholic Christian world.

The ancient Via Appia began at what is today Porta Sebastiano, and originally only went as far as Capua. It was then extended past Benevento and Taranto to

Equestrian Statue of Emperor Marcus Aurelius in Rome.

Brindisi in 190 BC. Around AD 113, Emperor Trajan added yet another ancillary road that led through Bari.

The 540-km-long (336-mile) basalt route, lined as it is by countless ancient tombs, temples, villas, ruins and even early Christian catacombs, can still be driven today and is considered 'the longest museum in the world'. The road initially takes you out of Rome and into the hills of the Colli Albani where, in the Middle Ages, popes and Roman nobles had numerous villas and castles built – collectively known as the Castelli Romani. From Velletri, the Via Appia continues in almost a dead straight line to what is

The Ponte Sant'Angelo bridge in Rome leads over the Tiber to the Castel Sant'Angelo, built in AD 139 as a citadel, prison and papal residence.

The 13th-century Cathedral of Matera (Apulia) is maintained in the late Romanesque style. The ancient town is famed as "Sassi di Matera".

today Terracina on the Tyrrhenian Sea, then through Gaeta and inland towards Cápua.

From here, there is still an access road to the former Greek city of Neapolis, known today as Naples. This is home to the infamous Mount Vesuvius, a still-active volcano that once destroyed Pompeii and Herculaneum, and whose next eruption remains a concern for some geologists. For the time being, the view from the crater's rim provides a wonderful view of the bustling city of Naples and the Island of Ischia in the Gulf of Naples.

From Naples, the journey continues along the sea around the Gulf to Sorrento. Since the time of the Roman emperors this picturesque area has been a meeting place for aristocracy. The southern side of the Sorrento Peninsula is where the steep cliffs of the Amalfi Coast begin, with its quaint, pastel-coloured villages nestled between the azure sea and the brilliant yellow lemon trees. At the end of the famous Amalfitana coastal road lies Salerno, where the actual Mezzogiorno begins.

The stunning coastal road then continues on to Paestum, with ancient golden-yellow Greek temples that are some of the most beautiful examples of their kind in Europe. Indeed, the Greeks settled in southern Italy long before the Romans and left some magnificent relics of a blossoming civilization. After Sapri the route leaves the coast and heads east through the inland province of Basilicata towards the Gulf of Taranto. At Metaponto on the gulf, the route again swings inland towards Matera, whose 'sassi' – former ancient cave dwellings – are a UNESCO World Heritage Site. Ta-ranto marks the starting point for the journey through the 'Land of the Trulli', whose capital is Alberobello. After passing through Ostuni you finally arrive in Brindisi, where one of the two ancient port columns is a reminder of how important this city at the end of the Via Appia once was for the mighty Imperium Romanum.

Remains of a colossal statue of Constantine the Great in the Palazzo dei Conservatori in Rome.

1

On the trail of the ancient Via Appia: this route begins in Rome and follows the famous highway of classic antiquity to Cápua, where it was later extended to Benevento, Taranto and then Brundisium (Brindisi). The stations recall the country's important historic periods.

1 Rome For a detailed description of the myriad attractions here, see pp. 226-227.
Porta Sebastiano used to be known as Porta Appia because this ancient city gate marked the start of the Via Appia. The area around the porta includes the burial site of the Scipios, the famous Temple of Mars and the tomb of Cecilia Metella on the cypress-lined road to Frascati.

2 Frascati This is the most famous town of the Castelli Romani. Its glorious location, numerous patrician villas (e.g. the 17th-century Villa Aldobrandini), its exceptional white wine and 'porchetta', crispy grilled suckling pig, all contribute to

this renown. And the popes enjoyed it all, which is why Frascati was their long-time summer residence before they moved to Castel Gandolfo. Roughly 5 km (3 miles) east of the city are the ruins of the ancient Tusculum, the favourite abode of Cicero, one of Rome's greatest orators and philosophers. A few smaller places around Frascati are also worth a visit. The main attraction of the Grottaferrata, 3 km (2 miles) south of Frascati, is the castle-like monastery of San Nilo, founded in 1004, with frescoes from Domenichio (17th century). It's worth taking a small detour into the Alban Hills (Colli Albani – 740 m/2,427 ft) to see the township of Rocca di

Travel Information

Route profile
Length: approx. 650 km (404 miles), excluding detours
Time required: 10–12 days
Start: Rome
End: Bríndisi
Route (main locations):
Rome, Frascati, Velletri, Latina, Terracina, Gaeta, Cápua, Naples, Sorrento, Salerno, Paestum, Rotondella, Metaponto, Matera, Taranto, Martina Franca, Bríndisi

Traffic information:
Drive on the right in Italy. Speed limit in built-up areas is 50 km/h (31 mph), on highways 130 km/h (81 mph). International licences are required unless you have a new photocard licence from a European nation. Spare

bulbs and warning triangle required.

When to go:
The best times to travel are spring and autumn, as temperatures are pleasant. In summer, temperatures can rise to over 40°C (105°F), though by the sea it is often cooler with the breezes. For current weather conditions at many holiday destinations visit:
www.italy-weather-and-maps.com

Information:
www.italiantourism.com
www.justitaly.org
For accommodation and events:
www.slowtrav.com/italy

its annual 'Infiorata' – on the Sunday after Corpus Christi a carpet of flowers adorns the Via Italo Belardi all the way up to the church of Maria della Cima. The flowers come from the neighbouring town of Nemi, which is also a local strawberry-growing center.

6 Velletri The southernmost of the Castelli Romani communes is Velletri, located at the edge of the Via Appia Antica. Like Frascati, it is known for its excellent wines, but apart from this there are architectural attractions including the Piazza Cairoli with its 50-m-high (164-ft) Torre del Trivio from 1353, the Palazzo Communale from 1590, and the cathedral, which was completed in 1662.
The Via Appia then continues from Velletri to Latina.

7 Latina This township is a good starting point for a day trip to the lovely forests and lakes of the Circeo Nature Park, which stretches over the mountainous promontory of Monte Circeo. At the tip of the peninsula is the alleged grotto of the sorceress, Circe, from Homer's *Odyssey*.
From Latina, the route leads into the coastal town of Terracina.

8 Terracina This town, which is today a famous spa resort, was once an important Roman trading town. Evidence of this can still be seen here.

1 The impressive complex of St Peter's Square, Rome, a masterpiece created by Bernini between 1656 and 1667. The obelisk in the middle of the square was erected in 1586 with the help of horses and winches.

2 An icon of Rome and a popular meeting place – the Spanish Steps. They get their name from the Piazza di Spagna.

Papa, some 8 km (5 miles) south-east of Frascati. Monte Cavo at 949 m (3,114 ft) provides a wonderful view out over the province of Lazio. The town of Marino is also lo-cated roughly 8 km (5 miles) away to the south of Frascati. During the wine festival on the first weekend of October, wine flows from the Fontana dei Mori instead of water!

3 Castel Gandolfo This small town, idyllically located on

Lake Albano (Lago Albano), has been the summer residence of the popes since 1604. The Papal Palace (1629–69) and other impressive homesteads like Villa Barberini and Villa Cyco, are the defining buildings in the area. The Piazza, with the Church of San Tommaso and a stunning fountain by Bernini, is also worth seeing.

4 Albano Laziale High above Lake Albano, the legendary Latin Alba Longa is said to have

once been located here before the rise of Rome even began. The remains of a villa belonging to the famous general Pompei-us is still open to the public. In Arrica, the neighbouring town designed by Bernini, it's worth visiting the Palazzo Chigi and the church of Santa Maria dell'Assunzione (1665) at the Piazza della Republica.

5 Genzano This small town between the Via Appia Antica and Lago di Nemi is famous for

Rome

The 'Eternal City', with its unparalleled artistic treasures and architectural monuments from basically every period of Western culture, is the center of the Catholic world and at the same time the lively and vibrant capital of Italy - you just have to see Rome at least once in your life!

Rome, built on seven hills around the Tiber River, obviously has a long and eventful history that has left endless marks on the city. Its neighbourhoods, squares, monuments, buildings and architectural treasures have been built in every style imaginable. Today, not all seven of the ancient hills are recognizable in the sea of houses, but from the Piazza del Quirinale on the Quirinal, the highest of these hills, you can get a fantastic view over the entire city. It is said that Rome was founded in 753, but the first traces of settlement are clearly older. In fact several centuries before there was significant activity here. The year 509 BC, for example, was a importance in the 19th century when Italy was reunited and Rome was made the capital of the Kingdom of Italy.

Ancient Rome includes several mustsees such as the Forum Romanum, the main square of the Old City; the Colosseum with its four-storey arena; and the Pantheon, the domed masterpiece of ancient architecture.

In the Vatican City is St Peter's Basilica, the domed, Renaissance-style monument; the Vatican museums and galleries, probably the largest collection of art in the world; the Sistine Chapel ceiling, painted by Michelangelo; and the Santa Maria Maggiore with original mosaics from the 5th century

Left: The view of Ponte Sant'Angelo and the Castel Sant'Angelo.
Top: Nicola Salvis' masterpiece, the Trevi Fountain, was completed in 1762.

dramatic one in which the Roman Republic was established – and one oriented towards expansion.

Rome soon became the mistress of the Mediterranean and ultimately, during the time of the emperors, the ruler of the known world. The Age of the Popes began after the fall of the Roman Empire. Rome then became primarily a religious center. However, the city eventually regained political (exclave of the Vatican). Be sure to visit the Villa Giulia, once a papal summer residence with the national Etruscan museum.

The baroque square of Piazza Navona, the baroque fountain Fontana di Trevi, and the Spanish Steps are great meeting places.

For day trips, take the Via Appia to the catacombs of San Callisto and San Sebastiano, or go to Tivoli.

The devastating bomb attacks during World War II actually had one fortuitous result – they uncovered a number of ancient sites, including a section of the Via Appia and the original foundation of the Roman Forum.

The cathedral is from the Middle Ages and is located on a former temple site. It contains some artistic treasures such as a mo-saic floor dating back to the 13th century. The spectacular coastal road leads from here to your next coastal town.

9 Gaeta The Old Town, whose silhouette is dominated by the Aragonian fort and the Church of San Francesco, has a picturesque location on a small peninsula. However, the town is particularly worth visiting for the unique bell tower in the 12th-century cathedral – its bricks are fired in bright colours. The small Church of San Giovanni a Mare, dating from the 10th century, also contains a small oddity – the builders wisely designed the floor on a slope so that the sea water could run off again at high tide. For a long time Gaeta was a fortress for the kingdom of Naples.

After a few kilometers, the road leaves the coast and heads inland towards Cápua.

10 Cápua When it was initially built, the first 'section' of the Via Appia ended here in Cápua. This former Etruscan center, with its enormous amphitheater from the 1st century AD, was destroyed after the collapse of the West Roman Empire and rebuilt by the Lombards in the 9th century. The cathedral's bell tower dates back to this time. The Museo Campagna on the nearby Palazzo Antignano houses numerous discoveries from the city's ancient burial sites. The tour now leaves the Lazio landscape and continues on towards Campania.

11 Caserta Just a stone's throw away from Cápua is the town of Caserta, sometimes boastfully called the 'Versailles of the South' – Bourbon King Karl III built the monumental French-style Palazzo Reale here. The palace is grouped around four large interior courtyards and is an impressive five storeys high. The whole complex – declared a UNESCO World Heritage Site – is 247 m (810 ft) long, 184 m

The ancient Via Appia

The most famous of ancient Rome's legendary roads was named after its builder, Appius Claudius Caecus, and was designed using large hexagonal blocks laid on an extremely solid foundation. First constructed as a military transport route, it was later used more heavily for trade. It originally led from the Porta Sebastiano in Rome to Cápua, but was extended through Bene-vento and Taranto to Brindisi in 190 BC. As Roman road architects mainly preferred straight lines, the road actually runs 'perfectly straight', despite steep rises in the Alban Hills and the Pontine Marshes. The Via Appia is 4.1 m (13 ft) wide, enough for two large transport wagons to pass each other at the time. You can still drive its complete length of 540 km (336 miles).

area; and the star-shaped Castel Sant'Elmo (14th–16th century) on Vomero Hill, just opposite the former Carthusian monastery of Certosa di San Martino. The Palazzo Reale and the Teatro San Carlo (1737) are also worth visiting.

Next to the Gothic Duomo San Gennaro (13th century) is the Gothic church of Santa Chiara (14th century), burial place of the Anjou kings with an interesting cloister. Behind the church Della Madre de Buon Consiglio is the entrance to the catacombs from early Christian times with frescoes dating back to the 2nd century. After the caves take a ride on the Funicolari, cable cars that bring you to the higher parts of the city.

The Museo Archeologico Nazionale has some priceless discoveries including the 'Farnese Bull' from the Baths of Caracalla in Rome and the mosaics from Pompeii depicting Alexander the Great's battle. A must on the way to Sorrento is Pompeii, which documents the devastating powers of Mount Vesuvius like no other place on earth.

13 Sorrento A beautiful coastal road leads you around the Gulf of Naples to Sorrento, with gorgeous views over the sea on the opposite side of the peninsula from Capri. The Roman emper-

1 The view over the Bay of Naples with the yacht port and Vesuvius in the background.

2 One of the important country villas of the ancient city of Pompeii – the Villa dei Misteri. Its wonderfully colourful paintings (80–30 BC) depict occult celebrations.

3 The church of San Francesco di Paola in Naples was modelled after the Roman Pantheon. Its cupola is 53 m (174 ft) high.

3

(604 ft) wide and has 1,200 rooms with 1,800 windows.

No less extraordinary are the 120-ha (297-acre) baroque gardens with statuaries and water features including the Great Waterfall, which are a mighty 78 m (256 ft) high!

Somewhat in contrast to this extravagance here is the modest medieval mountain town of Caserta Vecchia 10 km (6 miles) to the north-east. There is a

Norman cathedral here that was consecrated in 1153.

From Caserta, it's roughly 40 km (25 miles) to Naples, originally founded as Neapolis by the Greeks in the 7th century BC.

12 Naples Italy's third-largest city is often considered the 'most Italian' in the country. It is probably the noisiest and most hectic, but also the most likeable of Italy's big cities, where

washing lines still hang over the narrow alleys and the gap between rich and poor provides a somehow fascinating cultural mix.

The Spaccianapoli (literally 'split Naples'), a boulevard that cuts right through the city, widens at the turn-off to the north-south axis, Via Toledo, and leads you into the Piazza del Gesù Nuovo. At the center of the square is a 34-m-high (112-ft) baroque column dedicated to the memory of plague victims from the 17th century. Opposite this is the church of Gesù Nuovo, dating from the 16th century. The Old Town of Naples, with its 300 churches, castles and town houses, was declared a UNESCO World Heritage Site in 1995.

In addition, there are three castles in the center of the city: Castel dell'Ovo from 1154, the residence of the Normans and Hohenstaufen of Swabia; Castel Nuovo (1279–82) in the port

ors had villas and temples built in this small town upon high, steep rock faces as if on their own natural throne.

Sorrento experienced a Renaissance in the 18th century, when it was inundated by artists. Today, the birthplace of the poet Torquato Tasso in 1544 is one of Italy's most popular health resorts and artist colonies. A marble statue in the Piazza Torquato Tasso pays homage to the poet.

The iconic 14th-century cathedral is worth seeing for its inlay work alone, and the Villa Communale provides wonderful views out over the Gulf of Naples. Another popular holiday destination in the area is the medieval town of Massa Lubrense, south of Sorrento.

⑭ Positano One of the most beautiful spots on the Amalfi Coast is at the beginning of the Amalfitana. Famous for its picturesque location on two slopes of the Monte Angelo a Tre Pizzi (1,443 m/4,738 ft), Positano has been transformed from a once quaint fishing village into a sophisticated spa resort. Dominating the scene over Spaggia Grande Beach is the glazed cupola of the Church of Santa Maria Assunta.

⑮ Amalfi The cultivated fields dotting the Amalfi Coast, itself a UNESCO World Heritage Site, stretch out along the southern side of the Sorrento peninsula. Amalfi, today a lovely resort with a population of 6,000, was an important maritime republic between the 9th and 11th centuries that competed with the likes of Genoa, Pisa and Venice – it was home to 50,000 people back then. The rowing regatta held every four years between these former rivals is now the only legacy of those times. In the 14th century, Amalfi was extensively destroyed by a

heavy storm tide. Little of its history has been preserved.

In the middle of the maze of alleys is the monumental cathedral dating back to the 9th century. It was built in 1203 in an Arab-Norman-Sicilian style. Two former monasteries have been converted to luxury hotels where the likes of Henrik Ibsen and Ingrid Bergmann have stayed.

A worthwhile day trip from Amalfi takes you into the Valley of the Mills where some of Europe's oldest paper mills were constructed. Make sure you see the wild Castania forests on Monte Lattari, which form the impressive hinterland of the Amalfi Coast.

⑯ Salerno The capital of the province and gulf of the same name had its heyday under Norman rule in the 11th/12th centuries when it was home to the Scuola Medica, Europe's first medical school. The Duomo San Matteo, with its 56-m-high (184-ft) campanile, was also built during this time. After passing between the Roman lions you enter a large

forecourt with arcades of twenty-eight ancient columns brought from Paestum. The crypt is a gem of baroque marble inlay work. The Castello di Arechi towers over the city.

⑰ Paestum In 1752, road workers on the southern bend of the Gulf of Salerno came across the ruins of the ancient city of Poseidonia, which was founded by the Greeks in 600 BC and later called Paestum by the Romans. After being extensively destroyed by the Saracens in the 9th century, it was forgotten until the road came.

The imposing temple complexes (the Temple of Neptune, Temple of Ceres, Temple of Hera) have now been excavated and preserved.

Other attractions include the 4.7-km-long (3-mile) city wall, a forum, the Via Sacra and a Roman amphitheater. Herds of placid buffalo now graze between the monuments and supply milk for the reputedly best mozzarella in the world.

⑱ Agrópoli South of Paestum is Agrópoli, a fishing town that clings to a rock cape. It has picturesque alleyways, ancient

steps, a Saracen castle and more wonderful views of the gulf. East of Agrópoli, the hilly Parco Nazionale Del Cilento surrounds Monte Cervati (1,898 m/6,227 ft). You can go hiking, enjoy the serenity of the idyllic mountain village of Castellabate, or bathe in the turquoise-blue bays at Capo Palinuro.

Circling the promontory separating the Gulf of Salerno and the Gulf of Policastro, you finally arrive in Sapri. From here, the route leaves the southbound coastal road and heads east overland to Brindisi, the historic end terminus of the Via Appia. Just under half way to Metaponto, about 30 km (19 miles) out of Sapri, you should take a detour south at Lauría into the Parco Nazionale del Pollina, which preserves under its symbol, the Bosnian pine.

The rugged landscape of the Basilicata is home to some lovely verdant forests, and peaks like Monte Pollina (2,248 m/ 7,376 ft). Two of this region's specialities are the rare stone pines and the Apennine wolf.

⑲ **Metaponto** Founded by the Greeks, this ancient city on the Gulf of Taranto used to be called Metapontion before it fell to the Romans. It was also where the philosopher Pythagoras died in 497 BC. Numerous artefacts from excavations in the surrounding area are exhibited in the Museo Nazionale. The ruins of four temple complexes, the agora and amphitheaters are located in the Parco Archeologico. Drive to the Lido di Metaponto for a swim.

⑳ **Matera** Matera owes its fame to its 'sassi' – medieval cave dwellings dug into the steep tuff walls of the Gravina (gorge). Inextricably nestled into one another, houses later built in front of them stretch up the western slope. The caves were originally inhabited by Benedictine and Greek monks who built chapels, halls and altars and painted priceless historic frescoes. Farmers later followed their example. Almost 20,000 people lived here in incredibly tiny spaces and in very primitive conditions until the start of the 1950s – sometimes even with their animals. To eradicate them as a source of 'national shame', the sassi inhabitants were eventually relocated. Since the 1970s the structures were restored and made into a very popular tourist attraction. The town's other sights include the Norman-Roman cathedral (13th century), the Castello Tramontano (1515) and the Chiesa del Purgatorio (1770) with macabre

1 The Duomo di Sant'Andrea in Amalfi was rebuilt in Romanesque style in the 11th century. An impressive perron leads from the Piazza Duomo up to the church.

2 The Costiera Amalfitana near Positano – pastel-coloured houses cling to the steep slope in terraces.

3 The Temple of Neptune in Paestum was built in 450 BC and is one of the best-preserved Greek temples in all of Europe.

Amalfitana

The coast road running along the Sorrento Peninsula is considered by many to be the most beautiful in Italy. Hewn mercilessly from the steep cliff walls, the 45-km-long (28-mile) route makes its way along the sea through narrow serpentines and hairpins providing you with non-stop panoramic views over the azure blue sea and the Costiera Amalfitana. Villages dot the coastline like pearls amid lemon groves and vineyards, while the sturdy houses cling to the cliffs and cover the dramatic slopes. The road serves as a connection for the villages between Nerano and Salerno.

depictions of purgatory. In 1993, UNESCO declared the city with its two sassi areas a World Heritage Site.

The route heads through Castellanetta towards the coast near Chiatona. The next stop on your trip is Taranto.

㉑ Taranto Also originally a Greek settlement (Taras), Taranto became one of the richest and most powerful cities in Magna Graecia in the 4th century because of its colour production using the spiny dye-murex snail. Most of its inhabitants were still Greek at the time of Emperor Augustus.

Taranto is divided into three sections connected by two bridges. The Old City is perched on a small rock island and is still quite charming despite a long decline. It is dominated by the towers of the Castello Aragonese (15th century). The Museo Archeolo-gico Nazionale is really worth seeing, with its precious gold and silver treasures. The cathedral in the Città Vecchia (Old City) was built in the 12th century but later remodelled. Its cave-like crypt and ancient marble columns are worth a look.

㉒ Martina Franca Further down the road you cross the Zona dei Trulli and reach the town of Martina Franca. In contrast to the nearby trulli style, this town is defined by baroque and rococo buildings like the Palazzo Ducale (1668–1742). The Church of San Martino, built from 1747–75, has a beautiful altar and is located at the gorgeous Corso Vittorio Emanuele. A detour to the trulli after Alberobello is a must (see sidebar left).

㉓ Ostuni The 'white' town lies at the eastern edge of the Zona dei Trulli, just 6 km (4 miles) from the sea. The pic-

turesque village is full of tiny alleyways and terraced white houses sprawl over its three hills. The late Gothic cathedral (15th century) and the town hall at the Piazza della Liberta (14th century) are also worth visiting.

㉔ Bríndisi The ancient city, Brundisium, has been the terminus of the Via Appia since 190 BC. Its original icons were two 19-m-high (62-ft) marble columns down on the waterfront. As back then, Bríndisi continues to be a gateway to the eastern Mediterranean – it isn't much further to Greece and 'Asia Minor' from here.

A plaque on the Colonna Romana pays homage to the poet Vergil who died here in 19 BC. Not far from the Colonna Romana is the cathedral square complex, a 12th-century work that was later given a baroque look in 1743.

Other churches include the Temple Church of San Giovanni al Sepolcro (12th century) and, further west, the church of the same name with a Norman cloister. The Church of Santa Maria del Casale has striking frescoes and the castle on the Seno di Ponte was built under Friedrich II from 1227.

1 The cave dwellings in Matera are divided into an upper and lower district, which are in turn made up of Sasso Barisano and Sasso Cavoso. Over thousands of years, new caves and houses were continually dug into the tuff in the two horn-shaped rock gorges. A total of 150 rock churches have been preserved here.

2 Trulli are the round white houses made of stone with a cone-shaped roof that is really a false dome. The architecture is unique to Apulia.

Rome The city gate of Porta Sebastiano, constructed around 312 BC, marks the start of the Via Appia and was once known as the Porta Appia. The area surrounding the ancient city gate is home to burial sites of the Scipios, the famous Temple of Mars and the tomb of Cecilia Metella.

Vatican City This 'city within a city' covers an area of 44 ha (108 acres) and has 400 permanent residents whose leader is the Pope. The Vatican's 'territory' spans the Vatican itself, the Papal Gardens, St Peter's Basilica and St Peter's Square, as well as some basilicas outside the Vatican and the summer residence of Castel Gandolfo.

Frascati Fabulous villas and the white wine of the same name have made the former papal summer residence famous. It also has some historic buildings to see.

Castel Gandolfo This small town on Lago Albano has been the papal summer residence for 300 years. The Papal Palace (1629–69) and some grand estates such as the Villa Barberini and the Villa Cyco define the town.

Gaeta Visit the colourful cathedral tower (12th C.) and the Church of San Giovanni a Mare (10th C.) in this ancient town neatly perched on a promontory.

Cápua The city, destroyed after the fall of the West Roman Empire, is home to an enormous amphitheater (1st century AD) and an interesting museum.

Genzano This small town on Lago di Nemi is famous for its 'Infiorata' – every year on the Sunday after Corpus Christi, the Via Italo Belardi turns into a carpet of flowers.

Caserta The Palazzo Reale (1752–74) has 1,200 rooms with 1,800 windows. It is sometimes rightly called the 'Versailles of the South.' No less impressive is the 78-m-high (256-ft) waterfall in the palace garden.

Naples 'Italy's most Italian city' is noisy and hectic but its location on the coast, the narrow alleyways and small steps of the Old Town, and its wealth of artistic treasures easily compensate for that.

Pompeii This former provincial capital was buried under a meter of pumice and ash following the eruption of Mount Vesuvius in AD 79. Around three-fifths of the ruins have been unearthed since the 18th century. Nowhere else can Roman domestic culture be so vividly experienced.

Matera Cave dwellings called 'sassi', numerous chapels and buildings from the early Middle Ages buried into the tuff slope have made this picturesque area famous. Old caves were later 'modernized' with facades.

Alberobello Thousands of trulli – including a church and a two-storey stone house built in the typically Apulian style – define the look of this unique area.

Capri This oft-praised isle in the Gulf of Naples is only very small, but thanks to its location and the 'Blue Grotto' it has a mighty reputation on the Mediterranean.

The Amalfi Coast The 45-km-long (28-mile) road on the southern coast of Sorrento is considered Italy's most beautiful coastal stretch. The serpentine route itself is as spectacular as the views it affords.

Amalfi The 9th-century cathedral dominates the Old Town here. A regatta held every four years commemorates Amalfi's past as an important maritime republic.

Paestum This city was founded by the Greeks in the 7th century BC and later destroyed by the Saracens. Its ruins from the 5th century BC are the most important Hellenistic sights on the Italian mainland.

The port of Vieste in the north-east with medieval ramparts and a church

Around the Adriatic

The Realm of the Winged Lion

Sometimes rather sparse, sometimes lush Mediterranean vegetation – but always a view of the sea. Journeying along the Adriatic through Slovenia, Croatia and Italy you will encounter medieval towns, art and culture in spades, as well as tiny rocky coves and beaches stretching for miles.

The northern reaches of the Mediterranean Sea were originally named after the ancient Etruscan town of Adria on the Po Delta, which today is a good 40 km (25 mi) inland to the south-west of Chioggia and is now only linked to the sea by a man-made canal. The town was taken over by the Greeks after the Etruscans, and since that time the mouth of the Po has moved eastwards at a rate of up to 150 m (164 yds) per year. The Adriatic is actually a shallow arm of the Mediterranean, reaching depths of no more than 1,645 m (5,397 ft) between Bari and the Albanian coast.

Venice, the first stop on your journey around the Adriatic, is a trip in itself. The gondolas, palaces and unique cultural monuments of the lagoon city are the result of its rise to power in the 13th century, when influential patrons attracted the greatest artists of the age. It was the Renaissance in particu-lar that shaped not only the city but also the entire look of coast's culture. For it is not only at the start of the journey through the autonomous re-gion of Friuli-Venezia Giulia

Fresco in the Capella degli Scrovegni in Padua.

that you will encounter Venet-ian towns. Venetian architec-tural jewels are also scattered along the adjoining coastline of the Istrian Peninsula as well as along the entire Croatian coast. Many foreign cultures have laid claim to Istria over the centuries due to its fortuitous geographical position.

With 242 km (150 mi) of coast-line and idyllic medieval towns, the peninsula has now devel-oped into a popular holiday destination, with tourism pro-viding the coastal residents with a lucrative livelihood.

Between Istria and the main-land is the Kvarner Gulf, which includes the islands of Cres, Lošinj, Krk, Pag and Rab, but the lively port city of Rijeka is

The Church of San Giorgio Maggiore in Venice, built between 1559 and 1580 and designed by architect Andrea Palladio.

of the Gargano Peninsula in Apulia, shining by night like a lighthouse.

Piran, Slovenia, is a sailing port that juts into the Adriatic with buildings from the Venetian era.

the starting point for our journey along the Croatian coast. The coastal road is lined by relatively barren landscape, an intense mix of light, sea and limestone. All the more surprising, then, that the valleys behind the ridge are so fertile, protected from the infamous *bora*, an icy autumn wind. Vineyards and lush Mediterranean vegetation are pleasing to the eye and provide a refreshing contrast to the lunar landscape of the limestone cliffs. With its steep coastline, the Adria Magistrale is considered one of the most dangerous stretches of road in Europe. On the other hand, there are many interesting destinations and worthwhile attractions that can only be reached via this route. And, with the Serbo-

Croatian War having left very few scars along the coast, tourism has undergone a revival in recent years. As a result, the service sector has also become the most important economic engine for the whole coastal region.

The ferry from Dubrovnik to Bari links the Croatian and Italian coastlines, which are at once similar and different. The section along the Italian side of the Adriatic covers a total of five regions: Apulia, Abruzzi, the Marches, Emilia-Romagna and Veneto, each with an individual culture and landscape. The settlement of the area goes back a long way.

The Etruscans, the Greeks, the Venetians and the Romans all established towns throughout this coastal region. And the

coast itself is as diverse as the region: the rugged cliffs of the Gargano Peninsula rise dramatically from the water while south of Ancona the foothills of the Apennines protrude into the ocean. The tourist centers beyond Rímini are very different again. There, sandy beaches stretch for miles and have mutated into centers of mass recreation.

Veneto, on the other hand, paints a very different picture with canals, lagoons and tidy little islands off the coast at about the same latitude as the university town of Padua.

The defiant St. Nicholas Monastery on the island of Korčula off the Dalmatian coast.

An incomparable landscape combined with cultural diversity are what characterize this tour around the Adriatic, but a number of things remain constant as you pass through Italy, Slovenia and Croatia: the idyllic nature of the coastlines and clear seas, dramatic rock formations and cliffs, the gentle valleys and the tantalizing coves with magnificent beaches.

1 Venice (see page 237) Following one of the undisputed highlights of this tour right at the outset, namely a visit to Venice, you continue along the B14 as far as the intersection with the B352.

2 Aquiléia Aquiléia was one of the largest and richest towns in the ancient empire of Augustus, but today it is home to just 3,400 inhabitants. The remains of the Roman town as well as the Romanesque Basilica of Our Lady, with its magnificent 4th-century mosaic floor, have both been declared a UNESCO World Heritage Site. Visitors can get an idea about the glorious past.

3 Údine It was only in the late Middle Ages that this former Roman settlement developed into the region's main city. The influence of Venice can be seen throughout the town, as well as on the Piazza Libertà, whose loggias and the splendid clock tower (1527) truly make it one of the loveliest squares in the world. The Renaissance Castello di Údine towers over the Old Town and the Santa Maria Annunziata Cathedral (14th century) features master-

1 The imposing baroque church Santa Maria della Salute on the Grand Canal has a foundation of more than one million piles.

Travel Information

Route profile
Length: : approx. 2,125 km (1,320 mi)
Time required: at least 3 weeks
Start and end: Venice
Route (main locations): Venice, Trieste, Pula, Rijeka, Split, Dubrovnik, Bari, Pescara, Ancona, Ravenna, Padua, Venice

Traffic information:
The motorways in Austria, Switzerl and Italy all require a vignette. You also need to carry the Green Insurance Card with you.
Warnings of live landmines have been issued in Croatia; these warnings should obviously be heeded when making excursions into the coastal hinterland between Senj and Split as well as in the mountains south-east of Dubrovnik!
Information regarding the ferries from Cres and Rab as well as to Bari:
www.croatia-travel.org
www.croatiatraveller.com

Entry requirements:
Slovenia, Croatia, Bosnia-Herzegovina require a valid personal identity card or passport. In Bosnia-Herzegovina you need to register with the police for a stay of over 24 hours.

Information:
Here are some websites to help you plan your trip:
www.traveladriatic.net
www.slovenia.info
www.croatia.hr
www.ciaoitaly.net
www.venetia.it

Venice

A visit to the magnificent lagoon city is simply unforgettable, regardless of the time of year.

If you can somehow avoid the high season when thousands of tourists jam the narrow alleys around Piazza San Marco, you are lucky. But Venice (a UNESCO World Heritage Site) is so extraordinarily beautiful that it is a treat all year round. As a maritime power, Venice was once the queen of the eastern Mediterranean. The city is unique, and not least because of its medieval architectural design that is an amalgamation of Byzantine, Arab and Gothic elements.

This capital of the northern Italian province of Venezia includes over one hundred islands in a sandy lagoon in the Adriatic. The city is linked to the mainland via causeways and bridges, and was built on piles. There are over 150 bridges and 400 canals. Originally, Venice was a refuge built after the invasion of the Huns, and its inhabitants actually remained independent for centuries. They even managed to take over the legacy of Ravenna in the eighth century, but by the 15th century, the flow of world trade had shifted, leaving the former queen without its foundation.

Sights here include: the Piazza San Marco, city center for the last thousand years; the Basilica di San Marco with its priceless décor; the Doge's Palace, a masterpiece of the Venetian Gothic; the Grand Canal with the Rialto Bridge; the Church of Santa Maria Gloriosa dei Frari; the Scuola Grande di San Rocco, the Galleria del L'Accademia with collections of Venetian paintings from the 14th to 18th centuries, and the other islands of Murano, Burano and Torcello.

Top: Gondolas bobbing on the Canale di San Marco. Middle: The Grand Canal is 3.8 km (2.4 mi) long and lined with magnificent palaces. Bottom: The Piazza San Marco and the Basilica di San Marco.

ful altar pieces and frescos by Giambattista Tiepolo.

With its high limestone cliffs dropping sharply to the ocean, the Riviera Triestina has very little in common with the rest of the Italian Adriatic. Continuing from Údine via Monfalcone to Trieste along the B14 you get a taste of the craggy, bizarre landscape that awaits the traveller in Dalmatia.

④ Trieste This Mediterranean port was part of Austria for over five hundred years, from 1382 until 1918, when the city was annexed by Italy after World War I. Open squares and cozy cafes are testimony to the former presence and influence of the Austro-Hungarian monarchy, before it lost influence as a center of trade and culture. The atmosphere of the Grand Canal with its small boats is dominated by the imposing Sant' Antonio Church (1849).

⑤ Koper und Piran The Slovenian coast is only 40 km (25 mi) long and yet three towns here offer you virtually all of the aspects of the sea and seafaring you could want: Koper, the country's trading port, Izola the fishing port and Piran, where the beachgoers sun themselves.

Formerly an island, Koper is now linked to the mainland by a causeway. The center of the historic Old Town has a Venetian flair and is dominated by the Titov trg and the Praetorian Palace, the cathedral and the bell tower. One palace loggia on the square has been converted into a relaxed coffee house. Izola was also built on an island and before being later linked to the mainland. There are ample signs of a Venetian past here too, but Izola is primarily a fishing village and port.

Piran, on the other hand, is one of the loveliest towns along

the Adriatic, and lives primarily from tourism. The town's focal point is Tartini Square, lined by a semi-circular row of old buildings on the one side and with views of the small fishing port on the opposite side. In Piran, the best thing to do is go for a stroll and let yourself be enchanted by the delightful details of the loggias, fountains and wells.

The onward journey now takes you onto Croatian soil.

⑥ Umag The craggy west coast of Istria, from Savudrija to Rovinj, has lively coastal resorts, fishing villages and small Vene-

tian towns on the seaside that feature a varied landscape. The road initially travels through reddish, open countryside where you arrive in the "breadbasket" of Istria, the focal point of which is the lovely town of Umag. This former Venetian port on a spit of land has a historic Old Town that is surrounded almost completely by the sea. In the Middle Ages, Umag – then still an island separated from the mainland – belonged to the Bishop of Trieste.

The route then continues along small, scenic roads along the coast to Poreč with marvellous views on the sea.

⑦ Poreč Headlands covered in pine forests, lagoons with crystal-clear water and craggy cliffs of marble are the hallmarks of the 70-k-long (43-mi) riviera between Poreč and Vrsar, and it is no surprise that the little town of Poreč, originally settled by the Romans, has developed into Istria's tourism center. The main attractions include the towers of the former town walls, the 15th-century bell tower and the Euphrasian Basilica with its elaborate décor and fine mosaics – the most significant monument to Byzantine sacral architecture from the 3rd to 6th

ture with arcade arches up to 33 m (108 ft) in height. Pula's undisputed landmark is of course also a UNESCO World Heritage Site.

10 Labin The journey now takes you along the east coast of Istria to the north-east.
The E751 crosses the Raša Valley, which is a steep canyon in places, and then climbs rapidly up to the delightful medieval town of Labin, high above the sea. The stretch along the winding east coast is now dominated by Ucka, Istria's highest mountain at 1,400 m (4,593 ft). This is the beginning of the Opatijska Riviera, with the charming 19th-century seaside resorts of Lovran and Opatija. Brestova marks the end of the Istria region at Kvarner Bay.

11 Opatija Belle Époque styles, blossoming gardens and elegant coffee houses are all traces of the Austro-Hungarian monarchy here in Opatija. After being designated as a spa in 1889, this seaside resort developed into an urban work of art. In addition to the obvious beach pursuits, Opatija offers splendid walks along the 8-km (5-mi) waterfront promenade. European high society used to meet in Angiolina Park (1885) in the town center, and the glamour of those days can still be relived with a walk under the acacia, cedar and lemon trees.

centuries. In order to reach the medieval coastal town of Rovinj by car you will need to round the Limski zaljev bay on the E751 and, after a very short drive through the interior, turn off to the west of the peninsula.

8 Rovinj Insiders know that this coastal village, with its Venetian bell tower, numerous brightly painted houses, charming alleyways, and myriad swimming options is one of the country's loveliest. The rocky island has been settled since antiquity and was a prosperous fishing and trading center under the Venetians.

A stroll through the Old Town should begin at the waterfront promenade with its lovely views. The unique flair of Rovinj's center is formed by the Trg Tita Square, which opens out onto the waterfront with welcoming cafés, a town museum and a splendid late-Renaissance clock tower. The imposing St Eufemija baroque church (1736) with its bell tower is also worth visiting.
The route now returns to the E751 in order to reach the next stop. After passing through the very impressive limestone landscape you ultimately reach the southern part of Istria in a

winegrowing area interspersed with stone walls.

9 Pula This port and industrial town with its imposing Roman arena is located at the southern end of the peninsula. Pula had developed into a prosperous provincial capital even during the era of Emperor Augustus. With its 62,400 residents, it is today still the peninsula's cultural and economic center. Visitors are drawn by the museums and the ring-shaped Old Town laid out around the castle hill, but the most impressive sight remains the amphitheater, a huge struc-

1 Sailing yachts with the historic town of Trogir in the background. The medieval Old Town is enclosed by an impressive town wall.

2 Old Town Rovinj, dominated by the 60-m (199-ft) campanile.

3 The port of Piran has charming townhouses dating from the Venetian era, mirrored in the water.

12 Rijeka The port and industry town of Rijeka often serves only as the starting point for a drive along the coastal road. But that would not do the city justice. One of its attractions is the 33-m-high (108-ft) bell tower of the St Marija Cathedral (13th century, façade from the 19th-century), known as the "Leaning Tower of Rijeka" due to its angle. There are also a number of museums and the pedestrian zone lined with boutiques and shops. Be sure to visit the Trsat fortress (13th century), which towers above the town affording a fantastic panoramic view of the mountains and the sea.

The journey continues along the Croatian coast on the E65, also known as Adria-Magistrale, a 600-km (373-mi) stretch between Rijeka and Dubrovnik that follows the coastline almost the whole way, passing through a unique landscape comprising limestone mountains, shimmering, crystal blue water and – typically – bright sunshine.

Anyone with time for a longer detour should turn off at Kraljevica towards Krk and cross over at Valbiska to the island of Cres with its impressive, barren lunar landscape.

13 Crikvenica This seaside resort is situated about 30 km (19 mi) away from Rijeka. In the summer it attracts tourists with a wide sandy beach and the 8-km-long (5-mi) waterfront promenade, which extends as far as Selce.

A visit to the aquarium is also worthwhile and provides an insight into the wealth of Mediterranean fish and plant life. About 30 km (19 mi) further on is the town of Senj. From there it is worth taking the detour to the Plitvice lakes, roughly 90 km (56 mi) away.

Back on the coastal road this stretch is lined with small towns inviting you to stop over. The ferry port of Jablanac is located halfway between Rijeka and Šibenik and from here it is worth taking a detour to the scenic island of Rab – the crossing only takes ten minutes.

14 Zadar The Dalmatian capital boasts some historic buildings from the Venetian era such as the circular St Donatus Church and the campanile of St Anastasia's Cathedral dating

from the 12th and 13th centuries. The ruins of the medieval town fortress and the Roman forum are also worth visiting.

15 Šibenik This charming port is dominated by the glistening white cathedral by Jura Dalmatinác (1441). The talented builder spent most of his life working on his masterpiece, which is a unique embodiment of the transition from the Gothic to the Renaissance style. The apses contain a row of seventy-four heads, each of which displays an individual vitality and are especially intriguing.

The surrounding landscape is a bit more hospitable here than the northern section of the coastal road. The vegetation also becomes more Mediterranean.

Close to Šibenik is the start of the Krka National Park, a singular landscape of natural springs, babbling brooks and tumbling waterfalls – the realm of Croatian fairies and water sprites. The route continues via Primošten. Wine has been produced in this area for centuries, with elaborate walls of white stone built to protect the vines from the cold winds of the *bora*.

16 Trogir The charming Old Town of Trogir is situated on a small island. The winding alleys

seafaring republic of Ragusa. The Old Town, which features a mix of Renaissance and baroque buildings, winding alleys and a wide main street lined with cafés, is surrounded by mighty walls that open up toward the sea in only a few places. Basically impregnable for centuries, the town nevertheless faced near complete destruction on two occasions: from a strong earthquake in 1667, and from shelling by the Yugoslavian army in 1991. Fortunately, the bombed-out roofs of the public buildings were rebuilt with a great deal of effort, such that the townscape has largely been restored.

Other attractions include testimonies to the golden 15th century when Ragusa vied with Venice for power. The Rector's Palace with its arcades, harmoniously round arch windows and baroque staircase dates from this era, as does the completely intact town wall with a total length of 1,940 m (2,122 ft).

Kotor, Montenegro, is roughly 90 km (56 mi) from Dubrovnik, but the small medieval town is worth the detour. Bari, on the east coast of southern Italy, can be reached from Dubrovnik on a 16-hour ferry crossing.

⑳ Bari The capital of Apulia (331,600 residents) was initially

and a cathedral by the famous master builder Radoan transport visitors back to the Middle Ages. The town, which only has 7,000 residents, was once a Greek and then a Roman colony before becoming Croatia's political and cultural center from the 9th to 11th centuries, as is evidenced not only by the very impressive cathedral (13th–16th century), but also by the many splendid churches and palaces.

The magnificent Old Town has since been declared a UNESCO World Heritage Site.

⑰ Split The stunning port of Split, with 188,700 residents, is the cultural and economic center of Dalmatia and has numerous museums and theaters. It is out on a peninsula dominated by Marjan hill. The Old Town has a curious mixture of Roman, medieval and modern buildings, with the impressive Diocletian Palace (built at the turn of the 4th century) and the 13th-century cathedral – the entire Old Town was declared a UNESCO World Heritage Site. Unfortunately, it suffered significant damage during the Serbo-Croatian War, but that is slowly being repaired.

⑱ Makarska-Riviera This stretch of the Croatian coast becomes narrower and narrower as the journey progresses,

until there is only the Biokovo mountain range separating the coast from Bosnia-Herzegovina. This is home to the once popular seaside resort area known as the Makarska Riviera, which was a passenger liner stop back in the 19th century. Sadly, a great many of the historic buildings from that era were destroyed by an earthquake in 1962.

The high mountain ridge results in a mild climate that has inspired wine grape and olive cultivation. The picturesque fishing villages, pleasant pebble beaches and pine forests invite visitors to stop in.

A few miles before Donta Deli there is a turnoff leading to the Pelješac Peninsula. You can catch ferries from here to the island of Korčula. In order to provide Bosnia-Herzegovina with access to the sea, Croatia had to surrender a tiny piece of its coast. The road to Dubrovnik therefore passes through another border crossing.

⑲ Dubrovnik Viewed from the air, this town looks as if it is clinging to the rocks like a mussel. In the Middle Ages, Dubrovnik was known as the

1 The Biokovo Mountains form a wonderful backdrop for sailing yachts in one of the coastal resorts on the Makarska Riviera.

2 The Old Town of Split.

3 Sveti Ivan fortress is one of Dubrovnik's most popular photo motifs. The Old Town and the port create a picturesque backdrop.

4 View over the sea of buildings in the Old Town of Dubrovnik looking toward Lovrijenac fortress.

founded by the Romans and was long subject to changing rulers. Foreign trade with Venice and the Orient brought wealth to the city, which still has a historic Old Town of Byzantine origin. Large parts of the region surrounding Bari are used for agriculture, in particular olive cultivation.

The onward route takes you along the Autostrada 98 for a few miles before turning off at Ruvo di Púglia onto a smaller road towards Castel del Monte.

㉑ Castel del Monte This hunting castle from 1240, also known as the "Crown of Apulia", towers up from the plain and can be seen from quite a distance. The castle was built according to the laws of numerical mysticism by the German Staufer Emperor Frederick II (1194–1250) who had a passion for science and magic. The symmetrical, octagonal castle has a ring of octagonal towers, so that the only variations are those brought about by the changing daylight, an impressively active design element within the building.

The route continues along an equally small road to Barletta and from there 39 km (24 mi) along the coast to Manfredónia. A few miles further on it continues up to Monte S. Angelo.

The journey now takes you past two lagoons: Verano and Lesina. At Térmoli the route joins the N16. Térmoli itself holds little appeal, but the road now twists through the hilly, coastal landscape, revealing consistently good views. Inviting coves and picturesque villages like Vasto or Ortona perched on the cliffs tempt a stopover.

㉒ Vieste and the Gargano Peninsula The spur of the Italian boot consists of a wild lime-

stone massif (1,000 m/3,281 ft) that is mostly uninhabited. Monte San Angelo is the highest town on the Gargano Peninsula at 850 m (2,789 ft). You have a wonderful view of the plateau and the Gulf of Manfredónia from the town, which has been an important southern Italian pilgrimage destination ever since the apparition of the Archangel Michael in a nearby grotto at the end of the 5th century. A 12th-century bishop's throne and other valuables adorn the

grotto, which is shielded by bronze gates from Constantinople (1076).

Vieste is on the eastern tip of the peninsula. It has splendid beaches and a lovely medieval Old Town where the traditional outdoor *mignali* (staircases) are linked by narrow archways.

㉓ Pescara The largest town in the Abruzzi region always seems to be bustling. Large sections of the town were sadly destroyed in World War II but they have been rebuilt with

generous, open architecture. Only a very small historical Old Town still exists now around the Piazza Unione. The town's attractions include its fine sandy beaches and the annual jazz festival in July, where legendary musicians like Louis Armstrong have performed. Pescara is at the mouth of the river of the same name.

㉔ S. Benedetto del Tronto Italy's largest fishing port is a lively and vibrant place. The town's icons include the splen-

En route to Pésaro there are a number of historical villages inviting you to stop a while, including Senigallia, the first Roman colony on the Adriatic coast. The Old Town there features the imposing Rocca Roveresca fortress.

26 Pésaro At the exit from the Foglia Valley is the industrial town and port of Pésaro. The Old Town, with its Palazzo Ducale (15th–16th centuries) on the Piazza del Popolo is worth visiting. Continuing now toward Rímini the, coastal strip becomes noticeably narrower and the hinterland more mountainous. From Pésaro it is worth taking an excursion to the Old Town of Urbino 35 km (22 mi) to the south-west.

27 Cattólica to Rímini This is where you will find the tourist strongholds of the Adriatic, coastal resorts which, with their sandy beaches stretching for miles, a diverse range of sporting opportunities and vibrant nightlife are focused on entertaining the masses. Rímini's history goes back a long way, however, so make sure you enjoy that aspect too.
Having first gained major significance as an Etruscan port,

cliffs, forests and narrow pebble beaches. It is worth taking some detours inland from here, for example to Loreto, perched like a fortress on a hill above Porto Recanati.

25 Ancona The foothills of the imposing Monte Conero drop down to the sea in steps while Ancona, the attractive regional capital of the Marches, sits down at sea level on the natural port. Although the port and industry town with 98,400 residents was originally founded by the Greeks and boasts a rich history as a seafaring republic, its historical monuments unfortunately tend to be second rate.
In Ancona you should immerse yourself in the port atmosphere, which actually might be a welcome change from all the beach time and medieval towns. The San Ciriaco Cathedral (dating from the 11th–14th centuries) is perched high above the town. The Byzantine-influenced building is one of the most impressive Romanesque churches in Italy.

1 Castel del Monte is visible from a distance, rising up from the plain. The two-storey castle was built in 1240 by the German Staufer King Frederick II and is one of the most fascinating buildings from the Middle Ages.

2 Typical for the Apulia region, the Old Town of Vieste is dominated by white stone buildings.

3 The Gargano National Park also protects the high, rocky coastline of the peninsula of the same name. There is a series of caves and grottos to be visited.

did, palm-lined promenades, the elegant villas and a long sandy beach. The fishing museum and the fish market are also worth a brief visit. The steep Riviera del Conero, with the Monte Conero promontory, features stunning limestone

Rimini is divided into two districts that could hardly be more different. While the site of the Roman town is still recognizable in the Old Town, the coastal section is one of the liveliest seaside resorts on the Adriatic. After San Marino there is a tiny scenic road for about 20 km (12 mi) that leads past Rímini. You can also take the SS72.

28 Ravenna Art metropolis as well as an industrial city, Ravenna is a multifaceted place surrounded by the nature reserves of the Po Delta region. Indeed, as port in Roman times, imperial Ravenna was once directly on the coast. But the port silted up and the location's importance dwindled. Only when the marshlands were drained in the 19th century did the economic recovery begin. Further impetus came in 1952 with the discovery of natural gas.

Ravenna draws visitors with its early Christian churches and the charming Old Town. The numerous cultural monuments include the San Vitale and Sant' Apollinaire Nuovo churches; the mosaics in the Sant' Apollinaire Basilica in Classe; the Orthodox baptistery; the Arian baptistery; Galla Placidia's mausoleum; and the tomb of Ostrogothic King Theoderich. Santa Maria in Porto fuori, the Sant' Orso Cathedral and Dante's tomb date from later eras.

From Ravenna the route then takes you to Chióggia, where the unique coastal landscape south of the main Po Delta has been made into a lovely nature reserve. The lagoons and hidden channels as well as the vast fields of the open plain are quite beautiful. Along the river causeways anglers can try their luck with the legendary Po catfish.

29 Chióggia Gracious palaces with their "feet in the water",

three canals with boats and a number of charming bridges, those are the things that justify this baroque lagoon town's nickname of "Little Venice". Initially founded by the Romans, Chiógga was once very powerful but was ultimately overshadowed by La Serenissima for many centuries. In addition to enjoying the charming Venetian ambiance, it is also worth visiting the baroque St Maria Assunta Cathedral. Lovely beaches are to be found at Sottomarina and Isola Verde.

30 Padua This ancient university town on the edge of the Euganean Hills is the last stop on our tour around the Adriatic. The long arcade corridors and historic buildings characterize the town's appearance and Padua is one of the loveliest of the Italian towns from antiquity.

The main attractions are the Cappella degli Scrovegni, where Giotto painted his most important series of frescos in 1305, in a simple chapel; and the magnificent Basilica di Sant' Antonio from the 15th/16th centuries, which is still one of the country's most important pilgrimage destinations to this day.

Other buildings that are significant for their art history and ought to be visited are the 12th century-Palazzo della Ragione, the former Augustinian Eremitani Church (13th century) with frescoes by Mantegna, the Santa Giustina Church (16th century) and the monument to the military leader Gattamelata, an equestrian statue by Donatello, most of whose works are otherwise to be seen in Florence. It is worth taking a detour to the Abano Terme and Montegrotto Terme hot springs to the southwest of town, two oases of relaxation. The springs are a blazing 80°C (176°F).

1 The mosaics in the apse at San Vitale in Ravenna, a true gem of Byzantine art, date from the first half of the sixth century.

2 Giotto's famous cycle of frescoes in the Capella degli Scrovegni (1305) in Padua depicts scenes from the life of Christ.

Padua This ancient university town is arguably one of Italy's loveliest. Its particular attractions include the Cappella degli Scrovegni with Giotto's cycle of frescos (1305), and the Basilica di Sant'Antonio (15th/16th centuries), which is visited by millions of pilgrims every year.

Venice The "Queen of the Eastern Mediterranean" is a combination of splendor and disrepair, land and water, Gothic, baroque and Renaissance. The list of attractions includes the Canal Grande, the Piazza San Marco, the Bridge of Sighs, the Accademia and the Palazzo Ducale.

Opatija The blossoming gardens, coffee houses and the waterfront promenade in this spa resort town are all reminiscent of the Austro-Hungarian monarchy.

Murano and Burano Two islands in the Venice lagoon are especially noteworthy: Burano, a fishing island with bright buildings and small lace-making workshops, and Murano, the embodiment of quality glasswork since the 13th century.

Rovinji The best view of this Istrian port is from the sea. The Venetian influence is easily recognizable in buildings such as the campanile, the splendid late-Renaissance red clock tower, the waterfront promenade, the Church of St Euphemia and the countless cafés.

Pésaro, Cattólica, and Rímini The Palazzo Ducale in the Old Town of Pésaro is a beautiful sight. Cattólica, on the other hand, attracts visitors with its long beaches. Nearby Rímini is one of the most popular sea resorts in Italy.

The Plitvice Lakes The sixteen turquoise-colored lakes and over ninety waterfalls provide a superb nature experience here.

Split This port is the cultural and economic center of Dalmatia. The center boasts Roman sites such as the Palace of Diocletian and severla other medieval buildings such as the cathedral.

Ravenna Once the capital of the Ostrogothic King Theoderich the Great's empire, this town is primarily known for its early Christian-Byzantine churches.

Gargano The spur of the Italian boot is made of limestone mountains reaching an altitude of up to 1,000 m (3,281 ft). Monte Sant' Angelo is the highest.

Trogir Winding alleyways and a cathedral (13th–16th centuries) characterize the old heritage-protected town situated on an island. The numerous churches and palaces make the former political and cultural center of Croatia between worth seeing.

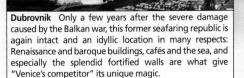

Castel del Monte The hunting castle of the Staufer Emperor Frederick II is visible from a distance and is enchanting with its perfect octagonal symmetry and strict simplicity.

Dubrovnik Only a few years after the severe damage caused by the Balkan war, this former seafaring republic is again intact and an idyllic location in many respects: Renaissance and baroque buildings, cafés and the sea, and especially the splendid fortified walls are what give "Venice's competitor" its unique magic.

Kotor This medieval town in Montenegro has a 4.5-km-long (2.8-mi) wall that is 20 m (66 ft) high. One of the town gates is from the ninth century and the cathedral is from the 14th.

Korčula This mountainous island is famous for its sword dancers and lush vegetation. The sights in the capital of the same name include the cathedral and All Saints Church.

Italy

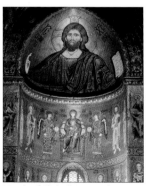

Remains of ancient civilizations: the amphitheater in Taormina.

Sicily: in the footsteps of the Greeks, Normans, Arabs and Staufers

Italy's largest island offers such great cultural diversity that it seems to embody an entire continent. Classic Greek temples, Norman cathedrals and baroque palaces have transformed the island into a larger-than-life open-air museum of art and cultural history. Nature in turn provides a powerful complement to the scene, offering dramatic rocky coasts and superlatives like the home of Europe's largest volcano.

On the edge of Europe, yet at the center of the Mediterranean world – there is no better way to describe Sicily's role in history. For lovers of antiquity, this island, formerly also called Trinacria, between the Ionic and the Tyrrhenian seas is a piece of Greece. For the good citizens of Milan and Turin, it is a stumbling block in front of the Italian boot that is dominated by shadowy powers and slowing down the pace of the country's progress. For Sicilians, despite the fact that many of its people suffered under the feudal conditions and were forced to emigrate due to the pressures of poverty, it will always remain "terra santa" – their sacred homeland – and it is all too often being kicked around by the Italian boot.

Historically, when so-called "world" politics revolved more or less around the Mediterranean, Sicily was the strategic crown jewel at the heart of the battle for dominance of this

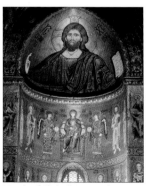

Mosaic of Christ in Monreale Monastery.

preeminent domain. In early antiquity, it was the Greeks, virtually dragged along by the Phoenicians, who colonized the island and made Syracuse the center of the ancient world – before the era of the Roman empire. They were then followed by the Romans, Vandals, Byzantines, Arabs, Normans, Staufers, Aragonese and Neapolitans. Many of these conquerors ruthlessly plundered the country and fought bloody wars on its soil. By contrast, the Arabs cultivated growth between the 9th and 11th centuries by planting citrus and mulberry trees, sugarcane and date palms. They made the island into a gateway for Europeans to experience their more

The Church of San Giorgio Maggiore in Venice, built between 1559 and 1580 and designed by architect Andrea Palladio.

The Concordia Temple in the Valle dei Templi near Agrigento dates back to the 5th century BC.

highly developed civilization. Almost all of them, however, left behind stone reminders of their presence. The result is that, in terms of cultural and art history, Sicily now presents itself not as just an island, but as a continent in miniature, a rich fabric of tradition contained in one island. From the classic Greek temples at Agrigento, Segesta and Selinunt to the Norman-era cathedrals of Monreale, Palermo and Cefalù, or the baroque Old Towns of Noto, Ragusa and Modica: Sicily has all these styles in their purest forms.

Of course it is not only these and other civilizations that fascinate today's tourists on a visit to the "Continente Sicilia". The land and the people leave an equally inspiring impression. Whether you come in the spring, when a paradisical sea of flowers cloaks the entire island with its aromas, or in the summer, when the gruelling heat parches the soil, Sicily rarely fails to enchant. Its ancient beauty, which neither earthquakes, volcanic eruptions nor outbreaks of human violence have been capable of destroying, looks destined to remain.

The juxtaposition of contrasts, passions and an almost fatalistic lethargy; the either–or, friend or foe, love or hate, life or death attitude is an essential element of the Sicilian mentality. On the piazzas of Palermo or Catania, life pulsates chaotically and yet elegantly. The other side of the coin, however, can be seen in the economy and politics. The spirit of the Mezzogiorno, the Mafia, the bureaucracy and the corruption forms an unholy alliance, exercises a painful lack of consideration for nature.

But one thing is certain: This small piece of land nearly equidistant from the African and European continents, will undoubtedly awaken the senses of any visitor and enchant them with its exotic fragrances, vibrant hues and unique light. It will inspire a desire in you to return before you even complete the journey back across the Straits of Messina at the end of your trip.

Solitude can still be found on the Isola Salina, the second-largest of the Aeolian Islands. The agriculture mainly consists of vineyards and capers.

Driving around the largest island in the Mediterranean along 850 km (528 mi) of coastline provides visitors with an excellent overview of Sicily's rich history, the wealth of its historical monuments and the diversity of its landscapes. All of this is then complemented by detours into the island's interior and to the small neighboring islands.

① Messina Located just 3 km (2 mi) from the Italian mainland, this port town has served as a first stop for conquerors since it was founded by the Greeks in the 8th century BC. It is of course still the "gateway to the island", despite having been destroyed several times: in 1783 and 1908 by earthquakes, and by bombing in 1943.

Among the remnants of ancient civilizations are the small Norman church of Santa Annunziata dei Catalani. From the upper districts of the town, a beautiful view unfolds of the checkerboard layout of roads, the harbor installations, the infamous straits and the wooded hills of Calabria nearby.

The winding scenic road also affords some grandiose views while taking you around to the north coast. After some 80 km (50 mi) you arrive in one of Sicily's most famous pilgrimage destinations.

② Tindari From the top of the steep cliff 260 m (853 ft)

above the sea is a modern sanctuary with its striking black Madonna. The location affords some fantastic views down to the sandbanks and across to the Aeolian Islands. The views from the adjacent ruins of ancient Tyndaris are no less magnificent, where the remains of a theater, a Roman basilica, the residential districts and the town fortifications have been preserved. Along the busy SS113, the journey continues toward the west, passing sandy beaches, rocky cliffs, seaside resorts and industrial complexes. After 130 km (81 mi) you finally come to Cefalù, located on a narrow spit of land.

1 The charming port of Cefalù is surrounded by the picturesque fishing quarter and lined with small houses used since medieval times.

2 In Tindari, the ruins of an ancient theater, the Teatro Greco, are situated high above the steep rocky coast on the Tyrrhenian Sea in the north-east of Sicily.

Travel Information

Route profile
Length: approx. 850 km (530 mi), without detours
Time required: 8–10 days
Start and finish: Messina
Route (main locations):
Cefalù, Palermo, Segesta, Trápani, Selinunt, Agrigento, Ragusa, Noto, Syracuse, Catania, Taormina

Traffic information:
The speed limit in town is 50 km/h (31 mph), on country roads outside of town 90 km/h (56 mph) and on motorways 110 or 130 km/h (70 or 80 mph). Seatbelts are required only in the front seats of the car. The blood-alcohol limit is .08.

When to go:
Spring and autumn are the best times to go. Starting April to mid-May, the flowers are in bloom all over the island (20–25 °C/68–77 °F). Summer temperatures can be extremely hot, but in autumn, the water and air temperatures typically stay at a comfortable 20 °C (68 °F) until November. Winters are brief, mild and only moderately rainy.

Information:
Here are some websites to help you plan your trip.
www.bestofsicily.com
www.initaly.com
www.sicilian.net

Palermo

During the First Punic War, Palermo was the main base for the Carthaginian fleet. Stationed here, Carthage flourished in unparalleled ways even during periods of Arab, Norman and Staufer rule. Superb architectural treasures have been preserved from all of these eras.

In Palermo's Old Town, Byzantine churches stand next to mosques, baroque and Catalan estates, neoclassical barracks and Arab pleasure palaces. Among the highlights are the vast cathedral and the Norman Palace with its Cappella Palatina, richly adorned with mosaics; the churches of San Cataldo, La Martorana, San Giovanni degli Eremiti; the La Zisa Palace; the Teatro Massimo; the catacombs of the Capuchin Convent; and the National Gallery and the archaeological museum.

One of Europe's most splendid imperial cities only two hundred years ago, Palermo was seemingly abandoned after World War II. In the 1990s, however, the "beautiful city" shed the stigma of Mafia corruption and, after a long malaise, is being busily renovated. Success can be seen in the vibrant markets, elegant promenades and charming piazzas.

The cathedral, 1184, is known officially as "Santa Maria Assunta".

3 Cefalù Cowering under a mighty limestone face, this small fishing town would be worth a stop just to see its Oriental-style Old Town and the sandy beach. After all, it boasts the ruins of an ancient sanctuary, Arabic washhouses and a delightful private art collection in the Museo Comunal Mandralisca.

All of this, however, pales in comparison to Cefalú's cathedral. The foundation stone for Sicily's oldest religious building, which dates back to Norman times, was laid in 1131, by King Roger II. The façade alone is impressive enough to etch itself forever in your mind, with its Romanesque vaulted portal and the defensive posture of the mighty towers. The tall, narrow interior is simply brilliant. Even during the lifetime of its patron, master craftsmen from Constantinople came to create the magnificent golden mosaics in the choirs.

4 Bagheria In the 17th and 18th centuries, this village was the favorite summer resort for the aristocratic families from the nearby town. Constant sea breezes here promised relief from the heat amidst idyllic lemon and orange groves, inspiring numerous baroque country manors to be built. Some of these palaces can still be visited today, including the Villa Palagonia with its superb Mannerist sculptures.

From Bagheria, it is about 14 km (9 mi) to Palermo.

5 Palermo (see page 249)

6 Monreale A visit to Palermo is unthinkable without an trip up to the small bishops' town of Monreale just 8 km (5 mi) away. The lofty environs of Monte Caputo make for spectacular views of the Sicilian capital and its neraly perfectly

round bay, the Conca d'Oro. The main sight, however, is the cathedral. In 1172, William II, King of Sicily, commissioned a Benedictine Abbey here, around which a town soon began to develop. In its center, he had a cathedral erected, a basilica with three aisles that was meant to symbolize the triumph of Christianity over Islam. At a length of 102 m (112 yds) and a width of 40 m (44 yds), it is Sicily's largest church, and rests on eighteeen ancient columns. It is home to the sarcophagi of kings William I and II, and has superb bronze portals and marble floors. The cathedrals's most impressive elements, however, are the unique mosaics, which cover an area of 6,300 sq m (67,788 sq ft), telling the stories of the Bible in exemplary splendor.

The cloisters feature a remarkable 216 pairs of columns. West of Palermo, the Tyrrhenian Sea is occasionally hidden from view as the SS113 leads into the island's interior, to Segesta.

7 Segesta In antiquity, the Elymians, supposed descendants of the Trojans, were said to have settled in this now uninhabited mountainous landscape. What remains of this ancient tribe's town are a majestic but unfinished Doric

temple and a gracefully situated amphitheater.

8 Trápani The provincial capital, spread out across a narrow spit of land, forms the western end of the SS113 and the A29. Drepanon, as Trápani was called in ancient times, was a naval base for the Carthaginian and Roman fleets. It flourished under the rule of the Normans and Staufers, and opened its arms to all Mediterranean peoples as a sanctuary of religious freedom. At the height of its powers it was also a main trading port for salt, fish and wine. The numerous splendid buildings in the baroque Old Town testify to its former prosperity, and the Museo Regionale Pepoli has a wealth of archaeo-

logical treasures. The pilgrimage church of Santuario dell' Annunziata, a colossal structure in Catalan Gothic style, and an excursion to Erice or San Vito lo Capo are worthy destinations here as well.

9 Aegadian Islands These three islands (the mythical "Aegades" of Homer's tale), are situated off the western tip of Sicily. Each one of thes former pirate strongholds is remarkable. They make for an interesting day trip from Trápani. Maréttimo is a pristine paradise for hikers. On Lévanzo you can admire the Stone Age rock paintings in the Grotta del Genovese. Favignana is known for the mattanza, a ritual tuna hunt in the spring.

in the provincial capital, which initially makes a rather ambivalent impression. Its slopes have been developed in a fairly unattractive manner with high-rise blocks and industrial complexes. But hidden in the primarily baroque Old Town are quite a few cozy spots and architectural gems, in particular the Norman cathedral in the center. The Old Town itself is also pleasantly void of the uncomely growth of modern buildings.

⑮ **Valle dei Templi** The "Valley of the Temples", or to be more precise, this protracted mountain ridge, fascinates with its harmonious melding of ancient architecture and Mediterranean landscape. In the 5th century BC, this town rose to prominence as the second most powerful city on Sicily after Syracuse. The monumental Doric temples that adorned ancient Akragas are strung next to one another like pearls on a necklace.

Via the harbor and industrial town of Gela – which is worth a stopover for its ancient Greek fortifications and the archaeological museum – your journey continues to south-east Sicily, a region of barren karst mountains and baroque relics. Vittoria and Comiso are the first two towns along this route into the interior (SS115), and they offer a taste of the sumptuous architecture to come.

⑩ **Marsala** This town's name is now synonymous with a dessert wine, but its port, founded by the Phoenicians near the Capo Lilibeo, Sicily's westernmost tip, has more to offer that just a drink. It features a tidy baroque Old Town with a lively piazza, a Norman cathedral, a museum featuring Flemish tapestries, and a Roman archaeological excavation site. The city owes its Oriental appearance to Mars al-Allah, or "port of God", from its time under Arab rule after 827.

⑪ **Mazara del Vallo** This former administrative capital of the Val di Mazara, an emirate with a majority Muslim population, has two faces: a rather unsightly side in the form of a vast fishing port, and a more attractive side in the form of a baroque Old Town with an idyllic piazza and an opulently adorned cathedral. Roughly 3.5 km (2 mi) west of the little town of Castelvetrano is another architectural jewel: the tiny domed Santa Trinità church, built by the Normans more than 900 years ago.

⑫ **Selinunte** This city, which thanks to its wheat trade was one of Sicily's most important Greek towns, was founded in the 7th century BC by the Dorians before being destroyed by the Carthaginians in 250 BC. Despite numerous earthquakes and the plundering of ancient sites for building materials, impressive remains have been preserved on the vast field of ruins. A total of nine temple complexes have been excavated on the acropolis and two other hills. Some have been reconstructed and represent perfect examples of the monumental sanctuaries of the ancient Greek empire.

You follow the coastline southeast now, taking a delightfully scenic road to the next stops: Sciacca, where a thermal hot spring rises from the sulfurous soil that was rated so highly even back in Roman times; and a short detour into the interior, to Caltabellotta, a spectacular "falcons nest" tucked up against the 1,000-m-high (3,281-ft) rock face. From the Norman castle ruins that stand here you get breathtaking panoramic views across large parts of the island. Back at the coast, after about 12 km (8 mi) you arrive at the next ancient sight.

⑬ **Eraclea Minoa** The few foundations and the beautiful theater in this town, which was founded in the 6th century BC, are situated on a plateau with strikingly white, 80-m (262-ft) limestone cliffs that plunge dramatically down to the sea.

⑭ **Agrigento** About 30 km (19 mi) farther along you arrive

1 Clouds darken the sky above the acropolis of Selinunte.

2 The interior of the cathedral of Monreale, south-west of Palermo.

3 The Doric temple of Selinunte, built in 490–480 BC, was probably dedicated to Hera.

4 Caltabellotta is on a rocky ridge almost 1,000 m (3,281 ft) high.

16 Ragusa This town was already an important center at the time of the Siculians, the ancient inhabitants of eastern Sicily. Following the devastating earthquake of 1693, Ragusa was completely rebuilt. The nooks and alleyways of its eastern part, Ragusa-Ibla, are jammed onto a narrow spit of rock while the San Giorgio Basilica towers above. The western half of the city is one hundred years younger than the rest, and here you will find the cathedral, splendid palaces and the Museo Archeologico Ibleo. Both districts are superb examples of a baroque styles.

17 Módica The venerable small town of Módica hugs the steep slopes of two karst gorges in an even more picturesque fashion, and is similarly dedicated to an omnipresent baroque architectural style. Its main attraction is San Giorgio Cathedral. All these stops, however, are but a prelude for the delights that await you just 50 km (31 mi) to the east from here.

18 Noto Founded on the low foothills of the Iblei Mountains, this small town is considered the most exemplary work of urban art created in the Sicilian "post-quake baroque" style. The main axis of the grid of roads, which cover the slope in terraced steps, is formed by the Corso Vittorio Emanuele. The stucco-adorned façades of the Franciscan church, Capuchin convent, San Nicolò Cathedral, the town hall and the archbishops' palace, combined with artistic staircases, parks and squares all create a dramatic display that is virtually beyond comparison. It is also delightfully morbid: all of the splendor and elegantly golden-yellow hues are threatened by imminent decay, and the sandstone

and gypsum are crumbling. The preservationists and restorers cannot keep up.

19 Siracusa (Syracuse) At first glance, the faceless new structures of Syracuse make it hard to believe that 2,300 years ago this provincial capital was home to more than one million inhabitants, and that it was once the mightiest of the Greek towns in southern Italy. It was a center of trade but also of philosophy and the sciences.

A walk through the picturesque Old Town, however, is indeed an eye-opener. For on the tiny island of Ortigia, which has been the historic heart of Syracuse since it was founded by the Corinthians in around 740 BC (and still is the center), many remains of its early heyday can easily be found: a temple of Apollo, for example, or the Arethusa springs, and a Doric temple that was transformed into the present cathedral in the 7th century AD.

Some parts of the ancient acropolis on the mainland have also been preserved. The archaeological park there features, among other things, a Roman and a Greek theater, a multitude of catacombs, the giant altar of Hiero II, hewn out of the soft chalky rock, and a

large grotto known as "the ear of Dionysus".

In addition to the relics from antiquity, attractions from the Middle Ages and more recent times, the regional gallery and the Castello Maniace, built under the Staufer King Friedrich II, are also worth a visit.

20 Catánia As the crow flies, Sicily's second-largest town is less than 30 km (19 mi) away from the summit of Etna, and has often had to endure the wrath of its active neighbor. During its 3,000-year history, lava currents and earthquakes have repeatedly destroyed the city. After a devastating quake at the end of the 17th century, Catánia was rebuilt according to original plans in late-baroque style using dark lava stone. The cathedral stands out among the numerous ostentatious palaces and churches.

The municipal museum inside the Castello Ursino, the Roman

theater – Bellini's birthplace –, the Teatro named after him, and the larg baroque church of San Nicolò are all worth a visit too.

From Catánia, a detour via Nicolosi to Mount Etna is well worth your time.

21 Taormina The journey now continues toward its grand finale, half way from Catánia going north toward Messina, in the most-visited town on the island, Taormina, where a fabulous location on a rocky cliff high above the sea and an ancient amphitheater have attracted droves of tourists since the 19th century.

1 The Old Town of Ragusa-Ibla, with its baroque buildings and Byzantine fortifications.

2 The ruins of a Greek amphitheater in Taormina, with Mount Etna and the rocky bay in the background.

Segesta In antiquity, the Elymians, who were supposedly descendants of the Trojans, had settled in these remote hills of Sicily. Of the former town founded by that people, an incomplete Doric temple and the semicircle of an amphitheater have been preserved.

Cefalù The cathedral in this fishing town is the oldest sacred Norman building on Sicily (1131). Other attractions here include an Arab washhouse, the ruins of an ancient sanctuary as well as the art collection in the Museo Comunal Mandralisca.

Taormina Impressive churches, monasteries, palaces, narrow alleyways, piazzas, the ancient theater and the coastline with Mount Etna as a backdrop has made this Sicily's most-visited town for centuries.

Palermo Sicily's capital is unique because of the structures left behind by Normans, Arabs and Staufers. It also has great museums and eerie catacombs.

Monreale The cathedral in this small episcopal city is Sicily's largest place of worship. Founded in 1172, it is adorned with rich mosaics. The views of Palermo from Monte Caputo cannot be matched.

Aeolian Islands The highlight of this volcanic island group is the still-active Stromboli volcano. Here: Filicudi Island.

Catánia The second-largest city in Sicily was rebuilt in the baroque style after an earthquake at the end of the 17th century.

Selinunte Large parts of this ancient city have not yet been excavated, but the restored acropolis and the widely scattered heaps of rubble leave visitors to imagine the vast size of this former settlement.

Valle dei Templi The valley of the temples is, in fact, a mountain ridge atop which the sacral buildings of Akragas – Sicily's most powerful city after Syracuse in the 5th century BC. The temples blend in nicely with the landscape.

Noto This late-baroque town has a remarkable gridiron road layout, and is known for its magnificent stucco-adorned façades.

Caltabellotta A number of striking rock pinnacles rise dramatically above this little village, each of them topped by castles or churches. Excellent views unfold across the island to Mount Etna and you get a birds-eye look at the town itself.

Ragusa This town was rebuilt in baroque style after an earthquake leveled it. A basilica dominates the Ragusa-Ibla quarter. The cathedral and the archaeological museum are in the younger part of town.

Mount Etna Erupting with amazing regularity, this is the highest volcano in Europe at 3,323-m-high (10,903-ft). It is fairly safe to approach, but the lava streams have destroyed some of the fertile agricultural areas as well as winter sports and protective structures on the flanks of the crater.

Greece

Classics of antiquity up close

Greece is the cradle of western civilization, and it is no surprise that the legacy of the ancient Greeks and its classic antiquities have inspired waves of fascination in the country. But a trip to *Hellas* is more than just a journey back through time: Greece is also a place of great natural beauty, with impressive mountainous landscapes, idyllic islands, wild coasts and pristine white-sand beaches.

The Parthenon on the Acropolis was built under Kallikrates and Iktinos in 447 BC, dedicated to the goddess Athena Pallas.

One-fifth of Greece's total area comprises islands. No place in the entire country is farther than 140 km (87 mi) from the sea, and the 14,000 km (8,700 mi) of coastline offer endless possibilities for spectacular hiking, swimming, sailing or just relaxing on the beach. On the mainland and the Peloponnese, less than one-third of the land is suitable for farming.

Agriculture is therefore concentrated on the plains of the country's north-east. The national tree of Greece, for example, the olive tree, can thrive up to elevations of around 800 m (2,625 ft), and does so on the mainland as well as on the islands.

Greece's mountainous landscape and its proximity to the sea have obviously shaped civilization here for millennia. The most significant evidence of this is that, throughout the country's long history, the combination of mainland and archipelago prevented the formation

The Virgin Mary in a Meteora monastery.

of a central power. Instead, small city-states were the natural entities created here since ancient times, despite the fact that these were more easily conquered and ruled by foreign powers than a centralized structure might have been.

When the Roman Empire broke up in AD 395, Greece was part of the Eastern Roman Empire (Byzantium). It became Christian very early on. After the Crusades (11th–13th centuries), and in some cases well into the 16th century, large parts of the country fell under the rule of the Venetians, whose legacy can still be seen in various place names and architecture. In 1453, the Ottomans seized Constantinople and later large parts of Greece. When it came to beliefs, the Turks were tol-

The island fort of Bourtzi protected Nauplia from enemies attacking from the south.

The spectacular "Shipwreck Beach" on the north-west coast of Zákinthos. This southernmost island in the Ionic Sea was called the "Flower of the Levant" by the Venetians.

erant, and their Greek subjects enjoyed religious freedom. The Orthodox Church thus became a unifying and protective force for all Greeks during the Ottoman era. Isolated from the important cultural and intellectual developments in the rest of Europe, Greece remained untouched by the Renaissance, Reformation and Enlightenment.

National pride, which emerged in the late 18th century, finally led to revolution in 1821, but it was quashed by the Turks. It was not until 1827 that the Greeks, with help from the British, French and Russians, were able to shake off Turkish rule and proclaim a sovereign state. After independence in 1830, the Greeks made Bavarian Prince Otto von Wittelsbach

the king of their nation as Otto I, after which a number of German architects worked in Athens to ensure the nation was transformed into worthy capital of the new Greece after centuries of decline.

At the time, however, some areas of Greece were still under Turkish rule, which again led to wars with the Turks – with varying success – and it was not until the early 20th century that Crete and a number of other Aegean islands were returned to Greece.

As a travel destination, Greece is often presented with deep blue skies above a turquoise sea, with whitewashed houses on a hillside above a quaint port – and not incorrectly. Regardless of whether you are hopping around the more than

2,000 islands or exploring the mainland, Greek hospitality is an exceptional national quality here, and the traditional cuisine based on rustic recipes wants to be tasted. A word of

warning, however: their driving can be rather "adventurous" at times. Some think the middle of the road belongs to them, even on curves, so make sure you drive with caution!

Such vibrantly colored fishing boats are typical of many Greek port towns.

This journey through the Greece of antiquity will take you through majestic mountains and glorious coastal landscapes to the most important remnants of this ancient civilization, as well as to the legacies of Roman, Byzantine and Venetian eras on the southern mainland, Attica and the Peloponnese peninsula.

1 Athens (see pages 258–259)

2 Cape Sounion From Athens, you initially head about 70 km (43 mi) south along Highway 91 to the outermost point of the peninsula. The lovely beaches at Voúla and Vouliagméni are worthwhile spots to stop along the Attic Coast between Piréas (Piraeus) and Soúnio. At the bottom of the cape is an amazing temple dedicated to Poseidon, god of the sea, from 444 BC. It provides stunning views down to the Saronic Gulf. From Cape Sounion, the route continues north along the eastern side of the peninsula. Then, east of Athens, you take Highway 54 toward Marathón. The Marathón Plain was where the Greeks defeated an army of Persians in 490 BC. On the day of the battle, a messenger in a full suit of armour brought news of the victory to Athens and the 42-km (26-mi) stretch became the reference distance for the modern marathon. Following the coastal road to the north, you can make a detour to Évia (Euboea) Island near Halkída, which is home to a 15th-century mosque.

Travel Information

Route profile
Length: approx. 1500 km (932 mi)
Time required: 3 weeks
Start and finish: Athens
Route (main locations): Athens, Cape Sounion, Thebes, Delphí, Corinth, Nauplia, Sparta, Máni, Methóni, Olympia, Patras, Corinth, Athens

Traffic information:
Greece has a good network of well-maintained roads. You should have a green insurance card with you. Speed limits are as follows: highways 110 or 120 km/h (70 or 75 mph), rural roads 90 km/h (55 mph), in town 50 km/h (30 mph).

When to go:
The best seasons in Greece are spring between March and May, or autumn from October to November. Summers are extremely hot and dry.

Accommodation:
Greece offers a wide variety of accommodation, from domátias (guestrooms for rent) to expensive luxury hotels. For more information check out: *www.gnto.gr*

Information:
Here are some websites to help you plan your trip.
www.gogreece.com
www.in2greece.com
www.greeka.com

picturesque mountain landscape on the steep slopes of Mount Parnassus, the town was considered by the ancient Greeks to be the center of the world. The Oracle of Delphí in the Sanctuary of Apollo was a regular center of consultation between the 8th century BC and AD 393.

The most famous sites of ancient Delphí include the amphitheater from the 2nd century BC, with a stunning view of the Temple of Apollo from 200 years earlier; the Holy Road; and the Sanctuary of Athena Pronaia with the Tholos, a famous circular temple. The Archaeological Museum's many sculptures and a reconstruction of the sanctuary is also worth a visit. The highlight is the life-size bronze charioteer, which had been dedicated to Apollo as a reward for a victorious chariot race in 478 BC. From Delphí, it is worth making a 220-km-long (137-mi) detour to the Metéora monasteries (see pp 326–327) in the mountainous heart of northern Greece.

Anyone wanting to omit the detour north will initially follow the same route back to Thíva, then continue along Highway 3 toward Athens as far as Asprópirgos before finally turning off west onto a small road that runs parallel to the coast. The route follows Salamis Bay, where the Greeks defeated the Persian fleet in 480 BC. Past Mégara, you will

❸ Thebes From Halkída, Highway 44 heads to Thíva, the new name of ancient Thebes, which is today an insignificant provincial town. The few historic remnants from what was once the mightiest city in Greece, in the 4th century BC, are on display in the Archaeological Museum. Continuing north-west you will pass the tower of a 13th-century fort built by Franconian crusaders. Heading towards Delphí, you initially take Highway 3 and then turn onto Route 48. The city of Livádia lies in the middle of vast cotton fields. After Livádia you will get some spectacular views over Mount Parnassus to the north-west.

❹ Ósios Loukás After about 13 km (8 mi), a road turns off southward toward Distomo, and a 13-km-long (8-mi) street leads to the Ósios Loukás Monastery, considered one of the most beautiful Greek Orthodox monasteries from the Byzantine era (10th century). It houses some magnificent mosaics from the 11th century. Another 24 km (15 mi) down the often steep and winding Highway 48 and you arrive in Delphí.

❺ Delphí Evidence of Delphí's magic can be seen in both its mythology and in its beautiful natural setting. Located amid a

1 View from the south over the Acropolis, with the imposing Parthenon in the center of the complex and Mount Lykabettos on the right in the background.

2 Three of the twenty columns were rebuilt at the Tholos, a round building at the Sanctuary of Athena Pronaia in Delphí.

Athens

The Greek capital is a pulsating, modern metropolis with three million inhabitants, approximately one third of whom live in the greater Athens area. The city's most recognizable icon is visible from afar and is the epitome of ancient Greece: the Acropolis.

Athens is a city of contrasts: chaos on the roads, traffic jams, complicated environmental problems and oppressive smog polluting the entire valley, while the greatest ruins from antiquity, especially the Acropolis, still stand tall on the south side of city center, affording wonderful views.

Athens' most famous site is the mighty Acropolis – a UNESCO World Heritage Site –, the castle hill of the ancient city that was converted into a holy district around 800 BC and mainly used to worship the goddess Athena, the city's patron saint. The Acropolis sits atop a steep, rugged, 156-m-high (512 ft) pale limestone plateau and was an important place of refuge for the population in times of need. The early beginnings of a castle wall already existed in the 13th century BC.

After the old temple was destroyed by the Persians in 480 BC, the complex of monumental marble buildings with the Propylae gate construction, the small Temple of Nike, the imposing Doric Parthenon (447–432 BC), and the Ionic Erechtheum with its Caryatid Porch were all created in the first half of the 5th century BC, the time of Pericles. The most extensive damage to the Parthenon dates back to the 17th century when a Venetian grenade hit the Turkish powder warehouse in the Parthenon and sent the roof flying into the air.

Important sculptures and reliefs are also on display in the Acropolis Museum. The main attractions below the Acropolis are the Theater of Dionysus, where the dramas of Aeschylus, Euripides and Sophocles premiered in front of an audience of 17,000; and the Roman Odeion (AD 160), a construction commissioned by the wealthy Athenian, Herodes Atticus.

The Acropolis project ultimately required a huge sacrifice from the Athenian taxpayers: the total costs were more than 2,000 ancient gold talents, an enormous sum of money for a city-state the size of Athens. Clustered around the Agora, the ancient market place from 600 BC and the center of public life for centuries, you will find the Doric Temple of Hephaistos, or Theseion (449–440 BC); the Attalos Stoa portico, once an artisans' center with discoveries from the ancient Agora, now reconstructed as a museum; the octagonal Tower of the Winds (1st century BC), formerly a clepsydra and sundial with a weather vane; the Roman Agora, from around the birth of Christ; and the adjacent Fethiye Mosque (15th century) that commemorates the fall of Constaninople in 1453.

The New Acropolis Museum, designed by Bernard Tschumi, is built over an extensive archaeological site, the floor, outside and inside, is often transparent using glass and thus the visitor can see the excavations below. The museum also provides an amphitheatre, a virtual theatre and a hall for temporary exhibitions. In the first two months since the museum opened, it was visited by 523,540 people (an average of 9,200 a day).

Plaka, the picturesque Turquish Town quarter features narrow alleyways, small shops, cafés and taverns, are several Byzantine churches, such as the beautiful Little Mitropolis (12th century) and Athens' oldest Christian church, the 11th-century cross-in-square Kapnikarea church on the fashionable Ermou shopping street.

Also worth seeing is the Panagía Geogoepíkoös cross-in-square church (12th century) at the Plateía Mitropóleos, as well as a small bazaar

mosque and the ruins of the Roman Library of Hadrian at Monastiraki Square.

Around the bustling Syntagma Square in modern Athens, you should see the Parliament building (Voulí), built by the architect Friedrich von Gärtner in 1842; the national garden created in 1836 with exotic plants; the Numismatic Museum in the home of German pioneer archaeologist Heinrich Schliemann (1871); the ruins of Hadrian's Gate and the Temple of Zeus (Olympieion) dating back to Roman times; the ancient Kallimármaro Stadium, reconstructed for the first modern Olympic Games in 1896; the National Archaeological Museum with a unique collection of ancient Greek art; the Museum of Cycladic Art; the Byzantine Museum; and the Benáki Museum (Byzantine works, Coptic textiles).

The surrounding area features: the Kaisariani Byzantine monasteries with the St Mary's Church, built around 1000, and 11th-century Dafni, which has some ornate gold leaf mosaics in the main church, UNESCO World Heritage Site.

It is worth taking a day trip out to Piraeus, Athens' port since ancient times, with the Mikrolimano fishing port, Hellenic Marine Museum and the Archaeological Museum. Also visit the Poseidon Temple on Cape Sounion, 67 km (42 mi) away, and the islands in the Saronic Gulf with the Temple of Apollo and the Temple of Aphaia, the island of Poros with its charming scenery, and the artists' island of Hydra.

In the 5th century BC, Pericles was able to gain support from the citizens Athens for the city's most ambitious building programme: the construction of the Acropolis, initially with three temples.

get some spectacular views of the Gulf of Aegina.

6 **Corinth** Some 25 km (16 mi) down the road you see the first glimpses of Corinth, considered Greece's most beautiful city in its heyday during the time of Emperor Hadrian in the 2nd century AD. Apart from the breathtaking Corinth Canal, the main attractions include the Temple of Apollo (44 BC), the Temple of Octavia and the Lechaion Road. A number of excavations document the sheer size of this ancient city, which was leveled by an earthquake in 375 and again in 551.

From Corinth, take Highway 70 along the north-eastern coast of Peloponnese to Epidauros.

7 **Epidauros** Ancient Epidaurus was a sanctuary of Asklepios, the god of medicine, and a city famous for its imposing amphitheater (4th century BC), which is very well preserved and well known for its unique acoustics.

8 **Nauplia** About 40 km (25 mi) further west is Nauplia. After the Greek War of Independence, this was temporarily the capital of the Kingdom of Greece, from 1829–1834. The port for centuries the constant target of enemy attacks, which prompted the construction of the two forts of Akronafplía and Palmídi in the north, and the island fort of Bourtzi in the south. The stylish Venetian quarter was built at the end of the 17th century.

9 **Tiryns** This fort dates back to the 14th or 13th century BC and perches atop an 18-m-high (59-ft) cliff above a once swampy plain. The imposing walls of the fort are made of blocks of stone that are 2 to 3 m long (7-10 ft) and weigh up

to an impressive 12 tonnes (13.2 tons). According to Homer, only giants – cyclops in this case – could have built the 700-m-long (2,297-ft), 8-m-thick (26-ft) wall. The town of Árgos is 13 km (8 mi) away.

From there, it's worth making a detour north to Mycenae. A small road turns off at Fihtí. Back in Árgos, the route heads west through Arcadia to Trípoli, and from there 60 km (37 mi) through the historic Laconia landscape to Sparta.

10 **Sparta** Ancient Sparta was a city-state that once superseded Athens in importance. By contrast, the modern 19th-century Spárti has little to offer. Apart from its acropolis (outside the city center), it's worth visiting the Archaeological Museum with Roman mosaics from the 4th and 5th centuries.

11 **Mistrás** The neighbouring town of Mistrás at the foot of 1

was founded near ancient Sparta in 1249, and is said to have had a population of 50,000 in its heyday, around 1700.

The unique Byzantine ruins of the city, which is located on a steep hillside, display impressive buildings from the 13th to 15th centuries, including some interesting churches, a monastery and the Despot's Palace.

Above the town, clinging to the mountainside, is a fort from the

13th century (Kástro) built by crusaders from Franconia.

Back in Sparta, take Highway 39 to the town of Hania 47 km (29 mi) away and from there, it's 75 km (47 mi) to Monemvassiá. From the intersection, it's downhill to Gythio, the gateway to the Mani Peninsula, the middle of the three fingers of the Peloponnese peninsula. Its west coast is rich of cultural jewels to be discovered.

Diroú, which can be explored by boat. In Areópoli, old residential towers have been converted into guesthouses.

⑬ The west coast of the Peloponnese From Areópoli, you continue to follow the coast north to Kalamáta. This city is located at the Bay of Navarino, where a united English, French and Russian fleet defeated the Ottomans in 1827. The beaches here are lined with dunes that stretch along the west side of the western finger of the peninsula. A small detour branches off from here to the port town of Methóni 13 km (8 mi) away. The route heads north along the coast for 15 km (9 mi) before Pírgos, where the picturesque but very winding Route 76 turns off and heads through mountainous Arcadia to Andrítsena, with the Temple of Bassae from the 5th century, and Karitena, with a bridge over the Alfíos, from the 15th century. This same road takes you back to Kréstena and over the Alfioó River to Olimbía (Olympia).

⑭ Olympia Traces of earlier settlement here date back to as early as the 2,000 BC. In ancient times, the town was a religious sanctuary of Zeus and a sporting cult site. It was here that the first Olympic Games were held no later than 776 BC.

All of Olympia's significant religious sites are found within the "Altis", a walled holy district. The sporting competitions took place outside the Altis, and the

⑫ Máni Peninsula This peninsula south of the route from Gythio to Areópoli is also known as Deep or Laconian Máni. The trip around Máni is about 90 km (56 mi) and initially heads past the Castle of Passavá (13th century) on the largely uninhabited mountain-

ous eastern side. The peninsula itself remains largely in its original state, but many of the villages are deserted today. From Páliros, on the southern tip, the route heads north to Vathia with its tower houses. The village has the most impressive location on the west coast, and

the 17-km-long (11-mi) stretch between Geroliménas and Pígros Diroú is famous for its Byzantine churches from the 10th to the 14th centuries.

In the north-west near Kíta and Mamína are some interesting stalactite caves, the most impressive of which is Pírgos

1 The tower houses of Vátheia, not far from Cape Ténaro on Máni.

2 One of Mistrás' Byzantine churches.

3 Limeni, the port of Areópoli on Máni.

sites include a stadium for runners, the hippodrome (for chariot races) and the training sites of Gymnasion and Palaestra. Other attractions are the Pryentaion, where the Olympic torch was lit and the Heraion, a temple dedicated to the goddess Hera. The Olympic torch is still lit in front of this temple before all Olympic Games. The Echo Hall, a foyer with two naves, was famous for its sevenfold echo. Columns at the ruins ofthe Temple of Zeus from 450 BC testify to the vast size of the former building. Olympia's Archaeological Museum is one of the best in Greece.

North of Pírgos you will drive along a road lined with olive trees, vineyards and sugar cane plantations.

⑮ Zákinthos Ferries to this, the southernmost of the Ionic Islands, operate from the port town of Kilíni on the northwest coast of the Peloponnese. you can easily drive around the island in one day. Almost all of the Venetian buildings in the main town were destroyed in

an earthquake in 1953, but the Agios Dionísos Church (1925) and the traditional Arcadian houses are worth seeing. The Blue Caves on the North Cape can be accessed by boat from Agios Nikólaos. Another of the island's attractions is the beach shipwreck on the north-west coast, while Laganás Bay in the south is a breeding ground for loggerhead turtles, which are considered an endangered species and protected.

⑯ Patras From Lehená, take Highway 9 to Patras. It is worth making a detour here to the lagoons along the coast. Stretching through this area is one of Europe's largest wetlands where swamps, stone pines and dunes are used by migratory birds as a stopover point on their travel from Europe to Africa. There is a visitors' center at Lápas.

The naval Battle of Lepanto took place in the strait northeast of Patras, the third-largest city in Greece with no notable attractions. Yet history was made here when Don Juan

d'Austria, the natural son of Emperor Charles V, defeated the Ottoman fleet in 1571.

⑰ Diakoftó Rather than taking Highway 8, we recommend you follow a small rural road along the coast. For a little diversity along the way, it is worth taking a ride on the cog railway from Diakoftó some 40 km (25 mi) east of Patras to Kalávrita at a height of 700 m (2,297 ft). The journey over this 22-km-long (14-mi) stretch with fourteen tunnels and a number of bridges takes about one

hour and travels through picturesque mountains. Don't miss the famous Méga Spíleo Monastery on your way back to Corinth. The monastery, which is said to be the oldest in the country, was where the Greeks began their revolution against the occupation of the Ottomans..

1 The octagonal fortress tower on the island of Boúrtzi near Methóni dates back to the 16th century.

2 Ruins of the former sporting grounds in ancient Olympia.

Metéora These monastery buildings are perched atop rock towers up to 300 m (984 ft) high, date back to the 14th/15th centuries, and sure live up to their name, "Floating Rocks". Five of the complexes are still inhabited.

Delphí The city of the Oracle perches on the steep slopes of Mount Parnassus with an amphitheater, the Temple of Apollo and an archaeological museum.

Aráchova In summer, this village near Thebes and Delphí attracts hordes of visitors with its wine, cheese and woven products.

Athens One-third of all Greeks live in the metropolitan area of their capital (since 1834). Athens hosted the 2004 Olympic Games. Numerous antiquities on the Acropolis plateau and in the National Archaeological Museum attest to Athens' former importance.

Euboea A diverse coast and a mountainous interior with numerous gorges characterize Greece's second-largest island, large parts of which have still barely been discovered by tourism.

Corinth This port city, which has been fortified for 2,700 years, has impressive ruins, including the temples of Apollo and Octavia, and a famous canal that opened in 1893.

Marathon A museum and the burial mound of fallen Athenians recall the victorious Greek battle against the Persion invaders in 490 BC.

Zákinthos The main attractions here are the breeding grounds for loggerhead turtles in Laganás Bay – and of course the pristine beaches.

Temple of Poseidon One of the most famous landmarks of the Aegean is Cape Sounion, adorned with a sanctuary for the god of the sea since 445 BC.

Epidaurus The highlight of this ancient cult site and healing town is Greece's best-preserved amphitheater from the 3rd century BC. It seated 12,000 people.

Monemvassia The "Gibraltar of Greece" is a fortified island town characterized by medieval and Venetian architecture that can be reached by a bridge.

Methoni This former Venetian port city is one of the largest on the Peloponnese and was protected by this fortress tower.

Máni Pensinsula This rugged mountainous area has no noteworthy ports or beaches, but interesting watchtowers characterize many of the region's old villages such as Váthia, pictured here.

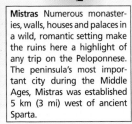

Mistras Numerous monasteries, walls, houses and palaces in a wild, romantic setting make the ruins here a highlight of any trip on the Peloponnese. The peninsula's most important city during the Middle Ages, Mistras was established 5 km (3 mi) west of ancient Sparta.

The tombs of Hasan Pasa Kümbet at Ahlat, on the northern shore of Lake Van.

Turkey

Temples, mosques and gorgeous coves

Olive orchards, beaches and the snow-capped peak of Mount Ararat – Turkey welcomes visitors with an enormous wealth of scenery and landscapes. Beyond that, cultural landmarks and monuments of numerous empires spanning more than nine thousand years play a huge role in making your trip to Turkey an unforgettable experience.

Your journey through the Republic of Turkey begins in a surprisingly rural setting. Istanbul's lively arterial roads are full of all sorts of businesses, but they soon give way to the green fields of East Thrace, a totally different landscape where traditional tearooms, bazaars and caravanserais coexist with modern highways, cargo vessels, Roman ruins and monuments like those in Gelibolu (Gallipoli)

National Park. It was here that Turkish troops managed to defeat the British and Australian Armies after months of fighting in 1915 – all under the command of Mustafa Kemal Pasha, later to become known as Atatürk, 'Father of the Turks', founder of modern Turkey.
All along the Mediterranean shores of western Anatolia, the 'Coasts of Light', there are historical sites of ancient Greek

Head of Medusa in the ancient city of Didyma.

and Roman culture in all their breath-taking beauty. Among them are Pergamon, Ephesus and Milet, some of the most

incredible examples of art and architecture from those times. The Hellenic mathematicians and philosophers living in Ionia, on Asia Minor's western frontier, transformed that city into one of the cradles of European civilization.
On the south coast between Marmaris and Alanya you will be delighted by the plentiful beaches where water sports and relaxation are high on the agenda. For more adventurous travellers, there is also rafting, paragliding, cave excursions and mountain climbing. With a bit of searching you can find secluded coves and pristine natural settings. Between the Olympus Mountains and the

A strange sight – wind and rain have exposed these tuff pillars near Göreme in Cappadocia.

The Hagia Sophia in Istanbul is a masterpiece of Byzantine architecture. The building is no longer used for religious purposes, but as a museum.

coast, a region of fishing villages, farms and winding pathways has been converted into a holiday destination where sensitive infrastructure and environmental considerations were taken into account right from the beginning. The project, known as the 'South Antalya Project' or 'Kemer project', has been called a 'total success'. The motto was 'Less is More', and it seems to have worked with the upmarket boutiques and hotels. East of Anamur Castle, built on a magnificent location above the sea, your 'Turkey adventure' can really finally begin. Very few people come this far to see the wide horizons of eastern Anatolia. For hours, and over considerable distances, the land appears completely empty, with low-lying,

dust-coloured villages barely standing out from the surrounding countryside. Yet this easternmost region of Turkey is where you find the country's largest lake, Lake Van, and its highest peak, Mount Ararat. Due to Ararat's remote location, however, we recommend you visit Nemrut Dagi in the Taurus Mountains, a man-made mountain with a 2,000-year-old king's tomb. Lake Van and the town of Van, on the other hand, are worth a longer visit. In central Anatolia you can experience Muslim culture at its most intense, especially in the highlands between the Taurus Mountains to the south and the Pontic Mountains at the Black Sea. Towns like Sivas or Konya are centers of Islamic mysticism.

Cappadocia, a must-see, is home to the bizarre erosion landscape around Nevsehir and Göreme. The tuff formations are a truly fantastic experience, both in terms of nature and culture. Byzantine monks once sought shelter here from Muslim Arab attacks. Today the

cave dwellings and churches form a giant open-air museum. An even older culture exists near Ankara, Turkey's modern capital. The Hattusas ruins are now a UNESCO World Heritage Site – one of a total of nine UNESCO Cultural and Natural Sites in Turkey.

The Celsus Library in Ephesus with its restored façade.

Turkey – a travel adventure even today? Beach-hopping along the west and south coasts is no problem at all – it's pure enjoyment. But what a bold contrast to the dust clouds on some of the dirt roads in eastern Anatolia! This journey takes you from touristy coastal towns to the central Anatolian hinterland, a fascinating excursion through the cultural and natural landscape of this diverse nation.

1 Istanbul This city of three names – Byzantium, Constantinople, Istanbul – was the mistress of two empires that both decisively shaped the history of the Mediterranean for almost two thousand years – the East Roman or Byzantine Empire and its direct successor, the Ottoman Empire. Art treasures from every era of its history as well as the variety and vitality of modern Istanbul make the city an ideal destination for lovers of art and culture.

In the Old Town between the Golden Horn, Bosporus and the Marmara Sea there are a few things you shouldn't miss – Hagia Sophia, the religious center of ancient Byzantium built by the emperor Justinian I from 532 to 537. It has a magnificent dome and some beautifully preserved mosaics. Hagia Eirene goes back to pre-Constantine times, the current building having been erected in the 8th century. The Archaeological Museum has an interesting collection of antique exhibits.

In the Ottoman city center be sure to visit – Topkapi Sultan's Palace, a spacious compound with magnificent buildings structured by courtyards and gates; the well of Sultan Ahmed

III (1728); the Sultan Ahmed Mosque – the 'Blue Mosque' (17th century); the Hippodrome, an antique carriage race track; the Museum of Turkish and Islamic Art; the Sokollu Mehmet Pasa Mosque (16th century); the Mosaic Museum; the beautiful ancient steam baths of Haseki Hürrem Hamam (1557) and Cagaloglu Hamam (18th century); Sogukcese Sokagi, a road lined with restored timber buildings from the Ottomans; and the High Gate, a rococo gate.

In the Old City check out: the Grand Bazaar, the world's largest indoor market; the Egyptian Bazaar, a book bazaar; the New Mosque (17th century); the Rüstem Pasa Mosque dating from the 16th century with its colourful tiles; the Beyazit Tower, a fire tower from 1828; the Beyazit Mosque (16th

Travel Information

Route profile
Length: approx. 6,000 km (3,730 miles), excluding detours
Time required: 8–12 weeks
Start and end: Istanbul
Route (main locations): Istanbul, Edirne, Çanakkale, Troy, Pergamon, Izmir, Ephesus, Bodrum, Fethiye, Antalya, Alanya, Silifke, Şanliurfa, Diyarbakir, Van, Göreme, Konya, Ankara, Safranbulo, Bursa

Traffic information:
Beware of the three-lane system where the middle lane is used for overtaking in both directions! The middle lane is not always empty! Speed limit outside towns is 90 km/h

(56 mph), inside towns it is 50 m/h (31 mph).

When to go:
Spring and autumn in general; due to relatively long winters in Eastern and central Anatolia, however, not before April/May and not after September. On the coasts, you can travel as early as March and as late as September.

Information:
www.turkeytravelplanner.com
www.travelturkey.com
www.turizm.net
www.exclusivetravelturkey.com

The Selimiye Camii Mosque, built by Selim II, was called Sinan's masterpiece by none other than the great architect himself. This terrific building has a giant dome that possesses enchanting harmony and grace. Back on the coast, Sarköy is the center of the wine-growing area on the northern shore of the Marmara Sea. Leave the E90 at Bolayir towards the east to get there.

Towards the south, the E90/550 ends in Eceabat, where you can catch one of the several ferries that cross the narrow Dardanelles each day to Çanakkale. The straits are only 1,200 m (1,300 yds) wide.

④ Çanakkale Burly 15th century fortifications, a marine museum and a reconstruction of a World War I minelayer leave no doubt about the military importance of the Dardanelles. Along the quays there is a row of cafés, shops and restaurants to explore. Away from the bustle of the port, the constant currents ensure that the waters are clean enough for swimming. We recommend Güzelyali on the southern shore of the Dardanelles.

⑤ Troy (Truva) This is where Heinrich Schliemann celebrated the discovery of the 'Priamos Treasure' and Homeric Troy in 1871. Archaeologists are still at work today but, due to a lack of written records, there is still no absolute certainty that this actually is the Troy of Homer's epics. An interesting and attrac-

1 The Temple of Hadrian in Ephesus is decorated in lavish relief.

2 Ortaköy Mosque, one of Istanbul's grand religious buildings.

3 The ruins of Hercules Gate in Ephesus, vestiges of a former imperial power.

century); Nuruosmaniye Mosque (18th century); the Constantine Column from AD 330; and the Sultan Süleyman Mosque.

At the edge of the Old City visit the Hagios Georgios (1720), the cast-iron Church of St Stephen (1871), Tefur Palace (11th century), some ruins of the Theodosian wall (5th century), the Mihrimah Mosque (16th century), the Chora Church and the Victory Mosque.

Following Highway 03, this dream route first takes you across the Bosporus through the gentle, fertile hills of Thrace. There is peace and quiet in the fields and villages of this ancient agricultural region.

② Lüleburgaz The Romans knew it as Arkadiopolis but modern Lüleburgaz is a modest town on National Road 100. It does have a place of interest, however – in the 16th century,

the architectural genius Sinan (1490–1578) built a mosque here for a pasha.

③ Edirne From 1365 until the conquest of Constantinople in 1453, the former Adrianople (Turkish: Edirne) was the capital of the Ottoman Empire. Buildings dating back to the sultanate and an historical town center with picturesque wooden houses have been well preserved throughout the ages.

tive exhibition presents the excavation findings.

6 **Assos** The Bagi Peninsula, an alternatingly flat and mountainous strip of land with plentiful forests, separates the Marmara Sea from the Gulf of Edremit. More densely populated in the past than it is today, the coastal road (not the E87!) takes you past the overgrown remains of a few ancient sites – Alexandreia Troas, a port town near Gülpinar; the temple walls of the Apollon Sminteion sanctuary; and, at dizzying heights with fantastic views above the southern seashore, the ruins of old Assos (around three thousand years old). At the foot of the mountain is the tiny picturesque port of Behramkale.

7 **Ayvalik** After passing through Edremit on Highway 550, the main town on the 'Olive Riviera', you come to the tourist destination of Ayvalik with its seaside promenade, Old Town alleyways, diving resorts and twenty-three islands just off the coast. Further inland are some wine-growing villages tucked in among the hills. Farmers, vintners and innkeepers have recently joined forces here to prevent the opening of a gold mine because of the environmental damage that it would most likely cause.

After turning off the E87 further inland, follow the signs for Pergamon (50 km/31 miles).

8 **Pergamon** The rulers of Pergamon used the steep slopes of the local rock plateaus, some up to 300 m (1,000 ft) high, to build the 'acropolis' of their capital city. Today, the acropolis' altar to Zeus can only be admired in Berlin's Pergamon Museum, but there are still abundant ruins in this ancient town of kings. Bergama, the modern city at the foot of the

castle mountain, also contains some historical ruins.

9 **Izmir** Cosmopolitan and full of energy, Izmir's two million people make it the only big city on Turkey's west coast and the country's most important port. Its bazaar is still as lively as ever. The parks, promenades and baths of Balcova provide a charming Mediterranean atmosphere, along with the lovely beaches of the Çesme Peninsula.

From Izmir, there are two ways to reach the sinter terraces at Pamukkale – through the mountains via Sardes and Salihli (210 km/130 miles) or more quickly via Aydin on Road 320 (270 km/168 miles).

10 **Ephesus** This city of ruins near the town of Selçuk really defines the concept of ancient – the Lydians and Carians worshipped the mother goddess of Kybele here long before Greek

traders and settlers arrived on the Ionian coast and built their own temple to Artemis in the tradition of the mother goddess.

In approximately AD 129, Ephesus became the capital of the Roman province of Asia. At the time it had about 200,000 inhabitants. Archaeologists have been able to reconstruct more of Ephesus' temples, streets, baths and living quar-

ters than any other site in Turkey. The city port, however, has silted up over the centuries and the sea is now several miles away.

Not far from Kusadasi is the important Ionian town of Milet.

11 **Milet** Like Ephesus and Priene, the trading town of Milet had to be relocated several times because its port was threatened by silt buildup.

Today the former port is hardly visible among the ruins, which nearly disappear into the flood plains of the Meander River (Büyük Menderes). Only one field with a mighty theater, an agora (square) and the walls of the baths have survived. The area that was once the largest town in ancient Greece is now home to frogs and storks. Historically, however, the cities of Thales, Anaximander and Anaximenes formed the center of philosophy and mathematics in the empire (the renowned Milesian School).

Road 525 first takes you to the forested region around Lake Bafa before reaching the well-preserved temple of Euromos. South of Milas you take National Road 330 to Bodrum, a pleasant drive with plenty of opportunities for excursions and breaks.

12 Bodrum This former fishing village is now a tidy white-washed town on a striking blue bay. Its center is the Castle of the Knights of St John (1413). If you want, you can hire a gulet, one of the traditional sailing vessels from these parts, to take you out to a secluded bay for a picnic.

13 Knidos/Datça The road now takes a sweeping curve along Gökova Bay, which is almost 80 km (50 miles) long, through Milas, Yatagan, Mugla and Marmaris, and out onto the 'pan handle' of the Datça Peninsula. A national park here covers an area of roughly 1,500 sq km (580 sq mi) and protects the local forests and bays from the sadly unbridled development taking place in the area.

From the fishing and holiday village of Datça you can take a boat across to Knidos, a town

founded in 400 BC at the end of the peninsula. Among the sights of this important antique trading and military post are an acropolis and the temples of Aphrodite and Demeter.

Leaving Marmaris behind we now drive through forested landscapes, over mountains and rivers, back along the coast, and then past Lake Köycegiz and some antique sites (Kaunos Rock Tombs) to the small town of Fethiye. National Road 400 starts here and follows Turkey's south coast. The rock tombs at Fethiye are well worth a climb at sunset. Ölü Deniz has attractive clear waters and an 'almost' white sand beach. It is the most famous bay south of Fethiye.

14 Phaselis On your way to Olimpos National Park you will be amazed by the antique Lycian town of Xanthos, miles of hotel-free beaches around Patara, the ancient towns of Kalkan and Kas, and the island world of Kekova with its submerged city.

A short detour from National Road 400 then takes you to Phaselis, an ancient port with a unique atmosphere. The ruins of three ports, an amphitheater, an agora and bath houses make this town, situated at the foot of an impressive mountain range, a worthy stop.

15 Antalya This town has been called 'Smiling Beauty of South Turkey'. In only two decades, this lovely place has become the undisputed tourist destination of southern Turkey. From the

1 Sunset over the sinter terraces of Pamukkale.

2 Kaunos: Lycian rock tombs near the holiday destination of Dalyan.

3 Beautiful beaches for bathing and snorkelling near Fethiye.

terrific mountain backdrops, city beaches and bustling nightlife to lively bazaars and outstanding museums, Antalya has everything the tourist's heart desires. In springtime you can go skiing in the mountains and take a plunge in the sea later all in one day, or you can take trips to Termessos National Park or the ancient town of Termessos. Golfers are drawn to nearby Belek, Turkey's upmarket golf center.

16 Manavgat/Side Just one hour east of Antalya is the ancient port of Side, now home to idyllic sandy beaches. In Side and the provincial town of Manavgat a little further inland you have a vast range of accommodation to choose from.
Using this area as a base, there are interesting trips to Köprülü Canyon National Park and the Manavgat waterfalls. Thrillseekers can take organized rafting tours on the Köpru River.

17 Alanya This is the third holiday destination on the south coast after Side and Antalya. The impressive red Seljuk castle on a steep rock outcrop above the town has 146 towers, stunning views and offers romantic sunsets. It's definitely Alanya's biggest attraction. The town's palm-lined alleyways and subtropical flora are wonderful for relaxing strolls, and Alanya's extensive beaches are well-suited to all kinds of sports and activities. Not long ago, one of Turkey's most beautiful stalactite caves – Dim Magarsi – was made accessible to the public.

18 Anamur From here, the distances between towns will start getting longer. Blasted out of coastal cliffs, National Road 400 is made up of a never-ending series of breathtaking sea views. Spiny, fragrant scrubland dominates the landscape while trees

are rare in the area. The town and castle of Anamur, however, are strikingly different – on the flood plain of the Dragon River you'll find lush green fields.
Greek settlers established the port of Anamurium as far back as 400 BC at this southernmost point in Asia Minor, and for a long time their trade with Cyprus flourished. The remains of a palestra (sports stadium), an odeon (theater) and baths several floors high still bear witness to these times.
The inhabitants of Anamurium were eventually driven out by Arab invasions in the 7th century. In the 12th and 13th centuries the town was resettled. Soon thereafter, Anamur Castle was built by a ruler of the Karaman principality. With its battlements and gallery, thirty-six towers and three courtyards, this is one of the most impressive medieval fortifications in all of Anatolia.
Its exposed location also makes it unforgettable – right above the the rocky coastline, the waves crash against the mighty ramparts of an impressive castle. Later Ottoman rulers added

a mosque, a bath and a well to the courtyards.

19 Silifke In 1190, Frederick I Barbarossa ('Red Beard') wanted to take this town during the third crusade, but one day in June a few miles outside of it he drowned in the Göksu River. Silifke, which was founded around 300 BC by Seleukos I Nikator, is the most unchanged of any town on Turkey's south coast. It is set against the majestic backdrop of the Cilikian Mountains close to the sea and makes a good base for a handful of day trips and excursions to islands, caves and ancient sanctuaries. Among the town's sights are the Roman ruins of Olba and Diocaesarea (Ura/

Uzuncaburç) set in some terrific scenery; the Byzantine monastery of Alahan; and also Cennet ve Cehennem ('Heaven and Hell'), two deep, round rock valleys.

20 Adana This area is dominated by the nearby Taurus Mountains, which rise to an impressive 4,000 m (13,000 ft). Between Adana and the sea are the Çukurova Plains with their endless fields of cotton. Turkey's largest mosque was recently constructed on Adana's Seydan River. In recent decades, 3,500-year-old Adana has grown to become Turkey's fourth-largest city. Its thousands of shops, bazaars and minarets are typical of the historical Old Town while

eastern shore was called Tuspa. It was the capital of the Urartu Kingdom, famed for its highly skilled metalworkers and grand fortifications. The Armenian church (915–921) on Ahtamar Island sits amid quaint olive groves and is definitely worth a visit for its stucco work and frescoes.

Your route to Sivas circles Lake Van and goes through some wonderful mountain scenery past Elazig, the Keban Reservoir to the north and Divrigi, whose large mosque is a UNESCO World Heritage Site.

㉕ Sivas This town's architecture is impressive, above all the intricately decorated gates of the Gök Madrasah. The 'Mukarnas', little niches in the building, are decorated to look like stalactites. Depictions of plants and animals cover the walls of these niches, giving them a labyrinth feel. The financial means for such intricate ornamentation were provided by Sivas' fortuitous location – the main trade routes to and from Russia, Egypt, Iran and southeastern Europe all pass through here.

㉖ Kayseri In ancient Rome, Kayseri was called Caesarea. At the time it was the capital of Cappadocia. The modern town sprawls out onto the plains at the foot of the Erciyes Dagi Mountain, whose mighty summit reaches 3,916 m (12,848 ft) and is always covered in snow.

1 Panorama of Cappadocia with bizarre tuff towers near Göreme.

2 The impressive, 1,000-year-old Armenian church on Ahtamar Island in Lake Van.

3 Nemrut Dag˘ı with its remnants of monumental heads of humans and eagles.

the new city is home to tree-lined boulevards, modern banks and high-rise buildings.

After passing Kahramanmaras, Adiyaman and Kahta, your route ascends the desolate mountain regions of the Taurus Range.

㉑ Nemrut Dağı The monumental eagles and statues sitting curiously at 2,150 m (7,050 ft) above sea level have become the leading icon of adventurous, exotic Turkey. The tomb monuments, which continue to baffle scientists to this day, were erected by King Antiochos I of Commagena (an Anatolian state around the birth of Christ). Today there are only ruins where cities once thrived.

Two of the tomb's three original terraces have been well preserved, with fragments of statues seemingly randomly placed around the site. Their heads gaze out over the land towards the rising sun. Greek as well as Oriental gods were worshipped here.

Road 875 now takes us via Adiyaman west of the Atatürk Reservoir to Şanliurfa.

㉒ Şanliurfa On the vast plains of Upper Mesopotamia, a rock promontory bears the ruins of an ancient fortification. Soldiers serving under Alexander the Great founded this city and gave it the Macedonian name Edessa. Şanliurfa was an important place for early Christianity

as well as for Arab scholars. Its spring was already sacred to the Greeks and to this day there are sacred Muslim carp swimming in it ('Abraham's Pond').

From Şanliurfa, National Road 360 takes us to Diyarbakir, the largest town in eastern Anatolia.

㉓ Diyarbakir To this day, the Old Town here is surrounded almost completely by the original Roman-Byzantine walls of basalt rock. East of these walls is the legendary Tigris River. Palaces, mosques and madrasahs (Koranic schools), caravanserais, churches, lively bazaars and modern boulevards all give this city its many faces. You reach Lake Van in the east by taking a winding mountain road for about 250 km (160 miles).

㉔ Van Lake Van covers an area of 3,750 sq km (3,225 sq mi), is located at an altitude of 1,600 m (5,250 ft) and is surrounded by mountain ranges more than 4,000 m (13,000 ft) high. Roughly 3,000 years ago, the town of Van on the south-

The Old Town of this industrial city has a lot to offer to lovers of art and architecture. The buildings from the heyday of the Seljuk Empire (11th–12th centuries) are worth seeing, along with those from later centuries. The mosque of Huand Hatun, a Seljuk princess, is well worth a visit with its madrasah, large baths and the mausoleum of the benefactress.

27 Nevsehir/Göreme The former is a predominantly modern town, but its Seljuk castle on the local mountain and its mosque and madrasah (Koranic school) are worth seeing. These were donated by a Grand Vizier of the Ottoman Empire in the 18th century, who was initially lauded but later decapitated. For many visitors, however, the town is simply a good starting point for excursions to the picturesque lunar landscape of Cappadocia. The cones, obelisks and tuff pillars here are the result of erosion over millions of years as well as extensive use by local people as cave dwellings, monks' habitations and lookout posts. Cappadocia is basically one big open-air museum with a terrific setting for this unique 'natural architecture' and some good hiking.

28 Konya The crusaders marvelled when they arrived in Konya in the Middle Ages, and modern Konya keeps up the tradition of beauty with wide boulevards and more parks than any other town in central Anatolia. Lovers of historic architecture and sculpture will find many precious stone carvings on the mosques and madrasahs of this former Seljuk capital.

The monastery of the Mevlevî dervish order (Mevlânâ Tekkesi) has been a museum since the order was outlawed by Atatürk back in 1925. For centuries this

was a center of the Mevlânâ sect. The Huzuri Pir Hall ('Presence of the Saint') is always filled with crowds of visitors wanting to touch their hands and lips to the sarcophagi of Celâleddin and his closest followers. The founder of the order came from Persia, lived in Konya for almost half a century and died in 1273. There are several museums in Konya with outstanding collections. Don't miss them if you have enough time to visit.

The road across the Anatolian highlands to Ankara 300 km (185 miles) away is well developed and easy to drive. You cross a deserted, dry plain with some impressive mountain scenery. From March to May the plains are in full bloom and the colourful carpets of wild tulips are one of the most popular themes of Turkish art.

Between Cihanbeyli and Kulu, you drive along the Tuz Gölü salt lake (1,500 sq km/580 sq mi). Tuz Gölü is one of the richest salt beds in the world. In the summer it shrinks to a bog with salty white edges.

29 Ankara This town was crucial in the Turkish National War of Liberation, which saved the country from being divided up among the victorious powers of World War I. At the time, around 1920, this small town only had about 30,000 inhabitants. By 1980, there were two million and today there may be as many as four million. Only a fraction of this city actually dates back more than eighty years.

Atatürk's decision to move the capital into the Anatolian plains 600 km (375 miles) away from the Aegean coast at first seemed absurd to many people, but it was a way to make Ankara (the Roman Ankyra) the instrument and symbol of a new orientation for the country. The move was designed to bring not only the Aegean Coast but the whole of Turkey closer to Europe. The ploy seems to have worked, at least in this young metropolis.

The German architect Hermann Jansen was responsible for much of the town planning in modern Ankara. For an en-

counter with the 9,000 years of Anatolian history, be sure to visit the Museum of Anatolian Civilization.

Allow at least two days for an excursion to Hattusas (Turkish: Bogazkale), the almost 4,000-year-old capital of the Hethitan kingdom, which has a number of palaces and temples.

Heading north, a winding road takes us into the Köroglu Daglari and Ilgaz Daglari forests. The route to the Black Sea coast then ends among some gentle, hilly scenery in Kastamonu on the northern slopes of the Pontic Mountains.

30 Kastamonu Numerous terraces and the well-proportioned Ottoman mosques dating from the 15th and 16th centuries are among the town's noteworthy sights. Sultan Suleyman the Magnificent's chef and storehouse overseer was the architect of Yakub Aga Külliyesi, a stately mosque with a central dome and neighbouring madrasah. Even more impressive than its mosques, however, are Kastamonu's two-

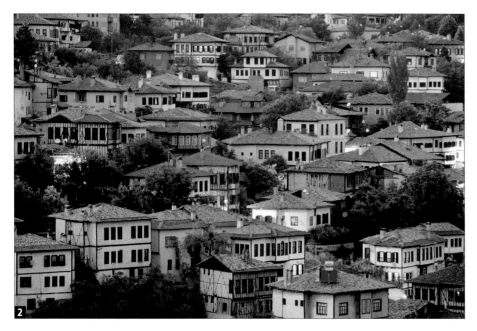

National Road 650 south towards Bözüyük. After roughly 120 km (75 miles) you follow National Road 200 (E90) northwest, which takes you to Bursa (another 120 km/75 miles), your last stop on the tour before we head back to Istanbul.

32 Bursa Its location on the slopes of Mount Uludag combined with the magnificent architecture of its palaces, mosques and mausoleums all make Bursa one of the most beautiful towns of the former sultanate. The city's monuments have been well preserved in park-like settings amid the urban surroundings. The former inhabitants of Prusa ad Olympum, its ancient predecessor, had long ago learned to appreciate the local hot springs. The town received its nickname from Mount Uludag, the 'Mystical Olympus'. In 1326, Bursa became the capital of the Ottoman Empire.

Bursa is now a large city, but in winter Mount Uludag provides ski resorts and a gondola that takes you to the top. Some pastel-coloured houses adorn the Old Town, and there are some babbling fountains beneath green cypresses. Due to its elevation the climate is pleasant even in summer, making Bursa a nice final stop on your way back to Istanbul.

Taking National Roads 575 and 130 you will pass through Gemlk. From Kocaeli (Highway 04), it is only 240 km (150 miles) back to Istanbul.

UNESCO World Heritage Site in 1994, this town has been more famous than Kastamonu, its neighbour to the east. The 'Saffron City' had its heyday in the 18th century, at a time when it was the trade hub for this much sought-after yellow plant dye that was used as a spice, medicine and, above all, dye for various foodstuffs. The 'Konak' houses here have been lovingly maintained and restored; most of them are built with two storeys around a central courtyard and brick roofs. The Old Town (Carsi) is easy to explore on foot, and a little further out on a hill in Baglar are the summer residences of some wealthier families. In the Carsi there are a few worthwhile museums as well as crafts workshops, a lively bazaar, typical tearooms and hotels, often in historic buildings.

Taking National Road 755 south from Safranbolu you'll arrive at National Road 100 (E80) at Eskipazar after about 60 km (37 miles). When you get to Gerede, the road becomes Highway 04. At Sakarya, take

and three-storey timber-framed houses, or 'Konaks'. The ground floors were made of stone, with bays and mostly flat roofs. The small river in the valley terminates in the Kizilir-mak River a little to the east, which in turn flows into the Black Sea.

31 Safranbolu Since its Old Town was designated a

1 The Mevlânâ Monastery in Konya has been the destination of pious pilgrims for centuries.

2 Traditional houses on the slopes of Safranbolu.

3 The Kocatepe Mosque in Ankara was consecrated in 1987.

Pergamon This temple was begun by Emperor Trajan and completed by his successor, Hadrian, on the highest point of the ancient city of kings on the castle hill of modern Bergama. The Pergamon Empire reached its peak after the death of Alexander the Great and later fell to Rome without a fight.

Assos There is a terrific view across to the island of Lesbos from the ruins of the Temple of Athena, which is on the town hill of Assos where Aristotle used to teach. It is worth driving down the steep hill to the stone houses, tea terraces and port of Behramkale.

Ephesus Few modern libraries can compete with the glorious columns of the Celsus Library. Built to commemorate the Roman Proconsul in the 2nd century AD, it is probably the most beautiful ancient library still standing.

Pamukkale The limestone terraces of Pamukkale ('Cotton Castle') are now gleaming white again. They were recently renovated after years of neglect. The cascading formations are formed by hot spring water with a high lime content.

Kaunos The unique rock tombs in south-west Turkey go back to the Lycians who presumably came from Crete even before the Greeks did. The picture shows tombs in a steep rock face near the fishing village of Dalyan, not far from Bodrum.

Turkish wine-growing around the Marmara Sea Wine has ever been grown around Şarköy and Mürefte. Annual harvests reach about 75,000 tons. Professional wine tastings have led to improve local wines in terms of both variety and quality to compete with Raki, a traditional anise-based liqueur from nearby Tekirdag.

Istanbul The Blue Mosque, with its six minarets (a very unusual number) was named after a Turkish speciality – the roughly 21,000 mostly blue tiles, which are indeed very intricately made. The 'Blue Miracle', right next to the Hagia Sophia in Turkey's capital, took five years to build between 1609 an 1616.

Bodrum This town has a modern-Mediterranean feel, but the castle of the Order of the Knights of St John was built here in 1413.

Aphrodisias Once a center for stone carving it is now an archaeological Mecca.

Fethiye Famous mainly because of the nearby dream bay of Ölü Deniz as well as numerous islands and beaches, Fethiye itself is a charming place with lively bazaars and picturesque mosques.

Antalya This city of half a million people has its share of parks, long beaches, ancient architecture and old-town romance, all of which contribute to its well-deserved nickname – the 'Smiling Beauty of South Turkey'.

Safranbolu Near the Black Sea and the coal mines of Zonguldak, the old quarters of Safranbolu have been preserved, with 'Hanes' (traditional trading houses with a central courtyard), restored wooden and stone houses and narrow alleyways on the cosy slopes that shape the town.

Ankara This former one-horse town is now one of the country's most modern cities. Kocatepe Camii Mosque (above), was built between 1976 an 1987 and is one of the country's largest. Many public buildings were inspired by Bauhaus architectural styles in the 1930s at a time when the budding Turkish state sheltered a number of architects persecuted in Nazi Germany.

Konya Mevlânâ Mosque recalls the preacher Mevlânâ Celâleddin Mehmed Rumi (1207–73), in whose name the Mevlevî order of dervishes was founded when he passed away. Konya, the capital of Islamic mysticism in Turkey, was also the capital of Seljuk knights and is now a modern metropolis.

Nevsehir/Göreme Many of the rock towers in the volcanic tuff landscapes of Cappadocia look like massive pieces of Swiss cheese. Above and below ground, both natural erosion and the human desire for shelter have been responsible for the carved-out sections in the rock. Innumerable caves, tunnels and even entire church halls such as Uçhisar (above) were constructed.

Divriği This town's most famous building is Ulu Camii, the Great Mosque, a UNESCO World Heritage Site built in 1240–41. It has portals designed in different styles. The north gate is adorned with large-scale depictions of plant themes.

Elazığ Tucked in among the rocks and rivers around this town is the Byzantine castle of Harput, which is over 1,000 years old. The Keban Baraji reservoirs, part of the East Anatolian Project on the Tigris and Euphrates rivers, are very close by.

Sivas This old trading post became rich as a stop on the trade routes between Russia, Egypt, Europe and Iran. Its most beautiful treasures are the madrasahs (Koranic schools) decorated in Seljuk style: stalactite vaults, birds and plants, palm fronds, animal heads, and above them the tiled minarets that once shone so brightly.

Şanlıurfa In the Old City of Urfa (its older name; before that it was called Edessa), the Halilür Rahman Mosque is worth a visit for its decorative stone carvings. The picture shows the pond that backs up to the little mosque.

Uzuncaburç Less than an hour from Silifke are the remains of the ancient twin cities of Olba and Diocaesarea. Their city gates, aqueducts and ruins are a magnificent sight against the backdrop of an untouched mountain landscape.

Nemrut Dağı The large heads and other stone monuments on the eastern terraces of Antiochos I of Commagena's monumental king's tomb date back to the 1st century BC. This place in the lonely, bare highlands is one of the most spectacular tombs in the world.

Lake Van The Armenian church on the island of Ahtamar in Lake Van is over a thousand years old. Its partially well-preserved reliefs and frescoes of biblical tales make it one of the most fascinating buildings in East Anatolia. The lake is surrounded by mountains more than 4,000 m (13,000 ft) high.

An impregnable and unique rock face – the Maharajas of Marwar.

India

Rajasthan and the 'Golden Triangle'

Rajasthan means 'Land of the Kings', yet many villages in this region of India live in extreme poverty. Exploring the land of the Rajputs, you very quickly realize one irony about this 'desert state' – there is a lot more green than you might think. And where else does India dazzle with such vivid colours and magnificent palaces as in Rajasthan?

Due to Rajasthan's size and diversity, it can be difficult to decide what to do first after arriving in Delhi. Despite being the capital of the state, the glorious Maharaja city of Jaipur is not always the first stop. Instead, many visitors are initially, and naturally, drawn to the Mughal city of Agra in the state of Uttar Pradesh, which makes up the other corner of India's 'Golden Triangle' (Delhi-Agra-

Jaipur). After all, it is the home of the immediately recognizable Taj Mahal, the white marble mausoleum built by Mughal Emperor Shah Jahan for his favourite wife Mumtaz Mahal. The Islamic building has ironically become the most visible icon of India despite Hinduism being the dominant religious and ethnic identity factor in this culturally multifarious country. About eighty-two percent of the people living in India are Hindus – the rest are an ethnic mix of Muslims, Christians, Sikhs, Buddhists and Jains.

Vivid colours and ornaments – that's Rajasthan!

Continuing westwards to Jaipur, now the capital of the whole of Rajasthan and barely four hours away from Delhi on the new motorway, you pass through Mathura, the legendary birthplace of the god Krishna and a holy pilgrimage destination for Hindus. Again, though, one is struck by the number of large mosques here. You will see this type of religious coexistence almost everywhere in Raj-asthan, not just in the so-called 'Golden Triangle'. The mighty walls of the Maharaja's fort bear witness to the centuries of power struggles between the Rajput dynasties and the Mughal emperors. Part of the legacy of the Rajputs are

Fort Meherangarh in Jodhpur on the edge of the Thar Desert, residence of

The Taj Mahal: a monumental marble grave built by Shah Jahan on the Yamuna River in Agra not far from the 'Red Fort'. The mausoleum took twenty-two years to complete and houses the sarcophagus of the Mughal emperor's favourite wife, Mumtaz Mahal, who died giving birth to their fourteenth child in 1631. His own sarcophagus followed in 1666.

their former hunting grounds, which are now some of India's most beautiful national parks and reserves. East of the long Aravalli Range near Bharatpur, for example, are three fabulous ones – Keoladeo Ghana, Sariska and Ranthambore. In the latter two it is possible to witness tigers in the wild, especially in the 400-sq-km (154-sq-mi) Ranthambore National Park.

West of the Aravalli is the semi-arid Thar Desert, which extends far into Pakistan. Former caravan routes through the Thar have become tourist tracks in recent decades. The camel safaris to the sand dunes around Jaisalmer and Bikaner are a whole new riding experience and visits to desert villages, carpet weavers and potters are interesting. The indigenous po-pulation of this region, the Bishnoi, have been carefully cultivating native flora and fauna for 600 years.

Rajasthan is not all rustic – the engineering feat of the century, the Indira Ghandi Canal, brings water from the Himalayas and the Punjab into the Thar. Stony desert soil becomes farmland and the desert shrinks. Modernity has also changed transportation – instead of running on a narrow gauge, trains are now rolling into the desert on standard Indian gauge.

Looking for remnants of the magic of 'a thousand and one nights'? You'll find it in more than a few places – Rajasthan tempts visitors with bazaars, temples and palaces from Alwar to Jaipur, from Udaipur to Jodhpur, from Bikaner into the Shekhawati land of 'painted cities'. Rajasthan also provided the model for Heritage Hotels, which are now all over India but nowhere as prevalent as in Rajasthan. Heritage Hotels are opulent palaces, glamorous merchants' houses (havelis) or relaxing country houses that have been turned into hotels by their owners. In some of them, royal personages stay under the same roof as normal hotel guests. From a comfortable bed to extreme luxury, every taste is catered for at Heritage Hotels – again a piece of 'a thousand and one nights' in Rajasthan.

A camel safari is almost a must – campfires under the starry sky included.

Opulent columned halls, defiant fortifications, tombs of Muslim saints and Indian Maharajas – the first stops on your journey to India offer some of the greatest architectural sights this ancient land has to offer. The state of Rajasthan, which is roughly the size of Germany, awaits you with magnificent fortresses, decadent palaces and the unique landscape of the Thar Desert.

1 Delhi (see pp. 280–281). From Delhi our journey leads us in two or three hours on mainly good roads to Agra, the former capital of the Mughal emperors. Roughly 150 km (93 miles) south of Agra, a town called Mathura is a worthy stop on our route.

2 Mathura East of Mathura's town center you'll see the broad Yamuna River lined with ghats (steps) and cobblestone streets. It is a pilgrimage destination for hundreds of thousands of Hindus. The reason for this ist that Mathura is the birthplace of Krishna, and therefore one of the holiest cities in India. Apart from Ganesha, the son of Shiva who provides success and wealth, Hindus worship virtually no other god more than the flute-playing Krishna. Mathura's many temples were destroyed by Muslim conquerors, in particular Mahmud of Ghazni in 1018.
Sculptures from the school of Mathura dating back to around 100 AD are of remarkable quality and depict gods and 'Yakshis' – semi-divine beings. They are on display in the Archaeological Museum of Mathura.

3 Agra For quite a long time this city was chosen by the Mughal emperors as their capi-

tal, which makes the number of extravagant buildings hardly surprising. The Taj Mahal, which Shah Jahan built as a tomb for his favourite wife, Mumtaz Mahal, is known as one of the most beautiful buildings on earth.
Also well worth a visit here is of course the Red Fort, the two tombs Chinika Rauza and the slightly older Itmad-du-Daulah (a finance minister had them erected during his lifetime). The miniature example of the latter may have inspired the architect of the Taj Mahal.
Only 37 km (23 miles) to the south-west of Agra we find the ruins of another Mughal capital, albeit a shorter-lived one.

4 Fatehpur Sikri Akbar the Great was one of the most successful among a succession of very successful Mughal rulers. His reign lasted from 1556–1605 and his influence helped extend the empire throughout most of India.
For years Akbar waited in vain for the birth of an heir, and it was only after a pilgrimage to the Muslim saint Shaik Salim Chisti that his wife bore him a

Travel Information

Route profile
Length: approx. 3,200 km (1,988 miles), excluding detours
Time required: 4–6 weeks
Start and end: Delhi
Route (main locations):
Delhi, Mathura, Agra, Fatehpur Sikri, Bharatpur, Alwar, Sariska, Jaipur, Ajmer, Pushkar, Ranakpur, Udaipur, Chittaurgarh, Mount Abu, Jodhpur, Jaisalmer, Bikaner, Mandawa, Neemrana

Traffic information:
Drive on the left in India. Because of the chaotic traffic, rental cars are always rented with a driver. Reliable agencies offer qualified drivers and top-notch vehicles.

When to go:
The best time to visit Rajasthan is from October to March when the weather is milder and many of the important festivals take place.

General information:
www.rajasthantourism. gov.in
www.rajasthantourism india.com
www.rajasthaninfo.org
Visa information:
www.india.gov.in

and was made a national park in 1979 with a focus on conserving the tiger. There is plenty of space for the tigers to live peacefully in the jungle here – they are actually rather afraid of people.

Failing a tiger sighting, you may catch a glimpse of beautifully spotted Chital deer, Chowsingha antelope, hyenas, a pack of wild boar or very likely a pack of rhesus monkeys.

There are also Mughal forts and temples both within and around the park. Take Highway 8 via Shahpura 100 km (62 miles) to Jaipur where you will be greeted first by magnificent Fort Amber.

⑦ Jaipur This old town, also known as the 'Pink City' for the colour of its facades, was planned on a nine-part rectangular grid in 1727 – very rational and geometric town planning. At the same time, the nine old-town quarters of Jaipur symbolize the Brahmin Hindu cosmos. The open-air observatory Jantar Mantar at the palace also fits in well with this cosmic association and is one of the main attractions here. You can even walk on some of its 'instruments', which are made of brick.

son. Out of gratidude for this gift and due to his victories over the Rajputs, Akbar had a new residence built on the spot where Shaik Salim Chisti had prophesied him a son – Fatehpur Sikri, the 'City of Victory'. Built on a waterless plateau above the plains west of Agra, this city was abandoned soon after it was built. It remains nearly fully intact and is a place of particular fascination to this day. An hour from Agra you suddenly find yourself behind an enormous gate in the halls of an abandoned palace and in courts surrounded by columns. Individual marble structures are

em-bedded like jewels into the sumptuous red sandstone architecture.

Pilgrims stream to the domed tomb of Shaik Salim Chisti, decorated with exquisite stone carvings. Children squat in the shadow of the mosque with their books and their teachers. Tourists admire the reception hall where Akbar discussed the possibility of a common religion ('Din-I-Ilahi') with the representatives of different faiths within his empire.

A trip to the Keoladeo Ghana National Park is well worth it for nature lovers and it is not too far from Bharatpur. In

Bharatpur a street turns off in the direction of Dig to the north and from there it is 80km (50 miles) to Alwar via the town of Nagar.

⑤ Alwar Set into the rocky Aravalli Mountains, Alwar is an old trading center with a royal palace and relatively few foreign visitors. Agra, Jaipur and the nearby national parks provide more of a draw for tourists than the ancient royal residence of Alwar, a town that received mention in India's great Mahabharata Epic from the 2nd century BC. All of this makes the city and the Rajput palace and gardens even more authentic.

Oddly, many of the palace's rooms serve the banal purpose of storing government files, which are stacked to the ceiling in places. Only the fifth floor has a museum with some of the hunting trophies, silver tables, meter-long scrolls and works of the Bundi school of painting.

⑥ Sariska National Park This reserve covers an area of about 800 sq km (308 sq mi) roughly 37 km (23 miles) south of Alwar,

1 The triple-nave reception hall in the Red Fort in Agra, built by Akbar in 1565–73, represents glamorous 16th-century architecture.

2 A symbol of India – tigers in the Sariska National Park.

3 Jaipur's most photographed sight is the five-storey Hawa Mahal, meaning "Palace of the Winds" from the late 18th century.

4 The magic of an old town on the edge of the mountains – the 19th-century city palace of Alwar sits above the temple pond.

279

Delhi

Delhi has always been an important strategic town on the north Indian plain. Approximately as old as Rome, over the centuries this city was made the capital of many an empire. Since the end of British colonial rule in 1947, Delhi is the political center of the Republic of India.

With its crowded bazaars, countless rickshaws and rumbling overcrowded buses, no traveller to Delhi would ever doubt that the population here has increased dramatically over the last century to its present 14 million.

A billion of people are governed from here. Indeed, Delhi has many faces. One leftover from colonial rule is the expansive capital of India, New Delhi. Its broad avenues are home to ministries, the parliament, the pres-

idential palace and magnificent museums, all of which form the center of power for the apparatus of government.

Edwin Lutyens and Herbert Baker designed the circle of arcades that is Connaught Place in the heart of New Delhi in the first part of the 20th century. The circles and 'spokes' around it form Connaught Circus.

High-rise buildings from the last two decades tower over this attrac– tive shopping and commercial area. Lutyens and Baker created New Delhi

in a style that mixed neo classicism with Indian Palatial.

Old Delhi, the old town, with its bazaars, temples and many mosques, is focused between the Yamuna River and the rail lines and has grown massively over centuries. Even if you have little time to spend in Delhi, we highly recommend a wander through the street bazaars of Chandni Chowk to experience the hustle and bustle of sellers, carts, cows and children – it certainly eclipses any department store adventure.

The two main monuments of Old Delhi are quite close to one another. The first is the Jama Masjid (Friday Mosque), India's largest, with a minaret that you can climb. The 'Mosque with a View of the World' – its original name – was commissioned by Shah Jahan, grandson of the great Akbar. By no coincidence, he was also responsible for Old Delhi's other feature attraction, a fortification and palace for the great Mughal rulers, the Red Fort. The Persians stole the legendary 'Peacock Throne' from its imperial halls and other conquerors removed the inlaid jewels from the columns and walls. Despite these thefts, a wide variety of art works from all the great epochs of Indian art can be found in Delhi. The National Museum displays great sculptures and miniatures, and nowhere else can you find as much contemporary Indian art and traditional arts and crafts as in Delhi. The Craft Museum is a good example, located in a village complex near the ruins of Purana Quila – said to be the location of Delhi's oldest city, Indraprashta. Basically, it's all here – numerous museums and parks, fine dining, luxurious shopping, theaters and cinemas.

Almost three million people a year also visit another temple, this one designed in the shape of a lotus flower with twenty-seven marble leaves: the Bahai House of Worship. The Bahai believe in uniting the faithful of all religions.

Everyday life in Delhi is dominated by contrasts – cosmopolitan and traditional, dire poverty and fairy-tale riches, bizarre and comfortable. Indeed, what most urban dwellers around the world take for granted has only just become reality in Delhi – a metro – and new satellite cities are springing up regularly in the surrounding countryside.

The gate of the Red Fort. The fortification is surrounded by a sandstone wall and is almost a kilometer long and over 500 m (1,640 ft) wide.

Jaipur, which is the western point of the 'Golden Triangle' (Delhi-Agra-Jaipur), is home to over two million people and is thus the only town with over a million inhabitants in Rajasthan. To this day the city is full of palaces.

The first Maharaja of Rajasthan to convert Rambagh, his summer palace, into a hotel was Sawai Man Singh II in 1957. Since then his aristocratic brethren all over India seem to have adopted the 'Palace and Heritage Tourism' concept.

Jaipur is also a center for jewellery, jewels, precious inlaid marble and all sorts of other arts and crafts.

⑧ Ajmer A defiant fortress built upon a stark rocky plateau overlooking a walled city, the model for many cities in this area where for centuries it was necessary to defend against the repeated attacks of ambitious conquerors. At Fort Taragarh in Ajmer, there is not much left of the often 4-m-thick (13-ft) walls built by a Hindu ruler some 900 years ago.

But Ajmer presents itself as a lively, pulsating city in many respects. It is home to many schools and universities and a pilgrimage destination for pious Muslims and Jains. In fact, about a quarter of the more than 400,000 inhabitants are Jains. Following the example of British public schools, the still highly regarded Mayo College in Ajmer was founded in 1873 for the sons of the Rajputs.

The Dargah Sharif Mosque Center is even older and was developed around the tomb of Khwaja Moinuddin Chisti, who was a friend of the poor. In memory of his works, two enormous iron vats of food are still provided for the needy at the entrance to the holy district. Even Emperor Akbar made a pilgrimage to Ajmer.

1

A more recent building that is worth a visit is the Nasiyan Temple from 1864, built by the Jains. A two-storey hall fantastically depicts the heavenly cosmos of the Jains, including golden temples and the airships of the gods. About 11 km (7 miles) from Ajmer you'll come to Pushkar.

⑨ Pushkar The name Pushkar means 'lotus blossom'. But in this case we are not talking about just any lotus blossom. It is the one that Brahma allegedly dropped to the floor to create Pushkar Lake. That is why the little town of Pushkar with its 15,000 inhabitants is one of the holiest sites in India.

Half surrounded by mountains, this little town with tidy white houses and the fresh green fauna of a nearby oasis possesses a majestic beauty. Unfortunately, it has been so overrun by tourism in the last few years that Pushkar's priests, beggars and numerous self-appointed Sadhus ('holy men') have developed a business sense to accompany their piety.

2

They constantly invite travellers to the 'Puja', the washing ceremony, which takes place at the fifty-two ghats, the steps down to the lake. Then without delay they demand payment with rupees or, even better, dollars. The 'Little Varansi' at Pushkar Lake is therefore best visited in the morning – the temples open early. The view from the hill with the Savitri Temple, dedicated to Brahma's wife, is especially beautiful. It can be

reached after a good half-hour hike.

From Pushkar you'll need a day of driving through winding mountain landscapes to get to Ranakpur. On the way, you'll be tempted to take a detour to one of the biggest forts in Rajasthan – the 15th-century Fort Kumbhalgarh. The 36-km (22-mile) wall around the perimeter of this fort is said to be second only to the Great Wall of China in length and

protects a total of 360 temples – 300 Jains and the rest Buddhist. You get a splendid view of the Aravalli Mountains from atop the wall.

⑩ Ranakpur Completely different from Pushkar, this holy temple town of the Jains typically allows you to enjoy its treasures in peace and quiet. It is set back from any larger neighbours in a forested valley with family farms, two reser-

voirs and a handful of hotels. One of these is the Maharani Bagh Orchard Retreat, a former fruit garden and picknicking spot of the Maharaja of Jodhpur. It is just an hour's walk from the Jain temples and the pilgrim hostels.

Before climbing the steps to the temples you will be required to remove anything you have that is made of leather or other animal products. The four temples here date from the 15th and

16th centuries. Three of them are dedicated to the 'forerunners' Adinath, Parsvanatha and Neminath, and the fourth is dedicated to the Sun god Surya. Take a look at the unique stonework on the hundreds of columns and domed prayer halls. Flowers are placed before the pictures of Jain saints and music echoes through the rooms.

It is now a good 80 km (50 miles) to Udaipur, the biggest city in the south of Rajasthan.

⑪ Udaipur Also known as the 'Queen of the Lakes', Udaipur is considered by many to be the most beautiful city in Rajasthan. Today it has 400,000 inhabitants, and from its founding in the year 1568 it was constantly under the rule of the Sisodia Maharanas until Indian independence in 1947. The title Maharana ('Great King') is equivalent to Maharajah. In the old realm of Mewar, the Sisodias took the top position in the royal hierarchy of India, and their influence is still felt today. Nearly 500 years ago

they were responsible for many of the reservoirs and artificial lakes that were built in the area.

In the midst of the most beautiful of these, Lake Pichola, summer palaces were built on two islands opposite the mighty towering complex of the city palace. The bigger of the two island palaces became world famous as the Lake Palace Hotel. The list of celebrated guests is endless. The nightly spectacle of the lake bathed in lights is best enjoyed from one of the roof terrace restaurants in the old town.

Parks like the 'Garden of the Ladies of Honour' (Saheliyon ki Bari) contribute not only to the charm of Udaipur when the lotus ponds and roses are in bloom, but also reveal the artistic sense and craftsmanship present here. Behind the city palace and in the small side streets are countless studios and shops where you can witness hundreds of indigenous artists and craftsmen that still specialize in the miniature paintings of the old academies and the skilled carpet weaving of the region.

⑫ Chittaurgarh Seven mighty gates once secured the ascent to the plateau over the Berach River 100 km (60 miles) to the east of Udaipur. On the plain below is a city of 75,000 inhabitants founded in the 8th century and once the capital of Mewar. The steep walls of the rocky plateau rise to 150 m (492 ft), but despite its formi-

1 In 1567 Maharana Udai Singh ordered the creation of Lake Pichola when he declared Udaipur the capital of Merwar. The Lake Palace Hotel is on an island in the lake.

2 Pushkar: India's holiest of lakes is supposed to have developed from Brahma's lotus blossom.

dable gates and walls it was still conquered three times by Mughal armies. Each of these invasions culminated in a 'Jauhar' by the women and children – the heroic ritual of collective suicide by throwing themselves onto burning pyres. The men then committed 'Saka': battling to their last breath.

Dozens of sprawling palace and temple ruins, a narrow 15th-century 'victory' tower, which you can climb, and some pavilions and ponds are all that is left of the glory and decline of this medieval residence.

Back in Udaipur the journey continues via Som straight through the Aravalli Mountains to the north-west in the direction of Abu Road. When the heat begins to hit the plains in April, the hotels in Rajasthan's 'hill station' Mount Abu begin to fill up. Close to the border to Gujarat, Abu Road winds its way to 1,200 m (3,937 ft) where you can live comfortably in this mountain village (20,000 inhabitants) even in the summer.

⑬ **Mount Abu** The hilly forest and hiking areas, Nakki Lake, the splendid view from 'Sunset Point' and a protected wildlife area for leopards, bears and red deer, all quite close to the center of town, make Mount Abu an enjoyable diversion for tourists, particularly if you've come in hotter months. The Dilwara temples outside of Mount Abu are well-known among art lovers.

On a par with the Jain temples of Ranakpur, the skilful stone carvings and sculpture in the five main temples here (11th–18th centuries) are even considered by some to be the best Jain work ever done.

To the left and right of Abu Road heading towards Jodhpur there are a number of Rajput residences, small country pala-

ces with gardens usually near a village, and some former 'havelis' in their modern guise as 'Heritage Hotels'. Among the 'havelis' are the Ghanerao Royal Castle, Karni Kot Sodawas, Bera, Bhenswara, Sardasamand, Fort Chanwar Luni and Rohet Garh.

⑭ **Jodhpur** In stark contrast to the rural landscape along the road, Jodhpur is Rajasthan's second-largest city and has more than 800,000 inhabitants. It is also the south-eastern point in the great 'Desert Triangle'. Once you are in town, the streets of Jodhpur are dominated by hectic traffic and lively trade in the bazaar. But high above it all stands the mighty Meherangarh Fort, built by the Rathore rulers, more than 120 m (393 ft) above the Old Town alleys in the north-west of the city. The fort's palaces are known for their superb filigree stone patterns and spacious courtyards.

Across the city on Chittar Hill is the magnificent Umaid Bhawan Palace, the last of the monumental residences built by the

Rajput (1929–43). Museums, markets, arts and crafts and antiques await you here.

⑮ **Jaisalmer** For many people, the most lasting impression of their desert travels in Rajasthan is the moment the honey-gold walls of Jaisalmer appear above the sandy plains. Since the 12th century the ninety-nine bastions of these fortifications have dominated the hills of the city of Jaisalmer.

Even until far into the 19th century, the caravans of the spice and silk traders travelled in and out of the city. Ironically, it was the faraway Suez Canal that made the difference. By boosting sea trade with Europe it more or less put an end to the overland business. As a result, Jaisalmer's wealthy traders and their fairy-tale mansions with opulent facades, bay windows and balconies became a thing of the past virtually overnight.

After the tumultuous division of India and Pakistan in 1947, Jaisalmer's strategic location on the western border gave it renewed significance and India soon invested in streets and railways. Yet the conversion from the narrow-gauge railways to the Indian wide-gauge system is actually a recent development, and one that greatly benefited tourism. Since the 1990s the industry has grown dramatically, and the population of Jaisalmer has doubled to 40,000 in the last decade. Jaisalmer is now the center of desert tourism in India and a main gathering point for camel drivers and thousands of souvenir sellers. The adventure is not all lost, however, on a trip to Desert National Park west of the city, which includes oases and deserted medieval cities like Kuldhara and Kabha. The Akal Wood Fossil Park, located 17 km (11 miles) south of Jaisalmer on the road to Barmer, has fascinating fossilized tree trunks 180 million years old.

In just two hours from here you can also reach Pokaran, a small desert town with only 20,000 inhabitants.

🔟 **Pokaran** The name of Pokaran went through the international press in 1998 when the Indian government demonstrated its status as a nuclear power by carrying out several test detonations near the neighbouring town of Khetolai. But what is also worth seeing in Pokaran is the fort built in the 14th century, whose imposing walls are an example of a private restoration initiative.

The family of the Thakur Rajputs has been living in this fort for thirteen generations and has installed not only a Heritage Hotel but also a small museum, which specializes in archaeology and folklore. When the owner can spare the time, he willingly explains to his guests how the neglected rooms of the palace are being restored to former glory.

🔟 **Gajner Wildlife Sanctuary** This well-preserved old palace on the lake is surrounded by old trees and almost seems haunted. The grounds, which are only 30 km (18 miles) west of the large city of Bikaner, were once used by their owner as hunting territory until India's conservationists and biologists pressed for the creation of a nature reserve under the auspices of 'Project Tiger'.

The primary objective of the reserve was obviously to protect and increase the number of species living here. The secondary objective was to increase tourism in the area. The Gajner Wildlife Sanctuary is now a paradise for birds and wild animals, and the Gajner Palace itself was turned into a Heritage Hotel. The rooms are decorated with antiques and enjoy a view of the bird-lake activities including boating, golf, cycling and hiking. However, during longer stretches of drought or a non-existent monsoon, there is nothing to be done – the lake dries out and the birds move on.

🔟 **Bikaner** The main roads to Bikaner, an old city of the Maharajas with a current population of about 500,000, have improved over the years as more and more palaces have recently converted to hotels. But the contrast between the present and the past, between bazaar alleys and shanty towns is more stark than in Jaipur or Udaipur.

1 The Meherangarh Fort towers high above Jodhpur.

2 The Indira Ghandi Canal flows into the Gadi Sagar, the temple lake of Jaisalmer.

The forward-planning Maharaja Dungar Singh had an electricity network installed comparatively early, in 1886. His successor then had schools, hospitals and canals built. A mighty ring of walls surrounds Junagarh Fort, which was built towards the end of the 16th century. Its mirrored cabinets, delicately decorated chambers and its opulent coronation hall make it one of the highlights of Indian palatial architecture in the region. Away from the city on a visit to India's only state camel-breeding farm you get to see first-hand why 750,000 of the five million camels worldwide live right here in Rajasthan.

A slightly unusual facet of Hindu culture presents itself to visitors about 30 km (18 miles) south in Deshnok at the Karni Mata Mandir, a temple with silver doors and marble reliefs. Rats are worshipped here as holy animals and run around uninhibited. According to legend, they are the souls of dead poets and singers.

⑲ Mandawa There are no big cities in the Shekhawati region east of Bikaner and north of Jaipur. Mandawa, founded in 1790 and now the tourist center of the area, is accordingly modest in size. Comfortable accommodation is limited here. The best option is the former Rajput palaces where the owner often lives in a separate wing. The Roop Niwa Palace in Nawalgarh is an option, or try the 18th-century Castle Mandawa.

Desert sands blow around the walls of the former fort of Mandawa (begun in 1760), behind which the Rajput Rangir Singh continues to restore the decaying splendour of palace halls and boudoirs to provide space for more visitors. No room here is the same as another. Exploring Mandawa you can find several large 'havelis' (Gulab Rai and Saraf, for example), a deep well with steps leading down to it, or a few antiques and arts and craft shops.

Mandawa is a convenient starting point for excursions into the partly green, partly desert landscape around the city and to a dozen other typical Shekhawati villages. The neighbouring village of Nawalgarh about 25 km (15 miles) away has more 'havelis' than any other town in the Shekhawati region. Several open their doors to visitors. The Poddar Haveli Museum from the 1920s has around 750 images on its facade, not counting the painted passages in the inner courtyard, as well as collections of musical instruments and historical photographs.

The drive to our last destination, Neemrana, takes around six hours (225 km/140 miles). Take the turn-off about 15 km (9 miles) north of Behror on Highway 8 between Jaipur and Delhi.

⑳ Neemrana For those who enjoy castles and exotic living, Neemrana is a very desirable destination. Some years ago a Frenchman and an Indian turned medieval Fort Neemrana above the village into a Heritage Hotel. With a sure sense of style and every detail of attention to the needs of their guests, they created an array of terraces, balconies, rooms and suites that spoil the visitor's eye. From the city of Neemrana it is another 120 km (74 miles) via the Delhi-Jaipur Highway back to Delhi.

1 The 'Pushkar Mela' is not the only big camel market in Rajasthan. Nagaur, north of Jodhpur, is also famed for its own gathering, which takes place once a year in January or February.

Jaisalmer With ninety-nine bastions, Jaisalmer towers 80 m (263 ft) above the Thar Desert. It was the residence of the Bhati Rajputs, a contested headquarters for caravan trade.

Fort Amber One of India's most beautiful, the Amber Palace (17th/18th century) in the fort of the same name is adorned with mirrors, marble halls, imposing gates and grand views of the stark mountains outside. The Mata Temple has a black marble depiction of Kali.

Delhi Mughal Emperor Shah Jahan had the Red Fort (Lal Quila) built between 1639 and 1648. The most beautiful of its buildings is the reception hall Diwan-I-Khas. Also worth seeing in Delhi are the Jama Masjid Mosque, the tomb of Mughal Emperor Humayun, the Lodi graves and the Qutb Minar minaret.

Jodhpur In front of the steep rock of Meherangarh Fort sits the 'Jhaswant Thada', a white marble palace built in memory of Maharaja Jhaswant Singh II to honour his progressive policies.

Fatehpur Sikri This city was founded by Akbar the Great in 1569 at the zenith of Mughal power in India. The Jama Masjid (Friday Mosque) is the center of the city's holy district.

Desert National Park This national park in the Thar Desert is a superb example of the ecosystems here and the rich variety of species (Dorkas gazelles, desert lynx, giant Indian bustards).

Sariska National Park Formerly the hunting ground of the Maharaja of Alwar, this region is alive with tigers and dense forest. Located in the Aravalli Range, it became a national park in 1979.

Ranakpur The 15th/16th-century temples built by the Jains contain unique halls with superb stone-carvings and domes considered among the most important masterpieces in all of India. They belong to a well-educated sub-culture in India.

Agra The Red Fort (1565–73), built as a fortification with deep and broad trenches, soon became an example of imperial luxury and prestigious architecture. It is accentuated with large courtyards, palaces, and opulent columned halls like the triple-nave marble hall of Diwan-I-Am shown here.

Udaipur The city palace of the Maharanas of Mewar, the oldest dynasty in Rajasthan, has been continuously expanded since it was built in the 16th century. It is still inhabited by the family.

Jaipur The 'Palace of the Winds' was built with stone lattice windows to allow the ladies of the court to see without being seen.

Gwalior Fort The enormous walls of this mighty fortress rise high above the town. It contains the Man Singh Palace, built around 1500, and four other palaces.

Taj Mahal Tomb and monument of a great love: the great Mughal Emperor Shah Jahan had this mausoleum built in Agra for his wife Mumtaz Mahal, who died giving birth to their 14th child.

The stupa in Boudhanath is 40 m (131 ft) high, the tallest in all of Nepal.

Nepal and Tibet

On the Road of Friendship across the Roof of the World

The path over the main crescent of the Himalayas easily makes it into our list of dream routes. After all, you cross part of the highest mountain range in the world, passing turquoise-coloured lakes and endless high steppe regions that are still traversed by nomads with yak, goat and sheep herds. Add monasteries perched on impossible bluffs and you've got an unforgettable journey. Our route begins in Kathmandu, meanders through central Nepal and ends in Lhasa on the Kodari Highway.

Foreigners have only been allowed to visit the previously sealed-off country of Nepal since 1950. Much has changed culturally since then, but fortunately the fascination that the country inspires has not. About a third of the country is taken up by the Himalayas, the highest point of which lies on the border to Tibet – Mount Everest, at 8,850 m (29,037 ft). Between the protective Mahabharat Range in the south and the mighty main crest of the Himalayas in the north lies the valley of Kathmandu, which contains the three ancient and royal cities of Kathmandu, Patan and Bhaktapur.

Even in the age of the automobile the spirit of times past is palpable in the capital, and Kathmandu continues to impress vis-

Buddha statue Amithaba/
Tashilhunpo Monastery.

itors with its royal palace and the hundreds of temples, statues and beautiful woodcarvings on the facades and monuments. The second of the ancient royal cities, Patan, lies on the opposite shore of the Bagmati. Once again, a former royal palace and over fifty temples remind us of Nepal's glorious past. South-east of Kathmandu lies Bhaktapur, where the alleys and streets are dominated by Newari wood-carvings.

Before you start off from Bhaktapur towards Lhasa, it is worth undertaking a journey to Pokhara in the north-west, on the shore of the Phewasees at the bottom of the Annapurna Massif. Via Lumbini, the birth-

'Om mani padme hum' – Tibetan monks gather for communal prayer in the Sakya monastery near Lhaze.

Sagarmatha National Park with its grandiose mountain landscape is listed in the UNESCO World Heritage register.

place of Buddha, and Butwal the round trip leads you to Bharatpur, the gate to the Royal Chitwan National Park, and eventually back to Bhaktapur. The Kodari Highway then brings you over the main ridge of the Himalayas into Tibet. Along this panoramic route you are constantly under the spell of 7,000 to 8,000-m-high (22,967 to 26,248-ft) mountains. In Tingri, for example, you finally experience Mount Everest. The journey here can become arduous at times, as the highway leads over passes where the air is rather thin – over 5,000 m (16,405 ft) above sealevel on the Lalung-La Pass. Tibet, 'The Land of Snow', has been closely linked to China since the 13th century. The current Tibet Autonomous Region (TAR) of

China has an extremely low population density – roughly 2.5 million Tibetans, and 350,000 Chinese live on 1.2 million sq km (463,000 sq mil) of land. The Chinese dominate the economy, politics and government. Since the 9th century, Tibetans have followed Lamaism, a Tibetan variant of Buddhism whose religious and political head is the Dalai Lama.

The route through Gutsuo, Tingri, Lhaze, Yigaze, Gyangze and Nagarze into the city of Lhasa is lined by Lamaist monasteries – at least, the ones that weren't destroyed by the Chinese cultural revolution. Sakya is one of the oldest monasteries in Tibet and the 15th-century Buddhist monastery of Tashilhunpo has also been preserved – the latter contains a 26-m-high (85-ft)

bronze Buddha. Dont' miss the Kubum monastery in Gyangze, a monumental complex of temples with pagodas, stupas and palaces.

Lhasa, the 'Place of the Gods', lies at an elevation of 3,700 m (12,140 ft) and was chosen by Songsten Ganpo (620–49), the

first Tibetan king, as his royal residence. Where today the Potala Palace looks down on the city, Ganpo had built a fortification that later became Tibet's theocratic center of power, including all pictorial works and national treasures – the icon of Tibetan religiosity.

Prayer flags on the Road of Friendship near Xigaze.

The Road of Friendship was built only twenty years ago, stretches 950 km (590 miles) and connects Nepal and Tibet. Apart from beautiful villages and monasteries that represent hundreds of years of history, it is the grandiose mountain scenery that so impresses travellers.

1 Kathmandu This ancient royal city at an elevation of 1,300 m (4,265 ft) is the centerpiece of the Kathmandu Valley. Its many palaces, temples and monasteries mirror the centuries-old traditions and history of the Nepalese kingdom.

Even back in the 10th century this city, which is located at the confluence of the Bagmati and Vishnumati rivers, was an important marketplace that eventually developed into a religious, cultural and political center competing with Patan and Bhaktapur ultimately to become the sole royal city. The Old Town presents the visitor with a plethora of streets and alleys where people, carts, bicycles, rickshaws and cars struggle to negotiate their way through the honking and screaming of the traffic.

In the center of the city is Durbar Square, which the Nepali call Hanuman Dhoka. Here there are Buddhist and Hindu temples and shrines as well as the old royal palace where for centuries Malla and Shah kings resided. The oldest parts developed in the 16th century include the great inner courtyard Nasal Chowk, or coronation court.

In the center of the Hanuman Dhoka is the Jagannath Temple, one of the most beautiful examples of Nepalese temple architecture. The Shiva Temple was built in 1690 and is flanked by two Vishnu temples and the Vishnu Parvati Temple with its two enormous drums.

After the Hanuman Dhoka is the Basantapur, which has been taken over by countless souvenir sellers.

Some of the most startling buildings on the square are the nine-storey Basanthapur Pagoda, with beautiful wood-carvings, and the richly decorated palace of Kumari, a living goddess.

Surrounding the old town are more UNESCO World Heritage Sites – about 5 km (3 miles) from the center is the Boudhanath Stupa, the largest shrine of Tibetan Nepalese people; west of Kathmandu is the Swayambunath Stupa, dating from the 14th century; and on the eastern edge of the city is the temple of Pashupatinath with the sacred Lingam.

2 Patan Over the years Patan (or Lalitpur), which has been famous for its metalworks for centuries, has almost completely melded with Kathmandu and is only separated from it by the Bagmati River. The Old Town here is particular worth visiting due to its royal palace. The more than fifty temples in Patan that are at least three storeys high were erected using either traditional wood or stone. The most important Shiva shrine is the five-storey Kumbeshvra Temple, not far from the 'Golden Temple'.

3 Bhaktapur Situated about 15 km (9.3 miles) from Kathmandu, Bhaktapur was founded in the 12th century and life here still seems to flow at a mostly rural pace. The potters' market is full of locally produced goods and there are wood-carvers all around town. The main sights are at Durbar Square around the royal palace. The magnificently gilded Sundhoka Gate connects the two wings of the palace and simultaneously marks the entrance to the Taleju Temple, the main shrine within the palace.

Travel Information

Route profile
Length: approx. 900 km (559 miles), excluding detours
Time required: 2–3 weeks
Start: Kathmandu, Nepal
End: Lhasa, Tibet
Route (main locations): Kathmandu, Patan, Bhaktapur, Pokhara, Lumbini, Bharatpur, Dolalghat, Nyalam, Gutsuo, Lhaze, Xigaze, Nagarze, Lhasa

Traffic information:
Drive on the left in Nepal, on the right in Tibet. The condition of the roads is generally very bad. So-called 'highways' are often full of potholes and asphalt is often missing. Landslides are common during monsoon season and after heavy rains.

Trekking:
The best time for trekking is after the monsoons. Any other time is too cold.
A trekking permit is required separately for each region (except the Langtang, Annapurna, Everest region). They can be acquired from the immigration offices in Kathmandu or Pokhara. From about 3,000 m (10,000 ft) altitude sickness may be a factor.

General information:
Nepal general info:
www.visitnepal.com
www.nepal.com
Tibet general info:
www.tibet.com
www.tibet-tour.com
Buddhism/Hinduism:
www.thamel.com

④ Langtang National Park
North of Kathmandu and Patan
is Langtang National Park. The
southern entrance near Dhunche is about six or seven hours
away. The park, which covers
an area of 1,710 sq km (660 sq
mi), gets its name from the
7,245-m-high (23,771-ft) Langtang Lirung peak and runs from
Dhunche to the Tibetan border.
Luxurious pine, birch and rhododendron forests are home to
musk deer, collar bears, small
pandas, snow leopards, tahrs,
and rhesus and langur monkeys. Starting from Kathmandu, a four-day trek leads you to
the sacred lakes of Gosainkund
via the monastery of Sing Gom-
pa, which lies at an elevation of
more than 4,400 m (14,436 ft).
Back in Kathmandu the serpentine drive takes you through
mountain landscapes on a road
of varying quality into Pokhara.

⑤ Gorkha On your way back,
you can make detour to the
Gorkha valley just before you
reach the town of Mugling. The
drive passes through green rice
plantations set in a fascinating
mountain landscape on its way
to the village of Gorkha at
1,000 m (3,300 ft), which is over-
looked by a fortification from
the 17th century. The giant
mountains Dhaulagiri, Ganesh
Himal and Manaslu present an
overwhelming panorama.
Ghorka has an important place
in Nepalese history. In 1768, King
Prithvi Narayan Shah conquered
Kathmandu from Gorkha, then
proceeded to Patan and Bhaktapur, thereby laying the foundations for his royal dynasty.

⑥ Pokhara Only on the last
few kilometers to Pokhara does
the road flatten out into a
broad valley. Nepal's third-
largest city lies at an elevation
of 800 m (3,150 ft) on the
shores of Lake Phewa. In stark
contrast to the surrounding
mountainscape, the subtropical
climate here has produced
ample vegetation. For many
trekkers the city is the 'Gateway
to the Himalaya'. From Pokhara
you get a magnificent view of
the central Himalayas, which
are now only 30 km (18 miles)
away. Peaks that you can see
from here include Dhaulagiri at
8,167 m (26,796 ft), the Annapurna Massif and the sacred
mountain of Machapuchare at
6,977 m (22,892 ft).
The sights nearby include the
dripstone cave at Batulechaur,
the ravine of Seti and Devin's
fall. The seven-storey fortification of Nuwakot arguably
offers the most beautiful view
of Dhaulagiri, Annapurna and
Manaslu. The winding road to
Lumbini leads down through a
richly forested mountain landscape. After Butwal the scenery
flattens out, giving way to rice
fields and willows that come
right up to the street.

⑦ Lumbini The birthplace of
Siddharta Gautama, Buddha's
birthname, is surprisingly off
the beaten track. Excavations
have been taking place in this
previously forgotten place
since the 1970s. Finds include
Emperor Ashoka's column from
the 3rd century, which was only
discovered in the jungle in
1896, and the Maya Devi Temple, both grouped around a
sacred pool of water in which
Buddha's mother (Maya Devi)
allegedly bathed shortly before
his birth.
To head for the Royal Chitwan
National Park from here, drive
back to Butwal and from there
to Bharatpur.

**⑧ Royal Chitwan National
Park** This large national park
covers 932 sq km (360 sq mi)
and is bordered by the Rapti,
Reu and Narayanif rivers. The
park is dominated by jungle
and grasslands that are home

1 The fertile Kathmandu valley is
the economic and population center
of Nepal.

2 Trekkers ascend to the
Thorung-La Pass when traversing
the Annapurna.

3 The Deorali Pass cuts through
the Annapurna Himal.

to elephants, rhinos, Bengal tigers, leopards, gaurs, sloth bears, gavial crocodiles, fresh-water dolphins and more than 400 types of birds. A variety of options for enjoying the park are available to visitors here – elephant safaris, rafting boat rides or guided tours.
The road back to Kathmandu leads through Bharatpur and Hetauda to Kathmandu.

9 Dolalghat The Chinese gave the beautiful Kodari High-way its nickname – 'The Friend-ship Road' – when they built it in 1967. The route connects Nepal with Tibet and travels 114 km (71 miles) from Bhakta-pur via Dolalghat to the border town of Kodari.
After a three-hour drive from Bhaktapur you arrive at the village of Dolalghat by the Sun Kosi at a modest elevation of 643 m (2,110 ft). The village is situated at the junction where the Bhote Kosi and the Indrawati rivers form the Sun Kosi (Golden River), which flows to the west along the Mahabharat. Dolalghat is pri-marily known as a jumping-off point for white-water rafting trips on the Sun Kosi.
Near Dolalghat a road leads to the Sagarmatha Nature Reser-ve. Once you have arrived in Kodari at 1,660 m (5,446 ft), the 'Friendship Bridge' takes you over the Bhote Kosi to Zhang-mu. The route now follows Highway 318 all the way to Lhasa.

10 Nyalam On a clear day you get a magnificent view from Nyalam (4,100 m/13,452 ft) of the Xixabangma Feng at 8,012 m (26,287 ft) rising up to the west. All around the old town are typical flat-roof clay houses, makeshift shacks of the Chinese inhabitants. The drive continues past snowcapped mountains 6,000–8,000 m

1

(19,686–26,248 ft) high until you finally reach the Lalung-La Pass at 5,200 m (17,061 ft), which leads to the Tibetan plateau. Here you'll find the vil-lage of Gutsuo, which has accommodation and provisions as well as a small hospital.
Tingri is known for its fantastic view of Cho Oyu at 8,153 m (26,750 ft), Mount Everest at 8,850 m (29,037 ft), Lhotse I at 8,516 m (27,941 ft) and Makalu I at 8,463 m (27,767 ft). We recommend you head south from here towards Rong-buk Monastery.

11 Lhaze Beyond Tingri the road winds down to Lhaze at 4,030 m (13,222 ft), which has a hotel, restaurants, a gas station and a monastery. This village is right on the road that leads west of the sacred mountain of Kailash and is located in a fer-tile valley whose green fields

2

provide colourful contrast to the arid Tibetan plateau.

12 Sa'gya The fortified monas-tery of Sakya was founded in 1073 and was the original monastery of the Sakya Order. Of the original 108 chapels in the north wing, only one is left

today. A white stupa stands nearby on the mountain's edge. The southern monastery is enclosed by mighty walls with four watchtowers, as the Sakya dynasty had to defend itself against many enemies. Head-ing to Xigaze you cross the Tso-La Pass at 4,500 m (14,765 ft)

292

cent example of Tibetan architecture.

From Gyangzee to Lhasa the road leads past little villages through fertile valleys where yaks graze at leisure. Then you must traverse the Karo-La Pass at 5,045 m (29,906 ft). The landscape is of overwhelming beauty here. On the way you'll see the Karo-La glacier, stunning waterfalls and mountain streams. You then descend the serpentine pass via Lungmar to Ralung with its monastery dating from 1180 and continue on to Nagarze.

15 Nagarze The village of Nagarze at 4,200 m (13,780 ft) sits between the snow-covered Noijin Kangsang at 7,100 m (23,295 ft) and the sacred lake of Yandrok Tso, one of the biggest and most beautiful lakes in central Tibet. The street runs along the shore for several kilometers passing grazing horses, yaks and goats. A visit to castle ruins and the 13th-century Samding Monastery is worthwhile. The way to Quxu leads over the Kampa-La Pass at 4,898 m (16,070 ft), then it is just 20 km (12 miles) into the valley.

16 Quxu The bridge over the Yarlung was opened in the mid 1970s and provides a connection between western and eastern Tibet. The place itself is a good starting point for trips to the monasteries of Gonggar and Samye to the east. North of Quxu is the region of Nethang, which houses the monastery of the same name founded by

1 View of the Tashilhunpo monastery near Xigaze.

2 The Kumbum Chorten in Pälkhor Chode Monastery near Gyangze is Nepalese in design.

3 Yandrok Tso is one of the largest lakes in Tibet.

where you have a good view of Everest on a clear day.

13 Xigaze After the devastation of the Cultural Revolution, only the foundations of the once impressive fortifications of the Tsang Dynasty kings (16th/17th century) are left. Today the main sight in Xigaze, former capital of Tibet, is the Tashilhunpo Monastery, home of the Panchen Lama that once housed 6,000 monks. Founded by the first Dalai Lama in 1447, the complex at the bottom of the Drölma consists of red and ochre-coloured buildings whose gilded roofs glimmer from afar.

14 Gyangze This small town at 4,070 m (13,354 ft) on the north shore of Nyangchu still gives a traditional Tibet impression with its white facades and colourful eaves, windows and door frames. Towering over the city is an impressive Dzhong (fortification) from 1268, which offers a splendid view of the walled monastery city of Pälkhor Chode (15th century). The extensive grounds are dominated by octagonal Kumbum Chorten and the Nepalese-influenced stupa is a magnifi-

1

Atisha (982–1054), an Indian Buddhist. Now we head back to the Tibetan capital through the Lhasa Valley.

17 Drepung About 10 km (6 miles) north of Lhasa is a monastery dating from 1416 that used to be the biggest in Tibet with 10,000 monks. As the religious and political center of the Gelugpa School (yellow-cap sect) its abbots were decision-makers in religious as well as political matters. Before the Potala became their residence it even housed the first five Dalai Lamas. Despite the destruction by the Chinese Red Guards, the main buildings of the monastery have remained unharmed, including Ganden Palace, the four theological faculties and the great congregation hall. Today some 600 monks are living here again.

18 Lhasa The capital of the Tibet Autonomous Region lies on the Lhasa River (Kyichu) at an elevation of 3,658 m (12,002 ft) and was founded in the 7th century. Originally the residence of the Tibetan kings

2

(7th–9th centuries) it became the seat of government of Lamaistic theocracy under Dalai Lama rule. For centuries Lhasa was a 'forbidden city' to foreigners. It even closed its doors to Sven Hedin, the famous explorer of Asia. In the heart of the old town you'll find the two-storey Jokhang Temple from the 7th century, the oldest Buddhist monastery in Tibet and akin to a national shrine. All roads in Lhasa therefore lead to the Jokhang temple, which is also once again home to monks.

Nearly as old as the Jokhang is the Ramoche Temple with fortified walls, which goes back to the times of the Chinese

princess Wencheng. Unfortunately, the Red Guards destroyed or stole many of the statues here during the Cultural Revolution.

Many associate Lhasa with the Potala Palace towering impressively over the city with its thirteen storeys (110 m/361 ft). Its facade alone is 360 m (1,181 ft) long and it reputedly houses 999 rooms with 130,000 sq m (1,399,308 sq ft) of living quarters. The part of the palace painted white houses administration and storage space while the red part was the residence of the Dalai Lama up to his flight in 1959. Since then the palace is only has been used as a museum. Opposite the Potala

is the cave temple Drolha Lubuk with depictions of Buddhist deities that reputedly created themselves. The summer palace of the Dalai Lama, Norbulingka, is also in the west of the city and was originally built on an even larger scale. On the northern edge of the city is the monastery of Sera, and on the road to Sichuan (approximately 45 km/30 miles east of Lhasa) you will reach the monastery of Ganden.

1 View from the Jokhang Temple, the heart of Tibetan culture in Lhasa.

2 Monks during communal prayer in the Ramoche Monastery in Lhasa.

Lake Phewa Fishing, rowing, and swimming – this lake leaves no wishes unfulfilled, and you have a view of Annapurna.

Kathmandu In the 'City of the Gods' it is mainly Durbar Square, a colorful bazaar surrounded by wood and brick buildings, that is well worth a visit.

Lhasa The 'Red Palace' of the Potala was commissioned by the fifth Dalai Lama in the 17th century. The white buildings were added in the 19th century. The palace has some 999 rooms and thirteen storeys. Since the occupation of Tibet by China and the flight of the Dalai Lama, the palace is used only as a museum.

Annapurna Massif The tenth highest peak in the world was first ascended in 1950. It is surrounded by mountains that often seem higher than the peak that gives the region its name. Especially outstanding is the sacred, and thus unconquered, Machapuchare.

Royal Chitwan National Park This park can be explored on the back of an elephant or in a rafting boat. It is known for its 400 rhinoceroses as well as tigers, gavial crocodiles, leopards and buffalo.

Bhaktapur Time seems to have stood still in this beautifully restored town situated at the east end of the Kathmandu Valley. Highlights include the Dattatraya Square and the temple pagodas on Taumadhi Square.

Sera Elaborate religious ceremonies are still held in this former monastery and university village on the edge of Lhasa.

Mount Everest At 8,850 m (29,037 ft) this is the highest mountain in the world, and is locally known as Chomolungma or Sagarmatha. The first successful ascent was in 1953 by Edmund Hillary and Sherpa Tenzing Norgay.

Xigaze Tibet's second-largest city is home to a the 15th-century monastery. The Panchen Lama residence survived the Cultural Revolution.

Gyangze This village southwest of Lhasa has a monastery worth visiting (Pälkhör Chode). The Kumbum Stupa is considered Tibet's most beautiful sanctum.

Lumbini Siddharta Gautama – aka Buddha – was born here in southern Nepal in the 6th century BC. Visit the sacred garden and the Maya Devi Temple.

Sagarmatha National Park This park, located in the Khumbu region at the base of Mount Everest, is home to a variety of rare animals like the black bear, snow leopard and musk deer.

Tengpoche Until a fire in 1989 this monastery at 4,000 m (13,124 ft) in the Khumbu Valley was the largest in the region. It is still well worth seeing.

Samye This rebuilt temple is part of the oldest Tibetan monastery. It was built around 770 and is situated in the mountains on the north shore of Yarlung Zangbo Jiang.

The courtyard at the Ayutthaya
statues of the sitting Buddha.

Thailand and Malaysia

Pulsing cities and tropical natural paradises

South-East Asia – teeming urban centers and quiet villages, tropical rainforests and idyllic white sand beaches, historic sites and modern daily life.
A trip along the region's North-South Highway will show you the many diverse faces of the region and immerse you in local life with all of glorious scenery and culture.

Starting in Thailand's mountainous north, this route first takes us down to the fertile plain of the Mae Nam Chao Phraya River and its many tributaries in Central Thailand. The Menam Basin, also nicknamed Thailand's 'rice bowl', has been the country's most densely settled economic region since the time of the first Thai kingdoms. South of the Thai capital of Bangkok, the highway then takes us onto the Malay Peninsula, which stretches 1,500 km (930 miles) between the Indian Ocean (Andaman Sea) and the Pacific Ocean (Gulf of Thailand and South China Sea).

At its narrowest point, the Isthmus of Kra, the peninsula is a mere 50 km (31 miles) wide. Its backbone is formed by a mountain range that reaches its highest elevations in Malaysia at more than 2,000 m (6,500 ft).

The tropical plants and animals of Thailand and Malaysia are almost unbeatably varied and abundant. Nevertheless, in

Sculpture at the entrance to Batu
Caves, a place of worship.

recent years the once so prevalent tropical rainforests have had to give way to large-scale plantations, rice paddies and urban sprawl. Only in mountainous regions and individual national parks can you still find real virgin rainforests with their wealth of plants and animals. You'll find giant trees, wild orchids and epiphytes, and these South-East Asian rainforests are also home to several species of apes as well as snakes and tigers.

As the climate of the area is very favourable, large areas of both countries have been devoted to agriculture. In some places in Thailand there are rice paddies as far as the eye can see, and in

temple is lined with innumerable

Penang Island is 285 sq km (110 sq mi) in size and located just off Malaysia's west coast. It is connected with the mainland by the Penang Bridge.

Petchaburi: In 1860, Rama IV had his summer palace of Phra Nakhon Khiri ('Heavenly Mountain City') constructed in this magnificent location. The palace is on a hill 92 m (302 ft) high.

Malaysia there are massive oil palm and rubber tree plantations.

Being one of South-East Asia's most ancient kingdoms, Thailand has a large number of historic sites dating from different periods in its history. Many of these monumental buildings, such as those of Sukhothai and Ayutthaya, are very well-maintained. Their size and the skill employed in their construction are truly impressive.

Malaysia and Singapore, by contrast, claim much shorter histories. Their oldest historic sites date from the colonial period. These days places like Georgetown, Melaka and Singapore have numerous preserved and restored colonial buildings that provide visitors

with a lively impression of this bygone era. All three states have ethnically diverse populations, and this variety makes the region all the more attractive. In Thailand a majority of around 80 percent of the population is Thai, in Malaysia 50 percent are Malay, and in Singapore 70 percent are Chinese. The remainder of the Thai population is made up of mountain tribes and Chinese descendants. Malaysia and Singapore also have large Indian populations. The Chinese, who account for a very small percentage of the population of Thailand, for example, exercise significant influence on the regional economy and local trade. In fact, they make up the vast majority of South-East Asia's economical-

ly powerful. Yet despite the region's ethnic diversity and the corresponding cultural and traditional differences, people mostly live together in harmony and welcome foreign visitors with all the legendary Asian friendliness. A journey from

northern Thailand to Singapore via Malaysia thus becomes a journey through a very diverse region in terms of scenery, ethnicity and culture. You will be both surprised and enchanted by the ever-changing human and natural landscape.

Wat Mahathat was once the spiritual center of the Sukhothai kingdom.

The North-South Highway of the Thai-Malay corridor – if you want to get to know this exciting region, we recommend the long and winding road from Chiang Mai in northern Thailand to Singapore at the southern tip of the Malay peninsula. The road leads through tropical landscapes and urban centers for more than 3,250 km (2,020 miles).

1 Chiang Mai The Thais call Chiang Mai the 'Rose of the North'. Thailand's second city is the tourist center of northern Thailand. Using Chiang Mai as a base, you can take trekking tours into the mountains and visit the hill tribes who live in them. Under King Mengrai this settlement, founded in 1292, became the capital of the Lanna Kingdom and an important center for Theravada Buddhism. The king and his successors built the majority of the numerous temples (wats) in the so-called Lanna style. The most important among them are Wat Phra Sing (1345), Wat Chedi Luang (c. 15th century) and Wat Chiang Man. The quadratic center of the Old Town, with its picturesque alleyways and traditional houses, is surrounded by well-preserved trenches that today separate the historic city center from modern Chiang Mai.

Outside the Old Town you'll find the National Museum with its large and beautiful terracotta collection, a small ethnological museum and numerous other temples.

Nature and art lovers should make sure to pay a visit to the densely forested national park Doi Suthep Doi Pui, 16 km (10 miles) north-west of Chiang Mai. The park is the home of Doi Suthep, the most important Buddhist temple in northern

Thailand, situated at an elevation of 1,600 m (5,250 ft) above sea level. Precisely 304 steep steps lead up to it.

Taking Highway 11 south you now drive through some lush green hills and mountains and pass some steep valleys with carefully maintained fields and rice paddies.

2 Chae Son National Park This is a mountainous national park around 50 km (31 miles) further south-east. Its forests are home to black bears, wild boar and monkeys as well as some rarely seen tigers.

The main trail through the national park starts in Khuntan and after an 8-km (5-mile) hike it takes you up to the summit of Yot Se (1,373 m/4,505 ft). From there you have some wonderful views of the surrounding mountain scenery.

3 Mae Ping National Park Rafting tours and boat trips are the main reason that so many people come to visit Mae Ping National Park, located west of

Highway 1. By car you get to it via Lamphum (30 km/19 miles south of Chiang Mai) on Highway 1. By car you get to it

ways 106 and 1087. The park is roughly 100 km (62 miles) away. Most visitors take a two-hour

Travel Information

Route profile
Length: approx. 3,250 km (2,020 miles), excluding detours
Time required: at least 3 weeks
Start: Chiang Mai
End: Singapore
Route (main locations): Chiang Mai, Bangkok, Ratchaburi, Hat Yai, Georgetown, Kuala Lumpur, Singapore

Traffic information:
Drive on the left throughout South-East Asia. Roads are generally in decent condition. Tolls are often charged on highways.
Singapore: Tolls are charged via an electronic device obtainable from car rental companies.
All three countries require international driving licences.

When to go:
North: November to February
East coast: Avoid the rainy season from October to February
West coast: April to October

Information:
Thailand:
www.thaiwave.com
www.gothailand.com
Malaysia:
www.allmalaysia.info
www.tourism.gov.my
Singapore:
www.visitingsingapore.com
www.stb.com/sg/

To find reasonable prices check the various national airline home pages at:
www.thaiair.com
www.malaysiaairlines.com
www.singaporeair.com

toric park and so many other attractions that you can easily spend several days here.

At the heart of the historic park is the Old Town, which is surrounded by a wall 1.6 km (1 mile) by 2 km (1.3 miles) long. The royal palace and the Wat Mahathat (13th century) temple alone encompass an area of more than 16 ha (40 acres). The complex is completely surrounded by a trench.

6 **Kamphaeng Phet** Founded in 1347, Kamphaeng Phet used to be a royal garrison town. In the north are the town's historic quarters, and in the south you will find the modern town. Surrounded as they are by a moat, the historic quarters give you an idea of what Old Sukhothai might have been like. The National Museum and the temple compound with Wat Phra Kaeo and Wat Phra That are also worth seeing.

7 **Nakhon Sawan** The most interesting thing here is not the provincial capital itself but the confluence of the Mae Nam Ping and Mae Nam Yom rivers. They come together in this region to form the Menam Chao Phraya, whose flood plains are the most fertile and densely populated region in Thailand.

All you can see for miles are the thousands of rice paddies,

boat ride on the Ping River from Doi Tao Lake, which takes them into the park. From there they carry on to the village of Ko. In addition to a whitewater ride and some impressive limestone cliffs and caves, this national park offers a good insight into the different plants and animals living in the rainforests.

4 **Lampang** What is fascinating about this 7th-century town are its temples, tradition-al houses and an old market with a variety of different architec-tural styles represented in the surrounding buildings. In the 19th century Lampang became a center for teak production. The town's brightly painted horse-drawn carriages date from this era and they are still Lampang's standard form of public transport. The town's most important temple is Wat Phra Kaew Don Tao. In the south-west you'll find one of northern Thailand's most beautiful temples – Wat Phra That Lampang Luang, dating from the 15th century.

Leaving Lampang, you take Highway 1 to the south. The mountains soon give way to more gentle hills that eventually flatten out towards the plains of the upper Menam Basin. Rice is cultivated in expansive paddies here for as far as the eye can see.

From Tak you can take a worthwhile excursion on Highway 12 to Sukhothai, the former capital of Thailand, which is 80 km (49 miles) away.

5 **Sukhothai** UNESCO declared the ruined city of Old Sukhothai a World Heritage Site in 1991. With more than forty temples, this city recalls the heyday of the Sukhothai kingdom, the most powerful in the Menam Basin between 1240 and 1320. Founded in 1238, the city was the capital of the first Thai nation for more than 120 years. The large compound stretches over 70 sq km (27 sq mi) and includes an his-

1 Buddha statues several meters high at the Ayutthaya temple compound north of Bangkok.

2 The temples at Chiang Mai in north-eastern Thailand were constructed between the 13th and 16th centuries.

3 Ruins of a Bot (ceremonial hall) north of the main chedi in the Wat Mahathat temple compound in Sukhothai.

dotted here and there with hills and mountains. From Nakhon Sawan take Highway 32 through the fields and hills towards Ayutthaya.

8 Ayutthaya From 1350 to 1767 Ayutthaya was the capital of Siam (Thailand). Historical sources claim that it was Asia's most impressive city at the time. Visitors from Europe back then were overwhelmed by its splendour and many said that they had never seen anything to equal it. The kings of thirty-three different dynasties ruled the country from here until the city was razed to the ground by the Burmese in 1767.

The historic Old Town is located at the confluence of three rivers and completely surrounded by water. The most impressive sights are located on the island in the middle of these three rivers. Among them are the temples of Wat Na Phra Men, which was not destroyed in 1767, and Wat Phra Si Sanphet with its three chedis.

From Ayutthaya, it is only around 40 km (25 miles) to Bangkok.

9 Bangkok (see p. 303).
From Taksin Bridge the highway sweeps west along the bay onto the Malay Peninsula. West of Bangkok you can visit

Nakhon Prathom with its giant temple compound and Kanchanaburi with the famous 'Bridge Over the River Kwai'. Both sights are relatively close to Highway 4. Carry on southbound along the east coast (west side of the bay). Around 20 km (13 miles) after Ratchaburi, a road turns off to Thailand's largest national park, Kaeng Krachan National Park, which is well worth visiting.

10 Kaeng Krachan National Park Thailand's largest park is surprisingly unknown among travellers despite the fact that its dense, evergreen tropical rainforests cover mountains

The 'Bridge Over the River Kwai'

Not far from Kanchanaburi is the 'Bridge Over the River Kwai', which was made famous by the novel by Pierre Boulle. During World War II the Japanese constructed a railway line here. Its construction cost the lives of 16,000 allied prisoners of war and around 100,000 local labourers, most of whom died of starvation, malaria and cholera. The current bridge is a reconstruction.

forest. It has some very good hiking among the impressive limestone cliffs and the numerous waterfalls, which are the park's principal attractions.

Among them are Nam Tok Sip Et Chan, where the water cascades down eleven glorious levels. With a bit of luck you might even find a specimen of the world's largest flower, a species of Rafflesia with a diameter of around 1 m (3.5 ft).

After Thap Lamu (see sidebar right for a worthwhile excursion to the diving paradise of the Similan Islands) the road runs along the Khao Lak coast riddled with lonely beaches against the backdrop of the extensive tropical monsoon forests of Khao Lak National Park. Past the turn-off for the incredibly touristy island of Phuket you can carry on to Phang Nga, the starting point for trips into the Phang Nga Bay.

⑫ Phang Nga Bay This bay's dense mangrove forests make it one of Thailand's most impressive regions. It is protected as a national park and has some bizarre, partly overgrown limestone rocks that rise up to 350 m (1,150 ft) out of the clear azure waters. Many of the rock faces have karst caves and tunnels.

The most important stations on a boat trip in this bay are Panyi, a village on stilts, the Suwan-Kuha caves with a reclining Buddha, and some other stalactite caves. To the east, the karst landscape continues on the mainland and into the Khao Phanom Bencha National Park north of Krabi.

that rise to 1,200 m (4,000 ft). The park is home to tigers, Malaysian bears, leopards, tapirs and elephants as well as gibbons and langurs. The next 370 km (230 miles) south of Ratchaburi run along the east coast before you get to Chumphon where Highway 4 changes to two lanes and you switch to the west coast for another 350 km (217 miles).

At Kra, the Malay Peninsula narrows to only 50 km (31 miles) wide. Soon after that you will arrive in Khuraburi and the next national park in the midst of a tropical mountain landscape.

⑪ Khao Sok National Park This hilly national park with luscious rainforests is regarded as Thailand's most beautiful

1 Wat Arun on the shores of Chao Phraya in Bangkok.

2 Phuket, Thailand's largest and most popular island, is 48 km (30 miles) long.

301

13 Krabi Most visitors come here because of the dream beaches and limestone cliffs in the area to the south and west of town. These are the 'beach images' that most people have come to associate with Thailand nowadays and some are truly spectacular.

Krabi, which is surrounded by karst cliff formations, has 21,000 inhabitants and is a good jumping-off point for boat trips into Phang Nga Bay; the famous Phi Phi Islands 40 km (25 miles) south with their magnificent beaches, steep karst rock faces and good diving; and a host of other white sand beaches and islands.

The temple compound of Wat Tham Sua with its beautiful view of the bay and the surrounding countryside is located on a rock outcrop 8 km (5 miles) north of Krabi.

From here we carry on across the southern Thai plains, which are among the most fertile in the country.

14 Hat Yai For many Thais this city is a shopping paradise because there are a lot of goods smuggled from Malaysia in the shops and markets.

West of the town center at Wat Hat Yai Nai is the world's third-largest reclining Buddha at 35 m (115 ft) long and 15 m (50 ft) tall. From Hat Yai you can do a little detour to Songkhla about 25 km (16 miles) and the lakes on the east coast north of town. A short drive south to Sadao takes you to the Malay border where the road turns into Malaysia's Highway 1. As an alternative to the North-South Highway, which is a dual carriageway, you can take the old road, which mostly runs parallel to the new one.

15 Alor Setar The state capital of Kedah is located in the

middle of a wide, fertile plain with picturesque rice paddies. The region is known as 'Malaysia's rice bowl'.

The town landmark, the Zahir Mosque (1912), is one of the largest and most beautiful in Malaysia. With its very slender minarets and onion domes it embodies beautifully everyone's mental image of an oriental mosque spreading spiritual atmosphere.

16 Penang Island The tropical island of Penang, which is up to 700 m (2,300 ft) high in places, is located in the Gulf of Bengal

1 Phang Nga Bay is famous for its karst rocks rising out of the sea.

2 Ko Phi Phi comprises the islands of Phi Phi Don and Phi Phi Ley. They are popular because of good diving and the film *The Beach* (Ley).

Bangkok

With its roughly twelve million inhabitants, Bangkok is Thailand's largest city and its cultural, political and social center. The city's most important sight, the Grand Palace with the temple of Wat Phra Kaeo, is located on the eastern shore of the Chao Phraya River. These two form the center of spiritual and worldly power in the kingdom.

As many as ten percent of the Thai population lives in and around the capital, which as a result suffers from high levels of pollution, heavy traffic and incessant noise.

These days Bangkok is certainly one of the most lively and exciting metropolises in South-East Asia. Every day three million cars, trucks, motorcycles and bicycles fight their way through the city labyrinth. Some through roads have been constructed on stilts, but expensive road tolls are charged for their use and they do nothing to enhance the city's beauty. The numerous palm-lined Khlongs that once gave Bangkok the nickname 'Venice of the East' are only visible in some of the outer districts like Thon Buri or around Wat Arun. Many of the principal sights are far away from each other and it can be quite an adventure to get from one to the next. The Old City's main sights include the King's Palace (1782) with the Dusit Throne Hall, Amarinn Winichai Hall, Inner Palace and Sivalai Gardens; a city wall 1,900 m (2,078 yds) long that surrounds the 'city within the city' housing Wat Phra Kaeo, Thailand's most sacred temple with its golden chedi and Emerald Buddha; Wat Po with its golden Buddha, Bangkok's oldest temple and a center for traditional medicine; and Wat Saket on the Golden Hill with a good view over the city. The most important museums are the National Museum with exhibits on the history, arts and crafts of Thailand and the National Gallery, the largest gallery for contemporary Asian art. In Chinatown discover the Songwat Road, a 200-year-old Chinese trade center, which exudes 19th-century flair; the Buddhist shrine of Leng Noi Yee; bustling streets and places such as Kao-Market and Pak-Khlong-Market); Yaowarat Road or Wat Traimit. Sights in the Dusit governmental center are Dusit Park with its museums; the Wat Banchamabophit temple; Worth seeing in the town center are the old foreigns' quarter with the Assumption Cathedral (1910), the Oriental Hotel, and the Jim Thomson House, a traditional Thai living quarter with museum.

Top: King's Palace and Wat Phra Kaeo in Bangkok.
Bottom: View of the city center and Chao Phraya.

and connected to the mainland by a bridge. Visitors from around the globe are attracted to the beaches at its northern end and to Georgetown, its lively capital.

With Chinese shopping streets, narrow alleyways, numerous temples, magnificent clan houses (such as Khoo Kongsi) and colonial buildings such as Fort Cornwallis (18th century) it always makes for a pleasant stroll.

⑰ Kuala Kangsar For more than 150 years Kuala Kangsar, located 110 km (68 miles) further south, has been the residence of the Sultans of Perak. This pleasant town on the wide Perak River has two cultural monuments worth seeing – the former sultan's palace of Istana Kenangan built in 1926, and Masjid Ubudiah, which was built 1913–17 and whose golden domes and minarets make it one of the country's finest mosques.

⑱ Ipoh The state capital of Perak has 500,000 inhabitants and owes its economic rise to the profitable tin deposits in the area. These were exploited well into the 1980s. Ipoh seems quite provincial for a city its size. The Kinta Valley to the north and south of the town is dominated by steep, partly forested limestone cliffs. There are some caves with Buddhist sanctuaries here.

⑲ Kellie's Castle On a small hill above the Kinta Valley are

South of Ipoh the highway runs along the foothills of the Cameron Highlands. These highlands enjoy comparatively moderate temperatures and their gently sloping hills are home to a long tradition of tea cultivation. In some places the plantations extend right up to the highway.

the ruins of Kellie's Castle. Construction began in 1915 for a

1 The temple of Kek Lok Si, also known as the Temple of a Thousand Buddhas, is in Georgetown on the island of Penang. Construction began in 1890.

2 Tea plantations in the Cameron Highlands in Malaysia at 2,000 m (6,500 ft). These highlands are renowned for their pleasant climate.

Singapore

The city state of Singapore is located on a small island in the Malacca Straits at the southern tip of the Malay Peninsula. It was founded as a trading post in 1819 and in the space of only a few years became South-East Asia's most important traffic hub as well as a major financial center.

Singapore is Asia's cleanest city and it has the best air quality of any of the world's large urban centers. The city charges high fines for environmental offences such as throwing away cigarette ends, and there are also high road tolls, horrendous car taxes and strict limits on registration quotas for new vehicles. With this draconic set of measures, the local government has long since managed to effectively ban cars from the city. Its outstanding public transport network makes it very easy to get to any point within the city limits quickly.

Singapore's population of roughly 4.5 million people is two-thirds Chinese, while the remainder is a mix of mostly Indian and Malay people. During the colonial period each of these ethnicities had its own neighbourhood, each of which has been meticulously reconstructed in recent years. Their markets, shops and restaurants are particularly full of atmosphere in the evening. The most colourful markets are in Little India.

Present and future coexist peacefully in this city. The commercial center is home to one skyscraper after another, the airport is one of Asia's busiest and the container terminal is the largest in the world. But quite a number of historic buildings survive to keep Old Singapore alive. Many of the colonial buildings in this neighbourhood along the Singapore River, where the city was founded in 1819, have also been meticulously restored over the years. They now house government buildings as well as a handful of museums and a small concert hall.

Sentosa Island, located just off the main island, is one of Singapore's most popular tourist destinations. In fact, its countless leisure attractions make it really quite similar to Disneyland. If you are seeking some peace and quiet in nature, you can retreat to the heartland of Singapore Island. It is hard to believe but even in this modern city there is still a small area of the island's original tropical rainforest. Bukit Timah Nature Reserve protects that last remnant very strictly. At Sungei Buloh Nature Park there are more than 120 species of birds living in the mangrove swamps. Singapore Botanic Gardens and Singapore Zoological Gardens enjoy good reputations around the world. Sights in the Colonial Core include Padang with the Supreme Court, the Victoria Theater (1862), the Old Parliament House (1826–27) and City Hall (1929), the famous Raffles Hotel (1887) and Fort Canning Park. Chinatown also has a number of interesting sights to behold – Sri Mariamman Temple with its seventy-two Hindu gods, the Jamae Mosque (1830), Boat Quay with its romantic seaside promenade, and Thian Hock Keng Temple (1839), the oldest of the Chinese temples in Singapore. Sights in Little India and Kampong Glam include the Sultan Mosque, the city's largest mosque; Istana Kampgong Glam, the former sultan's palace; Arab Street; several temples, including Leong San See Temple (1917), Sakya Muni Buddha Temple (Temple of a Thousand Lights), and Sri Srinivasa Perumal Temple (1855); and Orchard Road, a lively shopping street.

A Singapore's view of Orchard Road, central street.

Scottish plantation owner who never returned from a trip home to Europe in 1926. It is said that his ghost has haunted the castle ever since. Further south the highway rolls past some seemingly endless plantations of rubber and oil palm.

⑳ Kuala Lumpur Malaysia's largest city (1.3 million inhabitants) is this South-East Asian country's political and economic center. Today there is nothing that recalls the 'Muddy River Mouth' (the translation of its name) of the old days.

No other Malaysian city is quite as outspoken about the fact that the country is aiming to distinguish itself as an up-and-coming industrial nation. Its modern hotels and high-rises such as the Petronas Towers, which house the headquarters of many companies, banks and institutions, illustrate this aim impressively.

Kuala Lumpur is an attractive city because it balances lively urban elements with a healthy amount of greenery in the center and suburbs.

Its chief attraction, however, lies in its multicultural mix of people – Chinese, Malay and Indian peoples with very different cultures, traditions and lifestyles all seem to carry on in peaceful coexistence.

Tucked in below its modern skyline are the city's older sector: the administrative buildings of the former British colonials, the mansions of the tin barons, and traditional Indian and Chinese neighbourhoods.

㉑ Melaka A visit to historic Malacca is truly a journey into Malaysia's past. Unlike most other places in the country, this town looks back upon a long history. For a long time Melaka was an international port and transportation center for sea trade with China, and was coveted by the likes of the Portuguese, Dutch and British.

The former presence of these colonial powers is still demonstrated by the ruins of the mighty Portuguese castle, A Famosa, Dutch buildings around Red Square and many British colonial buildings.

In Chinatown on the other side of the Melaka River you'll find the most original part of town with houses more than 200

years old. Many of them were built in the so-called Chinese baroque style, a mix of Chinese architectural elements and colonial and classical European borrowings. Between Melaka and Johor Bahru the flat landscape, dense plantations and mangrove swamps mostly obstruct any view of the Malacca Straits.

㉒ Johor Bahru The southernmost town on the Malay Peninsula is the capital of the Johor Sultanate. Many locals have become rich here due to its proximity to Singapore. Numerous historic streets have been razed to the ground and replaced with modern blocks. A causeway takes you across to the island of Singapore, which is located in the Malacca Straits.

㉓ Singapore For more detailed information on this interesting city, (see p. 305) with sightseeing tips.

1 Life in the center of Singapore never stops. In the foreground is Boat Quay on the southern banks of the Singapore River.

2 Buildings in the Dutch Quarter, such as the Christ Church Melaka dating from 1753, recall the city's colonial period in the 18th century.

Chiang Rai Rice is the most important staple food in Asia. Whereas mountain rice is cultivated on terraces and does not require irrigation, water rice grows mainly on flood plains and near the mouths of large rivers such as this one near Chiang Rai.

Ayutthaya At its zenith, this former capital of Siam was one of the most magnificent cities in Asia. To this day the ruins of its numerous palaces, halls, fortifications and temples and its countless stupas and Buddhas continue to recall this era in a most impressive fashion.

Phuket This island used to be an important trading post for European merchants. Its magnificent bays and palm-lined beaches now make it a first-class tourist destination.

Phi Phi Islands This archipelago located about 50 km (31 miles) south of Phuket has some excellent diving and some bizarre rock formations in the Ko Phi Phi Marine National Park.

Penang Its dream beaches have turned this tropical island into Malaysia's best-known tourist destination, but it also has some interesting colonial buildings and temples. The picture shows the Buddhist temple Kek Lok Si located in a southern suburb of Georgetown, the island's capital.

Singapore Founded as recently as 1819 as a trading post, Singapore has quickly become one of the most important traffic hubs and financial and commercial centers in South-East Asia. The picture is of Orchard Road, the city's main artery.

Melaka Under the name of Malacca, this town was an important transportation center for trade with China. This can still be seen today in its numerous European-style colonial buildings and an extensive Chinatown.

Chiang Mai Thailand's second-largest city has some famous temple compounds built in the Lanna style: Wat Phra Sing, Wat Chedi Luang, Wat Chiang Man, and Wat Phra That Doi Suthep a little further out. It is also a center for outstanding arts and crafts.

Sukhothai The extensive palaces and temples of the Sukhothai Kingdom (13th–14th centuries) extend over an area of 70 sq km (27 sq mi). In 1991 the compound was declared a UNESCO World Heritage Site. The picture shows a Buddha at Wat Mahathat.

Bangkok This city of twelve million inhabitants is the political, cultural and social heart of Thailand. One of its main sights is the Old King's Palace and Wat Phra Kaeo, the most important temple in Thailand. The traffic here can be horrendous, but the nightlife can still entertain.

Kuala Lumpur A testimony to the dynamic nature of Malaysia's capital are the Petronas Towers, until recently the highest buildings in the world. They were inaugurated in 1998.

Tioman This tropical island, which is accessible by plane or express boat from Singapore, has every ingredient of a dream holiday: white sandy beaches, reefs and coral gardens, and mountains and forests that are home to monkeys and reptiles.

Central Asia and China

On the Silk Road from Bukhara to Xi'an

For more than a thousand years, Europe and Asia were connected primarily through the ancient 'Silk Road' trade route. The importance of this caravan route was not, however, only restricted to the trade of goods. It also provided the backdrop for a lively exchange of culture and ideas between the Mediterranean, Central Asian and Chinese realms.

When silk products originating from the Han and Tang dynasties of China (200 BC and 7th century, respectively) were discovered in Iran, Syria and Italy, the significance of this sought-after commodity immediately became clear. 2,000 years ago, silk was as expensive as gold in Rome. Julius Caesar drew extra attention to himself when he attended theater performances

wearing silken robes. At the time, the Romans believed that silk grew on trees and was combed from the leaves as a fine fluff. The Chinese, on the other hand, did not want to reveal the secrets of silk production, for it ensured their powerful monopoly in the trade. They were able to maintain this upper hand for centuries until, as legend has it,

monks smuggled silkworm eggs and mulberry seeds out of China in hollow bamboo canes and brought them to the East-

ern Roman Empire in the 6th century.
Western products that the Chinese had never heard of were,

A Kyrgyz family in their yurt, the round tents lined with carpets used as dwellings by the nomads.

The Lamaistic monastery of Ta'er Si is 26 km (16 miles) south of Xining in the Qinghai province.

Fort Jiayuguan in Gansu was built at the eastern end of the Great Wall and fitted with gates adorned with towers. It has a wall over 10 m (33 ft) high and 733 m (2,356 ft) long.

in turn, taken back to China – perfumes, pearls, grapes, pomegranates, walnuts, sesame, coriander and incense. Another incentive for the Chinese to keep the trade route alive was the acquisition of the highly regarded Fergana horses. The Romans paid for the silk not only with jingling coins, but also with gold, glass, wool and African slaves, who were very desirable in China at the time. The high price for silk is understandable if you take into account that, at the time, the Silk Road passed through thirty-six dominions, each demanding their own customs duties. During the Tang Dynasty (618–907), the Chinese were particularly open to foreigners. At that time, the Chinese upper

class was interested in music and instruments from Central and West Asia, as well as the handicrafts from the West. Clothing, metal and glass products, and even sculpture were all influenced by the West. The cultural exchange between East and West also helped develop astronomy, calendars, mathematics and medicine. Mediterranean acrobatics and circuses, the game of polo from Persia, as well as exotic songs and dances were all extremely popular. Chinese poetry and painting also incorporated influences from the West and thus developed new styles during the period.

The Silk Road was also a place where new and old religions were evangelized. In the first

century AD, Buddha's teachings spread from the kingdom of Gandhara in north-west Pakistan through the Central Asian khanates to the Middle Kingdom. The teachings of Zara-

thustra, as well as Manichaeism, Nestorianism and Islam, were later transported on this road through Central Asia to China, where they all found followers.

The wooden figure in the Haizang Temple in Wuwei, an oasis town in the Gansu province.

1

In addition to the spectacular desert landscapes of the Kysylkum and Takla Makan, high mountain regions such as the Tian Shan between Tashkent and Ürümqi or the Qilian Shan south of the Hexi Corridor await you along the eastern Silk Road.

① Bukhara During the European Middle Ages, this oasis city at the edge of the Kysylkum was one of the most significant religious and economic centers of the Islamic world, boasting 350 mosques and more than 100 madrasahs. The old city's most important sights include the Ulughbek madrasah (the oldest mosque in Central Asia), the Khalif-Niazkul Mosque (Chor Minor) with four 17-m-high (56-ft) towers, and the Ismail-Samani mausoleum (9th/10th century).

The Kaljan Mosque (1127) minaret is also an impressive sight at 47 m (154 ft). A navigational light used to guide approaching caravans a thousand years ago, and the tower provides you with a striking view of the old town. A museum of local history and popular art is today located in the citadel Ark (7th–8th century), once the castle of the Emir of Bukhara. Bukhara owes its existence to the Zarafshan river, whose waters feed the irrigation canals of oasis gardens; the main city canal, the Shachrud; and the Labihauz (1620), a large basin in the center of the city. The latter used to provide the city's inhabitants with water, as no irrigation system could be implemented owing to the narrow streets and alleys. In the old days, water bearers brought water to the courts and bazaars in leather buckets. Nowadays, after a long day exploring the old city,

you can sit and relax on a bench outside the tearooms, eat excellent food and soak up the atmosphere.

Out on the old Silk Road you enter the desert steppe and the shifting sand dunes of the Kysylkum. As was the case west of Bukhara, the sun beats down relentlessly on the vast cotton fields along the road here. Summer temperatures can reach 45°C (113°F), while in winter they fall to -25°C (-13°F) – these variations are typical of this landlocked area.

② Samarkand At an altitude of 725 m (2,379 ft), Samarkand is situated in the foothills of the Pamiro-Altai. Upon entering the city, the apartment blocks and factories do not initially reflect the glorious past of one of Central Asia's most important cultural and trading cities, and one of the oldest inhabited cities in the world. Having sur-

vived the imperial conquest of Alexander the Great and the destruction inflicted by Genghis Khan's troops, Samarkand has continually been rebuilt.

Today, its architectural monuments (15th–17th centuries) give it an almost fairy-tale feel

and in 2001 it was selected as a UNESCO World Heritage Site. Attractions include the Registan, or main square of Old Samarkand; the famous Gur-e Amir, cemetery and family mausoleum of the notorious conqueror Timur Lang; Shah-i-

Travel Information

Route profile
Length: approx. 4,800 km (2,983 miles), excluding detours
Time required: about 6 weeks
Start: Bukhara, Uzbekistan
Finish: Xi'an, China
Route (main locations): Bukhara, Samarkand, Tashkent, Kokand, Bishkek, Issyk Kul, Almaty, Ürümqi, Turpan, Astana, Minghoshan, Jiayuguan, Zhangye, Wuwei, Lanzhou, Xi'an

Traffic information:
Drive on the right on this trip. It is not always possible to drive from Tashkent into the Fergana Valley. Those using a diesel-powered vehicle must pay a weight tax upon entry.

Information:
www.centralasiatravel.com
www.dostuck.com
www.eurasianet.org
www.fantasticasia.net
www.marcopolo.uz/en/

der to Hungary. Samarkand lay at the heart of his dominion. He provided his place of birth, Kesh, with irrigation systems and thus called it Shakhrisyabz, or 'green city'. It is also where Timur built his summer residence, Aq-Saray, the 'White Palace'. As a result of his great successes (often looked upon with derision in the Persian and Arab regions that he conquered), an imposing monument was dedicated to the city's great son in the main square in front of the ruins of Aq-Saray.

④ Tashkent Highway 39 takes you to the Uzbek capital of Tashkent, located in the foothills of the Tian Shan. This is a place where two worlds collide: where traditional Asia meets the modern world, mud houses meet towering glass palaces, veiled women meet children in fashionable designer clothing, the colourful bazaars meet the supermarket, narrow alleyways meet vast leisure parks, and Islamic domes with decorative patterns meet colourful neon signs.
The city acquired its modern-day image in the 1970s. An earthquake in 1966 nearly destroyed the entire city, leaving around 300,000 people homeless and only very few historic buildings still intact. Soviet architects took advantage of

Zinda, or 'Tomb of the Living King; the glorious Bibi-Khanym Mosque; and the Ulughbek observatory, dating back to the early 15th century. Some 90 km (56 miles) south of Samarkand is Shakhrisyabz.

③ Shakhrisyabz The now exalted Timur Lang, known as Tamerlane in Europe, was born around 1330 in the immediate vicinity of Shakhrisyabz. He established a kingdom which, at his death in 1405, stretched from northern India to Damascus, and from the Chinese bor-

1 A glimpse of the artistic dome in the Tilla-Kari (the 'one decorated in gold') madrasah in Samarkand, Uzbekistan.

2 Three madrasahs from the 15th–17th centuries line the Registan, the main square of Samarkand – Ulugh Bek, Tilla-Kari and Sherdar.

3 Muslim arts have been taught in the Mir Arab madrasah in Bukhara (1530–1536) for over 400 years.

this and built a city with surprisingly numerous green areas in its place.

Since the country's independence in 1991, Tashkent's planners have been trying to give the modern buildings more of an Uzbek look. There are also several new monuments in memory of important persons in Uzbek history. At Amir Timur Square, you immediately notice the imposing monument of the kingdom's founder, Timur, on horseback. Increasing tourism means Tashkent is today a popular starting place for trekking tours in the Tian Shan mountains or the Pamir range.

Tashkent used to be a junction in the old Silk Road – the northern branch led through Bishkek, while the older, southern route first takes you into the Fergana Valley before travelling east through some difficult, dangerous mountain passes. Nowadays, the road into the Fergana basin is occasionally closed owing to fear of terrorist attacks.

⑤ **Kokand** Green mountainsides, clear blue lakes and fer-

tile plantations all await travellers in the Fergana Valley, whose diverse interior even includes deserty sections. Sheltered from cold, northerly winds by high mountain ranges, the valley provides optimal climatic conditions for agriculture. Minimal rainfall (25–30 cm/ 10–12 in per year) means the fertile oases are watered by a complex network of canals, and modern industry was really first introduced when the region was taken over by the Russians. Today, visitors see a Fergana basin that is well-settled and intensely cultivated. Kokand is located directly on the old caravan route. An earlier colony was destroyed by the Mongolians in the 13th century.

The city today, which was the religious center of the valley until the 19th century, offers sights such as the 19th-century Khan's palace, the Jummi Mosque and the mausoleums at the cemetery, all well worth seeing. One of the small silk factories at the edge of the city or in the surrounding area also make for an interesting visit. The route leads through Andi-

jan to the Kyrgyz border. Osh, an ancient city said to be 3,000 years old, has now become the second-largest city in Kyrgyzs-

tan and is a well-known pilgrimage site. Passing through Uzgen, with three mausoleums from the 11th and 12th cen-

cal grid layout of Russian 'colonial' cities. Today, over 600,000 people live in this city, Kyrgyzstan's political, economic and cultural center. Bishkek is home to universities, museums, theaters and industrial plants. South-east of the capital is one of the country's main attractions, the Issyk Kul.

7 Issyk Kul This high mountain lake at 1,608 m (5,276 ft) is lined with sandy beaches and encircled by snow-capped mountains. Despite the snowy mountains, however, the lake never freezes, hence its name, meaning 'warm lake' in Kyrgyz. From Balykchy on the western shore, the southern frontage road leads to Karakol at the eastern end of the lake. Its main attraction is the Buddhist-style Dungan Mosque, built in 1910 completely out of wood, with no metal nails used at all. On the way back to Bishkek is another captivating mountain lake south-west of Issyk Kul, the Song Köl, over 3,000 m (9,843 ft) above sea level.

1 The Tian Shan mountains stretch for 2,500 km (1,554 miles) through Central Asia. The highest peak is Pik Pobeda at 7,439 m (24,407 ft), on the Kyrgyz-Chinese border.

2 The 16th-century Kukeldash Madrasah in Tashkent is decorated with brightly coloured faiences.

3 A regional museum now stands at the site of the former palace of Khudoyar Khan of Kokand.

4 The beautifully decorated yurts of a Kazakh family.

5 Nestled in the impressive mountain landscape of the Tian Shan is Issyk Kul, the highest lake in Kyrgyzstan at 1,608 m (5,276 ft).

turies and a tall minaret that stands 27 m (89 ft) high, you will then come to Kara Kul before reaching Bishkek. Several 3,000-m-high (9,843-ft) passes must be overcome on the way to the Kyrgyz capital.

If the road through the Fergana Valley is blocked off, or for those who do not want to travel through the mountains, there is an alternative route along the northern edge of the mountain range. This well-built road leads for 450 km (280 miles) through Kazakhstan. In the footsteps of the old Silk Road, the route first heads north towards Shymkent, crossing a recreation area in the foothills of the Tian Shan before heading west. East of

Shymkent, the Khrebet Karatau, or 'Black Mountains', which reach elevations of 1,000–1,500 m (3,281–4,922 ft), must be traversed. These foothills of the mighty Tian Shan are sparsely covered in grassy vegetation.

The southern outskirts then follow the 'Starving Steppe' through the Muyunkum Desert. Here, the terrain rises from some 300 m (984 ft) in the north to around 700 m (2,297 ft) in the south-east. Occasionally you will witness barchans (shifting sand dunes). The arid land is used as a winter pasture, and groundwater close to the surface enables farming in some areas. After crossing the border into Kyrgyzstan at the

town of Merke, the Kyrgyz capital of Bishkek is another 100 km (62 miles). This country's impressive mountains, idyllic lakes, deep valleys and fertile basins have earned it the nickname 'Switzerland of Central Asia'.

6 Bishkek This city lies in the fertile yet earthquake-prone Chu Valley at the foot of the Kyrgyz Alatau (Ala-Toosu in Kyrgyz), at altitudes ranging from 750 to 900 m (2,461–2,953 ft). From 1929 to 1990, the city was known as Frunse in honour of a Russian general. The Russians had conquered a fortress founded here in the early 19th century and set up a military settlement in the typi-

1

Heading east now from Bishkek towards Almaty you will be confronted with some extremely diverse scenery. Oddly enough, winds coming from the north- and south-west bring plenty of rainfall to the windward side of the mountains, yet basins and valleys remain dry and have to be irrigated.

About 30 km (19 miles) from Bishkek you will come to another border crossing, this time into Kazakhstan. The numerous border checks on the northern route of the historic Silk Road are a tedious legacy from the collapse of the Soviet Union.

The next destination is the former capital of this vast country, Almaty (formerly Alma-Ata).

2

3

8 Almaty Caravans have been making stops here since ancient times, though there are no traces of this history in this modern administrative and industrial city. In 1854, the Russians constructed a fort where several mountain streams from the Tian Shan converge. The city, at 700–900 m (2,297–2,953 ft) has the typical grid layout of Russian cities. Its few tourist sights include the 19th-century cathedral in Panfilov Park, one of the largest and tallest wooden buildings on earth. The high mountain ice stadium, Medeo, is located at 1,680 m (5,512 ft) in the moun-

tain's foothills. The long road to Ürümqi is marked by desert-like river valleys and steep passes over high mountains. Taking a well-built mountain road through the Korgas Pass you cross the Chinese border, which has only been reopened since the 1980s. The journey through the Borohoro Shan mountains, with valley glaciers up to 20 km

(12 miles) long, is a diverse one. Glacial mountains 5,000 m (16,405 ft) high never cease to captivate travellers.

After a few monotonous stretches over wide, desolate plateaus at the edge of the Dzungaria, you reach Ürümqi at the northern side of the Tian Shan. Vehicular travel on the road through to the 5,000-m

Tian Chi A day trip out of Ürümqi into the Bogda Shan mountains 50 km (31 miles) to the east is well worth doing. Tian Chi, or Heaven Lake, has motorboats ready to take you around.

The lake is at a height of 1,900 m (6,234 ft) and located at the base of the always snow-capped Bogda Feng, a peak 5,445 m (17,865 ft) high.

When the snow melts in springtime, the depth of this relatively shallow lake suddenly reaches 90 m (295 ft). Dome-shaped yurts on the shore can provide overnight accommodation.

(16,405-ft) Chinese section of the Tian Shan has only been possible since 1955. From Tashkent on, the mountain chains and foothills of the Tian Shan accompany travellers along the Silk Road.

There is no rainfall in the basins between these imposing, landlocked mountains, but coniferous forests still exist at altitudes of over 1,600 m (5,250 ft). The mountains form the border between the extremely arid Tarim Valley to the south and the more humid Dzungaria north of Ürümqi.

Ürümqi This industrial city located at 870 m (2,854 ft) above sea level is the capital of the Xin Jiang Autonomous Region and home to 1.2 million people. Ürümqi is surrounded by a fertile oasis landscape and was an extremely important trading center on the Silk Road. This is reflected in the exhibits at the Qu Bowuguan Regional Museum and in the lively bazaars. The symbol of Ürümqi is the 900-m-high (2,953-ft) Red Mountain (Tiger Head Mountain).

1 The slopes of the Tian Shan mountains around Ürümqi.

2 The 'Precious Pagoda of the Red Mountains' in Ürümqi.

3 Bogda Shan peaks reflected like a painting in the Tian Chi.

4 The minaret of the Emin Mosque in Turpan.

11 Turpan Through desert valleys, the route heads 100 km (62 miles) down into the Turpan Valley, which the Chinese controlled over 2,000 years ago for the purposes of preserving safety on the Silk Road. Approximately 150 sq km (58 sq mi) in size, Aydingkol Hu (Moonlight Lake) lies at the deepest point of the valley (154 m/505 ft below sea level). During the hot summer months, temperatures here rise to 47°C (117°F). Even when it rains, the rainfall very rarely reaches the ground – most of it evaporates on the way down. For this reason, no more than 16 mm (0.63 in) of rainfall is recorded each year. In addition to its fame as the source of the famous Hami melons, the oasis city of Turpan is also known for the grapes grown here for raisins. It is a good starting point for a series of interesting day trips: about 10 m (6 miles) west are the ruins of Jiaohe Gucheng, and east of Turpan is the Bezeklik Qianfo Dong (Caves of the Thousand Buddhas) in the Murtuq Gorge.

12 Flaming Mountains (Huoyan Shan) This mountain range owes its name to the steep mounds of red sandstone rock, which look like they are on fire in the gleaming sun. Here in the Xin Jiang Autonomous Region, the climate is extremely continental, with ice-cold winters and hot, dry summers.

On the way to the Flaming Mountains, the road passes homesteads made of yellow clay bricks and enclosing large interior courtyards. During the hot summer, these courtyards, which are mostly overgrown with creepers, are the scene of everyday family life.

13 Gaochang Gucheng About 47 km (29 miles) southeast of Turpan at the foot of

the Flaming Mountains are the ruins of a city dating back to Tang times (618–908). The outline of the entire complex is still very recognizable even today. Sections of the once 5-km-long (3-mile) wall made from stamped mud also still exist and are up to 8 m (26 ft) high in some parts, despite the relatively extreme conditions in these parts. It once surrounded a settlement 1.5 sq km (0.5 sq mi) in size that was divided into an external, internal and palace city. An entrance gate, the foundations of a pagoda and a temple hall are all well-preserved, and some brick buildings were rebuilt in parts.

14 Astana In the immediate vicinity of Gaochang Gucheng are the tombs of Astana (Uygur for capital). Even though the ancient tomb complex, containing some 400 tombs, was built between the 3rd and 8th centuries AD, the mummies are still very well preserved because of the hot, dry climate. 2,000 books and documents were also discovered in the tombs.

Along with the coin, ceramic and silk findings, they are further proof of the enormous wealth this region possessed in the Silk Road's heyday.

The road follows the old trade routes along the northern edge of the eastern Tarim Basin

through the oasis town of Hami to Minghoshan in what is today the Gansu Province.

15 Minghoshan (Dunhuang) It is in this famous oasis city, where fruit and cotton are cultivated in abundance thanks to

clever irrigation, that the northern and southern forks of the Silk Road leading around the Taklimakan Desert converge. In the past, if travellers heading east on the Silk Road had reached Mingoshan, it meant they had survived virtually every kind of danger, be it nature, thieves or highway robbers. This meant the opposite was true for travellers heading west with their caravans. Minghoshan was the last safe haven in Chinese-protected territory. It is thus no surprise that wealthy travellers between the 4th and 14th centuries were told of supernatural powers here, and their donations helped to equip the Magao cave monastery in opulent style.

Mogao Ku This monastery complex is located in a river valley between the San Wei and Ming Sha mountains about 25 km (15 miles) from Minghoshan. Nearly 500 caves were unearthed here, with walls covering a total surface area of 45,000 sq m (484,200 sq ft). The illustrations are not just evidence of their creators' religious beliefs, but also depict a multitude of themes from everyday life.

The entire complex, including murals, reliefs and sculptures from the 8th century, is considered one of the most important examples of Buddhist art in China and was declared a UNESCO World Heritage Site in 1987.

Yueya Quan and Mingshashan The Minghoshan area's second-largest tourist sight are the dunes around Crescent Lake (Yueya Quan), which is fed by an underground reservoir. These flawlessly formed crescent dunes extend to the oasis gardens on the outskirts of town and are proof that the desert is near. You also get an amazing view of the eastern foothills of the Taklimakan Desert from the 200-m-

high (656-ft) dunes of the Mingshashan, the 'Singing Sands'. The next stretch of the journey via Anxi leads partly through semi-desert and partly through the steppe. Your next destination is Jiayuguan in the southeastern foothills of the Jiayu mountains. This is where you meet up with the western end of the Great Wall of China.

Jiayuguan This impressive fortress was built in 1372 and was the most remote western fort of the Ming Dynasty along the Great Wall. Over the centuries, it protected the strategically important Jiayu Pass between Qilian Shan and Bei Shan.

The fortress itself comprised a double wall with watchtowers in each corner and two double gates with 17-m (46-ft) watchtowers in the east and west. The wall in the inner city is 733 m (2,356 ft) long and 10 m (33 ft) high. In 1507, another 40 km (25 miles) was added to the wall, which was especially well fortified on the west side where the enemy was expected to attack. Archers shot the attackers from the small towers. The entire 24,000-sq-m (258,240-sq-ft) structure was built out of stamped mud and clad with bricks.

The Silk Road then continues towards Lanzhou through the Hexi Corridor along the Great Wall, surrounded by deserts and semi-deserts in the north

1 The Murtuq Gorge east of Turpan with the Caves of the Thousand Buddhas in Bezeklik.

2 The Mogao Grottoes with wooden porches near Minghoshan (Dunhuang) contain paintings, scripts and cult objects.

3 The western end of the Great Wall at the Jiayu Pass near Jiayuguan.

and lined by the steep Qilian Shan mountains in the south. 'Hexi' means 'west of the Huanghe.' This natural transportation link is 1,000 km (621 miles) long and 100 km (62 miles) wide. The connection only became a safe transport route after the Han emperor Wudi fortified the passes, built the Great Wall on the north side and put a function-ing administration in place, all more than 2,000 years ago. The corridor was located in a crucial position for relations and trade between Central Asia and China, and the cultural, linguistic and religious influences flowed from both sides.

19 Zhangye The first stop is Zhangye, a place Marco Polo described as a metropolis on his one-year sojourn here. Great Buddha Monastery, built in 1098 in the center of the city, was one of the places he visited. With its 34-m-long (109-ft) reclining Buddha, the mona-stery continues to be Zhangye's main attraction. The next section of the journey towards the south-east through the loess landscape is a diverse one, and must have been even more so

in earlier times. Mulberry trees, the basis for silk production, once flourished here where today there is only wasteland.

20 Wuwei Wuwei was, and still is, a strategically important settlement in the Hexi Corridor, and was established as the regional capital as early as 115 BC. To defend against attacking Huns, Han Emperor Wudi developed a plan to breed gov-ernment studs here, but the farmers did not know anything about horse breeding. Wudi brought horses from areas such as the Fergana Valley and mixed them with local breeds. A galloping bronze horse from the time of the Han Dynasty was discovered in a tomb near Wuwei. This masterpiece is the main attraction of the Wuwei Museum.

21 Lanzhou Lanzhou, the cap-ital of the Gansu province, is located where the Hexi Corri-dor leaves the road and contin-ues over the Huang He. It stretches from west to east along both banks of the Huang He. The best view of the 'Orchid City' is from the hills of the White Pagoda (Baita Shan)

on the northern riverbank. When in Lanzhou, it's worth visiting the Park of the Five Wells (Wuquan Gongyuan) on the southern side of a hill with its 600-year-old temple com-plex. In summer and autumn, you can take a boat ride on Lake Liujiaxia to Binglingsi Shiku, the cave temple of the Thousand Buddhas. It is one of the most impressive Buddhist cave temples in China. Here, a 60-m (197-ft) rock face soars out of the reservoir, from which a 27-m (89-ft) figure of the Buddha and numerous grot-toes and alcoves were fash-ioned. Craftsmen worked on

the complex between AD 513 and the mid 19th century, when it was suddenly forgot-ten. Wooden galleries and steps connect the grottoes in the rock face, and their forms are shown in frescoes and murals.

From Lanzhou, it is also worth allowing a couple of hours for a detour 300 km (186 miles) west to the Lamaistic mona-stery Ta'er Si. It is located 26 km (16 miles) south of Xining and is one of the six monasteries of the yellow-capped sect.

22 Tianshui This route initially heads through well-main-

3

The road runs parallel to Wei Hei towards Baoji in the Shaanxi province, an early center for breeding silkworms. It continues downhill through a rolling, fertile loess landscape, terraced in some parts and badly eroded in others, into the densely settled Wei Valley. Finally, you reach Xi'an, the starting or ending point of our section of the historic Silk Road.

㉓ Xi´an Today's provincial capital was also China's capital, known then as Chang'an, for over 1,000 years under a series of eleven dynasties. A visit to the colourful Neolithic settlement of Banpo Bowuguan illustrates how the region has been continually inhabited since ancient times. The historic city's mighty wall has been preserved from the 14th century and still surrounds the historic old city today. The bell and drum tower, pagodas and temples, as well as the Great Mosque, have all been very well preserved. However, only very few of the old living quarters survived the frenzy to modernize, which sacrificed large parts of the historic old city to create an autonomous inner city.

Roughly 85 km (53 miles) northwest of Xi'an near Qian Xian is an important necropolis from the Tang Dynasty (618–906). It contains the tombs of the third Tang Emperor Kao-tsung (649–683), who was buried here in the Liang mountains. Xi'an's biggest attraction is, however, the grave mound of the Emperor Qin Shi Huangdi, which towers 47 m (154 ft) above the plains not far from the city in the Lintong district. The tomb itself has still not been opened.

Just 1.5 km (0.9 miles) west of this is one of the main tourist sites of the route, where the 7,000-strong army of terracotta warriors, which was meant to protect the tomb, was uncovered in 1974.

1 Scenery near Lanzhou with 4,000-m (13,124-ft) peaks of the Qinling Shan range.

2 The Temple of the Great Buddha near Zhangye, an early garrison city on the old Silk Road.

3 Terracotta Army warriors, which the first emperor of China had erected not far from his tomb.

tained mountain roads to Tianshui, where a mountain towers up on the slopes of the Qinling Shan south of the city. The mountain resembles a haystack and is for this reason called Maiji (wheat storer). It is famous for the sculptures in its grottoes (Maijishan Shiku) which are some of the most significant Buddhist grottoes in China.

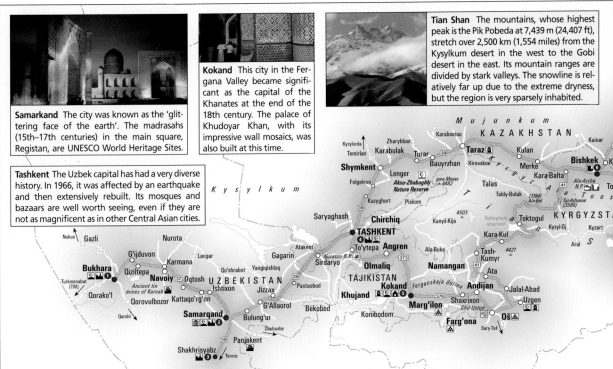

Samarkand The city was known as the 'glittering face of the earth'. The madrasahs (15th–17th centuries) in the main square, Registan, are UNESCO World Heritage Sites.

Kokand This city in the Fergana Valley became significant as the capital of the Khanates at the end of the 18th century. The palace of Khudoyar Khan, with its impressive wall mosaics, was also built at this time.

Tian Shan The mountains, whose highest peak is the Pik Pobeda at 7,439 m (24,407 ft), stretch over 2,500 km (1,554 miles) from the Kysylkum desert in the west to the Gobi desert in the east. Its mountain ranges are divided by stark valleys. The snowline is relatively far up due to the extreme dryness, but the region is very sparsely inhabited.

Tashkent The Uzbek capital has had a very diverse history. In 1966, it was affected by an earthquake and then extensively rebuilt. Its mosques and bazaars are well worth seeing, even if they are not as magnificent as in other Central Asian cities.

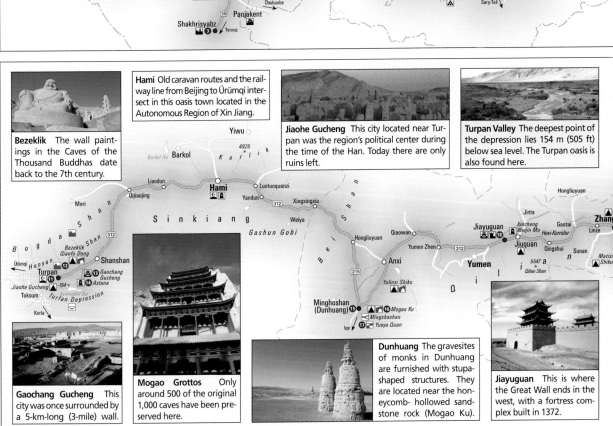

Hami Old caravan routes and the railway line from Beijing to Ürümqi intersect in this oasis town located in the Autonomous Region of Xin Jiang.

Jiaohe Gucheng This city located near Turpan was the region's political center during the time of the Han. Today there are only ruins left.

Turpan Valley The deepest point of the depression lies 154 m (505 ft) below sea level. The Turpan oasis is also found here.

Bezeklik The wall paintings in the Caves of the Thousand Buddhas date back to the 7th century.

Gaochang Gucheng This city was once surrounded by a 5-km-long (3-mile) wall.

Mogao Grottos Only around 500 of the original 1,000 caves have been preserved here.

Dunhuang The gravesites of monks in Dunhuang are furnished with stupa-shaped structures. They are located near the honeycomb-hollowed sandstone rock (Mogao Ku).

Jiayuguan This is where the Great Wall ends in the west, with a fortress complex built in 1372.

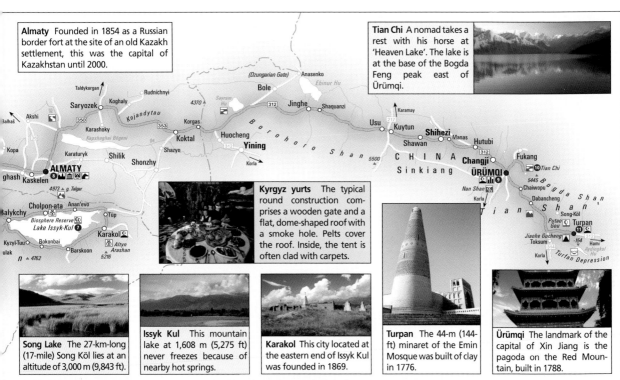

Almaty Founded in 1854 as a Russian border fort at the site of an old Kazakh settlement, this was the capital of Kazakhstan until 2000.

Tian Chi A nomad takes a rest with his horse at 'Heaven Lake'. The lake is at the base of the Bogda Feng peak east of Ürümqi.

Kyrgyz yurts The typical round construction comprises a wooden gate and a flat, dome-shaped roof with a smoke hole. Pelts cover the roof. Inside, the tent is often clad with carpets.

Song Lake The 27-km-long (17-mile) Song Köl lies at an altitude of 3,000 m (9,843 ft).

Issyk Kul This mountain lake at 1,608 m (5,275 ft) never freezes because of nearby hot springs.

Karakol This city located at the eastern end of Issyk Kul was founded in 1869.

Turpan The 44-m (144-ft) minaret of the Emin Mosque was built of clay in 1776.

Ürümqi The landmark of the capital of Xin Jiang is the pagoda on the Red Mountain, built in 1788.

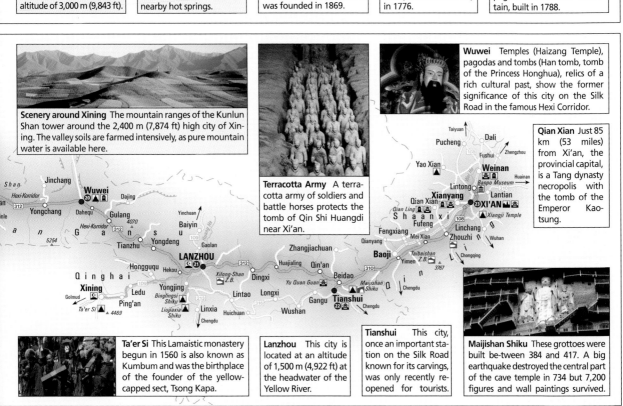

Scenery around Xining The mountain ranges of the Kunlun Shan tower around the 2,400 m (7,874 ft) high city of Xining. The valley soils are farmed intensively, as pure mountain water is available here.

Terracotta Army A terracotta army of soldiers and battle horses protects the tomb of Qin Shi Huangdi near Xi'an.

Wuwei Temples (Haizang Temple), pagodas and tombs (Han tomb, tomb of the Princess Honghua), relics of a rich cultural past, show the former significance of this city on the Silk Road in the famous Hexi Corridor.

Qian Xian Just 85 km (53 miles) from Xi'an, the provincial capital, is a Tang dynasty necropolis with the tomb of the Emperor Kaotsung.

Ta'er Si This Lamaistic monastery begun in 1560 is also known as Kumbum and was the birthplace of the founder of the yellow-capped sect, Tsong Kapa.

Lanzhou This city is located at an altitude of 1,500 m (4,922 ft) at the headwater of the Yellow River.

Tianshui This city, once an important station on the Silk Road known for its carvings, was only recently reopened for tourists.

Maijishan Shiku These grottoes were built be-tween 384 and 417. A big earthquake destroyed the central part of the cave temple in 734 but 7,200 figures and wall paintings survived.

Kakadu National Park in the Northern Territory of Australia is characterized by broad lowlands and dry sandstone plateaus.

Australia

On Stuart Highway through the 'Red Centre'

The Stuart Highway stretches 3,200 km (1,987 miles) from Adelaide on the south coast all the way across the legendary outback, the 'Red Centre' of the continent, to Darwin in the north on the Timor Sea. Along this dream route you pass some of Australia's most impressive natural sights. Indeed, long portions of the journey are devoid of any signs of life, much less human settlements, but it is precisely this emptiness and solitude that make this journey so fascinating.

The starting point for the adventure across the entire Australian continent is Adelaide, known as the 'greenest town' in the country. Today, tree-lined streets in this tidy city have replaced the rugged seaport where, in 1836, about 550 German settlers arrived bearing grape vines and a

vision for the future. The heart of Australian wine production is now concentrated in a handful of picturesque regions including the Adelaide Hills, the Barossa Valley and the Clare Valley.

Port Augusta, 317 km (197 miles) further north, is the real starting point of the Stuart

Aborigine with impressive and a bit scaring body paint.

Highway. It is named after John McDouall Stuart, an explorer who in 1862 became the first white man to cross the conti-

nent from north to south. At one time known for being one of the country's most hazardous roads, the highway, which has been surfaced now since 1987, has become a fully developed traffic route. Parts of the road can become impassable after unusually heavy rainfall. The first stretch of your route, from Port Augusta to Glendambo, is marked by dried-out salt lakes that are visible from the road. The first real town to the north after Port Augusta is Coober Pedy in the Stuart Range, a relatively inhospitable area where dramatic sandstorms are commonplace. It was here, in the 'opal capital of the world', that the

The Kakadu National Park covers almost the entire catchment area of the South Alligator River, which crashes over the cliffs of Twin Falls and Jim Jim Falls.

The Stuart Highway leads hundreds of kilometers through the desert landscape of the 'Red Centre'.

first opal was discovered by chance during the gold rush of 1915.

In general, between Port Augusta and Darwin what may look like a town along the highway on the map is often nothing more than a road-house where you can buy fuel, spend the night and stock up on basic food supplies. One of these is the Kulgera Road-house, just 'across the border' in the Northern Territory.

There are only 185,000 people living in this massive state (six times the size of Great Britain), and half of them live in Darwin. Coarse, rocky terrain and the endless spinifex grass steppe cover the land as far as the eye can see. The land is rusty red for hundreds of kilometers, with termite hills shimmering dark

red in the hot sun. Roughly 80 km (50 miles) over the border at Erlunda, the Lasseter Highway turns off towards Uluru National Park where two of Australia's famous landmarks are located – Uluru (Ayers Rock) and Kata Tjuta (The Olgas).

The most important city in the area is Alice Springs in the Macdonnell Ranges, a town that is also the geographical center of the country and a hub for trips to many well-known national parks – Finke Gorge, Watarrka and the West Macdonnell Ranges. The next tourist highlight on the way to 'Top End' are the bizarre spheres of the Devils Marbles. Tennant Creek has been known as 'Gold Town' ever since the short gold rush in 1932. At Renner Spring one finally leaves the arid plains of

the 'Red Centre' behind and the coastal savannah comes into view. From the town of Katherine you can reach the Cutta Cutta Caves Nature Park as well as the Nitmiluk National Park with the spectacular canyons of Katherine Gorge. At Pine Creek,

you have a choice between taking the road to Darwin or the drive through Kakadu National Park towards Jabiru.

Either way, after 3,200 km (1,987 miles) of hard going, you have finally reached the 'Top End'.

The giant red kangaroo measures up to 2 m (6.5 ft) when standing on its hind legs. It normally hops at 19 kph (12 mph), and up to 70 kph (44 mph).

Shortly after starting out from Adelaide, the Stuart Highway leads straight into the outback. Ayers Rock and Alice Springs lie at the halfway point of the route. The landscape turns into savannah in the far northern sections, and numerous national parks give travellers an idea of the Northern Territory's flora and fauna.

1

1 Adelaide With more than a million inhabitants, Adelaide lies on the north and south sides of the Torrens River. The city's many parks, gardens, historic arcades and churches give it a very European flair. Yet despite all this, Adelaide is often considered a bit of a backwater by people from other Australian cities, or is even called 'wow-serville', but this seems off the mark.

Every two years one of the world's most important cultural festivals takes place here – the Festival of Arts, held in the Adelaide Festival Centre. It is a tolerant and multicultural city with several museums along the 'Cultural Mile', including the Art Gallery of South Australia, the Ayers House Historical Museum (one of the most attractive colonial buildings in Australia), the Migration Museum on the history of immigration, and the South Australia Museum, with a good collection of Aboriginal tools, weapons and everyday items.

For a great view of the city go up to Montefiori Hill. Then take a break in the enchanting Botanic Gardens. If you feel like a swim, take one of the nostalgic trams down to Glenelg or Henley Beach. A worthwhile day trip is the drive into the Adelaide Hills or to the Barossa Valley. The first vineyards were planted here in 1847 by a German immigrant, Johann Cramp. Today in the Barossa Valley, 40 km (25 miles) long and 10 km (6 miles) wide, there are over 400 vineyards producing wines that have slowly but surely gained recognition around the world. One of the year's cultural highlights is the Vintage Festival with music, sauerkraut, brown bread, apple strudel, and of course wine.

Another interesting detour takes you to Kangaroo Island, 113 km (70 miles) south-west of Adelaide, which can be reached via the Fleurieu peninsula with its inviting sandy beaches. Australia's third-largest island is 155 km (96 miles) long and 55 km (34 miles) wide. You will come face to face here with the kangaroos that gave the island its name. In the Seal Bay Conservation Park, thousands of sea lions bask on rocks in the sun. In Flinders Chase National Park, koalas lounge in the eucalyptus trees.

The real trip to the far north begins on Highway 1 from Adelaide. On the northern banks of Spencer Gulf is the industrial port town of Port Pirie, 250 km (155 miles) from Adelaide. Enormous grain silos bear witness to the extensive wheat farming in this region. Zinc and silver ore are processed here too, as is lead.

About 65 km (40 miles) further north, on the way to Port Au-

Travel Information

Route profile
Length: approx. 3,200 km (1,987 miles), excluding detours
Time required: 3 weeks
Start: Adelaide
End: Darwin
Route (main locations): Adelaide, Port Augusta, Coober Pedy, Alice Springs, Wauchope, Tennant Creek, Katherine, Pine Creek, Darwin.

Accommodation:
Aside from signposted campsites, it's always possible to spend the night in a highway 'roadhouse'.

Traffic information:
Drive on the left in Australia. The Stuart Highway is completely tarmac from Adelaide to Darwin. In general, the driving conditions on auxil-

iary roads east and west of the highway are good. International driving licences are required for some nations. If you want to explore the outback, a four-wheel drive vehicle is recommended. There are service stations and rest areas about every 200–300 km (124–186 miles) along the highway. Speed limits are 50 km/h (30 mph) in town and 100 km/h (62 mph) outside towns. The blood alcohol limit is 0.05 percent and there are severe penalties if it is exceeded.

Information:
Australian Government
www.dfat.gov.au
General information:
www.australia.com
National Parks:
www.atn.com.au/parks

gusta, it is worth taking the scenic detour into Mount Remarkable National Park at the south end of the Flinders Range.

From the 959-m-high (3,146-ft) Mount Remarkable you can get

ground church in Coober, as well as underground bed and breakfast accommodation. Be sure to pay a visit to the lovingly restored Old Timers Mine while you are here.

Eventually, the Lasseter Highway makes its way west at Erlunda towards the Yulara Resort and the Visitor Centre of the Uluru and Kata Tjuta National Parks (1,325 sq km/511 sq mi).

If you are looking for outdoor adventure, turn left off the highway onto a track towards Chambers Pillar, a 56-m-high (184-ft) sandstone monolith that early settlers used as a point of reference and in which many explorers have carved their names and dedications.

5 Ayers Rock The Aborigines call this massive rock mountain Uluru (863 m/2,831 ft above sea level) and cherish it as a sacred place. Subsequently, since the path to the top is one of sacred significance, they 'kindly ask' that people do not climb it – but they do not forbid you to do so. Instead, they ask you to admire it from below as you stroll along the 9.4-km (5.8-mile) 'base walk'. The rock itself measures 3.5 km (2.2 miles) by 2.4 km (1.5 miles), and extends several kilometers down into the earth. It rises to 348 m (1,142 ft) above the steppe landscape like a whale stranded on a deserted beach. Due to its high iron content it changes colour with the movement of the sun – from crimson, rust, pink, brown and grey to a deep blue. After rainfall it even goes a silvery shade – a perpetually impressive show that will dazzle any visitor.

1 Uluru, also known as Ayers Rock.

2 At the base of the Stuart Range lies Coober Pedy, the 'Opal capital of the world'.

a fabulous panoramic view of the entire region.

After another 70 km (43 miles) along Spencer Gulf, the industrial port town of Augusta awaits you and marks the actual starting point of Stuart Highway (Highway 87).

2 Port Augusta This town is often called the 'Gateway to the outback'. In preparation for the trip, a visit to the Wadlata Outback Centre is highly recommended. A few historically important buildings including the Town Hall (1887), the Court House (1884) and St Augustine's Church, with lovely stained-glass windows, are worth seeing. The Australian Arid Lands Botanic Gardens north of town familiarize you

with the flora and fauna of the outback.

A short detour to the nearby Flinders Ranges National Park is an absolute must.

3 Pimba This little town is right next to the enormous Woomera military base. Interestingly, the 'restricted area' on the base contains the largest uranium source in the world. Australia's largest natural lakes can also be found outside of Pimba. These salt lakes are only periodically filled with water and are the remnants of what was once a huge inland sea. In the dry season they transform into salt marshes or salt pans. To the east of Stuart Highway is Lake Torrens, in the national park of the same name, which

covers an area of 5,800 sq km (2,240 sq mi). Frome Lake and Eyre Lake are also in the park. Further west is Lake Gairdner, another salt lake that is part of a separate national park.

4 Coober Pedy In 1915, fourteen-year-old Willie Hutchinson and his father discovered Australia's first opal completely by chance, about 270 km (168 miles) north of Pimba. The name Coober Pedy originates from the Aborigine 'kupa piti' (white man in a hole). Since then it has been overrun with pits up to 30 m (98 ft) deep and giant slag heaps that, due to consistent demand for opals, are constantly being expanded. In fact, 70 percent of the world's opal mining takes place in the Coober Pedy area. The raging sandstorms and intense heat in the area have compelled nearly half of the 3,000 inhabitants to live in 'dugouts', underground homes built in decommissioned opal mines. The often well-furnished apartments maintain consistent temperatures between 23°C and 25°C (73°F and 77°F) and can be up to 400 sq m (4,305 sq ft) in size. There is even an under-

1

6 The Olgas Known as Kata Tjuta by the Aborigines, the Olgas (1,066 m/ 3,497 ft above sea level) are a similarly spectacular sight. Kata Tjuta, meaning 'many heads', is 32 km (20 miles) to the north-west of Uluru and comprises a group of thirty geologically similar, mainly dome-shaped monoliths that spread over an area of 35 sq km (13.5 sq mi), the highest point peaking at 546 m (1,791 ft). It would appear that the Olgas were once a single mountain that eroded over time into individual hills. The Valley of Winds traverses a stark mountain range through which either seasonal icy winds blow or burning hot air turns each step into a torturous affair.

7 Henbury Back on Stuart Highway the journey continues to the north. Approximately 2,000–3,000 years ago a meteor impacted not far from Henbury, leaving twelve distinct craters. The largest has a diameter of 180 m (560 ft) and the smallest just 6 m (20 ft).

At Henbury, the Ernest Giles Highway splits off towards Watarrka National Park. It is a dirt track until it joins the Laritja Road where it becomes tarmac and eventually leads to the Kings Canyon Resort.

8 Watarrka National Park and Finke Gorge National Park The centrepiece of the Watarrka National Park is Kings Canyon on the west end of the George Gill Range. With walls that rise to 200 m (656 ft), the canyon looks as if it were manmade.

A number of Aboriginal rock paintings and carvings adorn the rugged canyon facades. The Aborigines aptly call the beehive-like eroded sandstone dome the 'Lost City'. Kings Canyon is best visited on foot by taking the Kings Creek Walk. From the resort, the Meerenie Loop (a dirt road) leads to the Aborigine town of Hermannsburg. On this slightly daunting stretch of road you'll cross low sand dunes that lead up to the base of the Macdonnell Range. East of the old Hermannsburger Mission, Larapinta Drive turns south and for the last 16 km (10 miles) it runs through

2

the dried-out Finke riverbed to Palm Valley. This last section is only really accessible with four-wheel drive vehicles. The main attraction of the Finke Gorge National Park is Palm Valley, home to more than 3,000 species of palm trees – all of them unique to this area – that line the picturesque watering holes.

The route then leads via Hermannsburg and Larapinta Drive to the turn-off for Namatjira Drive, which will take you further to the north-west.

9 West Macdonnell National Park The Tropic of Capricorn runs straight across these mountains to the east of Alice Springs, which rise to heights of 1,524 m (5,000 ft). The principal attractions of the park are the numerous gorges that lie on a fault line alongside Larapinta Drive and Namatjira Drive. The most spectacular one is near Alice Springs and is called Simpsons Gap. The Standley Chasm, with depths of up to 100 m (328 ft), only gets sunshine for twenty minutes in the middle of the day.

Ellery Creek Big Hole, Serpentine Gorge, Ormiston Gorge (giant blocks in Ormiston Pound) and Glen Helen Gorge

are 133 km (83 miles) further down the road. The small lake there is sacred to the Aborigines because the mythical giant water snake is said to live there. The return route or continuing drive to Alice Springs follows the same road.

⑩ **Alice Springs** The geographical centre of Australia is about 1,700 km (1,055 miles) north of Adelaide and 1,500 km (931 miles) south of Darwin. Alice Springs was founded in 1872 and its main attractions are the carefully restored Old Telegraph Station (1872) and the Flying Doctors centre from

which medical assistance has been organized to serve the outback since 1939. You can enjoy a magnificent view of the nearby Macdonnell Range from Anzac Hill.

The famous Camel Cup takes place in July when up to fifteen dromedaries take part in a hard desert race. At the comical Henley-on-Todd regatta in springtime, 'oarsmen' race each other on foot in bottomless boats along the usually dry Todd River.

North-east of the town is the Trephina Gorge National Park in the East Macdonnell Range. It can be reached via the paved

Ross Highway. Eucalyptus trees grow alongside watering holes tucked between the steep walls of the gorge. A dirt track to the N'dhala Gorge Nature Park also branches off the Stuart Highway. Another track leads to Maryvale, the last outpost of civilization in the Simson Desert. From there it is about 58 km (36 miles) to Chambers Pillar. On the way to the Devils Marbles near Wauchope, the view to your right overlooks the Davenport Range, another national park. To the north of the West Macdonnell Range there are Aborigine reserves on both sides of Stuart Highway, for example the Pawu Aboriginal Land west of Borrow Creek. It was not until the end of the 20th century that the lands were returned to the indigenous people.

⑪ **Devils Marbles** These eroded granite spheres look as if a mightier power had scattered them across the rocky plateau with mathematical precision. It seems as if the slightest breeze could blow them away. The Aborigines believe the marbles

to be rainbow water snake eggs.

⑫ **Tennant Creek** When the last gold rush began in Australia in 1932, Tennant Creek was known as 'Gold Town'. Within a few years, however, it became more of a ghost town until it was eventually reawakened by the discovery of nearby silver and copper mines. The Nobles Nob Mine and the Tennant Creek Stamp Battery Museum recall the short-lived bonanza. Some 11 km (7 miles) northwest of here are the Devils Pebbles, another scattering of granite boulders. A roadside memorial for John Flynn, the founder of the Flying Doctors, lies some 20 km (12 miles) in the same direction.

⑬ **Renner Springs** Further along the route towards Katherine, north of Helen Springs, the road takes you to Renner Springs. This small town marks both the climatic and geographical border between the outback of the 'Red Centre' and the savannah of the northern coastal areas.

Newcastle Waters to the north was once an important telegraph station and crossing point for livestock herds.

⑭ **Daly Waters** Still further north, it is definitely worth making a stop in Daly Waters, where the oldest pub in the Northern Territory has been wetting whistles since 1893. For

1 Chambers Pillar rises 56 m (184 ft) over the Simpson Desert.

2 The Finke River eroded the steep ravine in Finke Gorge National Park.

3 As if the gods had tossed them – the Devils Marbles.

4 Bizarre rock formations in the West Macdonnell Range.

327

decades, travellers have left various utensils here – from tickets for the legendary Ghan Express to autographed underwear. These are now all carefully arranged to decorate the walls of the pub. In this hot, dry environment, a cold beer tastes even better than in other roadhouses along the highway.

The next stop is Larrimah with its historic train station. From there it's on to Mataranka where you should not miss out on a refreshing dip in Mataranka Pool in Elsey National Park, roughly 9 km (5.5 miles) away. Accommodation is also available at the Mataranka Homestead Resort.

The thermal hotsprings are surrounded by paperbark trees, from which hang long strips of bark. The Aborigines used this bark for thousands of years as wrapping for their food. From Mataranka it's now only 110 km (68 miles) to Katherine on the banks of the Katherine River, a river that never dries out.

⑮ Katherine This town offers limited attractions, but there is a nostalgic train station dating from 1926 and the first biplane used by the Flying Doctors is on display here. Nature lovers in particular stop in Katherine because the Cutta Cutta Caves Nature Park is just 24 km (15 miles) away to the south-east. The stalactite and stalagmite formations in the caves are an important refuge for rare bats and tree snakes.

⑯ Nitmiluk National Park This impressive network of canyons formed over thousands of years by the Katherine River is one of the greatest natural wonders of Australia – Katherine Gorge. Red-brown limestone canyon walls rise up to 100 m (328 ft) above the river. The best way to view them is from a sightseeing boat that

embarks in Katherine, or you can explore the river by canoe when it is not the rainy season. During the rainy season the otherwise calm river turns into a raging torrent and is not really navigable.

Biologists often marvel at Katherine Gorge for its unbelievable variety of wildlife – freshwater crocodiles live here, along with more than 160 species of birds and numerous butterfly species. All in all, nine of the thirteen gorges in the park are open to visitors.

Edith Falls is a particularly spectacular natural phenomenon. You can reach the falls by either taking the rough 75-km (48-mile) track, or the more comfortabe Stuart Highway. Smaller pools and waterfalls invite sun-weary visitors to take a refreshing swim.

⑰ Pine Creek This town, 90 km (56 miles) north-west of Katherine, was once a hot spot for gold diggers. Today it's a supply station for those on their way to Darwin, or the starting point for

excursions to the Kakadu National Park to the east. If you would like to visit that world-famous national park, leave the Stuart Highway at Pine Creek and take the Kakadu Highway towards Jabiru. You will find the park visitor centre there and can plan your trip.

⑱ Kakadu National Park Covering an area of 20,000 sq km (7,800 sq mi), this national park in Arnhem Land is one of the largest and most attractive in the Northern Territory of Australia. The scenery shifts from

the tidal zone at Van Diemen Gulf and the flood plains of the lowlands to the escarpment and the arid plateaus of Arnhem Land. The most impressive attraction is the escarpment, a craggy 500-km-long (310-mile) outcrop with spectacular waterfalls such as the Jim Jim Falls, Tain Falls and Twin Falls, which are at their best towards the end of the rainy season. The name of the park comes from 'Gagudju', which is the name of an Aboriginal language originating in this flood-plain region. Biologists have counted

their homes in the morning and evening sun while protecting them from the midday sun.

The Tabletop Range escarpment is a spectacular sight where waterfalls like Sandy Creek Falls, Florence Falls, Tower Falls and Wangi Falls cascade down the ridge even in the dry season. The unique environment around the falls has developed its own unique spectrum of monsoon rainforest wildlife.

⑳ Darwin Due to its proximity to the South-East Asian countries to the north of Australia, Darwin has developed into a culturally very diverse city, which is reflected in its numerous markets and restaurants. One of the specialities here is the daily, slightly odd Aquascene Fish Feeding at Doctor's Gulley. At high tide various fish swim onto land to be fed by hand from humans. Wonderful white sand beaches can be found on both sides of the scenic port town of Beagle Gulf. Since the destruction caused by Tornado Tracy during Christmas of 1974, the city of Darwin has changed dramatically. After the storm, almost nothing was left of the historic 19th-century buildings apart from the Old Navy Headquarters, Fanny Bay Jail, the Court House, Brown's Mart and the Government House with its seven gables. Your journey across the mighty outback ends here, on the coast at the doorstep to Asia.

1 The Arnhem Land Plateau escarpment in Kakadu National Park.

2 Magnetic termite mounds, bizarre yet clever constructions in Litchfield National Park.

3 Kakadu National Park: The falls cascade into the depths along the 500-km (310-mile) edge of the escarpment.

1,300 plant, 10,000 insect, 240 bird and seventy reptile species, including the feared saltwater crocodile. The rare mountain kangaroos, wallabies and one-third of the country's bird species are also native to this area. Due to its great diversity, this impressive park has been made into a UNESCO World Heritage Site.

There are over 5,000 Aborigine rock paintings here, the most famous of which are on Nourlinge Rock, Ubirr Rock and in Nangaluwur. The paintings, some of which date back as many as 18,000–23,000 years, not only demonstrate the area's climate change, but are also a striking portrayal of the culture of the Aborigines, who have allegedly lived on the continent here for 50,000 years. The best time of year to visit the park is in the dry season from May to November, as the roads are otherwise impassable.

The Arnhem Highway leads back through Cooinda and Jabiru to the Stuart Highway. From Noonaman the road leads south before heading west through Batchelor into Litchfield National Park.

⑲ Litchfield National Park The main attractions of this park are immediately visible – the open eucalyptus forests, the thick rainforest around the escarpment, and the massive, skilfully crafted gravestone-like mounds of the magnetic termites can reach heights of 2 m (6.5 ft). Due to the extreme midday heat the termites have cleverly aligned the long side of their mounds with the north-south axis in order to warm

Kings Canyon Aboriginal rock paintings line the steep walls of this spectacular canyon.

Kata Tjuta The name means 'many heads' in the Aborigines language. This group of thirty-six rock monoliths in the middle of the steppe in central Australia is also known as The Olgas.

Uluru Like a beached whale, the 348-m-wide (1,142-ft) outcrop, named Ayers Rock by Europeans, emerges stoically from the red outback landscape. A mythical and sacred place for Aborigines, Uluru is an essential element in the divine acts of the ancestors who created life on earth.

Coober Pedy Opals have been mined at the foot of the Stuart Range since 1915. Nearly 70 percent of the world's opals are mined here. Many people live in underground dwellings owing to temperatures above 50°C (122°F).

Dreamtrack For Aborigines, Australia's landscape is filled with traces of the creators. Songs and dances tell the complex stories of the creators and how the giants became the contours of the land.

Adelaide The capital of South Australia was founded in 1836 between the beaches of Gulf St Vincent and the Mount Lofty Range. It was named after Queen Adelaide.

Barossa This is the collective name for Barossa Valley and Eden Valley, the best wine-growing region in Australia, originally settled by Germans in the mid 19th century.

Finke Gorge National Park In this park, 12 km (7.5 miles) south of Hermannsburg, you will find the beautiful Palm Valley. Thanks to the tropical climate, many rare palm trees grow here, some as high as 25 m (82 ft).

Chambers Pillar Various tracks lead to the 56-m-high (180-ft) reddish-yellow sandstone rock south-east of Henbury. The pillars were used as an orientation point by early colonists who had gone astray in the desert.

Flinders Ranges This 400-km (248-mile) range begins north of Clare Valley and passes between Lake Torrens and Lake Frome. The national park extends deep into the outback and includes the famous Wilpena Pound.

Fleurieu Peninsula This headland to the south of Adelaide boasts a series of beautiful beaches, bays and ports. Divers and snorkellers enjoy Port Noarlunga on the north-east side, and surfers head for the high breakers on Waitpinga Beach.

Map labels:

Tennant Creek
MacDonnell Ranges
Mt.Hay 1250
Claraville
Mt.Zeil 1511
Mt.Liebig 1524
West MacDonnell N.P.
Sounds of Starlight Theatre
Trephina Gorge N.P.
N'dhala Gorge N.P.
Alice Springs
Hermannsburg
Watarrka N.P.
Finke Gorge N.P.
Santa Theresa
Kings Canyon
Orange Creek
Urrampinyu Jijiltjarri A.L.
Henbury
Maryvale
Wallara Ranch Roadhouse
Chambers Pillar
Northern Territory
Lake Amadeus
Angas Downs
The Olgas (Kata Tjuta) 1066
Mt.Ebenezer Roadhouse
Erldunda
Yulara
Uluru - Kata Tjuta N.P.
863
Ayers Rock (Uluru)
Curtin Springs
Kulgera Roadhouse
Tieyon
Agnes Creek
Granite Downs
Iwantja
Mimili
Marla
Wellbourn Hill
Mintable
Arckaringa
Mt.Willoughby
San Marino
Stuart Range
Mabel Creek
Coober Pedy
Opal Deposit
Ingomar
South
McDouall Peak
The Twins
Mount Eba
Bulgunnia
Bon Bon
Wymiet
Gosses
Purple Downs
Bosworth
Australia
Wilgena
Kingoonya
Glendambo
Parachilna
Woomera
Lake Torrens N.P.
Lake Gairdner N.P.
Pimba
Wonoka
Bookaloo
Flinders Ranges N.P.
Hawker
Cariewerloo
Quorn
Port Augusta
Wilmington
Peterborough
Kalgoorlie
Whyalla
Mt.Remarkable N.P.
Port Germein
Jamestown
Port Lincoln
Port Pirie
Crystal Brook
Port Broughton
Snowtown
Broken Hill
Spencer Gulf
Auburn
Kulpara
Port Wakefield
Mildura
Ardrossan
Barossa Valley
Virginia
Gawler
Yorke Peninsula
Adelaide
Morphettville Racecourse
Cape Spencer
Port Noarlunga
Hahndorf
Melbourne
Fleurieu Peninsula

Darwin The port on the northern edge of the 'Top End' benefits from a sub-tropical climate. The few historic buildings include the Old Navy Headquarters, Fannie Bay and Brown's Mart.

Wangi Falls The waterfalls in Litchfield National Park crash spectacularly into the depths. It is safe to bathe in the bay.

Litchfield National Park This park is known for its magnetic termite mounds, which are cleverly designed to take advantage of the sunshine.

Tennant Creek The second-largest town on the Stuart Highway was once a telegraph post on the Overland Telegraph Line. Gold was found here in 1932.

West Macdonnell Ranges The highest peak in this craggy mountain range to the east and west of Alice Springs is Mount Liebig, at 1,524 m (5,000 ft).

Alice Springs At the heart of the 'Red Centre': 1,700 km (1,055 miles) from Adelaide and 1,500 km (931 miles) from Darwin.

Cutta Cutta Caves Nature Park Rare bat species live alongside equally rare snakes in limestone caves 25 km (15 miles) south-east of Katherine, a jumping-off point for the park.

Devils Marbles The 170-million-year-old red granite blocks near Wauchope were formed by the constant temperature changes from glowing heat to icy cold.

Aboriginal rock art Rock carvings, rock and cave paintings, drawings of animals, sand designs, totem poles, carvings that feature and wickerwork are all part of Aborigine culture. The designs in their stone paintings were applied using ochre, charcoal and limestone.

John Flynn Memorial This memorial, located 20 km (12 miles) north of Tennant Creek, is dedicated to John Flynn (1880–1951), founder of the Flying Doctors back in 1939. The service was the most effective way to provide medical assistance to people in the outback.

Nourlangie Rock The Aborigine rock paintings at Nourlangie Rock in the Kakadu National Park are examples of the so-called 'X-ray style'.

Kakadu National Park Stone plateaus, waterfalls, flood plains and the South Alligator River characterize this park's landscape, one of Australia's best-known attractions in the 'Top End'.

Nitmiluk National Park Some of the highlights of this park are the rivers and ravines of Katherine Gorge, which go down to depths of 100 m (328 ft).

Davenport Range National Park Waterfoul and giant red kangaroos have found refuge in the mountains and steppes of this park.

Trephina Gorge National Park This park in the East Macdonnell Range is famous for its quartz cliffs and the eucalyptus stands that box in the Trephina Gorge watering holes.

Map labels:

Cape Hotham
Darwin
Crocodile Farm
Aboriginal Rock Art
Kakadu A.L.
Oenpelli
Point Stuart
Ubir
Territory Wildlife Park
Noonamah
Jabiru
Uranium Mine
Cooinda
Nourlangie Rock
Batchelor
Bark Hut Inn
Kakadu A.L.
Wangi Falls
Adelaide River
Kakadu N.P.
Litchfield N.P.
Hayes Creek
Jim Jim Falls Twin Falls
Elsherana
Hot Springs
Pine Creek
Nitmiluk N.P.
Ferguson River
Katherine Gorge
Oulloo
Jawoyn A.L.
Dorisvale
Wagiman A.L.
Beswick
Katherine
Elsey N.P.
Kununurra
Cutta Cutta Caves
Matarank
Gorrie
Hist. Railway Station
Larrimah
Daly Waters
Burketown
Hidden Valley
Dunmarra
Northern
Newcastle Waters
Beetaloo
Lake Woods
Territory
Renner Springs
Helen Springs Roadhouse
Banka Banka
Brunchilly
Phillip Creek
John Flynn Memorial
Warumungu Aboriginal Land
Mount Isa
Warrego Mine
Three Way Roadhouse
Tennant Creek
Nobles Nob Mine
Karlantijpa South A.L.
Epenarra
Devils Marbles
Wauchope
Davenport Range N.P.
Hatches Creek
Numagalong
Murray Downs
Barrow Creek
Pawu A.L.
Stirling
Mount Skinner
Ti-Tree
Woodgreen
Napperby
Aileron
Bushy Park
Alcoota
Mt.Zeil 1511
Mt.Hay 1250
West MacDonnell N.P.
Sounds of Starlight Theatre
Claraville
Trephina Gorge N.P.
N'dhala Gorge N.P.
Alice Springs

Australia

The Pacific Highway – from the Blue Mountains to the Gold Coast

As you travel along Australia's colorful Pacific coastline, you will soon appreciate why Australians call their homeland "the lucky country". The national parks transport visitors into a magical, largely unspoilt, subtropical wonderland. The stunning and romantic Blue Mountains, formed on a sandstone plateau, reach elevations of more than 1,000 m (3,281 ft) and feature magnificent primeval rainforests that are millions of years old. The coast is dotted with interesting towns and unfathomably long beaches.

New South Wales, proudly named the 'Premier State', offers one of the most attractive sections of the Australia's Pacific coast. Not only is it the oldest state in the country, it is also has the largest and densest population, and the strongest economy. Common theory says that navigator and explorer Captain Cook gave the state its name in 1770, as the coastline reminded him of his homeland of Wales. With its heavily populated areas and developed landscape, New South Wales now forms a stark contrast to the vast empty expanses of the rest of the Australian continent. Indeed, it would be hard to beat the variety offered along the seaboard between Sydney and Brisbane. The steep slopes and deep wooded gorges of the Blue Mountains, cloaked in their signature bluish haze, are some of the most impressive sights in Australia. Combine that dramatic landscape of bizarre rock formations with

Border Ranges National Park is home to tall palm ferns and strangler figs.

Australia competes with places like Hawaii and California as one of the world's surfing meccas.

Sydney Harbour Bridge is a magnificent construction. The city's iconic building is the striking Opera House, opened in 1973, and declared a UNESCO World Heritage site in 2007.

the lush subtropical rainforests on the coastal plains nearby, with their huge variety of plant and animal life, and you could hardly ask for more. Lamington and Border Ranges National Parks on the border with Queensland have huge trees wrapped in vines, strangler figs and tree ferns. In fact, the entire string of national parks along the coast is a UNESCO World Natural Heritage Site, designated as East Coast Temperate and Subtropical Rainforest.

The Eastern Highlands run parallel to the coast, falling away dramatically to the east where the Great Dividing Range gives way to a fertile coastal plain. The plain begins to widen to the north, traversed by estuaries that have formed countless bays and inviting sandy beaches. The major towns and cities are concentrated in this region. The Gold Coast, in the south of Queensland, has developed into a very popular holiday area for both locals and tourists. Favourable wind conditions and endless beaches make it a paradise for surfers in particular, but sun worshippers will be more than satisfied as well.

Nestled in the romantic valleys at the edge of the highlands are Australia's oldest vineyards, including the Lower Hunter Valley west of Newcastle. Of the cities along the Pacific coast, Sydney holds the number one slot, with myriad examples of impressive modern engineering and architecture and a huge variety of cultural attractions. The southeast coast of Australia is best explored from the Pacific Highway. It connects the Bruce Highway, heading north from Brisbane, with the Princes Highway, which heads south from Sydney.

Eastern Australia's coastal waters are home to many species of shark.

The Pacific Highway connects Sydney in New South Wales with Brisbane in Queensland. The Highway mainly runs parallel to the coast, and roads off of it lead to the most famous sights and attractions along the eastern Australian seaboard. These include the mountains of the Great Dividing Range, idyllic vineyards in Hunter Valley, coastal rainforests and the holiday paradise of the Gold Coast.

1

1 Sydney (see pp. 336–337) Sydney is in the center of Australia's south-eastern coast. The 2000 Olympic Games are now a thing of the past, but there is no shortage of activities for everyone. It is unlikely you'll be bored in Sydney, unless none of the following strikes your fancy: fabulous restaurants, huge shopping centers, a spectacular variety of cultural attractions and events, a fascinating history exhibited in various museums and buildings, stunning city beaches, and a range of national parks right at your doorstep.

2 Ku-Ring-Gai Chase National Park This park is situated on a sandstone plateau traversed by rivers. Its northern border is formed by Broken Bay, an estuary of the Hawkesbury River. The park encompasses a classic Sydney landscape of beaches, bushland, eucalyptus forest and heath land, and boasts a huge network of waterways to keep canoeists and anglers happy. The well-preserved rock paintings and engravings by the Gurringai Aborigines, who once lived here and gave the park its name, are well worth seeing. Follow the route inland via Sydney along the Great Western

Highway (Hwy. 32) toward the Blue Mountains.

3 Blue Mountains National Park For many years the Blue Mountains, part of the Great Dividing Range, formed an insurmountable barrier for people living along the coast. The first successful crossing of the mountain range was not made until 1813, finally allowing access to much-needed pastures in the west.

Sydneysiders flock to the Blue Mountains for their magnificent cliffs, gorges and caverns. The Three Sisters rock formation and the Jenolan Caves are just two of the many attractions that lure city dwellers and travelers to theses mountains. Putty Road, between the small gold-rush towns of Windsor and Singleton, passes through the northern Blue Mountains and along the eastern boundary of Wollemi National Park.

4 Wollemi National Park This is the largest park of its kind in New South Wales, a huge wilderness area covering

5,000 sq km (1,930 sq mi) that is for the most part unspoilt and even very isolated in parts. The park features deep sandstone

Travel Information

Route profile
Length: approx. 1,100 km (684 mi) without detours
Time required: min. 1 week
Start: Sydney
End: Brisbane
Route (main locations):
Sydney, Blue Mountains National Park, Port Macquarie, Yuraygir National Park, Byron Bay, Gold Coast, Brisbane

Traffic information:
The Pacific Highway connects the two largest cities on the east coast, Sydney and Brisbane, and serves the major holiday regions in Queens-

land. Be prepared for a high volume of traffic in the densely populated coastal areas at weekends and during holidays.

Information:
Here are some websites to help you plan your trip.

General:
www.australia.com
New South Wales:
www.visitnsw.com.au
Queensland:
www.queenslandholidays. com.au
Sydney: www.sydney.com.au
Weather: ww.bom.gov.au

gorges and wonderful pristine landscapes along the Colo and Wollemi rivers. Basalt outcrops reach heights of over 1,200 m (3,937 ft), and rainforests thrive on the mountains and in the valleys.

Visitors can choose from a variety of activities including bush-walking through the wilderness, rock climbing or canoeing along the rivers. In 1994, David Noble discoverd the first living Wollemia pine tree in the park – 2-million-year-old fossils had been found, but no living specimens.

At Singleton, north-east of the park, join Highway 15 and head east through the Upper Hunter Valley, a region famous for horse breeding and vineyards, to one of Australia's most famous wine regions, the Lower Hunter Valley.

⑤ Lower Hunter Valley Cessnock is the main town at the

heart of the this wine-producing region. Farms and vineyards are nestled among gently rolling hills, and to the west you can just make out the foothills of the Great Dividing Range. Grapes have been cultivated in the fertile soil of this region since the 1830s, and there are around 140 wineries in the valley, most of them open to visitors. Among the most famous are Lindemans, Tyrrell's Wines and Wyndham Estate. In stark contrast, the main industries in nearby Newcastle, the second-

largest city in New South Wales, are steel, coal and shipping. Around 40 km (25 mi) north of Newcastle, it is worth making a stop in Port Stephens, the 'dolphin capital of Australia'.

⑥ Port Stephens Droves of tourists come to this port to enjoy a trip on a dolphin-watching boat to see the 150–200 dolphins that make Nelson Bay their home. Between May and July, and September and November, pods of whales also swim past the coast here,

among them killer whales, minkes and humpbacks.

Port Stephens is also famous for Stockton Beach, some 33 km (21 mi) long, where you can even take your four-wheel-drive for a spin in the sand.

Myall Lakes National Park is 60 km (37 mi) to the north and is the largest lake area in New South Wales.

⑦ Port Macquarie Founded in 1821 as a penal colony, Port Macquarie is one of the oldest towns in Australia. The Port Macquarie Museum and Courthouse, St Thomas' Anglican Church and the Roto House, all built in the 19th century, are still standing today. Since the 1970s, tourism has boosted the town's fortunes remarkably, and it is also popular among retired Australians, who enjoy the town's relaxed atmosphere. There are plenty of swimming and surfing beaches and a wide variety of other water sports in general on offer.

Heading north along the Pacific Highway, you enter increasingly humid and damp regions, home to dense rainforests. The route then leaves the coastal highway at Kempsey for another detour into the impressive Great Dividing Range. You travel via Bellingen and Dorrigo on the way to New England National Park.

⑧ New England National Park Covering an area of 300 sq km (116 sq mi), this park is situated on the escarpment of the New England Plateau at an

1 The fine blue haze that gives the Blue Mountains their name is formed by an oily mist released by the eucalyptus trees.

2 The magnificent 'Three Sisters' rock formation south-east of Katoomba is a landmark in the World Heritage Blue Mountains park.

335

Sydney

The oldest and largest city on the Australian continent, Sydney, the capital of New South Wales, has a population of over four million and is Australia's leading commercial and financial center. Numerous universities, museums and galleries also make Sydney the cultural center of the south-east coast.

In 1788, when the first wave of settlers – mostly convicts and their guards – came ashore under the command of Captain Arthur Phillip, none of them could have imagined that Port Jackson would one day become one of the most beautiful cities in the world. Admittedly, back in those days there was none of the laid-back, almost Mediterranean charm of present-day Sydney. Life for convicts and soldiers was rough and tumble. But things began to change towards the end of the 18th century with the first free settlers. Several gold-rushes then followed, the first of which took place in 1851.

Sydney's expansion first began with the arrival of European and then of Asian immigrants, a mixture that characterizes the city's present-day multicultural atmosphere. It is also a major financial center, and for most visitors to Australia it is the first stop on their tour of the fifth continent. From 250 m (820 ft) up on the viewing platform of the 305-m (1,001 ft) Sydney Tower, you get a magnificent view of the skyline, the port, the smart residential suburbs, the Pacific coast and, further inland, the Blue Mountains – not to mention the city's second great landmark, the Harbour Bridge. This amazing construction forms a graceful arc across the bay at a height of 134 m (440 ft) and with a span of 503 m (1,650 ft) over the water.

The best place to begin your tour of the city is the port, with the Harbour Bridge and the Opera House within striking distance. You could also start by people-watching from one of the many cafés, listening to the street musicians or taking a boat trip around the port. The Rocks area is a must for shoppers and pub-goers. From the city center, an elevated railway takes you to Darling Harbour and its myriad attractions. On the somewhat quieter side, the Botanic Gardens feature a cross-section of Australian flora in a tranquil and relaxing setting far from the crowds.

Chinatown is on the south side of town and, like most Chinatowns around the world, has its own unique charm that reflects the relationship and proximity to Asia. Cabramatta, an outlying district some 30 km (18.5 mi) west of the city, is the Vietnamese equivalent of Chinatown. Other districts worth visiting include Victorian-style Paddington, east of downtown, and the nightclub district, Kings Cross.

Top: Sydney Tower rises between the roofs of the Sydney Opera House. The viewing platform is 250 m (820 ft) up.
Bottom, left: Sydney and its Harbour Bridge, one of the most stunning views in Australia.
Top, left: The Sydney Opera House, an modern expressionist masterpiece, designe by Jorn Utzon, appears like pile of orange peels at the edge of the Harbour.

1

elevation of 1,400 m (4,593 ft). It encompasses one of the largest rainforests in New South Wales and features snow gum trees in the upper regions, temperate rainforest vegetation at the middle elevations, and subtropical rainforest with tree-high ferns at the base of the plateau. Drive up to Point Lookout at 1,562 m (5,125 ft) for a wonderful view of the highland escarpment and the Bellinger Valley.

On the return journey to the coast it is certainly worth making a detour to Dorrigo National Park (see sidebar left). From Dorrigo, the Waterfall Way takes you back to the coast.

Coffs Harbour boasts a series of attractive beaches and is one of the most popular holiday resorts in the state. Banana plantations have been the mainstay of the region's agriculture for more than one hundred years, and reflects the

gradual change in climate from subtropical to tropical. Just a few miles north of Coffs Harbour, the Pacific Highway heads inland toward Grafton.

⑨ Grafton This country town, nestled on the banks of the Clarence River, is known as the 'Jacaranda capital of Australia', and its wide, elegant streets are lined with these beautifully fragrant trees. The Jacaranda Festival takes place when the trees bloom in late October or early November. Grafton was founded by lumberjacks around 1830, with cattle farmers following later. When gold was discovered in the upper reaches of the Clarence River, the town developed rapidly and a busy river port flourished around 1880. Traces of the town's late 19th-century prosperity can be seen in a number of well-preserved buildings on the north side of the river.

2

A track from Grafton leads to Wooli, the gateway to Yuraygir National Park, about 50 km (31 mi) away.

⑩ Yuraygir National Park This national park encompasses the longest stretch of pristine coastline in New South Wales. It

perfectly shows how the coast looked before it became so densely populated and boasts remote sandy beaches, heaths, swamps and lagoons.

The national park has some excellent walking trails and offers perfect conditions for both surfers and anglers.

the city of the same name at its heart, is home to a plethora of luxury hotels, holiday complexes, motels, holiday apartments, guesthouses and comfortable youth hostels like nowhere else in the whole country. It offers an unrivaled variety of sporting and leisure activities, and more opportunities for entertainment and shopping than you are likely to find anywhere else. This section of coastline begins on the border with New South Wales and stretches to Coomera, south of Brisbane. The subtropical climate, with temperatures ranging from 22°C to 28°C (72°F to 83°F), and an annual quota of 300 days of sunshine, attracts over three million visitors per year.

14 Surfers Paradise The first holiday development in the Gold Coast's best-known resort opened in 1923. It was called 'Surfers Paradise Hotel' and just a few years later the entire area adopted the name. The town flourished in the 1950s, mostly because of the triple-S factor: sun, surf and sand.

Buildings sprang up, and today the whole length of lovely, sandy beach is lined with a strip of hotel and apartment complexes. With all the leisure and sporting activities, entertainment and a lively nightlife on offer, Surfers Paradise just seems to get more and more popular.

15 Coomera The northern end of the Gold Coast is now home

12 Byron Bay This surfer, hippie enclave-cum-holiday resort gets its name not from the famous poet, but from his grandfather, John Byron, a renowned navigator in the 1760s. It has a mild and sunny climate, splendidly long beaches and perfect wind conditions, all of which have made this surfing paradise into one of the most popular seaside resorts on the north-east coast of New South Wales.

If you don't feel like exploring the beaches of the neighboring Gold Coast to the north, take a detour into the hinterland instead. Some 50 km (31 mi) north of Byron, in Murwillumbah, the Summerland Way turns off into the spectacular Border Ranges National Park.

13 Gold Coast Nothing compares to this unique seaside as the destination no. 1 all over Australia. The Gold Coast, with

11 Yamba This 19th-century fishing village is about 60 km (37 mi) further north, and has become an angler's paradise. The beautiful beaches offer myriad water sports options, and there are rewarding fishing spots on the Clarence River, in the nearby coastal lakes and along the coast. Angourie Point, just 5 km (3 mi) south of Yamba, is one of the best surfing beaches in the country. The Pacific Highway now heads north along the seemingly endless string of white-sand beaches toward Byron Bay, about 120 km (75 mi) away.

1 The most powerful lighthouse in Australia is on the Cape Byron headland, 107 m (351 ft) above the ocean.

2 The Lower Hunter Valley has been home to the Lindemans Pokolbin winery since 1870.

to a string of leisure and theme parks. Dreamworld, right on the Pacific Highway, offers thrilling rides. Not far to the south is Movie World, a movie theme park. Wet'n'Wild offers aquatic fun, while Sea World, Australia's largest marine park, entertains visitors with a variety of shows featuring dolphins, sea lions, and aqua ballet.

Before reaching Brisbane, make a quick detour into the hinterland to the south-east of the city. From Coomera a minor road takes you 90 km (56 mi) to Highway 15. Main Range National Park is 15 km (9 mi) to the south.

16 Main Range National Park
This national park covers an area of just under 200 sq km (77 sq mi) and features impressively high mountains, steep escarpments and plateaus. It forms the western border of the Scenic Rim, a spectacular semicircle of mountains that runs from here to Lamington National Park, south-west of Brisbane. The range is protected by an almost uninterrupted chain of national parks.

The park features a variety of vegetation, from rainforest in the humid, protected areas, and eucalyptus woodland at higher altitudes and on the dry slopes, to montane heath on the escarpments of the plateau and on the mountain peaks. The different zones provide habitat for the various animals that are endangered elsewhere by clearcutting and bushfires.

Leaving Main Range National Park and its many forest and bushland hiking trails, it is only another 120 km (75 mi) on Highway 15 to Brisbane and the end of the Pacific Highway.

17 Brisbane
The capital of Queensland is on the Brisbane River, a few kilometers west of the point where it flows into the Pacific. With a population of 1.5 million and a modern, expanding economy, Brisbane enjoyed a boom in the 1980s, triggered by EXPO 88, the World Fair, which was held on the Brisbane River. These days, Brisbane does not take part in national competitions for Australia's best city. It is confident that it would win hands down anyway. Tourism and agriculture have meanwhile made Brisbane an affluent city, with a variety of cultural institutions including the Queensland Cultural Centre, several exhibition halls, concert and theater venues, and parks. The relatively small inner city area is easy to explore on foot, but for added charm and speed, try the old-style tram.

The Sunshine Coast to the north and the Gold Coast to the south both epitomize the Brisbane lifestyle – sun, sand, surf.

1 Monuments to the tourist boom: high-rise hotels line the beach at Surfers Paradise on the Gold Coast.

2 Boats moored off the banks of the Brisbane River against the skyline of Queensland's capital.

Lamington National Park Five hundred waterfalls, subtropical rainforest and diverse birdlife make this the most popular park in Australia.

Border Ranges National Park This park contains the remnants of a former shield volcano. Its subtropical rainforests are a UNESCO World Heritage Site.

Dorrigo National Park Various trails and the Skywalk take visitors through subtropical rainforest and eucalyptus woodlands filled with orchids, ferns and birdlife.

Jenolan Caves/Blue Mountains The impressively lit Jenolan Caves in the Blue Mountains are among the largest limestone caverns on the continent.

East Coast Temperate and Subtropical Rainforest Parks Wet eucalyptus forests typify the vegetation in the temperate and subtropical latitudes of Australia's Pacific coast. Mosses and ferns also grow in these zones.

Kanangra Walls Walks along the clifftops and ledges next to the vertical drops afford some breathtaking views – and might give you vertigo.

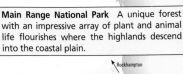

Main Range National Park A unique forest with an impressive array of plant and animal life flourishes where the highlands descend into the coastal plain.

Rockhampton
Glasshouse Mts.
Beerwah
Mundubbera
Bongaree
Moreton I. N.P.
Woodford
Miles
Esk
Toowoomba
Moree
Ipswich
BRISBANE
Queensland
Main Range N.P.
Movie World
Coomera
Sea World
Goondiwindi
Dreamworld
Surfers Paradise
Warwick
Beaudesert
Gold Coast
Lamington N.P.
Tweed Heads
Kingscliff
Woodenbong
Border Ranges
Murwillumbah
Stanthorpe
N.P.
Brunswick Heads
Byron Bay
Sundown
N.P.
Girraween N.P.
Broken Head
Lismore
Mallanganee
Tenterfield
Ballina
Goondiwindi
Woodburn
1524
Baryulgil
Bundjalung
Mt.Bajimba
Washpool
N.P.
Angourie
Glen
N.P.
Yamba
Innes
Maclean
Nymboida N.P.
Yuraygir N.P.
Grafton
Wooli
Tyringham
Dorrigo
Australian East Coast
N.P.
Cathedral
Dorrigo
Woolgoolga
Rock N.P.
Coffs Harbour
Wollomombi
New England N.P.
Urunga
Oxley Wild
Rivers N.P.
Bell Brook
Macksville
Temperate and Subtropical
South West
Werrikimbe N.P.
Rocks
Tamworth
Kempsey
Hat Head N.P.
Yarrowitch
Telegraph Point
New South
Port Macquarie
Wauchope
Bonnie Hills
Wales
Rainforest Parks
Crowdy Bay N.P.
Wingham
Harrington
Mt. Barrington
Taree
Tamworth
1554 Gloucester
Muswellbrook
Tuncurry
Nabiac
Denman
Bungwahl
Singleton
Bulahdelah
Myall Lakes N.P.
Wollemi N.P.
Maitland
Hawkes Nest
Cessnock
Karuah
Port Stephens
Blue Mountains
Putty
N.P.
Yengo N.P.
Lower Hunter
Newcastle
Valley
Dubbo
Lithgow
Budgewoi
Three Sisters
Wisemans
The Entrance
Windsor
Ferry
North Avoca Back Reef
Katoomba
Ku-Ring-Gai Chase N.P.
Jenolan
Penrith
Caves
SYDNEY
Kanangra-Boyd
Liverpool
N.P.
Nattai N.P.
Royal N.P.
Canberra
Stanwell Park
Nowra
Wollongong

Surfers Paradise The array of leisure activities, sports and entertainment leaves no time for boredom in what is probably Australia's best-known seaside holiday resort.

Byron Bay The lighthouse offers a magnificent panoramic view over land and sea.

Surfers' coast Australia's coasts offer surfers ideal conditions for their sport and some of the world's best surfers come from here. It's ususally possible to rent boards if you want to give it a go.

Port Macquarie This sunny coastal town is one of Australia's oldest settlements. It is popular with all ages and a paradise for water sports enthusiasts.

Port Stephens This port is famous for its dolphins. Take a boat out into the bay and in no time you'll be joined by a handful of these lively creatures. You can even swim with the dolphins in the safety of a drift net. It is a magical and unforgettable experience.

Hunter Valley The vineyards in Australia's oldest wine-growing region give visitors the chance to sample some of the excellent local varieties.

Sydney The oldest and largest city in Australia is one of the world's belvoed ports – even more so after the 2000 Olympic Games. In just two hundred years, Sydney has grown from a miserable penal camp into the most important economic center on the continent.

The snow-capped summit of Aoraki/Mount Cook is sacred to the Maori.

New Zealand

The South Island: glaciers, fiords and rainforests

Visitors to New Zealand's South Island can expect some absolutely fabulous scenery. You will enjoy one spectacular view after another as you travel along the coast or to the highest peaks in the interior. Some of the more remote regions are difficult to reach, making for a great diversity of plant and wildlife. The island's mountains, lakes and rivers are ideal for those in search of outdoor adventures.

Many consider that New Zealand's South Island embraces the whole range of the world's landscapes in perfect harmony. In the sun-drenched north, the Tasman Sea's large waves pound the shore, while you can relax on the sandy beaches in its sheltered bays. Further south, the agricultural flatlands of Canterbury Plain spread across the eastern side of the island. Although the South Island is much larger than its northern counterpart, it is much less densely populated. Large areas of the interior are almost uninhabited. Only five percent of New Zealand's Maori population lives on the South Island, so there are far fewer Maori sacred sites than on the North Island. On the east coast, you will find two lively, cosmopolitan cities with a distinctly European flavour: Christchurch and Dunedin. Christchurch still boasts colonial buildings and extensive parks and is often described as the

Brown kiwi.

most English city outside England, with good reason. As you stroll through the port city of Dunedin with its many Victorian-Gothic buildings and its lovely parks, you will be reminded of its Scottish heritage: the very name of the city derives from the Gaelic name for the Scottish capital, while the names of some of its streets and quarters will transport you briefly to Edinburgh. Further to the south and west, the plains give way to more hilly country, which rises to form the snow-covered peaks of the Southern Alps. This mountainous region, which forms the backbone of the South Island, is accessible by only a few roads. The highest

Coastal landscape near Akaroa on the Banks Peninsula, south-east of Christchurch.

Milford Sound, with its steep forest-clad rock faces, is one of the major attractions in New Zealand's South Island.

mountain in the Southern Alps is Aoraki/Mount Cook, originally named after Captain Cook, the British explorer. Five powerful glaciers flow from its summit (3,764 m/12,350 ft) down into the valley. In the Maori language, the mountain is known by its more poetic name Aoraki (Cloud Piercer).

The south-west of the island is one of New Zealand's most attractive regions, and Queenstown, on the northern shore of Lake Wakatipu, makes a perfect starting point for exploring it. Several fiords, such as the famous Milford Sound, penetrate deep into the island. There are some dramatic waterfalls, Sutherland Falls among them, and a number of impressive dripstone caves. Fiordland National Park at 12,000 sq km

(4,632 sq mi) is the country's largest protected area and a designated UNESCO World Heritage Site, a status it certainly deserves. It is home to a wide range of bird species. This route takes you to a number of large mountain lakes, known collectively as the Southern Lakes Region, which includes Lakes Te Anau, Wakatipu and Wanaka. A little further north, in Westland National Park, fifty-eight glaciers flow down from the mountain tops almost to the west coast. The Franz Josef and Fox Glaciers are the most famous, but the South Island has around three hundred such ice-flows, some of which can be several kilometers long. Owing to the island's high levels of precipitation, the coastal areas are usually covered in jungle-like rain-

forests. Following our route northwards along the west coast, you will come across villages that look much the same as they did at the time of the New Zealand gold-rush, which lured many people to seek their fortunes in the area in the 1860s. When it came to an end,

some communities, such as Greymouth, switched to coal-mining to sustain their economy. Agriculture continues to play an important role. Although the large majority of the population lives in the towns and cities, farming is vital to the economy of the South Island.

Countless islands, bays and fiords break up the coastline in the north of the South Island.

The South Island is full of amazing scenic contrasts. It has every imaginable variety of landscape: from sandy beaches to jagged mountains, from rocky shores to impressive glaciers and from dense rainforests and expanses of southern beech to meadows and pastures.
The island also has a good road network.

1 Picton Our trip around the South Island starts from this pretty port in the far north of the island. It is here that the ferries arrive from Wellington. It usually takes around 3.5 hours to travel across the Cook Strait and through Queen Charlotte Sound to reach the former whaling station of Picton. Sailing ships anchor regularly in the picturesque bays of the fiord, and you can take boat trips to the most beautiful destinations along the magical coastline around historic Picton.
Picton itself is more than just a stopover on the way to the heart of the South Island. The Picton Community Museum, dedicated to the discoveries of Captain Cook and to the heyday of whaling, offers an excellent introduction to the history of the island. A number of museum ships are anchored permanently in the port, the main attraction being the *Edwin Fox*, the last survivor of a large fleet that brought thousands of immigrants from Europe to New Zealand. The Seahorse World Aquarium gives a wonderful overview of local marine life. There's an interesting excursion east to Robin Hood Bay, although the route involves some very steep roads, and is a

challenge for both cars and drivers. It takes twenty minutes to reach the Karaka Point peninsula where the fortifications of a former Maori settlement are worth visiting.

2 Marlborough Sounds The fiords north of Picton are full of islands, bays, caves and a maze of waterways. Valleys in the area were flooded when the sea level rose after the last ice age. What were once hills are now mere islands jutting out of the sea. The coastline is 1,500 km (932 mi) long. You will enjoy constantly changing views on the hiking trails, including the Queen Charlotte Track, which is 67 km (42 miles) long and can also be tackled by mountain bike. A trip through the sounds by boat or kayak is a very special experience, and you will find several places where you can hire boats (and bikes). The region's famed Queen Charlotte Drive is the most scenic road. Allowing for stops, you should complete the winding 35-km (22-mi) route in around three hours. It is a well-signposted road, ending up in

Havelock, known for its green-shell mussels, from where you can continue to the next destination on our route, either back via Picton or via the vineyards in the Wairau Valley.

3 Blenheim This town enjoys around 2,600 hours of sunshine per year, making it one of the

Travel Information

Route profile
Length: approx. 2,500 km (1,500 mi) without detours
Time required: 2–3 weeks
Start and end: Picton
Route (main locations): Picton, Christchurch, Aoraki (Mount Cook) National Park, Invercargill, Fjordland National Park, Queenstown, Westland National Park, Karamea, Picton

Traffic information:
Cars drive on the left in New Zealand. The blood-alcohol limit for driving is .05. In metropolitan areas, the speed limit is 50 km/h

(31 mph); outside the towns it is 100 km/h (62 mph).

When to go:
In the southern part of the country, some higher altitude roads may become impassable during the winter (June to September) and sometimes also in early spring and late autumn. The best time to travel is December to March.

Information
www.newzealand.com
www.tourism.net.nz

Weather
www.metservice.co.nz

country's most sun-drenched spots. Almost everything in Blenheim revolves around wine and the region's mild climate is perfect for growing vines. West of Blenheim, New Renwick Road, Middle Renwick Road and Old Renwick Road take you to some of New Zealand's most famous vineyards, such as Highfield Estate, Allan Scott Wines and Estates and Stoneleigh Vineyards. Blenheim hosts a famous wine festival during the second week of February, featuring wine, food and entertainment.

New Zealand's only salt production plant is located 35 km (22 miles) south of Blenheim; its salt heaps are visible for miles. Highway I now hugs the water, running between the shore and the Seaward Kaikoura Range, parallel to the coastline.

❹ Kaikoura In the 19th century, this town was a famous whaling station. Nowadays, only a few whalebones serve as a reminder of bygone days, such as those you can see in the Garden of Memories. Fyffe House has carvings made of whale teeth. Kaikoura Bay itself is spectacular, set against the backdrop of the coastal mountains reaching nearly 3,000 m (10,000 ft). It is a perfect spot for whale watching. Warm and cold ocean currents meet in the coastal waters, and you can enjoy spotting sperm whales, orcas and several species of dolphin, all of which come to feed on the plentiful supplies of fish. Remember to look up from time to time to spot great albatrosses with wingspans extending to more than 3 m (10 ft). Only a few miles south of Kaikoura, you come to the Maori Leap Cave. Large numbers of bird and seal skeletons were discovered in this lovely dripstone cave. As you travel further south you will begin to notice more and more vineyards.

❺ Waipara This town is now the center of a relatively new wine-growing area. Vines have only been cultivated here successfully since the 1980s. Many vineyards are located along the smaller roads leading off the main route. If you are coming from Kaikoura, the Main North Road takes you to Glenmark Wines and Torlesse Wines. Take Reeces Road to Daniel Schuster Wines and MacKenzies Road to Fiddler's Green Wines. Chardonnay, Pinot Noir and Sauvignon Blanc grapes are cultivated in the area, together with Gewürztraminers.

Many vineyards offer wine tastings. At Christchurch Information Centre, you can even book a trip in a horse-drawn carriage through the vineyards.

❻ Christchurch The largest city on the South Island was founded as recently as 1850. Today, it is the political, economic and cultural hub of the island. Thanks to its lovely, sweeping parks and well-kept gardens, it is also known as the 'garden city'. Its clubs and cricket grounds and late 19th-century English-style architecture make Christchurch the 'most English town outside England'. Try to park your car on the outskirts as, despite its size, the center of town is easily manageable on foot. Enjoy a sightseeing tour on one of the lovingly restored trams that make regular stops in the city center.

The city is laid out in a grid pattern, and as a result it is quite easy to find your way around. Cathedral Square is dominated by the massive cathedral (1864– 1904), the city's landmark. Inside this monumental church, you'll find an exhibition on the history of the Anglican Church in New Zealand. You can climb halfway up the steeple (65 m/215 ft) to enjoy a beautiful view of the city. South of

1 The Inland Kaikoura Range runs parallel to the Seaward Kaikoura Range from north-east to southwest. The Clarence River divides the ranges.

2 Historic trams in Christchurch city center.

3 The mountains of the Seaward Kaikoura Range on the Kaikoura Peninsula run all the way down to sea level.

Cathedral Square is City Mall, the city's main shopping street. Many visitors also take a boat trip on the River Avon which winds its way across the city in numerous loops, with lovely weeping willows growing along its banks. In marked contrast to Christchurch itself is the mountainous Banks Peninsula just south of the city on the Canterbury Plains; the region is volcanic in origin. The port town of Lyttleton and the summer resort of Akaroa with its quiet beaches are also worth visiting.

7 Aoraki/Mount Cook National Park This National Park is one of the absolute highlights of a trip to the South Island of New Zealand, and not simply because of its altitude. The park was established in 1953 and covers an area of 700 sq km (270 sq miles). In addition to Aoraki/Mount Cook itself (3,764 m/12,350 ft), there are thirteen mountains, all at altitudes of more than 3,000 m (9,843 ft), including some very famous peaks such as Mount Tasman (3,498 m/11,477 ft). Forty percent of the park's surface area is covered in glaciers and high levels of precipitation around the mountain peaks provide a continuous supply of snow and ice. The Tasman Glacier flows directly from the summit of Aoraki/Mount Cook. It is some 27 km (17 miles) long and up to 3 km (2 miles) wide, making it the longest glacier in the country.

It will take you some time to get here from Christchurch, but you will find spectacular scenery along the way. Driving across the Canterbury Plains, you first reach Timaru, where you turn north-west onto Highway 8. From Twizel, take Aoraki/Mount Cook Road (Highway 80) to Aoraki/Mount Cook village. This access road is

sealed and generally in good condition. It climbs slowly, taking you along the western shore of Lake Pukaki in which, on a clear day, you can see the reflections of the park's giant mountains. The village sits at an altitude of 762 m (2,500 ft) amid the fabulous mountain scenery, and has all the amenities you are likely to need, including an information center. An alternative route takes you inland from Christchurch via Sheffield and Mount Hutt to Fairlie along Highway 8, and then follows the route already described. One of the highlights of the National Park is a visit to the lower part of the Tasman Glacier, which you can reach via the road to Blue Lake. After about 8 km (5 miles), park your vehicle and climb for around thirty minutes until you reach the Tasman Glacier viewpoint. From here, you can see the Aoraki/Mount Cook range in all its glory. At higher altitudes, skiers can enjoy a number of ski resorts that remain open throughout the year. The visitor center can provide you with detailed information on what to do in the National Park. Several hiking trails start here, too, and they are well signposted although very stony in places.

8 Twizel This town at the junction of Aoraki/Mount Cook Road and Highway 8 started out as a builder's campsite erected to service the construction of a hydroelectric dam. As part of this project, several lakes were created, including Lake Pukaki and Lake Tekapo in the north-east. The dam was highly controversial at the time, but one positive consequence was the development of the Mackenzie Hydro Lakes recreational area, which now provides ideal conditions for water sports. The lakes are full of fish, and you can hire boats from various places. Another attraction in Twizel is the Kaki Visitor Hide where ornithologists can observe the wading kaki (black stilt), one of the country's rarest birds, undisturbed.

Just 25 km (16 miles) south of Twizel you come to Omarama, whose north-west thermals make it a perfect spot for glid-

ers and paragliders. The 'Clay Cliffs' 10 km (6 miles) west of Omarama are a geological phenomenon but this jagged, rocky landscape with its many stone pinnacles is relatively difficult to get to. Our route now follows Highway 8 south to Cromwell at the eastern flank of the Southern Alps.

9 Cromwell This town is located at the point where the Kawarau and Clutha rivers meet and started out as a settlement for gold-diggers. The gold-rush arrived in Cromwell in the 1860s but quickly moved on to the west coast. At the end of the 19th century, the last of the pioneers left town. Part of the settlement was flooded when the dam was built, but some buildings of historical significance were moved to higher ground and restored to create Old Cromwell Town. At a few kilometers west of Cromwell is the

3

Milford Sound This fiord is 16 km (10 miles) long and becomes wider as it makes its way inland. Tall mountains surround the coastline of the South West New Zealand World Heritage Site, known in Maori as Te Wahipounamu, and rise suddenly above the waterline, their slopes covered in rainforests. Mitre Peak (1,692 m/6,437 ft), with its remarkable conical shape, is one of the most-photographed spots in New Zealand. The mountain peaks are reflected in the clear, still waters of the fiord.

From the town of Milford, located on the south-eastern shore of Milford Sound, you can arrange a boat trip on the fiord, or even book a cruise for a few days and really explore the area from the sea. From a zoological point of view, the diversity of fish species is very interesting. The heavy rains in the area mean that above the water that flows into the fiord from the sea there is a permanent layer of fresh water, several meters deep, providing an extraordinary environment in which both freshwater and saltwater fish can thrive.

Milford Track (54 km/33 miles) is one of the most famous hiking trails in the country. It begins at Glade House at the northern tip of Lake Te Anau and runs through the Clinton Valley, past Sutherland Falls

Goldfields Mining Centre, which gives you a real flavour of just how labour-intensive the process of gold-mining can be. You can also enjoy a trip along the Kawarau River in a kayak or rubber dinghy.

From Cromwell, Highway 8 follows the valley of the Clutha River for the most part. It rejoins Highway I in Milton. It is then worth taking a detour north to Dunedin along the south-east coast (see side panel, p. 468). Heading south, at Balclutha you will join Highway 92 to Invercargill, located on the southern tip of the island. The Cathedral Caves are worth a quick stop along the way, as are the Purakaunui Falls, where the river of the same name cascades from a height of over 20 m (66 ft).

10 Invercargill New Zealand's most southerly town boasts tree-lined avenues and sweeping parks, including Queen's

Park, which has an area of 10 sq km (4 sq miles). The town's Scottish heritage is clearly visible today, and many roads are named after Scottish rivers. The Southland Museum and Art Gallery is renowned throughout the country and includes Maori works of art and a natural history exhibition that includes impressive fossils and petrified tree trunks. Next stop is Bluff, around 30 km (18 miles) south of Invercargill. This small village at the southern tip of the island is home to a large fishing fleet and terminus for the ferries to Stewart Island. The Bluff Maritime Museum houses objects related to the history of whaling. Our next destination is the country's largest National Park, covering 12,000 sq km (4,632 sq miles) of the island's south-westerly tip.

11 Fiordland National Park Its wide lakes, fourteen deep fiords and snow-capped moun-

tains have made this National Park world famous. The park's protected area is traversed by around 500 km (311 miles) of hiking trails, among them the spectacular Milford Track. Our first point of call is Te Anau on the shore of Te Anau Lake. From here, a two-hour boat trip takes us to the fascinating underworld of the Te Anau Caves ('Glowworm Caves'). A drive along the Milford Road (120 km/75 miles) between Te Anau in the south and Milford Sound in the north, one of the scenic highlights of New Zealand, is an unforgettable experience. On both sides of the road, you can see the diverse landscapes of New Zealand's southern tip in all their glory and variety: luxuriant forests, jagged mountains, torrential mountain rivers, roaring waterfalls and tranquil lakes. The Milford Track passes Sutherland Falls which, at 580 m (1,900 ft), was once thought to be the world's tallest waterfall. A trip to the south to see Doubtful Sound is well worth while, although the journey from Manapouri to Doubtful Sound involves two boat trips and a drive across Wilmot Pass. Several dolphin species live in the coastal waters.

1 Aoraki/Mount Cook National Park is part of the UNESCO World Heritage Site Te Wahipounamu.

2 Lake Tekapo, east of the Aoraki/ Mount Cook range, is surrounded by forests and high mountains.

3 The fiords and forests of the Fiordland National Park are quite breathtaking.

347

1

and up to the fiord. When booking, do bear in mind that the track is only walkable from November to March. From Milford Sound, you return to Te Anau, where you pick up the eastbound Highway 94. The rivers near Lumsden are famous for their wealth of trout. From Lumsden, you follow Highway 6 to the north. In Kingston, at the southern shore of Lake Wakatipu, you can take a 75-minute ride on the Kingston Flyer, a vintage steam train.

⓭ **Queenstown** This town at the northern shore of Lake Wakatipu is one of the South Island's biggest tourist attractions. The town center is spread out around the Queenstown Bay. Queenstown Gardens are located on a peninsula that extends far into the lake. If you are looking for an oasis of peace and tranquillity in what is a very busy town, you have come to the right place: the gardens' fir tree-lined lawns and rose beds are a quiet haven. The Mall is a popular meeting point for locals and visitors alike. Along this bustling shopping street, you will see some well-preserved colonial buildings, among them Eichardt's Tavern (1871).

At Underwater World, you can observe some of the local marine life. The Kiwi and Birdlife Park shelters several endangered bird species. The Skyline Gondola takes you up to Bob's Peak (450 m/1,475 ft), with its fantastic view of the town and the surrounding area.

⓮ **Wanaka** This lakeside town lies around 55 km (34 miles) as the crow flies from Queenstown and sits at the southern tip of Lake Wanaka. Its proximity to Mount Aspiring National Park and to the lake itself makes this a very attractive spot. The Transport and Toy Museum located near the airport is definitely worth visiting – its collection of vehicles and toys comprises more than 13,000 exhibits. And if you want to take a break from all this wonderful scenery, you can head for Stuart Landsborough's Puzzling World in Wanaka.

⓯ **Mount Aspiring National Park** Wanaka is the gateway to this National Park. Northwest of the town, a small road follows the Matukituki river right into the park which, at 3,555 sq km (1,372 sq miles) is New Zealand's third largest. At its heart is Mount Aspiring

2

(3,027 m/9,932 ft), shaped like a pyramid, hence its nickname of 'New Zealand's Matterhorn'. The scenery consists of tall, snow-capped mountains. There are numerous densely forested valleys and picturesque river plains. Several hiking trails allow you to explore the beauty of the park on foot. The Dart Rees Track is well-known and makes an ideal trek lasting several days through mountainous terrain. However, do note that you have to be in very good physical shape if you plan to attempt it. Less demanding but still worth doing is a hike on the Rob Roy Valley Trail along the Matukituki River. Keas, a species of mountain parrot, and timberline wrens are just two of the bird species you might spot in the park. You may be lucky enough to see keas at close range but the

wrens tend to stick to higher altitudes. Many waterbirds live along the rivers and lakes.

⓰ **Lake Hawea** From Wanaka, on the next leg of our journey to the coast, Highway 6 runs between Lake Wanaka and Lake Hawea(140 sq km/ 54 sq miles). Surrounded as it is by impressive scenery, this lake, with its clear blue waters, is one of the most beautiful on the South Island. It is 410 m (1,345 ft) deep, which means it is actually below sea level. Its abundance of trout and salmon makes it one of New Zealand's most popular fishing grounds.

You might want to stop en route for a rest and enjoy the view at the Cameron Creek Lookout. On the far side of the Haast Pass (563 m/1,847 ft), you will pass Thunder Creek Falls,

at a height of 30 m (98 ft). The road now runs along the Haast River, and once you get to Haast you'll have made it to the west coast.

⑰ Westland National Park This 1,176-sq-km (454-sq-mile) park stretches from the Okarito Lagoon on the island's west coast inland to Mount Tasman (3,498 m/11,475 ft), one of the highest mountains in the New Zealand Alps. Its variety of wetlands, lakes, rainforests, glaciers and rocky landscapes make this National Park particularly attractive. The west coast still bears witness in places to the 1860s gold-rush. Gillespies Beach on the coast is a former gold-miners' settle-

ment, and traces of the era are still visible today. A beautiful hike along a former mining track leads down to a beach with a seal colony.

Access roads such as Docherty Creek Road and Forks Okarito Road link Highway 6 to the west coast. The shore of Lake Mapourika is a popular spot for a picnic on the main road. Further south, you will find Lake Matheson, which is probably New Zealand's most photographed lake.

⑱ Franz Josef Glacier Like Fox Glacier to the south, this glacier stretches from its feeding point at more than 3,000 m (9,840 ft) to about 300 m (984 ft) above sea level, where the coastal rainforests grow right up to the edge of the glacier. Named after the Austrian Emperor Franz Josef, it is around 13 km (8 miles) long and forms part of Westland National Park. There are some dangerous crevices, so hiking across the glacier is only permitted as part of a guided tour. During the last two centuries, the ice has advanced on a number of occasions, but then always receded to its current level. The melt waters form the Waiho River, on which Franz Josef Village is located. A road

takes you to a car park, and from there it is a one-hour tramp to the glacier gate at the lowest point of the ice flow.

⑲ Hokitika In this charming town, which you reach via Highway 6, the Hokitika Heritage Walk will take you to some interesting 19th-century buildings. An old ship is also open for visits. The West Coast Historical Museum is dedicated to the gold-rush era, as is the historical open-air museum at the recreated 1860s gold-mining town, known as Shantytown, located about 10 km (6 miles) south of Greymouth.

⑳ Greymouth This town had its heyday during the 19th-century gold-rush. When the region's deposits were exhausted, coal mining replaced gold

1 Mist drifts over Lake Wanaka.

2 View from Bob's Peak over Queenstown and Queenstown Gardens on Lake Wakatipu

3 Dense lowland rainforest covers the karst formations of the Paparoa National Park.

4 The Pancake Rocks near Punakaiki are one of the geological highlights of Paparoa National Park.

digging as the town's principal source of revenue. However, Greymouth's development was severely restricted by recurrent heavy flooding. The History House Museum displays some interesting photographic documentation of the town's history and the Left Bank Art Gallery features Maori arts and crafts. If you are looking for something a bit more exciting, why not try floating through the network of the Taniwha Caves on inflated inner tubes.

㉑ Paparoa National Park This National Park covers 300 sq km (116 sq miles) and protects the karst formations of the Paparoa Range, which runs parallel to the coast. Its most popular attractions are the Pancake Rocks and the blowholes close to Punakaiki, a coastal village. The Pancake Rocks are huge limestone pillars, so-named because they look like pancakes piled one on top of the other. Heavy seas force water through the blowholes – funnels carved out by the surf – and it shoots up into the air in powerful jets. This karst area is entirely covered in subtropical rainforests that

flourish thanks to the warm ocean currents in this part of the west coast. Dolomite Point Walk is a hiking trail that takes you right to the heart of this virgin forest and just fifteen minutes down Truman Track you come to a wild and romantic piece of coastline with a waterfall and several caves.

Continuing to the north, you reach Westport, which serves as an ideal base for a range of outdoor activities in the area. For thrill-seekers, the local underground rafting is particularly spectacular; accompanied by a guide, you can drift along underground waterways and visit hidden caves. A three-hour hike on Cape Foulwind Walkway takes you to a seal colony in Tauranga Bay.

㉒ Karamea In Westport, you leave Highway 6 and take Highway 67 to the north. The coastal town of Karamea is the starting point for several hikes into the Kahurangi National Park, of which the 15-km (9-mile) Heaphy Track is one of the most popular. North of Karamea, you reach the Oparara Basin with its monumental limestone cliffs. There is also an extensive and intricate network of caves known as the Honeycomb Hill Caves. Inside the caves are the bones of nine species of the now extinct wingless – and therefore flightless – moa bird. It boasts the most varied collection of subfossil bird bones ever found in New Zealand. The caves have some huge passages and enor-

mous chambers to explore. You will need to book a guided tour. Another scenic highlight is Oparara Arch, a natural rock arch, some 43 m (141 ft) high and 220 m (241 yds) long.

From Karamea, take Highway 67 back to Westport and then follow Highway 6 to Matupiko and Nelson. From either place, you can pick up a road to Abel Tasman National Park and Cape Farewell. Eroded granite sculptures, sandy bays and estuaries all feature in this National Park. Return to Picton along the shore of the Tasman Bay.

1 Rocky coastline at Wharakiri Beach near Cape Farewell.

2 At Tasman Bay near Nelson.

Abel Tasman National Park Endless beaches and jungle-like rainforests – this National Park named after the Dutch explorer boasts some spectacular contrasts.

Marlborough Sounds Quiet bays and green hills are typical of the scenery at the South Island's northernmost tip. There are also some impressive dripstone caves on the coast.

Kaikoura Range In the north-east of the South Island the land gradually rises up from the coast to jagged mountains — a hiker's paradise.

Paparoa National Park In the course of millennia, wind and waves have carved out the bizarre shapes of the Pancake Rocks – a breathtaking landscape.

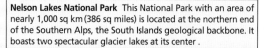

Nelson Lakes National Park This National Park with an area of nearly 1,000 sq km (386 sq miles) is located at the northern end of the Southern Alps, the South Islands geological backbone. It boasts two spectacular glacier lakes at its center .

Christchurch The impressive Christchurch Cathedral is located in the center of this city with its many typical parks.

Westland National Park Massive glaciers – among them the famous Franz Josef and Fox Glaciers – extend down the slopes of the Southern Alps.

Aoraki/Mount Cook National Park Much of this park, named after New Zealand's highest mountain (3,764 m/ 12,350 ft), is covered by glaciers.

Keas These mountain parrots are at home in the South Island's high country. Keas were named after the typical hooting noise they make while flying.

Te Wahipounamu The coastal scenery of the South Island's south-west is incredibly varied and intricate. In places rainforests run all the way down to the shoreline.

Dunedin A touch of Scotland in New Zealand: magnificent town houses, massive churches and lovely extensive parks make Dunedin so attractive.

Lake Wanaka This is one of several lakes at the eastern slopes of the Southern Alps. In summer, it is a popular water sports resort.

Milford Sound One of the landmarks of Fiordland National Park is the distinctive shape of Mitre Peak (1,692 m/6,437 ft), with its steep rock faces rising abruptly out of Milford Sound.

Queenstown Sloping down to Lake Wakatipu, in front of the 'Remarkables' – this is Queenstown. This former gold-diggers' settlement is now a popular holiday resort.

Purakaunui Falls The Purakaunui falls cascade down more than 20 m (66 ft) of rock faces and make a deafening roar.

Map labels:

Puponga · Cape Farewell · Collingwood · Abel Tasman N.P. · Marlborough Sounds · Kahurangi N.P. · Nelson · Wellington · Karamea · Matupiko · Picton · Havelock · Blenheim · Westport · Cape Foulwind · St.Arnaud · Cape Campbell · Paparoa N.P. · Murchison · Nelson Lakes N.P. · Mangamaunu · Reefton · Punakaiki · Pancake Rocks and Blowholes · Springs Junction · Kaikoura · Maori Leap Cave · Greymouth · Kumara Junction · Culverden · Hokitika · Arthur's Pass N.P. · Inland Kaikoura Range · Seaward Kaikoura Range · SOUTH ISLAND · Springfield · Sheffield · Waipara · Franz Josef Glacier · Gillespies Beach · Mount Hutt · Christchurch · Westland N.P. · Mt.Cook N.P. · Mount Cook · Canterbury Plains · Akaroa · Haast · Ashburton · Banks Peninsula · Lake Pukaki · Lake Tekapo · Geraldine · Southern Alps · Twizel · Fairlie · Canterbury Bight · Lake Wanaka · Clay Cliffs · Omarama · Timaru · Te Wahi- · Mt. Aspiring N.P. · Milford Sound · Lake Hawea · Wanaka · Lindis Valley · Oamaru · Sutherland Falls · Queenstown · Cromwell · Moeraki Boulders · Fiordland N.P. · pounamou · Te Anau · Palmerston · Doubtful Sound · Manapouri · Raes Junction · Dunedin · Otago Peninsula · Monowai · Lumsden · Gore · Milton · Larnach Castle · Owaka · Balclutha · Puysegur Point · Invercargill · Purakaunui Falls · Waikawa · Cathedral Caves · Bluff · Stewart Island

Colourful kilims draw tourists to the small market town of Taddert in the Atlas Mountains, far away from the Atlantic Coast.

Morocco

Royal cities, kasbahs and oases

The magic of Oriental medinas and palaces, the austere beauty of the Atlas Mountains, the bright white of the port cities, the green of the Saharan palm oases, and the colours and aromas of 'a thousand and one nights' in the souks of the royal cities make this tour an experience for the senses.

Tangiers is the starting point on the Strait of Gibraltar. Strolling through the maze-like medina (old Arab quarters with tiny streets), you get a sense of the special Arabic-Spanish atmosphere that made Tangiers a jet-setters' haunt in the 1960s. East of the city, the rugged mountains of the Rif slope gently back towards the Mediterranean coast. Tétouan, with its well-preserved medina, and the small, picturesque moun-

tain town of Chefchaouen are two fascinating stops on your way south. To the south of the Rif mountains, the columns and gates of the ruined Roman city of Volubilis soar above golden cornfields. Not far away, the holy city of Moulay Idriss clings to the hillside as if painted on with watercolours. Moulay Idriss I brought Islam to Morocco in the 8th century and founded the first dynasty here. His mausoleum in the city's holy

quarter is the most important pilgrimage site in the country. Nearby is the royal city of Meknès with its sturdy walls, storehouses and palaces. Fez was the first royal city under

Olive sellers in Meknès.

Moulay Idriss II and his Idriss Dynasty. Above the labyrinth of alleys, squares, markets and palaces, the minarets of countless mosques rise up towards the heavens. The architectural treasure of Fez, its colourful, aromatic souks (marketplaces) around the mausoleum of Idriss II, the palace area of the Dar el-Makhzen, and the dignified Kairaouine Mosque make this city of trade and science over a thousand years old, an Oriental gem. Heading south through the densely forested areas of the Middle Atlas, you pass Ifrane and Azrou and the Col du Zad. Vegetation in this area now becomes more scarce and the nearby desert begins to ex-

The Sultan's love nest – Menara Pavilion, in the garden of the same name, on the outskirts of Marrakech.

Tinerhir is one of the largest oases on the Route of the Kasbahs. Many 19th-century clay tighremt (family castles) and kasbahs (forts) are found in the lush palm gardens.

pand. From Ar-Rachidia onwards, the route follows the palm-filled valley of Oued Ziz on its way to Erfoud, a garrison city that is the jumping-off point for tours into the majestic Erg Chebbi Desert, a dream landscape of extraordinary golden sand dunes.

From Erfoud, you now follow the famous Route of the Kasbahs where mud fortresses tower above the palm tree oases of Tinerhir and Boumalne Dadès. Both towns lie at the mouth of wildly romantic gorges that lead deep into the mountainous realm of the High Atlas. A day trip south through the Drâa Valley passes Ouarzazate to the old oases of Agdz, Zagora and Tamegroute.

Ksar Aït Ben Haddou is probably the most frequently photographed movie set in Morocco. The mud city was abandoned by its inhabitants and is to be restored under the UNESCO protectorate. Over the Tizi-n' Tichka pass, the route continues north through the 3,000-m (9,843-ft) High Atlas to the royal city of Marrakech. Here, the minaret of the Koutoubia Mosque soars high above this ancient city, and goods from every land fill the souk. From Marrakech, our dream route heads towards the Atlantic, but before reaching Agadir it briefly breaks south into a landscape where erosion has created some amazing formations. Tafraoute and the Valley of Ammeln in the Anti-Atlas display the ancient world of the Berbers. The route now passes through the silver city of Tiznit and the resort of Agadir, and follows the Atlantic coast towards Essaouira. The port town protected by many forts has a beautiful medina. Further north, the modern metropolis of Casablanca is home to the largest, most magnificent mosque in the Maghreb, while the foundation and base of the Hassan Tower minaret tell of a similarly ambitious mosque project in nearby Rabat that was started in 1150 and never completed. Passing through Larache and Asilah you arrive back in Tangiers.

Horsemen and guards passionately show their might in an historical reenactment of a ferocious battle.

Our tour through Morocco uniquely combines culture with nature. In addition to royal cities, the journey includes oldstyle earthen fortresses against the backdrop of the Atlas Mountains as well as resorts on the stunning Atlantic coast.

1 **Tangiers** Founded in Roman times, the first impression made by this port city on the Strait of Gibraltar is one of a hectic Oriental marketplace. High over the city, the former royal palace is enthroned in the kasbah, which also houses the Archaeological Museum with exhibits from Volubilis. From Tangiers, the N2 winds its way south-east through the foothills of the Rif mountains.

2 **Tétouan** The largest city in the Rif is a UNESCO World Heritage Site for its architecture, which is heavily influenced by Andalusian styles and indeed was part of Spain until Moroccan independence in 1956. Within the walled medina you will see numerous vaulted arch alleyways, and many houses with windows covered in wrought-iron bars.

Tétouan's souk is the fourth largest in Morocco. On market days, countrywomen from the Rif bring their products into the city.

The fully restored N2 heads south through the cedar- and holm-oak-covered Rif mountains.

3 **Chefchaouen** The white houses of the medina here clutter the mountainside like building blocks, with the high peaks of the central Rif mountains in the background. In 1492, many Jews and Muslims settled here following their expulsion from Spain during the Reconquista. Even today

you cannot help but notice the Spanish influence in the architecture of the picturesque labyrinthine alleys in the medina. After crossing the Rif you reach Ouezzane and follow Highway 417 to the N3 intersection, then head first north-west travelling from Sidi-Kacem, and then south to Volubilis (180 km/ 112 miles).

4 **Volubilis** The ruins of this former Roman settlement lie at the foot of the Djebel Zerhoun. Founded in the first century BC, Volubilis was the capital of the Roman province Mauretania Tingitana until AD 285. The city became prosperous through the olive oil trade as well as by selling wild animals for Roman arena events. A mere 2.5 km (1.5 miles) away from Volubis is the pilgrimage site of Moulay Idriss.

5 **Moulay Idriss** Your first stop here should be the 'Terrace', a vista point with fantastic views over the maze of the medina with its mosques surrounding the central sanctuary mausoleum of Idriss I. A direct descendant of the prophet Mohammed, Idriss I founded this town around AD 788, succeeded in converting the Berber people to Islam and subsequently formed the first Moroccan dynasty. Passing now through an idyllic hill land-

Travel Information

Route profile
Length: approx. 3,100 km (1,926 miles), excluding detours
Time required: 21–25 days
Start and end: Tangiers
Route (main locations): Tangiers, Tétouan, Volubilis, Meknès, Fez, Erfoud, Route of the Kasbahs, Ouarzazate, Drâa Valley, Marrakech, Tafraoute, Agadir, Essaouira, Casablanca, Rabat, Tangiers

Traffic information:
Drive on the right in Morocco. It is advisable to avoid travelling after dark as there are often unlit carts, cyclists or pedestrians on the road at night. It is imperative to pay attention to signs, which are unfortunately not always very clear. Between the big

cities in the north, the roads are usually asphalt and also relatively wide.
The speed limit for rural roads is 100 km/h (62 mph), and 40–60 km/h (25–37 mph) in built-up areas.
Drivers are strictly forbidden from drinking alcohol.

When to go:
The weather is mild all year in the north, a bit cool in winter. Southern beaches can be foggy in summer. October to April is good for the lowlands with temps of 30°C.

Information:
General and travel:
www.morocco.com
wikitravel.org/en/Morocco
www.arab.net/morocco/
www.visitmorocco.org

scape, you will come to the royal city of Meknès just 28 km (17 miles) away.

⑥ **Meknès** Moulay Ismail, who chose Meknès as his royal city at the end of the 17th century, was a megalomaniac ruler and his monumental buildings are testimony to this.
The Ville Impériale, surrounded by mighty walls, the magnificent city gate Bab el-Mansour, the Heri es-Souani storehouse used as a stable and granary, and finally the lavishly decorated mausoleum of the ruler are all part of the city's UNESCO World Heritage offering. The medina, with its colourful souks, is labyrinthine and intimate in comparison. Among the Old City's maze of alleys, the Medersa Bou Inania conceals a special gem of neo-Moorish architecture. Just 70 km (43 miles) down the N6 is Fez.

⑦ **Fez** Fez el-Bali, the old Fez, sprawls like a labyrinth in the basin beneath the Marinid fortress. In AD 809, Idriss II deemed the town a royal city. Since then, Fez has become a modern metropolis. Madrasahs and palaces, the mausoleum of the city's founder and the venerated Kairaouine Mosque are adorned with a real fusion of Arabic-Berber decorative art, with carvings, mosaics and gypsum stucco work. In the souks, spice merchants, cobblers, carpet sellers and goldsmiths vie for customers' business while sheep and goat skins are made into leather in the tanners' quarter. From Fez, the N13 continues south into the foothills of the Middle Atlas.

⑧ **Ifrane** After roughly 60 km (37 miles) you will be pleasantly surprised by picturesque mountain scenery that many say is quaintly reminiscent of Switzerland. The health resort of Ifrane could just as easily be in the European Alps. Gabled houses, cool, fresh mountain air, a few nearby ski lifts – this is what Morocco's alpine holiday destinations look like. Morocco's most prestigious university is in Ifrane, and the royal family also owns a magnificent palace here. Enjoy a typically Moroccan pastry, the Cornes de Gazelle, before the upcoming 300-km-long (186-mile) stretch through the Middle and High Atlas.
The N8 and, from Azrou onwards, the N13 wind lazily through the impressive cedar forests. With a bit of luck, you will encounter some Barbary Apes. Once you've passed the 2,178-m (7,146-ft) Col du Zad, the landscape becomes more sparse and after the mining city of Midelt, the route winds its way through the enchanting eastern foothills of the High Atlas. North of Ar-Rachidia, the road continues up along the spectacular Gorges du Ziz.

⑨ **Ar-Rachidia** This town at 1,060 m (3,477 ft) is an important traffic and trade junction in southern Morocco. Surrounded by oasis gardens, it is the epitome of a typical oasis, but with the added backdrop of the majestic High Atlas. The town itself is rather modern and functional, with very few traces of traditional architecture. This is where the Tafilalt oases begin, fed by the Oued Ziz originating in the Atlas, and where the current royal family resides, the Alouites. The N13 follows the river past oasis gardens and small settlements until it reaches Erfoud 74 km (46 miles) away.

⑩ **Erfoud** Founded by the French only in 1917, Erfoud still looks like a desert garrison city with barracks, modern headquarters and wide, dusty streets. It is the center of the exotic Tafilalt, the largest valley oasis and the most popular green site of Morocco.
Many souvenir dealers have specialized in selling various fossils from the Atlas Mountains at the edge of the Sahara. From here you travel another 22 km (13.5 miles) south

1 The lavishly decorated Bab el-Mansour, completed in 1732, leads to the palace city of Meknès.

2 In the center of Moulay Idriss is the green-brick mausoleum.

3 The sand dunes of Erg Chebbi in the south of Morocco tower up to 100 m (328 ft) high.

4 Tourists can take camel rides from Merzouga into the dune landscape of the Erg Chebbi.

through the fascinating desert landscape.

⑪ Rissani Some 3,000 inhabitants populate the narrow, often vaulted-arch alleyways of the medina beyond the town gate. If a market is held on a Sunday, oasis farmers and cattle breeders from the surrounding villages fill the main town square.

It is interesting to do a day trip to the oasis of Rissani, the mausoleum of Moulay Ali Cherif, the founder of the Alouite dynasty, and to Ksar Abbar, whose mud walls are decorated with Islamic geometric patterns. In contrast, the ruins of the once most important trading city in southern Morocco, the legendary Sijilmassa, are disappointing. 100,000 people lived and traded goods here from the 11th to 15th centuries, acquiring caravans from the sub-Saharan African kingdoms of the south. Only a few mud walls have been preserved underneath the desert sand.

From Rissani, you can also make a detour to the sand dunes of Erg Chebbi near Merzouga. Otherwise, return to Ar-Rachidia on the same route through Erfoud and travel west on the N10.

⑫ Tinerhir The majestic range of the High Atlas accompanies the route in the north, while a grey-brown plain sprawls out to the south. You will then see what looks like an oversized molehill. These are the entry craters of the ancient 'foggaras' underground irrigation system. In the canals, water from the High Atlas is channelled into the arid foreland to irrigate the fields. The system must be serviced regularly and cleared of stones and refuse – a dangerous task that is usually carried

out by the unlucky descendants of former slaves.

At the mouth of the Gorges du Todra, at 1,342 m (4,403 ft), Tinerhir, the 19th-century kasbah, keeps watch over the town with its old mud houses around the rosé-coloured minaret of the mosque. The deep-green oasis gardens sprawl around the town, pomegranates, tomatoes, carrots and clover growing in the shade of the palm trees to feed the livestock.

Following the southern edge of the High Atlas, the route continues west to Boumalne Dadès, 53 km (33 miles) away. In the south, the Djebel Sarhro mountain range now draws near. You'll begin to see more and more mud kasbahs, constructed for the safety of the trade routes and to guard the oases. At the turn of the 20th century, the infamous Pasha of Marrakech, El-Glaoui, built these kasbahs to safeguard his domain and station his loyal troops.

⑬ Boumalne Dadès This oasis at 1,586 m (5,203 ft) is also tucked into the opening of a deep mountain gorge formed

by the Dadès. It accompanies the road from Boumalne to Ouarzazate. The Dadès Valley is also called the Route of the Kasbahs because of its many mud castles. The small market town is made up of several tighremt, Berber family castles built from mud and guarded by four towers, over which the well-fortified kasbah kept watch from high on the plateau. Some tighremt are still inhabited.

Fruit and olive trees as well as vegetables grow in the oasis gardens but palm trees are rarely seen at these heights. Boumalne Dadès is the starting point for day trips to the Gorges du Dadès and the

Djebel Sarhro. This high desert mountain range is home to Bedouin folk who roam between the mountains and river oases of the Dadès and the Drâa with goats and camels. Kasbahs and ksars (villages) line the road west to El Kelaa M'Gouna just 24 km (15 miles) away.

⑭ El Kelaa M'Gouna Just 10,000 people live in this settlement at an altitude of 1,467 m (4,813 ft). They farm the oasis gardens whose most valuable asset is the Damascene Rose (see sidebar at right).

El Kelaa M'Gouna is also under the watchful eye of an old kasbah originally built by El-Glaoui

facades decorated with delightful geometric patterns and artistic palaces at the entrance towers, but also clear traces of decay. Restoration of the castles and granaries is progressing only very slowly due to complicated land tenures.

From Aït Ben Haddou, a rugged track that is only navigable with off-road vehicles leads through spectacular scenery to Telouèt, parts of the road following the Asif Mellah River and traversing dramatic mountain passes along the way. You reach the town more easily by going back down the N9 and following it into the mountainous region of the High Atlas. The slopes are stony and stark, but in the valleys green terraced fields line the mountain streams and dark-brown mud houses cling to the hillside. In contrast to the tighremt in the Dadès Valley, the houses here are basic and almost bare.

After 65 km (40 miles) of sometimes narrow serpentine roads, you climb 2,280 m (7,480 ft) to the Tizi-n'Tichka pass. Just 2 km (1 mile) further on, the route branches off towards Telouèt.

⑰ **Telouèt** The journey now leads to one of Morocco's most unique kasbahs 20 km (12 miles) down the road. Telouèt was the headquarters of the Glaoua, a powerful subgroup of the Atlas Berbers that controlled much of the southern part of Morocco. Their most famous patriarch, El-Glaoui, also the Pasha of Marrakech,

to control trade routes. Like other towns along this route, there is also a river here, the Assif M'Goun, that comes down from the High Atlas Mountains and flows into the Dadès River. On the 94-km (58-mile) stretch heading toward Ouarzazate, the road is bordered by the High Atlas in the north and the Djebel Sarhro in the south. A series of kasbahs, sometimes in the midst of green palms and other times on stark mountain ledges, once again provides photo opportunities. Of particular interest is the oasis of Skoura with its reddish-brown mud castles.

⑮ **Ouarzazate** Shortly before reaching Ouarzazate, 'The Door of the Desert' (1,160 m/ 3,806 ft), the abandont waters of the Barrage El Mansour Eddahbi glimmer like a mirage in the otherwise bleak landscape.

The golf course, with its deep-green lawn alongside the dam, is an equally unusual sight. You then reach the Taourirt kasbah, one of Morocco's largest mud settlements and a small city in itself. The mud walls conceal numerous dwellings as well as the palace of Pasha El-Glaoui, where two rooms are open to the public.

Ouarzazate itself is a modern city without any charm as such, but it is an important stopping point thanks to its excellent offering of hotels and restaurants. It owes its nickname of the 'Hollywood of Morocco' to the local film studios that have produced numerous international films in the south of this picturesque country, to mention only a few blockbusters such as Babel, Gladiator,

Cleopatra or Seven Years In Tibet.

The N9 leaves the city to the north-west towards Marrakech. Approximately 26 km (16 miles) out of Ouarzazate a sign points you to the ksar Aït Ben Haddou.

⑯ **Aït Ben Haddou** The 9-km (5.5-mile) access road here ends at one of Morocco's most beautiful vista points looking out over a rocky plateau – the silvery gleaming Asif Mellah River snakes through the valley below while mud castles and storehouses of the ksar on the other side of the valley are piled on top of each other like honeycomb on the hillside. Above it all are the ruins of the kasbah.

Cinema-goers will recognize the landscape here. In addition to David Lean's *Lawrence of Arabia* and Orson Welles' *Sodom and Gomorra*, a good many other movies have been filmed here. At high tide, mule herders guide tourists over the river, while at low tide it is possible to cross on foot.

Strolling through the narrow alleys of the ksar, in parts lined with palm trunks, you'll see

1 Mud kasbahs and ksars side by side in the Dadès Valley.

2 Markets are held every Wednesday at the large square n Boumalne Dadès.

3 The Route of the Kasbahs, an important caravan route.

had the former family home converted into a magnificent mud castle but it has been falling to ruin since his death in 1956. Inside, valuable wooden inlays on doors and ceilings, as well as stucco ornaments on the walls, are exposed to the elements without any form of protection. Storks nest in the spires. El-Glaoui was opposed to King Mohammed V and had made an agreement with the French. As a result, his property was abandoned by the state. Back on the main route N9 it's another 20 km (12 miles) to the market town of Taddert.

⑱ Taddert You must drive very carefully here, as children selling minerals and fossils often jump out into the road suddenly to stop passing cars. Taddert is famous for its grill restaurants and takeaway food stores, where you can take a break and still enjoy the panoramic views of the High Atlas.

Around this striking valley, the peaks of the High Atlas reach 4,000 m (13,124 ft) and even in summer the weather is pleasant and cool. The N9 then winds its way down again, passing pine plantations that are an attempt by the state to reforest the eroded hillsides.

After just 40 km (25 miles) you will arrive at the Haouz plain, one of the most fertile areas of Morocco. The fields have abundant crops, and early vegetables are grown in the many greenhouses. It becomes clear now that Marrakech is approaching as greater signs of settlement appear and traffic becomes increasingly chaotic.

The clay walls of the 'Red City' can be seen from afar. The N9 opens out into the multi-lane Route des Remparts, which forms a ring road that almost completely encircles the mythical town of Marrakech.

⑲ Marrakech Some 750,000 people live in Marrakech, 'Pearl of the South'. This vibrant city is surrounded by palm groves and gardens and bordered by the often snow-capped peaks of the High Atlas mountains. With its colourful souks, time-honoured mosques, ornate mausoleums, magnificent palaces and lively night-time bustle on the Djemma el Fna, the almost 1,000-year-old city attracts tourists and locals alike. Marrakech was founded in 1062 by the Almoravids, a strictly orthodox dynasty with a strong connection to the origins of Islam. In 1126–1127, it became the capital of the Almoravid Kingdom.

In the centuries that followed, Marrakech was constantly competing with Fez for the seat of the Sultan. Ultimately, trans-Saharan trade restored Marrakech to its former prosperity and French colonization in the 20th century further shaped the city. Architectural highlights include the 12th-century Koutoubia Mosque and the magnificent 16th-century mausoleum of the

Saadier, with its impressive marble floors and numerous gravestones decorated with calligraphy. Similar in opulence is the 14th-century Medersa Ben Youssef in the medina. The city wall, built of clay bricks, is another unique monument interspersed with lavishly decorated gates.

You can take a worthwhile and relaxing excursion around the 'Remparts' and a detour to the Jardins Majorelle by calèche, or carriage. The villa and garden of the artist Majorelle form a perfect scene of varying blue and green hues.

Apart from wandering your way through Morocco's largest souks, the undisputed highlight of Marrakech is a visit to the Djemma el Fna, the city's main square and one that is used by both tourists and locals alike. Amid the bustling food and drinks stalls, the square transforms into a street performers' stage when the sun sets. The nightly shows include acrobats, story-tellers, Chleuh dancing boys, magicians, snake charmers

After 160 km (99 miles), the pinkish houses of Tafraoute come into view, sprawled out in a gorgeous mountain valley.

22 **Tafraoute** Some 1,000 m (3,300 ft) up, and surrounded by a palm oasis, Tafraoute is the main hub of the Ammeln, a subgroup of the Chleuh. From here, it is possible to make detours on foot or by car to villages such as Oumesnat (get back on the P509 heading north, then turn left after 6 km/4 miles), where one of the region's traditional stone houses is open to interested visitors as a museum. Approximately 3 km (2 miles) south on the S7146 gravel road you then come to a valley full of strangely eroded granite with an array of rock drawings. From Tafraoute the asphalt S7074 heads up and over the 1,200-m-high (3,936-ft) Col du Kerdous into another valley to Tiznit about 114 km (72 miles) away.

23 **Tiznit** This city of silversmiths initially disappoints with its modern outskirts, but a lively souk atmosphere reigns around the Place Mechouar. The Tiznit silversmiths are famous for the quality of their work. They make jewellery as well as traditional dagger accessories.

Your route now heads north, and another 90 km (56 miles) on the N1 takes you through flat, stark terrain until you reach the town of Agadir.

1 The peaks of the High Atlas are covered with snow until spring.

2 Seemingly calm dealers haggle over the most valuable objects at the carpet bazaar auctions in Marrakech.

3 At the end of the 16th century, artisans displayed their fantastic artistic skills at the Saadier graves in Marrakech.

and even traditional medicine peddlers.

The N10 heads south through Asni over a pass in the High Atlas that initially leads through green promontory landscape before finally entering an increasingly sparse mountain region due to the arid climate.

20 **Tizi-n'Test** After approximately 100 km (62 miles) it is worth stopping at the 12th-century Almohada mosque, Tin Mal. The almost square building, with four corner towers

and a crenellation, is more reminiscent of a fortress than a place of worship. Shortly after that begins the steepest and most winding part of the route to the 2,093-m (6,867-ft) Tizi-n'Test Pass, which you have completed after 35 km (22 miles) before arching back towards the valley. The views of the mountains are amazing. You reach Taroudannt after a total of 230 km (143 miles).

21 **Taroudannt** 'Marrakech's younger sister' is completely

surrounded by a mud wall with storks nesting on the pinnacles. In the medina it is worth visiting the Place Assarag where Berbers from the surrounding region hold a market on Thursdays and Sundays. This is the start of the maze of souks, which all still have a very original feel. In Taroudannt you'll have the opportunity to stay in one of the most beautiful hotels in Morocco, the 'Salam'. Leaving the city heading west on the N10, the route now crosses Morocco's most important agricultural region, the Souss plain. In Aït Melloui, just before reaching the spa resort of Agadir, you turn off onto the P509 and head south-east towards Biougra.

In a steady climb, the route crosses the quilt-like mountain landscape of the Anti-Atlas where prickly pears and argania spinosa are the main vegetation, along with the odd almond tree. Storage chambers of the Chleuh Berbers, so-called Agadire, sit on top of table plateaus above the villages.

24 Agadir This spa resort was rebuilt after a devastating earthquake in 1960. The modern city, located on a wide sandy beach lined with hotels, is a pleasant place to stop before taking the N1 coastal road and heading north to Essaouira. It winds its way along a dramatic, steeply sloping coastline and is bordered with argania groves with a particular attraction – goats climbing to the tops of the trees to nibble at the leaves.

25 Essaouira This port city, a former artists' colony, is also known as the "White City". Its stout walls and the Scala Fortress bring a slightly Portuguese flavour to it, but it was founded in 1760 by the Sultan Mohammed Ben Abdallah and today, it figures among the UNESCO World Heritage Sites.

Fishmongers at the port, the souk where beautiful thuja-wood furniture is sold, and the many art galleries with their dreamy images of the Gnaoua make the city an extremely popular destination. The N8 heads inland for a while through argania groves before branching off on the N1 to the intersection with Highway 204, which then continues west and ends in Safi (148 km/92 miles).

26 Safi This port city is famous for pottery. North-east of the old city, factories and shops are grouped opposite the Bab Chaaba on 'potters' hill'. Safi's blue-glazed ceramics are in high demand. Heading further north on the narrow but spectacular P121 coastal road you will pass Oualidia, where the Atlantic forms a peaceful lagoon behind a sand bar that

is ideal for bathing. About 144 km (89 miles) on, the brilliant white walls of El-Jadida come into view.

27 El-Jadida Behind the fully preserved city wall with numerous bastions lies a lovely and authentic medina, whose main attraction is the Portuguese cistern, a water reservoir covered by groined vaults. Only 16 km (10 miles) north is another port town of particular charm, Azemmour, with a colourful

market every Tuesday. From there it's another 100 m (62 miles) along the coastal road to Casablanca.

28 Casablanca This metropolis of 3 million people, formerly known as "Dar El Beida", is particularly worth a stop to take a look at the Hassan II Mosque and the neo-Moorish center, which originates from the French colonial era. The route to the nation's capital Rabat continues for 95 km (59 miles)

3

4

along a lovely coastline through the very popular resorts of Mohammedia and Skhirat Plage.

㉙ Rabat Along with the twin city of Salé, Morocco's capital has more than 1.5 million inhabitants, yet it is a pleasant experience thanks to the elegant villa neighbourhoods. In the 12th century, Rabat became the Ribat el Ftah Fortress under the Almohada rule. Buccaneers later settled there and the

pirate 'republic' of Rabat-Salé spread terror on the high seas between the 17th and 19th centuries. In 1956, Rabat became the capital of independent Morocco. The historic heart of the city is the Oudaïa, a kasbah on a bank above the Bou Regreg River. The 12th-century Bab des Oudaï, decorated with magnificent stone masonry, leads to a maze of partly vaulted alleys to a platform with a view over neighbourig Salé. East of the kasbah are the 200

pillar bases and the minaret of the Hassan Mosque designed by Yacoub el-Mansour. The charming minaret is often compared to the Giralda in Seville.

Opposite this is the impressive neo-Moorish mausoleum of Kings Mohammed V and Hassan II built in 1967.

The archaeological museum with the most beautiful finds from the Moroccan excavation sites is well worth a visit as well as the Marinid necropolis of Chellah south-east of Rabat. From Rabat, the N1 heads north through Ksar-el-Kebir on its way to Larache.

㉚ Larache The French poet, Jean Genet, is buried in the cemetery of this picturesque port town. The excavation site of the Roman Lixus with an amphitheater and the ruins of the ancient fish-processing fac-

tory lies 4 km (2.5 mi) further north. Tangiers is another 87 km (54 mi) on the N1 along the Atlantic coast. After 84 km (52 mi), it's worth taking a detour of about 9 km (5.5 mi) to Cap Spartel, and to the Hercules Grottoes with an exceptional view of the sea from a natural crevice shaped like the African continent.

1 Aday, one of the Ammeln villages in the vicinity of Tafraoute.

2 Agadir Tasguent, a storage chamber in the Anti-Atlas.

3 The metropolis of Casablanca has numerous colonial buildings that are worth seeing.

4 Essaouira, the 'White City' on the sea, was previously an artist colony and is today a popular tourist destination on the Atlantic coast.

El-Jadida The white city walls of this Atlantic coast town were only built in the 19th century. The medina houses a Portuguese cistern with tapering Gothic arches where Orson Welles once filmed scenes from his epic film version of *Othello*.

Rabat The Moroccan capital, with 1.7 million inhabitants, has a picturesque location at the mouth of the Bou Regreg River. The Ouadaï kasbah forms the foundation of the royal city.

Tangier This port city on the Strait of Gibraltar was once the meeting place for Bohemians. The atmosphere of that time can be somewhat relived over a glass of mint tea at one of the many cafés.

Safi At the edge of the medina, potters manufacture ceramics typical of the region in their traditional workshops. The old port city of Safi, guarded by a formidable kasbah, has so far barely been touched by tourists.

Essaouira Although this fishing town appears more Portuguese than Moroccan, it was in fact founded by Arab peoples. Its special atmosphere is adored by alternative lifestyle enthusiasts and artists. The traditional hypnosis rituals of the local Gnaoua are famous here.

Casablanca This metropolis of over 3 million people is home to an awe-inspiring place of worship in honour of Allah and the kings. With capacity for 12,000 people, the Hassan II Mosque is the largest in the Maghreb.

Marrakech The 'red' royal city is surrounded by lush oasis gardens. In the labyrinthine medina, souks entice would-be buyers with their Oriental scents and colours. Every evening in the Djemma el Fna, the street performers' square, people gather to watch acrobats and snake charmers.

Agadir After a devastating earthquake in 1960 destroyed this Atlantic Berber settlement, only the kasbah on the hill remained unscathed. After this, the city was rebuilt. Today, Agadir is primarily known as a spa and holiday resort.

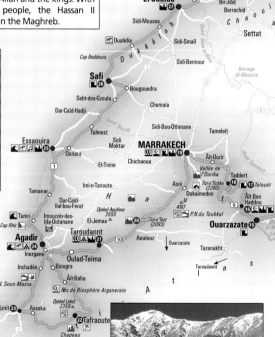

Ouarzazate This kasbah in Taourirt, on the outskirts of the garrison city, once belonged to the mighty Pasha El-Glaoui.

Aït Ben Haddou This UNESCO-protected ksar is at risk of falling into ruin. The former inhabitants abandoned the old mud castle and live in a modern village opposite.

Tafraoute Many houses in this oasis city are pink like the granite rock of the Ammeln Valley. Morocco's best almonds thrive in this valley.

Drâa Valley A sea of palms, ordered fields, oasis villages and kasbahs line the Drâa on its way through the arid south. In earlier times, the mud city of Zagora was the starting point for caravans making the 52-day trans-Sahara trade journeys to the legendary city of Timbuktu. The Drâa originally flowed out into the Atlantic, but today it barely makes it to Mhamid in the Sahara.

High Atlas These mountains between the Middle Atlas and the Anti-Atlas form the border between fertile Morocco and the desert. The highest peak is the Toubkal at 4,167 m (13,672 ft).

Tétouan Morocco's Spanish legacy becomes evident in the Ville Nouvelle of this Rif mountain town. This is the Place Hassan II. The Moorish tradition is reflected in the medina with its vaulted alleyways.

Chefchaouen This picturesque Rif town, surrounded by mountains reaching 2,000 m (6,562 ft) in height, is a popular summer resort. Rif countrywomen in colourful dress come to the market on Mondays and Thursdays.

Volubilis Between AD 42 and 285, Volubilis was the capital of the Roman province of Mauretania Tingitana. The ruins of the basilica, Capitol Temple, the triumphal arch and the villas with their filigree mosaic floors tower over the fertile landscape of northern Morocco.

Moulay Idriss The founder of the Idriss dynasty is entombed in the holy city. Fleeing the 'thousand and one nights' sultan, Harun al-Rashid, he sought refuge in Morocco where he was made leader by the Berbers.

Rissani Water and date palms in the Tafilalt oasis near Rissani ensure survival in the desert.

Meknès The builder of Meknès, Sultan Moulay Ismail, had a fondness for monuments that is reflected in the mighty gates and palaces as well as in the ruler's luxurious tomb complex.

Fez The royal city's medina is a unique work of art, with plenty of Moorish architecture and lively souks. The finest leather is dyed by hand in the tannery pools shown here.

Merzouga The Great Western Erg near Merzouga is a unique sand dune landscape.

Gorges du Ziz At first glance, the southern edge of the High Atlas appears arid and desolate, but in the mud -walled villages along the Ziz Gorge, farmers grow myriad crops near the river.

Vallée du Todra The Todra weaves its way through steep rock faces from the High Atlas down into the Dadès Valley where thousands of palm trees line its banks. The cool gorge is a popular destination for rock climbers and hikers.

Skoura A whole row of well-fortified, ancient-looking kasbahs with decorative brick patterns on their corner towers create a striking contrast to Skoura's other spectacle, its sea of lush palm trees.

Gorges du Dadès In the deep gorges not far from the 'Route of the Kasbahs', farmers make use of every square meter of fertile land. Tomatoes, alfalfa and sorghum are grown on plots of all sizes.

Tinerhir Numerous kasbahs watch over the oasis gardens of Tinerhir at the mouth of the Gorges du Todra in the Dadès Valley. The old trade route passing through here was host not only to caravans, but also to war tribes, against whom the oasis farmers had to defend themselves.

Egypt

The pyramids of Giza are the only ancient wonder of the world still standing today and attracting thousands of tourists every year.

A journey through the Kingdom of the Pharaohs

The pyramids of Giza are the most powerful emblem of ancient Egypt. The pharaohs who built them instilled the fabulous structures with dreams of immortality. Egypt's cultural legacy was also influenced by Christianity and Islam. In the desert, time-honoured monasteries are evidence of the religious zeal of the Copts, who are still very much alive today. The various Muslim dynasties gave Cairo its numerous mosques.

Egypt gives visitors an insight into an exotic realm situated at the crossroads of African, Asian and European civilizations, and which is indeed an intersection of myriad cultures. Obviously the monumental tombs and temples are still a subject of fascination today, but their mysterious hieroglyphics and ancients scripts also captivate our curiosi-

ties. The ancient societies of Egypt and the pharaohs began over 5,000 years ago. Most of the monuments from the time of the pharaohs run along the Nile. Along with the pulsating metropolis of Cairo, the 300-km (186-mile) stretch between Luxor and Aswan offers history buffs a multitude of impressive sights. Luxor's attractions in-

The golden mask of young King Tutankhamun.

clude the Valley of the Kings, the tremendous temple complex of Karnak and the funerary temple of the female pharaoh Hatshepsut.

Further south, the temples of Edfu and Kôm Ombo are evidence of the fact that even the Greek and Roman conquerors of Egypt succumbed to a fascination with the Pharaonic culture. Near Aswan, history and the modern world collide. The construction of the Aswan Dam meant the old temples were at risk of being submerged. It was only at great expense that they were relocated in the 1960s. The most famous example of this act of international preservation is the two rock temples of Abu Simbel.

Over 95 percent of Egypt's total surface area is desert that covers more than one million sq km (386,000 sq mi). Only very few

The four colossal figures of Pharaoh Ramses II tower 20 m (65.5 ft) before the façades of the rock temple of Abu Simbel.

The long avenue of ram's-headed sphinxes in front of the temple of the god Amun in Luxor is particularly impressive at dusk.

of the 75 million inhabitants earn their living in the oases of the western deserts, on the shores of the Red Sea or on Mount Sinai. The vast majority of the population live close together in the Nile valley. As early as the 5th century BC the Greek historian Herodotus wrote that 'Egypt is a gift of the Nile'.

The hot climate and the Nile's summer floods, which are nowadays controlled by the Aswan Dam, mean that farmers harvest two to four times a year depending on the crop being cultivated. This enables production of the country's basic food supply despite a rapidly increasing population.

In ancient times the Nile delta in the north of Egypt consisted of five branches bringing fertile alluvial soil with the ever plentiful waters. However, over the course of thousands of years the landscape has changed drastically. Today there are only two remaining branches that stretch from the north of Cairo through Lower Egypt to the Mediterranean Sea and water traffic on the river is now divided up with the help of an extensive canal network.

The Nile delta, which covers an area of 24,000 sq km (9,264 sq mi), is Egypt's most important agricultural region producing everything from corn, vegetables and fruit to the famous Egyptian long-fibre cotton. In the 19th century, Alexandria benefited enormously from this 'white gold' and developed into a modern, Mediterranean port city.

Cairo is located at the southern tip of the delta and connects Upper and Lower Egypt. The nation's capital dazzles visitors with the most diverse of sights. The pyramids in Giza in the west tower above the modern city. In the city center minarets, church towers and high-rise buildings vie for the attention of wor-shippers as Christians and Muslims make their way to prayers. Meanwhile, people of all backgrounds and nationalities stroll along the Nile in this, the 'Mother of the World' as locals have come to call their rich city.

The minarets of Cairo silhouetted in a glowing red-gold sunset.

From the Mediterranean to the 'Nubian Sea', Egypt is home to a plethora of sites that are loaded with history. You'll experience both ancient and modern worlds through-out the approximately 1,400-km (870-mile) journey and the route follows large stretches of the country's oldest traffic route, the Nile. The trip only branches off into the desert between Alexandria and Cairo.

① Alexandria Alexander the Great, after whom this town was named, founded Alexandria in 332 BC. Home to the Ptolemaic Dynasty (323–330 BC), it became the capital of Egypt and gained a great reputation as a center of scholarship and the sciences. The Temple of Serapi, the famous library and the lighthouse were the icons of the city.

However, after being conquered by the Romans its monuments fell into decay and Alexandria only prospered again under the leadership of Mohammed Ali (1805–1849). Fundamental city sanitation measures were introduced at the end of the 20th century and have restored the attractiveness of this important port city. Discoveries dating back to the time of Egypt's last ruler, Cleopatra, were recovered from the eastern port basin and made worldwide headlines.

With a population of close to five million, Alexandria is the country's second-largest city. Its beaches are very popular. Alexandria's eastern sprawl almost reaches the city of Rashid (Rosetta), where French esearchers discovered the famous trilingual Rosetta Stone (now in the British Museum in London) at the end of the 19th century. This stone helped to decipher hieroglyphic scripts that had proved impossible to understand.

South-west of Alexandria you turn off coastal road 55 towards one of the most important early Christian pilgrim sites on the Mediterranean.

② Abu Mena The martyr Mena was murdered in AD 296 under orders from the Roman emperor, Diocletian, and was buried here, some 50 km (31 miles) from Alexandria. Soon after that the well near his grave was said to possess heal-

Travel Information

Route profile
Length: approx. 1,400 km (870 miles), excluding detours
Time required: 14–20 days
Start: Alexandria
End: Abu Simbel
Route (main locations): Alexandria, Cairo, El-Minia, Assiût, Luxor/Thebes West, Edfu, Aswan, Abu Simbel

Specifics: Special safety regulations apply for off-road journeys, and some stretches can only be driven with an accompanying convoy. Night journeys are to be strictly avoided.

Traffic information:
The speed limit for cars in built-up areas is 50 km/h (31 mph), and 100 km/h (62 mph) on highways and rural roads. In the cities, Egyptian drivers take up the whole road but in rural areas be careful of forms of traffic such as donkeys, water buffalo or camels. Normally only parking lights are used at night. Oncoming cars briefly turn their headlights up to high beam. Always drive defensively!
Those entering and leaving in their own vehicle must be prepared for customs checks.

When to go:
October to May

General information:
www.egypt.com
www.ancientegypt.co.uk

ing powers. In the 5th century a large public bath was built that attracted tens of thousands of faithful to its magical waters. The ruins of churches, monastery complexes and pilgrim quarters that were rediscovered in 1905 are now UNESCO World Heritage Sites, though they are severely threatened by rising ground-water levels. In 1959, the new monastery of Abu Mena was built. The highway-like desert road 11 takes you further south.

③ Wadi el-Natrun About 110 km (68 miles) south of Alexandria you'll come to a val-

ley that is 22 m (72 ft) below sea level in the desert area west of the delta. Nitrate (sodium bicarbonate) extracted during the time of the pharaohs gave the valley its name, which means Nitrate Valley.

Surrounded by olive and date palm groves, four of the once more than fifty monasteries are still standing. In the 4th century, hermits would gather around spiritual leaders like the holy Makarios forming what would be the first monasterial communities. The oldest of these monasteries, built in the 4th century, is the Deir el-Baramus in the north of the valley. The

monks of the Deir Amba Bschoi and the Dei res-Suryan also accept non-Coptic guests.

Back on the desert road you'll pass Medînet es-Sadat, one of the planned cities built under the rule of President Anwar Sadat (1970–1981). These satellite cities were built in circles in the desert around Cairo. Industrial plants created jobs and kindergartens, schools, parks and leisure activities topped off the activities.

Taking the northern section of the ring road that circumvents most of Cairo's traffic will bring you to the Nile relatively quickly.

④ Cairo In Arabic, Egypt's capital is called Al-Qahira, 'The Victorious One'. It is home to some 20 million people and counting. Throughout its long history, the Egyptian metropolis has had many different looks, the city center having shifted from the Nile to the citadel in the foothills of the Moqattam mountains and then back to the Nile.

A Nilometer at the southern tip of Roda Island is testimony to

the Egyptian capital's dignified age. Long before it was given the name of Cairo in the 10th century BC, priests serving ancient Egyptian gods set up wells all over the country to measure the level of the yearly Nile flood and then calculated taxes.

Opposite the island on the eastern bank was one of the country's most important inland ports, Per Hapi en Junu. When the Romans fortified the port, the early Christians made use of the well-protected area to build their first churches here. In the 'Candles Quarter' directly next to the Mari Girgis metro station, the Moallka Church, dedicated to the Virgin Mary,

1 Alexandria stretches for miles along the Mediterranean coast.

2 The Sultan Hassan Mosque in Cairo is a place of worship, mausoleum and educational site.

3 Some of Egypt's oldest monasteries are found in the Wadi el-Natrun – Nitrate Valley.

rises high upon the foundations of the Roman fortress.

Over a period of 600 years, Fatimids, Ajjubids, Mamlucks and Osmans had elegant mosques, palaces, commercial establishments, wells and schools built in Cairo. Salah ed-Din, who came to power in AD 1171, had his residence moved to the citadel, but Al-Qahira remained the lively center of the city. Even today, visitors are still fascinated by the bustling bazaars of the Khan el-Khalili. City planners were again kept busy under Mohammed Ali's reign, who used Paris as a model to transform Cairo into a modern metropolis in the 19th century. Art-nouveau facades between the Midan el-Opera and the Midan Talaat Harb are evocative of these times.

Nowadays, the glass facades of hotels, government offices and shopping malls distinguish the modern heart of Cairo. Residential and office buildings twenty to thirty floors high loom large along the river where the property is most expensive.

Further on from the center are the old quarters such as Heliopolis or Maadi, filled with elegent villas and green parks. Then there are the concrete jungles of closely packed residential areas for the rest of Cairo's locals. And at the base of the citadel sprawls the Islamic Old Town with its hundreds of mosques.

5 Giza The provincial capital of Giza is a close relative of Cairo located on the western bank of the Nile. The three great pyramids of the pharaohs Cheops, Chephren and Mykerinos stand regally on a limestone plateau over the city. The rulers had them constructed in the 3rd millennium BC as tombs to withstand the ages. The blocks piled on top of each other to create the tremendous moun-

tain that is Cheops' pyramid weigh an average of 2 tonnes (2.2 tons) a piece. Even without the finely sanded coating they originally had, the pyramids are a majestic and awe-inspiring sight. They used to stand almost 147 m (482 ft) high, but they have shrunk over time by 10 m (33 ft).

In the Middle Ages, Cairo's master builders helped themselves to the almost endless quarry. Part of the coating has been preserved on the neighbouring pyramid of Chephren. Significantly smaller in size at just 65.5 m (215 ft) is the tomb of Mykerinos, which appears to have missed out on this detail and is humbled by the presence of its formidable neighbours.

The Sphinx lies to the east of these three monuments. Carved out of existing rocks at its location, the Sphinx embodies the divine rising sun. A shrine built of blocks of rock soars before its paws. Directly next to it, Chephren had his valley temple constructed out of pink granite and alabaster.

6 Memphis The first capital of Egypt, its administrative headquarters, the largest garrison

city, and the sacred place of the god Ptah – Memphis covered a lot of bases throughout the course of its long history. Today not much is left of this former cosmopolitan city.

Its palaces and residences of clay bricks have long been reclaimed by the earth and transformed into fertile farmland. The monumental figure of Ramses II and the alabaster sphinx are the only legacy of the city's former glory. They are housed in the open-air museum among palm groves near the small village of Mitrahina on the south-western edge of Giza.

7 Sakkara One of Egypt's largest cemeteries sprawls in

the desert approximately 20 km (12 miles) south of Giza. Great tombs of kings were already being constructed here in the early civilizations of the pharaohs. But this cemetery only gained in significance when the first pyramid was built under Djoser's reign (around 2750 BC). Its architect, Imhotep, invented the idea of using stone as a building material and laid the foundations for a tradition that now goes back three thousand years. The step pyramid subsequently attracted many other rulers and dignitaries who had their tombs erected here. The tomb of Ti, with its illustration of the entombed man hunting in the papyrus coppice, is one of

number of churches is a noticeable feature of the city's skyline. Minia is home to a great many Copts.

11 Beni Hassan From the western bank of the Nile approximately 25 km (15.5 miles) south of El-Minia you can take a boat to the graves of the princes of Beni Hassan. These structures were hewn into the precipice during the 11th and 12th dynasties between 2000 and 1755 BC. The murals on the walls depict interesting scenes: children dancing and playing with balls, craftsmen, mythical creatures in the desert and the famous wrestling scenes of Egyptian soldiers practising martial arts. The choice of themes is an indication of the independence and creativity of the ancient provincial rulers.

12 Ashmunein/Hermopolis On the western bank 8 km (5 miles) north of Mallawî are the ruins of Ashmunein. This is where Thot was worshipped, the god of wisdom. Statues of baboons are still testimony to his cult where they were one of the sacred animals. In Christian times a St Mary's basilica was built over the ruins of a Ptolemaic temple.

13 Tuna el-Gebel This graveyard of Ashmunein is located in the adjacent desert area west of town. The large, underground burial complex for the sacred animals of Thot is rather unusu-

3

the largest and most beautiful private tombs from the Ancient Kingdom (2750–2195 BC). Almost a thousand years later, General Haremhab had his 'Eternal House' constructed here before becoming pharaoh in 1320 BC and acquiring an even more magnificent tomb in the Valley of the Kings. Another 10 km (6 miles) further south the lane turns off toward the next field of pyramids.

8 Dahshûr Snofru was the father of the pharaoh Cheops who set up the 'Pyramid Experimentation Field'. In fact, two of these mighty constructions originate from his reign. The Red Pyramid gets its name from its

red-coloured limestone. Compared to Cheops' majestic edifice, it crouches much lower in the desert landscape.
Snofru's master builders had become cautious following serious problems at the preceding building some 2 km (1 mile) further south – fissures had formed inside the so-called bent pyramid, meaning it had to be completed with a softened, sloping angle. Further to the south-east are the 'Black Pyramids'.
Amenemhet III had them built around 1800 BC using a completely different method. The frame was a cross-shaped limestone shell on top of which a mighty mountain of mud bricks was piled.

After 45 km (28 miles), road 2 runs parallel to the Nile to the turn-off for Meidum.

9 Meidum Snofru also carried out work here at the edge of the fertile valley of Faijûm. The ruins of the shell-design pyramids look like gigantic sand cakes. There are some famous murals from the graves of the neighbouring royal suite – the Meidum Geese can be admired in Cairo's National Museum.
Back on road 2 the route heads further south through smaller settlements before reaching the provincial capital of Beni Suêf after 42 km (26 miles). Here we recommend you drive over the bridge to the eastern bank of the Nile where a quicker desert road makes the rest of the journey to El-Minia a lot easier.

10 El-Minia With some 250,000 inhabitants, El-Minia is one of the busiest cities in Middle Egypt. As an administrative headquarters, a university town and an industrial center it provides employment for people from the surrounding areas while also acting as a popular starting point for interesting sightseeing tours. The large

1 A desert camel ride in front of the pyramids of Giza.

2 The sphinx, part human, part lion, was worshiped as a representation of the morning sun god as it crouches in a hollow before the Khafre pyramids.

3 Colourfully bridled camels wait in Sakkara.

al and includes a wide array of mummified animals in addition to ibises and baboons. Even crocodiles and fish were found in the maze of crypts.

Priests at the temple of Thot were also laid to rest here. The tomb of the high priest Petosiris from early Ptolemaic times displays ancient Egyptian and Greek art side by side.

The journey continues south through Mallawî and over a narrow lane near the village of Deir Mawas towards the banks of the Nile. A boat can take you to the other side of the river where off-road vehicles are ready to take visitors to the very widely scattered tourist sites.

14 Tell el-Amârna In around 1350 BC, Akhenaten founded the new capital of Akhetaten, meaning the 'Horizon of Aten', in an expansive valley. Palace complexes and residences for the new elite were built along with new temples for the only god, Aten. Luckily for archaeologists, the city was abandoned after the heretic king's death and despite heavy destruction the excavations at the start of the 20th century revealed that many of the unique artworks from this time were still intact. The famous bust of Queen Nerfertiti (today in the Egyptian Museum in Berlin) was discovered on 6 December 1912.

15 Assiût After travelling approximately 75 km (46.5 miles) through the many villages and towns along the Nile you will eventually reach the next provincial capital on the trip, Assiût. Here, the long desert road turns off towards the oases of Kharga and Dakhla where a 19th-century dam regulates the Nile floods.

We recommend you go back over the bridge to the less developed eastern bank before continuing on.

16 Sohâg/Akhmîm These two sister cities 120 km (74.5 miles) south of Assiût are connected by one of the few Nile bridges. Outside Sohâg on the western bank are the ruins of Deir el-Abjad, the 'White Monastery', evidence of Egypt's early Christian history. Many of the blocks used to build the Deir el-Abjad and the accompanying church originate from pharaoh-era constructions. The monastery, which housed up to 4,000 monks in its heyday, became famous under its abbot Schenute (AD 348–466), the father of Coptic literature, who fought fiercely against the still existing ancient Egyptian cults and traditions.

On the western bank it's another 50 km (31 miles) on the main road until a sign at Balyana points to the turn-off to Abydos.

17 Abydos In ancient Egypt's early days, Abydos was already of paramount significance as a burial site for kings and princes. It was the main cult town for the god of life, death and fertility, Osiris, and one of the country's most important pilgrimage destinations. The belief in life after death is illustrated in tomb complexes, funerary temples and memorial stones.

Greatly worshiped as the rightful judge and ruler of the afterlife, Osiris also symbolized the hope for resurrection. The funerary temple of Sethos I (1290–1279 BC) is an impressive sight with a series of very ele-

gant reliefs. After Nag Hammâdi, another 35 km (22 miles) south, the main road 2 continues along the eastern bank. The stretch on the western bank leads through rural areas and a number of villages. Following a bend in the Nile that sweeps around to the east, you will reach the turn-off to the temple of the ancient goddess Hathor in Dendera after approximately 60 km (37 miles).

18 Dendera Hathor was celestial goddess of a great many things including love, music and debauchery. She was very popular among the Egyptians. Her temple, which was fitted with proper public baths, was visited by pilgrims in their droves even until Roman times. The 'caring mother' aspect of the great goddess was embodied through her sacred animal, the cow – the reason Hathor was often depicted as a woman with cow ears. The

astronomical images on the ceilings of the entrance hall and the so-called animal circle in an oratory on the roof are some of the interesting details of this Ptolemaic-Roman temple. Crypts embedded in the masonry were used as secret storage places for valuable cult devices.

From Dendera the journey continues over the bridge to the eastern bank towards Qena, one of the country's best-tended provincial capitals. A 160-km (99-mile) route through the eastern desert to Safâga on the Red Sea begins here. Luxor is just 60 km (37 miles) away to the south.

19 Luxor The city of Luxor is one of the main destinations for tourists visiting Egypt. It has had its own international airport for many years with commercial as well as chartered traffic. There is a wide selection of hotels to

suit all budgets here. Tourism is the region's main source of income and employment.

Right in the center of the city the columns of the Temple of Amun loom large. Built during the Amenhotep III (1390–1353 BC) and Ramses II (1279–1213 BC) eras, this extremely important temple in the history of Egyptian priest- king worship is particularly spectacular at dusk when its reliefs are accentuated. It is connected to the second temple for Amun by a 3-km (1.8-mile) avenue lined with sphinxes. This impressive complex, Al-Karnak, spreads over an area of approximately 30 ha (74 acres) and is the largest ancient religious site in the world, second only to Giza in terms of visitors. The Al-Karnak complex inudes the secondary temples of the lion-headed Mut, the mother goddess, Montu the god of war and Maat the goddess of truth as well as a holy

forum. The temple complex was under construction for nearly 2,000 years. The great columned hall is an impressive site with a total of 134 gigantic papyrus columns towering over a vast area of 5,000 sq m (5,980 sq yds). Numerous discoveries from both temples and other surrounding sites are displayed in the interesting Luxor Museum and include the blocks from a Temple of Aten dating back to the reign of the later ostracized pharaoh Amenhotep IV. The museum's treasures include statues from the time of Amenhotep III and Haremhab discovered in 1989 in the Luxor Temple.

A small mummification museum below the road along the Nile gives an overview of the preservation process.

⑳ **Thebes West** The area on the opposite side of the river is home to one of the most

famous cemeteries in the world. In a remote basin of crum-bling limestone mountains, pharaohs of the New Kingdom (1540–1075 BC) had their tombs built in what became known as the Valley of the Kings.

The world public got its first glimpse of this in 1922 when Howard Carter discovered the still unlooted tomb of the young King Tutankhamun. The small tomb's opulent adornments are today exhibited in the National Museum of Cairo. In the valley itself, people continue to marvel at the incredible murals whose bright colours are still preserved in some areas. Painted on the walls of the long passages and in the coffin chambers, these murals describe Ra the Sun god's journey through the night to the sunrise. The pharaohs hoped to take part in this journey and the daily rejuvenation that went with it.

The funerary temples built at the edges of the fertile land here were used for the cultish care of the pharaohs in the afterlife. The most unique of these was constructed for the female pharaoh Hatshepsut (1479–1458 BC). Divided into three monumental terraces, the perfectly symmetrical modern-looking building is nestled in the valley of Deir el-Bahri.

Officers, priests and other dignitaries built their own magnificent tombs on the path leading to the Temple of the Pharaohs as well as on the northern and

southern mountainsides. The reliefs and murals in these cave tombs, ranging from very small to imposingly large depending on their wealth, often depict scenes from everyday life.

Believing in eternal life, the tomb owners are shown having frivolous parties with their family and friends. Important stages of their careers are also illustrated. The artisan colony of Deir el-Medina is quite famous for its colourful tombs, where religious themes are shown on the walls. The Valley of the Queens is home to the tombs not only of the great pharaohs' wives, but also of the young princes of the kingdoms. The tomb of Nefertari, the royal wife of Ramses II (also known as Ramses the Great), was restored at great expense here. Only very few parts of this funerary temple have been preserved, mainly because his successor, Ramses III, used blocks from the older construction to build his temple in Medînet Habu.

㉑ **Esna** Just 60 km (37 miles) south of Luxor down the main road on the eastern bank is Esna. Cross the bridge to the western bank. Keep in mind that the bridge is closed twice a day to let the cruise ships pass.

1 Restoration work renewed the grandeur of the terrace temple of Hatshepsut.

2 These monumental figures of Amenhotep III in Luxor are as famous as the Colossi of Memnon.

3 In the second courtyard of the funerary temple of Ramses III in Thebes, reliefs depict a procession of Min, the god of fertility.

4 Luxor: In some parts of the Temple of Ramses III in Medînet Habu, the colours still retain their original brilliance.

Deep under the bustling bazaar are the remains of a Roman temple to the god of creation, Khnum. You can only see the atrium with its columns of plants. Other parts of the temple are possibly still underneath the modern buildings above.

22 El Kab The journey continues back over to the eastern bank, where rock tombs on the eastern side of the mountains draw you to a halt after some 35 km (22 miles). El Kab was a significant place early on, being the cult site of the goddess of Upper Egypt, Nechbet. Two of these tombs are of historic interest – that of Ahmose Son of Ibana who was a naval commander during the reign of Ahmose I (roughly 1550–1525 BC) and helped expel the Hyksos who had occupied Lower and Middle Egypt for more than 100 years. He even documented the event in an inscription due to its far-reaching effects for the whole of Egypt. His grandson, Paheri, earned the respect of the royals by educating the prince under the reign of Thutmosis III. On his tomb he is depicted with the king's son on his lap. South of the graves the Wadi Hilal opens up and its entrance is marked with small temple buildings.

23 Edfu It is just another 30 km (18.5 miles) to the country's best-preserved ancient Egyptian temple. On the outskirts of the vibrant city of Edfu on the west bank of the Nile is a massive Ptolemaic temple that is still surrounded by a mighty clay brick wall. Horus, with his human body and falcon head and one of the longest surviving cult gods in Egypt, was worshipped here. As the son of Osiris, who was murdered by his brother Set, it was his job to get revenge on his father's death. Horus thus came to represent

new beginnings and was the guarantor for law and justice. The pictures in the temple's tower gallery make reference to the mystery theater performances that took place every year depicting the battle between Horus and his father's murderer. The temple's inscriptions contain very precise instructions for the priests in their important task of reconstructing the ancient Egyptian cults.

24 Gebel el-Silsila A good 40 km (25 miles) south of Edfu are the sandstone formations of Gebel el-Silsila close to the banks of the Nile. In the time of the pharaohs, sandstone was quarried on both the banks for their many construction projects. Today the mountains further south give way to fertile land where sugar cane is the predominant crop processed in local refineries. After the Aswan Dam was built, this region became the home for resettled Nubians.

25 Kôm Ombo The picturesque remains of the mighty double temple of Kôm Ombo

rise up next to the banks of the river. Built in Ptolemaic-Roman times for the falcon-headed Horus and the crocodile-shaped Sobek, the extraordinary details on this temple include the depiction of the Roman Emperor Trajan who dedicated medical devices to the deity, Imhotep.

Crocodiles, kept by the priests as the sacred animals of Sobek, were carefully mummified after their deaths and buried near the temple. A few exam-

ples of these can be seen today in a small chapel dating back to the time of Hadrian.

26 Aswan Aswan is considered one of the most beautiful cities in Egypt because of its location at the first Nile cataract. Numerous small islands made from granite blocks worn smooth by the water rise up out of the river. A sailing trip in a traditional felucca should be part of a visit to the Nubian capital. Elephantine Island, the actual birthplace

3

27 **Philae** The temple complex of the goddess Isis is sitated on an island between the two dams that is only accessible by boat. This was one of the monuments moved to higher ground before the dam was built. Isis' followers continued to render homage to their goddess in the Ptolemaic temple until the 6th century AD. The first hall of columns was transformed into a church of St Stephen under the reign of Emperor Justinian to replace old Egyptian beliefs.

28 **Kalabsha** Directly south of the High Dam on the western bank is the new location of four ancient temples. A boat ride takes you to the Temple of Kalabsha.

During its relocation by German archaeologists, blocks from an older temple were discovered inside the walls. These blocks have been put back together and are today displayed as the Kalabsha Gate in the Egyptian Museum in Berlin. The temple, which was built in Roman times, was built for the god Mandulis, a Nubian version of the falcon god, Horus. At its southern edge are blocks containing prehistoric petroglyphs depicting giraffes and elephants, thus providing information on the essentially humid climate of the times 5,000 years before Christ. The columns and statues of the temple of Gerf Hussein are a stout reminder of the time of Ramses II. Reliefs in the rock

of the city, lies in the center of Aswan. Taking a walk through the excavations around its southern tip transport you back to the early times of the ancient Egyptian settlement of Abu, which means 'ivory'. German and Swiss archaeologists discovered Egypt's earliest cult site here – one of the recesses between the granite blocks dedicated to the goddess Satet. Over the centuries these humble beginnings were developed into an impressive temple. From

the end of the Old Kingdom, rulers of this border town had their tombs constructed in the mountainside on the western bank. Steep slopes lead to the burial sites. The ruins of the Simeon Monastery, home to a great many monks between the 7th and 13th centuries, are also located on the western bank. Looming large on a nearby hill is the Fatimid mosque-style mausoleum of the 48th imam of the Shia Ismaili Muslims, Aga Khan III (1877–1957).

South of the city two dams seal off the Nile Valley. The older dam was built as a water-regulating mechanism between 1898 and 1902, while the second is known as the High Dam (Sadd Ali). It holds back the waters of the Nile to Lake Nasser, which is 500 km (311 miles) long. Its construction (1960–1971) had economic, developmental and political consequences. After the US and Britain backed out of the financing of the project, President Nasser decided to nationalize the Suez Canal to pay for the dam. This led to the Suez Crisis and tensions between Egypt and the West. Egypt subsequently accepted an offer from the Soviets to finance the dam.

As part of the construction of the Aswan High Dam, the flood-threatened area of Nubia was explored and a number of monuments moved to other locations. New areas of settlement were developed for Nubia's population in Egypt and Sudan. The Nubian Museum was opened in 1997 and has a memorial to their history.

1 A natural granite threshold cuts through the river valley and shapes the landscape near Aswan.

2 The Temple of Horus in Edfu has gigantic columns.

3 The Temple of Isis in Philae was relocated to higher ground on a neighbouring island.

temple of Beit el-Wali, which were relocated just 100 m (328 yds) west of the Kalabsha Temple and created in the same era, are much more elegant in comparison. The graceful kiosk with Hathor column capitals was originally located at the Kertassi quarry and promised divine protection for the men working there.

㉙ Neu-Sebua The asphalt road now stretches through the desert west of Lake Nasser. Abu Simbel is about 300 km (186 miles) from Aswan. Halfway down, an access road leads to the shores of the lake near New Sebua, where you can see three temples at their new locations.

The largest of the three was named for the sphinx figures in front of it – Wadi es-Sebua means 'Valley of the Lions'. Ramses II appears arrogantly on the temple walls; inside, he sits on an equal level with the gods. The Temple of Ad Dakkah was dedicated to Thot, the god of wisdom. Thot had travelled to Nubia as a messenger from the gods to entice Tefnut to Egypt, the daughter of the Sun god Ra. The scene of an ape dancing in front of a lioness plays on this divine myth.

The Chapel of el-Maharraka is still small and incomplete. In Roman times its location marked the border between the Roman Empire and the Kingdom of Meroë whose capital was unearthed north of Khartoum. Finally, it's back on the main road for another 40 km (25 miles) to the south until the next road turns east.

㉚ New Amada When Thutmosis III (1479–1426 BC) was pharaoh, Egypt had expanded its empire to the south. The temple for Amun-Ra and Ra-Harakhte symbolizes the power of the Egyptian gods. In the

20th century archaeologists put the temple on a track and pulled it to this higher, drier bank.

The neighbouring temple of ed-Derr was also built by Ramses II. The scenes in the hall of columns are stunning. The third monument in New Amada is the small rock tomb of Pennut, a reputable administrator in the conquered province.

㉛ Toshka Canal This canal goes straight through the

desert for 50 km (31 miles) to Abu Simbel. It is the most recent land reclamation project. The hope is to create a new Nile Valley. Green open spaces seem to indicate success.

㉜ Abu Simbel The relocation of this rock temple in the 1960s made worldwide headlines. Four colossal figures of Ramses II were cut out of the rock and rebuilt at a site 64 m (210 ft) higher. Inside, the walls display images of historic battles and

ritual scenes. Pharaoh Ramses dedicated this smaller temple to his wife Nefertari and the goddess Hathor.

1 The Temple of Wadi es-Sebua is one of many buildings constructed under Ramses II in Nubia.

2 The southernmost destination for many travellers in Egypt is the famous rock temples of Ramses II in Abu Simbel.

Alexandria This city was founded by Alexander the Great in 332 BC and was once home to one of the most important libraries in the world, which was replaced in 2002 with a worthy successor.

Cairo In just a few decades the population of Egypt's capital grew from 3 million to over 20 million people – a real melting pot. In 1979, UNESCO declared the Islamic Old City a World Heritage Site.

Valley of the Kings Starting with the 11th dynasty, the pharaohs built their tombs on the western bank of the Nile near Thebes. It is still an enormous necropolis.

Temple of Queen Hatshepsut This temple near Deir el-Bahri is a spectacular sight below the 300-m (984-ft) rock face. Perfect symmetry well pre-dates the Parthenon.

Edfu The Temple of Horus is an example of Ptolemaic architecture located at the site of an older temple. Horus and Set, who killed his father Osiris, were impor-tant Egyptian deities worshipped here.

Abu Simbel The four mighty statues of Pharaoh Ramses II (c. 1200 BC) were relo-cated with the support of UNESCO when Egypt's President Gamal Abdel Nasser built the Aswan High Dam and Lake Nasser in the 1950s that would have flooded the ancient ruins.

Esna Far below today's ground level is the Temple of Esna, a significant monu-ment from Ptolemaic times (332–30 BC). The Nile Perch was worshipped here.

Philae The main temple in the complex on this island in the Nile near Aswan is dedicated to the goddess Isis and her son Horus.

Map labels:
Rosetta
ALEXANDRIA
Kafr el-Sheikh
Damietta
Port Said
Medinet el'Ameriya el Guedida
Damanhûr
Tanta
Tanis
Ismâilîya
55
Suez Canal
El-Alamein
Abu Mena
Sâdât City
Tûkh
11
Palace of Abbasi
Wadi el-Natrûn
19
CAIRO
El Agrud
Baharîja Oasis
Giza
Memphis
Sakkara
Suez
24
Dahshûr
Ain Sukhnah
Pyramid of Meidum
El Ghurdaqah
Pyramid of El Lâhûn
El Burumbul
Medinet el-Faijûm
Beni Suêf
Deir Samû'il
El Fashn
Beni Mazâr
Nile
Samâlût
Djebel at Tayr
El-Minia
El Fikriya
Beni Hassan
Hermopolis
Mallawî
Tuna el-Gebel
Deir Mawas
Tell el-Amârna
Dairût
Manfalût
El Badârî
Assiût
Dâw el Kabîr (Antaeopolis)
Tima
Kôm Ishqaw (Aphroditopolis)
Akhmîm
Kharga Oasis
Sohâg
Girgâ
Safâga
Deir el-Abyad
Dendera
Balyana
Qena
Abydos
El Quseir
Nag Hammâdi
Valley of the Kings
Qûs
Western Thebes
Karnak
Temple of Hatshepsut
Luxor
Kharga Oasis
El Kab (Nekheb)
Esna
Marsa Alam
Temple of Khnum
Kom el Ahmar (Nekhen)
Edfu
El Ridisiya Bahari
Temple of Horus
Silwa Bahari
Gebel el-Silsila
Kagug
Kôm Ombo
Daraw
Tombs of the Nobles
Aswân
Monastery of St Simeon
Temple of Philae
Medinet Sahara (Sahara City)
Aswân High Dam
Kalabsha
Lake Nasser
Kharga Oasis
New Sebua
Toshka project
New Amada
Abu Simbel
Wadi Halfa
SUDAN

The pyramids of Giza Built over 4,500 years ago (around 2700–2500 BC), Egypt's largest and most famous pyramids are found in the Cairo suburb of Giza. The mighty Sphinx next to the pyramids has the body of a lion and a human face. Nobody knows who destroyed its nose.

Dendera This temple complex was the most important cult site of the goddess Hathor. Her divine husband Thoh was also worshipped here.

Sakkara The step pyramid of the pharaoh Djoser lies in the middle of a large tem-ple area west of Memphis.

Luxor This city is the tourist center of Egypt. Looming large in the south of the city is the large temple complex where Amenhotep III immortalized himself at the end of an avenue lined with sphinxes.

Al-Karnak This vast tem-ple city near Luxor was built over 2,000 years ago and is one of the ancient wonders of the world.

Kôm Ombo This double temple is dedicated to the deities Sobek and Horus. Its magical location is captivating.

Aswan Egypt is domi-nated by the desert, but the Nile enabled civiliza-tion to prosper. A high-light of any Egypt trip is a cruise on the Nile to Aswan in a stylish feluc-ca, a traditional Arab sailing boat.

Oryx antelope can even survive

Namibia and Botswana

African big game and colonial history up close

Spectacular desert landscapes, charming colonial towns, bizarre granite realms, ancient rock art galleries, an impressive abundance of wildlife and the exotic cultures of the Himba and Bushmen. Despite its sparseness, Namibia is one of the most fascinating and diverse travel destinations in Africa. From here, two major rivers form the basis for a trip to Zambia and Zimbabwe, Namibia's neighbors to the east: the Zambezi River with Victoria Falls, and the Okavango River.

Your tour of Namibia starts in the capital, Windhoek, and then heads north. Past the wood markets of the village of Okahandja, the route continues on to the bizarrely formed massif of the Erongo Mountains before the Waterberg Plateau appears far away on the horizon. The plateau is home to a wide variety of rare wild animals such as black rhinos, leopards and sable antelope. The pretty colonial towns of Tsumeb and Grootfontein feature in the tour's next stage. This was where the 60-tonne (66-ton) Hoba meteorite crashed down some 80,000 years ago. The Transnamibiana then winds its

Astonishing San rock paintings in the Kalahari Desert.

way west towards Etosha National Park where elephants, gnus, zebras, giraffes, oryx, eland antelopes, ostriches, springboks and marabous can be seen at the watering hole on the stark steppe.

The Kaokoveld in the northwest is home to the Himba people, who are distinguished by their artistically styled hair. Opuwo, the main town in the Kaokoveld, is the last supplies station before the poorly maintained roads heading toward the Angolan border take you to the majestic Epupa Falls in the Kunene Region. On the way south, you'll visit the Twyfelfontein in Damaraland, a unique gallery of ancient Namibian rock art depicting animals, rituals and dances. Not far away, nature's artworks attract many visitors: the Organ Pipes, Burnt Mountain and the Petrified For-

in the arid Namib Desert.

Storm clouds over the nearly treeless Etosha Pan herald the approaching rainy season.

The star dunes tower up to heights of 350 m (1,148 ft) around the salt-pans of the Sossusvlei. At sunrise, the dunes are bathed in red light.

est. The route now proceeds towards the Atlantic through the vast basin of Messum Crater. Once there, a detour heads north to the Cape Cross seal colony. Sand dunes line the Atlantic coast, and the seaside resort of Swakopmund lures tourists with German colonial architecture and a red-and-white-striped lighthouse. The route then crosses the Namib, the oldest desert on earth, passes by the Naukluft and heads south to the sea of dunes around the Sossusvlei.

The Transnamibiana continues south along the Great Escarpment, where the Namibian High Plateau breaks off into the Namib Desert. The first German trade settlement, Lüderitz, is the destination on the next leg. The pastel-colored colonial town on the rugged Atlantic coast was founded in 1883. Twenty years later, diamonds were found in the desert nearby where today only the ghost town of Kolmanskop is reminds us of the golden years of diamond discoveries and mining in the what was at the time called German South-West Africa.

On the way back east, the 161-km-long (100 mi) Fish River Canyon is the next stop on your journey, where the vista point gives you a look down into the 500-m (1,641-ft) deep gorge: the world's second-largest canyon after the Grand Canyon. The Kokerboom (Quiver Tree Forest) near Keetmanshoop is the last stop on the way back to Windhoek.

A short flight will bring you quickly to the next exciting attractions in Zimbabwe and Botswana, Namibia's neighbours to the east: Victoria Falls, where the waters of the mighty Zambezi thunder 110 m (361 ft) down into a narrow gorge; and two renowned reserves in Botswana's Okavango Delta – the Chobe National Park and the Moremi Game Reserve.

The route then heads through the district capital of Maun and along the western edge of the Okavango Delta before briefly passing through a bit of Namibia. After driving through the Caprivi Strip, the circuit is complete when you arrive at the small town of Victoria Falls and then fly back to Windhoek.

Large herds of elephants roam Botswana's Chobe National Park.

1

From the farmlands of central Namibia to the stark wilderness of the Kaokoveld, from the wildlife of the Etosha Pan to the lunar landscapes of the Namib Desert, and from the colonial town of Swakopmund to the world's second-largest canyon, this 4,900-km (3,045 mi) tour shows you every facet of Namibia, culminating in a wonderful side trip to Victoria Falls and the Okavango Delta.

The street names and colonial architecture in parts of Namibia are reminders of the short-lived period when the Germans ruled the region they referred to as German South-West Africa, from 1884 to 1919.

1 Windhoek The capital of Namibia was not founded until 1890, when Curt von François built the Alte Feste (Old Fort). At the time the fort was the headquarters of the protection troops; today it is the national museum. In 1902, a rail connection to Swakopmund brought further development for the city, which was home to the German colonial administration until 1915. Windhoek remained the capital when Namibia gained its independence from South Africa in 1990. Those not wanting to stay the night in the city can drive to the

Daan Viljoen Game Park 24 km (15 mi) west and enjoy a first encounter with African wildlife.

The B1 heads north from the capital through seemingly uninhabited thorn bush savannahs to Okahandja 65 km (40 mi) away. Endless farm fences line both sides of the road.

2 Okahandja This town welcomes guests with its surprising greenness. For most of the year, a riverbed lined with gallery forests flows with underground water, supplying fields and gardens with sufficient moisture. Wood-carvers and cabinetmakers have been able to develop a sizable market here at both ends of town as well. Historic attractions include the train station, built in 1901, and the Rhine Mission Church, erected in 1876, the resting place of

several members of the German protection troops. Some important Herero chiefs are buried in a cemetery somewhat further away from Heroe's Street. Hereros from all over Namibia make

a pilgrimage at the end of August to this important historical and religious town to celebrate an annual memorial day. Traveling west for about 110 km (68 mi) along the B2 takes you

Travel Information

Route profile
Length: approx. 4900 km (3,045 mi)
Time required: 28–35 days
Start and end: Windhoek
Route (main locations): Windhoek, Waterberg Plateau Park, Etosha National Park, Opuwo, Epupa Falls, Twyfelfontein, Swakopmund, Namib, Lüderitz, Fish River Canyon Park, Keetmanshoop, Windhoek, Victoria Falls, Maun, Windhoek.

Transport information:
Traffic in Namibia is on the left! The permitted speed limit within townships is 60 km/h (37 mph), on paved roads 120 km/h (75 mph), and 100 km/h (62 mph) on unsealed roads. Caution: You must be careful of

animal crossings throughout the entire country.

When to go: Winter (June to September) is the ideal season for observing the wildlife, with daytime temperatures of around 20°C (68°F).

Particularities: The walk through the Fish River Canyon is only permitted in winter; you must also have a health certificate and be in groups of at least three. Hobas Lodge near the first lookout point has permits.

Information:
Nambia: *www.namibia tourism.com.na*
Botswana: *www.botswana-tourism.gov.bw*

to the farming town of Karibib. Roughly 28 km (17 miles) further on, a turnoff near Usakos brings you to the Ameib guest farm, just 16 km (10 mi) away at the foot of the Erongo Mountains and their impressive granite formations (entry fee).

③ **Erongo Mountains** The golden-brown granite domes of the 2,332-m-high (7,651-ft) Erongo Massif have been partially eroded to form bizarre sculptures. The Bull's Party rocks do actually look like bulls getting together for a meeting, and the elephant head is clearly visible in Elephant's Head rock. You can reach the most beautiful formations around 16

km (10 mi) from Ameib. The road is in good condition. A footpath leads you to Phillip's Cave, a natural overhang under which rock paintings such as the famous "White Elephant" have been protected from weather damage.

Before heading back to Karibib, it's worth looking to the west where the silhouette of the 1,728-m-high (5,670-ft) Spitzkoppe dominates the thorn bush savannah. From Karibib, head north on the C33.

④ **Omaruru** After a 64-km (40 mile) journey through the dry savannah, this small town also stuns visitors with its lush greenery. The Omaruru River

ensures sufficient moisture for the area.

The region here was a traditional grazing area for the nomadic Herero and their livestock. In 1872, emissaries of the Rhine Mission established a settlement here, which was then cut off and taken over by Herero warriors during the 1904 uprisings. Captain Franke, who had advanced in forced marchesfrom Gibeon, some 600 km (373 mi) away, was able to take the area back. In 1907, the Franke Tower was erected south of the dry riverbed as a signal tower in the event of another uprising.

⑤ **Otjihaenamaparero Farm** Another 65 km (40 mi) to the north, a short detour leads to some fossilized dinosaur prints. To get there, follow the D2414 at the hamlet of Kalkfeld. Turn off at the farm road towards Otjihaenamaparero Farm, about 30 km (19 mi) away. It's then a short walk through bushland to a sloping flagstone, on which you can clearly see the three-toed claw prints of several dinosaurs. The longest set of tracks extends for

more than 28 m (31 yds). They were created in the Jurassic period, probably about 150 million years ago.

The next stop is the town of Otjiwarongo. Here, follow the B1 south for 26 km (16 mi) and then turn off to the east onto the C22 towards Waterberg Plateau Park, which you will reach after 56 km (35 mi).

⑥ **Waterberg Plateau Park** The Waterberg mountain soars 200 m (656 ft) above the plains and is the remains of a once larger and higher plateau. Only a few massifs are left after the effects of erosion are taken into consideration. Fortunately, this 1,857-m-high (6,093 ft) plateau gets much more rainfall than the surrounding arid

1 The big and little Spitzkoppe are a challenge for climbers.

2 Erosion has exposed the granite rocks of the Erongo Mountains and formed smooth domes.

3 Thorn bush savannahs and bizarre stone formations are typical of central Namibia.

Omaheke Region, which means the nature reserve authorities were able to resettle wild game here whose original habitat was actually in the moister north of Namibia, in the Caprivi Strip. Sable antelope and black and white rhinos can be seen on safaris here, and the Cape griffon is among the rare birds living in the steep rock faces. Organized tours are the only way to see the plateau up close. The Waterberg is infamous as the setting for the "Battle of Waterberg" in which German troops under General Lothar von Trotha closed in on and killed the Herero gathered here in 1904. Estimates fluctuate between 20,000 and 60,000 Herero victims, most of whom died attempting to flee east through the Omaheke Desert. A cemetery with graves of colonial protection troops remembers the German deaths. There is no memorial for the Hereros. Back in Otjiwarongo, follow the B1 north-east before turning onto the B8 at Otavi. The city of Grootfontein is another 86 km (53 mi) away.

7 Grootfontein This pretty town at the foot of a castellated colonial fortress (now a museum) forms the eastern cor-

ner of a region characterized by large-scale mining and vast cornfields. The layers of stone are rich in natural resources, but copper mining is no longer profitable here. However, the water stored in the karst subsurface enables fruitful agriculture and regular harvests.
From Grootfontein, head back down the B8 for a little while before turning off onto the D2860. After roughly another 4 km (2 mi), turn onto the D2859. A sign will then show the way to the 60-tonne (66-ton) Hoba meteorite, which crashed down here 80,000 years ago. About 18 km (11 mi) further on, the road meets the paved C42, which you follow towards Tsumeb before hitting the B1. About 20 km (12 mi) north-west of Tsumeb on your left is the circular, 55-m-deep (180-ft) Otjikoto karst lake. After 50 km (31 mi) you reach the C38, which takes you to Etosha National Park.

8 Etosha National Park
You arrive at the boundary of the national park about 24 km (15 mi) after turning off the B1, and finally reach Namutoni after another 12 km (8 mi). The gleaming white Namutoni fort with its merlons was used as a

police station during the colonial period and today offers reasonably priced accommodation. Namutoni and the two other camps, Halali and Okaukuejo, open and close their gates at sunrise and sunset. No unauthorized persons can stay in the national park at night. However, the illuminated watering holes of the three camps are an excellent way to observe wildlife. The Okaukuejo water-

ing hole in particular is popular among the rhinos, but elephants, lions, hyenas, jackals and other hoofed animals can also be found here.
Etosha National Park was established by German Governor von Lindequist back in 1907. At the time, the park covered almost the entire northwestern part of Namibia, with a total area of 90,000 sq km (34,740 sq mi). In 1947, the

Kaokoveld broke away from the nature reserve to become the homeland of the Himba and Herero peoples. The park's size was again reduced in 1962 to create farmland. The actual inhabitants of the Etosha Pan and its surrounding area were originally the San Bushmen from the Heikom people, but when the park was created, they were prohibited from hunting and roaming in the region so their only alternative was to move further east to the "Bushman land" or work on the surrounding farms.

Today, the nature reserve is fenced in and covers an area of 22,000 sq km (8,492 sq mi). It has three entrance gates: the von Lindequist Gate in the east, the King Nehale Gate in the north and the Andersson Gate in the south-west. The speed limit in the park is 60 km/h (37 mph). Almost all the roads are open to cars, but leaving vehicles outside the fenced-in area is strictly prohibited.

Etosha's main feature is the Etosha Pan, a salt clay lakebed that covers about 5,000 sq km (1,930 sq mi) and whose water level depends on the season. The roads run along the southern edge of the pan and lead to a number of man-made watering holes, the Etosha Lookout and the "enchanted forest" west of Okaukuejo, where the almost leafless Moringa trees look like ancient giants. The vegetation throughout almost the entire park consists of light, salt-resistant plants. Bushes encircle the arid pan itself. To the east you will find palms and Mopane trees, whose foliage is popular among grazing giraffes, while grass savannahs stretch out to the west. Wild animals roam areas of the park according to the rainfall and the grass growth. In the dry season, herds prefer to stay at the artificial watering holes in the south, while in the rainy season, they head north and west and are harder to spot.

The local big game in Etosha include four of the "Big Five": elephants, rhinoceroses, leopards and lions. The habitat is too dry for the fifth: buffalo. The park has around 1,500 elephants and boasts an impressive 300 black rhinoceroses, which are better protected from opportunist poachers here than in the east African reserves. Apart from around 2,000 oryx antelope, more than 30,000 springboks also graze here with large herds of zebra and gnu, kudus, eland antelope and giraffes. Ostriches, secretary birds, Kori bustards and marabous are scattered throughout the savannah, while flamingos and pelicans dabble in the watery areas of the Pan. In actual fact, the population of roughly 500 lions is too large for the park, to the extent that they are displacing other predators such as cheetahs and leopards. However, with a bit of luck, you will still at least get to see some cheetahs. We recommend you stay at least one full day in the park. The watering holes are well marked, and the national park maps are helpful. Most importantly, be patient. At many watering holes, it's worth waiting a bit. Due to their good camouflage, you can only see lions once your eyes have adjusted to the grayish-brown surroundings. The Olifantsbad watering hole is considered a sure thing for elephant sightings, while lions often stay under the acacias of Ombika and near Okondeka.

Without any detours to the watering holes, it's roughly 140 km (87 mi) to Namutoni from Okaukuejo and another 17 km (11 mi) to Andersson Gate, where the C38 leaves the national park. Shortly before Outjo, after 84 km (52 mi), turn right onto the C40 and head west, following it through an increasingly mountainous, arid landscape, through the towns of Otjikondo and Kamanjab to the entrance of the luxurious Hobatere Lodge (220 km/137 mi from Outjo).

⑨ Hobatere Lodge This private game reserve, which forms part of the lodge, once belonged to the western portion of Etosha National Park. After the western border was determined, the adjacent areas were ceded to private tenants who were legally obliged to abide by the guidelines of the

1 Expansive grass savannahs with thorny umbrella acacias are typical of the northern part of Namibia.

2 Zebras and kudus crowd around a dried-up watering hole in Etosha National Park.

3 A rare sight: A pride of lions rests on the Etosha Pan. Lions typically prefer shady spots under trees or bushes.

reserve. The lodge offers safaris into this now "private" national park, as well as into the western part of the official national park, which is otherwise not open to individual visitors. After another 133 km (83 mi) or so you reach the turnoff of the C41, which heads toward Opuwo. Follow this for 60 km (37 mi) through the mountainous landscape of the Kaokoveld to the region's main town, Opuwo.

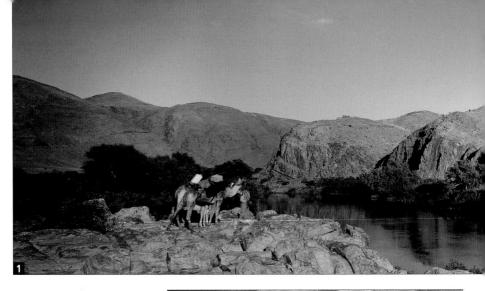

⑩ Opuwo This administrative town of the Kunene Region can no longer shake off its image as a garrison city. While under South African occupation, soldiers leading the war against the SWAPO independence fighters were stationed here. Although tourism has in the meantime begun bringing money to Opuwo, the town looks dilapidated. Either way, you can top up your supplies here and get the latest info on road conditions at the Information Center.

Those who want to visit a Himba village should stock up on gifts for the locals such as tobacco and cornmeal. The D3700, which can also be driven by passenger cars that have higher axle clearance than normal, takes you north-west to the Ehomba Range. After roughly 74 km (46 mi), you pass the village of Epembe, and from here you will follow the C43. On the D3701, which turns off north-west to the Kunene Region, you will only be able to travel with four-wheel-drive vehicles and you should in fact travel in convoys where possible.

About 35 km (22 mi) further on, in Okongwati, you have the opportunity to visit a Himba village. To get there, turn onto a narrow road heading right just before entering the town. The road ends at a Himba settle-

ment 11 km (7 mi) later. The locals charge an entry fee (or you can choose to give them gifts) to visit and take photographs of the village.

From Okongwati, it's another 64 km (40 mi) along a partly sandy, partly rocky road through the mountains into the Kunene Valley. In the rainy season, this part of the route is even a challenge with four-wheel-drive vehicles. The view from above the steep river valley over to the Kunene and the Epupa Falls is splendid.

⑪ Epupa Falls The cataracts and cascades of this 35-m-high (115-ft) waterfall fascinate visitors with their stunning location in the heart of a rugged mountain landscape. Palms, baobabs and Moringa trees form a beautiful contrast to the reddish-brown color of the stone. A simple campsite run by Himba is located on the banks of the Kunene, and various camps and lodges along the river organize rafting tours. However, it is best to avoid swimming because of the crocodiles.

This natural paradise is under threat from plans to dam the Kunene. The dam would produce enough electricity to allow Namibia to be self-suffi-

cient in terms of energy and potentially even supply neighboring countries with surplus power. Apart from the enormous costs of such a project, the consequences for humans and nature are incalculable. A whole valley would be flooded, destroying Himba ritual sites and pasture lands.

Follow the same route back to Opuwo and then continue south on the C43. The road, which is lined with Mopane and bloodfruit trees, heads slowly downhill but can also be managed with a normal vehicle when driven cautiously outside the rainy season. In some of the smaller settlements you will come across Himba as well as numerous Herero people in their Victorian garb. It is not

recommended that you enter the villages without a guide or visitor's permit.

After 135 km (84 miles) on the C34, turn westward onto the D3706. About 12 km (7 mi) further on, the merlons of the Sesfontein Fort pop out between the tops of the palms.

⑫ Sesfontein This fort was built among mountain wilderness in 1896, but was abandoned again in 1914, after which the complex fell into disuse until the early 1990s, when it was rebuilt as a comfortable lodge. Safaris to see the famous "desert elephants" can be organized from here, as well as from Palmwag Lodge 110 km (68 mi) further south. The elephants, which are somewhat smaller than Etosha

3

elephants, roam along the dry riverbed, sometimes even as far as the Atlantic. As there is almost no surface water here, they dig for water in the loose sand on the riverbank.

From Sesfontein, you continue your tour south on the C43 past the town of Warmquelle about 22 km (14 mi) away. Another 10 km (6 mi) on you'll get to Khowarib, with the gorge of the same name and a campsite run by the Damara. Not far from there you can buy traditional Damara handicrafts in the Anmire Traditional Village and gain an insight into the customs and practices of the people who, along with the San and Nama, are some of the oldest inhabitants of southern Africa.

The Palmwag Lodge also offers attractive accommodation in a charming setting. After roughly another 40 km (25 mi) the road will head toward the east and become the C39, from which you will again turn off 43 km (27 mi) later. After driving about 25 km (16 mi) through the dark cliffs along the D3254 (where the Huab intersects a ford), you will arrive at the D2612 and the D3214, which you take into the Twyfelfontein area.

⓭ **Twyfelfontein** This stone arena is slightly elevated on a plateau between mountains and is Namibia's most famous rock art site. It includes both etchings and paintings. All species of savanna animal are depicted on the rock faces, most of which are illustrated in a surprisingly natural state, while others appear more abstract. Interspersed with these are cryptic patterns made up of dots and lines. Only estimates can be given for the age of the paintings, but it is assumed they are between several thousand and a few hundred years old. At least part of them were created by the San.

Those wanting to stop in Twyfelfontein should also visit two other attractions in the surrounding area: "Burnt Mountain" owes its name to the hues of its rocks, which change from reddish to purple to pink, and the Organ Pipes are a series of basalt pillars made from solidified lava.

After 30 km (19 mi) back on the C39 you will pass the "Petrified Forest", with fossilized Monkey puzzle tree trunks measuring up to 30 m long (98 ft).

After desolate Khorixas, turn onto the C35 and head south. The road crosses Damaraland, a region with beautiful landscapes and many small-plot farms. On the right-hand side you will see the mighty Brandberg Massif, with the 2,573-m-high (8,442-ft) Königstein (King's Rock), soaring above the plain. Rock paintings were also discovered here, including the famous "White Lady". The route then heads through the western foothills of the Erongo Mountains to the fishing and holiday town of Hentiesbaai, about 235 km (146 mi) from Khorixas. The C34 turns off here to Cape Cross about 44 km (27 mi) away.

1 The 1,050-km-long (652-mi) Kunene forms the border between Namibia and Angola.

2 Endangered: The 35-m-high (115-ft) Epupa Falls are the focus of a controversial dam project.

3 Namibia's highest mountain, the 2,573-m (8,442-ft) Königstein, is part of the Brandberg Massif.

383

⑭ Cape Cross Seal Reserve

Occasionally, as many as 200,000 South African fur seals gather at this cape – the largest colony on the entire south-west coast of Africa. You can watch the animals after paying an entry fee, although it takes a strong stomach. Seals give off a pungent smell that penetrates the entire area. Not far away, a stone cross remembers Portuguese explorer, Diego Cão, who was the first European to land on this coastal stretch in 1486. From Cape Cross, follow the same road back to Hentiesbaai and then continue south to Swakopmund.

⑮ Swakopmund

This pretty colonial town on the Atlantic has about 20,000 inhabitants and was intended to compete with Walvis Bay, ruled by the British at the time. The settlement at the mouth of the Swakop River became part of German South-West Africa in 1892. Today it is a popular holiday destination for urbanites, and an important supplies stop before trip the Namib Desert, which begins south of the city.

⑯ Moon Valley und Welwitschia Plains

The Namib Desert starts right at the edge of the town of Swakopmund. It is part of the Namib Naukluft National Park, and those wanting to explore the park off of the main roads can only do so with a special permit from the Ministry of Environment and Tourism. The northern reaches of the park are dominated by the so-called Gravel Namib, sprawling gravel plains that occasionally feature granite formations or inselbergs (monadnocks).

The peculiar ecology of this gravel desert unfolds along the nature trail, Welwitschia Drive (only allowed with a permit). The route turns south from

the B2 onto the C28 about 3 km (2 mi) east of Swakopmund, and the rest of the route is well signposted. Information boards explain particularities such as lichen that can emerge after years without a drop of water to then flourish during the next rains. About 18 km (11 mi) down the road you reach the Moon Valley lookout. The black stone in the valley has eroded into some bizarre formations and really does look like a lunar landscape. Another highlight of the park is the Welwitschia Plains, a UNESCO World Heritage Site. The *Welwitschia mirabilis*, a desert plant that looks more like an untidy clump of leaves, is particularly prevalent in this part of the Namib. The largest specimen, which is protected by a fence, is said to be over 1,500 years old. From Swakopmund, it's just 31 km (19 mi) along the coast to Walvis Bay.

⑰ Walvis Bay

This settlement was founded by the Dutch in 1793. As the only deep-sea port on Namibia's coast until 1994, it actually remained a South

African enclave in Namibian territory. The town, with its flat bungalows surrounded by gardens, is home to a commercial port and its inhabitants live off fishing and sea salt extraction. Up to 120,000 birds live in the large lagoon to the north of town including flamingos, pelicans and a number of other migratory birds.

From here, the C14 leads you through the flat, monotonous landscape of the Namib Desert. The road follows the steep escarpment and continues into the mountains along a winding track which makes it a trhilling tour. You reach the turnoff to the Kuiseb Canyon after about 130 km (81 mi).

⑱ Kuiseb Canyon

The Kuiseb is one of several rivers that only runs at certain times of the year. The water originates in the Namibian highlands and crosses the Namib on its way towards the Atlantic.

Around one million years ago, the Kuiseb cut a narrow gorge into the foothills of the escarpment that became famous for a report by German geologists Henno Martin and Wolfgang Korn who hid from the South African authorities here for nearly three years when World War II broke out.

The C14 climbs the foothills of the escarpment over the Kuiseb Pass before heading south and passing through the fantastic

rich von Wolff, originally wanted to breed horses here, but was called to the front after the outbreak of World War I and was killed there two years later. The castle today serves as a museum with original furnishings.

Following the D0826 and D0831 for 43 km (27 mi) you will reach the C14. Continue along it for another 137 km (85 mi) until you reach Bethanie.

㉒ Bethanie It is worth making a stop at the Schmelen-House in this sleepy little town. The house was built in 1814 by a missionary, Heinrich Schmelen, who lived here among the Nama people in an effort to evangelize and convert them. About 22 km (14 mi) further on, the road meets the B4, which you follow westward for roughly 222 km (138 mi) as far as Lüderitz. The area near Garub train station is home to wild horses that are probably descendents of German soldiers' horses. The Namib Desert on the left of the road is a restricted area for diamonds. On the right you is the southern edge of the national park. Shortly before Lüderitz on the left-hand side is the former diamond mining settlement and now ghost town of Kolmanskop (see sidebar pg. 525).

㉓ Lüderitz You arrive in this pretty little town just a few miles after Kolmanskop. With its pastel-colored houses against the unreal backdrop of

1 Covering roughly 5 million ha (12 million acres), Namib Nakluft Park is Africa's largest nature reserve.

2 Flamingos find plenty of food in the Walvis Bay lagoon.

3 Gemsbok or oryx antelope are national animal of Nambia.

3

scenery of the Namib and arriving in the Naukluft. At the Büllsport guest farm about 145 km (90 mi) away, the D0854 turns off towards the entrance of the Naukluft, part of the national park of the same name.

⑲ Naukluft This massif, with peaks up to 2,000 m (6,562 ft), appears craggy and precipitous, but thanks to several springs, vegetation thrives in its valleys, and numerous species of birds nest in its mountains. The most striking inhabitant is the endangered Hartmann's mountain zebra. Multi-day hikes lead through the wilderness, and also include an adventurous 4x4 trail.

Back at Büllsport farm you reach Solitaire, 50 km (31 mi) north on the C14. On the C19 it is another 80 km (50 mi) to Sesriem, the starting point for trips into the Namib dunes, which stretch over 300 km (186 mi) from Kuiseb in the north to Koichab in the south, and 140 km (87 mi) into the country's interior.

⑳ Sossusvlei Sesriem is an elegant lodge near the deep, narrow Sesriem Canyon, and also the gateway to that part of the Namib Naukluft Park, where the famous dunes surround the Sossusvlei.

From Sesriem, an asphalt road initially heads along the mostly

dry bed of the Tsauchab River. Here, the dunes soar out of the plain to heights of up to 170 m 558 ft). The road ends after about 60 km (37 mi), and the next 5 km (3 mi) to the Sossusvlei through deep sand are either covered on foot or with a four-wheel-drive vehicle. A wall of star dunes surrounds the Vlei, which only contains water after good rainy seasons. Adventurous folks can climb the dunes along the ridge to get a fantastic panorama of the desert.

Follow the same road back to Sesriem and then turn to the south onto the D0826. On the right, the road is lined by the Namib dunes, and on the left by the Zaris Mountains. After 135 km (84 mi), the D0826 turns to the east. About 20 km (12 mi) later, a medieval knights' castle under palm trees appears as if out of the blue.

㉑ Duwisib Castle This castle was designed by architect Wilhelm Sander in 1909, who had erected many colonial buildings in south-western Africa. A German aristocrat, Hanshein-

the blue Atlantic, you almost feel as if you've been transported back to Scandinavia.

Most of the inhabitants live off fishing thanks to the still plentiful populations, and the clean Atlantic water also allows for some oyster farming. As the rivers have carried not only sediment but also some diamonds into the sea, diamond divers search for the precious stones off the coast. An old sailing ship brings guests to the Halifax Islands, where there is a nesting population of African penguins. From Lüderitz, head roughly 290 km (180 mi) further east through Goageb to Seeheim, which is really not more than just a train station. Follow the C12 to the south along the railroad tracks. After about 75 km (47 mi), turn right onto the C37. This will take you along a 5-km (3-mi) stretch of arid high plateau to the first vista point over the Fish River Canyon, which appears endless.

24 Fish River Canyon Measuring an impressive 161 km (100 mi) long and up to 550 m (1,805 ft) deep, this canyon is the second-largest in the world after

the Grand Canyon. From above, the two different levels of the canyon are clearly recognizable. The first is an indent in the high plateau that runs from north to south and is roughly 20 km (12 mi) wide. It was created by a subsidence during the Palaeozoic era approximately 500 million years ago. Roughly 200 million years later, glaciers once again deepened this rift during the Ice Age, and for the last 50 million years, since the Tertiary period, the Fish River has cut its way through the canyon, chiseling it out further over time and thus creating the narrow and deepest part of the present-day gorge landscape. A steep, shadeless path leads from the lookout down to the valley floor. Be sure to have proper shoes and plenty of water.

25 Ai-Ais Anyone who enjoys hiking can face a great challenge in the Fish River Canyon – it is 85 km (53 mi) from the lookout to the lovely Ai-Ais thermal hot springs at the southern end of the canyon. While walking through this

pristine landscape you will cross the quietly running river on several occasions. As you do, you pass several graves of German soldiers who once fought against the Nama here. You might even come across baboons, Hartmann's mountain zebras and small antelope.

Topping off the hike, which can really only be made during the cooler months, are the thermal hot springs of Ai-Ais, whose name equates to "hot water"

in the Nama language. The springs are a cozy 60°C (140°F) when it hits the surface, and the thermal spas are particularly frequented by people with rheumatic disorders. Ai-Ais also has a comfortable campsite.

From the lookout point, follow the same road back towards Holoog and turn south onto the C12 towards Grünau about 50 km (31 mi) away. After going 150 km (93 mi) north on the B1 you arrive in Keetmanshoop.

bred sheep and cattle. Today, they mostly work on the large farms, which primarily keep Karakul sheep here in the south.

The B1 heads north from Keetmanshoop. After 13 km (8 mi) you reach the gates of a farm where decorative quiver trees form almost an entire forest.

㉗ Kokerboom Forest Forest quiver trees, which belong to the Aloe family, owe their name to the fact that the San used their hollowed-out branches as arrow quivers. They are low-maintenance plants that prefer rocky subsurfaces and usually exist on their own – the forest here is thus rather unusual. The most beautiful photos are captured at sunset, when the unusual silhouettes of the trees stand out against the dark.

Just a few miles further on are giant granite taws known as Giant's Playground. After about 120 km (75 mi) along the B1, you pass the town of Gibeon, which became famous after a meteorite shower.

Over a huge area of 2,500 sq km (965 sq mi), you will find fragments weighing up to 650 kg (1,433 lb) from a gigantic meteorite that probably exploded before its landing.

In Mariental about 56 km (35 mi) further, you will see the foothills of the Kalahari in the east. The sand dunes run parallel to each other over hundreds of miles. Several lodges east of town organize interesting safaris and walks through the unique landscape led by San guides.

After 255 km (158 mi), your tour of Namibia returns to the capital, Windhoek, where you trade in your car for an airplane at the International Airport east of the city. The first destination of this next leg of the trip takes you to Victoria Falls in Zimbabwe, a UNESCO World Heritage Site, with national parks Hwange and Matetsi.

㉖ Keetmanshoop This settlement was founded as a Rhine Mission station in 1866. With its Imperial Post Office and Klipkerk, also built from dark granite, Keetmanshoop has some beautiful examples of German colonial architecture. The charming town has 16,000 inhabitants and is the administrative center of southern Namibia. It is the main town of the Nama. The Nama, like the San, clearly differ from Namibia's other African ethnic groups who are descendants of the Bantu peoples of Central and East Africa. They have lighter skin, high cheekbones and almost Asian features.

The Nama and San speak a language with clicking sounds, and ethnologists believe that these two Khoisan peoples were the actual original inhabitants of southern Africa. While the San were nomadic hunters, the Nama were sedentary and

1 The symmetrical tops of the quiver trees are adorned with yellow blossoms in June.

2 The magnificent Fish River Canyon in southern Namibia is the largest in Africa.

Epupa Falls The waterfalls of the Kunene are a fascinating natural spectacle in the arid Kaokoveld, the land of the Himba.

Himba Namibia's last nomads live as cattle herders in the north-west mountain region of the Kaokoveld. The animals represent a ritual link to their ancestors.

Cape Cross Up to 200,000 seals crowd the cliffs of the Cape Cross colony.

Etosha National Park Large herds of zebra and oryx can be found in the Etosha Pan when the animals come to man-made watering holes during the dry season.

Spitzkoppe Namibia's "Matterhorn" is popular among rock climbers. Bushman's Paradise is a densely overgrown site with San rock drawings.

Damaraland A stunning landscape and the ancient rock paintings of Twyfelfontein transport you back to the prehistoric and early times of Namibia.

Swakopmund A gem of German colonial architecture and a popular seaside resort. Apart from the Art Nouveau train station, many of the buildings from colonial times have been well preserved, including the lighthouse.

Walvis Bay "Whale Bay" is a paradise for ornithology enthusiasts as thousands of pink flamingos and pelicans live in the lagoon. You can also catch glimpses of the timid curlew sandpiper.

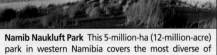

Namib Naukluft Park This 5-million-ha (12-million-acre) park in western Namibia covers the most diverse of landscapes, including the Naukluft Mountains, bleak gravel deserts and spectacular dune scenery.

Sossusvlei The world's highest star dunes are here. They measure up to 350 m (1,148 ft) and are clustered around the Vlei basin, which floods with water after the rainy season. It is a spectacular landscape.

Lüderitz This port town in southwest Namibia was founded in 1883 by Heinrich Vogelsang on behalf of Bremen businessman, Adolf Lüderitz. It was the beginning of the German South-West Africa colony. The pastel buildings look somewhat surreal here against the beautiful backdrop of the stormy blue Atlantic Ocean.

Kolmanskop The Namib Desert mercilessly reclaims its terrain. Where diamonds were once mined, ruins today sink into the sand.

Fish River Canyon The layers of stone in this pristine canyon transport observers well back into the history of the earth's creation.

Tsodilo Hills A true gem for scientists: San people have left behind drawings on the rocks in northern Botswana. The scenes depict hunting parties and ritual dances. The area is a UNESCO World Heritage Site.

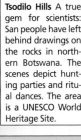

Windhoek The capital of Namibia has a charming Old Town characterized by both German colonial and post-modern architecture.

Khwai River This river meanders through the Moremi Game Reserve. The River Khwai Lodge located on its banks is one of Botswana's most exclusive hotels. From its bungalows, which stand on stilts, guests can relax and watch the wild animals at the river and even observe elephants bathing at sundown.

Victoria Falls These falls near the Zimbabwe-Zambia border have been a tourist attraction since the late 19th century.

Herero These former cattle herders became sedentary during colonial times. The women adopted the garb of female missionaries.

Moremi Game Reserve Luxurious lodges and a unique wealth of wild game make this Botswanan national park an exclusive experience. Lions can also be observed here at close range.

Zambezi National Park Crocodiles lurk for prey in the Zambezi River, but they retreat when elephants come to drink.

Duwisib Castle German Romanticism in the heart of the Namibian desert sand. Hansheinrich von Wolff had the castle built in 1909.

Baobabs According to San beliefs, the baobabs are said to be the result of a fight during the creation of the world.

Chobe National Park The gallery forests along the Chobe River are home to large herds of elephants as well as lions and leopards.

Kokerboom Forest These quiver trees still form a real forest near Keetmanshoop. Their branches were once used by the San to make arrows.

San The short hunters, often also known as Bushmen, are thought to be the original inhabitants of southern Africa.

Okavango Delta A landscape rich in wildlife has emerged where the mighty Okavango River ends at the northern edge of the Kalahari.

South Africa

Taking the Garden Route through the Garden of Eden

Our drive along the African continent's evergreen southern tip offers a series of enchanting natural spectacles. Animal lovers and amateur botanists will get their money's worth, as will wine-lovers, water-sports enthusiasts and fans of Cape Dutch architecture. Cape Town, a truly cosmopolitan city below the famous Table Mountain, is an experience of itself, while the drive back through the colourful Little Karoo Valley makes a fascinating contrast to urban life.

In many respects, the southern tip of Africa is really a world of its own. Well-groomed parklands, orchards, vineyards and forest jungles are all set against a backdrop of striking mountain ranges and breathtaking coastline. Beautiful beaches vie for attention with rugged rock promontories, seaside resorts and fishing villages on the oceanside. What's more, the region is blessed with a mild climate throughout the year and it rains regularly, so that the vegetation is abundant and colourful. It is no coincidence that the area is often called an 'earthly paradise' or that the English explorer Sir Francis

Drake called it the 'earth's finest cape' when he first came here in the late 16th century. The drive along the N2 coastal road (the Garden Route) from Cape Town to Port Elizabeth

Greater double-collared sunbird.

and returning through the stunning backcountry is one of the main highlights of any trip to South Africa. If at any time you want to leave your car behind, you can take a ride on the luxurious Blue Train, a rail line that runs parallel to the coastal road here as part of its route from Pretoria to Cape Town.

Without doubt, however, the chief attraction of this 'Garden of Eden' is its nature, which is at its most spectacular on the Garden Route between Mossel Bay and the mouth of the Storm River. Nature-lovers can make good use of a well-organized and expansive network of hiking trails that run along the

Table Mountain near Cape Town at sunrise – a classic scene taken from Blouberg Beach.

The Little Karoo's hot and arid climate makes it ideal for ostrich breeding. Most farms are located in the protected Oudtshoorn area in Western Cape. The town is home to the world's largest Ostrich population.

coast and through the forests. The area also offers plenty of opportunities to watch elephants, whales and a host of other exotic animals in their natural habitats. The Addo Elephant National Park is a good example of a wildlife experience. And for those who want nothing more than to sit on the beach and enjoy the consistently sunny weather, the entire south coast is a virtual paradise. Water sports are also fantastic in the dynamic surf of the Indian Ocean.

Up country from Cape Town, in the hills around Paarl, Franschhoek and Stellenbosch to the east, there are some magnificent vineyards where winelovers can taste some of the classier local wines. Culture and history buffs will enjoy the beautifully maintained villages from the pioneer days of European settlement, where Cape Dutch-style buildings and a few interesting museums recount a not-so-distant past when the Dutch East India Company established its first stations here, and both Amsterdam and London vied for this profitable new colony.

In the far west, against the commanding backdrop of Table Mountain, the lively metropolis of Cape Town provides a charming contrast to the pristine natural landscapes. Every year millions of visitors from around the globe are attracted by its lively markets, noble Wilhelminian architecture, elegant mansions set away from the coast, sandy bays and hip quarters like the 'Waterfront' with its trendy cafés, restaurants and boutiques. To get away from it all, you can take a spin along the scenic Chapman's Peak Drive towards the Cape of Good Hope on Africa's southern tip. The heather-clad countryside and colourful fishing villages in the area evoke scenes of Scandinavia. The beauty of South Africa is unrelenting as you move away from the coast to the starkly contrasting desert interior, where the arid steppe of Little Karoo is world-famous for its ostrich farms and stalactite caves.

Colourful beach huts like these in Muizenberg create a Scandinavian atmosphere. The sea resort is located 25 km (15.5 mi) south of Cape Town.

A drive from Cape Town to Port Elizabeth is definitely the crown jewel of a trip to South Africa. Starting in the metropolis at the foot of Table Mountain, this round trip takes you across the Cape Peninsula on the famous Garden Route along the south coast to Port Elizabeth, and from there back to Cape Town via the Little Karoo and the vineyards around Stellenbosch.

① Cape Town (see p. 394). Before heading out immediately from Cape Town on the N2, you should definitely take a day trip out to the famous Cape of Good Hope.

② Cape Peninsula 'The fairest cape in the whole circumference of the earth.' These enthusiastic words about Africa's rocky southern tip were uttered by none other than Sir Francis Drake, the second captain to circumnavigate the globe. Later generations of seafarers surely felt the words were nothing but mockery, as the Cape came to be feared for its storms and high waves, and dozens of ships have run aground on its reefs. Shipwrecks testify to the perils of the passage. In fact, you should check the weather before setting off in a rental car, and

remember to take a windcheater.
There are two ways to get out to the Cape – the route west of Table Mountain and the Twelve Apostles along the idyllic beaches past decadent mansions such as Sea Point, Clifton, Camps Bay and Llandudno, or the route further south-east via Kirstenbosch and Groot Constantia. They both reconnect at Hout Bay, a charming fishing town mainly famous for its langoustines.
Now take Chapman's Peak Drive to Noordhoek and carry on to Kommetjie and Scarborough, a pair of idyllic fishing villages on the small road to Smitswinkelbay. On the last 13 km (8 miles) you cross the southern part of the 'Cape of Good Hope Nature Reserve'. The low scrub and heathers of this reserve are distinctly remi-

Travel Information

Route profile
Length: approx. 1,800 km (1,120 miles), excluding detours
Time required:
at least 7–10 days
Start and end: Cape Town
Route (main locations):
Cape Town, Cape Peninsula, Hermanus, Swellendam, Mossel Bay, Knysna, Port Elizabeth, Oudtshoorn, Robertson, Paarl, Stellenbosch, Cape Town

When to go:
The best months for visiting are February, March and April when the long school holidays are over and the air and water are still pleasantly warm.

Traffic information:
Drive on the left in South Africa. Car rentals require a valid international driving licence. Petrol is always paid for in cash.

Blue Train:
A luxury alternative to the car is a ride on the legendary Blue Train from Cape Town to Port Elizabeth:
www.bluetrain.co.za

Information:
General:
www.gov.za
www.southafrica.net
Garden Route:
www.gardenroute.co.za
Cape Province:
www.tourismcapetown.co.za

3

4

3 Hermanus This picturesque town, founded by fishermen in 1855, is located on the northern shore of Walker Bay between Kleinrivierberge and the sea. It is famous not only for its many wild flowers, magnificent beaches and outstanding water-sports options, but also for its deep-sea fishing.

Many people from Cape Town come to spend their weekends in this holiday village where fishing boats, dreamy cottages and the old port give it the feel of an open-air museum.

During the winter, from July to November, Hermanus is a hot spot for whale-watchers from all around the world. They even have a bellman employed at the beach to ring when humpbacks, right whales or even orcas are sighted. Harold Porter National Botanic Gardens in the Kogelberg Nature Reserve west of the town have a good exhibition of Cape flora.

Before returning to the N2 take the scenic detour via Cape Agulhas. Passing through Bredasdorp, the R3l8 will take you back to the N2 and on to Swellendam.

4 Swellendam The country's third-oldest town was founded by the Dutch East India Company in 1745. It is located against the impressive backdrop of the Langeberg Mountain Range, whose ridge is called the '12 O'Clock Rock' by locals because at noon the sun is vertically

niscent of Scotland. You're likely to see antelope, ostrich, wildebeest and zebras and almost certainly some baboons. The last few hundred yards are covered by shuttle bus. Then it's 133 steps to Cape Point 200 m

(650 ft) above the waves where you get an absolutely magnificent view over the peninsula and False Bay – you'll know what Drake meant. The Cape of Good Hope is actually a few kilometers to the west, but the

view is much less spectacular from there.

Your return journey goes along a wild, rocky coastline via Simon's Town with its pretty Victorian center and the fishing ports of Fish Hoek and Kalk Bay. In the surfers' paradise of Muizenberg beach, the colourful huts recall times gone by.

After 20 km (12 miles) or so eastbound on Baden Powell Drive, which runs in a large arc along the flat beaches of False Bay, you get back to the N2. But at Somerset West you leave it behind again. For 60 km (40 miles) you then drive along the so-called Whale Route at the base of the Koeeberg mountains where lovely coastal scenery, and possibly some majestic marine mammals, will accompany you via Kleinmond to Hermanus where many city dwellers spend their week-end.

Chapman's Peak Drive

It may only be a drive of 10 km (6 miles), but you will never forget this scenic road cut directly into the steep coastal rock faces south of Hout Bay by Italian prisoners-of-war during World War II. Starting in an idyllic fishing port, the road winds its way around the colourful cliffs up to Noordhoek. From its highest point at 600 m (1,970 ft) above Chapman's Bay there is a breathtaking view across to Hout Bay, a rocky outcrop called 'The Sentinel' and the hills around Constantia.

1 Fishing ports like Kalk Bay dot the rocky western shore of False Bay.

2 Rocky coastline in the Cape Province.

3 The Cape of Good Hope – every globetrotter's dream.

4 Penguin colonies swimming in the ocean near Table Mountain.

Cape Town

To many globetrotters, the 'Mother City', as South Africans fondly call the oldest city in their country, is the world's most beautiful port city. It is mainly Cape Town's unique location against the imposing backdrop of Table Mountain that makes it special – on the cape where the Atlantic and Indian Oceans meet.

'Cape Town is different.' As any newcomer to this city will immediately notice, this simplistic and superficial advertising slogan really is justified, and in more ways than one. When the Dutchman Jan van Riebeeck moored in Table Bay for the Dutch East India Company on 7 April 1652, he and his handful of pioneers were the first white people ever to land here. They were met by Khoikhoi ('Men of men' in their language) and San ('Bushmen'). 'Hottentots' is a term given to the Khoikhoi by the Dutch to mean 'stutterer'. San in turn is Khoikhoi for 'outsider'. 'Bushmen' is more acceptable, but sometimes pejorative.

The fortifications on the cape quickly became a kind of 'tavern of the seas', a refuge and supply station for seafarers on the way between Europe and Asia. The city's backdrop is second to none. The entire 3 km (2 miles) of the mountain plateau are often draped in clouds and the city is sprawled out at its feet. Outside, in the port of Table Bay, cargo ships and sailing vessels ply the busy waters. The climate here is Mediterranean, with none of the drastic temperature changes that are so typical of the inland areas. A constant sea breeze seems even to blow away most germs and smog, inspiring the locals to gratefully call it the 'cape doctor'. Beyond its natural setting, the city's population is also far more cosmopolitan and multicultural than any other in sub-Saharan Africa.

Blacks, whites, Cape Coloureds, Chinese, Malays, Indians, Jews and countless immigrants from around the globe all contribute to the fascinating mix of colours, cultures and cuisine. A handful of must-sees while you are there are the Castle of Good Hope, which is more than 300 years old, the Bo Kaap Malay Quarter, the Houses of Parliament, Kirstenbosch Gardens, the South African Museum, the National Gallery, Signal Hill, a view from Table Mountain by cable car, and the busy waterfront by the port with its choice of stylish restaurants, boutiques and galleries. Meanwhile, Cape Town has become a favoured location for filmmakers.

And last but by no means least, do not forget Robben Island, home to the prison where Nelson Mandela was forced to wait half his life for Apartheid finally to come to an end.

Cape Town and Table Mountain at dusk.

birds is the pied buck (Bontebok), which gave the park its name. It is nearly extinct in the wild. If the weather is good, take a swim in the wonderful Breede River.

Just after the bridge across Kafferkuils River, exit the N2 once again and take a detour (about 20 km/13 miles) to Stilbaai at the coast.

⑤ Stilbaai Even prehistoric fishermen who settled in this area valued 'Still Bay' as a plentiful fishing ground. Its remarkably long beaches have turned it into a classic holiday resort. For nine months of the year the holiday cottages along its flat sandy shores remain closed up. Many of them are built on stilts. At the end of the school year, however, they come back to life almost overnight.

⑥ Mossel Bay Mossel Bay marks the beginning of the real Garden Route, where the N2 drops right down to the coast. It is also the location where explorers Bartholomeu Diaz and Vasco da Gama landed before 1500. Offshore oil and gas discoveries have added an industrial feel to this much-visited holiday village, but around the turn of the last century it

was briefly famous for the export of ostrich plumes. During the holiday season local beaches, which are separated by rocky outcrops, are crowded. Sun worshippers and swimmers go to Munro's Bay, Santos Beach and Diaz Beach, whereas surfers prefer The Point and De Bakke.In the historic town center, the Bartholomeu Diaz Museum Complex is well worth a visit. It houses a reconstruction of the vessel used by Diaz in 1488 when he was the first European to navigate the Cape. This reconstructed caravel is only 23 m (75 ft) long.

The neighbouring Shell Museum displays a large collection of seashells. A local curiosity is a 500-year-old milkwood tree that seafarers used as a 'post office'. They deposited their letters in a boot hung in the branches of the tree, where they would then be picked up by vessels bound for home.

1 Outeniqua Choo-Tjoe Train – bay to bay on steam power.

2 Mossel Bay is where the real Garden Route starts.

3 Coastline and wilderness – dream beaches for lazy strolls.

above it. Long alleyways of ancient oak trees are the town's landmark and in many places you can still feel a bit of atmosphere from the pioneer days. The town's biggest attraction is 'The Drostdy', the erstwhile residence of the bailiff (landdrost), which was built in 1747. This thatched mansion, which was renovated and enlarged between 1812 and 1825, now houses a stylish museum with

furniture and common household objects dating from the 18th and 19th centuries. An old post office and a vivid documentation of old arts and crafts complete the museum compound.

About 6 km (4 miles) south of Swellendam is Bontebok National Park, home to numerous very rare species of bird and various antelopes. The park is 18 sq km (7 sq mi). One of these

7 George The Garden Route's 'unofficial' capital is about 50 km (31 miles) further on, just away from the coast at the base of the Outeniqua Mountain Range. The range peaks at just under 1,600 m (5,250 ft). The name means something like 'they who bear honey'.

Moist sea air causes plenty of rainfall here, ensuring an abundance of verdant green vegetation. George is surrounded by forests and towards the sea there are some park-like landscapes. In the town center Cape Dutch and classical-style buildings stand alongside the oldest Catholic church in the country, 'Moederkerk', which is adorned with beautiful wood carvings. Next to it stands an almost 200-year-old oak. Slaves were once chained to it before being sold. A ride on the Outeniqua Choo-Tjoe Train across to Knysna goes through some striking coastal scenery and is a unique experience. The train crosses a long bridge (2 km/1.5 miles) over the Knysna Lagoon before entering the town of Knysna.

8 Wilderness National Park These days the resort town of Wilderness on the N2 does not really do justice to its name. About 12 m (7.5 miles) east of the Kaaiman River's deep gorge you are confronted with an excessive number of holiday cottages and hotels. But the town's fine sandy beach and the luscious forests in the surrounding countryside do make it a sight to behold.

The neighbouring Wilderness National Park is a stretch of coast around 20 km (13 miles) long interspersed with a number of lagoons and lakes surrounded by dense forests. It's a picture-book natural paradise that is most famous for its seabirds, but you can also go fishing, surfing, canoeing and

boating. A hike on Kingfisher Trail along the mouth of the Touw river is perfect for a day trip.

Just outside Knysna you pass the Goukamma Nature Reserve, a strip of rocky coastline that stretches 14 km (9 miles) and can only be explored on foot.

9 Knysna A hundred years ago this holiday resort located at the northern shore of a huge lagoon was the centerpoint of a tempestuous gold rush. These days it is mainly known for its oysters and the substantial forests nearby that have provided generations of local people with the economic base for a thriving timber industry. The forests are also home to a small herd of free-roaming elephants. A regional speciality is handcrafted hardwood furniture made from yellow wood, iron wood and stink wood.

The town's landmarks are two giant sandstone cliffs called 'The Heads', which tower above the small canal connecting the lagoon to the open ocean. West of Knysna is the Featherbed Nature Reserve, home to the rare blue duikers and a host of other rare bird species.

The most magnificent beaches in the area are called Brenton and Noetzie. The Elephant Nature Walk in Diepwalle State Forest offers some truly outstanding hiking. You get to it along the N9, which branches off inland a few miles after Knysna heading towards Prince Alfred's Pass and Avontour.

10 Plettenberg Bay There are some ideal opportunities for hiking in the forests of Kranshoek and Harkerville, approximately 30 km (18 miles) east of Knysna. A few minutes after that in the car take a look to your right off the N2 to see some truly fantastic scenery. Plettenberg Bay, with its almost 10 km (6 miles) of immaculate sandy beaches and crystal blue

waters, really is the essence of the 'South African Riviera'. From July to September there are whales calving within sight of numerous exclusive hotels.

11 Tsitsikamma National Park This national park, covering 5,000 ha (12,350 acres) of land, has everything that nature-lovers may desire – bizarre cliffs, lonely beaches, steep gorges and luscious vegetation if you make it further up country. Founded in 1962, the area also includes the rich coastal waters.

The Otter Trail, which starts in Nature's Valley and runs along the rocky shore for 42 km (26 miles) right up to the mouth of the Storms River, is one of the country's most attractive long-

serve, you have a magnificent view over Algoa Bay and there are some beautifully restored houses from the Victorian era as well as an old lighthouse.

The Museum Complex includes a snake park, dolphin shows in the Oceanium and a regional museum that promise a good variety of entertainment. Close by there are some exquisite beaches such as Kings Beach and Humewood Beach.

Instead of taking the same coastal route back towards Cape Town, we recommend driving the N62/60, which takes you further into the heartland of South Africa. This inland route branches off about 20 km (13 miles) west of Humansdorp, winding its way westwards past Joubertina, Avontour, Uniondale and De Rust – all of which are smart and tidy but otherwise unremarkable agricultural towns.

The landscape of the Little Karoo, as this interior plateau is called, extends over 250 km (155 miles) over a swathe of land about 60 km (40 miles) wide and is strikingly different to the coastal areas. This area, sandwiched between the Kouga and Swart Ranges to the north and the Outeniqua and Langeberg Ranges to the south, gets very little rain. There are colourful rock formations on either side of the road and large areas of the abundant fertile soil are irrigated. Over the years, ostrich farms have developed into an hugely important impetus for the local economy.

distance hiking trails. To do it you first have to acquire a permit – only the first 3 km (2 miles) from the eastern entrance are open to those without one. However, even within that distance you are fortunate enough to be able to visit the huge waterfalls and a spectacular hanging bridge that stretches 190 m (623 ft) over the chasm at a height of 130 m (427 ft). If you are into snorkelling, there is an underwater nature trail where you can go exploring the large variety of marine plants and animals.

⑫ Cape St Francis Near Humansdorp a road turns off to Cape St Francis on your right. This jaunt towards the coast is about 60 km (40 miles) and is

well worth doing for a few reasons. First is that the village at the end of the cape really does have a charm of its own with its whitewashed houses and black rooftops. Second is that the long beaches towards Oyster Bay and Jeffrey's Bay to the east are among the most beautiful in South Africa. The third reason has to do with the waves that break here. In the 1960s Jeffrey's Bay was made legend in the movie *The Endless Summer*, and the waves still break perfectly here, sometimes for hundreds of yards from the point into the bay. Watching the surfers on this world-famous wave is an enjoyable way to spend a day at the lovely beach.

Back on the N2 it is only 70 km (43 miles) to Port Elizabeth.

⑬ Port Elizabeth P. E., as the locals call this important port city, has the gold and diamond trade to thank for its rise. These days the heart of the South African car industry beats a little upriver in Port Elizabeth's 'twin city' of Uitenhage on the banks of the sizeable Swartkops River. Although 'Cape Detroit' is definitely not known for its scenic beauty, this port metropolis with its one million inhabitants still exudes its own personal brand of Victorian charm.

Its lively center and the starting point for guided tours is called Market Square, where the town hall is magnificent and the 'campanile' tower (52 m/ 170 ft) even has a viewing platform. From Park Donkin Re-

1 An especially spectacular stretch of coastline in Tsitsikamma National Park.

2 Subtropical climate and vegetation – the rain-forests in Tsitsikamma National Park.

3 Scene at a watering hole in Addo Elephant National Park.

14 Oudtshoorn This provincial town with 50,000 inhabitants is the 'urban center' of the Little Karoo. You can hardly imagine it these days, but in the late 19th century it was even a fashion hub and, at one point, a group of inventive farmers decided on a new tack for the fashion scene. They started large-scale ostrich breeding operations in this dry valley and subsequently managed to convince the haute couture of Vienna, Paris and New York that feather boas, capes or fans made from ostrich plumes were indispensable accessories for the fashionably up-to-date. At the height of the resulting boom around 750,000 birds were delivering 500 tonnes of feathers a year. Having become rich overnight, these ostrich 'barons', as they now called themselves, erected decadent mansions of stone and cast iron, the so-called 'feather palaces'. After a downturn lasting several decades, the ostrich business has recently regained some momentum in the wake of the low-cholesterol craze. Ostrich meat is now exported on a large scale, as is their leather. On some farms, you can try out specialities such as ostrich steaks and omelettes made from the birds' giant eggs, watch ostrich races or even risk a ride on one.

Located 30 km (18 miles) north of the town is an absolute five-star attraction – the Cango Caves. These are some of the world's most terrific stalactite caves and you get to see all their beauty during the course of a two-hour guided tour.

Ostrich farms and other plantations, neat towns with names such as Calitzdorp, Ladismith or Barrydale, and an imposing backdrop of mountain ranges

accompany you through this charming region. After passing Montagu, a charming center for growing fruit and wine at the western end of Little Karoo Valley with numerous historic buildings, the road winds its way up more than 6 km (4 miles) to Cogmanskloof Pass. It then goes through a tunnel under a jagged barrier called 'Turkey Rock' and carries on down into the wide and fertile Bree Valley.

15 Robertson This small town is blessed with a wonderfully mild climate and extremely fertile soil. High-quality apples, apricots and above all grapes grow here in luscious abundance. Wild roses, old oak trees and jacaranda trees grow by the roadside. A long sandy beach along the riverbank is reminiscent of the French Riviera. The area also has a plethora of accommodation in the form of holiday apartments or

around Church Street is considered to be the most complete collection of Cape Dutch architecture in the country. The town's oldest building is Oude Kerk (Old Church), which was built in 1743.

⑰ Paarl To reach this small town on the Berg River from Tulbagh follow the narrow, winding R44 via the jagged Bain's Pass. It is the industrial center of the wine-growing region and the seat of the wine-growers' co-operative KWV, which was founded in 1918 and now looks after more than 5,000 individual vintners. It stores more than 300 million litres (66 million gal) of wine, and more than three times this amount is processed here every year. There are guided tours that take you to five wine barrels alleged to be the largest in the world. Each of them holds

more than 200,000 litres (909,000 gal), was made without nails and weighs 25 tonnes (27.5 tons). The town was named after 'The Pears' ('De Paarl'), giant granite summits that sparkle in the sunlight after it rains. On one slope of Paarl Mountain, 600 m (1,970 ft) high, the Tall Monument, an imposing granite needle, commemorates the development and spread of Afrikaans, the Boer language.

Local vineyards such as Nederburg, Rhebokshof, Fairview, Backsberg or Kanonkop are considered the very best by wine enthusiasts.

1 Scenic Karoo landscape.

2 Ostrich plumes, meat and leather are sought-after export goods.

3 Irrigation turns the Little Karoo into a Garden of Eden.

campsites. Sheilam Cactus Garden is a must for hobby botanists. It is located 8 km (5 miles) outside the town and has one of the most comprehensive cactus collections anywhere in the world.

The next main town on the N60 is Worcester, which has few attractions apart from its botanic gardens and Kleinplasie Farm Museum, which invites you to take a touching journey back in time to the dai-

ly routine of an 18th-century farm.

There is a worthwhile detour here via Wolseley to the small town of Tulbagh, which is 70 km (43 miles) north of our route.

⑯ Tulbagh Also surrounded by extensive orchards and vineyards, Tulbagh was devastated by an earthquake in 1969 but has since been fully restored. The town center

18 Franschhoek This wine-growing town has some extensive vineyards with their typically large mansions. Huguenots fleeing from religious persecution in Europe at the end of the 17th century came to South Africa and settled in this picturesque valley. Farm names such as Dieu Donné, La Provence or Mont Rochelle testify to the pioneers' provenance.

A large monument at the exit of the village commemorates their achievements. The unusually large number of first-class restaurants, bistros and small inns also hints strongly at the town's French heritage.

19 Stellenbosch Nicknamed 'Boer Oxford' because of its venerable elite university, this town is the cultural heart of the winelands. In 1679 the governor Van der Stel established a border settlement on Eerste River. A stroll across the De Braak central square and along Dorp Straat, with its long rows of bright white, partly thatched buildings in classic Cape Dutch style, testify to its rank as South Africa's second-oldest town.

The Burgerhuis with its small town museum is worth a visit, as are the old stagecoach house, the Rhineland missionary church and the beautifully restored mansion of Libertas Parva, which houses an interesting wine museum as well as an art gallery.

Well-manicured lawns, shaded oak lanes and the botanical gardens right next to the university campus are definitely worth a leisurely stroll.

The hiking and bicycle trails through the surrounding vineyards are very well-signposted and nothing if not idyllic. They are certainly a safer option than driving if you have enjoyed some of the local wine! There are two routes back into Cape Town: either take the N1 back directly, or follow the road south to Somerset West and turn onto the N2 at the starting point of this journey - to be spoiled by choice!

1 The Stellenbosch vineyards grow some renowned high-quality wines.

2 It does not get more picturesque than this – the winery at

Boschendal is attractive not only because of its excellent wines, but also because of its excellent cuisine and meticulously maintained Cape Dutch architecture: a perfect detour for connoisseurs.

The Twelve Apostles The coastal road between Cape Town and Llandudno is also called Cape Riviera. The Twelve Apostles make a charming backdrop to any beach holiday on Camps Bay.

Paarl The town is said to be the cradle of Afrikaans. Alongside its museum and many historical buildings, the cellars of the KWV vintner's co-operative and the magnificent wineries are well worth a visit.

Addo Elephant National Park This protected area houses 200 addo elephants, which were nearly wiped out 100 years ago. It is also home to the last Cape buffalo herd.

Cango Caves The stalactite caves in the Swart Mountains are among the world's most impressive. The 'Big Hall' is 107 m (351 ft) long and 16 m (52 ft) high.

Cape Town Globetrotters say that this city, founded in the 17th century, is one of the world's most beautiful. Its port, its hillside houses and Table Mountain itself make a stunning sight.

Franschhoek This wine-growing town located in a picturesque valley was founded by Huguenots some 300 years ago. The French heritage is visible not only in an interesting museum and monument, but also in a large number of excellent restaurants and wineries.

Port Elizabeth This port city with its Victorian charm has gold and diamonds to thank for its rise. The museum compound includes a snake park and the regional museum is well worth visiting.

Chapman's Peak Drive The coastal road between Noordhoek and Hout Bay is one of the most spectacular in the world, with breathtaking views, such as this one looking east.

Kogelberg Nature Reserve This protected area west of Hermanus is the heart of the Cape floral kingdom.

Wilderness National Park East of George there is an extensive area of freshwater and saltwater lakes that are home to innumerable birds. Some of the lakes are connected via the Serpentine.

Outeniqua Choo-Tjoe Train A ride on this nostalgic steam train from George to Knysna across the Knysna lagoon is one of the highlights of the magnificent Garden Route.

Cape of Good Hope A visit to the southern tip of the Cape Peninsula is a must for any visitor to South Africa. Once seafarers had passed the 'Cape of Storms', they were safely on their way home.

Swellendam This small town was founded in 1745 and still exudes the pioneer spirit with its Cape Dutch buildings.

Bontebok National Park These days there are around 300 of the once-endangered pied buck roaming the park.

Tsitsikamma National Park This park of 5,000 ha (12,350 acres) has some bizarre cliffs, lonely beaches and a heartland rich in abundant vegetation.

Carved out by glaciers, Wonder Lake provides an impressive reflection of Mount McKinley, North America's highest mountain.

Alaska

Far North on the Alaska Highway

Americans like to call their 49th state 'The Last Frontier'. In Alaska, seashores, rivers, forests, mountains and glaciers remain almost untouched, brown bears fish for salmon, sea lions fight for territory, and herds of caribou trek across the tundra. But even this far north the cities are expanding, oil production is becoming a hazard for the wilderness and civilization is encroaching slowly but steadily on the pristine landscape. Fortunately, several national parks have been established, and this route takes you there.

When William Seward, the US Secretary of State, bought Alaska from the Russians for two cents per acre in 1867, this vast empty expanse of land was quickly derided as 'Seward's folly'. But the billions of barrels of oil that have since flown through the Alaskan Pipeline have more than earned the initial purchase price he paid.

In Alaska, there are eight national parks protecting the state's valuable natural resources. By area, the Alaskan peninsula in the north-west of the American continent is the largest state in the US. It measures 1.5 million sq km (1.3 sq mi), easily big enough to fit Western Europe into it.

From the Canadian border, which is 2,500 km (1,550 miles)

A walrus herd on the Alaskan coast.

long, the peninsula stretches nearly 4,000 km (2,480 miles) to the furthest of the Aleutian Islands on the western tip of the state. To the north of Alaska is the Beaufort Sea, to the west the Bering Straits, and to the south the Pacific Ocean.

The Pacific coast is broken up into innumerable islands, peninsulas and deep fjords that reach far into the interior. Mount McKinley is North America's highest mountain at 6,194 m (20,323 ft), and Juneau is the only state capital that is accessible only by boat, via the Alaska Marine Highway, or by plane. Of its highland plains, 40,000 sq km (15,000 sq mi) are covered by glaciers. North of

Mount Wrangell (4,317 m/14,164 ft) is an extinct volcano clearly visible from Glenn Highway, which connects Tok Junction with Anchorage.

Carved out by glaciers, Wonder Lake provides an impressive reflection of Mount McKinley, North America's highest mountain. Also named Denali, the "High One", it is perhaps the single most impressive mountain in the world.

the Arctic Circle, the permafrost soil only thaws to a maximum depth of half a meter, but agriculture is still possible in the Matanuska Valley.

Until 1942, there was no way to get to Alaska by land, and only when the Japanese threatened to close in on Alaska did the US government decide to build a road connection through Canada. On 9 March 1942, a total of 11,000 people began construction on this road, about 2,300 km (1,430 miles) long, between Dawson Creek in Canada to the south and Delta Junction to the north. Despite the huge difficulties encountered, this pioneer route was in use by 20 November 1942 after an impressively short construction period of only eight months. After the war it was handed over to the civil authorities and gradually improved. Today it is open year-round and in all weather conditions. It remains the only land connection between the USA and Alaska, and despite a tarmac surface along its entire length, the highway is indeed still a challenge. Be prepared for summer snowstorms, mudslides and washed-out bridges. The challenge has its rewards, however. Unforgettable scenery awaits you, often right by the roadside, where you occasionally see bears with their cubs, or elks with giant antlers. Fairbanks and Anchorage are modern cities, but even here the wilderness comes right to your doorstep. A trip into Denali National Park with the mighty Mount McKinley (6,194 m/20,323 ft) is a challenging and unique experience for any visitor.

If you want to get even closer to the 'real' Alaska, you can fly from Anchorage to King Salmon in the west and then take a hydroplane to Katmai National Park and Preserve. In July you can watch bears catching salmon from incredibly close range, a world-class sight. Or pay a visit to Kodiak Island with its massive Kodiak bears that weigh up to 500 kg (1,100 lbs) and reach heights of up to 3 m (10 ft). Wilderness in its purest form.

The Arctic tundra is home to small herds of shaggy musk oxen.

Our Alaskan dream route begins in Juneau, the capital. After a boat trip across to Haines we take the Haines Highway to the Alaska Highway as far as Border City Lodge where the route actually goes through Canada. Back in Alaska via Fairbanks and Anchorage, the route takes us to Homer on the Kenai Peninsula.

① **Juneau** Alaska's capital is located on a narrow stretch of coastal plain between Gastineau Channel and the steep slopes of Mount Juneau (1,091 m/3,580 ft). Right outside town are the towering Coast Mountains with spectacular glaciers.

In 1880, gold diggers Joe Juneau and Dick Harris first found gold in what is now the town's river. By World War II more than 150 million dollars' worth of the precious metal had been discovered in the area.

As early as 1906 the Alaskan state government was moved to this northern El Dorado. The mines have long been shut down now, and Juneau has become a quiet governmental town. More than half the town's population is involved in running the state.

Both of the town's most important sights are located on Franklin Street, the town's main road. One of them is the Red Dog Saloon, which was already infamous during the gold rush. The other is the Russian Orthodox Church of St Nicholas, which keeps a close watch over the moral fibre of the townsfolk. The church was erected by Rus-sian fur traders in 1894, making it the oldest Russian church in the southeastern part of Alaska. Another must-see is the Alaska State

Travel Information

Route profile

Length: approx. 3,000 km (1,850 miles), excluding detours

Time required: 3 weeks

Start: Juneau

End: Homer

Route (main locations): Juneau, Glacier Bay National Park, Skagway, Haines, Haines Junction, Whitehorse, Kluane National Park, Tok Junction, Delta Junction, Fairbanks, Denali National Park, Eklutna, Anchorage, Portage, Seward, Kenai, Homer

Traffic information:
Drive on the right in the USA. Speed limits in towns are 25–30 mph (40–48 km/h), and outside towns 65 mph (105 km/h). You must stop when you see a school bus with the indicators on.

In Canada, distances are indicated in kilometers, in Alaska in miles. Side roads are commonly unsurfaced – watch out for airborne gravel.

When to go:
The best time to go is from mid-May to late September.

The road into Denali National Park is only open from mid-June.

Information:
Alaska general:
www.alaska.com
www.travelalaska.com
Ferries in Alaska:
Alaska Marine Highway
www.dot.state.ak.us/amhs
Alaska Ferry
www.akferry.org
National Parks:
www.us-national-parks.net

Museum on Whittier Street, with an exhibition of indigenous Indian culture and a bit of history of the white settlements in the area.

The terrace on the State Office Building offers the best view of Juneau, the straits and Douglas Island just off the coast. An excursion to Mendenhall Glacier, about 20 km (13 miles) north of town, is a must. This glacier calves out of the 10,000-sq-km (3,650-sq-mi) Juneau Icefield, with a face 2.5 km (1.6 miles) long where it breaks off into the lake. The visitor center offers comprehensive documentation on the glacier, and you can go hiking along its edges.

2 Glacier Bay National Park You should not leave Juneau without taking a boat or plane trip to this national park 85 km (53 miles) away. Giant glaciers detach themselves directly into the sea here, and giant ice flows descend from mountains that tower above 4,000 m (13,000 ft). No fewer than sixteen glaciers terminate in this large bay, which was completely covered in pack ice as recently as 100 years ago. Since then, the ice has receded by more than 100 km (62 miles), faster than anywhere else on earth. These days, seals lounge on the ice floes of Glacier Bay, and humpback whales and orcas ply

the chilly waters, breaching, hunting and carrying on.

From mid-May to mid-September you can take day trips and longer excursions both by boat and by air from Juneau to Gustavus, a small settlement at the entrance to this huge bay. From Haines or Skagway you can also take scenic flights over Glacier Bay. The first leg on our route to the north is completed by boat.

3 Haines This town at the northern end of Lynn Canal used to be a Chilkat settlement. The Chilkats are a sub-tribe of the Tlingit Indians. Worth seeing are the old military outpost

'Fort William H. Seward', the Chilkat Center and a reconstructed Tlingit tribal house. Before carrying on, you should take the ferry across to Skagway (1 hour) at the end of Taiya Inlet and visit the former gold-diggers' settlement there.

4 Skagway When gold was discovered on the Klondike River in October 1897, the population of Skagway grew to more than 20,000 almost overnight as most gold seekers landed here before hiking along the Chilkoot Trail to the Yukon River. Between 1897 and 1898, a Wild-West-style town developed that has remained almost intact to this day. The town's Broadway Street is now an historical park. You can't miss the impressive Arctic Brotherhood building, with more than 20,000 wooden sticks decorating its facade, or the Red Onion Saloon, where the floor is still covered in sawdust. Every evening a play is performed in Eagles Hall, bringing the time of the gold diggers to life.

Although the gold rush was past its peak by then, the year 1900 saw the construction of a narrow-gauge railway across White Pass, between Skagway and Whitehorse. The most scenic stretch up to White Pass at 889 m (2,917 ft) is now maintained as a heritage railway

1 Mendenhall Glacier feeds - off the massive Juneau Icefield (10,000 sq km/ 3,860 sq mi). Its glacial tongue is 2.5 km (1.6 miles) wide.

2 Haines is located at the end of Inside Passage, where the Chilkat River flows into Lynn Canal, a fjord that stretches 145 km (90 miles).

3 In Glacier Bay National Park, glaciers have carved out some inviting beaches that are now popular with walruses.

and will give you some unforgettable views of this wild and romantic landscape. The different climate zones produce myriad vegetation, from wet coastal forests right up to alpine tundras at the top of the pass.

⑤ Haines Highway/Haines Junction From Haines, the Haines Highway winds its way across the foothills of the Alsek Range. At Porcupine it crosses the border into Canadian British Columbia, and just after that you get to Chilkat Pass at an altitude of 1,065 m (3,494 ft). West of the road, the Tatshenshini-Alsek Preserve connects Glacier Bay National Park to the south and Kluane National Park in the north.

Heading north, the nature reserve joins Wrangell-St Elias National Park back in Alaska. People on both sides of the border have worked together to create this park, the largest protected area on the North American continent. As the crow flies, it stretches more than 700 km (435 miles) from Gustavus at the southern tip of Glacier Bay National Park to Richardson Highway in the north. There are no roads anywhere in the park, but mountains up to 6,000 m (19,500 ft), massive glaciers and pristine forests.

The town of Haines Junction has 500 inhabitants and originally developed from what was once a soldiers' camp during the construction of the Alaska Highway. Here, the Haines Highway meets the Alaska Highway coming from Whitehorse, which itself is also worth an extra detour (111 km/69 miles).

⑥ Whitehorse This is where the exhausted gold diggers would arrive after crossing White Pass. Downriver from the large rapids they were able to

take a paddle steamer further north along the Yukon River. When the Alaska Highway was being built, Whitehorse developed into the largest settlement in the territory.

Today, at the McBride Museum, you can see old gold-digging and mining equipment as well as Indian arts and crafts. Old Log Church, built in 1900, houses an exhibition on the Yukon Territory's missionary history. The paddle steamer permanently moored at the southern end of Second Avenue is called the 'SS Klondike'. During the gold rush, it regularly plied the Yukon between Whitehorse and Dawson City.

Back at Haines Junction you take the Alaska Highway to Kluane Lake at the eastern end of Kluane National Park.

⑦ Kluane National Park North of Haines Junction the road rises up to Bear Creek Summit at 997 m (3,271 ft)

shortly before coming to Boutillier Summit at 1,000 m (3,281 ft). Just beneath the pass is Kluane Lake, the largest lake in the Yukon Territory at 400 sq km (155 sq m). The highway runs along its western shore.

The national park covers an area of 22,000 sq km (8,492 sq mi) and has plenty of untouched

nature including high peaks, huge glaciers and sub-Arctic vegetation. At 5,959 m (19,551 ft), Mount Logan is Canada's highest mountain. Down at more 'moderate' altitudes there are large populations of black bears, brown bears, wolves, mountain sheep, caribou and elk. Further to the west are the inaccessible Ice-

3

field Ranges. From the air these look something like a giant lunar landscape made of ice and snow. Given its extraordinary dimensions, it is hardly surprising that Kluane National Park was declared a UNESCO World Heritage Site as early as 1980, alongside Wrangell-St Elias Park, which borders it to the west.

There are very few places on the Alaska Highway to access Kluane National Park on foot, and you can never go any further than to the foot of the icy giants. As an alternative, it is well worth taking a scenic flight across this breathtaking mountain landscape. Small aircraft take off from the town of Burwash at the northern end of

Lake Kluane. Or maybe you are into old ghost towns? At the eastern end of Lake Kluane, a short access road takes you down to Silver City on the lakeshore. This old trading post, long since abandoned, really does give you that 'ghost-town' feel.

From Burwash Landing, the Alaska Highway winds its lonely way through a largely pristine landscape of mountains, forests and tundra all in seemingly endless repetition. Towards the west there are some impressive views of the mighty St Elias Mountains, Canada's highest mountain range. The road first crosses Donjek River, then White River and finally, just before you get to the Alaskan border, there is Beaver Creek, Canada's westernmost settlement with roughly 100 inhabitants.

In October 1942 the last section of the Alaska Highway was completed here.

⑧ **Tok Junction** Our first stop back in Alaska is Tetlin Junction, and after another 19 km (12 miles) you get to the small town of Tok.

Founded in 1942 as a soldier's camp when the Alaska Highway was being built, Tok is considered to be the gateway to Alaska. From here, Fairbanks and Anchorage are the same distance away.

The visitor center at the crossroads has an interesting exhibition of stuffed animals from Alaska, and Tok is also a center

1 The icy world of Wrangell-St Elias National Park is only visible from a helicopter or glacier plane.

2 A reflection of Mount Huxley (3,828 m/12,560 ft) in a temporarily ice-free pond in Wrangell-St Elias National Park.

3 Ice on lakes such as Kathleen Lake in Kluane National Park does not melt until late in the spring.

for husky breeding. Dogs-led races start here in winter and in the summer you can see teams practising on a 20-km (12-mile) track that runs parallel to the Alaska Highway.

From Tok Junction, the remaining 111 m (69 miles) of the Alaska Highway follow the mighty Tanana River. The broad flood plains on either side of the road remind us that the glaciers of the Alaska Range once extended all the way down to here.

9 **Delta Junction** We have now reached the northern end of the 2,300-km (1,430-mile) Alaska Highway. The terminus is located at the junction with Richardson Highway, where a visitors center offers all kinds of information about the construction of the highway and the Trans-Alaska Pipeline.

At Delta Junction the pipeline crosses the Tanana River in a wide arc and it is quite a sight in its own right. Its construction became a necessity when, in 1968, the USA's largest oil fields were discovered north of the Brooks Range in Prudhoe Bay. Starting in March 1975 about 22,000 workers were involved in the two-year construction of the line, which now extends 1,280 km (795 miles) straight through the heart of the penninsula and down to the port city of Valdez.

Half the pipeline was installed underground and the rest, nearly 700 km (435 miles) of it, is supported by a system of 78,000 stilts. The pipeline has to be continuously cooled in order to keep the 60°C (140°F) oil from destroying it. Another 153 km (95 miles) down Alaska's oldest highway, the Richardson Highway, you come to Fairbanks.

10 **Fairbanks** This city on the Tanana River owes its existence to the 1903 gold rush. Within

seven years 11,000 people had set up shop on its primitive campsite. In World War II, large military settlements and the construction of the Alaska Highway fostered an economic boom in the town. After 1974 the construction headquarters of the Trans-Alaska Pipeline were relocated here.

Today, Fairbanks is a modern city. The Otto William Geist Museum tells you everything about the history and culture of Alaska's indigenous people.

Before carrying on, take the opportunity to relax and enjoy Chena Hot Springs about 100 km (62 miles) east of the city, on oasis of peace.

11 **Denali National Park** Our next destination is the highlight of the entire trip – Denali National Park. To get there take the George Parks Highway from Riley Creek. If you want to see the 24,000 sq km (9,265 sq mi) of the park and the highest mountain in North America (Mount McKinley), you have to

12 **Eklutna** About 33 km (20 miles) outside Anchorage you pass the Indian village of Eklutna. The St Nicholas Russian Orthodox Church is oddly located right in the middle of an Indian Cemetery. There is also a Siberian chapel.

Bright wooden houses are set on the graves here, their eaves lavishly decorated with woodcarvings. The Indians believe they house the spirits of the dead.

Just south of Eagle River, it is worth taking a 20-km (13-mile) detour to visit Chugach State Park. From here you can do day hikes to the glaciers further up country.

1 Portage Glacier calving into the lake of the same name.

2 The snowy mountains behind the Anchorage Skyline. The wilderness starts right outside the city.

take one of the shuttle buses operated by the park authority. These regularly run the 140 km (87 miles) into the park to Kantishna at Wonder Lake. The trip takes eleven hours, and if you picked a sunny day, you will even get a glimpse of Denali, the High One, at a glorious 6,194 m (20,323 ft). The road

runs through some hilly tundra with mountains in the 2,000 m (6,560 ft) range.

At the park headquarters you can visit the dog pens where the park rangers breed huskies. During the summer they train them as sled dogs for winter when that is the only mode of transport allowed in the park.

The George Parks Highway now takes us towards Anchorage where you can experience Alaska Native Culture. Roughly halfway along it you get to the picture-book town of Talkeetna. You get yet another view of Denali from here. It is also the take-off point for scenic flights around the national park.

13 **Anchorage** This city owes its existence to the construction of the railway line between Fairbanks and the ice-free port of Seward on the Kenai Peninsula. Originally a builders' settlement established in 1914, Anchorage eventually developed into a modern aviation hub. It is now home to half of Alaska's entire population. As you enter the city via Glenn Highway you'll see thousands of small- and medium-size aircraft parked at Merill Field. Lake Hood is one of the largest hydroplane airports in the world.

14 **Portage** After 60 km (37 miles) on Seward Highway, you come to this town at the end of Turnagain Bay. At Girdwood, just before you get to Portage, is Alaska's northernmost al-pine ski resort at Mount Alyeska (1,201 m/ 3,940 ft). Take a chairlift up to 610 m (2,000 ft) and enjoy a view of the Chugach Mountain Range glaciers.

At the end of the bay is Portage Lake. There are usually some oddly shaped ice floes

bobbing on its deep-blue waters. On the far side, Portage Glacier drops into the lake like a giant wall.

15 **Seward** The natural deepwater port here is the economic engine of this town. The most important annual event is the Silver Salmon Derby in August, a salmon-fishing competition. You'll most likely want to check the Kenai Fjords National Park Visitor Center for information on the 780-sq-km (300-sq-mi) Harding Icefield. Leaving Kenai you first take Seward Highway back towards Anchorage be-

fore turning onto Sterling Highway at Moose Pass.

16 **Kenai** In 1791 the Russians built their second Alaskan settlement here. After 1846 it became the center of the Russian Orthodox Church in Alaska. The Holy Assumption Church and its three onion-domed spires are icons of the period, along with an old bible. The bible, like the other equipment in the church, was brought to Alaska from Siberia.

17 **Homer** Down on the southwest side of the Kenai Penin-

isula is the 'Halibut Capital', Homer, a quaint town nestled on the shore of Kachemak Bay. In this town at the end of Sterling Highway, it's all about fish. A giant fleet of vessels is always ready to set off for the next catch. If you are into fishing, rent a boat here or book one of the numerous deep-sea fishing tours to fetch your prey.

1 Portage Glacier calving into the lake of the same name.

2 The snowy mountains behind the Anchorage skyline.

Kodiak Island This island is home to the famous Kodiak brown bears, the largest carnivorous land animal in the world. They can weigh up to 500 kg (1,100 lbs).

Kenai Peninsula There are some large lakes on this mountainous peninsula that extends 200 km (135 miles) into the Gulf of Alaska.

Homer This port town on the Kenai Peninsula at the end of Highway 1 is a mecca for deep-sea fishermen.

Denali National Park The center of this park (24,000 sq km/9,265 sq mi), is Denali (Mount McKinley) at 6,194 m (20,323 ft). There are about 430 species of wild flowers here along with grizzlies, moose and caribou.

Anchorage The skyline of this boom town looks a lot like other American cities. Half of Alaska's population lives here and its airport is the eighth largest in the USA. Planes are an indispensable mode of transport in the remote regions here. Many people even have their own.

Chena Hot Springs This oasis of relaxation is located 100 km (62 miles) east of Fairbanks on Steese Highway amid the dense forests of the Chena Valley. A small access road takes you to the sulphur springs where you can enjoy the healing waters. But be careful of any black bears that might be in the car park.

Wrangell-St Elias National Park Two mountain ranges are protected by this park – the volcanic Wrangell Mountains and the St Elias Mountains with the striking Mount St Elias (5,489 m/18,009 ft).

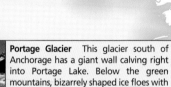

Kluane National Park Huge glaciers, sub-Arctic vegetation, bears, wolves, caribou and moose are all integral elements of this park in the Yukon Territory around Mount Logan (5,959 m/19,551 ft).

Portage Glacier This glacier south of Anchorage has a giant wall calving right into Portage Lake. Below the green mountains, bizarrely shaped ice floes with a bluish hue float aimlessly on the lake.

Haines This town at the mouth of the Chilkat River is an area where the Indians are famous for their totem poles.

Glacier Bay National Park In Alaska's southernmost national park there are no fewer than sixteen glaciers terminating in Glacier Bay. The bay is over 100 km (62 miles) long and has only been free of ice for the last 100 years.

Mendenhall Glacier This glacier, which is 20 km (13 miles) north of Juneau, Alaska's capital, is part of the gigantic Juneau Icefield, which measures almost 10,000 sq km (3,860 sq mi). The glacier tongue calves at a width of 2.5 km (1.6 miles) into Mendenhall Lake.

There are over 2,000 lakes in the 7,861-sq-km (3,034-sq-mi) Réserve Faunique des Laurentides north of Québec.

Canada

On the Trans-Canada Highway from the Great Lakes to the Atlantic

Eastern Canada is the country's historic core and heart of the nation. The French founded North America's first cities in Québec province, while modern Canada was launched on Prince Edward Island, which means that a trip through Canada's eastern reaches is also a journey through 250 years of history, not to mention some fascinating scenery.

When traveling from west to east through south-eastern Canada, you cross three vast and diverse regions. Initially you pass through the southern edge of the Canadian Shield, consisting of Precambrian volcanic rock interspersed with myriad lakes and smooth granite domes. The stone is up to 3.6 million years old, and owes its present-day appearance to glacial activity during the Ice Age.

The St Lawrence Lowlands, which start near the Great Lakes in southern Ontario and stretch as far as the mouth of the St Lawrence River into the Atlantic, were also shaped by the Ice Age. The easternmost reaches of this vast and distinctive area are formed by the Appalachian Mountains. They are the reason the coastlines of Nova Scotia and Cape Breton Island have so many tiny bays

and cliffs reminiscent of places like the west coasts of France and England.

European fishermen came to the east coast and to the St

Lawrence River as early as the end of the 15th century to take advantage of the summer catch, but it was not until 1534 that Jacques Cartier flew the

A grazing moose in Cape Breton Highlands National Park in Nova Scotia.

The thundering torrent of water at Horseshoe Falls, the Canadian side of Niagara Falls.

Ottawa's Parliament Building, the "Canadian Westminster", sits proudly over the Ottawa River, which is spanned by the Alexandra Bridge. It was built between 1898-1900 as a steel truss cantilever bridge for road and rail traffic.

French flag in present-day Montréal. It was actually the beaver, or more precisely its fur, that inspired the real development of permanent settlements in this region. Since every fashionista in Europe in those days wanted to wear a beaver-fur hat, Québec was founded as a fur trading center in 1608, and France's Finance Minister Colbert finally arranged New France as a royal colony modeled on the mother country.

As is often the case, however, the success attracted competition. In 1670, the British circumvented the sovereign French territory on the St Lawrence and founded the Hudson's Bay Company in the north. It soon became the most famous fur-trading company on the continent. After the Seven Years War, the Paris Treaty of 1763 forced France to cede New France to England. Since then, French is still spoken along the St Lawrence, but the French no longer had influence over Canada's political structure.

Today, although there are ongoing attempts in French-speaking parts of Canada, i.e. in Québec province and the adjacent regions of Ontario and New Brunswick, to secede, they are actually only a means of strengthening their own position and their cultural life. The accomplishments of secessionists thus far include a successful campaign to ensure French was declared the only official language in Québec in 1977.

For visitors coming from the west, it is always fascinating to observe how the first French traces suddenly appear in Ontario. Place names suddenly sound French and, when in the Old Town quarter of Québec, you feel as if you're no longer in North America but in a historic town of the Old World.

The 14-m-high (46-ft) Big Tub Lighthouse is on the Bruce Peninsula not far from Tobermory, a "veritable country in itself with a soul of its own".

413

The journey from the west bank of Lake Huron along the St Lawrence River to Nova Scotia is a journey through the land of "shimmering water" and heads beyond Québec to the craggy cliffs on the stormy North Atlantic. Although the trip passes through the most densely settled regions of Canada, the wilderness is never far away.

① Sault Ste Marie This "twin city" is located in both Canada and the United States, on a narrow promontory between Lake Superior and Lake Huron on the St Mary's River. The height difference between the two lakes is overcome by two locks from 1887 that are today listed as historic monuments. After a small detour to Tahquamenon Falls National Park in the west, your route follows the coast of the North Channel. At Sudbury, the Trans-Canada Highway branches off: Highway 17 heads directly to Ottawa while the south-western branch (Highway 69) runs along the east coast of Georgian Bay.

② Midland This small town has three main tourist attractions. One is Sainte-Marie among the Hurons, a Jesuit missionary station established in 1639 for the purpose of Christianizing Huron Indians. Laid out in the style of European monastic settlements, the mission has been restored to its original state. The second is Penetanguishene Discovery Harbour, a marine base that has also been partially restored. The third is Georgian Bay Islands National Park in the middle of the Thirty Thousand Islands (visitor center is in Honey Harbour).

A worthwhile detour now takes you from Midland around the southern tip of Georgian Bay to the Bruce Peninsula National Park (Hwy 6). For Toronto, leave the Trans-Canada Highway and take Highway 400.

③ Toronto (see page 416) From Toronto you should make the day trip to Niagara Falls, about 130 km (81 mi) away on the U.S.-Canadian border. Take Highway 400 to get there.

④ Niagara Falls The Niagara River plunges 50 m (164 ft) over a 675-m-long (2,215-ft) fracture line on the Canadian Side; on the U.S. side it is 330 m (1,083 ft) wide. Good observation points are Table Rock, to the west near the horseshoe-

Travel Information

Route profile
Length: approx. 3,500 km (2,175 mi)
Time required: 3 weeks
Start: Sault Ste Marie
End: Halifax
Route (main locations): Sault Ste. Marie, Toronto, Ottawa, Montréal, Québec, Charlottetown, Halifax

Traffic information:
Two different lines of the Trans-Canada Highway (TCH) run through northern Ontario: the northern line, which connects the most important mining and resource centers, and therefore leads through the breathtaking scenery of the Canadian Shield, with wild rivers, untouched lakes, numerous small pioneer settlements, and endless forests with their wealth of wildlife; and the southern line, which runs largely parallel to the US border along the Great Lakes (Lake Huron, Lake Superior).

Information:
Here are some websites to help you plan your trip.
Ontario:
www.ontariotravel.net
Québec:
www.bonjourquebec.com
New Brunswick:
www.tourismnbcanada.com
Nova Scotia:
www.novascotia.com
Prince Edward Island:
www.gov.pe.ca

itself. The second icon of Ottawa is the Château Laurier Hotel, built in 1912 by Grand Trunk Railway.

The most fascinating technicological attraction here is the lock staircase of the Rideau Canal, with a height difference of 25 m (82 ft). The Musée Canadien des Civilisations is also must.

7 Parc de la Gatineau This vast park, with sixty species of tree, is on the north-western edge of Hull. You can take beautiful walks here during the Indian summer, and 200 km (124 mi) of cross-country ski trails attract visitors in winter. Continuing along Highway 7, with a constant view of the Ottawa River, you arrive in Montréal after roughly 200 km (124 mi).

8 Montréal (see page 417) Québec is 250 km (155 mi) from Montréal, and Autoroute 20, part of the Trans-Canada Highway, heads along the southern side of the St Lawrence River.

9 Québec (see page 419) From Québec, Autoroute 20 runs parallel to the St Lawrence River before the 185 branches off to the south at Rivière-du-Loup and becomes the Trans-Canada Highway 2 in New Brunswick. The lovely scenic route initially follows the St John River Valley where fields and pastures characterize the landscape. Arriving at Grand Falls, west of Mount Carleton

shaped waterfall, or the Minolta Tower. Once back in Toronto, the route heads along highways 401 and 115 to the Trans-Canada Highway 7.

5 Peterborough The biggest attraction in this city on the Kawartha lakes is the Hydraulic Lift Lock from 1904. The lock is made out of a lock basin that can be pushed up or lowered 20 m (66 ft) together with the vessel. The Lang Pioneer Village is a rebuilt 19th-century pioneer village, while the Petroglyph Provincial Park features more than 900 Aboriginal rock drawings that are between five hundred and one thousand years old, depicting turtles, snakes, birds and humans.

6 Ottawa Canada's capital is happily mocked as the "Westminster in the Wilderness". The parliament building in English neo-Gothic style is the dominant edifice in Ottawa, and its 90-m (295-ft) Peace Tower has a carillon made up of fifty-three bells. The tower's impressive observation deck makes the city look like a miniature of

1 Toronto: View of the Skydome and CN Tower.

2 From the air you can see the Niagara River, Horseshoe Falls and Niagara Falls.

3 Old Town Montréal: the dome of the Marché de Bonsecours at the St Lawrence River.

Toronto

This metropolis on the northern shores of Lake Ontario owes its cosmopolitan character to the large number of immigrants who came here after World War II, and who gave the city its European-Asian composition.

Toronto is an extraordinarily lively city. Bustling Yonge Street is considered a shopping paradise and bold construction projects signal dynamic development, while traditional buildings such as the Holy Trinity Church are listed historic monuments.

Be sure to see: Ontario Place, a futuristic recreation center on Lake Ontario with varying exhibitions, an IMAX cinema and a ultra-modern children's playground; the Harbourfront Center; the converted warehouses on the piers with shops, restaurants, waterfront cafés, art galleries and theaters; and Queen's Quay and York Quay boardwalks.

Toronto Islands, connected to the city via a ferry, is a quiet refuge with tranquil canals, footpaths and a historic amusement park for children. The CN Tower was the highest free-standing building in the world until 2007. Its viewing platform provides a spectacular view from 447 m (1,467 ft). The dream-like and particularly interesting museums in town include the Art Gallery of Ontario, a modern art museum with the most famous works by Canadian artists, the Henry Moore Sculpture Center and classic paintings from Europe. There is also the Royal Ontario Museum, the country's largest museum with a wide variety of international exhibitions and a replica of a bat cave. The George R. Gardiner Museum of Ceramic Art specializes in pottery and porcelain, and is the only one of its kind in North America.

In 1995, the CN Tower, a true marvel of civil engineering, was classified as one of the Seven Wonders of the Modern World.

Montréal

Canada's second-largest city was founded by French Catholics in 1642. Due to its ideal location at the confluence of the St Lawrence and Ottawa rivers, Montréal rapidly grew to become a bustling trade center.

Vieux-Montréal, the picturesque Old Town quarter, has numerous historic buildings and narrow alleyways situated on the southern slope of Mont Royal that visibly remind you of the city's distinctly French character. In winter, locals flee to the Ville souterraine, the underground city with a network of tunnels, passages and shopping centers.

Sights worth visiting here include the Catholic Basilique Notre-Dame, an ornate church actually built by a Protestant Irish-American architect named James O'Donnell around 1829; the Pointe-à-Callière with the Musée d'Archéologie et d'Histoire, which remembers the site of the first settlement; and the Hôtel de Ville, the town hall built in French Empire Style, dating back to the year 1872. The Notre-Dame-de-Bonsecours Cha-

pel is, as the interiors of many model ships indicate, the sailors' church. The Musée des Beaux-Arts was opened as a museum for fine arts back in 1912, while the Biodome de Montréal, a museum dedicated to the environment is housed in the former Olympic velodrome and provides information on various ecosystems.

Montréal's skyline from the harbour, Canada's No. 1 container port.

417

Provincial Park, the St John crashes 25 m (82 ft) over a precipice. The next stop is the Hartland Covered Bridge, the world's longest covered bridge, measuring 390 m (1,280 ft).

🔟 **Kings Landing** The open-air museum at the St John River displays 19th-century life using thirty reconstructed buildings. Apart from various farmhouses and residential homes, there is a print shop, sawmill, blacksmith's shop, mill and a theater.

You arrive in the capital of New Brunswick 40 km (25 mi) later.

⓫ **Fredericton** This tranquil regional town at the lower reaches of the St John River was founded by French immigrants in 1732. The most important public buildings and the most beautiful Victorian houses are clustered around Queen Street and King Street. Learn about its history in the York-Sunbury Historical Society Museum.

Follow Highway 2 to the east until Route 114 branches off south toward the Bay of Fundy just beyond Sussex.

⓬ **Fundy National Park** The Bay of Fundy extends nearly 300 km (186 mi) into the country's interior and separates New Brunswick from Nova Scotia. Its unusual funnel shape produces

the world's largest tidal range, which can shift up to 16 m (52 ft) at the end of Cobequid Bay. At the northernmost arm of the Bay of Fundy is the national park of the same name, with its jagged coast cliffs. The sandstone formations at Cape Enrage are especially beautiful.

Back on Highway 2, you pass through Moncton and reach the star-shaped complex of Fort Beauséjour (Exit 513A at Aulac) at the northern edge of the Cumberland Basin wetland about 55 km (34 mi) away. The next stop is the Confederation Bridge, roughly 60 km (37 mi) down the road.

⓭ **Confederation Bridge** This bridge opened in 1997 and connects Prince Edward Island, also referred to as "P.E.I.", to the Trans-Canada Highway. It is the

1 The first-class Hotel Château Frontenac, perched high above the St Lawrence River, is the icon of Québec and one of the city's best addresses.

2 At 390 m (1,280 ft) in length, the Hartland Covered Bridge is the longest covered wooden bridge in the world.

3 High tide in Fundy Bay has formed the sandstone cliffs at Shepody Bay Beach.

Québec

The capital of the province of the same name is the heart of francophone Canada. More than 90 percent of its inhabitants speak French, and the townscape has also maintained its European flair.

Québec City is the only North American metropolis with a city wall, and the Old Town quarter's narrow alleyways even evoke a few memories of old Paris. Québec City has in fact been a UNESCO World Heritage Site since 1985. The settlement was founded here on the banks of the St Lawrence River back in 1608.

After the houses under Cap Diamant were repeatedly burned down, citizens of Quebec retreated to the hill and created the "Haute-Ville", the "Upper town", connected by a cog railway. Worth seeing here: the Escalier Cass-Cou, or "Breakneck Staircase", which connects the Haute-Ville with the Quartier Petit-Champlain in Basse-Ville, and the former market place Place Royale. The Musée de la Civilisation provides an insight into the city's development. At the eastern end of the city wall in Haute-Ville is La Citadelle from the early 19th century. Since 1920, it has been home to the Royal 22ième Régiment, the only French unit in the Canadian army. The Cathédrale Notre-Dame was built in 1647, and reminds visitors of French rule, while the Maison Chevalier shows how the wealthy families of the 18th and 19th century lived in Quebec.

Now a city landmark, the luxury hotel Chateau Frontenac, built in 1893, looks like a large European castle.

Québec City at dusk.

world's longest bridge over an ice-covered waterway at 13 km (21 mi). At a height of 60 m (197 ft) the crossing takes roughly ten minutes.

14 Charlottetown This hilly island is almost treeless, but green pastures and fertile farmland line the road. Charlottetown is considered the "Cradle of the Confederation", as it was here that the decision to unite Canada was made in 1864. The small regional town exudes Victorian charm with its old wooden and half-timbered houses.

15 Prince Edward Island National Park The country's smallest national park is 24 km (15 mi) north of Charlottetown. As the St Lawrence River is only 15 m (49 ft) deep here until far out in the sea, the water along the 40-km (25-mi) park coast is

a pleasant temperature. Less then 30 km (17 mi) east of Charlottetown, you can learn all about the lifestyle of European immigrants in the 19th century at the Orwell Corner Historic Village. From Wood Islands you head back to Caribou, Nova Scotia, on the mainland by ferry and from there along Highway 104 to the Canso Causeway, the road connection to Cape Breton Island. Highway 105 crosses the island, and from Sydney it's another 45 km (28 mi) to Louisbourg.

16 Louisbourg This small town on the east coast was the first French center of power in the New World. Tucked behind the 8-m-high (26-ft) walls of Fortresse de Louisbourg are around fifty historic buildings, from the governor's house to the soldiers' barracks. The road then heads along the coast past

Tahquamenon Falls National Park The Tahquamenon River crashes down roughly 20 m (66 ft), making it the highest waterfall in Michigan.

Sault Ste. Marie This town is an important stop on the St Lawrence Seaway. The numerous cataracts to Lake Huron are navigated these days by large locks.

Montréal Two thirds of the population in Canada's second largest city are French Canadians and continue to speak French today. The Île de Montréal island in the St Lawrence River forms the center of the metropolis.

Toronto The skyline of Canada's largest city is dominated by modern architecture, the most striking feature of which is the 553-m-high (1,814-ft) CN Tower.

Flowerpot Island A bizarre rock on Lake Huron.

Big Tub Lighthouse This lighthouse is the symbol of Bruce Peninsula National Park.

Niagara Falls The 50-m-high (164-ft) waterfalls comprise the American Falls and the Canadian Horseshoe Falls. Goat Island is tucked in between them.

Lake Ontario Covering an area of 20,000 sq km (7,720 sq mi), the easternmost of the Great Lakes is also the smallest. Its most famous city is Toronto.

Ottawa Canada's capital is also referred to as the "Westminster in the Wilderness". The neo-Gothic government buildings are the pride of the city.

Sydney and St Ann's through the mountains of the island's north-west and into the most beautiful national park of the Atlantic provinces.

⓱ Cape Breton Highlands National Park This impassable mountainous region with peaks up to 554 m (1,818 ft) immediately evokes images of Scotland. For hikers and mountaineers there are numerous trails and routes, while the 300-km-long (186-mi) Cabot Trail, a spectacular coast road around the peninsula is a joy for drivers.
Back on the mainland you follow Highway 104 and then Highway 102 from Truro to Halifax.

⓲ Halifax The Port of Halifax is the most important in the Atlantic provinces, and the Province House, completed in 1819, is the seat of parliament. Perched high up in the west is the old citadel, whose forts were built until 1856. The city's main landmark, however, is the clock tower from 1795. Halifax was home to Elisabeth Mann Borgese, an activist for protecting the world's oceans and the last surviving child of German literary giant Thomas Mann.

1 A fishing village on Prince Edward Island. With the Gulf of St Lawrence, the best fishing grounds are literally at your doorstep.

2 The Cabot Trail opens up the north of Cape Breton Island.

3 The fort of Louisbourg, built by the French around 1740, has been restored to its original condition.

4 The Canadian Coastguard Lighthouse on Cape Breton Island.

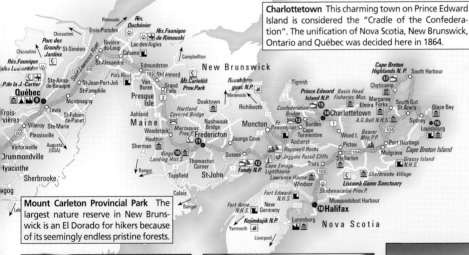

Charlottetown This charming town on Prince Edward Island is considered the "Cradle of the Confederation". The unification of Nova Scotia, New Brunswick, Ontario and Québec was decided here in 1864.

Cape Breton Highlands National Park This huge park is home to moose, beavers and over 250 species of birds.

Hartland Covered Bridge Built in 1901, this bridge is 390 m (1,280 ft) long and spans the St John River. It is the world's longest covered bridge.

Mount Carleton Provincial Park The largest nature reserve in New Brunswick is an El Dorado for hikers because of its seemingly endless pristine forests.

Québec This most recognizable icon of Québec city is the Château Frontenac with its many turrets and verdigris roofs. It was built on the site of the former governor's palace in 1893.

Réserve Faunique des Laurentides You can still spot moose, beavers and caribous in the mountainous region north of Montréal.

Cape Enrage Bizarre sandstones and a lighthouse characterize the cape in Fundy National Park.

Lunenburg This small town on the Atlantic was founded by Germans and Swiss in 1753, and is characterized by the old captain's quarters.

Old farmhouse in Grand Teton
the state of Wyoming.

Canada and the USA

On the Pan-American Highway from British Columbia to New Mexico

A journey through the North American West is a journey of contrasts. The route passes through mountain landscapes and open plains, pine forests and vast deserts, mining villages and megacities, and illustrates the impressive diversity of this enormous continent.

The full diversity of North America reveals itself in its entirety along the wide open stretches of the Pan-American Highway. From its begining on the Canadian Pacific coast to its end near the border between the USA and Mexico, this route initially travels in a south-easterly and then southerly direction. The roads on this long route are in exceptionally good condition but some of the side roads can be closed during the colder times of the year, especially in the north.

The northern section takes you through the Canadian provinces of British Columbia and Alberta as well as the US state of Montana. Larger towns are the exception here and the individual towns are often separated by large distances. Newer settlements originally developed from either trading posts or supply centers for the white fur hunters. There are also a number of old gold-digging locations along the Pan-American Highway, where visitors are taken back in time to the gold

rush of the 19th century. In some places there are also remnants of Native American Indian cultures, such as the impressive totem poles, longhouses

Mount Assiniboine after the first snow, located on the Great Divide.

and pueblos. The Canadian part of the route is loaded with absolutely breathtaking natural landscapes. Majestic, snowy mountains reflect in the shimmering turquoise hues of Rocky Mountain lakes. To the east of the highway Mount Robson rises to 3,954 m (12,973 ft) above sea level, the highest peak in the Canadian Rocky Mountains. Glaciers and waterfalls drop powerfully to great depths from high cliffs. The Pan-American Highway is also lined with vast expanses of forest. In a number of areas such as Banff National Park, the oldest National Park in Canada, the natural environment is protected from development. Further south the scenery changes.

422

National Park in the north-west of

Sunset over Jackson Lake and the granite mountains of the Teton Range.

Banff National Park will show you everything that makes the Canadian Rocky Mountains such an attraction – rugged peaks, dense forests, vast open spaces and scenic lakes like Moraine Lake, shown here.

In the distance you see the skyscrapers of Calgary, a modern metropolis built on wealth generated by oil and natural resources, and given a makeover for the 1988 Winter Olympics. Some three hours from Calgary are the spectacular lakes and mountains of Waterton-Glacier International Peace Park, a union of Glacier and Waterton National Parks.

The route continues through Idaho, Wyoming, Utah and Arizona. There are a number of remarkable contrasts here as well. Remnants of Native American cultures and the Spanish colonial era mix with modern cities and skyscrapers, and extensive forest areas stand in contrast to desert landscapes. A major highlight of this particular section of North America is Yellowstone National Park in Wyoming. Salt Lake City, the capital of Utah and the center of Mormonism, is also an Olympic city, having hosted the 2002 winter games. In the vast desert expanses of Utah and Arizona the light and landscape change dramatically with the movement of the sun, producing impressive interplays of colours and shadows, and the rocky landscape of the Colorado Plateau is also impressive in places like Bryce Canyon National Park. The Grand Canyon, stretching over 350 km (217 miles) of magnificent desert, is one of the most visited sightseeing attractions in the USA – some 4 million people come here every year.

Sunset Crater, the youngest of Arizona's volcanoes, can be seen near Flagstaff and is today a training area for astronauts. In the adjoining 'Valley of the Sun' to the south the towns appear like oases in the desert. The exclusive golf courses and fields exist only due to artificial irrigation. Phoenix, the capital of Arizona, still has a slight touch of the Wild West to it, but as a center for the aircraft construction and high-tech industries, the city is part of the modern world. Tucson, the 'City of Sunshine', has 350 days of sunshine a year.

Spirit Island in Maligne Lake in Jasper National Park – postcard views par excellence. It is the largest national park in the Canadian Rockies.

1

The North American section of the Pan-American Highway leads from the Pacific coast via the Rocky Mountains to the arid regions of the American south-west. The route is lined with natural beauty that is protected in a series of spectacular national parks.

① Prince Rupert The Pan-American Highway comes up with important cultural and historic sights right from the start. The creative carved totem poles of a variety of Indian tribes can be found all over the port town, and the pristine wilderness in the province of British Columbia awaits you just outside the city limits.

Highway 16 initially takes you through the Skeena Valley. At Hazelton it is worth taking a detour to the Gitksan Indian villages. The Ksan Native Village is an open-air museum with several longhouses. In Kitwancool you can see what is alleged to be the largest standing totem pole. After 242 km (150 miles) a small road branches off at Vanderhoof towards Fort St James to the north (66 km/41 miles)

② Fort St James National Historic Site On the eastern shore of the more than 100-km-long (62-mile) Stuart Lake is Fort St James, a town developed from what was originally a trading post founded in 1806. Actors re-enact scenes from the lives of 19th-century fur hunters during the annual summer festival in the reconstructed fort. For fishing enthusiasts there are a number of isolated lakes nearby to drop a line.

③ Prince George The Pan-American Highway crosses the Cariboo Highway (Highway 97) here. Once a satellite of Fort St James, Prince George grew into a lively town in the 19th century with the construction of a railway that brought new settlers and adventurers. The Railway Museum has an historic steam train on display.

④ Bowron Lake Provincial Park A little detour leads you through Quesnel and Barkerville (the center of a gold rush here in the 19th century) on your way to the wilderness around Bowron Lake. The drive over a gravel road at the end can be somewhat tedious but the effort is rewarded with fantastic landscape. The eleven lakes in the area are a major

Travel Information

Route profile
Length: approx. 3,200 km (1,988 miles), excluding detours
Time required: at least 3 weeks
Start : Prince Rupert, BC
End: Tucson, Arizona
Route (main locations): Prince Rupert, Jasper National Park, Calgary, Yellowstone National Park, Salt Lake City, Grand Canyon National Park, Phoenix, Tucson

Traffic information:
Drive on the right in US and Canada. Highways are also called Interstates or freeways. Speed limits vary in the individual provinces and states. Violations are met with stringent penalties. Air conditioning is essential in the southern US. The network of petrol stations and other supply facilities is good. This portion of the Pan-American Highway is in very good condition. In Canada some smaller roads are closed in winter. Closures are shorter the further south you go.

When to go:
The best time to go is summer when it is mild in the north and roads are open. Extreme heat in the southern US can be uncomfortable.

Information:
Canada:
www.trailcanada.com
USA:
www.travel-america.co.uk
National parks:
www.nps.gov/

majestically over what is the largest national park in the Canadian Rockies. It covers an area totalling 10,878 sq km (6,760 sq mi). You get closest to the natural beauty of the park either on foot or in a canoe, the latter of which is perfectly suited to the 22-km-long (14-mile) Maligne Lake.

The Icefields Parkway (Highway 93) is the next portion of the route and is a highlight of the Pan-American Highway. It runs 230 km (143 miles) along the gorgeous panoramic route at the foot of the glacial ridge of the Rocky Mountains and past the Columbia Ice Field, the largest ice field in North America. The Athabasca Falls and the Sunwapta Falls are also worth seeing.

7 Banff National Park The road then takes you past the smaller Yoho National Park and on to the shimmering turquoise waters of Lake Louise. Nearby Moraine Lake is somewhat quieter. There are more than twenty-four 3,000-m (10,000-ft) peaks in this national park.

Highway 1 turns off westwards near Lake Louise and heads over the Rogers Pass towards Glacier National Park.

8 Calgary The largest city in the area is Calgary on the western edge of the vast prairie. The approach from the west is especially impressive on days when the Chinooks, warm, dry autumn winds, are blowing down from the Rocky Mountains. They ensure grand views of the peaks towering behind

attraction for fans of canoeing. You can paddle through the entire lake landscape in the course of eight days. Back on the Pan-American Highway, after driving 270 km (168 miles) through Fraser Valley, you reach Tête Jaune Cache, the gateway to the lovely Mount Robson Provincial Park.

5 Mount Robson Provincial Park The highest mountain in the Canadian Rocky Mountains is Mount Robson at an impressive (3,954 m/12,973 ft). It is the king of this unique protected area (2,200 sq km/1,367 sq mi) and is beloved among hikers and mountaineers. High altitude glaciers, crystal-clear moun-

tain lakes, tumbling waterfalls and exhilarating pine forests characterize this jewel of the Rockies.

After 100 km (62 miles) on Yellowhead Pass you reach Jasper in the Jasper National Park.

6 Jasper National Park The huge mountains here tower

1 A mountain lake in Jasper National Park.

2 Boating on Maligne Lake in Jasper National Park.

3 The Calgary skyline – an up-and-coming metropolis.

the city and create the bizarre illusion that you could reach out and touch the mountains. The largest city in the province of Alberta can be seen from far away. The downtown high-rises, largely housing the offices of oil companies, banks and insurance companies, rise grandiosely against the backdrop of the mighty Rockies. The city has developed from an agricultural center to a modern metropolis that attracts a great deal of foreign capital. A milestone in this development was the hosting of the 1988 Winter Olympics. Isolated though it may be in the middle of Alberta, Calgary is well on its way to becoming a million-strong metropolis and is an important inter-regional traffic hub.

Landmark, symbol and the most important orientation point in the city is the Calgary Tower, standing at a proud 191 m (627 ft). The Olympic Saddledome ice sport arena provides an architectural link between tradition and modernity, and is one of the most advanced of its kind in the world. The design of the arena in the shape of a saddle also reflects the spirit of the Wild West, which is really brought back to life in July every year during the hugely popular ten-day Stampede, when the ten-gallon cowboy hats, cowboy boots and blue jeans dictate the dress code throughout the city. Rodeos and covered wagon races bring back the 'good old days'.

Heading south again, after 170 km (106 miles) you reach Fort Macleod. About 18 km (11 miles) north-west of the Fort is the World Heritage Site of Head-Smashed-In Buffalo Jump (see sidebar left). From here, take Highways 6 (via Pincher) or 5 (via Cardston) to reach Waterton, the entrance to another breathtaking Canadian national park.

1

2

⑨ Waterton Lakes National Park There are two national parks near the border between Canada and the USA – Waterton Lakes National Park in the Canadian province of Alberta, and Glacier National Park in the US state of Montana. In 1932 the two were combined as the Waterton-Glacier International Peace Park. For local Indians the entire area has always been known as the 'Land of the Shining Mountains'. Just after entering the park from the northeast (Highway 5 and 6) you reach Bison Paddocks. A few kilometers further down, a narrow road branches off to the west towards Red Rock Canyon, named as such due to the red sedimentary rock in the area. The route continues to the 2,940-m-high (9,646-ft) Mount Blakiston, the highest peak in the Waterton Lakes National Park. The Prince of Wales Hotel is one of the most striking buildings in the reserve, with stunning views of two lakes, Middle and Upper Waterton.

Access to Glacier National Park is via the Chief Mountain Inter-

considered one of the most beautiful mountain routes in the whole of North America. The journey then continues via Browning to Shelby. From here it is a further 82 km (51 miles) on Highway 15 to Great Falls.

11 Great Falls The city's sightseeing attractions include the Giant Springs, one of the largest freshwater springs in North America, and the Lewis and Clark National Forest, named after the explorers who traversed much of western North America at the start of the 19th century.

About 44 km (27 miles) northeast of the city is Fort Benton, founded in 1846 as a trading post on the upper reaches of the Missouri River. Continuing south you pass more springs, including White Sulphur Springs. Continuing to Yellowstone National Park it is worth taking a detour near Livingston to the battlefield of Little Bighorn 110 km (68 miles) away.

12 Yellowstone National Park From Montana you continue along the Pan-American Highway to the state of Wyoming, which boasts one of the continent's main attractions. Yellowstone National Park is indeed in a league of its own, not least because it is the oldest and largest in the USA. It

1 An ideal location – the historic Prince of Wales Hotel in Waterton Lakes National Park.

2 Sinopah Mountain in Glacier National Park is an almost perfect pyramid.

3 St Mary Lake in Glacier National Park, Montana.

4 Fascinating Glacier National Park is reached via Logan Pass.

national Highway which travels along the eastern side of the park. The road was built in 1935 and is in good condition but is only passable between mid-May and mid-September.

10 Glacier National Park Mount Cleveland, at 3,185 m (10,450 ft) the highest mountain in the national park (not to

be confused with the park of the same name in Canada), slowly comes into view after crossing the border. Dense pine forests in the low-lying areas are home to elks, grizzly bears, pumas and lynxes.

Shortly before reaching St Mary, the road, which is closed in winter, branches off to Many Glaciers. The scenic landscape

here, with a total of fifty glaciers, is criss-crossed by hiking routes, of which the Swiftcurrent Lake Nature Trail is especially impressive.

An 80-km-long (50-mile) road takes you from St Mary over the Logan Pass at 2,026 m (6,647 ft) to West Glacier. The route, which is only passable between June and mid-September, is

receives around 3 million visitors a year, and it is easily accessible by car, although some roads are closed between November and April. The Grand Loop Road meanders 230 km (143 miles) through the park. If you are approaching from the north it is worth making a short stop at Mammoth Hot Springs where information material and updates on the passability of the side roads are available from the park office. The significance of the reserve (8,983 sq km/5,582 sq mi) in the midst of the Rocky Mountains and the Grand Tetons was recognized early on as a natural treasure and was declared a national park in 1872. Mother Nature shows her most spectacular side on this high plateau, which ranges from 2,100 to 2,400 m (6,890 to 7,874 ft). The forces of the earth's core come to the surface in the Yellowstone National Park where the world's most impressive and powerful geysers can be seen. The highest of the roughly 300 geysers is Steamboat.

Approaching from the north you first reach the Norris Geyser Basin where, in addition to the Steamboat, the Echinus Geyser also puts on a show from time to time. A short distance further on to the south-west you reach the Fountain Paint Pot, a basin of bubbling red-brown mud. Upper Geyser Basin has the most geysers in the whole of the national park. It is therefore no surprise that this is where the highest number of visitors will be found. You can even set your watch by some of

1 Yellowstone River near the 94-m-high (308-ft) Lower Falls.

2 The tranquil river landscape is ideal bison territory.

3 In summer bison graze on the wide open spaces of the park.

4 Old Faithful Geyser in Yellowstone National Park.

5 A 34-km (21-mile) shoreline road provides access to Yellowstone Lake in the south-west of the park.

the geysers and can plan your arrival accordingly.

Old Faithful is one of the most 'punctual', displaying its skills almost every 80 minutes for a few minutes at a time, sending huge quantities of water about 50 m (164 ft) into the air. Other well-known geysers are Giant Geyser and Castle Geyser. And it's not just a visual experience. The accompanying noises as you approach are also fascinating. Make sure you stick to the marked pathways at all times as the unstable ground bubbles and hisses at many places in the park. Steam clouds sometimes even reach as far as the Grand Loop Road.

All of this is evidence of volcanic activity within the park. Violent volcanic eruptions are not to be feared, however, as the last major eruption took place around 600,000 years ago.

The waterfalls along the Yellowstone River in the south of the park are another striking attraction. At Upper Falls the river drops 33 m (108 ft) over the cliffs. At Lower Falls – only a few 100 m away – the drop is as much as 94 m (308 ft). The viewing points in the Lookout Point and Grandview Point parking areas offer especially dramatic views.

⓭ **Grand Teton National Park** From Yellowstone National Park, John D. Rockefeller Jr. Memorial Parkway takes you to a much smaller park, Grand Teton National Park (1,257 sq km/ 781 sq mi), which is often overshadowed by its famous neighbour. This is unjustified to say the least, however, as it also has a number of attractions on offer and is a more relaxed experience altogether.

The jagged peaks of the Teton Range, dominated by Grand Teton at 4,197 m (13,770 ft), are accompanied by glaciers that extend far into the steep valleys. The park's main axis is Jackson Hole, an 80-km (50-mile) valley through which the idyllic Snake River passes on part of its 1,670-km (1,038-mile)

journey to the Columbia River, which eventually flows through Idaho, Oregon and Washington into the Pacific. There are also a number of lakes in the valley. Teton Park Road takes you from

Jackson Lake to the south-east, the panoramic road offering continuously lovely views of the mountain landscape. Jackson Hole boasts one superlative in particular. In 1933 the lowest

430

temperature ever recorded in Wyoming, -54°C, was measured here. Even though it can be very cold in winter, such temperatures are obviously not typical. This park is open all year and the best time to go is between June and September. Most of the tourist facilities are closed in the winter but winter sports are popular here.

⑭ Jackson Situated on the southern rim of Jackson Hole, this is the ideal starting point for hikes in Grand Teton National Park as well as for whitewater rafting on the Snake River. And, with its Wild-West-style saloons and bars, Jackson is more than just a tourist staging post. The place retains an authentic Wild West atmosphere and can be a lot of fun. The Wildlife of the American West Art Museum has a worthwhile collection of paintings featuring the wild animals of the region. The cultural history of the local Indians is illustrated in the Teton County Historical Center.

A few kilometers south of Jackson a turn-off near Alpine heads west towards Idaho. Idaho Falls are a good distance beyond the state line. In addition to a Mormon temple that is worth seeing, the city is home to the Intermountain Science Experience Center, a first-class natural history museum.

Back on Highway 89 you continue south from Montpellier through the Wasatch Mountains, which emerge abruptly from the plains. The area, at more than 3,500 m (11,484 ft), is covered in snow all year and is a popular winter sport area for residents of Salt Lake City. One of the main attractions here is the large salt lake to the west of the road, which you can reach by making a detour on Highway 80.

⑮ Salt Lake City The capital of Utah is one of the largest cities along the Pan-American Highway. Initially it seems an intimidating location for a city, with the Great Salt Lake to the west, the Wasatch Mountains forming a natural border to the east, and the Great Salt Lake Desert stretching west to the horizon.

However, in the middle of the 19th century the Mormons were in search of just this type of environment, remote and inhospitable.

Yet the gold rush and the completion of the transcontinental railroad brought more and more people to the town, which had developed into a lively city by the start of the 20th century. A century later the city received further impetus from the Winter Olympics in 2002.

The classical Capitol building (1915) is visible from afar and is the city's primary landmark, but Temple Square is really

1 The Snake River flows through Grand Teton National Park.

2 The Teton Range reaches more than 4,000 m (13,124 ft) and gave the national park its name.

3 Salt Lake City, the capital of Utah founded in 1915, lit up at night against the background of the surrounding mountains.

where things happen here. The 4-ha (10-acre) square is considered to be the Mormons' 'holy square' and the temple is accessible only to members of the Mormon church.

The city's highest building at 128 m (420 ft) is the Church Office Building, also a Mormon building, which houses the central administration of this religious community. The view from the platform on the 26th floor is especially popular with visitors to the city.

16 Timpanogos Cave National Monument On the northern slope of the 3,581-m (11,749-ft) Mount Timpanogo are three caves that have been formed over a long period of time due to the porosity of the limestone that is characteristic of the area. The bizarre stalactites are a real sight to behold. The three caves are connected by a man-made tunnel and can be viewed as part of a guided tour.

Due to its extraordinary nature the entire area has been declared a National Monument.

17 Capitol Reef National Park The Pan-American Highway is well-maintained in Utah. After having covered more than half of this state you will reach some of the absolute highlights along this dream route. Leave Highway 15 at Scipio and turn off onto Highway 50 for around 30 km (19 miles). Highway 12 turns off at Salina to the next national park.

The Capitol Reef National Park is characterized by a colourful cliff face towering above the Fremont River. The Fremont River has cut its way deep into a geological shift known as the Waterpocket Fold. Parallel ridges rise out of the desert sands here in a wave formation over a distance of 160 km (99 miles). Water and wind have

1

fashioned the unique shapes, which invite comparisons with chimneys, roofs and even fortresses. There are also rock paintings from the Fremont Indians, which frequently depict animals.

Continuing along scenic Highway 12 you will reach Escalante where the road turns off to the south towards the Grand Staircase Escalante National Monument.

18 Grand Staircase Escalante National Monument Those in search of pristine nature will not be disappointed by this reserve between Bryce Canyon National Park to the south and west, the Capitol Reef National Park in the north, and the Glen Canyon National Recreation Area to the east. The National Monument was named after four towering layers of rock. The beauty of the landscape is characterized by gorges, rows of cliffs and plateaus and is best experienced from the dirt roads off the main highway.

The drive along the 200-km (124-mile) Burr Trail Loop wea-

2

ves its way through the entire area. Initially a tarred road, it takes you along Deer Creek and then through the rocky labyrinth of Long Canyon.

It later becomes a bit more challenging but is easily done with an off-road vehicle.

Back on Highway 12 head towards Bryce Canyon Airport. Shortly thereafter, Highway 63 turns off right to the Bryce Canyon Visitors Center.

19 Bryce Canyon National Park Unlike the rest of the landscape in the region, Bryce Canyon is not a canyon in the strict sense of the word. Rather, it is a series of crevices and smaller gullies. Some of the eroded gullies are more than

300 m (984 ft) deep. A lovely panoramic route takes you 30 km (19 miles) through the park, which was founded in 1928, and leads to the southernmost point, Rainbow Point. The drive and its many vista points constantly provide splendid views over the dense pine forests.

Many of the orange, salmon-pink or red rock formations have characteristic names, such as Sunrise Point, Inspiration Point, Thor's Hammer or Chinese Wall. The landscape is other-worldly and is especially impressive at sunset or sunrise. After Bryce Canyon it is worth making a detour some 100 km (62 miles) to the west to the Cedar Breaks National Monument. The turn-off to Cedar

City is a few kilometers after the junction of Highway 12 and Highway 89.

⑳ Cedar Breaks National Monument Founded by the Mormons in 1851, Cedar City's Iron Mission State Park and Museum, with more than 300 old vehicles, documents the pioneering spirit of the Mor-

mons. The Shakespeare Festival also takes place here every summer in the Globe Theater. The National Monument's dimensions may be somewhat smaller than those of Bryce Canyon but the colours are just as enticing. The next stop is Zion National Park, reached from the turn-off at Mount Carmel Junction (Highway 9).

㉑ Zion National Park This area was declared a national park in 1919 and has several entrances. The most important attractions are found in the southern part, and the Zion-Mount Carmel Highway (9) takes you via the plateau at the East Entrance 600 m (1,969 ft) downhill to the more deserty South Entrance.

The Canyon Overlook provides one of the best views of the heart of the national park, Zion Canyon, created by the Virgin River, a tributary of the Colorado River.

A tunnel built 255 m (837 ft) above the valley floor makes the drive to the Zion Canyon Visitor Center all the more dramatic. From here the Zion Canyon Scenic Drive follows numerous serpentine bends of the winding Virgin River for 12 km (7.5 miles). The most well-known hike in the park, the 2-km (1.2-mile) River Walk, starts at the end of the road and leads to the 600-m (1,969-ft) canyon walls. The waterfalls on the Emerald Pools Trail are also worth seeing, as are the Hang-

ing Gardens, a cliff overgrown with vegetation.

If you have time, take the park's southern exit and return via the Pipe Spring National Monument and the Pan-American Highway where the A89 turns off from Highway 89 at Kanab heading south. At Jacob Lake a side road leads to the northern entrance of the Grand Canyon (North Rim), or you can continue along the A89 to the next stop, Marble Canyon.

㉒ Marble Canyon Close to the town of the same name in the far north of Arizona is Marble Canyon, a prime example of the state's diverse natural beauty. The canyon is traversed by the Colorado River and is spanned by a road bridge. Turn onto Highway 89 where it joins the A89 and drive a short distance north towards Page. From here you can either continue to Glen Canyon Dam or make a detour to Antelope Canyon.

㉓ Lake Powell Since 1963 the Glen Canyon Dam has held back the Colorado River to create the 653-sq-km (405-sq-mi) Lake Powell, built to generate hydroelectric power.

The lake is now a haven for water-sports enthusiasts. There are also marvellous views of the sandstone formations whose perfectly flat plateaus look like they were measured with a ruler. On the southern shore is

1 Walls of rock in Capitol Reef National Park.

2 View over the countless needles of Bryce Canyon at twilight.

3 The Colorado River cuts through the horizontal layers of fascinating Marble Canyon.

4 A bold bridge over Marble Canyon.

1

the nearly 90-m-high (295-ft) Rainbow Bridge, considered the largest natural bridge in North America. The area around the lake was declared the Glen Canyon National Recreation Area in 1972.

㉔ Grand Canyon National Park This world-famous national park can be reached from the north via the turn-off at Jacob Lake and from the south via Cameron (Highway 64) or Flagstaff (Highway 180), both of which lead to the South Rim. The northern side of the canyon, which is 30 km at its widest point, is about 360 m (1,181 ft) higher than the southern side and the canyon walls drop nearly 1,800 m (5,906 ft) down to the Colorado River here.

As the northern Kaibab Plateau is significantly higher than the southern Coconino Plateau, the North Rim provides a completely different perspective of the

canyon landscape than the South Rim. Bright Angel Point provides a marvellous backdrop near the Grand Canyon Lodge. Shortly before this viewing point there is a 35-km-long (22-mile) road that branches off to the north to Point Imperial which, at 2,683 m (8,803 ft), is the highest point in the national park.

The southern part receives considerably more visitors. Grand Canyon Village is recommended as the starting point. From here a panoramic route provides access to West Rim Drive and East Rim Drive.

㉕ Flagstaff The drive from Cameron to Flagstaff passes the Wupatki National Monument with more than 2,000 historical sites once inhabited by Hopi Indians. Just outside Flagstaff is the 120-m-deep (394-ft) crater created in 1064 by a volcanic eruption. The volcanic cone is

2

called Sunset Crater Volcano because of its colour. The center of Flagstaff is characterized by red-brick buildings. It is worth paying a visit to the Lowell Observatory from which scientists discovered Pluto in 1930. The cultural highlight is the Museum of Northern Arizona with archaeological and ethnological displays.

㉖ Walnut Canyon South of town close to Interstate 40/

Route 66, head west to Walnut Canyon with its famous Sinagua Indian dwellings. More than twenty of the dwellings open to visitors were built into the cliffs in the 12th and 13th centuries, and some of them are in especially adventurous locations.

㉗ Montezuma Castle National Monument Once home to aboriginals close to the town of Cottonwood, the site was

declared a National Monument in 1906 and comprises the remnants of a Sinagua Indian dwelling that was fitted into the recess of a rock face 30 m

(98 ft) high. The Sinagua built twenty rooms in the dwelling more than 600 years ago and used ladders for access. An exhibition in the visitor center beneath the cliffs documents the Sinagua culture. The trailhead along Beaver Creek is also here.

From Cottonwood it is around 80 km (50 miles) to the junction of Highway 89 and Highway 60, which takes you to Phoenix.

28 Phoenix In Phoenix you join Interstate 10 going towards Tucson. The last stop before Tucson is an American Indian memorial.

29 Casa Grande Ruins National Monument Agriculture has been practised in the Gila River Valley south of Phoenix for thousands of years by intelligent irrigation systems. Local Hohokam Indian culture was already cultivating the land in

this area in 200 BC using sophisticated canal systems.

The most important remnants of this culture include the Casa Grande, or 'Big House', a four-storey clay building constructed at the start of the 14th century, the last period of the Hohokam. With walls 1.20 m (4 ft) thick it is more like a fortress, but was abandoned in the 14th century. The building can only be viewed from the outside.

30 Tucson After about three hours on the road you reach Tucson, the 'City of Sunshine'. The approach is an experience in itself. Once you have crossed the last chain of mountains outside the city, gleaming skyscrapers appear like a mirage, towering out of the Santa Cruz River valley. The colonial era neighbourhood lies in the shadows of these massive buildings exuding the flair of ancient times.

Due to its climate and mountainous surroundings, the city is a popular winter sports destination, especially during the 'cold' season when the temperature is a consistent 20 to 25°C (68 to 77°F). Tucson is situated in the Sonoran Desert where the Saguaro cacti reach heights of 10 m (33 ft). The contrast between the end of the North American portion of the Pan-American Highway in the desert and its start in the cold coastal forests.

1 Grand Canyon – view of the canyon from Toroweap Point.

2 The Wupatki National Monument is about 96 km (60 miles) south-east of Grand Canyon National Park and is a testimony to the American Indian way of life.

3 Montezuma Castle Valley and the ruins of an Indian pueblo.

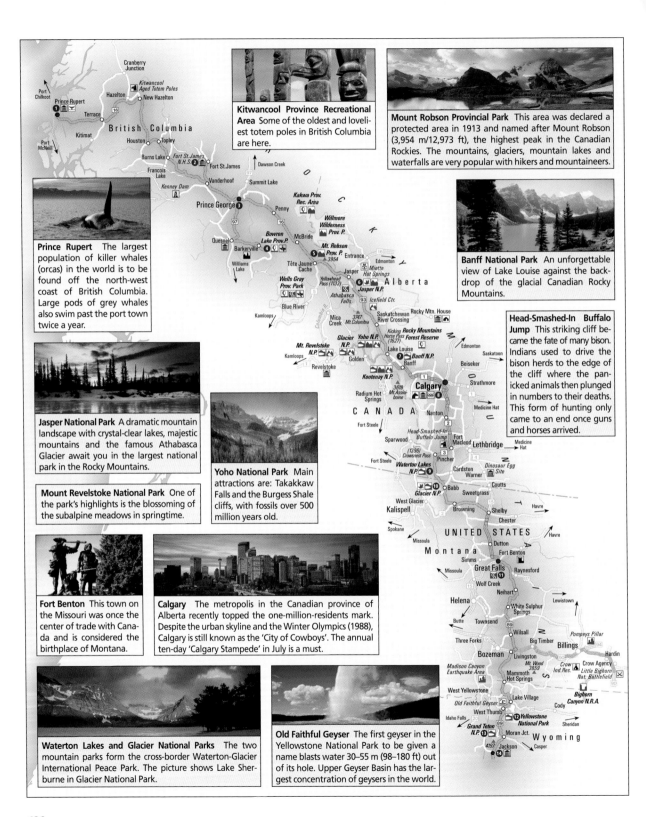

Kitwancool Province Recreational Area Some of the oldest and loveliest totem poles in British Columbia are here.

Mount Robson Provincial Park This area was declared a protected area in 1913 and named after Mount Robson (3,954 m/12,973 ft), the highest peak in the Canadian Rockies. The mountains, glaciers, mountain lakes and waterfalls are very popular with hikers and mountaineers.

Prince Rupert The largest population of killer whales (orcas) in the world is to be found off the north-west coast of British Columbia. Large pods of grey whales also swim past the port town twice a year.

Banff National Park An unforgettable view of Lake Louise against the backdrop of the glacial Canadian Rocky Mountains.

Head-Smashed-In Buffalo Jump This striking cliff became the fate of many bison. Indians used to drive the bison herds to the edge of the cliff where the panicked animals then plunged in numbers to their deaths. This form of hunting only came to an end once guns and horses arrived.

Jasper National Park A dramatic mountain landscape with crystal-clear lakes, majestic mountains and the famous Athabasca Glacier await you in the largest national park in the Rocky Mountains.

Yoho National Park Main attractions are: Takakkaw Falls and the Burgess Shale cliffs, with fossils over 500 million years old.

Mount Revelstoke National Park One of the park's highlights is the blossoming of the subalpine meadows in springtime.

Fort Benton This town on the Missouri was once the center of trade with Canada and is considered the birthplace of Montana.

Calgary The metropolis in the Canadian province of Alberta recently topped the one-million-residents mark. Despite the urban skyline and the Winter Olympics (1988), Calgary is still known as the 'City of Cowboys'. The annual ten-day 'Calgary Stampede' in July is a must.

Waterton Lakes and Glacier National Parks The two mountain parks form the cross-border Waterton-Glacier International Peace Park. The picture shows Lake Sherburne in Glacier National Park.

Old Faithful Geyser The first geyser in the Yellowstone National Park to be given a name blasts water 30–55 m (98–180 ft) out of its hole. Upper Geyser Basin has the largest concentration of geysers in the world.

Grand Teton National Park Elk roam the low-lying areas of the Teton Range, one of the most impressive mountain chains in the USA. The highest peak, Grand Teton, is 4,197 m (13,770 ft). Some of the mountains are covered with glaciers while former glaciers have formed deep lakes in the basins.

Salt Lake City The skyline of the Utah capital is dominated by the Capitol building (1915). Salt Lake City, venue for the 2002 Winter Olympics, is the center of the growing global Mormon community.

Grand Canyon The canyon in north-west Arizona was formed by the Colorado River cutting into the Colorado Plateau. The 350-km-long (217-mile) and up to 1.8-km-deep (1-mile) canyon is one of the most impressive natural wonders in the USA.

Phoenix Once an Indian settlement, Phoenix is today an important high-tech center. It boasts buildings from all eras, like this colonial-era mission church. The palms that grow throughout the city are characteristic of Phoenix.

Mission San Xavier del Bac This bright white mission church was completed in 1790 by Franciscans. It is an impressive example of Spanish mission architecture and one of the best-preserved churches in the whole of the United States.

Yellowstone National Park Geysers and hot springs – in this case Morning Glory Prismatic Spring – are the most spectacular attractions in the largest and oldest national park in the USA, situated in the Rocky Mountains at an altitude of 2,400 m (7,874 ft).

Capitol Reef National Park Rock needles tower over a sandstone cliff 150 km (93 miles) long.

Bryce Canyon National Park The forces of erosion make an impressive display here, especially in the Bryce Amphitheater.

Wupatki National Monument The largest and best-preserved pueblo ruins, built by prehistoric Indians, are to be found north of Sunset Crater in the midst of a desert landscape. In total there are around 2,000 Sinagua and Anasazi dwellings.

Meteor Crater Some 50,000 years ago a meteorite landed in northern Arizona. It left behind a crater with a circumference of 1.3 km (0.81 miles) and a depth of 170 m (558 ft). Because of its geological similarity to the craters on the moon it is used as a NASA training ground for astronauts.

Pima Air and Space Museum There are over 200 planes on display here at the south-eastern edge of Tucson.

Tucson The center of the second-largest city in Arizona, after Phoenix, is dominated by skyscrapers. A colonial-era neighbourhood with a number of adobe houses has been preserved in the shadows of the skyscrapers and makes a significant contribution to Tucson's charm.

USA

'The American Way of Life' between the Pacific coast and the Sierra Nevada

Sun, sea and tanned surfers. It's a popular cliché image that many people have of California and, as with many such clichés, it has an element of truth to it. But the Golden State on the west coast of the USA has myriad other facets as well – majestic mountains, ancient forests with giant redwood trees, superb alpine lakes, breathtaking deserts and one of the most beautiful coastal roads in the country, Highway 1. On top of that there are lively cities such as Los Angeles, San Francisco and San Diego.

'Go West, young man, and grow up with the country!' Since the middle of the 19th century this call has inspired countless people to seek their fortunes in the promised lands of California. Today, millions of tourists from all over the world are also drawn by the magic of this region on the West Coast.

Highway 1, with its magnificent views of the mighty Pacific Ocean, could easily be considered one of the most beautiful roads in the world. Yet the 'hinterland' offers equally spectacular natural wonders, from the rock walls and waterfalls of Yosemite National Park and the bizarre limestone formations of

Mono Lake to the glorious giant sequoias (redwood trees) scattered throughout the numerous parks around the state. They flourish wonderfully along the misty Pacific coast as well as in the cool Sierra Nevada mountains. Then there are arid regions such as the Mojave Desert which, at first glance, seem devoid of almost any life. After the brief, irregular showers of rain, however, the desert produces a magical

variety of plant life. Death Valley, somewhat off this tour's path, is surrounded by mountains rising to more than 3,000 m (9,843 ft) and evokes lunar landscapes of spectacular proportions. It also boasts such superlatives as the lowest point in the Western Hemisphere and the highest temperature ever recorded. European travellers are continually overwhelmed by the beauty of these magnificent natural landscapes.

In the late 1980s the Santa Monica Pier was restored to its former glory.

San Francisco by moonlight. The 2.7-km (1.7-mile) Golden Gate Bridge, at the entrance to San Francisco Bay, was completed in 1937 and links the city with Marin County to the north.

Population growth in Los Angeles in the mid-1900s depleted water levels in Mono Lake to such an extent that evaporation became faster than inflow. These exposed tufa towers are a result of these developments. Successful efforts are now being made to restore the lake's former state.

Indeed, Mother Nature has been generous to this Pacific region. Gold discoveries in 1849 brought about the first major wave of settlement. Hollywood, synonymous with the glamorous world of film, has the sunny Southern California climate to thank for its existence. Yet the same sun that draws tourists to the beaches also makes the hugely important agricultural business here a major challenge, one that is really only possible with the help of sophisticated and far-reaching irrigation systems. The Californians have artfully mastered their often tough environment and do not even seem too distracted or worried by the San Andreas Fault, repeatedly the cause of disastrous earthquakes in the state.

A tour through California brings to life the many places linked to the region's Spanish and Mexican legacy, like Santa Barbara, San Luis Obispo or Carmel, all of which play host to mission churches founded by Spanish monks along 'El Camino Real', the Royal Road. San Francisco, often considered the most 'European' city in the USA and a dream destination for people around the world, originally boomed after the discovery of gold in the foothills of the Sierra Nevada. It was only in the 20th century that its rival to the south, Los Angeles, grew to its current size – life without a car is inconceivable in this sprawling environment.

California's open-mindedness has often promoted important subculture movements that have even had global influence – the Beat Generation, the Hippies, the Gay Movement, rural communes, ecological movements and other milieus experimenting with alternative lifestyles. Not to be forgotten is of course Silicon Valley, the pioneer site of the digital revolution in the 20th century. As a whole, a trip through California reflects a wonderful sort of microcosm of what the 'American Dream' really means to many people.

El Capitan and the Merced River in a wintry Yosemite National Park.

1

In addition to numerous cultural highlights, our tour through California offers a look at some breathtaking natural landscapes. The Highway 1 drive from Los Angeles to San Francisco runs high above the spectacular Pacific coast for most of the way.

1 Los Angeles (see pp. 442–443). Our route begins in Los Angeles on Highway 101 (the Ventura Highway). From there, the most famous stretch of Highway 1 branches off at Las Cruces (called Cabrillo Highway here), a few miles beyond Santa Barbara. It covers an often breathtaking route over bridges or directly along the steep Pacific coastline, providing continuously spectacular views.

2 Santa Barbara Founded in 1782 as a Spanish garrison, the city's architecture fascinates visitors. After being reduced to rubble in 1925 by a heavy earthquake, the city took the opportunity to rebuild the entire downtown in Spanish colonial style, an example of

which is the County Courthouse built in 1929. From the bell tower you can enjoy a wonderful view of the city. Mission Santa Barbara, officially nicknamed the 'Queen of the Missions', also suffered severe damage in the 1925 earthquake and was initially restored before further rebuilding took place in the 1950s. The mission's characteristic combination of Roman, Moorish and Spanish elements became the archetype of the California mission style. The mission church is the only one of the original California missions that is still being used today as a church.

3 San Luis Obispo The heart of this tranquil little town at the base of the Santa Lucia

Mountains is the San Luis Obispo de Tolosa Mission, founded in 1772 as the fifth of more than 20 Californian

missions. One of the mission buildings adjoining the church has a museum with interesting and colourful art

Travel Information

Route profile
Length: approx. 2,500 km (1,554 miles), excluding detours
Time required: 3–4 weeks
Start and end: Los Angeles
Route (main locations): Los Angeles, Monterey, San Francisco, Eureka, Redwood National Park, Mount Shasta, Lassen Volcanic National Park, Lake Tahoe, Yosemite National Park, Sequoia and Kings Canyon National Park, Mono Lake, Mojave, Los Angeles

Traffic information:
Drive on the right in the USA. In autumn and spring you should enquire as to the condition of the roads in the national parks of the Cascade

Range (Mount Shasta, Mount Lassen) and the Sierra Nevada (Yosemite, Sequoia and Kings Canyon) as the roads close in winter. Toll roads along the route: the 17-Mile Drive on the Monterey Peninsula and the Golden Gate Bridge (travelling into San Francisco).

Information:
Detailed information on national parks in California: *www.nps.gov*
Information and departure times for ferries to Santa Cruz Island from Ventura: *www.islandpackers.com* and from Santa Barbara: *www.truthaquatics.com*
Napa Valley information: *www.napavalley.com*

works created by the Chumash Indians who lived in this Californian region.

④ Hearst Castle, San Simeon Hearst Castle, completed in 1947, is without doubt one of the classic tourist attractions along Highway 1. This bizarre 'castle', situated above the town of San Simeon, was built by one of America's legendary newspaper magnates, William Randolph Hearst. Gothic and Renaissance features are combined with Moorish ornaments, while the Neptune Pool bears traces of Ancient Rome. But the 155 rooms of this kitschy, decadent setting also host valuable art treasures, from Ancient Egyptian, Greek and Roman artefacts, and paintings from the Flemish, Gothic and Italian Renaissance eras, to baroque pieces and priceless books.

⑤ Big Sur The name refers to a 160-km (99-mile) stretch of coast-line between San Simeon and Carmel. Sections of this frequently untouched landscape are indeed easy to reach thanks to Highway 1, but there are still remote, deserted bays, a magnificently rocky coast and backcountry that is easily accessible via the state park North America's largest kelp forest (a type of seaweed) lies off the coast, as does the Monterey Canyon, which is similar in size to the actual Grand Canyon in Arizona. The unique attraction of this stretch of the highway is the Central Coast Range's sharp descent into the sea.
Architectural attractions include the 80-m (262-ft) Bixby Creek Bridge, an arch bridge dating from 1932.

⑥ Carmel This settlement at the southern end of the Monterey Peninsula was established as an artists' colony after the San Francisco earthquake of 1906, taking in the many Bohemians who left the destroyed city. The town retains this char-

acter even today. The most original house in the town is the Tor House, carved out of stone blocks and built by the poet Robinson Jeffers. During the heyday of the missions, the Mission San Carlos Borromeodel Rio Carmelo (Mission Carmel) was established in 1770 and served as a center of religious activities due to its proximity to the then capital of 'Alta California', Monterey. The old mission kitchen, garden and the housing have also been rebuilt according to the original design.

⑦ Monterey During the colonial era this city, with its significant center, was the capital of 'Alta California', the site of another famous mission.
The Monterey State Historic Park includes over thirty historic sites including the oldest

1 Highway 1 joins the 160-km (99-mile) Big Sur Coast between San Simeon and Carmel.

2 The pounding Pacific surf continues to erode the steep cliffs along the coast in Big Sur.

Los Angeles

The 'City of Angels' actually comprises several independent neighbourhoods and a multitude of massive freeways. Some traces of the Spanish past can still be seen today in the old town, while Hollywood has become a modern legend. On the periphery are the beaches – Santa Monica, Malibu and Venice.

Mann's Chinese Theater, a luxurious cinema in the style of a Chinese temple, was built in 1927 by Sid Grauman and was the scene of elaborate premieres during Hollywood's golden years. Legendary stars such as Elizabeth Taylor, Humphrey Bogart and John Wayne have been immortalized with their hand- and footprints in the cement in front of the entrance.

The best view of Los Angeles is from the Griffith Observatory on Mount a

exhibitions of note. The broad, palm-lined Sunset Boulevard takes you through Bel Air and Beverly Hills. Even the smog seems to have disappeared from this artificial luxury oasis with its waving palm trees, blossoming gardens and magnificent villas. There is hardly a single house without its own pool and tennis court. The rich and famous live behind these walls, and they don't seem to want company.

Numerous impressive skyscrapers dominate the skyline of downtown LA

adobe buildings from the 19th century in the old town. In this 'El Pueblo de Los Angeles', Olvera Street is the scene of an annual carnival with street artists and colourful stalls.

Union Station is the name of the magnificent railway station built in 1939 in the style of a Spanish mission. It was once a stop for legendary trains such as the *Daylight Special* or the *City of Los Angeles*. In the 1960s Venice Beach was the in-beach for spaced-out Beatniks and Hippies. Today it is frequented by countless street performers, skaters, rappers and bodybuilders. Front Walk is full of stalls selling T-shirts and sunglasses. The J. Paul Getty Museum at the Getty Center is more than just an architectural sensation. The millionaire's legacy includes valuable paintings, graphic arts, furniture and other

The Beverly Hills Hotel (1912) on Sunset Boulevard was thoroughly renovated in 2005. Marilyn Monroe was a frequent guest of the famous Polo Lounge. Italian and French designer names dominate the expensive fashion shops on nearby Rodeo Drive.

The famous pier in Santa Monica was built in 1909 and renovated in the 1980s to its former glory. Even the wooden carousel still operates. Three streets away, on the Third Street Promenade between Broadway and Wilshire Boulevard, is a pedestrian zone with the usual chain stores as well as exclusive boutiques. Malibu 30 km (17 miles) north of Santa Monica, once a private ranch, has been home to film stars and singers since the 1940s. The numerous beaches are popular with surfers.

1

government building in California, the Customs House, built in 1840. The signposted 'Path of History' takes you to all the important historic buildings. The Monterey Bay Aquarium presents the flora and fauna of the four large habitats of Monterey Bay – the kelp forest, the reef, the rocky coast and the outer bay.

Our journey then continues to San Francisco via the delightful seaside town of Santa Cruz.

8 **San Francisco** (see pp. 466-467). You depart San Francisco via its most famous landmark, the Golden Gate Bridge, towards the north, passing through Sausalito with its original houseboats and Victorian houses perched on the slopes above the North Bay.

After a short distance on Highway 101 along the waterfront, Highway 1 turns off towards the Pacific at the very affluent small town of Belvedere. From there it continues through the

2

fabulous Point Reyes National Seashore to Fort Ross, 19 km (12 miles) north of Jenner.

9 **Fort Ross State Historic Park** This fortified complex was founded in 1812 by Russian traders sent by the Tsars to supply their fellow fur hunters living in Alaska. The fort was abandoned in 1839 and part of the original complex still remains.

The Russian Orthodox chapel (1824) is especially attractive and the cemetery with its Russian crosses is also worth visiting.

10 **Mendocino** Fishermen from New England first settled here in 1852. Later adopted by artists as a place of residence, the town has a spectacular location high above the sea and still retains some of its East Coast character. It has often served as a set for Hollywood films.

Highway 1, still offering magnificent views of the Pacific, leaves the coast just north of Westport and joins up with Highway 101 again at Leggett.

11 **Humboldt Redwoods State Park** The 53-km-long (33-mile) Avenue of Giants was

originally built as a stagecoach road and runs through the park for about 1 km (0.6 miles) parallel to Highway 101. As the park's name indicates, redwood trees are the main attraction here, and you'll see them in all their colossal glory as they dwarf the humans that marvel at them. Loads of trails lead deep into the realm of the coastal giants. The trees are often more than 500 years old and they flourish in the mild, misty climate on the coast. Despite extensive deforestation in the past there are still dense clusters in places. One

oddity is the almost 100-m (328-ft) Chandelier Tree – it has a passage cut into it that is large enough for cars.

12 Eureka Today the most important industrial center on the northern Californian coast, this town was founded by gold diggers in 1850. The examples of Victorian architecture include the unusual William Carson Mansion, which resembles a haunted castle with numerous towers and gables. Local timber businessman Carson built it in the 1880s. Other must-sees include the Clarke Museum with its fine exhibits from the Victorian era exhibits and its excellent collection of Indian artworks.

13 Redwood National Park This national park (a UNESCO World Heritage Site), founded in 1968, protects some of the largest redwood forests in the world. It extends over a total of 125 km (78 miles) from

Arcata (north of Eureka) to Crescent City the (center of the national park). One of greatest drives in the world is through the Avenue of the Giants which parallels route US101. Historic Crescent City Crescent City was largely destroyed on 28 March 1964 by a tsunami with 6-m-high (20-ft) waves, caused by an earthquake in Alaska. In Crescent City you turn onto Highway 99, travelling for about 110 km (68 miles) via Grant's Pass into Oregon where Highway 199 joins Interstate Highway 5. Cave fans can stop off and visit the Oregon Caves on the way. The mighty Cascade Range begins with the climb up the 1,361-m (4,465-ft) Slskiyou Pass.

14 Mount Shasta This 4,317-m (14,165-ft) volcano towers over the much lower peaks around it. A mountain road with fantastic views climbs up to an altitude of 2,400 m (7,874 ft), but an ascent on foot to the

peak of the strato volcano should only be attempted by experienced mountaineers as it is extremely challenging for n amateur climber. On the south-western side of the mountain is the little village of Mount Shasta City with a ranger station. Highway 89 turns off to the south-east directly after Mount Shasta before making its way through the mountains of the Mount Shasta National Forest past the 40-m (131-ft) Burney Falls in Lassen National Forest. At Subway Cave, a 396-m (1,299-ft) lava pipe, a well-signposted road turns off to the south-west in the direction of Lassen Volcanic National Park, the entrance to which is near Manzanita Lake.

15 Lassen Volcanic National Park This national park takes its name from the volcano in the Cascade Range. The last dramatic eruption of the 3,187-m (10,457-ft) Mount Lassen took place in 1915 and

destroyed some 40,500 ha (100,076 acres) of land. The Bumpass Hell trail is especially impressive, with hot springs, mud pools and smoke columns highlighting the undisturbed tectonic activity in the area.

As Lassen Park Road, Highway 89 leads through the national park to Mineral where you turn east onto Highway 36 to Susanville. From there continue on Highway 395 between the Diamond Mountains in the west and Honey Lake in the east towards the south and over the border to Reno in Nevada. Here, Highway 80 turns off westwards to San Francisco.

Exit after 30 km (19 miles) at Truckee and then continue south to Lake Tahoe.

1 When it opened in 1937, the almost 3-km (1.9-mile) Golden Gate was the world's longest bridge.

2 Mount Lassen reflected off Manzanita Lake. The volcano erupted often between 1914 and 1921.

San Francisco

A unique location overlooking an expansive bay on the Pacific Ocean, historic cable cars, unique neighbourhoods like Chinatown and North Beach, bustling Market Street, Fisherman's Wharf and the Golden Gate Bridge have all made San Francisco, the 'Paris of the American West', into a revered travel destination.

The city was founded by the Spanish in 1776 and named Yerba Buena. Only in 1847 was the name changed to San Francisco after the famous San Francisco de Asís Mission was founded by Father Junipero Serra.

The city's most turbulent period began in January 1848 when gold was discovered in northern California. San Francisco became a base for many gold diggers heading north.

town in 1873. By 1880 there were already eight lines and since 1964 they have been protected as part of the city's heritage.

One of the USA's most well-known landmarks, the Golden Gate Bridge, opened for traffic in 1937 following four years of construction. Including its access roads, the bridge is 11 km (9 miles) long, and the pylons extend 228 m (748 ft) out of the water.

The characteristic triangular shape of the Transamerica Pyramid, also called "The Triangle", is clearly recognizable among the skyscrapers.

More than 40,000 adventurers and profiteers settled in the city in 1849 alone. It soon grew to become an important trading center, and has remained so even after the massive earthquake destroyed entire neighbourhoods in 1906.

Alcatraz lies in San Francisco Bay. The rocky island was discovered by the Spanish and named after the pelicans that used to inhabit the island. In the 19th century the US Army built a fort there, which was converted to a military prison in 1909. The first civil prisoners were brought in 1934 to 'The Rock', at the time considered the most secure prison in the world.

The famous cable cars were developed by Andrew S. Hallidie in 1869, the first of them rolling through

Following the California gold rush of 1849, Fisherman's Wharf was the primary mooring for commercial boats. Today it is geared toward shopping and tourism.

San Francisco's distinct neighbourhoods are a joy to explore. Chinatown, for example, between Broadway, Bush, Kearny and Stockton Street is the second largest Chinese community in the USA (after New York). The official entrance is marked by a large red-green gate at the junction of Grant and Bush streets. The first Star-Spangled Banner was raised in California in 1846 at Portsmouth Square.

The Transamerica Pyramid is the most astonishing landmark in the San Francisco skyline.

1

2

16 Lake Tahoe At an elevation of 1,920 m (6,300 ft), this alpine lake is 35 km (22 miles) long and 13 km (8 miles) wide. It reaches a depth of more than 500 m (1,641 ft) in parts and is one of the deepest inland lakes in the world. The majesty of this place is especially apparent from out on the lake itself. The border between California and Nevada actually runs through the middle of it. The 72-Mile Drive circles the lake, includes sightseeing attractions along the shore and is the access road to the state park there. On the southern shore is South Lake Tahoe, which attracts many visitors with its casinos. North of the city the replica of a 10th-century Viking fortress stands in Emerald Bay State Park. The backcountry offers perfect conditions for skiers. The 1960 Winter Olympics were held at Squaw Valley on the north-western side of the lake.

Highway 395 continues through the sparsely populated mountains to the eastern entrance of Yosemite National Park at Lee Vining. Highway 120 takes you over the Tioga Pass at an elevation of 3,031 m (9,945 ft) and heads west towards Tuolumne Grove 56 km (35 miles) away at the park's north-west entrance.

17 Yosemite National Park Not only is this one of the most famed national parks in the United States, it's also one of the oldest – the initial areas were originally declared a national park in the 1860s. This protected area was extended in around 1890, and in 1905 it was enlarged to its present size. Many of the main attractions here are in the 10-km-long (6-mile) Yosemite Valley, at the epicenter of the park – majestic peaks such as El Capitan or Half Dome, and the glorious Yosemite Falls, over 739 m (2,425 ft) high. Around 500 giant redwoods, some of them over 75 m (246 ft) high, can be found in Mariposa Grove on the park's southern border. The early summer blossoms of sub-alpine plants in the Tuolumne Meadows are a special treat. Glacier Point, at 2,138 m (7,015 ft), towers almost 1,000 m (3,281 ft) over the valley and offers spectacular panoramic views over large areas of the park. Get there via Glacier Point Road. The visitor center provides background details on the park and the Yosemite Museum gives you an idea of the history of the Miwok and Paiute Indians. The Pioneer Center is another museum made up of blockhouses from various parts of the park and documents the life of the early Wild West settlers. The approach to the adjoining Sequoia and Kings Canyon National Park is difficult as this is accessible only from the southern side. To reach it you

need to leave Yosemite via Highway 41 in the south and head to Fresno. From there Highway 180 leads to the Big Stump Entrance in the west of the national park.

⑱ Sequoia and Kings Canyon National Park These two national parks, which are administered as one entity, are perhaps less famous than their northern neighbour but they offer breathtaking scenery nonetheless: mountain forests, granite domes and giant canyons, including Kings Canyon, one of the deepest in America. The Sequoia National Park protects an impressive number of giant redwoods in various sections – Cedar Grove, Grant Grove and Giant Forest. The 'General Sherman' tree in the Giant Forest, standing at 85 m (279 ft), is said to be the largest tree in the world by volume and between 2,300 and 2,700 years old. Five of the world's ten largest trees are in

also this park. The viewing point at Moro Rock provides a fantastic panorama of the area and is reached via more than one hundred stone steps. If the 150-km (93-mile) detour is too far for you, then leave Yosemite Park via the same route, return to Highway 395, and then continue to the 'most beautiful lake in California'.

⑲ Mono Lake Due to Southern California's need for water since the early 1940s, the tributaries that once fed Mono Lake have been drastically depleted. Until 1994, when the lake was afforded official protection,

evaporation had exceeded inflow rates and the salt content of the lake rose to a level three times greater than that of the Pacific. This cycle turned the lake's islands into peninsulas and exposed the breeding grounds of a number of already endangered waterfowl to predators putting their future existence in danger. This problem has been reversed and the lake is recovering. For visitors, however, the lower water level makes the landscape on and around the lake even more attractive because the bizarre tufa pillars that formed under the water over

centuries now rise out of the water. On the southern shores there are a number of hiking trails leading the formations. The road then continues south through the scenic Owens Valley between the White Mountains and the Sierra Nevada. To the west is Sequoia and Kings Canyon National Park.
On the south-eastern edge of the park stands mighty Mount Whitney, at 4,418 m (14,495 ft) the tallest mountain in the continental United States, towering over the spaghetti-western backdrop town of Lone Pine.

1 Yosemite National Park. Even in winter, El Capitan and the 190-m-high (623-ft) Bridal Veil Falls make an impressive picture.

2 The bizarre tufa stone formations in Mono Lake were formed by underwater chemical reactions.

3 The Sequoia and Kings Canyon National Park in the Sierra Nevada Range.

Those heading for the desert can take Highway 190 from here to Death Valley National Park (80 km/50 miles). Death Valley hosts the lowest point in North America, Badwater, and is 193 km (120 miles) long. If you follow Highway 395 further south, the foothills of the Sierra Nevada are visible to the west, while to the east it becomes increasingly flat and dry. Parts of the Mojave Desert are used for military purposes, including the US Naval Weapons Center, for example, which occupies a huge tract of land between the now dry Owens Lake and Ridgecrest.

20 Red Rock Canyon State Park This park is located in the Paso Mountains at the far southern foothills of the Sierra Nevada and is a source of fascination with its canyons, bizarrely eroded rock formations and impressive display of colours – red, white and brown sandstone alternate with the white clay layers and dark lava tones. While the western side of the mountains rise gently, the eastern side dazzles with its steep cliffs. This landscape has been used as the set for so many Hollywood westerns that it evokes a feeling of déjà vu in

some visitors. South of the small town of Mojave you pass Edwards Air Force Base, internationally known as the space shuttle landing site. The NASA Dryden Flight Research Center is open to visitors but only by prior appointment. It was from here that Chuck Yeager took off in the aircraft that broke the sound barrier for the very first time on October 14, 1947.

The journey then continues via Highway 14 back towards Los Angeles. The San Gabriel Mountains, with peaks rising to nearly 2,000 m (6,562 ft), begin 100 km (62 miles) beyond the town of Mojave, located at the southwestern corner of the Mojave Desert, below the Oak Creek Pass. The mountain range borders the greater metropolitan area on its north-east side. North-west of San Fernando, Highway 14 joins Interstate Highway 5, which you will take back into Los Angeles before

finally exiting at the Hollywood Freeway (170).

21 Hollywood The view from Sunset Boulevard of the 'Hollywood' sign on the slopes of this Los Angeles district is world famous. The letters originally read 'Hollywoodland' and were erected in 1923 as an advertisement for a property scheme. However, they have now long been the symbol of a place synonymous the world over with the film industry, and of course its glamour and glitter. Made out to be the main streets of the city in many a film, Sunset Boulevard and Hollywood Boulevard are in fact relatively unspectacular, but there are a few places to get a feel for the stars of Hollywood's more appealing heyday.

The famous Walk of Fame is part of Hollywood Boulevard. Since 1960 more than 2,000 golden stars bearing names of

legendary film actors have been engraved and set in the pavements.

Today, the majority of the studios have moved to other parts of Los Angeles such as Burbank or San Fernando Valley. You can visit the final resting places of many movie stars and directors such as Cecil B. de Mille, Rudolph Valentino, Peter Finch, or Jayne Mansfield who are buried in Memorial Park. From Hollywood the route continues via Beverly Hills for a few kilometers to the beaches in Santa Monica or Venice. In nearby Anaheim, Disneyland attracts numerous visitors.

1 Since many desert tracks and roads, such as this one at Little Lake, run through remote areas, you should make sure the tank is full and you have sufficient water in the car.

2 A thunderstorm approaches over the Mojave Desert.

Redwood National Park Humans are dwarfed by the redwoods (sequoias) that can grow to 112 m (367 ft) – the tallest trees in the world.

Oregon Caves National Monument Visit a fascinating underground labyrinth of marble caves with bizarre shapes, created by water over thousands of years in the Siskiyou Mountains in southern Oregon.

Lassen Volcanic National Park Lassen Peak is within this national park. It is 3,187 m (10,457 ft) high and the only active volcano left in California. Sulphur leaks out of the ground in fizzing, stinking plumes at the Sulphur Works Thermal Area.

San Francisco The imposing Golden Gate Bridge is the landmark of this, the 'most European city in the USA'. San Francisco is a magnet for many subcultures with the motto 'live and let live'.

Yosemite National Park One of the first national parks in the USA boasts many attractions – rock faces like El Capitan with its extreme vertical face, or impressive waterfalls like Yosemite Falls (739 m/2,425 ft).

Big Sur Since the 1930s, Highway 1 has run directly along the steep coast, with fantastic views over the mighty Pacific.

Kings Canyon Majestic redwoods that reach heights of over 80 m (262 ft) are the main attraction in this wonderful park. Some of the trees have been here for more than 2,000 years.

Monterey This little town owes its fame to writer John Steinbeck, born in 1902 in neighbouring Salinas.

Mount Whitney California is the state of superlatives – Mount Whitney, at 4,418 m (14,495 ft), is the highest mountain in the USA, excluding Alaska.

Hearst Castle Newspaper tycoon William Randolph Hearst built himself a more than ample residence to house his collection of art treasures.

Disneyland Mickey Mouse's Empire has been drawing innumerable visitors since 1955 with its various theme parks.

Los Angeles The 'city in search of a center' displays its Mediterranean charm in many of its neighbourhoods, be it Malibu or Venice Beach on the coast, the celebrity neighbourhood of Beverly Hills or the slightly more bohemian Westwood.

Hollywood The reality of this town on the north side of Los Angeles is not as glamorous as the name might imply, but the Walk of Fame or Mann's Chinese Theater still evoke the golden age of American film.

San Diego A metropolis has arisen around the Old Town, and it radiates a holiday atmosphere thanks to a sunny climate. Balboa Park is certainly worth a visit, with museums and one of the world's most diverse zoos.

Map labels

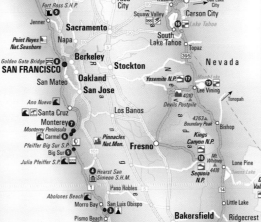

Coos Bay — Grants Pass — Eugene
Cave Junction — 199 — Medford — *Oregon*
Crescent City — Oregon Caves Nat. Mon. — Klamath Falls
Klamath — Siskiyou Pass (1361)
Klamath — Yreka — Klamath Falls
Redwood N.P. — *Klamath Mountains* — Mt. Shasta 4317
Eureka 12 — Mount Shasta 14 — 89 — Burney Falls
Humboldt Redwoods S.P. 11 — Shasta Lake — 299
Redding — Subway Cave — Lassen Volcanic N.P.
Leggett — 101 — Mineral — 15 — Susanville
Fort Bragg — Red Bluff — Alturas / Honey Lake
Mendocino 10 — 1 — Doyle
Point Arena — Ukiah — 395
Clear Lake — Yuba City — Truckee — Reno — Salt Lake City
Fort Ross S.H.P. 9 — Squaw Valley — Carson City — Lake Tahoe
Jenner — Sacramento — South Lake Tahoe — 16 — Topaz
Point Reyes Nat. Seashore — Napa — *Nevada*
Golden Gate Bridge 8 — Berkeley — Stockton — 395
SAN FRANCISCO — Oakland — Yosemite N.P. 17 — Mono Lake
San Mateo — San Jose — 19 — Lee Vining
Ano Nuevo — Santa Cruz — Los Banos — 4010 Devils Postpile — Tonopah
Monterey 7 — Pinnacles Nat. Mon. — 4263 Boundary Peak — Bishop
Monterey Peninsula — Carmel 6 — Fresno — Kings Canyon N.P.
Pfeiffer Big Sur S.P. — Big Sur 5 — Mt. Whitney 18 — Lone Pine
Julia Pfeiffer S.P. — Sequoia N.P. 4418 — Owens Lake
Hearst San Simeon S.H.M. 4 — Death Valley N.P.
Paso Robles — 14
Abolones Beach — Little Lake
Morro Bay — San Luis Obispo 3 — Bakersfield — Ridgecrest
Pismo Beach — 20 Red Rock Canyon S.P.
Santa Maria — Mojave
Jalama — Lompoc — Mission Santa Barbara — Mt. Pinos 2092 — Edwards Air Force Base — Barstow
Gaviota Beach — Santa Barbara 2 — Palmdale
Santa Cruz I. — Ventura — Getty Center — Hollywood 21 — Pasadena
Channel Islands N.P. — Oxnard — Santa Monica — **LOS ANGELES** 1 — Anaheim — Phoenix
Long Beach — Disneyland
Huntington Beach
Mission San Juan Capistrano
Oceanside — Escondido — Yuma
SAN DIEGO
TIJUANA — Ensenada
M É X I C O

USA
Route 66: The American Myth

The first continuous road link between Chicago and Los Angeles still evokes nostalgia today. It is synonymous with freedom and wide open country, cruisers and 'Easy Rider', neon signs and diners – in short, the symbol of a nation whose identity is characterized by being on the road. The West was all about promises and aspirations, a paradise on earth. 'Go California' was the motto – Route 66 was the way there.

The first link between the Great Lakes and the Pacific Ocean has been a continuing legend and the symbol of the American dream ever since Bobby Troup's 'Get your kicks on Route 66'. It was Horace Greely who popularized the phrase 'Go West, young man, and grow up with the country' in the *New York Herald Tribune,* and with it created the creed of an entire nation. What came of this creed and the people who later followed it through the Depression and droughts of the 1930s has nowhere been described as tellingly as in John Steinbeck's *The Grapes of Wrath* in which the Joad family heads out on what later became known as the 'Mother Road' to the West. The clash between dreams and reality remains part of the Route 66 legend today. What has since become a long forgot-ten chapter in the history of fast-moving America began less than 100 years ago as cars began to compete with the rail-ways. The 'National Old Trails Highway' developed from the first 'highways' in the individ-ual states and thus became the predecessor of Route 66. But the evocative name did not stand for much more than sand, gravel and strip roads. It was only on 11 November 1926 that the eight Federal states of Illinois, Missouri, Kansas, Okla-homa, Texas, New Mexico, Ari-zona and California completed the uniform 4,000-km (2,486-mile) route between Chicago and Los Angeles, and the high-way was officially opened as Route 66.

The start of Route 66 is marked by a signpost at the Michigan Avenue/Jackson Drive intersec-tion in Chicago. The idyllic countryside of Illinois begins directly after the suburban neighbourhoods to the west of town. Remote farms and tran-quil villages characterize Abra-ham Lincoln's home country. The Amish people's rejection of the technological age takes the traveller back into a bygone

Route 66 in Arizona.

View of the Chicago skyline by night from Sears Tower. Left in the background is the tapered 344-m-high (1,129-ft) John Hancock Center adorned with two antennae.

In the state of New Mexico Route 66 passes through a stark landscape of bizarre rock formations.

era. You finally reach the 'Gateway to the West' in St Louis where the road crosses the expanse of the Mississippi and through the 192-m-high (630-ft) steel archway designed by Eero Saarinen.

The gentle hills of the Ozark Mountains and the 'glitter world' of the Meramec Caverns are hard to resist. Upon reaching Oklahoma, the 'Native American State', you are finally in the mythical land of cowboys and Red Indians with its vast never-ending plains. The cowboys are still in charge on the giant cattle ranches in the area, and this applies to the 290 km (180 miles) where Route 66 crosses the narrow panhandle in northern Texas.

In New Mexico there is a whole new world waiting to greet the visitor. The special light in the valleys and canyons glows mysteriously on the red and brown cliffs and gentle mountains. Between Santa Fe and Taos you will experience an enchanted landscape with a harmonious combination of Spanish charm and Indian culture.

Next comes Arizona, which is not only the state with the largest Indian reservations, but also an area of spectacular rock formations in Red Rock Country, Oak Creek Canyon and of course the Grand Canyon. Intoxicated by the beauty of the landscape, you enter California, crossing the daunting Mojave Desert with its cacti as the last obstacle before heading down towards the Pacific. San Bernardino marks the start of the fertile 'Orange Empire'

Route 66 is slowly swallowed up by Los Angeles' sea of buildings. It ends in Palisades Park near Santa Monica which has a rich showcase of historic landmarks and modern art.

Mexican children pose in traditional costume in Santa Fe, New Mexico.

1

The first continuous East-West connection in the USA from Chicago to Los Angeles remains something of a legend today. Even though large parts of the original Route 66 gave way to more modern Interstate highways in the 20th century, there are still many original stretches where the legend lives on.

Chicago Including its outer suburbs, Chicago sprawls over 100 km (62 miles) along the southern shores of Lake Michigan. The city is a fantastic destination for anyone interested in the arts, architecture and music. Chicago was already an important transport hub and trading centre in the 19th century. Cattle and pigs were unloaded here at the largest livestock station in the country and driven to urban slaughterhouses, of which there are only a few remaining today.

In the 'Roaring Twenties', the 'Windy City' gained the dubious reputation of being a gangster metropolis, but Al Capone is all but legend now. The skyline of the new Chicago rose up out of the ruins of the old city and is proof of the determination, initiative of its residents. The 'Great Chicago Fire' of 9 October 1871 almost destroyed the city. Over 200 people died and more than 90,000 lost everything they owned.

State Street is considered the largest pedestrian zone in the world and attracts crowds with its department stores, boutiques, restaurants, cinemas and theatres.

Passers-by encounter a number of remarkable artworks on the pavements – a 16-m (52-ft) statue left to the citizens of Chicago by Pablo Picasso; 'Flamingo', the bright red giant spider by Alexander Calder in front of the Chicago Federal Center;

'Universe', a gigantic mobile by the same artist in the lobby of the Sears Tower; or 'The Fours Seasons', a 20-m-long (66-ft) mosaic by Marc Chagall in front of the First National Bank, a major Amer-

ican commercial bank formed in 1863.

Before starting off towards the south it is worth taking a detour to the town of Holland 110 km (68 miles) away. This carefully reconstructed village

Travel Information

Route profile
Length: approx. 4,000 km (2,486 miles), excluding detours
Time required: 3 weeks
Start: Chicago
End: Santa Monica
Route (main locations): Chicago, St Louis, Tulsa, Oklahoma City, Santa Fe, Albuquerque, Flagstaff, Barstow, Santa Monica

---

Traffic information:
Drive on the right in the USA. Maximum speed limits in built-up areas are 25 to 30 mph (40–48 km/h); on the highways 55–70 mph

(88–115 km/h). Speed checks (with tough penalties) are also conducted from the air. Drink-driving is strictly prohibited in all of the states here, with heavy fines. It is prohibited to carry open or even empty bottles or cans of alcoholic beverages in the car (not even in the boot).

Information:
Detailed information on the historical Route 66 as well as the most important sightseeing attractions can be found at:
www.historic66.com or
www.theroadwanderer.net

is a memorial to the region's Dutch immigrants.

The journey along the legendary Route 66 begins at the Michigan Avenue/Jackson Drive intersection in Chicago and from there Interstate Highway 55 takes you to Springfield. North of Springfield is the beautiful Chautauqua National Wildlife Reserve.

2 Springfield The capital of Illinois still has the aura of an idyllic country town today.

A little further north, New Salem was the home of the famous president (Lincoln) who lived here in humble circumstances from 1831–1837. The village has now been reconstructed as an open-air museum with staff in period costume who demonstrate how hard life was here 200 years ago.

In Springfield itself the focus is also on President Lincoln and his carefully restored house on Jackson Street is open to visitors, as is his law office on

Adams Street where he practised as a lawyer from 1843–1853. He found his final resting place in Oak Ridge Cemetery. Lincoln was a parliamentarian in the Old State Capitol in the Downtown Mall but since 1877 state business has been conducted in the opulent new Illinois State Capitol. Shea's Gas Station Museum imparts true Route 66 feeling.

The journey continues southwards via Interstate Highway 55 toward the bustling city of St Louis, which touts cultural experience with a unique French flair.

3 St Louis The largest city in the state of Missouri lies on the western bank of the Mississippi just before the confluence with the Missouri River. The Mark Twain National Wildlife Reserve was established on the river north of the city. The city was founded in 1764 by a French fur trader, Pierre Liguest, and it was fur traders who first brought wealth to the new settlement. Large parts of

the American west were then settled from here. It was also from here that the endless wagon trains began their journey across the prairies and it was to here that the riches of the grasslands and the Rocky

1 The port and skyline of Chicago. The Sears Tower (second from the left) was the tallest building in the world until 1998.

1 At the height of summer, the St Louis sun sets in the middle of the Gateway Arc.

1

Mountains were brought back and traded.

The 192-m-high (630-ft) Gateway Arch designed by the Finn, Eero Saarinen, is St Louis' primary landmark and is purposely visible from great distances. As a symbolic 'Gateway to the West', the arch is a reminder that this is where the great tide of settlers heading for the coast began their often perilous journey towards a better life. A short distance south of the Gateway Arch is the Old Cathedral dating from 1834 with its attractive mosaics and an interesting museum of the city's history in the basement. Market Street begins on the Gateway Arch axis and its notable tourist attractions include the dome of the Old Court House from 1864, the magnificent round building that is the Busch Memorial Stadium and the City Hall, based on its counterpart in Paris.

On Lindell Boulevard is the splendid St Louis Cathedral built in 1907 in Byzantine style.

It has a spectacular mosaic dome and is on the sight of the first cathedral to be built in the USA. You leave St Louis via Interstate Highway 44 and then make your way towards the town of Stanton.

④ **Meramec Caverns** A visit to the Meramec Caverns about 5 km (3 miles) south of Stanton is not to be missed. They are among the largest stalactite caves in the USA and include some fascinating formations. Some doubt that the famous bandit Jesse James and his gang used the caves as a hideout, but legends certainly tell of their presence here.

For the onward journey you continue down Interstate 44 to Springfield, Missouri.

⑤ **Branson** South of Springfield, the third-largest city in Missouri, are the Ozark Mountains, which attract a great number of visitors, particularly in autumn. The small town of

Branson is your specific destination reached via Highway 65. It is known as 'America's Biggest Little Town' and the new Mecca of American country music. As such, it has outdone legendary Nashville, Tennessee.

Traditional handicrafts and nostalgic events are staged in 'Silver Dollar City'. Highway 13 takes you to the Talking Rock Caverns, considered the most scenic of the 5,000 caves in Missouri. Those interested in history can make a detour to the Pea Ridge National Monument.

Back in Springfield continue along Interstate 44 westwards.

⑥ **Joplin** A part of the original Route 66 turns right from Highway 44 shortly before the small town of Joplin, Missouri. Continue through Joplin and shortly thereafter you reach the little town of Galena where time appears to have stood still. The whole town is like an open-air museum. The next little village is Riverton where the old Marsh

2

Arch Bridge, an arched concrete suspension bridge, was built in 1923 to span Brush Creek. Route 66 passed over this bridge until 1960. The next stop is Baxter Springs where under no circumstances should you miss a visit to Murphey's Restaurant in the Baxter National Bank, which was closed in 1952. Part of the decor comprises former bank furniture, and old cheques from the 1920s lie on the tables under glass.

⑦ **Miami** Here too, little appears to have changed on the

3

outside. Miami developed from a trading station set up in 1890. In 1905 lead and zinc brought a boom to the town. The main attraction is the Coleman Theatre, built in 1929, a cinema with magnificently crafted balconies and a ceiling lined with gold leaf. On the first floor there is a small exhibition about Route 66 and its history.

8 Tulsa The former 'Oil Capital of the World', Tulsa has long been stripped of this title, but some of the oil barons' art deco villas are still a sign of the city's former wealth. Waite Phillips' mansion still houses works of art from the Italian Renaissance. The original Route 66 follows Eleventh Street through downtown. Between Tulsa and Oklahoma City you can also travel along lengthy stretches of the historic Route 66, which maintain their rustic charm.

9 Oklahoma City Founded in 1889 – after Indian territories were opened to whites – the capital of Oklahoma owes its wealth to oil. There are still a good 2,000 wells within the city limits today, one of which is directly in front of the Capitol. The spirit of the Wild West is still alive and well in the National Cowboy Hall of Fame on Persimmon Hill, which includes the replica of an old western town called 'Prosperity Junction'. 'The American Cowboy Gallery' documents the life of the cowboys, and the 'American Rodeo Gallery' is dedicated to that long-standing western tradition. South-west of the city center is the historic neighbourhood Stockyards City, where you can get a feeling for the way things might have been in the heyday of the cattle business here. South of the city are the Wichita Mountains, a hiking area, and to the north-west the Washita Battlefield is found where Custer staged an attack on the Cheyenne Indians in the ongoing and tragic clash of cultures that took place in the area in November 1868. The journey continues via Interstate 40 westwards to Clinton.

10 Clinton The most interesting Route 66 museums on the whole trip are to be found here. Films, photographs and original exhibition pieces document the route's heyday. Beyond Clinton you stay on Interstate 40. Once you get to Amarillo, a detour on Interstate 27 leads to one of the most interesting canyons in the area.

11 Palo Duro Canyon State Park This canyon is surrounded by cliffs some 350 m (1,148 ft) high where remote Indian trails lead deep into the canyon to the most spectacular cliff for-

1 They're back: nostalgic diners and the cars to match.

2 Stark cliffs rise 350 m (1,148 ft) in the Palo Duro Canyon.

3 The Oklahoma City National Memorial was erected to commemorate the victims of the attack on the Alfred P. Murrah Federal Building in 1995.

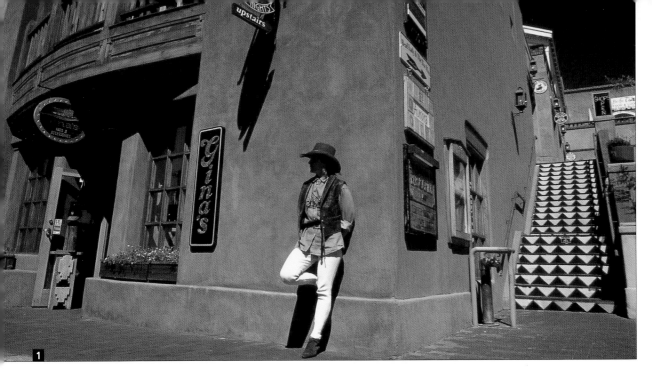

1

mations. Also called the 'Grand Canyon of Texas', Palo Duro is the second-largest canyon in the USA: 195 km (121 miles) long, 32 km (20 miles) wide and 243 m (797 ft) deep – a good warm-up for the real Grand Canyon in Arizona.

⑫ Amarillo Route 66 used to pass along Sixth Avenue in this Texas town, a street lined with some restored buildings from the route's heyday. The American Quarter Horse Heritage Center documents the history of the breeding of the American Quarter Horse. Cadillac Ranch 15 km (9 miles) to the west is a bizarre collection of old Cadillacs. There is a flint quarry further north, Alibates Flint Quarries National Monument. The route continues on Interstate 40 into New Mexico towards Albuquerque.

⑬ Fort Sumner Before reaching the little town of Santa Rosa, it is worthwhile taking a brief detour to the south on Highway 84 to Fort Sumner.

This is where 8,000 Navajo and Apache Indians were rounded up in 1864 and forcefully relocated to the fort to survive on their own. Many of them died. The visitor centre and adjacent museum tell the tragic story of this gruesome incident.

The town went down in American history a second time as it was here on 16 July 1881 that Pat Garrett shot the famous Billy the Kid. A small museum has been erected in his memory.

Back in Santa Rosa, continue to follow Interstate 40. To reach Santa Fe you need to leave the actual Route 66 at Clines Corners, the intersection of Interstate 40 and Highway 285, then head north toward Santa Fe.

⑭ Santa Fe The second-oldest city in the USA and the capital of New Mexico is characterized by both Indian and Spanish culture. There are eight large museums and a multitude of art galleries, jewellery shops and handicraft stores here. When the Spanish arrived in 1542, there was already a large Pueblo

2

Indian settlement here, which later revolted against the colonials and sent them packing. In the meantime, however, the Spanish made Santa Fe the capital of their new colony. Today the architectural mix of Indian, Spanish, European American and Mexican influences is the special attraction of Santa Fe's old town.

The famous Santa Fe Trail, an historic trading route running from Independence in the west of Missouri to Santa Fe, ends at the Plaza built in 1610 in the historic heart of the city. This is

also the site of the Palace of the Governors (1614), the governor's residence dating from the 17th century. The oldest buildings are situated south of the Santa Fe River in the Indian settlement of Barrio de Analco, established in the early 17th century by the Tlaxcala Indians. The Museum of Fine Arts shows the work of regional artists. Those especially interested in Indian culture ought not to miss the museums on Camino Lejo. The Museum of Indian Arts and Culture displays artworks from the Indian tribes of

New Mexico. The Museum of International Folk Art is one of the largest ethnographic museums in the USA, while the Wheelwright Museum of the American Indian is dedicated to all the Indian cultures of North America. The numerous interesting Indian pueblos in the area are worth visiting. The Interstate Highway 25 takes you directly to Albuquerque and back to the original Route 66.

⑮ **Albuquerque** The largest city in New Mexico is situated on the Rio Grande at an altitude of 1,600 m (5,250 ft) and is overshadowed by Sandia Peak. There is a 4-km-long (2.5-miles) exhilarating cable car ride that takes you up to 3,163 m (10,378 ft) above sea level.
Founded by the Anasazi Indians, who had already been living here between 1100 and 1300, the town was then settled by the Spanish at the beginning of the 18th century and they built what is today known as Old Town. About 170 years later the town was linked to the rail network. There is a series of museums worth visit-

ing here – the Albuquerque Museum has a collection of exhibits from the Spanish colonial era; nature fans will want to see the New Mexico Museum of National History, with exhibits on the natural history of the south-west (such as dinosaurs); and the largest collection of rock paintings is to be found in the Petroglyph National Monument north of the city. The Indian Pueblo Cultural Center north of Interstate 40 is an absolute must-see.

⑯ **Laguna Pueblo** About 10 km (6 miles) west of Albuquerque, north of Interstate 40, is a Keresan pueblo made up of six villages – Encinal, Laguna, Mesita, Paguate, Paraje and Seama. The site has been in existence since the middle of the 15th century. Colourful local pottery is on sale in every village. The St Joseph Mission on the lake in Old Laguna is also worth a visit.

⑰ **Acoma Pueblo** Roughly 48 km (30 miles) south-east

of the small town of Grant is Acoma, considered the most attractive pueblo far and wide. The village, which is also known as 'Sky City' because of its spectacular location, sits on top of a mesa (table mountain) 10 m (361 ft) above the plain.
The pueblo has been a settlement for over 1,200 years and is considered to be the oldest continually inhabited settlement in the USA. Today, there are only about fifty residents, most of the tribe's members

1 Indian and Spanish cultures characterize the beautiful Old Town of Santa Fe. The picture features Canyon Road.

2 Old Town Albuquerque shares Spanish and Indian origins.

3 The El Morro National Monument is a 60-m-high (197-ft) sandstone cliff. The numerous inscriptions have led to the cliff's nickname 'Inscription Rock'.

4 Acoma Pueblo sits on top of a majestic cliff plateau.

having moved to the villages on the plain. As the village is sometimes closed for religious ceremonies, it is best to enquire beforehand whether it is open to visitors. There is a fantastic view of the hinterland from the pueblo. West of Acoma is the El Malpais National Monument, famous for its bizarre rock formations and the more than 150 local bird species.

In the state of Arizona, Interstate 40 continues on more or less the old Route 66. At the town of Thoreau, Highway 371 branches off towards Crownpoint to the Chaco Culture National History Park. Continuing westwards, south of the road is the El Morro National Monument on Highway 53. Both the Indian tribes and the Spanish settlers have left their mark on the 60-m (197-ft) sandstone cliffs.

Sanders, in the 'Grand Canyon State' Arizona, is the starting point for a detour to the north.

⑱ Hubbel Trading Post West of Sanders you should not miss

the 50-km (31-mile) detour via Highway 191 to the Hubbel Trading Post. The trading post was founded in 1890 by John Lorenzo Hubbel in the middle of Navajo territory. The buildings date back to the turn of the last century and the Navajo have quality handicrafts on sale here. Back on Interstate 40, the next highlight is only 30 km (19 miles) away to the west.

⑲ Petrified Forest National Park This park, spread out over 379 sq km (236 sq miles), offers insight into a geological world that is 200 million years old. Around 100 species of fossilized plants and animals have been identified to date. The most impressive examples are the petrified tree trunks that were infused with quartz around 200 million years ago. Today their fractures glimmer with all the colours of the rainbow. The park, which extends both north and south of Interstate 40, is accessed via the 43-km (27-mile) park road and has two information centres,

one of which is located at the north entrance, directly accessible from Interstate 40. Pintado Point, right at the start of the park road, offers the best overview of the Painted Desert. All the colours of the glowing badlands are seen at their best from here. Blue Mesa Point, reached by the 4.8-km (3-mile) access road, offers a second spectacular overview. Agate House is an 800-year-old Anasazi pueblo, the walls of which are made of petrified wood that glitters in myriadcolours. The most beautiful of the petrified trees can be found in the southern part of the park. The Giant Logs Trail leads to Old Faithful, a conifer

tree that has a diameter of 2.9 m (9.5 ft).

The Rainbow Forest Museum ought not to be missed. The exhibition includes a variety of pre-Columbian Indian artefacts fashioned from petrified wood. At the southern end of the park you will reach Highway 180, which will take you directly to Holbrook and Interstate 40.

⑳ Winslow About 20,000 years ago a space 'bomb' landed a little further south of the village. The meteorite created a 180-m-deep (591-ft) crater with a circumference of around 1,300 m (4,265 ft). The visitor center has all the details about

the meteorite and has pieces of the celestial body on display. It is now a further 70 km (43 miles) on Interstate 40 to Flagstaff.

㉑ Sunset Crater Before visiting Flagstaff, it is worth making a detour to the north on Highway 89. On the eastern side of the highway is a bizarre volcanic landscape surrounding the Sunset Crater National Monument. The focal point of the volcanic area is the over 300-m-wide (984-ft) cinder cone of the Sunset Crater. It is the youngest volcano in Arizona and has been active for some 200 years. It first erupted in 1064 and the layer of ash

covered an area of over 2,000 sq km (1,243 sq miles). In 1250 the volcano discharged the red and yellow oxidized lava that today still causes the edge of the crater to glow with the colours of a permanent sunset. The area is accessed via Scenic Drive, with spectacular views of the spooky volcanic landscape. If you take the Sunset Crater National Monument park road a little further north, you soon reach another noteworthy Indian site.

㉒ Wupatki National Monument There used to be more than 2,000 settlements here that were part of the ancient

Indian Sinagua culture. The Indians settled in this region between 500 and 1400. The Wupatki Pueblo, dating back to the 12th and 13th centuries, is relatively well-preserved. The three-storey pueblo had more than 100 rooms, all ventilated by means of a sophisticated system of wall and floor openings. and could also be heated during the winter months.

You can learn anything and everything you want to know about the culture of the Sinagua Indians (Sinagua = sine, aqua = without water) in the visitor center.

㉓ Flagstaff This city on the southern edge of the San Francisco Mountains was founded in 1870 when gold diggers followed farmers and ranchers. The railway line followed as soon as 1882 and with the completion of Route 66 the transit traffic continued to increase. Flagstaff's sightseeing attractions include the Museum of Northern Arizona with a range of exhibits from the various cul-

tural strata of the Pueblo Indians. Flagstaff's real attraction, however, is its surrounding natural landscape. North of town are the fantastic San Francisco Mountains with the highest point in Arizona. Take a chair lift up the 3,854-m (12,645-ft) Humphrey's Peak.

South-east of Flagstaff is Walnut Canyon, 36 km (22 miles) long and 12 m (39 ft) deep, definitely worth exploring on foot. The canyon conceals around 300 Zinagua Indian cliff dwellings; they lived here from the 10th

1 Sinagua Indian dwellings used to cover the area that is now the Wupatki National Monument.

2 The Wigwam Hotel in Holbrook, Arizona. An affordable Indian tradition for modern nomads.

3 The 300-m (984-ft) cinder cone of the Sunset Crater is the product of Arizona's youngest volcano.

4 The historic railway station in Flagstaff dates from the 19th century.

century and built their dwellings solely under overhanging cliffs. From Flagstaff you can go directly to the Grand Canyon on Highways 89 and 64 or 180 and 64. On Interstate 40 follow the highway as far as Seligman and then take the Highway 66 turn-off. The most scenic stretch of old Route 66, which is still largely in its original condition, takes you to the next stop. Access roads lead to the Grand Canyon Caverns and to the Havasupai Indian Reservation. You then end up in central Kingman after crossing the Interstate Highway 40.

24 **Kingman** Between the Cerbat Mountains in the north and the over 2,500-m (8,203-ft) Hualapai Mountains in the south is a traffic interchange in the middle of a desert landscape. Nowhere else on the entire Route 66 has there been a greater investment in nostalgia than here. Old petrol stations and snack bars have been brought back to life, and road

signs and signposts have been saved from obsolescence. The entire town is full of unadulterated Route 66 nostalgia. In the Mohave Museum of History and Arts, with its extensive collection of turquoise jewellery, you learn that the area had already been settled by the Hohokam Indians some 1,300 years ago. The museum gives you a history of their work with the precious stones.

After Kingman you leave Route 66 and Interstate 40 (which goes towards Barstow), to pay homage to the spectacular Hoover Dam and legendary Las Vegas. Both are easy to reach via Highway 93. If you stay on Route 66 you can also visit Lake Havasu south of Kingman.

25 **Hoover Dam** This dam near Boulder City was once the largest embankment dam in the world. The 221-m-high (725-ft) and 379-m-wide (1,242-ft) construction, which is an amazing 201 m (659 ft) thick at its base, was completed in 1935.

The awe-inspiring structure holds back the waters of Lake Mead, a 170-km-long (106-mile) and 150-m-deep (492-ft) body of water. There is a large visitor centre on the dam wall where you learn about the dam's fascinating technical details. You can then take a cruise on Lake Mead with the paddle steamer *Desert Princess*. After 56 km (35 miles) on Highway 93 you eventually reach the city of Las Vegas, an international hub for weddings and winners of all kind.

26 **Las Vegas** The world's gambling capital is located in the middle of the desert and really only consists of hotels and casinos. No less than fourteen of the twenty largest hotels in the world are located here. More than 40 million visitors come to Las Vegas each year to seek their fortune and, more often than not, lose their money to the one-armed bandits and casinos. The big casino hotels stage elaborate shows, revues and circuses in order to provide entertainment for the non-

gamblers, or perhaps to raise the spirits of those who do try their hands. The individual casinos each have their own theme and these range from 'Stratosphere Tower' to the 'Venetian', complete with Doge Palace and Campanile, and the 'Luxor', evoking associations with Ancient Egypt with pyramids and pharaohs.

From Las Vegas, Interstate 15 rejoins the old Route 66 at Barstow. But before you reach Barstow, it is worth paying a brief visit to Calico, a ghost town that was once a very successful mining operation at the end of the 19th century due to the discovery of substantial reserves of silver and borax. The minerals here were extracted from more than 500 mines throughout the area. In 1907 Calico was instantly rendered a ghost town, when silver and borax prices dropped sharply.

27 Barstow This town to the east of the Edwards Air Force Base is situated in the middle of the desert and serves as a major supply centre for a huge yet sparsely populated hinterland. The California Desert Information Center is very interesting, providing a plethora of details on the Mojave Desert and its difficult living conditions. Following Interstate 15 you gradually leave the desert behind and reach the centre of the Californian citrus-growing region, San Bernardino County.

28 San Bernardino This city, almost 100 km (62 miles) east of Los Angeles, developed from a Franciscan mission founded in 1810. From here you really must do the 'Rim of the World Drive', a panoramic drive through a spectacular high desert and mountain landscape. It passes scenic lakes, reaches an altitude of 2,200 m (7,218 ft) and offers splendid views of the San Bernardino Mountains.

The Joshua Tree National Par with its amazing variety of wildlife and plants is a worthwhile detour from here, and while driving south. the entrance at Twenty-nine Palms can be reached via Interstate 10 and Highway 62.

The historic Route 66 takes you westwards from San Bernardino, just north of Interstate 10, past Pasadena (Pasadena Freeway) and on towards Los Angeles. Via West Hollywood and Beverly Hills you continue along Santa Monica Boulevard to the famous beach town of Santa Monica. Beforehand, if you want to visit the oldest of Disney's parks, Disneyland, take Interstate 15 and Highway 91 over to Anaheim.

29 Anaheim The ending 'heim' is indicative of the German origins of this settlement near the Santa 'Ana' River, where German immigrants settled in about 1857 to start citrus farming. Anaheim is in Orange County, around 60 km (37 miles) south-east of Los Angeles. The largest attraction is Disneyland, the leisure park founded by Walt Disney in 1955 and which brought an end to the country tranquillity of this once rustic town. It is worth continuing along Interstate 5 to San Diego, 150 km (93 mi) south along the coast.

30 Santa Monica In 1935, Route 66 was extended from Los Angeles to Santa Monica and since then has followed Santa Monica Boulevard, terminating at Ocean Boulevard in Palisades Park, where a modest signpost indicates the end of the 'Mother Road' or 'Main Street USA'.

1 South of Kingman are the Hualapai Mountains, over 2,500-m-high (8,203-ft).

2 In 1885 some 1,200 people lived in Calico, and sought their fortunes in one of the 500 silver mines. Calico became a ghost town after 1907 and some of the old buildings, here the old school, have been restored.

3 Downtown Los Angeles is characterized by skyscrapers.

Clinton, Oklahoma In addition to other exhibits, the Route 66 Museum displays a farming family's original loaded truck.

Wichita Mountains The mountain range south-west of Oklahoma City is a popular recreational area rich in flora and fauna.

Oklahoma City In front of the Capitol, an oil well and the sculpture of an Indian woman evoke the history and identity of the city.

Tulsa Downtown Tulsa has an impressive number of interesting art deco buildings. The art museums founded and sponsored by some of the oil magnates contain valuable collections and are worth a visit.

Washita Battlefield N. H. S. This site commemorates a battle between the US cavalry under Custer and the Cheyenne Indians.

Muskogee There are numerous historic buildings to be seen in the Old Town at the railway bridge over the Arkansas River.

Anadarko The Southern Plains Museum in the 'Indian Capital of the Nation' brings the culture of the Plains Indians and the Wild West back to life.

Pea Ridge National Military Park The bloody Civil War battle of 7 and 8 March 1862 in which 26,000 soldiers faced each other is commemorated near Rogers.

Los Angeles Palms between the skyscrapers remind passers-by that they are in the 'Golden State' and that Malibu and Venice Beach are not far away.

San Bernardino This is where the 'Orange Empire' begins, where oranges are grown as far as the eye can see.

Joshua Tree National Park This park near Palm Springs is dedicated to the cactus-like yucca trees. They were given their name by a group of passing Mormons who were reminded of a biblical story about Joshua pointing to the sky.

Calico Ghost Town This town, abandoned following the 'Silver Rush' in 1900, has been restored.

Grand Canyon The largest canyon in the world is about 1,800 m (5,906 ft) deep, up to 30 km (19 miles) wide and some 450 km (280 miles) long. The view of the giant canyon, with its colourful ridges, turrets and free-standing outcrops is overwhelming. At the bottom the Colorado River looks like a tiny little stream.

Hualapai Mountain Park This park near Peach Springs is located in a side valley of the Grand Canyon.

Sunset Crater This crater is part of a huge lava field in the San Francisco Peaks range and is 300 m (984 ft) deep. The best lava cones, flows and pipes are accessed from the panoramic drive.

St Louis The 192-m (630-ft) Gateway Arch is St Louis' landmark. You can take an elevator to the top of the steel archway built by the Finnish architect Eero Saarinen.

Chautauqua N.W.R. The game reserve in County Mason south-west of Peoria, almost 20 sq km (12 sq mi), is part of the Illinois River National Wildlife and Fish Refuges.

Lake Michigan The southern-most of the five Great Lakes of North America is 560 km (348 miles) long, 135 km (84 miles) wide and covers 58,000 sq km (36,041 sq mi).

Springfield The capital of Illinois was the domain of the late US President Abraham Lincoln until 1861. His former home is now a museum.

Galena Parts of this small town in Missouri are an open-air museum that takes visitors back in time to the 19th century.

Mark Twain National Forest This game reserve north of St Louis was set up as a result of the dams built to control the flow of the Mississippi. The river is an important flight path for migrating birds.

Chicago The third-largest city in the USA has the largest inland port, the busiest airport in the world, and extends over 100 km (62 miles) along the southern shore of Lake Michigan. The lakefront with its parks and skyline view of numerous skyscrapers are particularly impressive.

Painted Desert In the north of the Petrified Forest National Park the rocks glow with red tones.

El Morro National Monument The giant sandstone rocks in New Mexico feature inscriptions by the pre-Columbian Indians as well as pueblo ruins from the Anasazi Indians.

Acoma Pueblo Many of the basic adobe houses in the 'Sky City' of this pueblo – one of the oldest settlements in America – can be accessed only by a ladder.

Amarillo West of Amarillo at 'Cadillac Ranch' you can see Cadillacs standing on their heads.

Alibates Flint Quarries National Monument This national monument in Texas protects a site thousands of years old with valuable flint stones in the Red Bluffs above the Canadian River.

Palo Duro Canyon State Park You can visit the Panhandle Plains Historical Museum in this canyon south of Amarillo.

Petrified Forest National Park Here you can see the coloured stone of fossilized tree trunks and gain an insight into a world that is 200 million years old, a time when dinosaurs roamed here.

Albuquerque The largest city in New Mexico lies on the Rio Grande surrounded by mountains. The Spanish Old Town is as much of an attraction as the Pueblo Indian Cultural Center, which has dancing demonstrations at the weekends.

Monument Valley glowing red in the

USA

The "Wild West": cowboys, canyons and cactus

"Go West, young man…" – It is no coincidence that tourists in America's South-West still follow the old call made to pioneers and settlers. Virtually nowhere else in the world will you find more bizarre rock formations, wilder mountains, more breathtaking canyons, more remote cactus deserts, more impressive caves, or hotter valleys. The remnants of ancient Native American pueblo culture are also unique, and their adobe buildings and handicrafts still fascinate visitors from all over the world.

The American South-West stretches from the southern Rocky Mountains in the east to the Sierra Nevada in the west, and from the northern edge of the Colorado Plateau in Utah to the Mexican border in the south. Six states make up the region: Arizona, Nevada, Utah, Colorado, New Mexico and California. The north is dominated by the Col-

orado Plateau, which covers an area of roughly 110,000 sq km (2,460 sq mi) at elevations of 1,000 to 3,000 m (3,281 and 9,843 ft). The most impressive and most beautiful national parks are found here, including the Grand Canyon, Bryce Canyon, Zion, Arches and Canyonlands. There are a total of eleven national parks in the South-

West alone, as well as numerous monuments and state parks. The Organ Pipe Cactus National Monument near Why, Arizona, is even a UNESCO World Nature Heritage Site. Other national

The "Wild West" was Native American territory.

monuments are dedicated to ancient and historic Indian settlements. And if that isn't enough, there are also the national historic parks that are mostly dedicated to the pioneer days, such as the Hubbell Trading Post near Ganado, Arizona. In the south, the plateau stretches out to the Sonora Desert, which extends deep into Mexico. To the north is the Mojave Desert, home of Death Valley with the lowest point in North America. Temperatures of over 50°C (122°F) in the shade are not uncommon here. But anyone driving into the valley before sunrise will experience an unforgettable interplay of colours on the bizarre rock in places like Zabriskie Point.

Delicate Arch in south-east Utah is the symbol not only of Arches National Park, but also of America's entire South-West. The 13.7-m-high (45-ft) sandstone arch glows most impressively in the warm light of the evening sun.

evening light is for many people the epitome of Wild West romanticism.

The Colorado River is the dominant feature of the entire South-West and runs for over 2,300 km (1,429 mi). It originates in the Rocky Mountains, flows through man-made Lake Powell in Utah, continues to whittle away at the Grand Canyon as it has done for millions of years, and finally peters out before reaching the Gulf of California. The spectacular natural beauty of the American South-West was created over sixty-five million years ago when the pressure of the Pacific Plate formed the Rocky Mountains and the Colorado Plateau was pushed up. Giant fractures allowed stones more than a billion years old to emerge, after which erosion from rivers and the elements created the fantastic worlds of pillars, towers, arches, craters

and gorges. The rugged, mostly arid land was originally exclusively Native American territory, and the oldest traces of their ancient desert culture are some eight thousand years old. About three thousand years ago, sedentary peoples built multi-storey settlements called pueblos. The arrival of the Spaniards in the mid-16th century, however, marked the beginning of a drastic decline of their civilizations. In the 20th century, cities were built on former Native American lands.

The contrasts in the South-West are therefore remarkable: fascinating remnants of ancient cultures juxtaposed with raucous metropolises, puritan Mormon settlements near the glitz and kitsch of Las Vegas. One journey is really not enough to take it all

in, but anyone who follows the dream route laid out before you, starting in Los Angeles, following the Rio Grande northwards through New Mexico, exploring the wonders of Utah and then making a great arch

back towards the City of Angels via Las Vegas and Death Valley will experience at least a handful of the highlights. And, at the end of the trip, you will realize that the only option left is to come back and see more.

This Indian chief only wears his full feathered headdress on festive occasions. Much can be learned about a people from their folklore and legends.

1

This journey from Los Angeles through Arizona, New Mexico, Colorado, Utah and Nevada back to the Pacific takes you through impressive rock landscapes, deserts and metropolises, and includes a look into the thousand-year-old history of the Native Americans.

1 Los Angeles Your trip begins in the second-largest metropolis in the United States, Los Angeles. Approximately seventeen million people live in an area that stretches 71 km (44 mi) north to south and 47 km (29 mi) east to west. It is bordered in the West by the Pacific Ocean and in the north and east by high mountains. For some reason, however, the founders of the city, when they established the original Pueblo de Nuestra Señora La Reina de Los Angeles, chose a location 25 km (16 mi) from the coast. Today, L.A., the most common abbreviation of the city's name, is the most important industrial and services metropolis in the western United States, a status to which the film industry has contributed immensely. The first American film was shot here in 1910, and the first film with sound was made in 1927,

bringing world fame to Hollywood and Beverly Hills.

Today, the Hollywood Freeway separates the city's two main centers. El Pueblo in the northeast is the actual Old Town district, and the Civic Center in the south-west is the modern downtown. Chinatown borders the north of the Old Town, while Little Tokyo is located south of the Civic Center. The focal point of the historic center is the Plaza with the old mission church of Nuestra Señora La Reina, built by Spanish Franciscans in 1922. The picturesque Olvera Street unfolds as a Mexican street market and is also home to the city's oldest house, the Avila Adobe House, dating back to 1818. The focal point of the Civic Center district is the high-rise City Hall building, erected in 1928. The viewing platform on the 27th floor provides the best views of greater

Los Angeles. The Museum of Contemporary Art on Grand Avenue was designed by renowned Japanese architect Arata Isozaki and is a striking.

The section of Wilshire Boulevard between Highland and Fairfax avenues is known as the Miracle Mile and features interesting art deco build-

Travel Information

Route profile
Length: approx. 4,000 km (2,486 mi)
Time required: 4 weeks
Start and end Los Angeles
Route (main locations):
Los Angeles, Tucson, Alamogordo, Albuquerque, Aztec, Moab, Cameron, Las Vegas, Mojave

Traffic information:
The speed limit in towns: 25 to 30 mph (40 to 45 km/h), on open roads 55–65 mph (88–104 km/h). Strict speed checks with high penalties are often random.

When to go:
March to October is the best time. The desert blooms in spring, and in autumn the temperatures are a bit cooler

than in late summer, when it can be brutally hot.

Alcohol:
Drunk-driving is strictly prohibited in all states of the south-west. Open and even empty bottles or cans of alcoholic drinks are not permitted inside the vehicle. Alcohol consumption is prohibited in all public areas including the open road.

Information:
Here are some websites to help you plan your trip.
www. arizonaguide.com;
www.colorado.com
www.gocalif.ca.gov
www.newmexico.org
www.travelnevada.com
www.utah.com
www.us-national-parks.net

the city. The Rim of the World Drive heads up to an altitude of 2,200 m (1,367 ft) and provides magnificent views.

You then follow Interstate 10 east before joining Highway 62 and heading north-east towards the town of Twentynine Palms and the magnificent Joshua Tree National Park.

③ Joshua Tree National Park This park is living proof that the desert is alive. Apart from the striking Joshua trees, you will also find palm groves, cactus gardens and juniper bushes here. After exploring the park, you will come out on the south side where you will get back on Interstate 10 heading east towards Phoenix.

④ Phoenix The capital of Arizona, is a mix of the Old West and unrelenting modernization represented by a series of museums, cultural and recreational facilities, and a booming high-tech industry.

At an altitude of 369 m (1,211 ft), this city in the Valley of the Sun typically has three hundred sunny days a year. Thanks to countless irrigation systems – which supply water for agriculture as well as golf courses –, however, and despite its desert location, Phoenix is actually quite green. Along with the Piestewa Peak, the Camelback Mountains, which are the city's most famous icon, provide a good view over this urban sprawl in the Sonoran Desert. The suburb of Scottsdale is one of the city's best-known areas and is particularly popular for

1 Sunset over the Mormon "Trees of God" in Joshua Tree National Park.

2 These imposing candelabra cactuses are the symbol of Saguaro National Park.

ings. Of course, you should not miss Hollywood. Although very little of the former glitz and glamour of the neighborhood remains, Mann's Chinese Theater is still an eye-catcher designed in Chinese pagoda style. The cement blocks in the main courtyard have the footprints, handprints and signatures of more than two hundred Hollywood personalities. The theater also marks the start of the famous "Walk of Fame" on Hollywood Boulevard, a collection of over two thousand pink marble stars with the names of Hollywood greats embossed on brass plaques.

Not far from the Chinese Theater are a few museums: the Hollywood Wax Museum with famous actors and politicians; the Guinness Book of World Records Museum, dedicated to the world's most bizarre records; and the CBS film and television studios near the Farmers Market.

At Paramount Pictures you can get behind the scenes and even watch a live production if you are lucky. Sunset Boulevard begins at the Roosevelt Hotel, which hosted the first Oscars ceremony back in 1929. The point where it turns into Sunset Strip marks the start of Hollywood's nightclub district.

The route then heads southeast along the Hollywood and Santa Ana Freeways towards Anaheim, home of Disneyland.

② Anaheim The Disneyland amusement park is by far the most significant attraction in Anaheim, a town founded by German immigrants in 1857. The most interesting building in the city is the Crystal Cathedral, a steel pipe edifice built in 1980 with a shell of mirrored glass.

The route now follows Interstate 91 to San Bernardino, where you can make a detour to the surprisingly high San Bernardino Mountains north of

its luxury atmosphere and pretty Old Town quarter. Alongside the modern office towers and high-rise buildings, you can still find traces of the past in downtown Phoenix. The famous Heritage Square forms the center of the city and is lined with beautiful Victorian houses. The most famous of these is Rosson House, which dates back to the late 19th century like many of the other Old Town buildings. The square is part of Heritage and Science Park, which also includes the Arizona Science Center (with planetarium) and the Phoenix Museum of History. The Heard Museum has an extensive collection of prehistoric, traditional, and modern works by Native American artists from the South-West. The Phoenix Art Museum has artwork by international artists from the 15th to the 20th century, as well as modern art from America's western states.

The high culture of the Hohokam Indians, who irrigated the desert as early as AD 200, collapsed in the 15th century. The ruins of one of their settlements and some of their irrigation canals, are displayed in the Pueblo Grande Museum. Phoenix Zoo is one of the most famous zoos in the world and breeds many endangered species.

After visiting Phoenix, Interstate 10 takes you quickly south to the region around Tucson, the second-largest city in Arizona. Anyone looking to spend a bit more time getting to Tucson, however, should travel west on the I10 back to Buckeye and from there head south on Highway 85 to Why and the Organ Pipe Cactus National Monument. From there you can head east to Tucson on Highway 86 and take a detour through Saguaro National Park-West, just north-west of the city.

5 Saguaro National Park This park owes its name to the candelabra saguaro cactuses. These kings of the desert can live up to 150 years old, grow to a height of 15 m (49 ft) and weigh up to 8 tonnes (8.8 tons). The most beautiful specimens of this cactus can be found in both the East and West sections of the 338-sq-km (130-sq-mi) Sonora Desert park.

On the southern edge of the western section of the park, you should definitely not miss out on a visit to the Arizona Sonora Desert Museum, which has impressive displays of the desert's flora and fauna. You can also see many of the desert animals that most people never get a glimpse of.

6 Tucson The "City of Sunshine", surrounded by the Santa Catalina Mountains, has an average of 350 sunny days a year. Spanish missionaries built a mission station in 1775, on the site of an old Native American settlement, and it quickly became a Spanish-Mexican colonial town. It is now the second-largest city in Arizona after Phoenix. It has a sizable university and, with military bases in the area, it has also become a high-tech center.

However, there is also an Old Town district in modern Tucson where the Spanish colonial center was located, between Alameda and Washington streets. There are some meticulously

restored adobe houses that are representative of the old days. South of the historic Old Town is the Barrio Historico, originally the commercial quarter of the Spanish quarter. Today, many beautiful adobe buildings from the late 19th century are still in use here.

The Pima Air and Space Museum is an absolute must for aerospace enthusiasts. More than two hundred exhibits including airplanes, helicopters, ultra-light aircraft and all kinds of experimental devices are on display.

Fans of westerns will get their money's worth in Tucscon as well. They only need to drive about 21 km (13 mi) west of the city to Old Tucson Studios, built in late 19th-century style as the set for some classic western films such as *Gunfight at the O.K. Corral* and *Rio Bravo*. Only a few miles further south is the San Xavier del Bac mission.

Leaving Tucson you head east on Interstate 10. In Willcox, you can make a detour on Highway 186 to the Chiricahua National Monument, where innumerable rock pillars stand to attention like soldiers – eroded remains of a volcanic eruption several million years ago. The Apaches held their last stand against US Army troops in the remote gorges of this region. Back on Interstate 10 heading east, Stein's Ghost Town will appear near the Highway 80 turnoff. It is a typical example of a stagecoach-era town that was eventually abandoned by its inhabitants.

Today, Stein is basically a tourist attraction. East of Las Cruces, you leave Interstate 10 and head north on Interstate 25, taking Highway 70 to Alamogordo after about 11 km (7 mi).

7 Alamogordo This city has undoubtedly made history. In the nearby San Andreas Mountains, US forces set up the White Sands Missile Range where the

world's first atomic bomb, developed and built in Los Alamos, New Mexico, was detonated on July 16, 1945. Alamogordo now offers visitors both a technical and natural experience. Technology enthusiasts will be drawn to the International Space Hall of Fame, which covers everything from the early Mercury capsule to the Apollo Program, and from the Russian space capsule to the Skylab. If it was important to the discovery of outer space, it's in this museum.

Nature enthusiasts will enjoy an excursion to White Sands National Monument west of the city as it is home to a unique gypsum dune landscape with dunes as high as 18 m (59 ft). To get there take the 26-km (16-mi) Heart of Sands Drive.

8 San Antonio After circling the rocket testing grounds of White Sands, the road reaches the Rio Grande near San Antonio. A vast wetland area strad-

dles the river south of this small township.

The Bosque del Apache National Wildlife Refuge is accessible to visitors through the Bosque del Apache Loop. There are viewing towers along the road for observing wild animals.

Highways 60, 36 and 117 then take you through the Plains of St Augustin to Grants.

9 Grants South of this small town you will find the bizarre rock formations of El Malpais National Monument. Volcanic eruptions roughly four million years ago created the conditions for these fantastic rock structures. Lava covered the existing limestone, and erosion slowly shaped the canyons and uncovered the diverse stone layers. One of the highlights of a visit to the park is the Bandera Crater. It has several ice caves, the most impressive of which is the Candeleria Cave. The Big Tubes are the largest lava tunnels in the United States.

About 48 km (30 mi) south-east of Grants is the most beautiful pueblo far and wide, Acoma, or "Sky City". The village has a picturesque location on a rock plateau 110 m (361 ft) above the plain and has been there for about 1,200 years. Originally only accessible with ladders, the Spaniards called it "the best fort in the world". You can visit the pueblo as part of a guided tour. About 80 km (50 mi) east on Interstate 40 is Albuquerque.

10 Albuquerque This city on the Rio Grande is the largest in the state of New Mexico. The intersection of Interstates 40 and 25 was apparently so attractive that around one-third of the state's population now lives in this area. Albuquerque was founded in 1716, when thirty families initially settled here.

Albuquerque's real draw is therefore its Old Town with the Plaza from 1780, as well as the old trees and overall Spanish feel. Surrounding the square are some beautiful adobe buildings, in particular San Felipe de Neri Church (1706). Anyone interested in the city's historic development should visit the Albuquerque Museum, which houses the largest collection of Spanish colonial items. Opposite that is the New Mexico Museum of Natural History, with a history of the Southwest from early times to today.

After exploring this lovely town on the mighty Rio Grande, travel another 62 km (38 mi) or so north-east along Interstate 25 to Santa Fe.

11 Santa Fe The capital of New Mexico is the second-oldest city in the USA and, thanks to the mix of Indian and Spanish culture, also one of the most interesting. The Spaniards officially "founded" the city in 1609, albeit on a Pueblo Indian settlement that had already existed since 11th century.

Today, Santa Fe fascinates visitors with its charming adobe buildings made of yellowish-brown clay, wonderful Spanish colonial buildings, and modern adobe architecture. The bustling center is the Plaza, created in 1610, which once marked the end of the legendary Santa Fe Trail.

Highway 68 takes you to the Native American and artisan town of Taos roughly 112 km (70 mi) away.

12 Taos Often referred to as the "Soul of the Southwest", Taos presents itself as an artists colony dedicated to Native American and Mexican styles with more than sixty galleries.

1 The cliff settlement of the Anasazi Indians in Mesa Verde National Park was only accessible from above using vertical ladders that could be retracted in the event of danger.

2 St Mary's Basilica among modern high-rise buildings in Phoenix.

3 Taos Pueblo: the adobe houses here were built onto each other like honeycomb squares.

4 The San Xavier del Bac Mission is a perfect example of baroque church architecture in the Spanish colonial style.

The Artist Society was founded in 1912. The Tiwa tribe had a permanent settlement on the Taos Plateau for some 1,100 years before the Spanish arrived. The city center's picturesque Plaza reflects the colonial style. South of the square on Ledoux Street are the town's oldest and most beautiful adobe buildings.

The Harwood Museum displays interesting works by Taos artists from the last 100 years. Just under 5 km (3 mi) north-east of town is Taos Pueblo where 1,500 members of the Tiwa tribe still live. The village has existed since the 12th century and was always exclusively inhabited by Native Americans. The route now heads west through the southern foothills of the San Juan Mountains towards Farmington. At Bloomfield, a road heads south to the Chaco Culture National Historical Park in Nageezi.

13 Chaco Culture National Historical Park
Chaco Canyon was the spiritual, political and commercial hub of the Anasazi as early as the 10th century. The most important sights in the valley can be reached on by the circular route. The valley's main attraction is definitely Pueblo Bonito, which covered an area of 1,200 sq m (12,912 sq ft) and had 700 rooms for about 1,200 people spread over five levels. After returning to Bloomfield, head north on Highway 544 to Aztec.

14 Aztec Ruins National Monument
This is another Anasazi ruin. It was inhabited by up to 1,300 people in 450 rooms arranged in a semi-circle around a kiva (ritual and meeting room). It has now been completely rebuilt, making it the only place in the United States to provide real insight into a major Native American settlement.

Take Highway 550 to Durango and then continue on Highway 160 until you reach the next spectacular national park.

15 Mesa Verde National Park
The most beautiful and certainly the most impressive residential complex of the Anasazi is in this park. It is deservedly a UNESCO World Heritage site. Some of the pueblos, which cling impossibly to inaccessible rock overhangs, were built between the 10th and 13th centuries. They have over 100 rooms and many have several *kivas*. The entire area can be reached from Ruins Road Drive, which provides good views and insights but does not allow direct access. The best cave dwellings are in Cliff Palace, comprising over 200 rooms and twenty-three *kivas*. The Balcony House is similarly arranged and is only accessible via vertical ladders and a narrow tunnel pipe. Highways 160 and 191 take you to the Canyon de Chelly National Monument.

16 Canyon de Chelly National Monument
This canyon is roughly 300 m deep (984 ft) and is carved from red rock faces. From the canyon floor, freestanding formations such as Spider Rock at 243 m (797 ft) in height will dazzle any visitor. Over 100 Native American settlements up to 1,500 years old were found in the canyon. As in Mesa Verde National Park, the pueblos here were built into the rock like birds' nests.

The main gorge can be accessed by two roads: North Rim Drive and South Rim Drive. Both offer spectacular views way down into the canyon. Highlights of the park include the White House Ruin, an Anasazi pueblo made from shiny white limestone; the Mummy Cave, which was once used as a cult and burial site; and Antelope House, which has a rock drawing with an antelope motif.

Highways 191 and 160 will take you to Kayenta and the entrance to Monument Valley.

17 Monument Valley Navajo Tribal Park
In the middle of the Colorado Plateau, on the

border between Arizona and Utah, Monument Valley is home to spectacular rock formations that have been used as the backdrop for countless Westerns. Anyone traveling through here in the early morning or late evening will experience an amazing flush of color as the rocks glow in all hues of red, pink and purple.

This rugged land was a Native American hunting and settlement region for thousands of years and is now once again a Navajo reserve. The best view of the rock towers, which reach heights of 600 m (1,969 ft), is seen from the 27 km (17 mi) circle route. If you want to learn more about the lifestyle of the

desert floor like giant waves that extend over 160 km (99 mi) through the desert. Their exposed edges have been eroded away into a tangle of bulky domes formed from naked rock, steep cliffs and canyons. While the northern and southern parts of the park are less accessible and mainly prized by hikers, the easy-to-access middle section is home to the more rugged beauty of towering rock formations, among which the green Fruita oasis, created by the Mormons on the Fremont River, looks like an island in a vast ocean.

The most important part of the park is accessed on the 40-km (25 mile) Scenic Drive, which leads to the park's most impressive rock faces. The trip then follows Highways 24, 12 and 89 to Bryce Canyon National Park.

㉑ Bryce Canyon National Park This park extends over an area of 145 sq km (56 sq mi) on the fringe of the Paunsaugunt Plateau, whose cornices drop away 600 m (1,969 ft) over the delicately divided escarpments. At the bottom is the Paria Valley with a natural amphitheater shaped like a horseshoe. Erosion has carved deep ditches and furrows into the soft sandstone slopes that have resulted in finely engraved heads, needles and arches. In the early morning, this magical world glows in a spectrum of hues from pale yellow to dark orange. The rock amphitheatre can be accessed via the 27-km-long (17 mile) scenic drive around the upper rim.

Navajo, take a guided tour from the visitor center.

Your journey continues now over Monument Pass to Bluff. From there you take Highway 191 to Moab. The 211 takes you to the southern part of Canyonlands National Park, and the 279 goes into the northern portion from Moab.

⑱ Canyonlands National Park The national park covers an area of 1,366-sq-km (527-sq-mi) and includes the confluence of the Green and Colorado rivers, which have carved their way into 600-m (1,969-ft) gorges whose walls gleam in red and beige hues. Bizarrely shaped rock towers with chim-

neys and needles inspire the imagination of visitors. The park is so vast that you have to approach it from two sides. The southern half (Needles) has enchanting rock sculptures and formations. Parts of the Needles district are accessible via two paved roads while other trails requiring four-wheel-drive vehicles lead down to the river.

The northern part of the park (Island in the Sky) comprises the headland between the rivers. The gorges reach depths of up to 600 m (1,969 ft) on both sides and the view is breathtaking in the truest sense of the word. In the dry air, visibility usually reaches 150 km (93 mi).

From the Grand View Point at the south end of the park road, you will experience a truly unforgettable canyon landscape. A bumpy but wide road for four-wheel-drives also runs below the White Rim in the northern part of the park.

⑲ Arches National Park Almost a thousand natural stone arches in all imaginable shapes, as well as giant mushroom rocks, rock towers, pinnacles and cones make this 313-sq-km (121-sq-mi) national park something really special. You can enter the park via Arches Scenic Drive, a 29-km (18-mi) panorama road.

Back in Moab, you again follow Highway 191 as far as Interstate 70, which takes you west until the Highway 24 turns off going south at Green River. From there the road heads directly into Capitol Reef National Park.

⑳ Capitol Reef National Park This park covers an area of roughly 972 sq km (375 sq mi) around the Waterpocket Fold, whose ridges rise out of the

1 Canyonlands National Park was formed by the Colorado River.

2 Giant sandstone arches dot the rocky, mountainous landscape of Arches National Park.

473

1

East of Bryce Canyon, it's worth visiting the Kodachrome Basin State Park, which you can reach via Highway 12. It is home to splendid rock faces of red-and-white striped sandstone, towering rock chimneys and spindly rock needles that glow in all shades of red, especially at sunrise and sunset. A panorama trail takes you to the most beautiful formations whose rich colors can hardly be surpassed.

Back on Highway 12 and Interstate 89 you will head to nearby Zion National Park.

22 Zion National Park The vertical walls of the Virgin River Canyon break away steeply here at heights of more than 1,000 m (3,281 ft), forming solid pillars and deep recesses. The Mormons saw this as a "natural temple of God" back in the 19th century. Visitors feel like tiny ants but you can walk along the base of the canyon in areas where even the rays of the sun hardly ever shine. Only the southern part of the park (593 sq km/229 sq ft) is open to vehicles along the 29-km-long (18-mi) Scenic Drive. The rest of the park is accessible on more than 160 km (99 mi) of hiking trails. An absolute must is the Gateway to the Narrows Trail. Along the Weeping Rock Trail,

you will pass so-called "Hanging Gardens", a rock overhang covered in ferns.

The best panorama view over the entire canyon can be seen from Angels Landing, a cliff that drops away to a depth of 450 m (1,476 ft) on three sides. Your route follows Highway 89 past Marble Canyon to Wupatki National Monument back in Cameron, Arizona.

23 Wupatki National Monument Roughly 40 km (25 mi) south of Cameron, you come across the ancient pueblo of Wupatki on Highway 89. More than 2,000 Sinagua dwellings dating back to between the 9th and 14th centuries can be found in this arid desert landscape on the western edge of the Painted Desert.

A few miles further south of the pueblo ruins is Sunset Crater National Monument. The focal point here is the 305-m-high (1,001-ft) cinder cone of the Sunset Crater, the result of a massive eruption in 1065, followed by a second in 1250. The region can be accessed on the Scenic Drive with spectacular views over the volcanic landscape. Individual features are explained on the nature trail.

Highways 89 and 64 take you to the Grand Canyon.

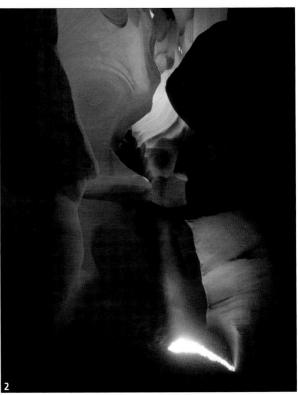

2

24 Grand Canyon National Park This park covers an area of 4,933 sq km (1,904 sq mi) and includes roughly 445 km (277 mi) of the mighty Colorado River, which has carved out a canyon that is up to 1,800 m (5,906 ft) deep with spectacular walls. At its farthest point, the canyon is 30 km (19 mi) wide, and the solid rock formations obviously make for unforgettable photographs. You can enter the Grand Canyon from both the northern and southern sides, but by far the most spectacular views can be seen from the southern side, which is also where the most important tourist facilities are located.

By contrast, Sequoia National Park to the west of Death Valley, is a completely different world comprising granite peaks, redwood forests and Alpine rivers.

28 Sequoia National Park Giant sequoias are the largest redwood trees by volume and only exist on the western slopes of the Sierra Nevada. Some specimens have a circumference of up to 30 m (98 ft) and live to be over 3,000 years old.

29 Mojave Highway 14 runs along the western edge of the Mojave Desert back to Los Angeles. Dry lakebeds, dunes and precipices accompany you here before you finally reach the Pacific in Santa Monica.

Due to the crush of visitors, the entire South Rim has been closed off to individual vehicle traffic and instead there are free shuttle buses which take you to all of the major vista points.
Back on Highway 64 and Interstate 40, you continue on to Kingman, where you take the turnoff to Highway 93 and head towards Hoover Dam.

25 Hoover Dam Just east of Las Vegas is the world's largest dam – until the Three Gorges project in China is completed. The Hoover Dam is 221 m (725 ft) high, 379 m (1,243 ft) wide, and roughly 200 m (659 ft) thick at the base. A feat of engineering in any era, the dam was completed in 1935. Lake Mead, which is 170 km (106 mi) long and up to 150 m (492 ft) deep, was the result of holding back the Colorado River here. The lake is a reservoir

for Las Vegas and a major recreation area.
After about 56 km (35 mi) on Highway 93 you will arrive in Las Vegas.

26 Las Vegas This glitzy city in Nevada has an almost magic appeal. Bugsy Siegel, an underworld king from the east coast, opened the first casino palace here, the Flamingo Hotel, almost single-handedly making Las Vegas a gambling Mecca. Gambling was legalized in Nevada as early as 1931, in order to create additional sources of income for the state. Special offers throughout the city now lure visitors inside as they stumble from one slot machine to the next. Since the legendary appearances of Frank Sinatra and Elvis Presley, the stages of Las Vegas have become a make-or-break setting for many artists, at least in the USA.

Of the twenty largest hotels in the world, fourteen are in Las Vegas.
East of the city is the Valley of Fire State Park. Death Valley, which is 230 km (143 mi) long and 26 km (16 mi), begins just 80 m (50 mi) west of the gaming paradise.

27 Death Valley National Park At 86 m (282 ft) below sea level, Badwater, in the middle of the park, is the lowest point in North America. It is the hottest and driest place in the United States. It recorded the hottest ever temperature in the Western Hemisphere, and the second-hottest in the world. In summer it can reach 57°C (135°F). Highlights include: Dante's View, the marvelous Zabriskie Point, Artist's Drive, Mosaic Canyon, the vast sand dunes and the Rhyolite Ghost Town.

1 The giant craggy rocks and table mountains in Zion National Park impress visitors with their different bands of color.

2 In Zion National Park, gorges are only 4 m (4 yds) wide, as here in Antelope Canyon.

3 The mighty walls of the Grand Canyon gleam magically in the soft light of the setting sun.

4 Las Vegas, the capital of gambling, is a city that never sleeps.

Las Vegas This has been the USA's gambling haven since 1931. The countless casinos give their all to outdo each other in an effort to lure more money from gamblers' pockets. Lavish hotel complexes, theaters and erotic shows provide entertainment and luxury around the clock.

Rhyolite Ghost Town This town on the edge of Death Valley reminds us of the Gold Rush. Its main attractions are a house made of beer bottles and a collection of gold-digger utensils.

Grand Canyon The Colorado River has carved a gorge through the Colorado Plateau up to 1,800 m deep (5906 ft), 30 km wide (19 mi) and 445 km long (277 mi). The view from the edge of the canyon sweeps over solid yellow-brown and milky white rock outcrops, pinnacles and towers. The layers in the canyon represent 1.7 billion years of the earth's history.

Death Valley This national park is a desert with impressive rocks, vast sand dunes and temperatures reaching 57°C (135°F). However, springs also allow for extensive flora and fauna. Rock drawings prove that the valley was already settled thousands of years ago.

Sequoia National Park The southern Sierra Nevada is home to a remote high Alpine region with majestic granite peaks, deep gorges, silent mountain lakes, small rivers and impressive forests.

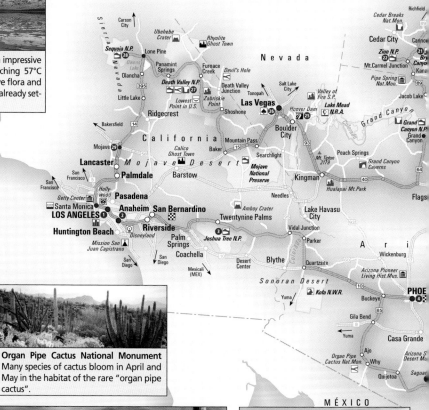

Los Angeles Freeways are the lifeline of Los Angeles, which covers 1,200 sq km (463 sq mi) and comprises many individual towns that have grown together. Stretching from Malibu to Santa Ana, and from Pasadena to Long Beach, the city's highlights include a visit to the film studios in Hollywood.

Organ Pipe Cactus National Monument Many species of cactus bloom in April and May in the habitat of the rare "organ pipe cactus".

Joshua Tree National Park This park south of Twentynine Palms is part of the Mojave Desert and is home to dried-up salt lakes and sparse vegetation with cactuses, junipers and yucca palms.

Sonora Desert This desert is full of surprises. The giant saguaro cactuses, for example are up to 150 years old and up to 15 m (49 ft) high. They flower in May. Everything else the desert has to offer is displayed in the Arizona Sonora Desert Museum in Saguaro National Park.

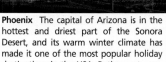

Phoenix The capital of Arizona is in the hottest and driest part of the Sonora Desert, and its warm winter climate has made it one of the most popular holiday destinations in the USA. Retirement communities such as Sun City have been established on its outskirts.

Marble Canyon Formed by the Colorado River, the color of the walls ranges from white to red depending on the position of the sun.

Bryce Canyon National Park This national park in Utah impresses visitors with a tangle of surreal-looking pinnacles and peaks. Here, the rock needles are bathed in the soft yellow and orange hues of the morning sun.

Arches National Park About one thousand freestanding stone arches are clustered here – more than anywhere else in the world – along with mushroom rocks, rock towers, pinnacles and domes of smooth sandstone. In the evening light, the red rocks look as if they are on fire.

Canyonlands National Park The fantastic rock landscape in this national park includes the confluence of the Green River and the Colorado River. The two have carved their way down to depths of 600 m (1,969 ft).

Mesa Verde National Park These historic residential settlements of the Anasazi Indians are set into rock niches and caves. Though protected, many of the rock dwellings and pueblos can be visited.

Monument Valley The table mountains and rock pillars formed by the wind are popular film sets. The valley is part of a Navajo reserve, and you can buy handmade Navajo silver jewelry at the Visitor Center.

Taos Pueblo The Pueblo Indians lived in these multi-storey flat-roofed houses more than one thousand years ago.

Acoma Pueblo This beautiful settlement with historic clay-brick buildings and winding alleys sits gracefully atop a plateau.

Albuquerque This city was founded in 1716, and has a lot of Spanish character, with adobe houses and baroque churches in the Old Town. Pictured here is the San Felipe de Neri Church from the early 18th century.

Mission San Xavier del Bac Founded by Spanish priests near Tucson, this church is located on the Tohono O'odham San Xavier Indian Reservation.

Chiricahua National Monument These charming rock landscapes near the Mexican border were once part of Apache hunting grounds.

White Sands National Monument This 600-sq-km (232 sq mi) dune landscape is made of white gypsum sand that glistens like newly fallen snow. Dunes rise to 18 m (59 ft) here. The US Army set off the world's first atomic bomb in the northern part of the desert on July 16, 1945.

Typical for Maine and the whole of

USA

From Bass Harbor Lighthouse in Maine to Cape Lookout Lighthouse in Maryland

A fairly narrow coastal plain stretches between the Atlantic Ocean in the East and the Appalachians in the West. Here on the East Coast the cities line up like pearls on a chain forming a massive conurbation that is also referred to as 'Boswash' (Boston to Washington). However, despite the high population densities there are still a number of remote natural landscapes to be found.

In 1620, when they disembarked from the *Mayflower* at Plymouth Rock in present-day Massachusetts, the Pilgrim Fathers could not have dreamt that they were playing 'midwife' to what is now the most powerful nation on earth, the United States of America. What they encountered was a largely untouched natural environment only sparsely populated by a number of Native North American tribes. Today the fascination of the US Atlantic coast derives not only from the bustling cities and the centers of political and economic power, but also from the peace and solitude of its idyllic natural setting. The mountain scenery of the Appalachians, which stretch from New England along the East Coast states to the south, can be demanding for hikers on parts of the famous Appalachian Trail. On the coast, beaches close to the metropolitan areas may be crowded, but further afield

George Washington crossing the Delaware, painting by Emanuel G. Leutze, 1851. The victory of Trenton was not the end of the Revolutionary War.

478

New England – rocky headlands with a picturesque lighthouse.

People all over the world recognize the New York skyline, the 'city that never sleeps'. The city has provided a better life for many an immigrant, but is also the scene of many a broken dream.

they are relatively untouched for miles and are a fantastic invitation to simply relax and unwind. Here you can also begin to imagine the courage the first settlers must have needed to set sail across the expansive ocean in their none-too-seaworthy sailing ships. The rich history can be seen at a number of places along the Atlantic Coast – from Plymouth Rock, where the Pilgrim Fathers landed, to Salem, where the witch hunts took place (described so exactingly by the writers Nathaniel Hawthorne in *The Scarlet Letter*, and Arthur Miller in *The Crucible*), on through to Boston, the starting point of the rebellion against England. The Declaration of Independence was proclaimed in Phila-

delphia, Pennsylvania, while Williamsburg presents itself as an historical picture book when actors in traditional costumes take to the streets to relive days of yore.

The eastern USA is also the political nerve center of the USA as a superpower: Washington, with the White House, Capitol Hill and the Pentagon, has formed the backdrop for the making and implementing of decisions with far-reaching historical impact. And then of course there is the city that, for many people, is the very embodiment of the 'American dream'. It's 'the city that never sleeps the 'Big Apple'. It's New York.

Nestled between the Hudson and East rivers, New York is a melting pot of folks with an

incredible diversity of languages, skin colours and religions, a shopping paradise with the most exclusive shops for the appropriate wallets, and a cultural center with the-

aters and museums of international standing. In short, it's a truly cosmopolitan city that captivates nearly every one of its millions of visitors and tourists from abroad.

The White House in Washington, seat of the US President and the nerve center of power. The original design by James Hoban remains intact.

1

The dream route travels through the forests of New England via Boston and New York to Washington. It returns to the coast via Virginia. All twelve of the East Coast states have one thing in common – a view of the endless ocean.

① **Portland** The route begins in the largest city in the state of Maine. Henry W Longfellow, a writer born here in 1807, often extolled Portland's attractive location on Casco Bay. Many parts of the city have been rebuilt after a series of disastrous fires. One of the few historical buildings left is the Wadsworth-Longfellow House, the oldest brick building in the city (1786). The Old Port, with its warehouses, new office buildings, and a variety of numerous shops and restaurants, is ideal for a relaxing stroll.

The route initially heads north via Rockland towards the Acadia National Park. Interstate 95 and Highway 1 run parallel to the coast and always offer wonderful views of the rocky cliffs and islands, scenic bays, and small port villages such as Bath, the 'City of Ships'.

② **Rockland** This city at the south-west end of Penobscot Bay calls itself the 'Lobster Capital of the World' and attracts visitors en masse at the beginning of August every year for its Maine Seafood Festival. Two lighthouses ensure a safe approach to Penobscot Bay: Rockland Lighthouse and Owls Head Lighthouse. Information about the lighthouses can be found at the Shore Village Museum. Highway 1 continues via the port town of Camden, especially popular with sailors and windsurfers, before passing through Belfast and Bucksport on the way to Ellsworth.

Travel Information

Route profile
Length: approx. 1,700 km (1,056 miles), excluding detours
Time required: at least 2 weeks
Start: Portland, Maine
End: Washington, DC
Route (main locations): Portland, Bar Harbor, Boston, Newport, New York, Philadelphia, Baltimore, Williamsburg, Cape Hatteras, Ocean City

Traffic information:
Drive on the right in the USA. There are numerous interstates, highways or freeways running parallel to one another along the North American coast and orientating yourself through them is not always easy. The typical speed limit (55–65 mph/ 90–105 km/h) can vary from state to state and breaches receive harsh penalties. Drink-driving is strictly prohibited.

Indian Summer:
A number of Internet sites in the New England states provide updates on the changing autumn colours during the so-called Indian Summer, which often occurs between early/mid September and the end of October:
www.gonewengland. about.com
www.foliagenetwork.com
www.state.me.us/doc/foliage

Information:
General
www.usa.gov
www.usembassy.gov
National parks
www.us-national-parks.net

the only port in New Hampshire, it is only 29 km (18 miles) to the next state, Massachusetts.

④ **Salem** This port town, founded in 1626 about 25 km (16 miles) north of Boston, achieved its tragic claim to fame when the devout Puritans of Salem staged a crazed witch hunt in 1692 where twenty people were brought to 'trial' and executed. The town has several museums dedicated to these woeful events – Salem Witch Museum, Salem Witch Village, Witch Dungeon Museum and the Witch House. The mansions, among the most attractive in the country, bear witness to the former wealth of this trading town. They also include the birthplace of author Nathaniel Hawthorne (1804–1864), and the House of the Seven Gables.

⑤ **Boston** (see p. 482). Via Interstate 3 it is 65 km (40 miles) to Plymouth which, due to its long coastline and more than 300 lakes and sprawling forests, is a populated commuter area.

⑥ **Plymouth** The port town is itself a milestone in American history – it was here that the *Mayflower* landed on 21 December 1620 after a perilous crossing, and it was here that the Pilgrim Fathers first set foot on American soil. A replica of the ship, the *Mayflower II*, is anchored in the port. The museum village Plimoth Plantation provides an interesting

Highway 3 takes you over a bridge to Mount Desert Island.

③ **Acadia National Park** Still outside of the National Park is the fishing village of Bar Harbor, once a popular summer resort among American millionaires. Today, stately mansions reminiscent of this era still line the coast. The National Park, set up in 1916, encompasses half of Mount Desert Island and also includes the smaller islands of Isle au Haut, Baker and Little Cranberry.

When timber companies began felling timber on the islands at the end of the 19th century, Bar Harbor's 'high society' bought the endangered land and donated it to the nation on condition that it be declared a national park.

The 500-m-high (1,640-ft) Cadillac Mountain is located within the park and attracts large numbers of visitors, especially during elusive Indian Summer days. The stark cliffs of Acadia National Park are constantly pounded by Atlantic surf. The

park coincidentally lies on a migratory bird route and can be explored on foot, by boat or by bicycle.

Back on the mainland, the return journey to Portland provides the opportunity to stop off at any of the quaint port towns on the coast road, stroll along one of the piers, or take a sailing trip on a windjammer. It is difficult to resist the fascination of the boats anchored so majestically in the ports, or a graceful cruise along the coast at full sail. From Portsmouth,

1 At the southern end of Mount Desert Island in the Acadia National Park is the Bass Harbor Lighthouse.

2 Today it is mainly yachts that are anchored in the Camden port in Maine. In centuries gone by the whalers made it a lively place.

Boston

The capital of Massachusetts resembles a giant open-air museum, a European enclave with historic buildings and winding streets amid a modern inner city with glazed office towers, world-renowned universities and leading research establishments.

It was in 1776 that the Declaration of Independence was first read out from the balcony of the Old State House in Boston, a red-brown brick building erected in 1712 as the seat of the English colonial government.

There has been a settlement on the hills around Massachusetts Bay from as far back as the 1720s. The settlement grew into an important port and became the economic and intellectual focus of the colony. The conflict with the colonial power exploded onto the public scene in 1770 when a number of citizens rebelled against the harsh tax policies of the British Crown and staged a boycott of all European goods. On 16 December 1773 the colonists met in the Faneuil Hall, where the "Boston Tea Party" was plotted: dressed as Native North Americans, they boarded three British ships and threw the tea bales into the sea. Paul Revere was to become a hero in the following war of independence that followed the evening of 18 April 1775

when he warned the citizens of the British arrival. The Paul Revere House, the oldest building in the city, has been converted into a museum, located a few blocks away from the Old North Church, which housed the two lanterns that gave Paul Revere warning of the approach of the British forces. The Freedom Trail begins at Boston Common. Today it is the city's green lung for people working downtown and for tourists.

The narrow Acorn Street in the romantic Beacon Hill area.

insight into the world of the first settlers. Not only does it have 17th century houses and tools on display, but actors also re-enact everyday life at the beginning of that century. The Pilgrim Hall Museum has artefacts from the Pilgrim Fathers on display, and Cole's Hill is the site of the graves of those who died in the first winter. From Cape Cod Bay the journey continues towards Hyannis on Cape Cod.

7 Hyannis The Steamship Authority ferries set off from Hyannis to Nantucket and Martha's Vineyard all year round.

8 Provincetown This little town at the northernmost end of the Cape Cod headland was founded by artists around 1900. Numerous writers and painters such as Edward Hop-per and Jackson Pollock lived there for a time. Today the town still retains its artistic flair. Spectacular Whale-watching trips by boat are also on offer in Provincetown.

Cape Cod's elbow shape dates back to the ice age. The retreating glaciers left behind some 365 lakes that are ideal for swimming, fishing and boating. The beautiful Atlantic beaches are extremely popular today, particularly thanks to their warm waters. If you have time you really ought to take a detour to the nearby islands of Martha's Vineyard and Nantucket.

From Falmouth to the south of the peninsula the route initially takes you along Buzzards Bay to Wareham. After crossing the Fall River, it then continues to Newport in Rhode Island (Highway 24).

9 Newport Founded in 1639, this town, which has 27,000 residents, is among the most beautiful places on the East Coast. Further along there are lovely views of the islands in the bay, with Providence lying at the northern end.

10 Providence The capital and economic center of Rhode Island was founded in 1636 by Roger Williams, whom the Puritans had driven out of Salem because of his reputedly heretical, i.e. cosmopolitan, views. The most impressive building in the town is the State House, built entirely of white marble and with the second-largest self-supporting dome in the world.

Coastal Road 1 leads through a series of quaint villages and along the lovely beaches to Mystic Seaport.

11 Mystic Seaport This reconstruction of a port village from the 19th century in the south-east of Connecticut has now become an open-air museum. Since the end of the 1920s around sixty historic buildings have been reconstructed as replicas of the originals. There are up to 430 historic ships anchored in the large museum port. One of the yards specializes in the repair of historical ships. The modern neighbouring town of Mystic is a small coastal resort with an aquarium worth seeing. A few kilometers west of Mystic is the port of New London, where the ferries to Long Island set out. Via Highway 25 along the coast of the Long Island Sound you can reach New York in around two hours.

12 New York (see pp. 484-485). If you want to discover the rural charm of the state of New York, then you are best advised to go for an outing to the Hudson River Valley, which stretches north from New York City to Albany.

13 Hudson Valley Pine forests sprinkled with lakes, farms and small villages are what characterize the landscape along the Hudson River. Given the wonderful views, it is not surprising that many of the well-to-do from New York have built themselves stately homes here with well-tended parks. 100 km (62 miles) north of Yonkers is New Paltz, founded by the Huguenots in 1692.

1 Brooklyn Bridge, linking Brooklyn and Manhattan since 1883.

2 Newport is home to magnificent mansions built at the close of the 19th century.

New York

New York City comprises Manhattan, Brooklyn, Queens, the Bronx and Staten Island. New York means the Statue of Liberty, the Empire State Building, the Chrysler Building, the Brooklyn Bridge, Broadway, Fifth Avenue, but also the ghettos of the now up-and-coming Bronx.

New York is sort of the 'capital of the Western world', a melting pot where immigrants from around the globe have gathered to become an intrinsic part of America's cultural fabric. Of course, many ethnic groups have retained their cultural identity by developing neighbourhoods such as Little Italy or Chinatown, just as they would in Palermo or Beijing. Indeed, New York gladly retreats into its 'villages', creating its own worlds in neighbourhoods such as Tribeca, Soho, Chelsea and Greenwich Village. Yet the chaos continues in Midtown and on the wide avenues: the wailing of police sirens, the honking horns of taxis and the pounding of jackham-

mers. The office towers rise up into the clouds. Be sure to check out Broadway, from the Battery in southern Manhattan as far as Yonkers and Albany in Upstate New York. It is the city's lifeline – in the financial district in the south and especially in the theater neighbourhood around Times Square.

One of the most famous buildings in the world, the Empire State Building (1929–1931), was built in art deco style and is 381 m (1,257 ft) high – with the aerial mast, 448 m (1,588 ft.).

Central Park, the green oasis in the mega metropolis, stretches from

59th to 110th Street over an area of 340 ha (840 acres). People of all kinds, leisure joggers, ball-playing teenagers, picnicking families and disabled variety artists make for interesting encounters.

The Rockefeller Center (1930–1940) is a giant complex with offices, television studios, restaurants and shops. Concerts and other events take place in the Radio City Music Hall (1930). The neo-Gothic St Patrick's Cathedral (1858–1887) is a replica of the cathedral in Cologne. The main train station, opened in 1913 as Grand Central Station after several years under construction,

was built in the beaux arts style and decorated with baroque and Renaissance elements. An artificial sky sprinkled with 2,500 stars stretches over the somewhat ostentatious main hall.

Once completed, the Chrysler Building (1930) was the highest building in the world for just one year. Specific aspects resemble the radiator grilles of the Chrysler cars of that period. The United Nations building (1949–53) looks over the East River. A number of works of art are on display in the entrance hall.

The financial district, Wall Street, takes its name from a solid protective wall intended to protect the Dutch Nieuw Amsterdam from enemies such as the English and the Native North Americans.

The Brooklyn Bridge is the most recognizable bridge in the Big Apple. Opened in May 1883 after sixteen years under construction, it is 1,052 m long (1,180 yds), excluding the access roads.

The Statue of Liberty stands out on Liberty Island (formerly Bedloe's Island), a small rock between Manhattan and Staten Island. In her right hand she holds a torch, in the left the Declaration of Independence. The statue became a symbol of freedom for immigrants on the approaching ships. The 'path to freedom' used to lead through Ellis Island where every immigrant was registered between 1892 and 1917. In the museum you trace the process from the luggage room to the Great Hall where checks were carried out.

With its winding, tree-lined streets, the famous artists' neighbourhood of Greenwich Village between 12th St, Houston St, Lafayette St and the Hudson River is reminiscent of the 'Old Europe' that early immigrants left behind. The Metropolitan Opera, or the 'Met', one of the most well-known opera houses in the world, is part of the Lincoln Center, a giant complex of theaters and concert halls. The Guggenheim Museum, built by architect Frank Lloyd Wright, was disparagingly referred to as the 'snail building' but there is no dispute over its art treasures. The new Museum of Modern Art (MoMa) complex was designed by the Japanese architect, Yoshio Taniguchi, and takes up an entire city block. Its galleries house the world's largest collection of valuable paintings from the late 19th century to the present.

View over night-lit Manhattan from the north.

The next section of the river is lined with historically significant properties. Springwood (Franklin D. Roosevelt Historic Site), the property where the later US President was born and grew up, is located there. Even more stately is the Vanderbilt National Historic Site, the palace built by the industrialist Frederick W. Vanderbilt in 1890 in the style of the Italian Renaissance. The trip along the Hudson Valley ends in Kingston, the gateway to the Catskills, an important recreational area for New Yorkers.

⑭ Philadelphia From the outskirts of New York the route continues towards Philadelphia, Pennsylvania. Up until the completion of the various government buildings in Washington, Congress was housed in the Congress Hall of this, the most historically significant city in the USA. The center of the city is the Independence National Historical Park, with Independence Hall where the representatives of the thirteen colonies signed the Declaration of Independence on 4 July 1776. The Liberty Bell, which was rung to mark the occasion, is housed in the Liberty Bell Pavilion. Numerous significant museums line the Benjamin Franklin

Parkway, including the Philadelphia Museum of Art, the Rodin Museum and the Franklin Institute Science Museum.
From here it is around 100 km (62 miles) along Highway 30 to Atlantic City, the 'Las Vegas of the East'. Back on Interstate 95, Baltimore in the state of Maryland is the next stop.

⑮ Baltimore This small city only has a few historic buildings left to show for itself after a large majority of them were destroyed by fire in 1904. Little Italy still gives some impression of how the city must have looked in the past. The renovated port area (Harbor Place) has become an attractive area again since the 1970s. Not to be missed are the National Aquarium, 19th-century Fort Henry and the *Constellation* in the docks, a triple-mast sailing ship

built in 1854. The outskirts of Washington extend far into surrounding Maryland and Virginia, and it is therefore not long before you encounter the first suburbs of the capital city 50 km (31 miles) away.

⑯ Washington (see p. 487). In Washington you leave the coast for a short while and travel along the Manassas (Highway 29) and Warrenton (Highway 211) towards Washington, Virginia. Shortly before you enter town, Highway 522 branches off to Front Royal. The broad cave complex, Skyline Caverns, near Front Royal lies at the edge of the Shenandoah National Park.

⑰ Shenandoah National Park You should plan five hours for the 170-km-long (106-mile) Skyline Drive through the national park because it is

worth making multiple stops at the viewing points to take a look at the Shenandoah Valley. The park covers a particularly scenic part of the Appalachians with the panoramic route ending in Waynesboro. From there it is another 60 km (37 miles) to Monticello.

⑱ Monticello This property, which once belonged to Thomas Jefferson (1743–1826), is located to the east of Charlottesville. Jefferson designed the building for the Monticello plantation in Palladian style. Construction began in 1770. After 100 km (62 miles) on

1 The Philadelphia skyline along the Delaware River at twilight.

2 Shenandoah National Park in Virginia includes the most beautiful sections of the Blue Ridge Mountains.

Washington

Washington, DC is the center of Western democracy and the seat of the US President, a focal point of political power.

The capital of the United States derives its importance from its central geographic location between the northern and southern regions of the original Thirteen Colonies – and also its proximity to Mount Vernon, home of first US President George Washington. Many of the city's buildings, including the Capitol Building, were set on fire during the war of 1812, and the city's present-day appearance is the result of a 'beautification plan' implemented at the end of the 19th century. Today DC is one of the most attractive travel destinations in the USA.

The Capitol sits on top of Capitol Hill opposite the Supreme Court and the Library of Congress. The White House has been the office and residence of the US President since 1800. The National Mall, a mile-long boulevard between the Capitol and the Washington Monument, is renowned for its cultural institutions. Numerous first-class museums such as the National Museum of Natural History and the National Air & Space Museum attract visitors all year round.

The Washington Monument, a 170-m-high (560-ft) obelisk made of granite and marble, commemorates the first president of the USA. The extermination of the Jews in World War II is documented in the United States Holocaust Memorial Museum. The Jefferon memorial is a circular colonnade. The Americans who fell in Vietnam are commemorated at the Vietnam Veterans Memorial.

The Capitol, built by Pierre Charles L'Enfant, has been the seat of the Senate since 1800.

Interstate 64 you reach Richmond, the capital of Virginia.

19 Richmond The State Capitol on Capitol Square, designed by Thomas Jefferson, is considered to be the first neoclassical building in the USA. Here you will find the only statue for which George Washington modelled in person. The Canal Walk on the northern bank of the James River is ideal for a leisurely stroll. With its Victorian houses the city has retained the flair of the Old South.

20 Williamsburg During the 18th century the town was the capital of Virginia. 'Colonial Williamsburg', as the town calls itself, is home to eighty-eight buildings restored as facsimiles of the originals. Parks in the style of the 18th century complete the scene. Highway 158 leads you to Point Harbor via Hampton, Norfolk and Chesapeake (Highway 64). The port town of Albermarle Sound is the gateway to the Cape Hatteras National Seashore. The nearby Wright Brothers National Monument commemorates the Wright Brothers' attempted flights in 1903.

21 Cape Hatteras National Seashore The 210-km-long (130-mile) group of islands off the east coast of North Carolina is known as the Outer Banks. The only road that goes there is the 150-km-long (93-mile) Highway 12, which connects the islands of Hatteras and Roanoke with each other.

The Outer Banks were once frequently targeted by pirates, and countless ships have been wrecked along the rocky coast. These days the often empty beaches, picturesque lighthouses and other monuments attract nature lovers, recreational sports enthusiasts and even the odd surfer. The majority of the islands are protected areas within the Cape Hatteras and Cape Lookout National Seashores.

On the return journey to Washington, DC take Highway 13 after leaving Chesapeake. At Salisbury turn off towards Ocean City (Highway 50) via Highway 611 and the bridge over Sinepuxent Bay. There you come to Assateague Island.

22 Assateague Island National Seashore Due to its exposure to wind and waves, this

island is constantly changing shape. A diverse animal and plant world braves the raw climate here. From the only small road on the island you can even see herds of wild horses roaming this narrow spit of windswept dunes and grass.

The return to Washington takes you via Highway 50. A bridge links the eastern side of Chesapeake Bay with quaint Annapolis, Maryland. Picturesque fishing villages, quaint historic towns and scenic

bathing spots line the shores of the bay. The founding of Annapolis, the capital of the state of Maryland, dates back to 1649. From Annapolis you are just a few kilometers away from Washington DC.

1 Not far from the busy American capital there are idyllic spots to be found on Chesapeake Bay.

2 The lighthouse at Cape Hatteras is popular with photographers.

Nantucket Island Prosperity here came in the 18th and 19th centuries from whale hunting, as documented in the Whaling Museum.

Boston The colonial revolt against the English hegemony began with the 'Boston Tea Party'. You still encounter traces of history in many of Boston's neighbourhoods. It is also home to important research institutions and universities such as Harvard University and MIT.

New York The heart of this megacity beats loudly in places like Times Square. Every year thousands of people gather here on New Year's Eve to ring in the new year together. Here, in the middle of downtown Manhattan, the impressive skyscrapers rise up into the clouds.

Philadelphia This is where the Declaration of Independence was signed and the constitution drawn up. Today the metropolis is an important commercial center.

Washington The main American political nerve centers are in DC: the White House, the Capitol and the Pentagon, seat of the Dept of Defense.

Shenandoah National Park This beautiful park contains part of the Appalachian Trail, which stretches from Maine to Georgia.

Monticello This classic Palladian mansion was once the home of Thomas Jefferson, the third US President.

Richmond This defiant granite building was constructed in 1894 and was for a long time the city hall in Virginia's capital.

Cape Lookout The lighthouse at Cape Lookout, built in 1859, rises above the shallows of Core Sound. It is characterized by its unusual decoration – black stripes on a white background.

Acadia National Park Mount Desert Island, with its impressive craggy coast, is home to majestic Cadillac Mountain, also part of this striking national park.

Bath The Maine Maritime Museum and the Bath Iron Works document the history of shipping and shipbuilding in the area.

Martha's Vineyard This is a popular getaway among East Coast urbanites and plays host to the summer homes of the elite.

Atlantic City This East Coast counterpart to Las Vegas attracts visitors with the promise of big winnings and glamorous shows. The boardwalk along the Atlantic is especially scenic.

Cape Hatteras Lighthouse The highest lighthouse in the USA has been warning ships of the shallows off Cape Hatteras.

Williamsburg The many old buildings in Williamsburg, such as the Governor's Palace, bring the colonial history of this coastal town back to life.

Mexico, Guatemala and Belize

Through the Kingdom of the Maya

Culture and beaches all in one – a journey through the Yucatán Peninsula. In the heartland of the Mayan region you can marvel at both ancient pyramids and Spanish-colonial-style baroque towns, while the white sand beaches of the Caribbean offer idyllic relaxation after your adventures.

The name of the peninsula separating the Caribbean Sea from the Gulf of Mexico originally arose from a misunderstanding. When the Spanish conquistadors first set foot on the peninsula at the start of the 16th century they addressed the indigenous people in Spanish. The Maya answered in their language: 'Ma c'ubab than', meaning 'We do not understand your words'. This later became Yucatán.

Three countries lay claim to the Yucatán Peninsula: the north and west belong to Mexico, the south-east coast and Barrier Reef to Belize, and the mountainous south-east to Guatemala. Detours from the route also take you to the most significant ruins in Honduras – Copán.
When the conquistadors arrived in Mexico they discovered a uniquely advanced civilization. The Maya had both a precise calendar and their own alpha-

bet. Their massive constructions – pyramids, palaces, places of worship – are all the more astounding given that the Maya had neither the wheel as a means of transport nor iron, metal implements, winches, pulleys, ploughs, or pack or

Mexico: a well-earned siesta in the afternoon.

draught animals. Mayan ruins are often located in the midst of tropical rainforests, are often overgrown and have only been partly uncovered. Sites that are easily accessible for tourists along the route we suggest here are Chichén Itzá, Tulum, Tikal, Edzná and Uxmal. The city of San Cristóbal de las Casas and the surrounding Indian villages in the south-west of the peninsula, Chiapas (Mexico), provide wonderful insight into the present-day life of the descendants of the Maya.
The Indian population of Mexico and Belize makes up around one-tenth of the overall population of each country. In Guatemala, however, half of all

San Miguel is the largest town on the holiday island of Cozumel off the coast of Cancún.

High above the Caribbean Sea sits Tulum, meaning 'fortress', a mighty wall that once encircled the Mayan town. The original Mayan name was Zama, meaning 'City of Dawn'.

citizens are of Indian origin. In Mexico and Guatemala numerous Mayan languages are also still spoken. The Spanish who first landed on the Yucatán Peninsula in 1517 greatly underestimated the scale of Mayan civilization and unfortunately destroyed a large part of their physical culture and records. In their place rose a series of colonial cities from the ruins of older Mayan settlements. The Spanish legacy includes baroque monasteries, cathedrals, palaces and large town plazas. The oldest cathedral in the Americas is in Mérida (1560), Campeche was once the most important port on the Yucatán Peninsula for goods headed to Europe, and there are important monasteries dating back to the 17th and 18th centuries in Antigua,

Guatemala. The route we recommend includes some of the most scenic nature reserves in Central America. On the northeast coast is the Sian Ka'an biosphere reserve (a UNESCO World Heritage Site) covering 4,500 ha (11,120 acres) of jungle and swamp as well as a 100-km-long (62-mile) coral reef. Belize is home to the Blue Hole National Park and the 300-km-long (186-mile) Belize Barrier Reef (also a UNESCO World Heritage Site). Guatemala is home to the Sierra de Las Minas biosphere reserve. Wild cocoa trees can still be found in the north-east of the peninsula and also in the mountainous regions of the south. Today the east coast, known as the 'Mayan Riviera', is a popular holiday destination – white sand beaches and the splendid

reef between Cancún in the north and Tulum Playa in the south provide ideal conditions for both snorkelling and diving. Yet swimming, diving, snorkelling and relaxing on the 'Mayan Riviera' are just some of the many options for an active holi-

day on the Yucatán Peninsula. If you go for a hike through the often still pristine tropical rainforests of the national parks and nature reserves in the interior of the peninsula, you will discover an unparalleled wealth of flora and fauna.

'The Old Man from Copán' sculpture in the ruined Mayan town of Copán in the Honduran forest.

The Yucatán tour goes through Mexico, Guatemala and Belize, with a detour to the ruins of Copán in Honduras. From the idyllic Caribbean beaches you head to the mountainous regions of Guatemala before visiting the Petén rainforest and the magnificent coast of Belize then heading back to the start.

1 **Cancún** The journey across the Yucatán Peninsula begins in Cancún on the north-east coast. The town's name derives from the name of the former Mayan settlement 'Can-Cune' ('End of the Rainbow'). Until the beginning of the 1960s Cancún was a tiny fishing village with barely 100 residents. The Mexican government then decided to create an international seaside resort, a project that met with massive success. Today more than 2.5 million tourists visit this town of 300,000 residents. South of the town the MEX 180 highway turns towards Mérida. The turn-off to the most architecturally significant Mayan site on the peninsula, Chichén Itzá, is well signposted, 40 km (25 miles) beyond Valladolid.

2 **Chichén Itzá** The largest and best preserved pre-Columbian ruins on the Yucatán Peninsula represented an important economic, political and religious center between the years 400 and 1260, with a population of about 35,000 people. The best-known building at the site is El Castillo, a 24-m-high (79-ft) pyramid. Other buildings worth seeing are the Templo de los Guerreros, the observatory (Caracol) and the Cenote de los Sacrificios, as well as the 168-m-long (180-yd) play-

ing field, the largest of its kind in the whole of Mesoamerica. Four 45° angle steps lead up to the El Castillo platform from where you will have a breathtaking view of the entire site.

3 **Mérida** At the turn of the 19th century, the capital of the Federal state of Yucatán was a center for the cultivation and production of sisal, a type of hemp. Magnificent town villas, spacious plazas and lovely parks are reminiscent of the town's heyday. Today it is an important industrial and commercial center. At Uman, 20 km (12 miles) south of the town, a road branches off from the MEX 180 to the Parque Natural Rio Celestún.

4 **Parque Natural Rio Celestún Nature Park** It is about 70 km (43 miles) to the small fishing village of Celestún

Travel Information

Route profile
Length: approx. 2,800 km (1,740 miles), excluding detours
Time required: min. 4 weeks
Start and end: Cancún
Route (main locations): Mérida, Campeche, San Cristóbal de las Casas, Antigua, Ciudad de Guatemala, Quiriguá, Tikal, Belmopan, Belize City, Chetumal, Tulum

Traffic information:
Drive on the right on this trip. Most of the roads in Mexico are decent. In Guatemala expect bad roads, apart from the Pan-American Highway and the main roads – best to travel by day. The roads in Belize are in relatively good condition. Caution during flooding in the rainy season!

Information:
Mexico:
www.mexicotravel101.com
Guatemala:
www.enjoyguatemala.com
Belize:
www.travelbelize.org

on the Bahia de Campeche coast. In addition to the white, sandy beaches, the waterfowl living here are the main attraction. Fishermen offer boat trips through the mangroves and to a petrified forest on the Isla de Pájaros. The same route takes you back towards the MEX 180. In Uman the MEX 261 branches

off towards Muna and Uxmal (60 km/37 miles).

⑤ Uxmal Archaeologists presume that the first stages of construction took place in the year AD 1. The majority of the buildings, however, date back to between the 7th and 10th centuries when parts of the peninsula were ruled from Uxmal. Uxmal is the best-known example of the Puuc civilization, represented by elongated buildings with attractive courtyards, facades decorated with stone mosaics and the conspicuous lack of cenotes (natural limestone pools) typical of this style. Indeed, it was the ability to build artificial cisterns that enabled the Mayans to settle in this arid region.

Opposite the entrance to Uxmal stands the 35-m (115-ft) 'Fortune Teller's Pyramid', with its oval foundation, dating from the 6th–10th centuries. The steep, 60° staircase up the pyramid has a safety chain for visitors to hold when climbing. From Muna it is then around 40 km (25 miles) to the MEX 180.

⑥ Campeche During the colonial era Campeche became an important port from which the Spanish shipped wood and other valuable raw materials back to Europe. The mighty city wall was reinforced with eight bastions (baluartes) to protect it from constant pirate attacks. From this significant port town on the peninsula we then follow the MEX 180S to Champotón, where we turn onto the MEX 261 towards Francisco Escárcega.

⑦ Calakmul The detour to Calakmul in the Reserva de la Biósfera Calakmul is around 150 km (93 miles). The reserve protects the largest continuous tropical rainforest area in Mexico and is also host to a number of important Mayan sites – Balamkú, Becán, Xpujil and Calakmul. After around 110 km (68 miles), at Conhuas, a road turns off the two-lane MEX 186 south towards Calakmul. During the rainy season the 60-km (37-mile) surfaced road, first built in 1993, is often passable only with four-wheel-drive vehicles.

Although it has not been extensively researched to date, this sprawling settlement, which was continuously inhabited from 500 to 1521, is one of the most important examples of a classic Mayan town and was declared a UNESCO World Heritage Site in 2002. Until the year 1000 Calakmul was the capital of a former kingdom. Thereafter it served merely as a cere-

monial center. The 50-m (164-ft) pyramid is the highest in Mexico and from the top is a breathtaking view of these overgrown rainforest ruins. There are around 100 pillars spread around the site, but more valuable archaeological treasures such as the priceless jade masks have been moved to the museum in Campeche.

Back in Francisco Escárcega take the MEX 186 to Palenque.

⑧ Palenque These ruins, covering an area of 6 sq km (4 sq mi), are about 12 km (7.5 miles) outside of town and surrounded by the last sicable area of rainforest on the peninsula. The town, which must have been an important trading center in the region, experienced its heyday between 600 and 800.

One important Mayan ruler is still known by name – Pacal the Great, whose reign coincided with one of the most splendid eras in Mayan history. Today only part of the site is accessible to visitors. Try to plan a whole day for it. Inside the most famous temple, the 20-m (66-ft) Templo de las Inscripciones (Temple of the Inscriptions), sixty steps lead 25 m (83 ft) down into the crypt. Similar to the Egyptian pyramids, the step pyramids of Palenque were also the tombs of rulers. The most valuable possessions are now on dis-

1 Uxmal: The Palacio del Gobernador from the 9th–10th century is considered a highlight of Puuc architecture.

2 Chichén Itzá: The Warriors' Temple is lined on two sides by '1,000 pillars' that originally supported a roof.

3 Chichén Itzá: The Warriors' Temple with Chac Mool in the foreground.

play in the Museo Nacional de Antropologica in Ciudad de Mexico. Opposite the Temple of the Inscriptions is the El Palacio, where the royal family lived, while other accessible temples are located on the other side of the Otulum River. One of the most important discoverers of ancient Mexican culture was the American John Lloyd Stephens, who visited the Yucatán between 1839 and 1841. According to his report, when Stephens first visited Palenque, 'a single Indian footpath' led to the archaeological site. He travelled all over the Yucatán with English draughtsman and architect Frederick Catherwood. Stephens recorded his impressions in travel journals while Catherwood captured his in drawings. On the way from Palenque to San Cristóbal de las Casas it is worth making a stop at the Agua Azul National Park. The more than 500 waterfalls are especially worthy of their name, 'blue water', during the dry period between April and May. They vary in height from 3 m (10 ft) to an impressive 50 m (164 ft). Beyond Palenque the road climbs gradually into the mountainous area of Montañas del Norte de Chiapas.

⑨ San Cristóbal de las Casas
This lovely little town at an altitude of 2,100 m (6,890 ft) carries the name of the Spanish Bishop of Chiapas, who was especially committed to the interests of the indigenous peoples. Particularly noticeable are the low-slung buildings in the town, a result of constant fear of earthquakes.

San Cristóbal is the center of one of Mexico's important cocoa-growing areas. The Mayans were already growing the wild plant as a monocrop before the arrival of the Europeans, and even used slave labour to work on their plantations. The striking terrace-like fields on these steep slopes (sometimes at an angle of 45°) date all the way back to the Mayans who built rows of stones running diagonally over the slope in order to fashion fields of up to 50 by 70 m (164 by 230 ft). The fields were enclosed by walls measuring over 1.5 m (5 ft) high.

Many visitors take trips from San Cristóbal into the outlying villages of the Chamula Indians, for example to San Júan Chamula (11 km/7 miles), or to Zinacantán, where the Tzotzil Indians live (8 km/5 miles).

Another worthwhile excursion from San Cristóbal is to Cañon El Sumidero, with fantastic views of gloriously coloured craggy cliffs that tower to heights of 1,000 m (3,281 ft). With a bit of luck you might even see crocodiles during a boat trip on the river.

From San Cristóbal to Ciudad de Guatemala the route follows the Pan-American Highway, known as the CA1 after the border. Around 85 km (53 miles) south-

12 Antigua This village in Panchoytal is situated in a tectonically active region at the foot of three live volcanoes – Agua (3,766 m/12,356 ft), Fuego (3,763 m/12,346 ft) and Acatenango (3,975 m/13,042 ft). In 1541, mud-slides from Agua destroyed the town of Ciudad de Santiago de los Caballeros founded by the Spanish in 1527, but it was rebuilt further north in 1543. Numerous religious orders settled in this Central American capital where monasteries, schools and churches were erected.

However, only parts of the Catedral de Santiago (1545) with its five naves have survived the earthquakes of the subsequent centuries. Nuestra Señora la Merced is one of the most attractive examples of the Churrigueresque style. Together with the awe-inspiring Palacio de los Capitanes Generales and the mighty Palacio del Ayuntamiento, the Capuchin monastery Las Capuchinas is an impressive example of Spanish colonial architecture.

The town was destroyed by strong earthquakes in 1717 and 1773, but the Spanish rebuilt it as La Nueva Guatemala and it later became present-day Ciudad de Guatemala. The previous capital was then simply called Antigua.

In 1979 the old city, which in the 18th century was one of the most beautiful baroque ensembles of the Spanish colonial era, and which still retains a great deal of flair today, was declared a UNESCO World Heritage Site.

1 Cleared ruins in the north of the Palenque archaeological site.

2 In Palenque, nine terraces lead up to the Temple of the Inscriptions.

3 One of the many waterfalls in the Agua Azul National Park.

east of San Cristóbal is Comitán de Dominquez. From there you can take an excursion to the Mayan site of Chinkultic.

You will reach the border at Paso Hondo after another 80 km (50 miles). On the Guatemalan side a mountain road leads via La Mesilla through the Sierra de los Cuchumatanes to Huehuetenango. The roads in the rugged mountainous regions of Guatemala are generally in bad condition and are often full of potholes. Turning off at Los Encuentros, Lago de Atitlan is one of the featured sights in these highlands.

10 Lago de Atitlan Three volcanoes – San Pedro (3,029 m/9,938 ft), Atitlan (3,535 m/11,598) and Toliman (3,158 m/10,361 ft) – are reflected in the water of this alpine lake, which lies at 1,560 m (5,118 ft). Alexander von Humboldt wrote of the beauty of this 130-sq-km (81-sq-mi) azure blue lake, describing it as 'the most beautiful lake in the world'. There are fourteen Indian villages located around the lake, some of which already existed prior to the arrival of the Spanish conquistadors.

Today the residents are farmers or make a living from selling traditional handicrafts. The famous Friday market in Sololá, high above the lake on the northern shore, is even frequented by hordes of Indians from the surrounding areas. The largest settlement is Santiago Atitlan at the southern end of the lake. In 1955 the government declared the lake and surrounding mountains a national park. At Los Encuentros a narrow road turns off towards Chichicastenango, 20 km (12 miles) further north

11 Chichicastenango This town, lying at an altitude of 1,965 m (6,447 ft) is characterized by its classic white colonial architecture. In the pre-colonial era the town was an important Mayan trading center. Markets are the main attraction and draw residents from the surrounding areas in their colourful traditional costumes, who come to sell their textiles and carvings. In 1540 a Spaniard erected the oldest building in the town on the ruins of a Mayan temple, the Santo-Tomás church. Each of the eighteen roads leading to it represents a month in the Mayan calendar, which comprised 18 months each with 20 days.

13 Ciudad de Guatemala The rebuilding of the residential town for the Spanish governor took place at a safer distance of 45 km (30 miles). Today, La Nueva Guatemala de la Asunción is still the economic and political center of Guatemala. It lies at 1,480 m (4,856 ft) and is the seat of several universities. The main sightseeing attractions include the cathedral (1782–1809), the National Palace (1939–1943) and the Archaeological Museum. Another important Mayan site is located in Tazumal, not far from Santa Ana in El Salvador, roughly 200 km (124 miles) away.

From the capital it is about 150 km (93 miles) on the CA9 to Rio Hondo where the asphalt CA10 takes you via Zacapa, Chiguimula and Vado Hondo to the border post at El Florido. About 12 km (7.5 miles) beyond the Guatemala-Honduras border is Copán. On the return journey along the same road, about 70 km (43 miles) beyond Rio Hondo, you reach another UNESCO World Heritage Site – the ruins of Quiriguá.

14 Quiriguá This Mayan town on the lower Rio Motagua saw its heyday between 500 and 800. Its layout is very similar to that of Copá, only 50 km (31 miles) away. Explorer John Lloyd Stephens discovered Quiriguá in 1840. Today the archaeological site at the edge of the Sierra del Espiritu Santo is still surrounded by thick jungle, and this is a major part of its attraction. The large mythical creatures carved in stone and the pillars measuring over 10 m (33 ft) in height, which constitute a high point of Mayan sculpture, are among the special attractions here. The highest pillar, E, is 10.5 m (34 ft) high and weighs 65 tonnes (71.5 tons).

Approximately 45 km (28 miles) beyond Quiriguá you leave the

1

2

CA9 and turn to the north-west towards Lago de Izabal. The lake, 590 sq km (367 sq mi) in size, is surrounded by dense rainforest. Between the largest lake in Guatemala and the Rio Dulce, lined by rainforest, is the Spanish Fort Castillo de San Felipe. The fortress was originally constructed in 1595 to defend the arsenals on the eastern shore of the lake from the repeated attacks of determined pirates plying the broad river.

The national road CA13 now crosses the foothills of the Sierra de Santa Cruz and continues via Semox into the lowlands of Petén. The small town of Flores on an island in Lago Petén Itzá

is a good starting point for a visit to Tikal.

15 Tikal National Park This 576-sq-km (358-sq-mi) national park is surrounded by dense forest and includes one of the most important Mayan sites on the peninsula. Together, the park and rainforest, one of the largest continuous forests in Central America with over 2,000 plant varieties, has been declared a UNESCO World Heritage Site. Between 600 BC and AD 900 as many as 55,000 people lived in Tikal. Today, many of the 4,000 temples, palaces, houses and playing fields are buried under the encroaching forest.

A climb up one of the pyramids, the most important of which are on the Gran Plaza, gives visitors an impressive view of the 16-sq-km (10-sq-mi) Tikal National Park. The Jaguar Temple, some 45 m (148 ft) high, houses a burial chamber where the ruler Ah Cacao lies at rest.

From Flores it is about 100 km (62 miles) to the border with Belize, and from there it is another 50 km (31 miles) to Belmopan, which has been the capital of Belize since 1970.

16 Guanacaste National Park 3 km (2 miles) north of Belmopan is the 20-ha (49-acre) national park named after the large

3

Blue Hole National Park

⑰ Blue Hole National Park
This 2.3-ha (5.7-acre) national park is a popular leisure area for the residents of Belmopan. Large areas of the park contain cave formations and are covered by dense rainforest. Sightseeing attractions include the 33-m (108-ft) collapsed crater that feeds a tributary of the Sibun River. It flows briefly above ground before disappearing into an extensive underground cave system. The 7.5-m (25-ft) 'blue hole' takes its name from its sapphire blue colour. Also within the park is St Herman's Cave, also used by the Mayans as evidenced by the ceramics, spears and torches that have been found inside.

⑱ Belize City Until 1970, Belize City was the capital of the former British Honduras. Today it is still the largest city in the country as well as an important seaport. St John Cathedral, the oldest Anglican cathedral in Central America, was built in 1812 from bricks that sailing ships from Europe had used as ballast. The British Governor lived at Government House starting in 1814 (today it is the House of Culture museum). The city is an ideal base for excursions to the Belize Barrier Reef, a renowned diving paradise.

⑲ Belize Barrier Reef System
The 300-km (186-mile) Barrier Reef is one of the longest in the northern hemisphere. The many islands and cays off the coast are covered with mangroves and palms. The cays that are within reach include Ambergris Cay some 58 km (36 miles) north of Belize City as well as the Turneffe Islands. The reef's main attraction is its underwater world, with visibility of up to 30 m (98 ft), the bird reserve, Half Moon Cay and the Blue Hole, a massive collapsed cave.

1 The Toliman and San Pedro volcanoes form an impressive backdrop to Lago de Atitlan in the Guatemalan highlands.

2 Universidad de San Carlos (1763) in Antigua.

3 Relief of a high priest in the Quiriguá Archaeological Park, also home to the tallest Mayan pillars.

Guanacaste tree (Tubroos). It grows in the south of the park and is one of the largest tree types in Central America. The many tree species in the park also include mahogany, the national tree of Belize. South of Belmopan is the Blue Hole National Park, on the road to Dangriga.

20 Altun Ha The ruins of Altun Ha are close to the village of Rockstone Pond. It is postulated that this Mayan ceremonial center was originally settled over 2,000 years ago. The Mayans built up much of their trading around Altun Ha. The most valuable finds from Altun Ha include a jade head of the Mayan Sun god that weighs 4.5 kg (9.9 lbs). Via Orange Walk the road continues through the lowlands of Belize to the Mexican port town of Chetumal and along the second largest lake in Mexico, Laguna de Bacalar (MEX 307), to Felipe Carrillo Puerto. Here an access road branches off to the Sian Ka'an biosphere reserve.

21 Tulum This ancient Mayan town is a popular destination on the peninsula, primarily due to its spectacular location on a cliff overlooking the sea. The

conquistadors were impressed by its imposing and protective walls. Five narrow gates opened the way into town. Outside the walls there were two ancient Mayan temple sites north of town. Tulum has always had a safe port from which pilgrims in the pre-Columbian era once travelled to the island of Cozumel to honour the Moon god Ixchel with sacrifices. After 1540 Tulum was engulfed by tropical vegetation and forgotten until 1840. From Tulum there is a road leading to the small fishing village of Punta Allen in the Reserva de la Biósfera Sian Ka'an. In the forest 48 km (30 miles) north-west of Tulum you can visit another ruins complex – Cobá.

22 Cobá You can reach the site of the ruins on the well-made road in half an hour. US archaeologists began the first

excavations of the complex (210 sq km/130 sq mi) in the 1920s, and further excavation projects that are still going on today began in the 1970s. Cobá also has a pyramid. From the top you can see smaller pyramids, temples, a series of procession streets, a playing field, pillars with life-size images of kings and queens, and of course dense forest. In Cobá you can see peccaris (wild pigs), iguanas, tortoises and the colourful toucan.

The 130-km (81-mile) stretch of coast between Tulum and Cancún is also known as the 'Mayan Riviera'. Small villages and bays such as Puerto Morelos provide swimming and diving opportunities for water enthusiasts. The seaside resort of Playa del Carmen is only a few kilometers south of the more upmarket Cancún, which is the start and end point of

this round trip through the Yucatán Peninsulua.

1 Belize's main attraction is the Barrier Reef. At just less than 300 km (186 miles) in length, it is the longest barrier reef in the western hemisphere. Divers will find unique coral, good visibility and more than 350 types of fish. Hundreds of small islands (cays) are scattered along the length of the reef.

2 Guanacaste National Park: The jaguar is the most well-known wild cat on the Yucatán Peninsula.

3 Tikal: Temple 1 is one of the most attractive pyramid tombs of the late classic Mayan period. It rises about 45 m (148 ft) above the central square. Around 55,000 people lived here in the town's heyday. It was abandoned in the 10th or 11th century.

Mérida The 'white town' was founded in the 16th century. At its center are the Montejo Palast and the cathedral, one of the first sacral buildings in Mexico.

Chichén Itzá The highlights of the complex in the northern part of the Yucatán Peninsula are the Kukulcán and El Castillo pyramids, probably constructed by the Mayas and the Tolteken. Close by is a deep cenote, an underground limestone well from which water rises and forms a pool.

Cancún With its magnificent beaches and tropical climate the former fishing village in the north-east of the Yucatán has become Mexico's most popular holiday destination. With 20,000 beds and night entertainment options, more than 2.5 million tourists visit the giant hotel town each year.

Uxmal The 'Fortune Teller's Pyramid' is a highlight of Mayan architecture. The name dates back to the Spanish era but does not have anything to do with the actual purpose of the construction.

Tulum Situated on a cliff over the Caribbean Sea south of Cancún, the ruins of this Mayan town are easily accessible for even the laziest of beachcombers.

Palenque This archaeological site in the middle of the rainforest is among the most attractive in Mexico. Many of the buildings date from the reign of King Pacal and his son, Chan Balum.

Altun Ha The largest archaeological site in Belize is made up of two plazas with temple and residential complexes. Important jade artefacts have been found here, including a magnificent axe.

Lago de Atitlan This lake in the highlands of Guatemala (1,560 m/5,118 ft) is tucked between the San Pedro, Atitlan and Toliman volcanoes.

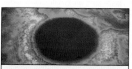

The Blue Hole In the Lighthouse Reef Atoll off the coast of Belize is one of the most beautiful coral reefs in the world. The Blue Hole has a diameter of 300 m (984 ft) and a depth of 125 m (410 ft).

Antigua The Spanish Governor used to rule Central America from this Guatemalan town. A number of baroque churches and palaces from the Spanish colonial era survived the earthquakes of 1717 and 1773, and are definitely worth seeing.

Tazumal Close to Santa Ana in El Salvador is the country's oldest Mayan settlement. The ruins of the 10-sq-km (6-sq-mi) complex with five temples were first cleared only 40 years ago.

Quiriguá The tallest and most artistic Mayan pillars can be found here. Their multitude of shapes evokes associations with the surrounding rainforest.

Tikal These ruins, buried in the jungle in the heart of the Mayan lowlands in present-day Guatemala, have inspired awe in many a visitor. Gustav Bernoulli discovered the ruins in 1877.

Skulls and bones in the Nazca Cemeterio de Chanchilla in Southern Peru.

Peru

With the Panamericana along the Peruvian Pacific coast

Peru was the heart of the Inca civilization, and its riches also made it the center of the Spanish colonial empire. Cuzco, at an altitude of 3,500 m (11,484 ft) in the Andean highlands, was founded as the Inca capital in the 12th century. From here, the Incas continued to expand until their empire reached from Ingapirca in Ecuador to northern Argentina at the start of the 16th century. The Inca themselves had built a road over 5,000 km (3,107 mi) long, setting up stations (tambos) a day's march apart where the travel-weary could stop get refreshments.

The Inca Road was an important communications and transport artery within their extensive dominions. For the most part it ran through the Andes, but there were also shorter, seemingly insignificant, routes along the Pacific coast in what is modern-day Peru. The Spanish, who had conquered the Inca empire under Francisco Pizarro in 1532, established the capital of their viceroyalty in Lima, on the coast, as early as 1535. However, for a long time Peru's economic heart remained in the country's interior, in the domains of the fallen Inca. Things have changed since then as the focus of power shifted to Lima. In modern times this shift has also been influenced by the Panamericana, which primarily runs along the coast. The ports and coastal towns (Chiclayo, Trujillo, Chimbote, Lima-Callao or Arequipa) have since become important industrial conurbations. The country's mineral resources, meanwhile, have become the backbone of the economy and are shipped from those ports.

Peru was the wealthiest and most important of Spain's Latin American colonies. The country's gold and silver mines – the most important of which were situated near Potosí, in the heart of the former Inca empire – yielded immeasurable volumes and hence almost every important colonial town boasts resplendent civil buildings and magnificent churches.

Then, as now, Peruvian society was characterized by one ele-

Representation of a Mochican chief.

The famous tomb of the "Lord of Sipán": the Moche ruler was buried together with two men and two women as well as magnificent weapons, gold clothing and valuable artworks.

Arequipa, the "White City", is home to numerous baroque monasteries, churches and palaces.

ment: a highly conspicuous contrast between rich and poor. Impoverished shanties stand next to magnificent palaces – those of the colonial era and those of the industrial age. About twenty-seven million people live in Peru, some 70 percent of them in the inhospitable coastal region and 25 percent in the highlands of the Andes. Only 5 percent live in the Selva, the Amazon lowlands. One-third of the population lives within greater Lima alone, and the cities continue to grow. As in most Latin American countries, Spanish is the official language in Peru but many Peruvians speak a different mother tongue. More than half of the country's inhabitants come from Indian families, so almost one-third of the

population speaks Quechua (the language of the Inca empire), and four percent speaks Aymara as their first language. A majority of the poorest people are "indígenas" – indigenous folk. It is estimated that four out of ten Peruvians live in abject poverty.

Peru is the third-largest country in South America after Brazil and Argentina. It is a country of contrasts with arid coastal deserts, impressive peaks in the central Andes region and the Selva, and tropical rainforests in the east that form part of the Amazon lowlands.

The Panamericana follows the coast for almost its entire length, passing mostly through inhospitable scree and sand landscapes. Almost no rain falls here because the humidity

coming from the ocean is only released as rain at a height of around 800 m (2,625 ft). The coastal deserts are dotted with occasional river oases where earlier civilizations and later

also the Spanish built their towns. Due to the cold Humboldt Current, however, the entire coast is very rich in fish populations and therefore still a popular area to settle.

View over Huascarán National Park from the statue of Christ in the town of Yungay, located in the Cordillera Blanca in central Peru.

Following the Panamericana through Peru means that you get to know one portion of the country, but will miss out on some mountain regions and rainforest. But the coastal route does provide an insight into the country's various cultures, which extend from the adobe pyramids of the Moche people to the desert images of the Nazca civilization and Spanish colonial-era buildings.

1 Piura The Spanish conquistadors founded this town on the northern rim of the Sechura Desert in 1532, and some of its colonial-era buildings have survived the years. Mostly, though, it is simply a suitable stopover before crossing the desert on the way to Chiclayo.
From Piura you drive through 220 km (137 mi) of bleak sand and stone landscape.

2 Chiclayo The fourth-largest town in Peru is the ideal starting point for visiting the region's archaeological sites. You start in Lambayeque 12 km (7.5 mi) to the north-west, which not only has a number of attractive colonial buildings, but also the Museo Tumbas Reales de Sipán. The museum holds wonderful collection of ceramics and textiles from Northern Peru, and exhibits from Sipán, Moche and Chan Chan.

3 Sipán With the tomb of the so-called Lord of Sipán, this town 32 km (20 mi) east of Chiclayo, the burial site of the Moche warrior, which has been fully reconstructed, is one of Peru's most interesting excavations. The dead ruler lay on the upper level of a 30-m-high (98-ft), six-storey pyramid,

beset by a number of decorative items and skeletons. The landscape becomes more fertile south of Chiclayo, with sugar plantations lining the road before the gray desert begins again at Chicama. It extends as far as Chan Chan about 30 km (19 mi) away.

4 Chan Chan This town was founded in the 12th/13th centuries as the capital of the Chimú realm. The Inca later conquered the Chimú empire in 1460, but its true decline, like many cultures here, came only with the arrival of the Spanish. Chan Chan comprises ten districts, each with a temple pyramid which, like the houses, are built from adobe (clay bricks). From Chan Chan, one of Peru's many UNESCO World Heritage Sites, it just a short distance to the city of Trujillo.

5 Trujillo For a city with 1.2 million residents, Trujillo's Old Town has an astonishingly charming colonial feel. Fortunately, many of the 17th- and 18th-century buildings have survived a number of earthquakes: the cathedral with the magnificent choir stalls is one of them, as are the aristocratic

Travel Information

Route profile
Length: about 2,600 km (1,616 mi)
Time required: at least 3 weeks
Start: Piura
End: Tacna
Route (main locations): Piura, Trujillo, Lima, Reserva Nacional de Paracas, Nazca, Arequipa, Tacna

Special note:
Protests and demonstrations with roadblocks have been a regular occurrence in Peru in recent years. Peru also has a pretty high crime rate (drug-related , robbery, kidnapping). Slum areas should be avoided, as should nighttime overland journeys.

The route follows the Panamericana, which runs parallel to the coast, but there are some worthwhile detours to sights in the country's interior. They bring you from Pisco to Ayacucho, from Nazca to Cuzco/Machu Picchu and from Arequipa to Lake Titicaca.
Roads near the coast tend to be well maintained. Farther inland that changes and you may need four-wheel-drive vehicles to get around.

Information:
Here are some websites to help you plan your trip.
travel.peru.com
www.justperu.org
www.peruatravel.com

8 **Chavín de Huántar** It is still not clear today whether Chavín was a town, a temple area or a pilgrimage site. What is clear, however, is that the complex was built around 800 BC and belonged to the Chavín civilization, which extended from Piura to Lake Titicaca between 1400 and 400 BC. At the center of the site is a 5-m (16 ft) monolith depicting a deity with clawed hands and a jaguar's head. The road now takes you via Callejón de Huaylas back to the Panamericana for the journey to Paramonga.

9 **Paramonga** This Chimú temple stands high up above the coast and affords a splendid view of the ocean. Its mighty walls made it impregnable. After a drive through the coastal desert you reach Lima about 200 km (124 mi) away.

10 **Lima** Lima is Peru's cultural, economic and political center with one-third of the total Peruvian population. The city has twelve universities as well as the oldest college in the Americas, founded in 1551. Lima is also Peru's capital, and is home to the seats of government and ad-

1 Tucume Moche is about 45 km (30 mi) north of Chiclayo. From Mirador you have a view over twenty-six clay pyramids, unwalled citadels and residential areas.

2 Only a few of the buildings at Chan Chan still bear evidence of the reliefs that once decorated the houses and walls.

3 Huascarán National Park is home to Nevado Huascarán (6,768 m / 22,206 ft), Peru's highest mountain.

4 Paramonga: a temple built of clay bricks, and a Chimú fortress built to defend against the Incas.

houses in the blocks around the central plaza. South of the town center there is a bridge over the Río Moche and 6 km (4 mi) further on you reach the pyramids of Moche.

6 **Moche** The largest of the pyramids at the foot of Cerro Blanco is the Huaca de Sol (pyramid of the sun), built in the 5th century using over 140 million clay bricks. It covers an area of 55,200 sq m (66,000 sq yds),

making it one of the largest pre-Columbian structures in all of South America, and has ornately decorated relief walls. The route now continues south along the Panamericana via Chimbote as far as Casma. Here you leave the coastal road and travel east to Huarás at 3,028 m (9,935 ft) in the Cordillera Negra (Black Range), almost 100 km (62 mi) away. This town is the gateway to the Huascarán National Park.

7 **Parque Nacional Huascarán** Nevado Huascarán, the highest mountain in the Peruvian Andes, forms the heart of this national park at an elevation of 6,768 m (22,206 ft). The park contains the core of the Cordillera Blanca (White Range), a snow-capped chain with more than two dozen peaks over 6,000 m (20,000 ft). Chavín de Huántar, yet another UNESCO World Heritage Site, is also within the park.

ministrative offices. The Port of Callao is the country's most important transport hub. As a city, Lima is literally overflowing: the very heavily populated outskirts are full of shanty towns and slums. After leaving greater Lima you reach Pachacámac after another 30 km (19 mi).

11 Pachacámac This excavation site was once the center of the Cuismancu empire, established in around 500 and later subjugated by the Incas. Pachacámac was founded in around 800 and was one of the largest towns in Peru when the Spanish arrived. The Inca built a stepped pyramid around 80 m (262 ft) high over the Cuismancu sanctuary. From the top of the platform you get wonderful panoramic views. The small museum has an interesting model of the now almost completely derelict town.

The Panamericana stays on the Pacific coast for the next 170 km (106 mi), passing a series of seaside resorts that serve as getaway destinations for residents of Lima during the December to April season and on weekends. Towns such as Punta Hermosa, Punta Negra, San Bartolo, Santa María and especially Pucusana, slightly back from the Panamericana, have great beaches. San Vicente de Cañete, a small market town surrounded by cotton fields, and Chincha Alta are the next two stops.

Chincha Alta is known for its distinctive Afro-Peruvian culture. It is home to many of the descendants of African slaves who were shipped in to work on the plantations in this area. The road branches off from the Panamericana to Tambo Colorado and Ayacucho, near Pisco.

12 Tambo Colorado The Peruvian coast boasts but a few Inca ruins. Tambo Colorado, whose name comes from the traces of

red on the walls, is one of the best preserved sites. The ruins are situated at an elevation of 530 m (1,739 ft) about 50 km (31 mi) from the Panamericana. It is not clear whether Tambo Colorado was a sun temple or a military base.

Anyone looking for adventure can continue along the road to Ayacucho, which climbs up into the mountains to an elevation of 4,600 m (15,093 ft) at Castrovirreyna after roughly 70 km (43 mi). The Andes here present a superb panorama.

Back on the Panamericana you soon reach Pisco.

13 Pisco The town of Pisco would not be as well known if it were not for the famous marc schnapps. Indeed, the Peruvian national drink, Pisco Sour, has turned the town into a tourist destination even though most of the distilleries are located around Ica, about 60 km (37 mi) further south.

The Old Town of Pisco has even developed its own port. It is now 15 km (9 mi) to Paracas, where the boats sail to the Islas Ballestas.

14 Islas Ballestas Because it is a sanctuary for tens of thousands of sea birds, landing on the islands is prohibited. You are only allowed to observe from the boat. The Islas Ballestas, Isla Sangayan and the neighboring Reserva Nacional de Paracas to the south (the Islas Ballestas are not part of the park) boast what is probably the highest density of sea birds in the world. The cliffs of this wild, craggy group of islands, pounded by the foaming blue-green waves of the Pacific, provide ideal nesting grounds – and shelter.

Until the mid-19th century, these sea birds were an indirect source of great wealth for the

region: their guano, meaning dung in Quechua, was the best natural fertilizer and fetched high prices on international markets before the rise of artificial fertilizers.

15 Reserva Nacional de Paracas This nature reserve is not just worth a visit for nature lovers, but for anyone interested in ancient civilizations – the peninsula was settled as early as 3000 BC. People here lived primarily from fishing and gathering mussels. In around 1000 BC maize, cassava, cotton and beans were cultivated by a community living here. It is considered the earliest example of a complex soci-

colossal geometric shapes and figures such as a monkey, a 46-m (50-yd) spider, hands and the Colibri, which also often appears on Nazca ceramics. The largest figures measure up to 200 m (219 yds) and some of them are incomplete. There are over one hundred overall and around thirty human or animal images in total. From the viewing platform you get a good look at three of the images: the hands, the lizard and the tree.

You are directly on the Panamericana, but even from the platform the lines, which are up to half a mile long, reveal real images. To really grasp their size and beauty, take a short sightseeing flight from the nearby airfield in Nazca. The figures are best seen from the air.

South of Nazca, the Panamericana initially takes you through a desolate desert landscape and past the Cementerio de Chauchilla, where the Nazca dead were preserved in this arid climate with an impressive method of natural mummification.

After 85 km (53 mi), the road reaches the Pacific again near Puerto de Lomas. To Camaná it is another 300 km (186 mi) through a desert of gravel that

the Paracas civilization was divided into two types: the cavernas graves date from the period 600 to 400 BC, while those from the necropolis date from 400 BC to AD 200.

On a slope north-west of the Bay of Paracas (best viewed from the sea) is the 120-m-tall (394-ft) "Candelabra" geoglyph. It is also known as the "Three Crosses", the "Trident" or the "Tree of Life". Its actual meaning remains unclear. Was it a navigational aid for ships? A fetish image? Or a stylized sign of the zodiac? Experts believe that the image derives from the same civilization as the Nazca geoglyphs, while others surmise it was only created in the 19th century.

16 Nazca You can make the comparison yourself with the Nazca Lines (Líneas de Nazca) some 150 km (93 mi) further to the south. They were created in the stony desert soil during the Nazca civilization. The creation involved clearing away the dark gravel of the top layer to a depth of up to 20 cm (9 in) over a width of 1 m (1.1 yds) to form

ety on the southern Peruvian coast. The museum in Paracas details the history of the settlement of the Paracas Peninsula, and displays the archaeological finds excavated on the peninsula since 1925, including mummies, wrapped in woven shrouds. Both the graves and the mummies had remained almost completely intact due to the location and the dry climate. Based on the burial grounds,

1 The wild, craggy, storm-battered coast of the Paracas Peninsula is a paradise for sea birds.

2 Isla Sangayan is an island off the coast of the Paracas Peninsula inhabited solely by birds and sea lions.

3 Despite its height, the peak of the Chachani Volcano near Arequipa is considered an easy climb at 6,080 m (19,948 ft).

4 The "Candelabra" geoglyph in Paracas, viewed from the ocean.

skirts the steep coastline. The route takes you up and down hilly stretches, and you roll past a series of bays with beautiful long beaches. There are a number of sleepy fishing villages on the way that only come to life when the regional bus makes a stop here.

17 Camaná With its attractive beaches, this small town has quickly become a popular seaside resort for the residents of Arequipa. Originally founded as the port for Potosí and Arequipa, the goods produced in Camaná are now shipped from the port further south.

18 Arequipa The "White City", or "Ciudad blanca", is the local nickname for Arequipa, and when you arrive at the central plaza you realize why: the shiny white cathedral and the myriad other white colonial buildings with their two-storey arcades. All of them were built from the white volcanic rock sillar quarried in the region and still used as a building material today.

The Old Town of Arequipa, which was founded in 1540 and experienced its peak in the 17th and 18th centuries, has been perfectly restored, an effort that earned it the title of UNESCO World Heritage Site in

2000. The two most important attractions are buildings of religious significance. The Jesuit church dates from 1698, and the decoration of its façade displays distinct Indian influences, as does Santa Catalina monastery, a "town within a town" with fountains, squares and courtyards. It was expanded in the 17th century to its present size of 20,000 sq m (215,2000 sq ft). Two volcanoes form the backdrop for Arequipa, at an elevation of 2,370 m (7,776 ft): Volcán Misti (5,835 m/19,145 ft), which is constantly smoking, and the higher but easier to climb Chachaní (6,080 m/19,948 ft). From Arequipa the route continues through the desert along the Panamericana to the south. Moquegua, a town situated in the river valley of the same name, is worth a short visit and is about 213 km (132 mi) away. It has a lovely Old Town center around the plaza with a number of well-restored churches and other colonial buildings. Torota, about 24 km (15 mi) away, also has a scenic Old Town.

You then come to Tacna after another 185 km (115 mi).

19 Tacna The last of the larger Peruvian towns before you reach the Chilean border used to belong to Chile, from 1880 to 1929. In 1880, during the so-called Saltpeter War, the Chileans conquered large parts of Peru and Bolivia in order to take control of the salt-producing regions of the desert. Chile gave the town of Tacna back to Peru in 1929 following a referendum.

The battlefield from 1880 can be visited on a hill above the town. The town center has two early works by André Gustave Eiffel: the cathedral at the plaza and the fountains.

From Tacna it is then 46 km (29 mi) to the Chilean border at Concordia.

1 Palm-lined Plaza de Armas in Arequipa where the 19th-century cathedral takes up the entire north side of the plaza.

2 Arequipa's volcano, Vocán Misti (5,835 m/19,145 ft) emits clouds of smoke nearly constantly.

Túcume Moche Pirámides
Many civilizations have lived in Peru's "Valley of the Pyramids" where twenty-six adobe buildings have been excavated.

Sipán The "Tomb of the Lord of Sipán", the 2nd/3rd-century Moche prince, and his companions is one of South America's most important archeological finds.

Chan-Chan The former Chimú capital is the largest archaeological site in South America. 100,000 people lived in the ten districts here in the 12th/13th centuries.

Parque Nacional Huascarán This reserve is home to the world's largest bromeliad variety. Nevado Huascarán at 6,768 m (22,206 ft) is the highest peak in Peru.

Paramonga This clay brick complex served as a Chimú fortress to defend against the Incas. Pizarro found it nearly completely intact. Seeing the Pacific and the Río Fortaleza from atop the ruins is an overwhelming experience.

Torata This town has a number of colonial buildings worth seeing, including the community church and the stone windmills. In addition to the Sabaya Inca center, Camata, the "Machu Picchu of Moquegua" is particular worth a visit.

Cañón del Colca This massive canyon north-west of Arequipa is 1,200 m (3,937 ft) deep, 70 km (43 mi) long, and is lined with volcanos as high as 6,000 m (19,686 ft).

Volcanos near Arequipa Misti, at 5,835 m (19,145 ft), and Chachani, at 6,080 m (19,948 ft), make for an impressive backdrop.

Lima Despite some disastrous earthquakes, the square-shaped Old Town in Peru's capital, founded in 1535, remains intact. Its unique gems include the Museo de Oro and the cathedral.

Arequipa The "White City" is one of South America's most important cultural and historical sites. Its idiosyncrasies include the Santa Catalina monastery and baroque churches and palaces.

Paracas This peninsula is known for its wealth of fish and birdlife, including flamingos and pelicans. Sea lions and seals also cavort in the cold Humboldt Current.

Reserva Nacional de Paracas The park is the only one of its kind in Peru, and encompasses a marine sanctuary. This picture shows the bird and sea lion island of Sangayan, also part of the reserve.

Nazca The bone-dry landscape is known for its giant geoglyphs. Here: an aerial view of the so-called "Astronaut".

Cementerio de Chauchilla This cemetery in the middle of the desert is a macabre conglomeration of plundered graves and pre-Columbian mummies.

Map labels: Guayaquil, Huaquillas, Machala, Cuenca, Tumbes, El Cisne, Loja, Bosque Petrificado de Puyango, P.N.Cerros de Amotape, ECUADOR, Máncora, Zapotillo, Macará, Talara, Sullana, Chulucanas, Paita, Piura ①, Vicús, Punta Negra, Motupe, P.N. de Cutervo, Pirámides Moche de Túcume, Cutervo, Lambayeque, Sipán ③, Chiclayo ②, Kuntur Wasi, Cajamarca, Pacasmayo, Ascope, Otuzco, Chan Chan ④, Pirámides Moche, TRUJILLO ⑤⑥, S.N. Calipuy, P.N.Calipuy, Cañón del Pato, Caraz, Yungay, Chimbote, Casma, Huarás, P.N. Huascarán ⑦, Chavín de Huántar, Sechín, Huánuco Viejo, Pucallpa, Callejón de Huaylas, Playa Grande, PERU, Bermejo, Paramonga ⑨, Barranca, Cerro de Pasco, Centinela, Lago Junín, Huacho, R.N.Junín, Junín, R.N. Lachay, La Oroya, Chancay, LIMA ⑩, Callao, Pasamayo, Pachacámac ⑪, San Bartolo, Concepción, Huancayo, Pico Alto, Pucusana, Sta.Rosa de Ocopa, Mala, Huancavelica, Cerro Azul, Catahuasi, San Vicente de Cañete, Incahuasi, Castrovirreyna, Chincha Alta ⑫, Ayacucho, Pisco ⑬, Huaytará, Islas Ballestas ⑭, Tambo Colorado, Pen.de Paracas, Ica ⑮, Huacachina, R.N.de Paracas, Nazca ⑯, Cahuachi, Cuzco, Líneas de Nazca, R.N.Pampa Galeras, Chauchilla, Cotahuasi, Lomas, Pampa de Cortaderas, Cañón del Colca, Sibayo, R.N.Salinas Aguada Blanca, Chivay, Juliaca, Atico, Vol.Chachani 6080, Vol. Misti 5835, Arequipa ⑱, Vol.Tutupaca 5806, Camaná ⑰, Torata, Mollendo, Santuario Nacional Lagunas de Mejía, Moquegua, Ilo, Ite, Tacna ⑲, La Paz (BOL), Arica, San Miguel de Azapa, CHILE, Iquique

507

Stone pillars at the sun gate of the ruined city of Tiahuanaca, south of Lake Titicaca. It sits 3812 m (12507 ft) above sea level on the border to Bolivia.

Peru and Bolivia

The Inca Trail

The Inca Trail connects the capitals of Peru and Bolivia and passes through culturally and historically significant sites in the highlands of the Andes Mountains. Travellers will be amazed by magnificent monuments dating back to early Inca civilization and Spanish colonial times.

The Inca Trail begins in the Peruvian capital of Lima, extends through the western cordilleras (range) of the Andes and runs right across Peru to Lake Titicaca. From there, one of the most spectacular routes in the whole of South America travels over Bolivian territory through the basin scenery of the Altiplano to the south-east and finally terminates in the eastern cordilleras of the Andes, in Sucre, the country's constitutional capital.

A fascinating natural environment, protected in a number of national parks such as the Parque Nacional Manú, provides a stunning backdrop for the region's cultural treasures.

At the beginning of the 16th century, before the arrival of the Spanish, the Inca Empire covered almost the entire Andes region, including parts of the Andean foreland. A large number of the architectural treasures of this advanced civilization have been preserved

Highland Indians with their llamas.

along the Inca Trail. The architectural highlights include spectacular temples and palaces as well as a series of fortresses built at impressively shrewd locations. Most of these huge buildings, such as the large sun

temple at Cuzco, were also built without significant technological assistance. A prime example of the strategic locations selected for Inca settlements is Machu Picchu, an extraordinary terraced site and one of the Inca's last places of refuge from advancing colonial troops.

Ironically, the Spanish never actually discovered this well-hidden settlement, which lies at around 2,800 m (9,187 ft). It was an American explorer who first discovered it in 1911. However, the discovery brought with it more riddles than answers regarding Inca culture. Lake Titicaca, which still has a healthy fish population, straddles the Peru-Bolivia border. It

A view of the ruins of Machu Picchu, a glorious terraced Inca city in the high Andes.

In Sillustani, a peninsula on Laky Umayo, the Colla cultures buried their important citizens under chullpas, or burial mounds, measuring over 10 m (6 ft) in height and dating back to the 13th century.

lies 3,812 m (12,507 ft) above sea level and is not only the largest lake in South America, it is also the highest navigable lake in the world. Close to its southern shores is the town of Tiahuanaco (also known as Tiwanaku) which, up until the 10th century, was the religious and administrative center of an important pre-Columbian civilization. The natural environment in the region around Lake Titicaca is also spectacular. Some of the highest mountains in the Andes are here, including the 6,880-m (22,573-ft) Nevado del Illimani south-east of Bolivia's largest city and administrative capital, La Paz.

Numerous remnants of the Spanish colonial era can also be seen here, in particular in the area around Lago de Poopó.

The Europeans were especially interested in the mineral wealth of the 'New World', and many Indians were forced to work as slaves in Spanish mines, many of them losing their lives in the process. At the beginning of the 17th century Potosí was the world's most important center for silver mining. As a result of its historical significance the town has been declared a World Heritage Site, together with Cuzco, Machu Picchu and the Old Town in Lima. The distinction is intended for both the time-honoured Inca sites and for some of the architectural achievements of the Spanish colonial rulers. In addition to these cultural and historical features, the diverse natural environment in this South American region has

also been given its share of attention – the Manú National Park, in the transition zone between the Amazon lowlands and the middle Andes, has also been declared a UNESCO World Heritage Site.

With its dramatic differences in altitude, the Inca Trail provides a wonderful cross-section not only of Peru and the northern reaches of Bolivia, but also of the history and natural environment of an entire continent.

Women with traditional headwear offer their produce at the market in Cuzco.

The Inca Trail runs from Lima on the Peruvian Pacific coast through countless Andean passes, majestic mountains and high plateaus on its way to Sucre in Bolivia. The route features both desert landscapes and tropical rainforests as well as high mountain lakes. The well-preserved Inca ruins make the journey an unforgettable experience.

1 Lima Our journey begins in the largest city on the Inca Trail, where traffic is characterized by the expected noise and chaos of a large urban center. Lima was founded by the Spanish in 1535 and they quickly established it as the focal point of their colonial empire in South America. In 1826 Lima replaced Cuzco as the capital and grew into a wealthy metropolis.

Some of the most magnificent buildings from this era – both palaces and churches – have since been beautifully restored to their original glory. The main cathedral (1535–1625) is located on Plaza San Martín in the historic Old Town, which itself has been declared a World Heritage Site in its entirety. The

tomb of the conqueror Francisco Pizarro, the founder of Lima, is also said to be somewhere in the city.

Lima is a junction for important transcontinental routes such as the Pan-American Highway. When you leave Lima heading east you will unfortunately encounter few inviting locations. Due to significant migration from the countryside, sprawling slums have developed on the outskirts of the city. Road conditions in the outer areas can be very bad at times. The multilane Pan-American Highway runs past these outskirts before heading south towards Pachacámac.

You will soon leave the coastal flats as the road climbs quickly

into the Andean foothills toward the market town of La Oroya. There are some steep, winding sections here. From there a detour (64 km/40 miles) heads north to Junín. Several memorials here com-

memorate the battle of Junín in 1824 between Simon Bolívar's troops and Spanish soldiers, one of many South American battles for independence. The journey then continues through the narrow

Travel Information

Route profile
Length: approx. 2,000 km (1,243 miles), excluding detours
Time required: 3 weeks
Start: Lima, Peru
End: Sucre, Bolivia
Route (main locations):
Lima, Ayacucho, Cuzco, Machu Picchu, Lake Titicaca, La Paz, Cochabamba, Oruro, Potosí, Sucre

Traffic information:
Drive on the right side. Road conditions vary considerably. Heavy rainfall and the resulting landslides can make some mountain routes impassable.

When to go:
The best time for travelling to the Andes is during the southern hemisphere winter (May to September), as the southern summer (December to March) is the rainy season. The temperature range between night and day is considerable.

Information:
Peru travel info:
www.peru.info/perueng.asp
Bolivian travel info:
www.boliviaweb.com
Peruvian and Bolivian embassies around the world:
www.embassyworld.com

100,000 people lived here during the heyday of the Huari Empire in the 9th century. The city was carefully planned and the grid-like layout of the streets can still be seen today. The well-organized Huari armies had a history of subordinating enemy peoples, but the city was ultimately abandoned in the 10th century.

Back on the main route we now head east past more Andean peaks towards Cuzco, the red tiled roofs of which can be seen from miles away.

⑤ **Cuzco** For many travellers, Cuzco is one of the most important destinations in Peru. With its scenic location in the Andes, relaxed atmosphere, easy access to its attractions, and especially as a base for tours to the Urubamba Valley and Machu Picchu, the city is indeed a highlight along the Inca Trail. For the Incas, Cuzco was the focal point of their empire and therefore the center of the world as they knew it. They established the city as a political, religious and cultural hub. Upon their arrival the Spanish knew of the city's importance but were dazzled by its wealth and grandeur. Unlike other Inca strongholds, the Spanish destroyed only a few of the buildings when they invaded Cuzco, and only the most significant structures with political or religious functions were razed. On those foundations the colonial rulers then erected a series of

1 Rooftop view of the Renaissance-style cathedral in Cuzco (17th century).

2 Near Cuzco, a high-altitude basin framed by snow-capped Andean peaks.

3 The Corpus Christi procession is one of the most important religious ceremonies in Cuzco.

Mantaro valley towards trade town Huáncayo.

② **Huáncayo** The Mantaro Valley is renowned for its numerous pre-Columbian ruins. It ends in Huáncayo, the largest town in the region. Maize, potatoes and vegetables are grown outside the town using irrigation and in some places the allotments seem to stretch beyond the horizon.

Huáncayo, at an altitude of roughly 3,350 m (10,991 ft), is an important regional trading center.

Today there is little left as a reminder that the town was once a center of the Inca Empire. It is now characterized by delicate Spanish colonial architecture.

The route now heads along a valley towards the south and the climate becomes milder

with the decreasing altitude. Prickly pears grow right up to the roadside, their fruit highly prized by the Peruvians.

③ **Ayacucho** This city, at an elevation of 2,760 m (9,056 ft), is an interesting combination of past and present. Ayacucho was at one time the capital of the Huari Empire, one of the first advanced civilizations in the Andes and, as such, a predecessor to the Incas.

The city was discovered and refounded in 1539 by Francisco Pizarro. It is known as the 'City of 33 churches' and religious ceremonies play an important role here. The Holy Week processions (Semana Santa) are among the most important of their kind in South America, drawing visitors from all parts of the country.

④ **Huari** Approximately 22 km (14 miles) north-east of Ayacucho is Huari, once the center of the culture of the same name (6th–12th centuries). Nearly

their own buildings, some stately in scale, others of religious importance.

The Plaza de Armas, for example, was constructed on the site of the former main square, Huacaypata, at the time 600 m (1,969 ft) long. Santo Domingo monastery was built from the ruins of the Coricancha sun temple. The Jesuit church La Compañía (1571) was constructed on the foundations of the grand Inca palace, Huayna Capac.

In 1950, parts of the city were destroyed by a strong earthquake. Fortuitously, however, the quake actually unearthed a number of Inca remains that had been previously hidden from view.

Cuzco's importance remains unchanged for the descendants of the Inca. The Quechua-speaking Indians hold colourful ceremonies in the city, in which the customs and traditions of their forebearers are relived, and yet Christian festivals are also celebrated with enthusiasm. The annual Corpus Christi processions in particular attract much attention. In 1983 the Old Town was declared a UNESCO World Heritage Site.

6 Sacsayhuamán Situated above Cuzco – about 3 km (2 miles) north of the city – are the remains of a mighty fortress. Between 1440 and 1532 the Inca built an imposing citadel here encircled by three concentric walls.

Sacsayhuamán can be reached on foot from Cuzco in just under half an hour. The path leads from the Plaza de Armas via the Calle Suecia, past San Cristobal church and via the old Inca path up to the fortress.

In their time the stone blocks, which are up to 5 m (16 ft) high and weigh 200 tonnes (220 tons), intimidated many a would-be attacker and thus ful-

filled their purpose as a demonstration of the power of their owners. The fortress is a main attraction in the Cuzco area. Today it is assumed that the fortress was built to control the most vulnerable entrance to the city. The complex includes a number of store rooms for food and an armory for weapons.

During the Spanish invasion, hundreds of Inca warriors barricaded themselves within the walls of Sacsayhuamán, right up until the bitter end. In addition to the heavy fighting, strong earthquakes have also caused significant damage to the structure. Today only about one-third of the fortress remains.

7 Pisac On a 32-km-long (20-mile) detour to the north you are led along a scenic road via the cult site Kenko, the 'Red Fortress' (Puca Pucara), and the

sacred spring of Tambo Machay in the idyllic village of Pisac, which can be reached by a metal bridge. Inca influences clash here with colonial era flair.

Market days in Pisac are full of activity. Souvenirs such as flutes, jewellery, and clothing made from llama wool are traded on the central plaza. Just as attractive, however, are the ruins of an Inca ceremonial site located 600 m (1,969 ft) above the village with a marvellous view.

8 Ollantaytambo At the end of the Sacred Valley, 19 km (12 miles) beyond the main town of Urubamba, is the village of Ollanta (2,800 m / 9,187 ft), named after Ollantay, an Inca military leader. The fortress, with its spectacular stone terraces, stands on a bluff above the village. The Inca began construction on the

well-fortified complex in 1460, but the project took much longer than planned. Ollantaytambo was not yet complete when the Spanish attacked in 1523.

Despite that, residents of Ollanta are still enjoying the benefits of the irrigation system developed back then by the Inca. Even during the dry season there was, and is, enough water available for agriculture.

Costumes worn by local residents are especially eye-catching and have hardly changed from those worn by their forefathers 500 years ago. The last few meters to the fortress have to be covered on foot.

While the landscape in the Cuzco hinterland is characterized by sparse vegetation, the scenery changes drastically as you head towards Machu Picchu. It becomes more tropical and the

4

monotone flora of the highlands gives way to dense rainforest. The road starts to wind pretty heavily now, with tight curves and an occasionally hair-raising climb up to the 'City of Clouds'.

⑨ Machu Picchu The 'City of Clouds', as Machu Picchu is also known, is about 80 km (50 miles) north-west of Cuzco. Surrounded by imposing mountains and set in the midst of a dense forest is the most significant and fascinating archaeological site in South America. It is spectacularly located on a high mountain ridge nearly 600 m (1,969 ft) above the Urubamba River. There is hardly any other site where the technical and mechanical skills of the Inca are demonstrated more tangibly than Machu Picchu, and it is therefore no surprise

that the site was declared a UNESCO World Heritage Site in 1983. It is also no surprise that myths and legends still surround this magical place today. In fact, its very origins remain unknown.

It is assumed that Machu Picchu was built in the 15th century. One theory holds that Machu Picchu served as a place of refuge during the Spanish invasion. Another theory supposes that the Inca relocated their political center to this barely visible and even more inaccessible site. One thing remains certain, however – the colonial Spanish were fully unaware of the existence of this city. The site was first discovered in 1911. The city's structure is still easily recognizable. Stone houses comprise one room only and are arranged around small courtyards. What might appear

simple at first is in fact the result of considerable technical and mechanical skill on the part of the builders. The structures are grouped around a central, more or less quadratic formation. The most striking buildings include the temple tower, or Torreon, and the Sintihuatana sun temple, with seventy-eight stone steps leading up to it.

From Machu Picchu you first need to return to Pisac via the same road, where another road then branches off toward Huambutiyo. On a narrow, gravel road you will then come to Paucartambo and Atalaya, jumping-off point for a visit to the Manú National Park.

From Pisac back on the Inca Trail you soon branch off onto a sign-posted side road heading north to Tipón. The gravel road here is typically in good condi-

tion. After about 4 km (2.5 miles) you will reach the ruins of the old city of Tipón at an altitude of about 3,500 m (11,454 ft).

⑩ Tipón Especially noteworthy here are the well-preserved terraces, where a sophisticated system of irrigation still enables productive cultivation of the land. It is now surmised that the Inca used the site as an experimental area for acclimatizing plants that otherwise only grew in lower-lying areas. On the onward journey from Tipón towards the south-east you pass the little village of Andahuaylillas where the 17th-century baroque church is worth a brief visit. The peak of Nudo Ausandate towers 6,400 m (20,998 ft) above you on the left.

⑪ Raqchi Located at the base of the Quinsachata volcano, this town hosts an important traditional festival every year on the 3rd Sunday of June. From a distance, the temple, which is dedicated to Viracocha, the most important Inca god, resembles a viaduct because of its 15-m-high (49-ft) walls. It provides an impressive backdrop for the festivities.

⑫ Sillustani The well-built road from Raqchi now leads south-east towards Lake Titica-

1 The walls of the Inca fortress Sacsayhuamán were intended to command the respect of attackers.

2 Ruins at the Inca ceremonial center of Pisac with the typical trapezoid doors.

3 The sun temple and stone terraces of the Ollantaytambo fortress.

4 View from the strategically situated village of Pisac down into the Sacred Valley of the Incas.

ca. Near the northern shore of the lake a road branches off to the right towards one of the architectural attractions on this section of the route – the burial mounds of Sillustani, a peninsula on Lake Umayo.

The mounds, known as chullpas, were constructed out of clay in the pre-Inca era and are up to 12 m (39 ft) high. They served as the burial sites of regional rulers. Some chullpas seem to defy gravity, with base diameters smaller than those of their tops.

It is known that the material for the burial mounds comes from quarries near the lake. Particularly noticeable here, too, is the precise working of the stone blocks, which were put together without the use of joints.

It is possible to drive around Lake Titicaca to the north and the south, and both roads run close to the shores almost all the way. You will reach Puno after about 32 km (20 miles) on the southern route of the Inca Trail.

⑬ Puno The location of this town, directly on Lake Titicaca, is striking enough in itself, giving you the impression that you are at the coast. Puno is considered to be a cradle of Inca civilization. One legend has it that the first Inca rose from the lake here to create the empire. The surrounding area used to be ruled from Tiahuanaco.

Puno, at an elevation of 3,830 m (12,566 ft), was founded by the Spanish in 1668 and quickly equipped with a number of Christian churches intended to evangelize the Indians living here. Part of this religious center remains today. Many Peruvians associate Puno with colourful folklore. Every year in February, residents stage one of the most well-known festivals in the country, named after the Virgen de la Candelaria. Lively markets are held on the Plaza Mayor, which is flanked by the cathedral completed in 1757. Boats depart from Puno's port to some of the islands on the

lake. The region around the city is used intensively for agriculture, and pastures for the llama and alpaca herds extend almost to the edge of the road. After a short drive you will reach Chucuito, a village with two colonial churches and an Inca fertility temple.

⑭ Lake Titicaca This is a lake in a class of its own. With a surface area of 8,300 sq km (5,158 sq mi), Lake Titicaca is the largest lake in South America and the border of Peru and Bolivia runs right through it. The water level lies at 3,812 m (12,507 ft).

But it is not only these record features that characterize this unique body of water. The scenery and the remains of Inca civilization in the area around the crystal-clear 'Andean Sea' constitute the real attraction of the lake, which belongs to both Peru and Bolivia. Ruins and ritual sites exist on the Isla del Sol (Island of the Sun) as well, which rises nearly 200 m (656 ft) out of the lake. The Incas created a variety of myths that proclaimed the island as their place of origin. The Templo del Sol (sun temple) in particular, situated on the highest point of the island, is still shrouded in mystery.

3

4

Isla de la Luna (Island of the Moon) is also worth a brief visit. In addition to the 'stationary' islands there is also a series of 'floating' islands, designed by the Uros people in the pre-Inca era and still surviving today (see sidebar on the right).

⑮ Copacabana Turn off the southern coastal road to the border town of Yunguyo. On the Bolivian side, between the Cerro Calvarío and Cerro Sancollani mountains, is the ancient fishing village of Copacabana, on the peninsula of the same name extending far out into Lake Titicaca.

Excursion boats to the islands of the sun and moon depart from here. The climate is rough and the water temperature is usually quite cool.

Copacabana is an important pilgrimage destination for Bolivians. On 4 August every year a large procession of pilgrims arrives for the Fiesta de la Virgen de Copacabana. The Virgin is also sanctified in the Moorish-style basilica (1820).

From Copacabana you can either return to the southern route via Yunguyo (crossing the border for the second time), or continue your journey without the border crossing by taking

the northern route around the lake towards La Paz.

⑯ Tiahuanaco The ruins of this city (also called Tiwanaku) lie about 20 km (12 miles) from the southern end of Lake Titicaca. The site used to be directly on the lake shore but the lake has become smaller over the centuries. Very close to the former ceremonial site is present-day Tiahuanaco, just a short drive from the ruins.

The first traces of settlement here have been dated back to approximately 1500 BC. Tiahuanaco was probably founded in around AD 300. It subsequently developed into the center of an empire that covered most of the region and whose cultural and religious influences extended far beyond Peru, even as far as northern Chile and Argentina. The civilization experienced its heyday between 300 and 900. It is meant to have been the most advanced civilization in the

central Andes. Around 20,000 residents lived together on only a few square kilometers. Agriculture was the most important economic activity in

1 The ruins of Machu Picchu are even impressive when shrouded in mist. Yet they lay hidden for several centuries without the help of this natural veil. Situated as it is 600 m (1,969 ft) above the Urubamba River on a high mountain bluff, this surprisingly well-preserved Inca ruin is reached only with difficulty.

2 On the Inca Trail, the Nudo Ausandate (6,400 m/20,998 ft) rises out of the high Andean plateau.

3 Many of the massive stone tombs in Sillustani, which are visible from great distances, have been partially destroyed by grave robbers or lightning.

4 A colonial church in Puno, at an altitude of 3,830 m (12,566 ft), on the western shore of Lake Titicaca.

Tiahuanaco, with nearby Lake Titicaca providing water for effective cultivation. Using an advanced system of canals, farmers here channelled lake water to their fields, which extended over an area of about 80 sq km (50 sq mi).

Most of the temples, pillars and monoliths were built between 700 and 1200. An important place of worship, in this case a step pyramid about 15 m (49 ft) high, is situated in the middle of the city. The most famous construction, however, was the sun gate, sculpted out of one stone that weighs almost 44 t (48 tons). Many buildings were removed by the Spanish who needed ready-made stone blocks for the construction of their own showcase buildings. Blocks from Tiahuanaco were used to build a number of churches in La Paz, for example. Only a few remains of the site survived the centuries of destruction and overall disregard for their cultural significance. It was only at the beginning of the 20th century that extensive excavations began. The site was reconstructed as precisely as possible to the original once archaeologists were able to clear sufficient remains of the buildings.

Ultimately, the site was declared a UNESCO World Heritage Site in the year 2000. However, there are still many unanswered questions. Why was the city abandoned? Was it due to climate change, or had the population become too large? Without any doubt, the stonemasonry in Tiahuanaco is among the most skilled in South America. Shortly before La Paz the road following the eastern shore of Lake Titicaca joins National Road 1.

17 **La Paz** The largest city in Bolivia, and the highest city in the world, is nestled impres-

sively among the slopes of a steep valley. The metropolis is not the constitutional capital but it is the seat of the Bolivian government – and the heartbeat of the country.

The city's neighbourhoods seem to cling to the mountain slopes and are striking even from afar. La Paz is situated at an elevation of between 3,650 and 4,000 m (11,976 and 13,124 ft). Those who can afford it choose to live in the low-lying suburbs as the climate is somewhat milder in the 'lower city' and the residents are more protected from the Altiplano winds.

If you arrive from the west, the road passes the international airport of El Alto. Temperatures in this now independent suburb are often up to 10°C (50°F) cooler than in the city center. From El Alto the road crosses a basin where many stop to enjoy the view of the city.

On the onward journey the colourful markets of the famous 'Indio neighbourhood' pop up on the right. Behind that is the Old Town, which has been able to retain its colonial era character. A wide boulevard passes straight through the entire inner city and while the various sections of it have different names, the locals simply call the road the 'Prado'.

From here it is not far to the sightseeing attractions such as

the cathedral, which was completed in 1933 and has capacity for 12,000 people. The Bolivian metropolis is a good base for tours to the Nevado del Illimani, the highest mountain in the country, to the east of the city.

18 **Nevado del Illimani** The journey to this 6,880-m-high (22,573-ft) mountain in the Cordillera Real can be tedious as the road leading directly to the base of Illimani is occasionally closed. The road to the small Indian village of Comunidad Uno is recommended as an alternate route. Climbers can start the ascent of the mountain from here too, and base camp is reached in about five hours of hiking.

in Bolivia after Lake Titicaca. Lake Poopó receives some of its water from the outflow of Lake Titicaca from the Río Desaguadero. The lake is very shallow in comparison to the up to 280-m-deep (919-ft) Lake Titicaca, with a depth of just a few meters. High levels of evaporation over the decades have caused a slow but consistent drop in the water level and surface area of the lake. Its swampy shores are only sparsely populated.

㉒ Laguna Tarapaya The road now heads south-east to another scenic highlight of the region, an almost perfectly circular lake with a diameter of some 100 m (328 ft) in the crater of an extinct volcano, Laguna Tarapaya. This thermal pool has a temperature of about 35°C (95°F). The Balneario de Tarapaya, at 3,400 m (11,155 ft), is a perfect place to relax, especially after long hikes at this altitude.

The onward journey is a steep climb towards Potosí, about 25 km (15 miles) away.

㉓ Potosí At just below 4,000 m (13,124 ft), Potosí was one of the wealthiest cities in all of South America between the 16th and 18th centuries. The

For locals the mountain is not only a symbol, it also represents an image of their country. With a little imagination you can recognize the outline of an Indian with wife, child and llama in the three peaks of the Nevado del Illimani. The southernmost of the three peaks is the highest and easily the most accessible, but it takes several days to complete the challenging hike.

Another awe-inspiring peak, the Mount Sajama volcano, lies to the west of the Inca Trail. From La Paz travel south-east to Patacamaya. From there a well-paved road branches off to the south-west. After 150 km (93 miles) on this road you reach the Sajama National Park in the center of which is the majestic 6,520-m (21,392-ft) volcano of the same name.

Back in Patacamaya, follow National Road 1, which has oil and gas pipelines running parallel to it. After 90 km (56 miles) turn off to the south-east at Caracollo, taking National Road 4 towards Cochabamba. The road passes a vast expanse of fertile farmland where grain, fruit and vegetables are grown.

⑲ Cochabamba In contrast to the raw climate of the highlands, the weather is much milder in Cochabamba, which is situated at 'only' 2,570 m (1,597 ft) above sea level. This city on the eastern slopes of the Andes has appropriately earned the name 'The city of eternal springtime'. The name Cochabamba, however, actually derives from the Quechua language and basically means 'swampy flatland'. It is home to a renowned university and, with about 600,000 residents, is one of the largest cities in Bolivia. Unlike most of the cities along the Inca Trail it has no pre-colonial history, having been first founded by the Spanish in 1574. Many Spanish immigrants settled here due to the comfortable climate. In the center of the city there are a number of houses and churches dating back to the city's early history. A poor-quality road leads from Cochabamba to the Tunari National Park, which extends to the mountain of the same name.

⑳ Oruro Back in Caracollo, continue for a few kilometers through some pretty bleak scenery until you reach the city of Oruro, elevation 3,710 m (12,173 ft). At the height of the tin-mining era, from the early 19th century to the middle of the 20th century, Oruro was one of the most important economic locations in Bolivia. That has changed since the mines were closed.

The locals' zest for life, however, remains the same and Oruro continues to be the center of the Bolivian carnival, which is celebrated here with sophisticated revelry. The dancers adorn themselves with colourful, ornately carved devil and ghost masks.

㉑ Lago de Poopó Only a short distance beyond Oruro is Lake Poopó. With a surface area of 2,800 sq km (1,740 sq mi), it is the second-largest lake

1 Market day on the main square in front of the cathedral in Copacabana.

2 Tiahuanaco, the sacred site and capital of an Andean culture of the same name that experienced its heyday between the 3rd and 9th centuries.

3 View over La Paz with snow-capped volcano.

4 Salar de Uyuni and Salar de Coipas, the two largest saltwater lakes in the Bolivian Altiplano.

wealth came from a mountain with relatively unspectacular looks, but of spectacular intrinsic value – the conical, 4,830-m-high (815,847-ft) Cerro Rico ('Rich Mountain').

The Spanish colonial rulers were fortunate enough to discover extensive silver reserves within this mountain, which they then proceeded to mine mercilessly. Tens of thousands of tonnes of silver were extracted but the lucrative mining activities had another side to them, namely Indian slave labour that led to countless deaths.

The silver mines have since been abandoned but tin-mining has become increasingly important in recent decades. Unfortunately for the people of Potosí, tin mining is not nearly as lucrative as silver.

Traces of the former wealth can be found in the city center – stately homes and churches from the Spanish colonial era, some of which have striking facades. The city and the neighbouring silver mines were declared a UNESCO World Heritage Site in 1987 and a bumpy road leads to the visitors' mine, located at an altitude of 4,300 m (14,108 ft).

Beyond Potosí the road (No 5) winds its way north. En route to the much lower-lying city of Sucre you descend some 1,400 m (4,593 ft) in altitude over a relatively short distance, with very steep gradients in places.

24 Sucre On the approach to the capital, at an altitude of about 2,600 m (8,531 ft), the glittering buildings of the 'White City' are visible even from a distance. Ivory-coloured baroque churches and religious buildings, whitewashed houses and regal palaces define Sucre, which was founded in 1538.

There are only a few Spanish colonial cities that are as well-preserved as this one. Buildings with stylish balconies and lovely arcades characterize the Old

Town, which was declared a UNESCO World Heritage Site in 1990. Even though Sucre has been the capital of Bolivia since 1828, there are only a few civil authorities here. The government and its ministries are based in La Paz.

The university here, founded in 1624, is one of the oldest in South America. Celebrated as the jewel of Bolivian colonial architecture, Sucre makes a fit-ting conclusion to the Inca Trail, running through two countries and two worlds.

1 A view over Potosí, the 'Silver City', towards the snow-capped peak of Cerro Rico.

2 The Universidad de San Francisco Xavier in Sucre has an impressive courtyard. Founded in 1624, it is one of the oldest universities in South America.

Lima With its two towers, the 16th-century cathedral here is one of the Peruvian capital's featured architectural treasures.

Pachacámac Located directly outside Lima are the remains of the temple complex of Pachacámac. One of the most important buildings in the complex was the 80-m-high (262-ft) sun pyramid, the ruins of which sit on top of an artificially constructed hill.

Machu Picchu These ruins represent the zenith of Inca architecture. Built in the 15th century, the city was situated on sophisticated terraces and its construction is profound evidence of highly accomplished technical skill and know-how. This unique complex is a UNESCO World Heritage Site.

Huari In its heyday (6th–10th century), the Huari Empire extended over almost the whole of Peru. Theories postulate that up to 100,000 people lived in this center of Huari power. The giant stone sculptures are testimony to their high degree of artistic ability.

Tipón Inca settlements such as Tipón arose around Cuzco. The remains of the now uncovered village are open to visitors.

Manú National Park This national park extends from the central Andes to the rainforest in the Amazon lowlands.

Sacsayhuamán Built at the end of the 15th century, this fortress is one of many outstanding examples of Inca architecture. It was impregnable for centuries.

Cuzco This city, at 3,500 m (11,484 ft), is characterized not only by buildings from the Inca era but also by those from the Spanish colonial period. The Renaissance-style cathedral (17th century) is an example.

Lake Titicaca The 8,300-sq-km (5,158-sq-mi) lake at 3,812 m (12,507 ft) belongs to both Peru and Bolivia. Descendants of the Uros people living on the lake are renowned for their 'floating' islands built from reeds.

Tiahuanaco So-called 'nail heads' portray priests on a temple wall of the former center of an Andean culture, Tiahuanaco. The town was founded in around AD 300.

La Paz The highest city in the world (4,000 m/13,124 ft) sprawls in a basin at the foot of the Andes. There are only a few old buildings, one of which is a prominent cathedral with capacity for 12,000 people.

Potosí Following the discovery of a silver mine in Cerro Rico in 1545, this town became one of the largest cities in the world. It then went into decline once the silver reserves were depleted around 1800.

Sucre Bolivia's official capital (La Paz is the seat of government) is home to one of the oldest universities in South America (1624).

A perfect volcanic cone in the Chilean Andes at the edge of the Atacama Desert, covering a 1000 km (600 miles) strip of land along the Pacific Ocean.

Chile

On the Panamericana Highway down the Chilean Pacific coast

"When God looked at the world He had created in seven days, He realized that there were a number of things left over: volcanoes, primeval forests, deserts, fjords, rivers and ice. He told the angels to stack them up behind a long mountain chain. Those mountains were the Andes – and that is how Chile came to be the most diverse country on earth."

That is how one legend describes the creation of Chile, also referred to by some as the "country with the craziest geography". Indeed, its proportions are record-breaking: the country covers more than 4,300 km (2,672 mi), from Arica in the north on the border with Peru to the border post in the southern Tierra del Fuego, and is never wider than 180 km (112 mi).

Chile has covers an area of 756,629 sq km (470,169 sq mi). The Panamerican Highway, known as the Panamericana in Chile, is the backbone of the country's infrastructure. It links the most important cities and, for the most part, runs straight through the central Chilean valley. Two roads branch off from the Panamericana to the east and the west, leading either

Guanacos (Lama guanicoe) are prized for their soft coats.

into the mountains or out to the coast. The majority of the more than fifteen million Chileans live in the three main regions: the so-called "Small North", central Chile around the capital, Santiago de Chile, and the so-called "Small South" between Temuco and Puerto Montt. The "Great North" region is a desert that extends for more than 1,000 km (621 mi) from Arica to the south of Antofagasta. It is a desert with ochre-colored mountains, snow-covered volcanoes, deep blue lagoons, green oases and white shimmering salt lakes. Known as the Atacama, it is one of the driest and most hostile regions on the planet. The aridity is caused by the cold Humboldt Current, an ocean current off the Pacific Coast of South America that flows northwards from the Antarctic. The low water

The majority of the high-rises in Santiago de Chile are in the newer areas of the city, such as here in Providencia.

Lago Chungara in the Parque Nacional Lauca is at an elevation of 4,570 m (14,994 ft), making it the highest lake in the world. It is home to over 130 species of bird.

temperatures result in the regular build up of fog, which largely prevents precipitation. Life exists here only at a few oases, but this coastal desert is definitely one of the most interesting destinations in Chile. It has also been one of the country's most economically important regions since the 19th century. The rich saltpeter deposits here were the catalyst for the so-called Salt-peter War between Chile on the one side, and Peru and Bolivia on the other. Other mineral resources are mined here as well, such as copper in Chuquicamata west of Calama, the world's largest opencast copper mine. Rainfall increases towards the south so that the desert landscape in the "Small North" is scattered with rivers and some agricultural production.

Central Chile around Santiago is the primary wine growing and agricultural region as well as the most industrialized area. Coastal towns like Viña del Mar, are popular summer resorts and Valparaíso is the country's most important port. The "Small South" is known as the lake district, with lakes strung from north to south along the Andes like a chain of pearls: Lago Villarrica, Lago Llanquihue and Lago Todos Los Santos – to name just a few of the major ones. Most of them are accompanied by towering volcanoes and surrounded by thick forests where the rare araucaria conifers grow. The "Large South" is also referred to as the "wild south". South of Puerto Montt and the Isla Grande de Chiloé is the beginning of a remote, almost

uninhabited region filled with glaciers, islands, fjords and cold rain forests – and of course a chilly climate. The best way to get there is via the Carretera Austral, a road built in the 1970s, that cuts through wilderness, skirts majestic fjords and

lakes, traverses raging white-water rivers, climbs mountains and sweeps across vast meadow landscapes, swamp areas and pristine forests before coming to an end in Puerto Yungay at the mouth of the Río Bravo on the Pacific coast.

A covered well in the village of Parinacota in the Parque Nacional Lauca in northern Chile. The park is home to a rich fauna of llamas and alpacas.

Chile is an "island on the mainland": In the north it is bordered by the driest desert on the planet; to the west are the crashing waves of the Pacific; to the east are the towering peaks of the Andes. In the south the narrow strip of land breaks up into islands and islets that get lost in the Antarctic Ocean. Anyone looking to experience the beauty of this country should travel along the Panamericana.

1 Arica The northernmost town in Chile is one of the country's oldest settlements. People have lived here at the mouth of the Río San José on the Pacific coast for thousands of years. The Spanish built a port here to ship the silver from the Potosí mines. The best view of town is from Morro, a 200-m-high (656 ft) rocky peak south of the center where can look down at the bustling fishing port and the Iglesia San Marcos (1875), one of Gustave Eiffel's early works. Beaches stretch for miles south of the town.

The Museo Arqueológico in the suburb of San Miguel de Azapa is worth a visit. It has Chinchorro mummies on display that are thought to be over 7,500 years old. In the mummification process, the Chinchorro removed all soft tissue and muscles from the corpse, hollowed out the skull and rebuilt the skeleton. The head was fixed to the body by means of a wooden stick and all cavities were filled and padded with straw and wool. There are two options for the onward journey south from Arica. The shorter follows the Panamericana (Ruta Nacional 5) which often hugs the Pacific coast and rolls over the coastal mountains towards the south.

You reach Humberstone after 265 km (165 mi). From there it is 40 km (25 mi) to Iquique. The longer, more interesting option takes you through the Chilean Altiplano, past 6,000-m (19,686-ft) volcanoes, salt lakes, geysers and some tiny villages. From Arica, Ruta 11 follows the Río Lluta Valley and initially runs parallel to the railway line that links Arica with La Paz, Bolivia. After a little more than 12 km (7.5 mi) you will be able to see the gigantic geoglyphs on the mountainsides depicting llamas, humans and other figures. You soon reach Poconchile with its attractive adobe church built in 1605. Like most of the village churches in Northern Chile, it has a freestanding, tiered bell tower. The roof and the door are made from the wood of the large candelabra cactuses that are visible all along the route.

2 Putre The scenic village of Putre at an elevation of 3,500 m (11,484 ft) is a green oasis in an otherwise desolate landscape and is the most important stop on the route from Arica near the Bolivian border. It is also the gateway to the Parque Nacional Lauca. Many visitors use a stop in the village to acclimatize to the elevation. Soroche, or altitude sickness, can make itself felt as of 3,000 m (9,843 ft). The village has about 1,200 residents, the majority of whom are Aymara Indians.

The village church was built in 1670. At 6,825 m (22,393 ft), the

Travel Information

Route profile
Length: approx. 4,300 km (2,672mi), with detours 6,500 km (4,050 mi)
Length: at least 5 weeks
Start: Arica
End: Puerto Yungay
Route (main locations): Arica, Iquique, Valparaíso, Santiago de Chile, Temuco, Villarrica, Valdivia, Puerto Montt, Coihaique, Lago General Carrera, Puerto Yungay

Traffic information:
The Panamericana is in good condition pretty much throughout, and parts of it even of highway quality. Difficult dirt roads are mainly in the north on the detours to and in Parque Nacional Lauca.

The Carretera Austral is a dirt road of good quality in all weather conditions. BUT, it is only accessible along its full length in summer because the necessary ferries only operate between December and February.

Health:
Tiredness and headaches are the initial, still harmless symptoms of elevation sickness. You should descend to the lower regions as soon as the first signs appear.

Information:
General:
www.sernatur.cl
www.turismochile.com
www.geographia.com/chile

dilleras rising up more than 600 m (1,969 ft) from the ocean. Above Iquique is a gigantic sand dune. The port is of economic significance as a reloading point, initially for guano, later for saltpeter and today for fishmeal. The center of Iquique is very compact, but atypical for South America as its cathedral is not right on the main plaza. Instead, the plaza boasts buildings that are testimony to the wealth created from saltpeter mining: the large, classicist Teatro Municipal, opened in 1890, the clock tower that has adorned the plaza since 1877, and the Centro Español with its elegant restaurant built in 1904. South of the plaza is Calle Baquedano a street with the town's loveliest wooden buildings as well as the Museo Regional. The latter provides an outstanding overview of the history of the "Great North".

The distance from Iquique to Antofagasta is about 480 km (298 mi). You have a choice between two routes: one climbs directly up into the coastal range from Iquique and follows the Panamericana. You can make detours from the main road to the Atacama and San

Nevado de Putre towers impressively over the village.

❸ Parque Nacional Lauca The road continues to climb the mountain into the national park and affords a terrific mountain panorama, particularly once you get to Lago Chungara at an elevation of 4,570 m (14,994 ft) on the border with Bolivia. The lake often reflects Las Payachatas, the twin icy volcanoes Pomarape in Bolivia that rise more than 6,000 m (20,000 ft) above the Altiplano plateau. From the national park the route continues south along the border, initially through the Reserva Nacional Las Vicuñas to Salar de Surire, a salt lake at an elevation

of 4,200 m (13,780 ft) where you can often see flamingos. The Parque Nacional Volcán Isluga covers 174,744 ha (431,792 acre) and begins south of the Salar. It includes part of the Cordillera Occidental and is dominated by the still active volcano of the same name (5,530 m/18,144 ft). You'll pass through a number of villages such as Isluga before reaching the southern edge of Baños de Puchuldiza National Park, a geyser field at an elevation of over 4,000 m (13,124 ft).

❹ Gigante de Atacama The "Desert Giant" geoglyph is on the Cerro Unitá just before Huara. The ground drawing is 86 m (94 yds) long and presum-

ably depicts an Indian ruler or a deity. From here it is just 70 km (43 mi) to Humberstone.

❺ Humberstone Once a boomtown and the economic center of the region, Humberstone is no more than a ghost town now. It was here that the saltpeter required to make gunpowder and artificial fertilizers was mined after 1872.

After a descent of 15 km (9 mi) down to the coast you reach the port of Iquique.

❻ Iquique The largest town in northern Chile, with 150,000 inhabitants, sprawls out on a narrow plain between the Pacific and the wall of coastal cor-

1 The Parque Nacional Lauca on the Chilean Altiplano lies at an elevation of some 4,000 m (13,124 ft) and is dominated by several 6,000-m (19,686-ft) peaks such as Parinacota.

2 A herd of llamas with Las Payachatas in the background, two volcanoes in the Chile-Bolivia border region. To the left is the 6,282-m (20,611-ft) Pomarape; to the right is the 6,342-m (20,808-ft) Parinacota.

3 The area near Iquique has cordilleras that rise 600–1,000 m (1,969–3,281 ft) almost directly out of the sea.

Pedro de Atacama at the María Elena turnoff (Ruta 24). The other option is to take Ruta 1 along the coast, which cruises past the seemingly neverending white sandy beaches.

7 La Portada On the coastal route about 20 km (12 mi) north of Antofagasta you reach La Portada, a rocky arch towering up out of the Pacific surf. The steep coast here is made up of shell limestone and is eroded away by the ocean. La Portada, however, is on top of the coastal cliffs, enabling it to withstand the waves. The area around the arch is a great place for watching pelicans and other seabirds.

8 Antofagasta The largest town in the north, with around 225,000 people, owes its wealth and development to the port from which Chile's abundant natrual resources from the desert are shipped throughout the world – formerly guano and saltpeter, today copper. There is no mistaking the English influence from the saltpeter era on the Plaza Colón in the town center where a miniature Big Ben stands. The plaza is surrounded by attractive neo-Gothic buildings such as the cathedral and the town theater with beautful vitraux inside.

Just over 900 km (565 miles) of desert open up south of Antofagasta. The famous Panamericana climbs up over the plateau before heading down again to the coast passing Parque Nacional Pan de Azúcar near the seaside town of Chañaral.

The nature reserve offers sandy beaches and vast desert areas for penguins, cormorants, pelicans and seals.

This is followed by the port of Caldera and the Panamericana then heads for the interior, passing through the mining town of Copiapó, which is in a rich silver and copper mining district, and has an outstanding Museo Mineralógico. After 350 km (217 mi) you reach the Pacific again near La Serena.

be navigated by rickety elevators that date back to the second half of the 19th century.

14 Isla Negra "Black Island" is a fishing village around 80 km (50 mi) south of Valparaíso. The largest and loveliest house in town belongs to Chilean winner of the Nobel Prize for Literature, Pablo Neruda. It is an imaginative structure directly on the Pacific coast, half family home, half castle.
From Isla Negra there is a road that connects you with the highway to Santiago.

15 Santiago de Chile The Chilean capital is the country's undisputed center. Founded in 1541, it is not only home to one-third of the entire population of Chile (around five million) but also to almost all of the country's important political, economic and cultural institutions. On a clear day, Santiago, affords wonderful panoramic views of the snow-covered peaks of the Andes and the rich green exapnse of the plains. It also boasts a number of especially lovely colonial buildings around the lively

9 La Serena Thanks to its expansive beaches, this town of 100,000 has developed in recent decades into one of Chile's most popular seaside resorts. But it is not only swimmers who head for La Serena. Founded in 1544, the town has a great deal of colonial character and yet owes much of its charisma to the conversions of the 1950s. The center boasts twenty-nine churches, most of them from the 17th to 19th centuries, an attractive market as well as a mineralogical and an archaeological museum.

10 Valle del Río Elqui The Río Elqui Valley extends east of La Serena and is a tropical paradise in the midst of the desert, with grapevines, fig and papaya trees growing between

the basically barren mountains. The valley is scattered with small towns like Vicuña, birthplace of Nobel Prize winner for Literature, Gabriela Mistral. Vicuña also boasts another draw: the Planta Capel where the country's best Pisco, Chilean schnapps, is distilled.

11 Parque Nacional Bosque de Fray Jorge South of La Serena, the onward journey takes you by Parque Nacional Bosque Fray Jorge, encompassing a wetland forest area close to the coast. The park has a special microclimate due to the rising coastal fog and the resulting humidity. On the stretch from the national park to Viña del Mar, wide beaches and charming seaside resorts like Los Vilos await you.

12 Cristo Redentor de los Andes Shortly before Viña del Mar it is worth taking a detour to the east on Ruta 60, which takes you high up into the Andes before crossing the border with Argentina. At an elevation of 4,000 m (13,124 ft) the statue of Christ, Cristo Redentor de los Andes, marks the national border in this rugged and majestic mountain landscape. Just a short distance down the road, on the Argentinean side, you will be able to enjoy probably the best view of Aconcagua peak at 6,959 m (22,832 ft).
Leaving the mountain world of the Andes to return to the Pacific, two very different but very appealing towns await your arrival.

13 Viña del Mar and Valparaíso These two towns have nearly merged into one larger entity. Viña del Mar is Chile's best-known coastal resort with wide beaches, lovely parks and expensive hotels. Valparaíso, on the other hand, is the country's largest port and the seat of the Chilean parliament. It stretches along a large bay and extends high up the mountain. The steep hillsides in town can

1 The icon of the Antofagasta region is La Portada, an archway of shell limestone.

2 The coastal landscape of the Parque Nacional Pan de Azúcar.

3 With its lovely beaches and its proximity to the capital, Viña del Mar is one of Chile's most popular and most beautiful coastal resorts.

4 The center of Santiago de Chile at dusk. In the foreground to the right is the Moneda, the seat of government.

5 The old town of Valparaíso extends right up the hillside. The steeper slopes are sometimes bridged by elevators.

525

plaza, and the sea of buildings downtown is dominated by high-rises.

It is easy to list the most important sightseeing attractions: the plaza with the cathedral, completed in 1789; the Palacio de la Moneda, which was built as a mint in 1799, but has been the presidential palace since 1846; and the Iglesia de San Francisco with its accompanying convent, which were built in the 16th century and are today the oldest buildings in Santiago. The city has suffered earthquakes and outbreaks of fire over the centuries. It is worth taking a day's excursion to the Maipo Valley (Cajón del Maipo), known for its fine wineries.

South of Santiago, the Panamericana traverses the long valley running through the center of Chile – the country's orchard and bread basket. The road is lined with vast plantations and large storage warehouses where it is not uncommon to see trucks being loaded with the apples, grapes and other fruit grown in the area. You pass Talca and Chillán before reaching a superb waterfall after 400 km (249 mi).

16 Salto del Laja The Panamericana crosses the Río Laja about 25 km (16 mi) north of Los Angeles. Just above the bridge the river, which is about 100 m (109 yds) wide at this point, drops nearly 50 m (164 ft) over a high rocky plateau, forming the Salto del Laja, Chile's largest waterfall. A short walk takes you directly to the falls.

17 Temuco The town of Pablo Neruda's birth has a population of about 250,000 residents, making it one of the largest towns in the south and the economic center of this primarily agricultural region. You can get

a taste of Chilean country life at the Feria Libre, the huge market to the south-west of the railway station where many Mapuche Indians from the region's more remote villages sell their wares. The Mercado Municipal is more tourist-oriented and mainly has handicrafts on offer. The Museo Regional de la Araucania offers details of the culture and history of the region and its inhabitants, the Mapuche.

Temuco is the starting point for a number of excursions into the Andes and so, instead of following the Panamericana further south, it is worthwhile taking a detour through the various national parks and the Andes as well as briefly crossing over into Argentina.

18 Villarrica South of Temuco, near Loncoche, there is a road that branches off the Panamericana to the east that will take you to Villarrica. This town's

location on one of Chile's loveliest lakes has made it into one of the country's most popular tourist destinations.

From here you can enjoy a wonderful view of the active volcano of the same name (2,847 m/9,341 ft) with its nearly symmetrical cone and tidy collar of snow beautifully reflected in the sizable lake.

Lago Villarrica is the northernmost of a string of lakes that extend south as far as Lago Llanquihue.

After passing the tourist town of Pucón, and between the Villarrica and Huerquehue national parks – the latter has extensive araucaria forests –, you will cross the border into the Argentinean Parque

the river where you will find all kinds of fish and seafood on offer. The next stop is Lago Llanquihue, 70 km (43 mi) south of Osorno. This marks the south end of the Chilean lake district.

㉒ Lago Llanquihue Covering 877 sq km (339 sq mi) this is the second-largest lake in Chile after Lago General Carrera. Llanquihue's deepest point is 350 m (1,148 ft) and, like most of the country's lakes it is glacial in origin, a so-called moraine basin edged with detritus deposited by the glaciers.
Towering above the lake is the 2,652-m-high (8,701-ft) Osorno volcano which, like the Villarrica volcano, has a nearly flawless cone shape. There are a number of popular tourist towns along the lake, a couple of which were founded by German immigrants including Puerto Varas and Fruillar, mostly famous for its open-air museum. Only a stone's throw away is Puerto Montt, a harbor town on the Seno de Reloncaví, the north end of the Golfo de Ancud.

㉓ Puerto Montt This town itself is not particularly attractive for visitors but it is a handy starting point for journeys into Chile's "wild south" and the island of Chiloé. On the outskirts of town it is worth visiting Angelmo, where one of Chile's largest handicraft markets is held. You will find mountains of thick, knitted pullovers,

Nacional Lanín and come to San Martín de los Andes, a small town that is a perfect jumping off point for exploring the Argentinean Andes. Not only does the "Seven Lakes Road" take you to more than seven lakes, it also passes torrential waterfalls and travels through thick forests to the Parque Nacional Nahuel Huapí.

⑲ Parque Nacional Nahuel Huapí This national park is one of the largest and most popular of its kind in Argentina. Lago Nahuel Huapí, a sizable glacial lake that covers an overall surface area of 500 sq km (193 sq mi), forms the heart of the park. The route continues past another lake to a further Andes park back in Chile.

⑳ Parque Nacional Puyehue The highest peak in this park is Puyehue, a still active volcano that rises 2,236 m (7,336 ft) and last erupted in 1960. The park is home to pumas and pudús (a type of small deer).
Passing the small town of Entre Lagos, "between" Lago Puyehue and Lago Rupanco, you will get back on the Panamericana at Osorno. Anyone still wanting to visit the port of Valdivia will need to continue about 100 km (62 mi) further north.

㉑ Valdivia Founded and named after Spanish conquistador Pedro de Valdivia in 1552, this is one of the loveliest towns in Chile. Valdivia today boasts a modern skyline after having been almost completely leveled by a series of earthquakes, including submarine, or offshore, earthquakes, in 1960. The main attraction here is the Mercado Fluvial on the banks of

1 Salto del Huilo Huilo is the most spectacular of Chile's waterfalls, plunging 100 m (328 ft).

2 The Parque Nacional Lanin in Argentina, here in a decidedly autumnal mood.

3 View over Lago Llanquihue towards the 2,652-m-high (8,701-ft) Osorno volcano.

wood carvings, as well as regional delicacies such as cheese, honey, liqueur, dried mussels and dried algae on offer. All kinds of seafood is also served from bubbling pots in the fishing port.

From Puerto Montt it is another 60 km (37 mi) to Pargua and Calbuco, where the ferries embark to Isla Grande de Chiloé. If you're lucky, you may be accompanied by dolphins.

For anyone wanting to skip this detour, the journey continues along the east coast of the gulf toward Parque Nacional Alerce Andino.

24 **Parque Nacional Alerce Andino** The Alerce Reserve extends along the Seno and the Estuario de Reloncaví. This pristine forest features the Alerce, or Patagonian Cypress (related to the redwood), large trees that can reach diameters of up to 4 m (13 ft), and heights of up to 50 m (164 ft). Many of the trees are around 1,000 years old.

Puerto Montt is also the starting point of the famous Carretera Austral, Chile's most scenic route into the remote south. For the most part, Ruta 7 is unpaved for over 1,000 km (621 mi) taking you through forests, around lakes, past fjords and by snow-capped peaks. There are only some 100,000 people living in the region, which covers about 150,000 sq km (57,900 sq mi). Even the first 200 km (124 mi) of the Carretera Austral from Puerto Montt to Chaitén are a tough haul. There are two expansive estuaries to be crossed: the one from Caleta La Arena to Puelche takes 30 minutes and the one from Hornopirén to Caleta Gonzalo takes five hours and includes entering Parque Natural Pumalín.

25 **Parque Natural Pumalín** This 270,000-ha (667,170-acre) nature reserve was created by Douglas Tompkins, a successful American businessman

focused on environmentalism. The sanctuary includes spectacular Pacific coast fjords, steep mountains and pristine forests. With 4,500 to 6,000 mm (177 to 236 in) of rain a year, the lichens and ferns compete with bamboo and fuchsia plants, while centuries-old giant alerce confiers continue to tower among the southern beech trees. There are hiking trails leading deep into this magical forest.

Next comes the small town of Chaitén before the road passes Lago Yelcho in the Río Yelcho Valley and heads on to some expansive meadowlands. The next point of reference is the settlement of La Junta, about 150 km (93 mi) south of Chaitén, followed by Puerto Puyuhuapi. This storybook pioneer village is the starting point for a visit to Queulat National Park and Isla Magdalena. It is also home to a handful of quaint, atypical wooden houses.

26 **Parque Nacional Queulat** This nature sanctuary encompasses 154,000 ha (380,534 acres) of unspoilt forest with wonderful ferns and lianas, bamboo trees and pangue plants. The latter are similar to rhubarb, with leaves easily reaching the size of an umbrella. The park rises up from the ocean in several plateaus until it reaches an elevation of 2,225 m (7,300 ft). There is a hiking trail to the Ventisquero Colgante glacier, or "hanging glacier". Its tongue protrudes threateningly over a saddle between two mountains.

On the way to Coihaique almost 200 km (124 mi) away it is worth taking a detour to Puerto Aisén, a port and starting point for boat cruises through the fjords, including the Laguna San Rafael. After the turnoff to Puerto Aisén the road follows the Río Simpson as far as Coihaique. The river's southern catchment area is protected in the Reserva Nacional Río Simpson.

27 Coihaique "The land between the water" is what the indigenous inhabitants called this place at the confluence of two rivers. Today it has 50,000 residents. A hiking trail leads to the Verde and Venus lagoons close to the Reserva Nacional Coihaique. After driving about 200 km (124 mi) through dense-ly forested lands you then come to Lago General Carrera near Puerto Murta .

28 Lago General Carrera With 1,840 sq km (710 sq mi) of coverage, this body of water on the border with Argentina is the largest lake in Chile and in the Patagonian Andes. The Chilean part of the lake is surrounded by the mighty peaks of the southern Andes: Cerro Campana (2,194 m/7,199 ft), Pico Sur (2,190 m/7,185 ft), Cerro Hyades (3,078 m/10,099 ft) and Cerro San Valentín (4,058 m/13,314 ft). The smaller Argentinean part, known as Lago Buenos Aires, is imbedded in the Patagonian lowlands. Following Río Baker you reach Cochrane after about 150 km (93 mi). From there it is still 120 km (75 mi) to Puerto Yungay.

29 Puerto Yungay This settlement at the mouth of the Río Bravo in the Mitchell Fjord was only founded in the 1990s for the construction of the Carretera Austral. It marks the end of your journey and its port provides an important link with the north.

1 The Villarrica volcano is 2,847 m (9,341 ft) high and has a near perfect conical shape.

2 The Carretera Austral road in the Río Baker valley.

3 Large ice blocks break off from the tongue of the Glaciar San Rafael with a loud crash, then drift through the 120-km-long (75-mi) Fjord Estero Elefantes.

Parque Nacional Lauca This nature sanctuary is on the vast, 4,000-m-high (13,124-ft) Altiplano home of snow-covered 6,000-m (19,686-ft) peaks. The shores of one of the highest lakes in the world, Lago Chungará (4,570 m/14,994 ft), are home to over 130 bird species.

Géiser el Tatio These geysers at an elevation of 4,300 m (14,108 ft) are always active in the early morning hours. Those who want to can swim in a warm water basin in the middle of the steppe landscape while icy temperatures prevail all around.

Chañaral This area around a mining town has numerous canyons and is influenced by the cold Humboldt Current. Due to the frequent coastal fog the interior is constantly dry.

Observatories Low humidity, clean air and starry nights prevail in the Chilean Andes, ideal conditions for observatories. Here, the Cerro Tololo Inter-American Observatory.

Viña del Mar The "Vineyard at the Sea" is Chile's most famous seaside resort, with nice beaches, old palaces, magnificent parks and the Casino Municipal. It is reminiscent of Nice and Monte Carlo.

Valparaíso "Paradise Valley", Chile's largest port, sprawls over a great many hills. The differences in elevation within the city are sometimes overcome with elevators.

Reserva Nacional las Vicuñas The vast vicuña herds are what gave this sanctuary on the Altiplano its name. The smallest of the Andean camel species (shoulder height 85 cm/33 in) produces fine, light wool and has thus far resisted all attempts at domestication.

Licancábur This volcano is on the border with Bolivia and is 5,916 m (19,410 ft) high. The deep crater lake and the sacrificial sites on the crater's edge make it an anomaly in the chain of Atacama volcanoes.

San Pedro de Atacama This adobe village on the northern shore of the Salar de Atacama is home to a church made partly of cactus wood. The bizarre landscape is magnificent, with glowing deserts and snowy mountains in the background.

Valle de la Luna "Moon Valley" is aptly named as it boasts a wealth of fantastic sand, salt and clay formations which, at sunset, appear indeed to be otherworldly.

Aconcagua The best view of Aconcagua, one of the highest mountains in the Andes at 6,959 m (22,832 ft), is from the pass where a number of Chilean winter sports resorts are located.

Santiago de Chile One-third of all Chileans lives in the capital city. Only a few colonial-era buildings remain, such as the Casa Colorada or the Posada del Corregidor. On a clear day you have an impressive view of the snow-covered peaks of the Andes.

Cajón del Maipo This valley situated in the foothills of the Andes is especially popular with wine lovers.

Chillán The valleys between Santiago and Osorno are popular among trekking and skiing fans. The town was destroyed by an earthquake in 1751.

Valdivia Despite damage from fires, this university town is one of the loveliest in Chile. Its various markets, in particular, still show the influence of German colonists.

Puerto Varas The legacy of immigrant Germans in the Lago Llanquihue area is clearly visible.

Isla Grande de Chiloé This island is 180 km (112 mi) long and 50 km (31 mi) wide. It is inhabited mainly by farmers and fishermen, and is famous for more than 150 wooden churches built by the Jesuits.

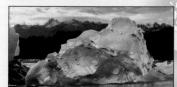

Laguna San Rafael A boat cruise from Puerto Aisén provides a close-up look at the impressive glacier tongue and the icebergs in the fjord.

Villarrica This volcano is 2,847 m (9,341 ft) and towers over the southern Chilean lake district.

Parque Nacional Villarrica With the volcano as a backdrop on Lago Villarrica, this national park is one of the loveliest of its kind in Chile.

Parque Nacional Lanín Lanín is an extinct volcano (3,776 m/12,389 ft) and the main highlight of this vast sanctuary.

Parque Nacional Nahuel Huapí The main attraction here is a glacial lake of the same name. The highest peak: Cerro Tronador (3,554 m/11,661 ft).

Osorno The snow-covered Osorno (2,652 m/8,701 ft), also known as Pise, towers behind Lago Rupanco and is a nearly perfectly shaped cone.

Lago Llanquihue Chile's second-largest lake covers 877 sq km (338 sq mi) and is up to 350 m (1,148 ft) deep. It is situated in the "Switzerland of Chile". The town of Frutillar still has many old colonial buildings as well as the "German Colonists' Museum".

Puerto Montt This port with 120,000 residents is the starting point for various journeys into Chile's "wild south" and to Isla Grande de Chiloé.

Salto Huilo Huilo One of the most spectacular Chilean waterfalls plunges 100 m (328 ft) into the abyss while the dense virgin forests surrounding it provide some fascinating hiking.

Isla Magdalena This barren island is inhabited by about 250,000 Magellan penguins that breed in October and March.

Parque Nacional Alerce Andino This park is home to Patagonian cypresses, which can grow up to 70 m (230 ft) in height.

Lago General Carrera The landscape around Chile's largest lake boasts very diverse vegetation and stunning vistas.

Coihaique This town is the ideal starting point for tours to the Cascada de la Virgen, pictured here.

The common rhea or nandu, a and in Argentinian Patagonia.

Argentina and Chile

Through the Pampas and Patagonia

Argentina is characterized by three major geographical regions that could scarcely be more different from one another – the endless Pampas, the high peaks of the Andes, and the plains of Patagonia with their steep isolated mountains and glaciers. Part of the Andes and some of the southern foothills of Patagonia near the Tierra del Fuego belong to Chile.

icas. The Andes Mountains mark the natural border between Argentina and neighbouring Chile. National parks have been established on both

sides of the border in magnificent mountain landscapes containing virgin forests interspersed with shimmering blue and green lakes and rivers of

Covering an area of more than 2.8 million sq km (1 million sq mi), Argentina is the second-largest country in South America after its signficantly larger neighbour Brazil. The Pampas, which make up the heartland of Argentina, are a vast green expanse on which isolated mountain ranges emerge like islands in an ocean, from Buenos Aires all the way to the western border with Chile.

One such 'island' is the Sierra de Córdoba, a range that rises west of Córdoba in the Cerro Champaqui to a height of 2,884 m (9,614 ft), indeed a considerable height, but that is nothing compared to the peaks west of Mendoza. There, the Cerro Aconcagua, or 'Stone Sentinel', towers to 6,963 m (23,000 ft) and is both the highest peak in the Andes and the highest mountain in the Amer-

An Argentinian gaucho herding his cattle on the Pampas.

flightless bird, lives on the Pampas

The tongue of the Perito Morena Glacier in Los Glaciares National Park is some 70 m (233 ft) high.

Like an impregnable fortress, the granite towers of the Torres del Paine in Chile rise from the plains of southern Patagonia. They are a favourite destination for adventurous trekkers from all over the world.

cloudy glacier water. The areas are a paradise for hikers and include the Lanín National Park, where dense forests of araucaria and Antarctic beech engulf the mighty Lanín volcano. At the base of this 3,747-m (12,290-ft) volcano is a deep blue lake, Lago Huechulafquén. While northern Patagonia occasionally offers gentle landscapes such as that of the Nahuel Huapi National Park, in the south the landscape becomes progressively more windswept and barren. The constant Westerlies bring humidity from the Pacific, falling as rain on the Chilean side of the Andes. They then sweep over the icy inland regions, glaciers and ice fields of Patagonia, which chill them

before they whip over the eastern plains.

The Andes open up here and there, revealing gaps between the peaks like the ones at Lago Buenos Aires – known as the Lago General Carrera on the Chilean side – and at the Los Glaciares National Park. Also typical of southern Patagonia are the isolated granite peaks that dominate the plains: the FitzRoy Massif and the Torres del Paine, for example.

It was not until the last ice age that the Strait of Magellan, once just a cleft in the Andes, split off from the mainland and created the island of Tierra del Fuego. This main island in the archipelago is 47,000 sq km (20,000 sq mi) with a landscape that clearly resem-

bles that of Patagonia. In the north is a broad plateau while in the south the last foothills of the Cordilleras reach heights of 2,500 m (9,000 ft),

finally sinking spectacularly into the sea at the notorious Cape Horn, whose perpetually stormy seas have been the bane of so many a brave sailor.

An impressive landscape of gorges and ravines east of San Carlos de Bariloche, a well-frequented holiday region in summer and winter.

From the Pampas through the mountains, past the granite massifs and glaciers of Patagonia, through the Strait of Magellan to Ushuaia, this dream route leads you all the way down through Argentina along the Pan-American Highway to the southern tip of Tierra del Fuego on Lapataia Bay.

1 Córdoba Argentina's second-largest city, with 1.5 million inhabitants, is known as 'La Docta', 'the Erudite', and it bears the nickname with pride. For it was here in 1614 that the country's first university was founded, and Córdoba still possesses excellent university faculties.

The city, founded in 1573, is surprisingly tranquil in its center. The plaza contains the arcaded Cabildo, the colonial-style government building, and the cathedral, built in 1574 in a mixed baroque and neoclassical style. A few steps further, through the pedestrian zone, you come to the so-called Manzana Jesuítica, the Jesuit quarter, with a Jesuit church and the first university buildings.

Passing through some dull suburbs, we leave Córdoba on Ruta 20 in the direction of Carlos Paz and reach the Sierra de Córdoba, which rises impressively from the Pampas to a height of 2,884 m (9,614 ft) in the Cerro Champaqui. At Villa Dolores, some 170 km (105 miles) south-west of Córdoba, you will leave the mountains behind and enter a flatter landscape that remains as such for the next 500 km (310 miles) until Mendoza.

2 Mendoza The green countryside around Mendoza is deceptive, as this city of 600,000 is located in a desert known as the Cuyo, meaning 'sandy earth'. Plentiful water from the nearby mountains has allowed the desert to bloom, and it is here that the finest Argentinian wines are produced.

Although Mendoza was founded as early as 1561, the city center is mostly modern because older portions have been repeatedly razed by earthquakes, most severely in 1861. All that remains is the Church of San Francisco, dating from 1638. The pedestrian area of the Calle Sarmiento, with its cafés and restaurants, and the suburb of Maipú, with bodegas that offer wine tastings, are worth a visit. From Mendoza, take a detour to the stunning Puente del Inca.

3 Puente del Inca The 'Inca Bridge', at a height of 2,720 m (9,000 ft), is a natural arch over the Río Mendoza that was formed by mineral deposits. Following the road westwards, you soon come to the best view of Aconcagua (see sidebar left). A dirt road then leads up to the old border zone on the Bermejo Pass at 3,750 m (12,500 ft). From there your climb will be rewarded by a wonderful view over the High Andes.

From Mendoza, Ruta 40 leads south. After about 300 km (190 miles) through the Cuyo, a road branches at El Sosneada to the west towards Las Leñas, Argentina's greatest skiing area. You will then head another 490 km (310 miles) south, parallel to the Andes, to Zapala.

This city has a museum displaying beautiful local minerals and

Travel Information

Route profile
Length: approx. 5,300 km (3,315 miles), excluding detours
Time required: 4 weeks
Start: Córdoba
End: Ushuaia
Route (main locations): Córdoba, Mendoza, Puente del Inca, San Carlos de Bariloche, Parque Nacional Los Glaciares, Parque Nacional Torres del Paine, Punta Arenas, Parque Nacional Tierra del Fuego,

Traffic information:
The trip mostly follows the Argentinian Ruta 40, which runs north-south along the eastern edge of the Andes. The highway is mostly surfaced, although a few of the side-roads in southern Patagonia are gravel. You will need to watch for oncoming traffic and pass close to it, otherwise loose stones flying up from the road could damage the windshield. It is generally not advisable to drive at night outside the cities.

Strait of Magellan:
There is a good ferry connection from the mainland to Tierra del Fuego; in summer, the ferries operate hourly.

More information:
www.ontheroadtravel.com
www.parquesnacionales.gov.ar
www.travelsur.net

area of 260,000 ha (650,000 acres) and is dedicated to the preservation of the alerces, gigantic evergreen trees that can reach heights of 70 m (235 ft) and have diameters of 4 m (14 ft). Some of them are estimated to be 3,500 years old. In the center of the park is the 78-sq-km (30-sq-mi) Lake Futalaufquén.

From the national park, Ruta 40 continues on to the south. It is 381 km (237 miles) from Esquel to Río Mayo, but shortly before this, Ruta 26 branches off to the east towards Sarmiento via the petrified forests, the Bosques Victor Szlapelis and J. Ormachea. To the west, Ruta 26 winds through the Andes to the Chilean city of Coyhaique. From this crossroads it is another 129 km (80 miles) south to Perito Moreno.

7 Perito Moreno This small town does not offer anything special, but it is the starting point for excursions to the milky, teal-coloured Lake Buenos Aires, the second-largest lake in South America after Lake Titicaca. The Argentinean side of the lake lies in the middle of the Patagonian plains; the Chilean side is surrounded by snow-covered peaks. You can cross the Chilean border at Los Antiguos, on the southern edge of the lake.

named. The 3,747-m (12,490-ft) volcano, which has a perfectly formed cone peak, is mirrored in glorious Lago Huechulafquén. It is the ideal backdrop for extended hikes. Back on Ruta 40, San Carlos de Bariloche is not far away.

5 San Carlos de Bariloche Bariloche was founded by Swiss immigrants, and is the 'Swiss side' of Argentina. The Centro Civico, the community center, is built to resemble a Swiss chalet. Best of all, the main shopping street features one chocolate factory after another, and all the restaurants have cheese fondue on the menu.

The first settlers sought and found a rural idyll here. Bariloche lies on one of Argentina's most beautiful lakes, Lago Nahuel Huapi, at the heart of the national park of the same name. The road leads further south through a magnificent mountain landscape until you reach Los Alerces National Park near the town of Esquel.

6 Los Alerces National Park This national park covers an

fossils. The distances are great in Argentina, but after another 156 km (100 miles) on Ruta 40 there is a road turning off to the west, leading to San Martín de los Andes, a little mountain town with the best approach to Lanín National Park.

4 Lanín National Park This park surrounds the extinct volcano for which the park is

1 Steppe as far as the eye can see – beginning just east of San Carlos de Bariloche, the vast Patagonian plains extend all the way out to the Atlantic Ocean.

2 A peak in the southern Pampas – the 3,680-m (12,266-ft) Cerro Payún south-east of Bardas Blancas.

3 Autumnal mood on Lake Nahuel Huapi in the national park of the same name.

Some 56 km (35 miles) south of Perito Moreno, the road forks, one branch leading to Cueva de las Manos (see sidebar right). It is another 239 km (148 miles) from Perito Moreno through the desolate Patagonian plains to the next settlement, Hotel las Horquetas, just a handful of houses in the Río Chico Valley. At an intersection here, a gravel road branches off to the west in the direction of Estancia la Oriental and Lake Belgrano. This is the route to the Perito Moreno National Park.

⑧ **Perito Moreno National Park** This is one of Argentina's most isolated and spectacular national parks. There are glaciers and shimmering mountain lakes with floating blocks of ice, and the park is teeming with wildlife such as pumas, foxes, wildcats, guanacos and waterfowl.

The second-highest mountain in Patagonia, Monte San Lorenzo (3,706 m/12,159 ft), is the home of the condor. The park can only be explored on foot or on horseback. There are hardly any roads or facilities – only campsites.

Tres Lagos is the name of the next crossroads on Ruta 40, about 235 km (146 miles) further on. At this point, Ruta 288 goes east towards the Atlantic. After another 45 km (28 miles) heading south is Lake Viedma. The road on this lake's northern bank leads westward and, on clear days, there is a fantastic view of the FitzRoy Massif.

⑨ **El Chaltén** This small town is the northern access point for Los Glaciares National Park, a dream destination for mountaineers from all over the world as it is home to the 3,375-m (11,072-ft) Mount FitzRoy. But it is not just for climbers.

Hikers will also find a plethora of activities. You can organize one-day or multi-day excur-

sions from El Chaltén. Back on Ruta 40, you pass through the Leona Valley and along the eastern bank of Lake Argentino to the junction to El Calafate in the Los Glaciares National Park.

⑩ **Los Glaciares National Park** There is considerably more activity at the southern end of this park, near El Calafate, than in the northern part. This is due to the spectacular glaciers that

can be much more easily accessed from here than from anywhere else. Large slabs of ice break off from the 70-m (230-ft) glacial walls, landing in the lake with an immense crash.

an east-west passage. Puerto Natales is the best starting point for a visit to nearby Torres del Paine National Park, and also a worthwhile stop for arranging various excursions. For example, you could take a boat ride on Seno de la Ultima Esperanza (Last Hope Sound) up to the border of the Bernardo O'Higgins National Park to Cerro Balmaceda (2,035 m/6,676 ft) with its impressive glaciers. Bird lovers should visit the town's old pier in the late afternoon. It's a meeting place for hundreds of cormorants.

12 **Cueva del Milodón** En route to the Torres del Paine National Park, it is well worth taking time to pay a short visit to Cueva del Milodón. To get there, go 8 km (5 miles) north out of Puerto Natales and head west. After 5 km (3 miles) you reach the cave where German immigrant Hermann Eberhard found remains of a huge dinosaur, a 4-m (13-ft) megatherium, in 1896. A replica of the creature by the entrance to the cave shows how it may have looked.

1 The drastic edge of the Perito Moreno Glacier in Los Glaciares is up to 70 m (230 ft) high. With a great roar, ice chunks the size of houses continually break off from its walls.

2 The icy blue-green waters of Lake del Grano in the Perito Moreno National Park.

3 Colourful sandstone cliffs near Sarmiento between Lake Musters and Lake Colhué Huapí.

4 The expansive green steppe in the Los Glaciares National Park with the Andes in the background.

5 The jagged peaks of the FitzRoy Massif tower over the rugged Patagonian plains.

The biggest of these giants is the Upsala Glacier, with a surface area of 595 sq km (230 sq mi). The most popular spot, however, is the Perito Moreno Glacier about 80 km (50 miles) from El Calafate, whose glacial tongue pushes out into Lake Argentino to such an extent that every few years it completely seals off the Brazo Rico, one of the lake's offshoots.

11 **Puerto Natales** The town, situated on the Ultima Esperanza Estuary, was the last hope of sailors who had got lost in the countless channels of southern Patagonia in their search for

⑬ Torres del Paine National Park The peaks of the Torres del Paine Massif rise dramatically from the windswept plain. These steep, seemingly impregnable mountains have granite peaks, the highest of which is Cerro Torre Grande at 3,050 m (10,007 ft), surrounded by the peaks of Paine Chico, Torres del Paine and Cuernos del Paine. This is Chile's adventure paradise. Visitors can choose between embarking on long hiking trails in the park, day-long tours, or a hiking trail around the entire massif. All these trails pass by bluish-white, opaque, glacial lakes with floating icebergs. They include Grey Glacier and the amazing Río Paine, which plummets into Lake Pehoe as a cascading waterfall.

The stunted trees brace themselves against the wind here, but in early summer the plains form a sea of flowers. In addition to guanacos, you will likely spot condors and sundry waterfowl. Remember to take warm clothing.

To the south of Puerto Natales, the route continues straight through the plains. Stubby grass grows on both sides of the road. You'll often see guanacos, rheas and sheep. This is Ruta 9 to Punta Arenas.

Some 34 km (21 miles) before the city, a road branches westwards. After 23 km (14 miles) you reach Otway Sound, home to a large penguin colony.

⑭ Monumento Natural Los Pingüinos There is another large penguin colony to the north-east of Punta Arenas, right on the Strait of Magellan. In the summer months, some 2,500 Magellan penguins, the smallest of the species, live in this colony. They only grow to between 50 and 70 cm (20 and 28 in) and weigh a mere 5 kg (11 lbs). They can be easily recognized by their black-and-white heads and the black stripe running across the upper part of their torsos.

⑮ Punta Arenas This city, founded in the mid 19th century as a penal colony, grew quickly and was an important port for ships plying the west coast of America until the con-

struction of the Panama Canal in 1914. Patagonia's profitable sheep-farming also made its contribution to the city's success, allowing wealthy inhabitants to build large sheep estancias (ranches) around the city center.

The Palacio Braun-Menéndez, today a museum, shows how the upper class lived in those days: walls covered in fabric imported from France, billiard tables from England, gold-plated fireguards from Flanders and Carrara marble decorations from Italy. Burials were no less regal here. The Punta Arenas cemetery contains the enormous mausoleums of the city's wealthier families. The Museo Regional Mayorino Borgatallo is also worth a visit.

From Punta Arenas you can drive 50 km (31 miles) back to the intersection of Ruta 9 and Ruta 255. Then follow Ruta 255 in a north-east direction until you reach Punta Delgada. From there, Ruta 3, which starts in Argentina, leads south and soon reaches the Strait, where a ferry transports travellers to Puerto Espora in Tierra del Fuego.

1 Guanacos, relatives of the llama, in a flowery meadow in the Torres del Paine National Park.

2 Rider on the Patagonian plains north of Punta Arenas.

One of the wonders of nature – a cluster of flowers, mainly lupins, in the Torres del Paine National Park, with snowy peaks in the background. This magnificent sight can be seen only in late spring and early summer.

16 Strait of Magellan/Tierra del Fuego In 1520, Fernando de Magellan was the first to sail through the Strait later named after him. As he skirted the mainland and the islands, he saw fire and smoke, hence the archipelago's name. The island group covers an area of 73,500 sq km (28,378 sq mi). Its main island, the western part of which belongs to Chile, covers an area of about 47,000 sq km (18,147 sq mi).

It is some 280 km (174 miles) from Puerto Espora to the Río Grande through vast, open countryside. At San Sebastián Bay, you can cross the border into Argentina. South of the Río Grande, the landscape changes – the valleys become narrower, the hills higher, and dense forests come into view. After about 250 km (155 miles), you reach Ushuaia and the adjacent Tierra del Fuego National Park.

17 Tierra del Fuego National Park Hikers will enjoy Tierra del Fuego National Park, which begins 18 km (11 miles) west of Ushuaia. It is easily accessible in its southern part but inaccessible in the north, and stretches along the Chilean border offering marshes, rocky cliffs and temperate rainforests.

Ruta 3, the Argentinean part of the southern Pan-American Highway, leads directly into the park and ends picturesquely at the Bahía Lapataía.

18 Ushuaia The southernmost city in the world is set between the icy waters of the deep Beagle Channel and the peaks of the Cordillera which, despite being only 1,500 m (4,921 feet) high, are always covered in snow. Originally founded as a penal colony, the city lives mostly from tourism these days. The Port of Ushuaia is proud to host large cruise ships on voyages through the Antarctic from November to March. The Museo Fin del Mundo has a collection depicting the early and colonial history of the region. If the weather is good, take a boat trip to the glorious 'End of the World', Cape Horn.

1 The Tierra del Fuego National Park entices adventuresome travellers with its expansive steppe, mountainous landscape and impenetrable jungles and rainforests.

2 Punta Arenas port in the Strait of Magellan.

3 View of Ushuaia port, the southermost city in the world. The foothills of the Darwin Cordillera rise up in the background.

Aconcagua The highest mountain in the Americas at 6,963 m (23,000 ft), Aconcagua is near Mendoza on the Chilean border. It was first 'officially' climbed in 1897. Today, 2,000 to 4,000 mountaineers enjoy it every year.

Mendoza This modern city of 600,000 also has a colonial past, though it has largely been destroyed by earthquakes. Mendoza has now become the hub of Argentina's flourishing wine industry. It has many well located wineries and bodegas.

Los Alerces National Park Massive alerces trees, some are believed to be over 3,500 years old, grow to a massive height and girth.

Villa el Chocón Jurassic Park in Argentina: dinosaur fossils and models are on show at Neuquén.

Los Glaciares National Park This park consists mainly of two formations, the high mountain landscape in the north, with the FitzRoy Massif, and the inland glaciers in the south, with the Upsala and Perito-Moreno Glaciers.

The Torres del Paine National Park The highest peak in the park is the 3,050-m-high (10,007-ft) Cerro Torre Grande, surrounded by Paine Chico, Torres del Paine and Cuernas del Paine.

Ushuaia This city, the southernmost in Argentina, lies on the Beagle Channel. The Museo del Fin del Mundo (End of the World Museum) displays exhibits from the prehistoric and colonial history of Tierra del Fuego.

Córdoba Argentina's second-largest city (1.5 million inhabitants) is home to the country's oldest university. The picture shows the cathedral and Cabildo in the central plaza of town.

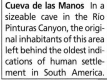

Cueva de las Manos In a sizeable cave in the Río Pinturas Canyon, the original inhabitants of this area left behind the oldest indications of human settlement in South America.

Nahuel Huapi National Park This park near Bariloche has several different landscape zones including the High Andes, rainforest, transitional forest and steppe.

Perito Moreno National Park The national park surrounding Lake Belgrano (the picture shows the broad Belgrano Peninsula) showcases wild and pristine Patagonian nature. Numerous indigenous animals live here, including pumas, guanacos, nandus, flamingos and condors.

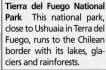

Tierra del Fuego National Park This national park, close to Ushuaia in Terra del Fuego, runs to the Chilean border with its lakes, glaciers and rainforests.

Punta Arenas Until the Panama Canal was built in 1914, this port town was of great importance at the tip of South America. Some of the typical houses from that period still remain.

The Los Pingüinos and Seno Otway Penguin Colonies Thousands of Magellan penguins live here near Punta Arenas in the summer. They are the smallest species of penguin in South America.

b = bottom
cl = clockwise
f = from
l = left
m = middle
r = right
t = top or to

Cover: G/Panoramic Images; 2/3 t.: Premium; 2/3 b.: Ifa; 4 l.: Premium; 4 m.: Ifa; 4 r.: Premium; 5 l. + m.: Ifa; 5 r.: Premium; 6/7 t.: Ifa; 8/9 t.: Getty; 8 m. - 12 r.: Corbis; 13 map(f. l. t. r., f. t. t. b.): 5 x Corbis, Premium, Laif, NN, Premium, Corbis; 14/15 - 16: Premium; 17 t.: Laif; 17 b. - 19 r.: Premium; 20 t.: Ifa; 20 b.: Premium; 21 map (f. l. t. r. cl): 4 x Corbis, 2 x Premium, Corbis, 2 x Premium; 22/23 + 22 m.: Premium; 22 b.: Getty; 23 m.: Premium; 23 b.: Ifa; 24 t. + b.: Premium; 25: Huber; 26/27: Premium; 26 l.: Corbis; 26 b.: Ifa; 27: Corbis; 28 t. + 28 m.: Ifa; 28 b.: Premium; 29 t.: Ifa; 29 m. - 30 m.: Premium; 30 b.: Ifa; 31 map (f. l. t. cl): Corbis, Premium, Corbis, Premium, 3 x Corbis, Ifa, Premium, 2 x Corbis; 32/33 - 32 b.: Premium; 33 m.: Corbis; 33 b. - 34 b.: Premium; 35 t. l. + t. r.: Corbis; 35 b. - 38 b.: Premium; 39 + 40: Corbis; 40/41 map (f. l. t. cl): Corbis, Ifa, 2 x Corbis, Premium, Corbis, 2 x Premium, 2 x Corbis, 3 x Ifa, 2 x Premium; 42/43: Corbis; 42 m. + 42 b.: Premium; 43 m.: Corbis; 43 b. + 44/45: Ifa; 44 l. + 45 b. l.: Premium; 45 b. r.: Ifa; 46/47: Klammet; 46 l.: Premium; 46 r.: Corbis; 47 l.: Premium; 47 r.: Corbis; 48 t.: Premium; 48 b.: Corbis; 49 map (f. t. t. b., f. l. t. r.): 2 x Ifa, Getty, Premium, Ifa, Corbis, Ifa, Getty, NN, 2 x Premium, 2 x Ifa; 50/51 - 50 b.: Ifa; 51 m.: Digitalvision; 51 b.: Premium; 52 t.: Klammet; 52 b. l. + b. r.: Corbis; 53 l.: DFA; 53 r. t. + r. b.: Laif; 54 t. - 54 b.: Ifa; 55 l. + r.: Corbis; 56 t.: Pix; 56 b. l.: Klammet; 56 b. r.: Nordis; 57 map (f. t. t. b., f. l. t. r.): Ifa, Premium, Corbis, Premium, Corbis, Ifa, Premium, Klammet, Ifa, Corbis, DFA, Ifa, laif, Corbis; 58/59: DFA; 58 m.: Ifa; 58 b.: Corbis; 59 m. + b.: Ifa; 60 t. + b.: Corbis; 61: Ifa; 62 t.: Nordis; 62 b.: Ifa; 63 t.: Premium; 63 m.:

Ifa; 63 b.: Premium; 64 l. - 64 r. b.: Corbis; 65 map (f. t. t. b., f. l. t. r.): 2 x Premium, 4 x Corbis, Nordis, DFA, Corbis, 3 x Premium; 66/67: Ifa; 66 m.: Corbis; 66 b. + 66 m.: Ifa; 67 b.: Corbis; 68 t.: Ifa; 69 t.: Corbis; 69 b. l. + b. r.: Premium; 70/71: Ifa; 71: Premium; 72 t. + b.: Corbis; 73 map (f. t. t. b., f. l. t. r.): Premium, 4 x Corbis, Premium, 3 x Corbis, Ifa, Premium, Corbis; 74/75: Dr. Zahn; 74 b. + 75 m.: Premium; 75 b.: Corbis; 76 t.: Mauritius; 76 b. + 77 t.: Huber; 77 b. l.: DFA; 77 b. r., 78 + 79: Huber; 80/81: Boettcher; 80 b. l.: BAV; 80 b. r. + 82/83: Huber; 82 b.: Premium; 83 b.: DFA; 84 t.: Laif; 84 m.: NN; 84 b.: Mauritius; 85 t.: Ifa; 85 b.: Mauritius; 86 l.: Premium; 86 r.: Huber; 86/87 map (f. l. t. cl): Premium; Huber, DFA, Dr. Zahn, Huber, 2 x Ifa, NN, Premium, DFA, 2 x Premium, 2 x Huber; 88/89 + 88 m.: Ifa; 88 b.: Bieker; 89 m. + 89 b.: Ifa; 90/91 + 90 b. l.: Huber; 90 b. r.: Ifa; 91 b. l.: Getty; 91 b. r.: Huber; 92/93: Premium; 92 b.: Huber; 93 b.: Corbis; 94/95: Ifa; 94 b. l.: Monheim; 94 b. r.: Huber; 95 b. l.: Romeis; 95 b. r.: Bieker; 96 t.: Mauritius; 96 b.: Romeis; 97 map (f. t. t. b. und f. l. t. r.): Huber, 2 x Getty, Ifa, 2 x Huber, Ifa, Laif, Ifa, Premium, Schilgen, Huber, Romeis, Freyer; 98/99: Huber; 98 m.: Bieker; 98 b.: Huber; 99 m.: Premium; 99 b.: DFA; 100/101: Romeis; 100 b.: Huber; 101 b.: Ifa; 102/103: Klammet; 102 b.: Romeis; 103 b.: Freyer; 104 t.: Romeis; 104 b.: Huber ;105 map (f. l. t. r., f. t. t. b.): Romeis, 2 x Huber, Romeis, 2 x Huber, Bieker, Ifa, Huber, Freyer, Ifa, Premium, Klammet; 106/107: Laif; 106 m.: Ifa; 106 b.: Premium; 107 m.: Ifa; 107 b.: Premium; 108/109: Huber; 108 b.: Corbis; 109 b.: Wackenhut; 110/111: Boettcher; 112 t.: Ifa; 112 b.: Premium; 113 + 114/115: Ifa; 114 b.: Huber; 115 b.: Premium; 116/117: DFA; 117 b.: Ifa; 117 m.: Westermann; 117 b.: Ifa; 118 t.: Tony Stone; 118 m.: Laif; 118 b.: Corbis; 119: Premium; 120 t. + b.: Ifa; 121 map (f. l. t. r., f. t. t. b.): Corbis, 2 x Ifa, Huber, Wandmacher, FAN, Huber, 2 x Ifa, Westermann, DFA, Stone, Corbis, Ifa; 122/123: Ifa; 122 m.: Premium; 122 b.: Huber; 123 m.: Premium; 123 b.: Mediacolors; 124/125: Premium; 124 b.: Ifa; 125 m.: Mediacolors; 125

b. + 126/127: Premium; 126 b. l. - 129 b.: Ifa; 130/131 map (f. l. t., cl): Ifa, 2 x Premium, Ifa, Monheim, Ifa, Premium, 3 x Ifa, 2 x mediacolors, Getty, Ifa; 132/133: Premium; 132 m.: Ifa; 132 b.: Corbis; 133 m.: Premium; 133 b.: Ifa; 134 t.: Premium; 134 b.: Monheim; 135 t. - 135 b.: Premium; 136 t. - 137 t.: Ifa; 137 b.: Monheim; 138 t.: Premium; 138 b.: Corbis; 139 t.: Premium; 139 b.: Corbis; 140 t.: Ifa; 140 b.: Premium; 141 map (f. l. t. cl): Monheim, 2 x Ifa, 2 x Premium, Corbis, Premium, Corbis, Monheim, Premium, Ifa, NN; 142/143: Ifa; 142 m.: DFA; 142 b. - 145 b.: Ifa; 146/147 + 146 b.: Corbis; 147 b. l. + b. r.: Ifa; 148 l. + r.: Corbis; 149: Ifa; 148/149 map (f. t. t. b., f. l. t. r.): Corbis, 7 x Ifa, Premium, 3 x Corbis, Ifa, Premium; 150/151: Monheim; 150 m.: Ifa; 150 b.: Corbis; 151 m.: Premium; 151 b.: Corbis; 152: Premium; 153 t. + b.: Herzig; 154 + 155: Premium; 156/157: Ifa; 156 t. + 157 m.: Corbis; 157 b.: Laif; 158/159 t.: Corbis; 158/159 b.: Premium; 160 t.: Laif; 160 b.: Corbis; 161 map (f. t. t. b., f. l. t. r.): Huber, Herzig, Corbis, Herzig, Premium, Corbis, Getty, 5 x Corbis; 162/163 - 163 b.: Ifa; 164 t.: Premium; 164 b. + 165 t.: Ifa; 165 b.: Mauritius; 166 t.: Huber; 166 b. - 168 t.: Ifa; 168 b.: Premium; 169: Huber; 170/171: Premium; 170/171 map (f. t. t. b., f. l. t. r.): 2 x Ifa, Huber, 3 x Ifa, DFA, 10 x Ifa; 172/173: Corbis; 172 m.: Ifa; 172 b. + m.: Corbis; 173 b. + 174: Ifa; 175 t. l. - 177 t.: Corbis; 177 b. l.: Laif; 177 b. r.: Ifa; 178/179 + 178 b. l.: Corbis; 178 b. r.: Ifa; 179 b.: Corbis; 180/181: Premium; 180/181 map (f. l. t. cl): 2 x Ifa, Corbis, Getty, Corbis, Ifa, Huber, Ifa, 4 x Corbis, Ifa, Corbis; 182/183: Premium; 182 m. + b.: Corbis; 183 m. + b.: Ifa; 184/185: Premium 184 b.: Corbis; 185 b.: Pix; 186/187 t. + b.: Premium; 188/189 t.: Ifa; 188/189 b.: Corbis; 190 t.: Premium; 190 b.: Corbis; 191 map (f. l. t. cl): Getty, 2 x Corbis, 2 x Ifa, 5 x Corbis, Pix, Ifa; 192/193: Premium; 192 m. + b.: Ifa; 193 m. - 195 r.: Premium; 196/197: Ifa; 196 b.: Premium; 197 b. - 199 b.: Ifa; 200 t.: Laif; 200 b.: Marc Frei; 201 map (f. t. t. b., f. l. t. r.): Premium, Ifa, Corbis, Ifa, 2 x Corbis, 2 x Ifa, Premium, Corbis, 4

x Ifa; 202/203: Premium; 202 m. + b.: Ifa; 203 m. - 206 b.: Premium; 207 b. l.: Corbis; 207 b. r. + 208 t.: Corbis; 208 b.: Ifa; 209 t.: Premium; 209 m. + b.: Corbis; 210 t.: Premium; 210 b.: Corbis; 211 map (f. t. t. b., f. l. t. r.): 2 x Premium, Corbis, Ifa, 2 x Premium, Corbis, Premium, 2 x Ifa, 2 x Premium, Corbis; 212/213 - 213 m.: Premium; 212 b.: Klammet; 213 m.: Premium; 213 b.: Laif; 214 t.: Premium; 214 b.: Corbis; 215 t.: Klammet; 216/217 t.: Corbis; 216 b.: Laif; 216/217 b.: Premium; 217 b.: Getty; 218/219 t.: Premium; 218/219 b.: Corbis; 220 t. + b.: Premium; 221 map (f. l. t. cl): Corbis, Laif, Klammet, Corbis, Premium, Laif, Premium, Jannicke, 2 x Premium, Klammet; 222/223: Ifa; 222 m.: Corbis; 222 b.: Mauritius; 223 m.: Corbis; 223 b.: Mauritius; 224/225: Premium; 225 b.: Getty; 226/227 + 227: Premium; 228/229 t.: Laif; 228 b.: Mauritius; 229 b. + 230 b.: Ifa; 231 t.: Corbis; 231 b.: Premium; 232: Corbis; 232 b.: NN; 233 map (f. t. t. b., f. l. t. r.): Premium, Getty, 5 x Corbis, Ifa, Mauritius, 2 x Corbis, Ifa, Premium, Ifa, Corbis; 234/235: Premium; 234 m. + b.: Ifa; 235 m.: Corbis; 235 b.: Laif; 236 - 237 b.: Premium; 238/239: Corbis; 238 b.: Premium; 239 b. + 240 t.: Corbis; 240 b.: Huber; 241 t.: Ifa; 241 b.: Huber; 242/243: Laif; 242 b. + 243 b.: Ifa; 244 t.: NN; 244 b.: Corbis; 245 map (f. l. t. r., f. t. t. b.): Corbis, Premium, Corbis, Premium, Ifa, Huber, Ifa, Corbis, Huber, Mauritius, Ifa, Getty, Premium; 246/247 - 246 b.: Ifa; 247 m. + b.: Corbis; 248 t.: Ifa; 248 b. - 250 b.: Corbis; 251 t. + b.: Ifa; 252 t. + b.: Corbis; 253 map (f. t. t. b., f. l. t. r.): Corbis, Ifa, 2 x Corbis, Ifa, 2 x Corbis, Ifa, 2 x Corbis, 2 x Ifa, Corbis, Ifa; 254/255: Premium; 254 m.: Corbis; 254 b. + m.: Ifa; 255 b.: Premium; 256/257 - 260 b.: Corbis; 261 b.: Ifa; 262 t.: Laif; 262 b.: Look; 263 map (f. l. t. cl): Premium, Ifa, Corbis, 4 x Ifa, Huber, Premium, Huber, Laif; 264/265: Premium; 264 m. - 265 m.: Ifa; 265 b. + 266/267: Premium; 267 b. l.: Ifa; 267 b. r. + 268/269: Premium; 268 b.: Laif; 269 b.: Ifa; 270/271: Premium; 270 b. + 271 b.: Ifa; 272: Corbis; 273 t. + b.: Ifa; 274/275 map (f. l. t. r.): Premium,

Huber, 4 x Ifa, Laif, 2 x Corbis, Premium, Corbis, 6 x Ifa, Corbis, Premium, Ifa; 276/277 t.: Premium; 276/277 b.: Getty; 276 b. - 278 t.: Ifa; 278 b.: NN; 279 t. - 282/283 t.: Corbis; 282/283 b.: Ifa; 284/285 t.: Corbis; 284/285 b.: Ifa; 286: Premium; 287 map (f. l. t. cl): 2 x Ifa, Corbis, mediacolors, 2 x Premium, Bronsteen, Corbis, Ifa, 2 x Corbis; 288/289: Corbis; 288 m.: Getty; 288 b.: Corbis; 289 m.: Premium; 289 b.: Corbis; 290, 291 t. + b.: Premium; 292/293 t. + 292 b.: Corbis; 293 t.: DFA; 294 t. + b.: Ifa; 295 map (f. l. t. r., f. t. b.): Ifa, 2 x Premium, 3 x Corbis, Premium, 4 x Corbis, Ifa, Corbis; 296/297: Ifa; 296 m.: Premium; 296 b.: Corbis; 297 m.: Ifa; 297 b.: Corbis; 298/299: Ifa; 299 m.: Premium; 299 b.: Corbis; 300/301 + 300: Ifa; 301 b.: Premium; 302 t. + b.: Ifa; 303 t.: Premium; 303 b.: DFA; 304 t.: Ifa; 304 b.: Corbis; 305 + 306 t.: Premium; 306 b.: Ifa; 307 map (f. l. t. cl): Corbis, Premium, Ifa, Corbis, 2 x Premium, 3 x Ifa, Premium; 308/309: Corbis; 308 b.: Zefa; 309 m.: Premium; 309 b.: K.-U. Müller; 310/311: Corbis; 311 m. + b.: Mauritius, 312 t. - 313 t.: Corbis; 313 b. + 314/315: Premium; 314/315 - 315 b. r.: Corbis; 316/317: Premium; 316 b.: Corbis; 317 b.: K.-U. Müller; 318/319: Premium; 318 b.: K.-U. Müller; 319 b.: Corbis; 320/321 map (f. l. t. r.): 4 x Corbis, Zefa, Corbis, Premium, 3 x Corbis, 2 x K.-U. Müller, Corbis, Premium, Corbis, K.-U. Müller, 2 x Corbis; 322/323 t.: Corbis; 322 m.: Ifa; 322 b.: Laif; 323 m.: Corbis; 323 b. + 324/325 t.: Premium; 325 b. + 326 t.: Corbis; 326 b.: IFA; 327 t.: Premium; 327 b.: Don Fuchs; 328/329: Corbis; 328 b.: Ifa; 329 b.: Corbis; 330 map (f. l. t. t. r. b.): 5 x Corbis, Ifa, Corbis, Look, Laif, Corbis; 331 map (f. l. t. r. b.): Corbis, Transglobe, Ifa, Corbis, 3 x Ifa, 5 x Corbis; 332/333: Ifa; 332 b.: Corbis; 333 m.: Ifa; 333 b. + 334/335: Premium; 335 b.: Corbis; 336/337 t. + b.: Ifa; 337 b. + 338/339 t.: Premium; 338/339 b.: Alamy; 340 t.: Corbis; 340 b.: Premium; 341 map (f. l. t. cl): 2 x Corbis, Premium, 2 x Corbis, Laif, Corbis, 2 x Premium, 2 x Corbis; 342/343: Getty; 342 m. - 343 m.: Premium; 343 b. + 344 t.: Ifa;

344 b.: Premium; 345 t.: Ifa; 345 u.: Premium; 346/347: Ifa; 346 b. - 348 t.: Premium; 348 b. + 349 t.: Ifa; 349 b.: Ifa; 350 t. + b.: NN; 351 map (f. l. t. cl): Corbis, Alamy, 3 x Ifa, Corbis, 2 x Premium, Ifa, Huber, Ifa, Premium; 352/352 t.: Ifa; 352 m.: Premium; 352 b.: Ifa; 353 M: Premium; 353 b.: Ifa; 354 t.: Getty; 354 b. + 355 t.: Ifa; 355 b. + 356/357: Premium; 356 b.: Corbis; 357 b.: Premium; 358/359 + 359 b.: Ifa; 359 b.: Laif; 360 t. - 361 t.: Ifa; 361 b.: Corbis; 362 map (f. l. t. r. b.): 4 x Corbis, Laif, Corbis, Getty, Corbis, Laif, 3 x Ifa, Corbis; 363 map (f. l. t. t. r. b.): Corbis, Mauritius, Premium, Ifa, Corbis, Premium, Corbis, 2 x Premium, Ifa, Corbis; 364/365: Huber; 364 m. - 365 m.: Premium; 365 b. + 366 t.: Ifa; 367 t.: Premium; 367 b.: Corbis; 368/369 t.: Ifa; 368 b.: Premium; 369 b.: Ifa; 370 t. + b.: Premium; 371 t. + b.: Ifa; 372/373: Huber; 372 b.: Laif; 373 b.: Stone; 374 t.: Ifa; 374 b.: Premium; 375 map (f. l. t. t. r. b.): Corbis, Getty, Ifa, Corbis, Ifa, Laif, Ifa, Getty, 2 x Corbis, Ifa, Corbis, Huber, Stone, DFA; 376/377 t.: Alamy; 376 m.: Premium; 376 b.: Schapowalow; 377 m.: Premium; 377 b.: Kunth; 378 + 379 t.: Corbis; 379 b.: Ifa; 380/381 t. + m.: Kunth; 380/381 b.: Premium; 382/383: Corbis; 382 b.: Premium; 383 b. + 384/385: Corbis; 384 b.: Ifa; 385 b. - 386/387: Premium; 388 map (f. l. t. r., f. t. b.): Premium, Corbis, Ifa, Kunth, 2 x Corbis, Kunth, Ifa, Corbis, 3 x Premium; 389 map (f. l. t. r., f. t. b.): Mediacolors, Corbis, 3 x Ifa, 3 x Corbis, 2 x Premium, 2 x Corbis; 390/391 - 392 t.: Ifa; 392 b.: Premium; 393 t.: Ifa; 393 m.: Corbis; 393 b. + 394: Ifa; 395 t.: DFA; 395 m.: Corbis; 395 b.: Ifa; 396 t.: Corbis; 396 b.: Ifa; 397: Premium; 398/399 t. + 398 b.: Ifa; 399 b.: Laif; 400 t.: Alamy; 400 b.: Ifa; 401 map (f. l. t. r., f. t. b.): Premium, 2 x Corbis, 2 x Ifa, Premium, Ifa, Corbis, 2 x Ifa, Premium, 3 x Corbis; 402/403: Ifa; 402 m. - 403 m.: Premium; 403 b.: Corbis; 404/405 + 404 b.: Premium; 405 b.: Mauritius; 406/407 t.: Corbis; 406 b.: Premium; 407 b. + 408 t.: Corbis; 408 b.: Premium; 410 t. + b.: Corbis; 411 map (f. l. t. r., f. t. b.): Corbis, Premium, Ifa, Corbis, 2 x Ifa, 6 x Corbis; 412/413 t. + 412 m.:

Premium; 412 b. - 413 b.: Corbis; 414/415 t. + 415 b.: Premium; 416: Corbis; 417 + 418 t.: Premium; 418 m. + b.: Corbis; 419: Getty; 420 t. + 421 b.: Corbis; 420/421 map (f. l. t. r., f. t. b.): Corbis, Premium, Corbis, Premium, 3 x Corbis, Premium, Corbis, Premium, 3 x Corbis; 422/423 t.: Premium; 422 m.: Ifa; 422 b.: Premium; 423 m.: Corbis; 423 b.: Ifa; 424/425 t.: Premium; 424 b.: Ifa; 424 m.: Premium; 425 u.: Ifa; 426/427 t.: Premium; 426 b.: Corbis; 427 m. - 429 b. l.: Ifa; 430/431 t., m. + b.: Premium; 432/433 t. + 432 b.: Ifa; 433 m. - 434/435 t.: Premium; 434 b. + 435 b.: Ifa; 436 map (f. l. t. r. b.): 2 x Corbis, Premium, Ifa, Corbis, Premium, Corbis, Ifa, Corbis, Ifa; 437 map (f. l. t. r. b.): 5 x Corbis, Ifa, Premium, 3 x Corbis; 438/439 t.: Getty; 438 b. + 439 m.: Premium; 439 b.: Corbis; 440/441: Premium; 441 b.: Corbis; 442: Mauritius; 443 + 444/445: Premium; 445: Corbis; 446: Premium; 447: Corbis; 448/449 - 450 b.: Premium; 451 map (f. l. t. cl): 2 x Corbis, Premium, Corbis, Premium, 3 x Corbis, Premium, Corbis, NN; 452/453: Premium; 452 b.: Ifa; 453 m.: Premium; 453 b. + 454/455: Ifa; 455 b. - 456/457 t.: Premium; 456 b. + 457 b.: Corbis; 458 t.: Premium; 458 b. - 459 b.: Corbis; 460 t. + b., 461 t.: Ifa; 461 b. - 462 b.: Corbis; 463: Premium; 464/465 map (f. l. t. cl): 3 x Corbis, Premium, Corbis, Premium, 6 x Corbis, Premium, Ifa, 2 x Corbis, Ifa, 6 x Corbis; 466/467 t.: Ifa; 466/467 b.: Getty; 466 b.: Ifa; 467 b.: Getty; 468/469: Premium; 469 b. + 470 b.: Ifa; 471 b.: Heeb; 472/473 t. + b.: Ifa; 474 t. - 475 b.: Premium; 476/477 map (f. l. t. r., f. t. b.): Ifa, Corbis, Stone, 2 x Ifa, Premium, 2 x Ifa, Corbis, 2 x Ifa, Corbis, 3 x Ifa, Kohlhaas, Ifa, Premium, Ifa, Premium, Ifa; 478/479 t.: Stockmarket; 478/479 b.: Corbis; 478 b.: AKG; 479: IFA; 480/481 - 483 b.: Corbis; 484/485: Premium; 486 t.: Huber; 486 b. + 487: Premium; 488 t. + b.: Corbis; 489 map (f. l. t. cl): 3 x Corbis, 2 x Premium, Corbis, Stone, 4 x Corbis, 2 x Ifa; 490/491 + 490 b.: Premium; 491 m.: Ifa; 491 b.: Corbis; 492/493 t.: Ifa; 492 b.: Kohlhaas; 493 b.: Premium; 494/495 t.: Ifa; 494 b.: Premium; 495 b. + 496/497: Ifa; 496

b.: Premium; 497 b.: Corbis; 498 t.: Ifa; 498 b. l. + b. r.: Premium; 498 b. r.: Premium; 499 map (f. l. t.cl): Corbis, 3 x Ifa, Premium, Ifa, Corbis, Ifa, Corbis, Ifa, 2 x Corbis, Stone; 500/501 - 500 b.: Corbis; 501 m.: Pix; 501 b. - 502 b.: Corbis; 503 t.: Laif; 503 b. - 506 b.: Corbis; 507 map (f. l. t. r., f. t. t. b.): 3 x Corbis, Laif, 3 x Corbis, Premium, Pix, 4 x Corbis; 508/509: Premium; 508 m. - 509 m.: Corbis; 509 b.: Premium; 510 t.: Corbis; 511 t.: Premium; 511 b.: Corbis; 512/513 t.: Premium; 512 b. l. - 515 t.: Corbis; 515 b.: Woodhouse; 516 t. - 518 b.: Corbis; 519 map (f. l. t. r., f. t. t. b.): Laif, Corbis, Premium, Corbis, Getty, Laif, Corbis, Mauritius, Corbis, Stone, 2 x Corbis; 520/521: Corbis; 520 m.: Digitalvision; 520 b.: Corbis; 521 m.: Premium; 521 b. - 523 t.: Corbis; 523 b.: Premium; 524 t.: Corbis; 524 m. - 524 b.: Corbis; 526/527: Premium; 527 b. l - 529 t.: Corbis; 530 map (f. l. t. cl): 2 x Corbis, Premium, 4 x Corbis, Ifa, 3 x Corbis; 531 map (f. l. t. r., f. t. t. b.): 5 x Corbis, Ifa, Corbis, Premium, 5 x Corbis; 532/533 t. + 532 m.: Premium; 532 b.: Corbis; 533 m.: Getty; 533 b. - 535 b.: Corbis; 536/537 t. + 536 m.: Premium; 536 b. - 540 b.: Corbis; 541 map (f. l. t. r., f. t. t. b.): Corbis, Ifa, 8 x Corbis, Ifa, Corbis.

IMPRINT

MONACO BOOKS is an imprint of Verlag Wolfgang Kunth

© Verlag Wolfgang Kunth GmbH & Co.KG, Munich, 2010

Translation: Silva Editions Ltd., Emily Plank, Katherine Taylor,

For distribution please contact:

Monaco Books
c/o Verlag Wolfgang Kunth, Königinstr. 11
80539 München, Germany
Tel. (49) 89 45 80 20 23
Fax (49) 89 45 80 20 21
info@kunth-verlag.de

www.monacobooks.com
www.kunth-verlag.de

Printed in Slovakia

All facts have been researched with the greatest possible care, to the best of our knowledge and belief. However, the editors and publishers can accept no responsibility for any inaccuracies or incompleteness of the details provided. The publishers are pleased to receive any information or suggestions for improvement.